SECULAR SAINTS

*"But the souls of the just are in the hand of God,
and the torment of death shall not touch them. In
the sight of the unwise they seemed to die: and their
departure was taken for misery: and their going away
from us, for utter destruction: but they are in peace.
And though in the sight of men they suffered torments, their hope is full of immortality. Afflicted in
few things, in many they shall be well rewarded: because God hath tried them, and found them worthy
of himself. As gold in the furnace he hath proved
them, and as a victim of a holocaust he hath received
them, and in time there shall be respect had to them.
The just shall shine, and shall run to and fro like
sparks among the reeds. They shall judge nations,
and rule over people, and their Lord shall reign for
ever. They that trust in him, shall understand the
truth: and they that are faithful in love shall rest in
him: for grace and peace is to his elect. But the wicked
shall be punished according to their own devices: who
have neglected the just, and have revolted from the
Lord."*

—Wisdom 3:1-10

The Holy Family, to whom this book is dedicated.

SECULAR SAINTS

250 Canonized and Beatified Lay Men, Women and Children

by

Joan Carroll Cruz

"Thou hast loved justice, and hated iniquity: therefore God, thy God, hath anointed thee with the oil of gladness above thy fellows."

—Psalm 46:8

TAN BOOKS AND PUBLISHERS, INC.
Rockford, Illinois 61105

OTHER BOOKS BY THE AUTHOR

The Incorruptibles
Eucharistic Miracles
Relics
Desires of Thy Heart

Soon to be published:
Eucharistic Miracles, Vol. II
Prayers and Heavenly Promises
(Compiled from approved sources by Mrs. Cruz)

Nihil Obstat: Rev. Reginald R. Masterson, O.P.
                  Censor Librorum

Imprimatur: ✠ Philip M. Hannan
                  Archbishop of New Orleans
                  September 6, 1988

Library of Congress Catalog Card No.: 89-50830

ISBN: 0-89555-383-X

Printed and bound in the United States of America.

TAN BOOKS AND PUBLISHERS, INC.
P.O. Box 424
Rockford, Illinois 61105

1989

This book is
dedicated with love
to
The Holy Family.

AUTHOR'S NOTE

A national Catholic magazine recently polled a thousand of its readers to learn what they believe about the Saints. The magazine reported that while recent news reports on the nation's Catholics have highlighted disagreements with traditional Church teachings, 67% of the survey's respondents said they prayed to the Saints as much, or more, than they did years ago. Sixty-eight percent of the respondents said they tried to imitate the lives of the Saints.

Mentioned as the four favorite saints were the Blessed Mother, St. Joseph, St. Francis of Assisi and St. Therese of Lisieux (the Little Flower). With the exception of the Blessed Mother and St. Joseph, who are in a unique category, we are left with a Franciscan brother and a Discalced Carmelite cloistered nun. While we can admire the virtues of St. Francis and St. Therese, the lifestyles of these two saints, and other saints of religious orders, are far removed, to say the least, from those of secular people.

Although the exact number of canonized saints is unknown, we know, of course, that the greater majority have been members of religious orders. We love them, we admire them, we wish to imitate them, but how can a mother with small children, a wife with a difficult husband, a young bride with in-law problems—how can they really relate to the nun who lived in the quiet of a cloister, the nun who lived in a community where everyone shared the work of the house? How can they relate to the saints of religious orders whose lives were arranged in an orderly manner and who had designated times for quiet prayer and who had little or no financial problems? One might wonder if these saints of the cloister would have merited their titles if they had remained in the world to face the conflicts and dangers confronted by ordinary lay people.

It is profitable, of course, for laymen to love these saints, to pray to them and to imitate their virtues as much as they are able. But it seems that laymen would draw more encouragement to advance in prayer and virtue and would derive more consolation in their trials by examining the troubles and temptations of those saints who lived and died as secular members of the Church.

St. Teresa of Avila suggests that "We need to cultivate and think upon, and seek the companionship of those saints who, though living on earth like ourselves, have accomplished such great deeds for God." Here, then, are the lives of 250 secular saints who have, so to speak, "lived on earth like ourselves." Represented here are single men and women, mothers and fathers, soldiers and servants, doctors and lawyers, the humble and the noble—all who have met the difficulties and challenges of the secular life and triumphed over them. Their virtues are to be admired, but most of all imitated. May we benefit from their example and from their prayers.

Joan Carroll Cruz

PREFACE

A Word about The Blessed Virgin Mary

A book about secular saints would be incomplete without mentioning the pre-eminent model for secular people, the Blessed Mother. But what could be said here that has not been mentioned about her already in numerous biographies and devotional works? We have only to delve into these to find a solicitous and understanding mother, a kindly and generous friend, a consoling companion, and a ready and willing intercessor with God.

Although it is known that Mary was free from sin, full of grace, blessed among women and the fairest honor of our race, yet, as we know, she was not exempt from countless trials and hardships. She, who was the model of saints throughout the ages, should be the particular ideal of secular people, since Mary was an exemplary member of our secular ranks. She was, of course, a young bride, a young mother, a housekeeper, a widow...

May this Immaculate Mother pray for us, that in our imitation of the Saints, we can advance in virtue and eventually join her and her sainted children in our heavenly homeland.

Marriage of the Blessed Virgin Mary and St. Joseph.

CONTENTS

xi

SECULAR SAINTS

"Then shall the king say to them that shall be on his right hand: Come, ye blessed of my Father, possess you the kingdom prepared for you from the foundation of the world. For I was hungry, and you gave me to eat; I was thirsty, and you gave me to drink; I was a stranger, and you took me in: Naked, and you covered me: sick, and you visited me: I was in prison, and you came to me. Then shall the just answer him, saying: Lord, when did we see thee hungry, and fed thee; thirsty, and gave thee drink? And when did we see thee a stranger, and took thee in? or naked, and covered thee? Or when did we see thee sick or in prison, and came to thee? And the king answering, shall say to them: Amen I say to you, as long as you did it to one of these my least brethren, you did it to me."

—Matthew 25:34-40

Chapter 1

ST. ADALBALD OF OSTREVANT

d. 650

As the son of a distinguished family, Adalbald spent much of his time in the court of Dagobert I and Clovis II and may have been the Duke of Douai. An ideal Christian noble, he was a general favorite among the courtiers.

While on an expedition in Gascony, Adalbald became friends with a noble lord named Ernold whose daughter, Rictrude, became Adalbald's bride. The wedding was performed with great pomp, but the union did not please certain members of the bride's family. Yet, in spite of a critical assessment of the groom by his in-laws and their dire predictions for the couple's future, the marriage proved to be a happy one. Early in their wedded life the young couple became interested in performing works of mercy and spent time visiting the sick, relieving the poor, feeding the hungry and converting prisoners.

Four children were born to them: a son, Mauront, and three daughters, Eusebia, Clotsind and Adalsind. All four children imitated their parents in the ways of virtue and acts of charity.

In the year 650, 16 years after his marriage, Adalbald was recalled to Gascony, never to return. When he reached the vicinity of Perigueux, he was attacked and killed by a number of his wife's vindictive relatives.

When news of her husband's death reached Rictrude, she was overcome with grief. Even so, she managed to obtain possession of her husband's body, which was buried with honor.

Following Adalbald's death and after her children were grown, Rictrude entered the double monastery for men and women at Marchiennes, which she had previously founded. This monastery was so arranged that the living accommodations and prayer areas were entirely separate. Only the chapel was shared, but even this was divided into sections. Accompanying Rictrude into the monastery were her two younger daughters, Adalsind and Clotsind, as well as her only

1

son, Mauront, who left the world and the Frankish court to receive the tonsure in his mother's presence.

Following Rictrude's death, Clotsind succeeded her mother as abbess of the monastery. The third daughter, Eusebia, entered the monastery of Halmage, which had been founded by her great-grandmother, St. Gertrude of Halmage.

The remains of St. Adalbald rested in the Monastery of St. Amand-les-Eaux in Elanone (Elnon), France, but afterward his head was taken to Douai. This we learn from an ancient manuscript of the Church of St. Ame, where there was, at one time, a magnificent chapel dedicated to Sts. Adalbald, Rictrude and their son, St. Mauront. Exhibited there for public veneration were statues of the holy trio. That of St. Adalbald was draped in a robe covered with lilies; St. Rictrude's statue was clothed in a Benedictine habit and held a miniature replica of the Abbey of Marchiennes in her hand; and St. Mauront was represented with a sceptre in his right hand and towers in his left.

The whole family—father, mother, three daughers and one son—are honored as saints of the Church. Also included in this holy gathering are Adalbald's grandmother, St. Gertrude of Halmage, and Rictrude's sister, St. Bertha, who after being widowed became a nun and the foundress of the Monastery of Blangy in Artois.

Chapter 2

ST. ADELAIDE

d. 999

The history of St. Adelaide (Adelheid) is dominated by the tenth-century power struggle and intrigue of certain parties for control of the Kingdom of Italy. Adelaide was born into this struggle, being the daughter of Rudolph II, King of Burgundy, who was at war with Hugh of Provence for the Italian crown. In 933 the rivals reached a peace agreement by which it was stipulated that Adelaide, the daughter of one rival, should marry Lothaire, the son of the other rival. Adelaide was then only two years old. Fourteen years later her brother, Conrad of Burgundy, arranged the marriage and thereby fulfilled the contract. This marriage produced one child, a daughter, who was named Emma.

As a result of this marriage, Adelaide's husband, Lothaire, was considered the King of Italy. However, Berengarius, the Marquis of Ivrea, came upon the scene and claimed the Kingdom of Italy for himself. When Lothaire suddenly died in 950, it was suspected that he had been poisoned by Berengarius, who succeeded him. Berengarius then attempted to force the widow Adelaide to marry his son, Adalbert. When she refused, Berengarius treated her with brutality and kept her in almost solitary confinement in the Castle of Garda. From there she was rescued by a priest named Martin, who is said to have dug a subterranean passage by which she escaped. Adelaide remained concealed in the woods until her friend Alberto Uzzo, the Duke of Canossa, heard of the rescue and conveyed her to his castle.

While this was taking place, the Italian nobles, having grown weary of Berengarius, invited Otto the Great of Germany to invade and seize the country for himself. Otto met little resistance and promptly defeated Berengarius. To consolidate his authority in Italy, Otto married Adelaide at Pavia in the year 951. Adelaide had been a widow for one year and was twenty years younger than Otto. Of Adelaide's

3

second marriage, five children were born: Otto II, Henry, Bruno and two daughters, who eventually became nuns.

Otto, it seems, had been married earlier to the daughter of Athelstan of England. Otto's son by this marriage, Rudolph, was jealous of the influence of his stepmother and her children and became a source of friction and rebellion. In spite of this, the German people accepted the gentle Adelaide and held her in the highest regard.

Berengarius once again instigated trouble in Italy, and when he finally invaded the States of the Church, Pope John XII appealed to Otto for help. When Otto took his forces across the Alps, Berengarius retreated. In 962 Otto was crowned emperor at Rome. Little is related about Adelaide for the following 10 years, until the death of Otto the Great in 973 and the succession of her son Otto II.

During the reign of her son, trouble once again brought Adelaide to prominence. Although Otto II had many worthy traits, he permitted his wife, Theophania, and other counselors to turn him against his mother. Some suspect that the daughter-in-law resented Adelaide because of the Saint's liberality to the poor. Because of the unpleasant atmosphere at court, Adelaide left and went to her brother, Conrad, at Vienna. She appealed to St. Majolus, Abbot of Cluny, to effect a reconciliation. This was eventually brought about at Pavia—with her son asking pardon on his knees for his unkindness.

Trouble once more shadowed Adelaide when Otto II died and left as his successor his son, Otto III, who was then an infant. The child's mother, Theophania, assumed the duties of regent. With her troublesome daughter-in-law in complete control and as yet unreconciled, Adelaide again left the court. When Theophania died suddenly in 991, Adelaide was recalled to serve as regent in her place.

Adelaide's administration was dependent upon the wise guidance of Adalbert of Magdeburg, St. Majolus and St. Odilo of Cluny, who wrote about the saintly regent. These holy men reported that Adelaide was forgiving to her enemies and proved herself generous in her dealings. She founded and restored monasteries of monks and nuns, maintained a peaceful religious atmosphere at court, and was zealous in her attempts to convert the pagans of the northern and eastern frontiers.

When she was 68 years of age, St. Adelaide died while on a journey to Burgundy to reconcile Rudolph III with his subjects. It was December 16, 999.

Although St. Adelaide is not mentioned in the *Roman Martyrology*, she is greatly revered in Germany, where her name appears on their calendars.

A fourteenth-century statue of St. Adelaide which is located in the cathedral at Augsburg, Germany.

A close-up view of a statue of St. Adelaide (which stands next to a statue of her second husband, Otto the Great of Germany). St. Adelaide is remembered for her wisdom and generosity when serving as regent near the end of the tenth century. The Saint was widowed at an early age and experienced difficulty with her daughter-in-law. She founded and restored monasteries, zealously converted pagans and won the high regard of the German people.

Chapter 3

BL. ADRIAN FORTESCUE

d. 1539

Sir Adrian Fortescue was born in 1476 to an old Devonshire family which traced its ancestry to the time of the Norman Conquest. His father, Sir John, held important posts at court; his mother was Alice Boleyn, a cousin of Anne Boleyn, whose marriage to King Henry VIII was to bring about the fall of the Catholic religion in England—as well as the martyrdom of countless Catholics.

Sir Adrian's early and middle life was that of a typical country gentleman of the time. He was a serious, thrifty man, careful in business, exact in accounts and a lover of the homely wit of the day. Because his family fortunes had been secured in earlier times, he was also a man of considerable wealth. He was a justice of the peace for the county of Oxford and assisted at the royal court. In 1513 he fought in France at the "Battle of the Spurs," and in 1520 he was in Queen Catherine's train when she went to Calais during the "Field of the Cloth of Gold." Always a religious man, Sir Adrian was admitted in 1532 as a "knight of devotion" of St. John of Jerusalem (the Knights of Malta). The following year he was enrolled at Oxford as a tertiary in the Third Order of St. Dominic.

Sir Adrian was also a married man and the father of two daughters by his first wife, Anne Stoner. Twelve years after her death he married Anne Rede of Boarstall, who bore him three sons.

During the time that King Henry VIII was persecuting Catholics as a result of his differences with the Pope concerning his marriage to Anne Boleyn, Sir Adrian seems to have behaved with prudence. But for reasons that have not been given he was arrested on August 29, 1534 and detained in the Marshalsea prison. He was probably released in the spring of 1535, the year during which St. Thomas More and St. John Fisher were beheaded for the Faith for refusing to side with King Henry VIII in the matter of his divorce and

7

remarriage. Because Catholics and priests were being arrested for their faith, Sir Adrian, well-known as a Catholic, must have expected the inevitable. During February of 1539, the expected occurred when he was arrested and sent to the Tower of London.

Parliament met in April, and Sir Adrian was condemned without a trial. It was claimed that he "not only most traitorously refused his duty of allegiance, which he ought to bear to Your Highness, but also hath committed divers and sundry detestable and abominable treasons, and put sedition in your realm." The nature of these treasons was never given. Condemned at the same time were Cardinal Pole and several others because they "adhered themselves to the Bishop of Rome." Catholic tradition has always held that Sir Adrian died for the same cause.

Bl. Adrian was beheaded with Bl. Thomas Dingley at Tower Hill on July 8, 1539. Since his death, his cultus has always flourished among the Knights of St. John. He was beatified by Pope Leo XIII in 1895.

In the church at Husband's Bosworth is preserved Bl. Adrian's *Book of Hours*. On the flyleaf he had written and signed a series of maxims, or rules, of the spiritual life. A few of these are the following:

Above all things, love God with thy heart.

Desire His honour more than the health of thine own soul.

Take heed with all diligence to purge and cleanse thy mind with oft confession, and raise thy desire or lust from earthly things.

Resort to God every hour.

Be pitiful unto poor folk and help them to thy power, for there you shall greatly please God.

In prosperity be meek of heart, and in adversity patient.

And pray continually to God that you may do all that is His pleasure.

If by chance you fall into sin, despair not; and if you keep these precepts, the Holy Ghost will strengthen thee in all other things necessary, and this doing you shall be with Christ in Heaven, to whom be given laud, praise and honour everlasting.

(Signed) Adrian Fortescue

Chapter 4

ST. AFRA

d. 304

In her native city of Augsburg, Bavaria (located in southern West Germany), Afra was a well-known prostitute. Her three servants, Digna, Eunomia and Eutropia, were also well-known for their disorderly lives.

However, when the persecution of Diocletian threatened, St. Narcissus, the holy Bishop of Gerona, was driven from his see and for a time lodged in the home of Afra's mother, Hilaria. During his stay he converted not only the mother, but Afra and her servants as well.

Realizing the gravity and the number of her sins, Afra became a sincere penitent and wept bitterly for the pain her sins had caused her Redeemer. She did all she could to make amends for them by giving what she had to the poor and by spending time in fervent prayer and penance.

When the citizens of Augsburg noticed the conversion and Afra's new occupation of aiding the poor, she came under suspicion of being a Christian when the persecution of Diocletian reached the city. She was arrested and brought to trial before a judge named Gaius, who knew of her former life of sin. He ordered her to sacrifice to the gods, to which Afra replied, "I was a great sinner before God; but I will not add new crimes, nor do what you command me."

Gaius then revealed that he knew Afra had been a prostitute, and he promised that her paramours would return and make her wealthy if she would only sacrifice to the gods. This and other offers were all rejected. Threats of torture were dismissed with the words, "Let this, my body, which has been the instrument of so many sins, undergo every torment; but let my soul not be contaminated by sacrificing to demons."

Gaius passed the sentence of death by fire. Executioners seized Afra, carried her to an island in the river Lech, and tied her to a stake. The prayer that Afra offered just prior to her death concluded with

9

the words, "By this fire, which is about to burn my body, deliver my soul from everlasting flames." The executioners then heaped a pile of dry vine branches about her and set them on fire. While Afra was still praying, the smoke billowed up and suffocated her.

Standing on the opposite side of the river during the martyrdom were Afra's faithful servants, who had followed her in the ways of sin and later had joined their mistress in her conversion to the Faith. When the executioners left, the three women went to the island—and with the martyr's mother, Hilaria, and some priests, they carried the body to the family's sepulchre, which was located two miles from the city.

Fleury, a church historian, informs us that the sepulchres of the ancients were often buildings large enough to contain rooms. While Hilaria and her company were in the sepulchre preparing to entomb Afra's body, Gaius was informed of what was taking place. He immediately dispatched soldiers with an order to demand the mourners to sacrifice to the gods or face death. When the soldiers could not persuade the group to comply, they filled the sepulchre with dry wood, thorns and vine branches, set fire to them, secured the door and left. In this way St. Afra, her mother and the three servants all died of suffocation and merited the crown of martyrdom on the same day.

In writing about St. Afra, St. Alphonsus de Liguori relates that we are grateful to such respected church historians as Fleury, Orsi and Massini for preserving the details of the martyr's life. St. Alphonsus also writes that:

> Penitent sinners may receive great encouragement from the consideration of the fortitude communicated to this penitent by the Lord, which enabled her to suffer martyrdom of fire; and also from the consideration of the wisdom given to her, by which she answered the insidious arguments that were intended to pervert her.

St. Afra, St. Hilaria and their three sainted companions are inscribed in the *Roman Martyrology* under the date of August 12. It has been firmly established that St. Afra, who died in 304, was venerated from the earliest times. This fact is also proved by Venantius Fortunatus, Bishop of Poitiers, who mentions St. Afra in his poem dedicated to St. Martin, which was written in the sixth century.

The remains of St. Afra rest at Augsburg in the Church of Sts. Ulrich and Afra, where she continues to be venerated.

Chapter 5

STS. AGAPE, CHIONIA AND IRENE

d. 304

During the persecution that raged against the Church at the beginning of the fourth century, the citizens of Thessalonica (now northern Greece) were asked to prove their rejection of the Christian Faith by eating meat that had been sacrificed to the gods. One day when Dulcitius, the Governor, was hearing the charges against certain Christians, his secretary, Artemesius, began to read a report that had been submitted by a public informer. The document read as follows:

> The pensioner Cassander to Dulcitius, Governor of Macedonia, greeting. I send to Your Highness six Christian women and one man who have refused to eat meat sacrificed to the gods. Their names are Agape, Chionia, Irene, Casia, Philippa, Eutychia, and the man is called Agatho.

Unknown to the informer, he could have lodged another complaint against three of the women, who happened to be sisters: Agape, Chionia and Irene. According to a decree issued by Emperor Diocletian, it was an offense punishable by death to possess or retain any portion of the Sacred Scriptures. Even their parents were unaware that the three sisters had portions of the sacred books which they studied in secret whenever time permitted.

Dulcitius asked the six women and one man standing before him, "Why will you not eat of the meat offered to the gods, like other subjects?" To this and other persistent questions, the three sisters, as well as the others, repeatedly answered that they could not cooperate because they were Christians and that they would rather die than offend the true God.

Among other questions, there was one asked of all who were taken captive: "Have you books, papers, or writings relating to the religion of the impious Christians?" Agape and Chionia answered that they

11

did have these forbidden papers, which they considered to be a treasure of great value. The sentence of Dulcitius came swiftly and angrily: "I condemn Agape and Chionia to be burnt alive for having, out of malice and obstinacy, acted in contravention of the divine edicts of our lords, the emperors and Caesars."

Irene was sent back to prison, but after the martyrdom of her elder sisters she was again presented to Dulcitius, who ordered her to reveal the names of the persons who had encouraged her to hide the papers relating to the doctrines of Jesus Christ. Irene's only answer was that Almighty God had commanded them to love Him unto death and that she would prefer to be burned alive rather than surrender the Holy Scriptures and betray the interests of God.

After declaring that neither her parents nor the servants nor the neighbors knew of the hidden Scriptures, Irene was given a sentence more cruel than the one given to her sisters. For refusing to relinquish the sacred books which she loved, it was ordered that she be stripped and exposed in an immoral house. When she was miraculously protected from abuse, she was martyred. One source claims that she was burned at the stake; another that she died from an arrow that struck her throat.

Chapter 6

ST. AGATHA

d. 251

St. Agatha, a native of Sicily, is said to have been a person of extraordinary beauty who belonged to a noble and opulent family. These attributes attracted a man named Quintianus, the Roman governor of the district. Having made a vow of virginity at an early age, Agatha rejected his proposal of marriage and all the attempts he made to force her to accept him. Offended by her constant refusals, Quintianus had Agatha arrested in compliance with the Emperor's edict against Christians.

When St. Agatha continued to resist, Quintianus schemed to weaken her by placing her in the care of Aphrodisia, an evil woman whose house was known for immoral activities. Because of Agatha's gentle upbringing and her firm faith, it was thought best to place her in the company of Aphrodisia's daughters, who have been described as silly, conceited girls. They had no useful occupation, but rather spent their time in idleness or foolish conversation. They were careful not to say or do anything that would shock Agatha, hoping that if she could be induced to fail in small matters such as assuming behavior comparable to theirs, she would eventually consent to larger improprieties.

The reputation of Aphrodisia was concealed from St. Agatha, who was told that in consideration of her noble birth, she was being placed in the woman's care and would remain with her until Quintianus consulted the Emperor about her future.

During the month that she stayed with Aphrodisia and her daughters, Agatha continued her usual prayers and devotions. But when she learned of the scheme to weaken her resolution to remain a virgin so that she would consent to marriage with Quintianus, St. Agatha informed Aphrodisia that she would continue to resist all their temptations and would stand firm in her innocence.

13

After it was realized that the plan had failed, Agatha was returned to prison—and Quintianus' anger. When next she appeared before him, she again refused his advances. This so infuriated Quintianus that he ordered her to be tortured. When this also failed, he commanded that her breasts should be cut from her body. He added that on no account should she be given food or drink, nor should a surgeon tend her, but that she should be allowed to die in the agony of her wounds. During the night, while the Saint was enduring great pain and fever, St. Peter is said to have appeared in a great light to comfort her.

When the saintly virgin did not die as he expected, Quintianus had her rolled on hot coals which were mixed with broken pieces of pottery. During this torture an earthquake shook the city and produced extensive damage. The people immediately recognized this as a punishment from God for the cruelty with which the Saint was being treated.

Agatha was returned to prison, and after suffering torments because of her wounds, she offered her soul to God and expired. This took place in the year 251 in the city of Catania, Sicily. Because Agatha died on February 5, the Church observes her feast on that day.

The Saint's name is mentioned in the Canon of the Mass, and she is venerated in the Churches of both the Greek and Latin Rite.

Above: A painting of St. Agatha of Sicily, who was cruelly tortured in the third century by the Roman consul Quintianus when she refused to marry him. The rebuffed consul subjected her to unspeakable torture, including cutting off her breasts and having her rolled naked over hot coals. An earthquake which struck the city at this time was viewed by the people as punishment from God for the cruelty inflicted upon the Saint. *(Painting by Zurburan.)*

Following page: The precious reliquary of St. Agatha at Catania, Italy, which contains incorrupt relics of her body.

15

Chapter 7

ST. AGNES

d. 304 or 305

The name Agnes, meaning "chaste" or "pure" in Greek, seems appropriate for one who is regarded among the foremost of the virgin martyrs of the primitive Church. Not only is she one of the most popular Christian saints, but her name is also commemorated in the Canon of the Mass.

Born in the City of Rome, the young Saint had a brief life. St. Ambrose (d. 397) claims that Agnes was 12 years old at the time of her death, while St. Augustine (d. 430) states that she was 13.

Pope Damasus (d. 384) informs us that immediately after the promulgation of the Imperial Edict against the Christians, Agnes voluntarily declared herself a follower of Christ. Another source maintains that her riches and beauty excited the young noblemen of the first families of Rome, who became rivals for her hand in marriage.

When Agnes refused all of them because of her vow of chastity, one of the young men spitefully reported to the Governor that Agnes was a Christian. When a judge could not persuade her to marry nor to renounce her faith, he threatened her with confinement in a house of immorality and death by fire. Agnes calmly listened to his threats and quietly proclaimed her confidence that God would protect her body from defilement. Her only concern was the defense of her modesty, since she was later disrobed before the gaze of a heathen audience. Her flowing hair is said to have sufficiently concealed her nakedness.

St. Ambrose reported in the sixth century what took place when Agnes entered the house of sin:

> When her hair was loosed, God gave such length and thickness to her flowing tresses that they seemed to cover her completely; and when she entered the cell she found an angel of

17

the Lord there waiting for her, who surrounded her with a dazzling light, by reason of the glory of which none might touch or look upon her. The whole room shone like the dazzling sun of midday. As Agnes knelt in prayer, Our Lord appeared and gave her a snow-white robe. The Prefect Symphonianus' son, the prime mover in the prosecution, came with some young companions to offer insult to the maiden; but suddenly falling on his face he was struck dead, and his terrified companions fled, half-dead with pain and terror. At Agnes' prayer the youth was restored to life and converted to Christianity. The people cried out that she was a sorceress and had raised him by magic.

The Prefect was disposed to release her, but feared the people and the Emperor; so he went away and resigned his office to the Deputy-Prefect, Aspasius by name, who confined Agnes to prison.

The prison in which the Saint was kept can be visited in the crypt of the Roman church, Sant' Agnese in Agone, located across from the Piazza Navona. In the vaulted chamber of the crypt are frescoes which depict the angels who accompanied and watched over St. Agnes.

St. Ambrose continues:

The Deputy-Prefect, Aspasius, commanded a great fire to be lighted [in the Piazza Navona] before all the people and caused Agnes to be cast into it. Immediately, the flames divided into two, scorching the people on both sides, but leaving the Saint untouched. The people ascribed this marvel to witchcraft, and the air was loud with screams and cries of "Away with the witch!" Then Aspasius, impatient at the excitement of the people, bade the executioner plunge a sword into her throat. When Agnes heard the sentence she was transported with joy and went to the place of execution more cheerfully than others go to a wedding.

St. Ambrose tells us in his sermon *De Virginibus* of the year 377 that, "This child was holy beyond her years and courageous beyond human nature...She stood, prayed, and then bent her neck for the stroke..."

The Saint died in Rome in the year 304 or 305. Burial was in the cemetery, afterwards called by her name, beside the *Via Nomentana*. After the death of Agnes, those who prayed at her grave were constantly harassed and wounded by non-Christians.

Among those who visited the grave was the Saint's foster sister, St. Emerentiana, who was still a catechumen and had not yet been baptized. She was, however, baptized—not in water, but in her own blood—when she was stoned to death because of her faith. Her body was laid close to that of St. Agnes, who had died two days earlier.

Over this grave Constantia, the daughter of the Emperor Constantine, erected a basilica, *Sant' Agnes Fuori Le Mura* (St. Agnes Beyond the Walls). Below the main altar of this basilica is found a silver shrine given by Pope Paul V (1605-1621) which contains the relics of St. Agnes and those of her foster sister, St. Emerentiana.

Since the fourth century the Saint's feast day has been observed on January 21. On this day each year two white lambs are offered in her basilica during High Mass and are cared for until the time for shearing. Their wool is woven into the pallia given to archbishops throughout the Church as symbolic of the jurisdiction that ultimately derives from the Holy See. A pallium, a band measuring two inches wide and decorated with six purple crosses, is placed over the archbishop's head and worn about his shoulders, falling in the front and back in the shape of a letter Y. The archbishop may wear the pallium only on special occasions, and it is always buried with him. The investiture of the Pope with the pallium at his coronation is the most solemn part of the ceremony and is a symbol older than the wearing of the papal tiara.

Although some claim that the Saint was killed by a sword thrust into her throat, others maintain that she was beheaded. Supporting this latter claim is the fact that the *Sancta Sanctorum* at the Lateran is in possession of the head of the Saint, which was discovered in 1901 when Pope Leo XIII gave permission for the examination of the treasury after it had been closed for a number of years. According to Dr. Lapponi, an archaeologist, the dentition (arrangement of the teeth) of the skull shows conclusively that the skull belonged to a child of about 13 years. As the result of other studies, the relic was declared to be authentic. It was further observed that the body was found without a head when the relics of the Saint were examined in her church in 1605.

St. Agnes is commonly represented in art with a lamb and a palm, the lamb being originally suggested by the resemblance of the word *agnus* (lamb) to the name Agnes.

This statue, created by sculptor Ercole Ferrata in 1660, represents St. Agnes (d. c. 304) extending her arms in prayer, unharmed by the flames leaping up around her. She had been sentenced to death by fire for refusing to marry and renounce her faith. The Saint is among the foremost of the virgin martyrs of the early Church. (*The statue is located in S. Agnese Piazza Navona, Rome.*)

20

Chapter 8

ST. ALBAN

d. 209

Regarded as the first Christian martyr of Great Britain, Alban was a prominent citizen of Roman Verulamium, a place now known as St. Albans, in Hertfordshire. Although St. Alban was a pagan, he offered hospitality to a priest who was fleeing from the persecutors. The Venerable Bede (673-735) reports in his *Ecclesiastical History of the English Nation* that:

> This man [the priest] Alban observed to be engaged in continual prayer and watching day and night; when on a sudden the Divine grace shining on him, Alban began to imitate the example of faith and piety which was set before him, and being gradually instructed by his wholesome admonitions, Alban cast off the darkness of idolatry and became a Christian in all sincerity of heart.

The priest remained several days with Alban before his whereabouts were discovered and reported to the authorities. Soldiers were sent to apprehend him, but:

> ...when they came to the martyr's house, St. Alban immediately presented himself to the soldiers, instead of his guest and master, in the habit or long coat which the priest wore, and was led bound before the judge. It happened that the judge, at the time when Alban was carried before him, was standing at the altar and offering sacrifice to devils. When he saw Alban, being much enraged that he should thus, of his own accord, put himself into the hands of the soldiers and incur such danger in behalf of his guest, he commanded Alban to be dragged up to the images of the devils.

St. Alban was told that since he had chosen to conceal a "rebellious and sacrilegious person" rather than deliver him up to the soldiers, he was to undergo all the punishment that the priest would have endured. Alban professed his willingness to suffer for the priest and made a noble declaration of his Christian faith. In an attempt to win him over, the judge ordered Alban to offer sacrifice to the devils—but Alban replied that all who offer sacrifice to the images would receive the everlasting pains of Hell. The judge was angered at the words and ordered that Alban be scourged. However, when the tortures did not change Alban's firmness in the Faith, the judge ordered his death.

As St. Alban was being escorted to the place of execution, he came to a river which ran between the wall of the town and the arena where he was to be beheaded. Since St. Alban and his guards could not cross the bridge because of the people who had assembled there to accompany the Saint, Alban remained on the shore of the river and prayed. Immediately the water "dried up, and he perceived that the water had departed and made way for him to pass." On seeing this miracle the executioner threw down his sword, fell at St. Alban's feet, and moved by Divine inspiration, he asked to suffer with the Saint. Both the soldier and St. Alban were martyred on the twenty-second day of June in the year 209.

Venerable Bede reports that afterwards, "A church of wonderful workmanship, and suitable to his martyrdom, was erected, in which place there ceased not to this day the cure of sick persons and the frequent working of wonders." After the Norman Conquest in 1066, a great new church was started using bricks which the Romans had used in other buildings. Still later a monastery was built, and finally a city under the name of St. Albans, which is located approximately twenty miles north of London.

Pitkin Pictorials Ltd., London

The shrine of St. Alban (d. 209), the first Christian martyr of Britain. Converted from paganism after observing a priest at prayer, St. Alban was martyred because he provided refuge to the priest. On the way to his execution, St. Alban and his guards were prevented from crossing a bridge by an assembly of people. He prayed at the river's shore, and the water miraculously receded. The soldier appointed to be St. Alban's executioner was immediately converted and was executed with him.

Chapter 9

BL. ALBERT OF BERGAMO

d. 1279

Blessed Albert's virtuous parents were peasant farmers in the little town of Villa d'Ogna, near Bergamo, Italy. Albert began his prayerful life at an early age, being only seven when he began to practice penance and perform works of charity. At about the same time, he also began his laborious work in the fields. While performing his chores, he kept himself in continual recollection and made use of the sights and sounds of nature to raise his mind and heart to God.

When Albert came of age, his father suggested that he marry. In obedience to his father's wishes he married a young peasant girl, with whom he lived for many years in perfect harmony. After a time Albert's wife, who remained childless, began to imitate him in his pious exercises.

However, upon the death of her father-in-law, Albert's wife underwent a sudden change of disposition and from then on became a continual trial to her husband. She bitterly reproached and criticized him for spending time in prayer and for his generosity to the poor. Bl. Albert is said to have possessed an unalterable sweetness and to have been patient and silent while enduring his domestic difficulties. After some time his wife died, leaving him a widower.

Sometime after Albert was widowed, a group of powerful nobles seized his property. He left the neighborhood and settled at Cremona, where he again worked as a farmer, earning for himself the title of "the diligent laborer." There he performed various miracles, and gave to the poor all that he could spare from his meager wages.

Albert placed himself under the direction of the Dominican Fathers whose monastery was near his lodging and was accepted into the Dominican Third Order. From then on he devoted himself to the care of the sick and poor, visiting them and performing useful services to relieve their distress. He also kept a prayerful vigil during their final agony and saw to their burial.

After occupying himself in this manner for many years, Albert felt himself called to undertake the life of a pilgrim. He is known to have traveled to the Holy Land at least once, to have visited the sanctuaries and shrines of Spain, and to have journeyed to Rome on nine occasions. He remained recollected during his travels, and as Proctor relates, he "beguiled the monotony of the way by singing hymns or reciting psalms."

After traveling for several years, Albert settled once more in Cremona and resumed his work among the distressed, welcoming into his poor home those in extreme poverty and travelers who needed rest and lodging.

When Albert was about 70 years old, he became ill and asked for the Last Sacraments. When the priest delayed in coming, it is said that the Holy Eucharist was brought to him by a white dove, which then disappeared.

Bl. Albert died on May 7, 1279. Those who were preparing a grave for him in the cemetery found it impossible to penetrate the ground with their tools. For this reason it became necessary to return the remains to the church. There, on the very spot where he had so often prayed, was found a vault which had been mysteriously prepared to accept his body. The poor who had so often benefitted from his generosity attended the funeral service, which was conducted by the Bishop with the assistance of the Dominican Fathers.

The veneration for Bl. Albert which soon developed was approved by Pope Benedict XIV, who also gave permission for a Mass and Office to be celebrated in Albert's honor by members of the Dominican Order and by the clergy of the Dioceses of Bergamo and Cremona.

Bl. Albert (d. 1279), a farmer near Bergamo, Italy, began at the age of seven to practice penance and perform works of charity. In his adult life, he demonstrated exemplary patience in enduring bitter reproaches from his wife for the time he spent in prayer and for his generosity to the poor.

Bl. Albert in prayer. From childhood, he kept himself in continual recollection while performing his chores, using the sights and sounds of nature to raise his mind to God.

27

Above: Bl. Albert, "the diligent laborer," is represented in this insignia as he received the Holy Eucharist from a white dove. Following Albert's death, cemetery workers were unable to penetrate the ground with their tools. When they returned his remains to the church, they found that a vault had been mysteriously prepared to receive his body.

Right: A statue of Bl. Albert.

This painting shows Bl. Albert on his deathbed (his nakedness symbolizing his poverty). Angels watch as he is given Holy Communion by a beautiful white dove.

Chapter 10

BL. ALPAIS

d. 1211

Alpais was a peasant girl who was born into lowly circumstances at Cudot in the Diocese of Orleans, France. Because of her family's humble situation, she was obliged to work with her father in the fields until she was stricken by a disease which may have been leprosy. Her biographer, a Cistercian monk of Escharlis who knew her personally, assures us that Bl. Alpais was cured of the disease during a vision of Our Lady. Later, due to the effects of another illness, she lost the use of her limbs and was confined to bed.

It was soon noticed that Bl. Alpais subsisted entirely on the Holy Eucharist. This was confirmed by the Archbishop after a commission which he organized had examined and tested the authenticity of her fast. In fact, Bl. Alpais seems to be the earliest mystic of whom it is recorded on reliable evidence that she lived for years on the Blessed Eucharist alone.

Because of Bl. Alpais' Eucharistic fast and her reputation for holiness, the Archbishop had a church built next to her home at Cudot so that, by means of a window, the invalid could assist at religious services.

Pilgrims, prelates and nobles came to Alpais for advice; even Queen Adela, wife of Louis VII of France, visited her three times. In 1180 the Queen made a substantial donation to the canons of the church, "for love of Alpais."

The honor which had been bestowed on Bl. Alpais from the time of her death was approved by Pope Pius IX in 1874.

Bl. Alpais (d. 1211) was a French peasant girl who may have been the earliest mystic to have lived for years on the Blessed Eucharist alone. She is remembered for her ability to advise pilgrims, prelates, nobles and royalty. *(Illustration taken from la Chronique de Nüremberg.)*

The tomb of Bl. Alpais, located at Cudot, France. Because Bl. Alpais was an invalid, the Archbishop had a church built next to her home at Cudot so that she could assist at religious services.

Chapter 11

BL. AMADEUS IX

1435 - 1472

Amadeus was the son of Duke Louis I of Savoy (now southeastern France) and Anne of Cyprus; he was born at Thonon in 1435. His grandfather, Amadeus VIII, was elected antipope in 1438 under the title of Felix IV, but he later renounced his claim and withdrew into the monastery of Ripaille, where he died.

While still an infant, Amadeus was betrothed to Yolande, daughter of Charles VII of France. It was hoped that through this alliance, peace between Savoy and France would be assured. In 1451, when Amadeus was 16, the marriage took place. The union proved to be a happy one, but of the couple's four sons and two daughters, most died at an early age.

Bl. Amadeus was handsome, accomplished, and endowed with exceptional graces. Unfortunately, he was subject all his life to severe attacks of epilepsy, which at times completely prostrated and incapacitated him. Following these attacks he would tell his attendants, "Why concern yourselves? Humiliations give access to the Kingdom of God."

In spite of this ailment, Bl. Amadeus was extremely austere in his private life and never excused himself because of his delicate health. He began every day with private meditation. He assisted at Holy Mass and received the Sacraments more frequently than was customary.

With his wife and children, Amadeus lived a secluded and happy life in the Province of Brescia, which had been given to him as his portion. But when his father died in 1465, Amadeus was called upon to govern Savoy and Piedmont (now northwestern Italy). He proved to be a kind and just ruler. During his seven-year reign, he was successful in reducing bribery and in preventing the oppression of the poor by the rich. So solicitous was he of the poor, and so often did he champion their cause, that Duke Galeazzo of Milan once humorously remarked that, whereas in the rest of the world it was better to be rich than poor, in the Duchy of Savoy it was the beggars who were favored and the rich who were less favorably dealt with.

Amadeus could not bring himself to refuse alms to anyone and is known to frequently have exhausted the contents of his purse. He once removed his jewelled collar, broke it into pieces and distributed the fragments.

On another occasion an ambassador was boasting of the numerous packs of hounds and the different breeds of dogs that were kept by his master for various forms of hunting. Amadeus listened patiently, then led the ambassador to a terrace outside the palace where beggars were eating at tables that had been set up for them. "These are my packs and my hunting dogs," Amadeus remarked. "It is with the help of these poor people that I chase after virtue and hunt for the Kingdom of Heaven." The ambassador observed that some were idlers, hypocrites, and undeserving. To this Amadeus replied, "I would not judge them too severely lest God should judge me likewise and should withhold His blessing."

Amadeus abhorred blasphemy and would not retain in his service anyone who used profane language. He was liberal toward churches, paying their debt and contributing funds for their beautification. On the occasion of a visit to Rome, he made donations to nearly every church.

Through his wise administration Amadeus was able to pay the debts of his predecessors, and he provided dowries and lands for three of his sisters. Instead of his many charities being a strain on the treasury, through the grace of God the amount of treasury was actually increased.

Amadeus had a forgiving nature and bore malice to no one, even those who offended him. An example of this occurred when the Duke of Milan, Francis Sforza, died and his son Galeazzo, in his haste to reach Milan quickly from Dauphiny, passed through Savoy incognito and was arrested when he was not recognized: Amadeus rescued him, treated him with honor and provided an escort to assist him in reaching Milan. But in spite of this kindness, Galeazzo was ungrateful enough to attack Amadeus' troops. However, Amadeus brought the conflict to an end, gained Galeazzo's friendship and even gave him his sister Bona in marriage.

Again, when his brothers rebelled against him on more than one occasion, Amadeus always forgave them and made excuses for them.

When his epileptic seizures became more numerous and undermined his health, Amadeus resigned the government into the hands of his wife. When his subjects rose in revolt, Amadeus was imprisoned. He was freed by King Louis XI of France, who was his brother-in-law. A few years later, when he was only 37 years old, Amadeus knew his death was approaching when his affliction became extremely burdensome. To the sorrow of his subjects, he arranged for his burial in the Church of St. Eusebius of Vercelli and appointed his wife to serve as regent over the state and over his children.

Amadeus received the Sacraments and died on Easter Monday, March 30, 1472 after instructing his children to "Be just, love the poor, and the Lord will give peace to your lands."

Chapter 12

BL. ANGELA OF FOLIGNO

c. 1248 - 1309

Angela was born in the City of Foligno, Italy, where she derived all the benefits of being reared as a member of a prominent family. She was married to a man of substantial means and became the mother of several children. In her early life she was careless and worldly, and according to her own account, her life was not only pleasure-seeking and self-indulgent, but was also sinful. One source tells that, "Forgetful of her dignity and duties as wife and mother, she fell into sin and led a disorderly life."

Quite suddenly Angela experienced a complete transformation—a sudden, vivid conversion in which the life she had thought harmless, she now saw in its true perspective as having been sinful. As a result of this, she earnestly wanted to make reparation by doing penance and performing works of mercy. She took as her model St. Francis of Assisi, and became a tertiary in the Franciscan Third Order.

As a tertiary she continued her normal life in the world, but now spent more time in prayer and penance—more than that which was prescribed by the Rule. Then, her life became one of great sorrow when death claimed her husband and her mother. Finally, one by one, all her children died. Brother Arnold, a Friar Minor, who was her confessor, tells how cruelly she suffered as blow after blow fell upon her. Her conversion had been so complete, however, that despite her great sorrow, she accepted her trial with complete resignation to the will of God.

Soon after these losses, Angela began to experience visions. In one of these she was reminded that if she meant to be perfect, she must sell all that she had and follow St. Francis in his absolute poverty. As a result of this vision, she sold a castle that was very dear to her.

Although Angela experienced many visions and ecstasies, Brother

Arnold wrote that she was ever humble, so that the greater the ecstasy, the deeper was her humility. The details of her mystical experiences were dictated to Brother Arnold, who recorded them in
a book entitled *(Book of) Visions and Instructions,* which contains
70 chapters.

We are also told that Bl. Angela experienced the mystical marriage
with Our Lord and bore on her body the wounds of the stigmata.
Although Angela always remained a lay person, a number of her
fellow tertiaries—both men and women—looked to her for guidance.
These also received her dying prayer as they stood around her
deathbed.

Bl. Angela died on January 4, 1309. Her remains are found in
the Church of St. Francis at Foligno, where the many miracles worked
at her tomb prompted Pope Innocent XII to sanction the veneration
paid to her. Bl. Angela of Foligno is considered one of the Church's
great mystics.

Above: This painting illustrates the fact that Bl. Angela of Foligno (1248-1309) achieved great heights of holiness; here this Franciscan tertiary and mystic receives the Holy Eucharist from an angel.

Right: Again, Bl. Angela is portrayed in humble reception of the Blessed Sacrament, which is given to her by an angel. Her confessor wrote that even though Bl. Angela experienced many visions and ecstasies, she was always humble. She is an example for all who wish to make a spiritual conversion.

Left: Bl. Angela spent her early life in worldly, self-indulgent behavior, but a sudden illumination revealed to her the sinfulness of her former life. She spent the rest of her days in prayer and penance, suffering with complete resignation the deaths of her husband, mother and all of her children. *(Painting by Scaramucci Ugo.)* *Right:* A statue of Bl. Angela of Foligno. *(Statue by Corradi Don Pietro.)*

40

The penitential practices of Bl. Angela are suggested in this work, created in 1669.

Bl. Angela's mystical union with Our Lord is represented in the above work by Marcello Oddi. On her body the beata bore the wounds of the stigmata. *(Convento di S. Francesco, Foligno.)*

A seventeenth-century representation of Bl. Angela of Foligno, one of the Church's great mystics.

Chapter 13

BL. ANNA MARIA TAIGI

1769 - 1837

The life story of this beata is distinguished by serious family trials, painful physical ailments, an intense spiritual life and extraordinary mystical gifts.

Her father was Louis Giannetti, a pharmacist who kept a shop in Siena; her mother, Mary Santa Masil, was a good Catholic of lowly fortune. Anna Maria was born on May 29, 1769, and was baptized the same day in the Church of St. John the Baptist at Siena. Her early childhood was happily spent in the city made famous 400 years earlier by St. Catherine.

But when Anna Maria was six years old, her father's business failed. She and her impoverished parents moved to Rome, where they found a home in the crowded *dei Monti* quarter. In this area there also lived St. Benedict Joseph Labre, whom Anna Maria and her parents undoubtedly saw on many occasions. When St. Benedict Labre died, the future beata was among the many children who ran through the streets crying, "The Saint is dead! The Saint is dead!" Anna Maria's mother prepared the Saint's body for burial, since she was accustomed to performing such acts of charity.

While Anna Maria's parents worked as domestics, she attended the free school which had been founded by St. Lucia Filippini. In this school her education included lessons in cooking and sewing— occupations that would greatly benefit her in later life. She learned to read, but she never learned to write. Her formal schooling ended abruptly when she contracted smallpox, which left its traces on her face. After recovering from the disease, she remained at home to perform the household chores, which greatly relieved her working mother.

Anna Maria is known to have received the Sacrament of Penance at the age of seven. At eleven she was confirmed in the Basilica of St. John Lateran, and at thirteen she made her First Holy Communion in the parish church of St. Francis of Paola. Although the family performed many pious practices, which included reciting their prayers together both morning and night and often saying the Rosary, their household was not particularly happy. Neither father nor mother ever adjusted to the failure of their business and the harsh life they were forced to endure as a result. The mother, it seems, found her lot particularly hard to bear, while Anna's father "vented his ill humor on the child, ill-treating her without reason."

Anna Maria's childhood did not last long. At the age of thirteen she was employed in a shop run by two elderly ladies. Engaged in winding silk and cutting out dresses, she returned home in the evenings only to take up other chores, which included washing the clothes, cooking the meals and cleaning the house.

In 1787 Anna Maria joined both her parents at the Maccarani palace, where all three were employed as servants. The burdens of poverty were eased considerably for the little family, and it was here that the attractive child matured into a great beauty. Her mistress, Maria Serra, joined Anna Maria's mother in frequently praising the girl's charms—until eventually Anna Maria was spending more and more time before her mirror. According to the Decree of Beatification, "The beautiful young girl early encountered the dangers that imperil chastity." Her first biographer, Msgr. Luquet, a friend of the family, states only that there was an "occasion" which made Anna Maria realize certain dangers and made her resolve to "shelter her virtue by giving it the safeguard of a chaste marriage."

After three years spent in the service of Madame Serra, Anna Maria met her future husband. He was not a man of wealth, as her mother had hoped, but was a lowly porter by the name of Domenico Taigi, who served at the palace of Prince Chigi. He was a handsome young man of medium height and healthy constitution— but, according to the Decree of Beatification, "His manners were rough and uncultured and his temperament unamiable." He nevertheless won the heart of 20-year-old Anna Maria. The marriage was solemnized six weeks later on January 7, 1790 by the parish priest of St. Marcel in the Corso. Many years later, after Anna Maria's death, her daughter Sophia testified for the Process:

My mother told me that if she arranged everything within forty days, it was because she did not want to be forever at home "warming the seat," but to get on with it once she was assured of a good and honorable future; delay could only bring boredom and danger. She never regretted her action. My father was a rough character, and anyone but my mother would certainly have repented of marrying such a man; but although he tried her patience sorely, she was always glad that she had married him.

During the first year of her marriage, Anna Maria succumbed to a bit of human weakness. To please her husband she engaged in a measure of vanity and took to wearing jewelry and pretty clothes. Nevertheless, she was always modest and was always a credit and joy to her proud husband. After these early years she met Fr. Angelo Verandi, a Servite priest who was to lead her from the vanities of the world to a life of sanctity. Although many charges have been justly levelled at Domenico, he seems to have been moved by grace at the time of Anna Maria's call to a life of self-sacrifice and virtue. In his deposition, Domenico, himself, stated what took place at that time:

> The Servant of God, while yet in the flower of her youth, gave up, for the love of God, all the jewelry she used to wear—rings, earrings, necklaces and so on, and took to wearing the plainest possible clothes. She asked my permission for this, and I gave it to her with all my heart, for I saw she was entirely given to the love of God.

At the age of twenty-one, when Anna Maria was the mother of a new baby, she received Domenico's permission to be received as a tertiary in the Trinitarian Order. During the first year of this profession she was granted an extraordinary favor that was to endure for forty-seven years. This privilege took the form of a constant vision of a luminous disc, somewhat like a miniature sun, that maintained a position above and before her. Atop the upper rays was a large crown of interwoven thorns, with two lengthy thorns on either side curving downward so that they crossed each other under the solar disc, their points emerging on either side of the rays. In the center sat a beautiful woman with her face raised toward Heaven. In this vision Anna Maria saw things of the natural, moral and divine order and could see present or future events anywhere in the world, as well as the state of grace of living individuals and the fate of the departed. The Decree of Beatification speaks of it as "a prodigy unique in the annals of sanctity." In this sun she also received answers to difficult theological questions and observed scenes of the life of Christ.

In addition to this perpetual vision, Anna Maria was blessed with frequent ecstasies, and was able to read hearts, work miracles of healing and predict future events. She was also blessed with various visions and occasionally was visited by St. Joseph, to whom she was particularly devoted. He appeared not as an old man, but as a strong, handsome young man, a little older than the Blessed Mother.

Although favored with these spiritual privileges, Anna Maria nevertheless remained a diligent housewife and a mother who in twelve years bore seven children, three of whom died in infancy. Another preceded his mother in death. We are told that Anna Maria herself placed her children in their shrouds.

Domenico tells how Anna Maria was faithful both to the practice of virtue and the duties of her vocation:

> I can assert in very truth that from the beginning of our marriage she never refused my rights, but never asserted her own. She contracted no debts, because she always guided her outlay by her income. If any of us fell ill she lavished every attention on us, to the extent of omitting, when necessary, her Mass and her devotions. As for me, I have always thought in the past and say now that God took this excellent servant from me because I was not worthy to have her.

Considering Domenico's many faults and the trials inflicted on Anna Maria by her parents, who lived with the Taigi family, one can say that the beata's life was one lengthy martyrdom and an exercise of continual virtue. For a description of Domenico's faults and shortcomings we have the words of his daughter Sophie:

> My father was as pious and earnest a man as one could desire, but of such a fiery, exacting, haughty and wild temperament as to amaze one. On coming home he would whistle or knock, and we had immediately to dash to open the door at the risk of breaking our necks. In fact, twice my sister Mariuccia fell down through rushing too quickly to meet him, and on one of these occasions she had one of my baby daughters in her arms.

If everything was not just as he wanted it he came in furious,
and would go so far as to snatch hold of the tablecloth, where
the dinner was served, and throw everything to the four winds.
Everything had to be prepared to the tick, the soup hot in the
tureen, the chair in place. He was as exacting in the matter of
his clothes and of everything else.

To gain the children's obedience, Domenico frequently resorted
to using a stick. One day, in order to avoid a beating, one of the
children ran from the house. In a rage, Domenico tossed an armchair
through a window. He was also given to using foul language in front
of the children, but in the end Anna Maria succeeded in curing him
of that habit through her patience and gentleness.

In addition to his exacting nature, fits of anger, impatience and
coarse manners, Domenico was also jealous and protective of his
wife. Domenico himself stated, "If I saw anyone annoying her I
saw to it that it cost him dearly." An example of this was the time
when Anna Maria, who was then pregnant, was going to church
in the company of her husband. It was a great feastday with many
people attending. A soldier, whose duty it was to keep order, nudged
Anna Maria into place. Domenico's temper was immediately aroused.
He attacked the soldier, verbally abused him, took away his carbine
and began to beat him. Witnesses succeeded in separating the two
before the soldier was seriously injured.

Domenico's temper was likewise provoked by women whose wag-
ging tongues spoke ill of his wife. He relates that:

> Although she was at pains to do good to all and sundry, there
> were people with whispering tongues who gave her no rest,
> whether it was because they were jealous at seeing so many per-
> sons of distinction at our house, or because the devil induced
> them to beset her. But I could not be with her everywhere. More-
> over, I saw that the Servant of God was pained when I took
> a hand in these matters, so in the end I said to her: "Do what
> you like and as you like; if you wish people to throw stones
> at you and to suffer thus at their hands, you are free to do so."

But there were times when Domenico could not restrain himself
against those who spoke against his wife. Once when he heard that
someone had referred to his wife by saying, "That sorceress has just
passed," he:

made a violent complaint to the woman's husband, and told
him that if he did not succeed in making his wife control her
tongue he would cut it out. The scatter-tongue, on coming home,
was so beaten by her husband that she had to stay in bed for
several days...Finally she [Anna Maria] paid a visit to the
woman, brought her some delicacies, prayed for her cure and
obtained it.

Domenico also told of a woman who "had the hardihood to cal-
umniate my wife's honor. I had the wretch put in prison, but my
wife was grieved about it and did all she could to obtain her release."

In spite of all her husband's faults, Anna Maria was devoted to
him—and there were times of gentleness and peace. Domenico again
praises his wife:

> I wish to say this, for the glory of God, that I lived for forty-
> eight years or so with this saintly soul and never did I hear from
> her a word of impatience or discord. We lived in a perpetual
> peace as of Paradise. I used to go home often dead tired and
> a little distraught after my day's work and difficulties with my
> employers, and she would restore my serenity of mind.

Besides being ever alert to her husband's changing moods, the
beata had in her household other difficult personalities—her own
parents. With Domenico always on the verge of resorting to anger,
Anna Maria's irritable mother apparently found pleasure in provok-
ing him. Anna Maria is said to have gone from one to the other
recommending patience. Anna Maria's mother became even more
difficult as she grew older. She was frequently impatient, but nevertheless, Anna Maria did all she could for her and watched over her
night and day when she became ill. When she died at the age of
seventy-three, her last moments were spent in the arms of her devoted
daughter.

Louis Giannetti, Anna Maria's father, was likewise difficult. After
Madame Serra died, Louis lost his position as servant and squandered his small pension roaming Italy. When this was gone he lived
at his daughter's expense—while refusing to enter her home. Anna
Maria found lodging for him and a position as a porter at an orphanage. When poor health made it impossible for her father to
work, Anna Maria somehow found ways to satisfy his needs. He
seems to have been disagreeable and to have made a practice of

complaining. Frequently in a bad temper, he was often found sitting on the stairs of his daughter's home. Since he refused to enter the house, Anna Maria joined him on the stairs to wash him, comb his hair, mend his clothes and feed him.

"My father-in-law was smitten with a horrible leprosy," Domenico wrote, but with all the care Anna Maria gave him in cleansing the repulsive sores and performing the other services for him, he was never known to have thanked her. She prepared her father for death and obtained the Last Sacraments for him. Domenico observed that "One would think that God gave the Servant of God such parents simply to put her great virtue to a keener test."

Because of Anna Maria's infused knowledge and high degree of sanctity, she was frequently consulted by distinguished persons, including Pope Leo XII, Pope Gregory XVI, Napoleon's mother, Cardinal Fesch and Sts. Vincent Pallotti, Gaspar del Bufalo and Mary Euphrasia Pelletier. Many, too, were the simple folk who wanted advice from her on temporal and spiritual matters or who wanted to ask for Anna Maria's prayers for a cure or a favor. But Anna Maria always knew where her first duties lay. Domenico noted:

> Sometimes, on coming home to change my clothes, I found the house full of people. Instantly my wife left everybody, lords and prelates, and hurried to receive me, to brush me down and to wait on me, with the greatest charm for me and the greatest satisfaction to herself. You could see that what she did, she did with all her heart—down to settling my shoe laces.

Throughout Anna Maria's life, difficulties seem to have constantly increased in number. When her son Camillo married, he brought his bride to live with him in his parents' already-crowded home, staying for two years. As if this were not enough, it is said that the daughter-in-law "was a difficult character, because she wanted to be the mistress." With her usual tact and charity, Anna Maria was successful in reminding the young bride of her proper position in the household.

Somehow Anna Maria maintained a schedule of prayer in spite of the clash of personalities, the overcrowded house, her many household responsibilities and the almost steady stream of visitors to her home. There were family prayers in the morning; after supper there was the recitation of the Rosary, the reading from the life of the

Saint of the day, and the singing of hymns. On Sundays the whole family attended Holy Mass, then the girls went with their mother to the hospital to perform acts of charity.

Anna Maria was also careful that her children received instructions in their faith and that they behaved properly. When it was necessary, her children were dutifully reprimanded. Her daughter Sophie related that "Mamma loved us all tenderly and with an equal love that had no favorites. She used the stick, if necessary, but in moderation, and preferred to make us go without our dinner or to put us on dry bread."

Anna Maria also taught her children the value of keeping busy. Sophie reported that "She herself was never idle a minute; she was always at work. She used to say: 'Laziness is the mother of all the vices.'" If Anna Maria taught the value of industry, she likewise gave a good example in this regard and maintained a busy needle. She made her husband's trousers and coats, and when he was unemployed she supported the family by making bodices, petticoats, half-boots and socks. She regularly worked from two to three hours after midnight; then, after only two hours sleep, she was up for early Mass and Communion. We are told that when illness forced her to stay in bed she set herself to mending linen, and never remained idle.

When the children were older, there were other problems. For a brief time Anna Maria's son Alessandro was imprisoned, which caused the beata great heartache. Later, when he married, he and his wife—who came from a poor family—found great difficulty in meeting their financial obligations. Anna Maria gently recommended employment for her daughter-in-law who, having little, nevertheless wanted to be maintained in a gentle lifestyle. In the end the beata taught both her daughters-in-law how to be thrifty and useful.

Anna Maria's younger daughter, Mariuccia, never married; and although in her youth she was reportedly vain and lazy, she died with a reputation for holiness, having survived her mother by forty-eight years.

Sophie was her mother's joy. She married well and became the mother of six children. When Sophie was widowed, Anna Maria welcomed her and her children into her household. Sophie died thirty years after her mother and was buried at her side in the Church of St. Chrysogonus.

To the troubles inflicted on Anna Maria by members of her family and the burden of her impoverished state, she added penances and mortifications. We are told that "She was self-denying, especially on Fridays," but she likewise fasted on Saturdays and on Wednesdays in honor of St. Joseph. Her portion of food was always meager, and she was inclined to an almost continual thirst, which she refused to satisfy completely. Domenico observed that she never drank water between meals, even in the heat of summertime, and that at dinner she drank only a few sips at a time so as to mortify her thirst. Additionally, Anna Maria wore articles of penance and suffered from several physical maladies including asthma, almost continual headaches, chronic rheumatic troubles, a hernia, and pains in the ears so fierce that the beata frequently wrapped a band around her head. She also had sharp pains in her eyes, which were particularly sensitive to light. Eventually she lost the sight of one eye, and in her last years she was all but blind in the other.

We learn of the beata's interior life from Cardinal Pedicini, as well as from Msgr. Natali and from her director of thirty years, Father Philip-Louis of St. Nicholas, a Discalced Carmelite. In addition to the sustaining vision of the miraculous sun, we are told that frequently, while she was engaged in simple household chores, Anna Maria would be seized by an ecstasy or a vision of Our Lord, and she was known to have occasionally levitated. She recognized souls in a state of grace by the sweet fragrance of their souls, and upon entering a church she knew immediately at which altar the Blessed Sacrament was reserved. She is known to have cured many by virtue of a prayer and the Sign of the Cross.

Often, at the moment of Communion, Anna Maria saw the Host come to life. Once she saw Jesus in the form of a child lying upon the petals of a white lily. He spoke softly to her: "I am the flower of the fields and the lily of the valley. In this crowd of people that you see in the church there are scarcely two souls truly sincere in their love. The others are equally ready to come to church or to go to the theater."

Frequently demons assaulted Anna Maria in ways that are reminiscent of those attacks experienced by the Curé of Ars. They often appeared in horrible forms and frequently disturbed her prayers by suggesting unclean imaginings and doubts against the Faith. The remedy used by the beata against the devils was the same as that recommended by St. Teresa of Avila—holy water.

Anna Maria's married life lasted forty-eight years. At the age of sixty-eight, on October 26, 1836, the beata took to her bed, never to leave it. For seven months she suffered an increase in her bodily ailments, yet we are told that she preserved a miraculous peace that never left her. After a vision of Our Lord, and after delivering a message to each of her children, she thanked Domenico for the care he had taken of her. Supported by the prayers of those around her and by a last absolution, Anna Maria died on June 9, 1837.

After a plaster cast had been made of her face, the body was placed in a leaden coffin and was buried in a cemetery on the outskirts of Rome. When Anna Maria's popularity became widespread and miracles were occurring through her intercession, her body was removed to the city in 1855, eighteen years after burial. Discovered incorrupt, it was still intact three years later when it was placed in the Basilica of San Chrysogono. The body is no longer incorrupt, but the bones are well arranged and enclosed in a representative figure clothed in the habit of a Trinitarian tertiary. This is seen in a glass-sided reliquary beneath an altar of the basilica. Also found there is a small museum containing articles the beata used during her life.

Among those who testified during the Process of Beatification was her husband, Domenico, who survived Anna Maria by sixteen years. The ninety-two-year-old Domenico gave his wife a glowing tribute, as did two daughters who gave evidence of their mother's heroic virtues.

Anna Maria was beatified on May 30, 1920 by Pope Benedict XV, who later designated her a special protectress of mothers.

A painting of Bl. Anna Maria Taigi (1769-1837), who for 47 years was granted the extraordinary favor of the constant vision of a luminous disc (*upper left*), in which a beautiful woman sat with her face raised toward Heaven. The vision revealed to the beata past, present and future events. She saw in the vision information of the natural, moral and divine orders, as well as the state of grace of living individuals and the fate of the departed.

The figure pictured above, encased in glass, contains Bl. Anna Maria Taigi's relics. It is located in the Basilica of San Chrysogono in Rome. Hardships she endured included a particularly difficult husband, an irritable mother, an ill-tempered father and two daughters-in-law who were overbearing and demanding. Bl. Anna Maria received numerous supernatural gifts, including the power to cure by prayer and the Sign of the Cross. She also levitated. Sometimes she was attacked by demons. She died in 1837 and was designated by Pope Benedict XV in 1920 to be a special protectress of mothers.

Chapter 14

ST. ANNE LYNE

1569 - 1601

It is the opinion of some, that had it not been for the close association that existed in Elizabethan England between the persecuted lay people and their hunted priests, the Catholic Church in England might have disappeared altogether. The government of the time realized this, and imposed the death penalty, not only on priests who were discovered, but also on every person convicted of willingly aiding, housing or maintaining them. The priests were undoubtedly heroic in remaining in England to perform their ministry, but also heroic were those people who secretly opened their homes to gatherings of Catholics for the celebration of Mass and the administration of the Sacraments. Many Catholic housewives opened their doors for these secret meetings, including St. Margaret Clitherow and St. Anne Lyne (also spelled Line).

Born in the town of Dunmow in the county of Essex a little before 1570, Anne Heigham was the daughter of wealthy Calvinist parents. When Anne and her brother reached their teens, they announced their intention of becoming Catholics, in direct opposition to the wishes of their parents. As a result, both were disinherited, disowned, and were made to leave the house.

Even though she was denied a dowry, Anne was happily married to a fervent Catholic, Roger Lyne. He, too, had lost a considerable fortune, but for a different reason—that of refusing to obey the authorities by not giving the slightest appearance of conforming to the Protestant church. Roger once said: "If I must desert either the world or God, I will desert the world, for it is good to cling to God." Shortly after his marriage, Roger was apprehended for attending Mass. Eventually released, he was permitted to go into exile in Flanders, where he died in 1594.

Anne did not follow her husband into exile, but continued the dangerous activity of harboring priests and permitting services to be secretly conducted in her home. Eventually Fr. John Gerard established a house of refuge in London for priests and other hunted Catholics. When he was thinking of finding someone to run the guest house, Anne came immediately to his mind: "I could think of no better person than Anne to take charge of it. She managed the finances, did the housekeeping, looked after the guests and dealt with strangers."

Fr. Gerard was arrested away from the guest house and was imprisoned in the Tower, but he made his escape at a time when the authorities were beginning to suspect Anne's unlawful activities. She quickly moved elsewhere and made her house a rallying point for neighboring Catholics.

On the feast of Candlemas, 1601, as Holy Mass was about to be celebrated in Anne's apartments by Fr. Francis Page, S.J., priest-catchers approached her house for an inspection. Immediately the priest unvested and mingled with the others; but when the authorities broke into the house, the altar prepared for the ceremony was all the evidence needed for Anne's arrest. She was indicted for harboring priests and was tried at the Old Bailey on February 26, 1601. Having been convicted of the charge, she was brought the next day to the gallows at Tyburn in London.

In the manuscript of the Duke of Rutland we read:

> The said Mrs. Lyne, carried next day to her execution...being further urged among other things by the minister that she had been a common receiver of many priests, she answered, "Where I have received one, I would to God that I had been able to receive a thousand." She behaved herself most meekly, patiently and virtuously to her last breath.

After kissing the gallows, reciting a few private prayers and blessing herself with the Sign of the Cross, she was hanged.

Two priests were executed along with St. Anne: Fr. Mark Barkworth, O.S.B. and her confessor, Fr. Roger Filcock, S.J.

Anne Lyne was canonized by Pope Paul VI in 1970 as one of the Forty Martyrs of England and Wales.

Chapter 15

BL. ANTHONY MANZI, THE PILGRIM

c. 1237 - 1267

Bl. Anthony was a native of Padua and belonged to a distinguished and wealthy family. As a child he was pious and practiced many Christian virtues. When Anthony was a young man his father died, leaving a considerable amount of money in the care of his only son. Anthony's zeal for the poor took precedence over his better judgment, and he promptly distributed the wealth among the needy, keeping nothing for himself or his two sisters.

Ridicule was heaped on Anthony's head as soon as his two sisters learned of his charity. Other members of his family, as well as his fellow citizens, reviled him in the streets and subjected him to all manner of indignities. Eventually Anthony assumed the clothing of a pilgrim, left his home town, and wandered about the countryside. During his travels he found a sick and saintly old priest, whom he tended and served for three years.

Upon the death of the priest Anthony resumed his wanderings and visited many shrines and holy places, among them Rome, Loreto, Compostela, Cologne and Jerusalem. When he returned home he received the same ridicule and abuse he had known before his departure. Even his two sisters, who had become nuns, were still mindful of the disgrace and suffering they had endured from their sudden impoverishment many years before.

Throughout his life Anthony fasted, took severe disciplines and wore a rough hair shirt. He always slept on the bare ground with a stone for his pillow. The colonnade of a church outside the walls of Padua served Anthony as a shelter until his death.

Soon miracles were worked at his grave, and the Paduans who had scorned him during his lifetime petitioned the Pope for Anthony's canonization. This, however, was denied when the Pope replied that it was enough for the City of Padua to have one St. Anthony, especially since the great St. Anthony, the Franciscan, had died a mere 36 years earlier. For this reason Anthony Manzi remains a beatus.

Chapter 16

BL. ANTHONY PRIMALDI

d. 1480

The city of Otranto in southern Italy was overrun in the year 1480 by the Turks, who rounded up a large group of the city's inhabitants and defenders and ruthlessly killed them. Archbishop Stephen Pendinelli was selected for a more cruel and painful death, being sawed into pieces by his heathen captors. When the Turks decided to torment the rest of the population they sacked homes, carried off the women and led approximately 800 men into a valley near the town. There the Turks offered the men the restoration of their liberty, their wives and their goods if they would renounce the Christian Faith and become Moslems.

The leader of the men was Anthony Primaldi, a shoemaker who was well-known in the city as an honest workman, an honorable citizen and a good Christian. Acting as spokesman, Anthony replied that they believed that Jesus Christ was the true Son of God and that they refused to renounce their faith in Him. The Turkish general threatened them with torture and promised them a painful death if they did not renounce Jesus and acknowledge the Moslem faith.

Some of the men began to weaken under the threats, considering, too, that the fate of their families might depend on how they would choose. But Anthony loudly addressed them: "We have fought for our city and for our lives. Now we must fight for our souls and for Jesus Christ. He died for us; we must die for Him." Anthony's appeal strengthened the men, who were then ordered to be beheaded.

After witnessing the bravery of Bl. Anthony, who was the first to die, all the other men likewise met their death while professing their faith. Their bodies were left unburied in the valley for twelve months while the Turks occupied the country, but when Otranto was retaken by Alfonso, Duke of Calabria, the Apostolic Nuncio, Bl. Angelo Carletti, ordered that some of the relics be transported to the cathedral.

In 1539 evidence was gathered from those who had escaped the massacre. One account of the Otranto martyrdoms reads:

> The witness replied that he was taken prisoner by one of the Turks and was led to a place outside the city called San Joanne de la Minerva, where about seventy men had been taken, bound, for execution. This was to frighten the witness, who was then only a boy; and one of the captain's servants said to him, "Be glad that you are not a man yet, for our lord would do the same to you." And the witness saw these men put to the sword on the spot, and killed with great cruelty...and there was one among them, their leader, Master Primaldi, a shoemaker, who exhorted and encouraged them all by his words, to accept their suffering and death for the love of our Lord Jesus Christ.

The veneration paid to the martyrs, and Bl. Anthony Primaldi in particular, was approved by Pope Clement XIV in 1771.

Chapter 17

BL. ANTONIA MESINA

1919 - 1935

Nestled in the mountainous interior of Sardinia is the little city of Orgosolo, which became the birthplace of Antonia Mesina on June 21, 1919. Her father, Agostino Mesina, who is described as being handsome, tall and lean, was a corporal in the cavalry whose assignment was to guard the rural areas around the community of Orgosolo. Antonia's mother, Grazia Raubanu, was noted for her great piety and her appreciation of her daughter Antonia, whom she frequently called "the flower of my life." There were ten children in the family, Antonia being the second-born.

Around the time of her birth, a disease known familiarly as the Spanish Fever was claiming the lives of many children. It became the practice during the epidemic for children to be confirmed at an early age. For this reason Antonia was confirmed shortly after her Baptism.

During her infancy and early childhood, Antonia was like all children, being lively and playful, as well as obedient and affectionate. When she was old enough to attend school she was described as being well-liked by both her teachers and the students. Her instructors also stated that Antonia was well-behaved, precise and studious. In addition to being punctual for class, she loved the duties she was asked to perform, and she exhibited a commendable spirit of sacrifice in bending to the wishes and welfare of her classmates.

Antonia received her First Communion at the age of seven, and at the age of ten she joined an organization for young people known as the Catholic Action. She was proud to be a member and encouraged many to join the group, saying that to belong was a beautiful experience and that it "helps one to be good."

It was during Antonia's school years that her mother developed a heart condition. Unable to strain herself or lift anything heavy,

Grazia found it necessary to depend almost entirely upon the help of the young Antonia, who was forced to leave school after attending elementary classes for only four years.

Taking over much of the household chores, Antonia helped her mother with the cooking, the care of the children, the cleaning and marketing. The washing of clothes and the carrying of water into the house also fell to her charge; these and her other responsibilities she performed willingly and diligently, as though she were much older. It was also noted that she was always ready to renounce her personal pleasures in favor of the needs of the family.

According to the testimony of family members and those who knew her, Antonia performed all her chores joyfully, and serenely accepted the family's modest economic condition and the hard work and sacrifice this entailed. She was also affectionate and tender with the other children in the family, and she was submissive and obedient to her parents. Her mother was proud to claim that Antonia "never once went against me."

One of Antonia's tasks was the weekly baking of bread. It was her custom to grind the grain, sift it, prepare the dough and gather wood for the baking.

On May 17, 1935, when Antonia was 16 years old, she asked her friend Annedda Castangia to accompany her into the forest while she gathered wood for the oven. While the two girls were strolling along the path toward the woods, Antonia asked Annedda if she would like to become a member of the Catholic Action. When Annedda said that she could not join because of the cost, Antonia encouraged her to join the group by saying that there were no expenses and that there were many spiritual benefits to be gained from the good works they performed and the catechetical instruction they received.

In a deposition, Annedda reported that she could remember details of what next happened as though she had just witnessed them. After gathering a sufficient amount of wood, the girls were preparing to return home when they noticed a teenaged boy along the path. Annedda recognized him as a student from her school, but since he turned onto a different path, the girls thought no more of him. In a few moments Annedda heard Antonia scream desperately for help. The youth had sneaked up behind Antonia, grabbed her by the shoulders and was attempting to force her to the ground. Annedda tells that Antonia broke away twice, but she was caught a third time and knocked down. The would-be rapist then grabbed a rock and struck Antonia repeatedly on the face and head. Mortally wounded, Antonia continued to resist.

Annedda screamed for help and ran to the nearest house to report what was taking place. The captain of the police was hastily summoned and he, together with other citizens, quickly rode into the woods on horseback. There they found the bloody and brutally wounded body of the 16-year-old Antonia. Her face was horribly disfigured from the fierce beating and was hardly recognizable as the formerly beautiful face of the virtuous little housekeeper they had always admired. After an autopsy, it was determined that Antonia's body had not been sinfully violated. Like Maria Goretti, Antonia had died a martyr of holy purity.

Antonia's companion identified the assassin; he was captured, tried and condemned to death.

During the Process for her beatification, Antonia's remains were exhumed from the local cemetery. A grand procession of the townspeople, led by the bishop and several priests, accompanied the relics to the Church of the Holy Saviour, where they now recline in a black marble tomb. Both the tomb and the memorial stone that marks the place of martyrdom are frequently visited by Antonia's devotees.

Antonia Mesina was beatified on Sunday, October 4, 1987 by Pope John Paul II. Also beatified during the same ceremony were Blessed Marcel Callo and Blessed Pierina Morosini—all three being twentieth-century laymen and martyrs.

Bl. Antonia Mesina (1919-1935), like St. Maria Goretti, died a martyr of holy purity.

Photographs of Bl. Antonia's mother and father. The Italian maiden was always submissive and obedient to her parents. She left school after only four years to take over the household chores for her mother, who had developed a heart condition. When Antonia was 16 years old, she and a friend, Annedda Castangia, were gathering wood in a forest when Antonia was brutally murdered by a would-be rapist.

Antonia Mesina was beatified in 1987.

Above: Annedda Castangia tells how her friend Antonia Mesina was grabbed from behind by her attacker.
Left: Francesco Coco, the judge at the trial of Bl. Antonia's murderer. The assassin was sentenced to death for the crime.

Chapter 18

ST. ARMOGASTES

d. 455

When Genseric, King of the Vandals, renounced the Catholic Faith which he had practiced from childhood, he set in motion a persecution against his subjects and those in his household who maintained allegiance to the Church.

Genseric's son, Theodoric, had in his service Lord Armogastes, who was a loyal Christian. When Armogastes refused to submit, he was promptly stripped of his honors and the dignities of the court. He was also cruelly tortured. During his ordeal cords were bound around his head and legs, but these are said to have broken of their own accord when Armogastes made the Sign of the Cross. This happened several times, even though stouter cords were used each time. Finally he was suspended by one foot with his head hanging down, but he still refused to deny his faith.

Theodoric, who was as vindictive as his father, then considered putting Armogastes to death, but the Arian priests persuaded him to abandon the plan since the Christians would then have reason to honor Armogastes as a martyr. Instead, Armogastes was banished to Byzacena to work in the mines. To further humiliate this noble lord, who had enjoyed the honors and privileges of the court, he was sent to Carthage, where he was ordered to mind cattle.

Armogastes considered it an honor to be thus employed while remaining true to his faith. After a time, when Armogastes realized that his end was near, he prepared himself by penance and prayer to meet his Redeemer. He instructed a devout Christian named Felix concerning his place of burial. Armogastes died during the year 455, on the day he had predicted.

Chapter 19

ST. ARTHELAIS

d. 570

There lived in Constantinople during the reign of the Emperor Justinian a beautiful and virtuous girl named Arthelais, the daughter of the pro-consul Lucius and his wife, Anthusa. Many young men proposed marriage, but the Emperor, on learning of Arthelais' extraordinary beauty and grace, sent messengers to her father requesting that the girl be turned over to him. Completely shocked by the request, the family decided that the only way to avoid dishonor was to escape from the Emperor's jurisdiction. Secret arrangements were made for Arthelais to journey to her uncle, Narses Patricius, in the City of Benevento.

Her father escorted her as far as Buda in Dalmatia, where he left her to complete the journey under the escort of three trusted servants. Hardly had the father left them when they were attacked by robbers. Arthelais was seized while the servants panicked and made their escape. After being held for three days, Arthelais was miraculously released and rejoined her escort. The vengeance of God is said to have fallen upon her captors.

Arthelais and her companions crossed the sea in safety, traveled from Sipontum to Narses, and then to Lucera, and finally arrived at Benevento, where her uncle was expecting her. From the Golden Gate of the city, Arthelais walked barefoot to the Church of Our Lady to offer her thanksgiving for her release and her safe arrival at her destination.

Arthelais then gave herself over to mortification and fasting.

At the age of 16 Arthelais died as the result of an intense fever and was buried in the Church of St. Luke. Unfortunately, three centuries ago St. Arthelais' church in Benevento was destroyed; it has never been rebuilt. Tragically lost were her relics and artistic representations.

Chapter 20

STS. AURELIUS AND NATALIA

d. 852

During the eighth century, when Spain first came under Mohammedan domination, the Christians were treated with tolerance, provided they did not abuse the Law of Mohammed or attempt to make converts from Islam. But during the ninth century, when the independent emirate at Cordova was established and the Emirs Abd-er-Rahman II and Mohammed I came into power, a vigorous persecution was directed toward all Spanish Catholics. One of the first to suffer was Aurelius, the son of a Moor and a Spanish woman who were both people of distinction. When both parents died during the childhood of Aurelius, he was placed in the care of his mother's sister, who educated him in the Catholic Faith.

When Aurelius reached maturity, there was some cowardice in his personality, since he conformed outwardly to Islam as far as his conscience would allow—but practiced the True Religion in secret. Despite this weakness, he is credited with converting his half-Moorish wife to the Faith. Known as Sabigotho, she received the name of Natalia at her Baptism.

The turning point in Aurelius' life occurred one day when he saw a Christian merchant named John being publicly ridiculed and scourged in the public square. John was afterward dragged through the city for having spoken of the falseness of the Mohammedan religion. Feeling compunction for his cowardice in hiding his own faith, Aurelius vowed to make a public confession of his beliefs.

However, he was concerned about what would happen to his wife and two children. In discussing the matter with his wife, he learned that she, too, wanted to make a confession of her faith. Together the two Catholics consulted the imprisoned St. Eulogius, Archbishop of Toledo (who was to face martyrdom in 859). St. Eulogius advised them that their profession of faith would probably result in their

71

martyrdom, and that, as a precaution, they should make provisions for their children's material and spiritual welfare by entrusting the two girls to Christian people.

Through the grace of God, St. Aurelius thoroughly overcame his former cowardice. He and his wife began fearlessly to practice their faith and live a life of prayer and mortification. Aurelius even opened his home to fellow Christians, who joined the couple in pious practices and attendance at Holy Mass.

It was during one of these services that Aurelius, Natalia and their companions were arrested. Charged by the magistrate with being apostates from Islam, Aurelius, with his wife and companions, went heroically to the place of execution, where they were all beheaded. Their martyrdom took place on July 27, 852.

St. Eulogius, the Archbishop who advised Aurelius and Natalia, had ministered to other Christians in prison, fortifying many who were condemned. He also wrote accounts of their lives, sufferings and deaths, thus leaving stories of many saints, including Sts. Aurelius and Natalia.

Chapter 21

BL. BARTOLO LONGO

1841 - 1926

When Bartolo Longo was being "ordained" a priest in the church of Satan, the walls shook with thunder, while cries of blasphemy from disembodied spirits were heard throughout the building. Bartolo was so frightened that he fainted, and for some days afterward, his mind was severely affected. His health also suffered, and he was to experience poor eyesight and digestive problems for the rest of his life.

How is it that this former priest of Satan became a virtuous man who was honored in St. Peter's Basilica by Pope John Paul II?

Bartolo Longo was born in Latiano, Italy on February 11, 1841 of a good Catholic family and received his early training in the Piarist school of Francavill Fontana. Not unlike many who later turn to cults and satanism, Bartolo continued the practice of his faith until he began his college studies. It was at the University of Naples, while studying for a law degree, that he was introduced to members of a satanic sect.

It was a time of national revolution for the unification of all Italy. The era was characterized by anticlericalism and opposition to the teachings and authority of the Pope. Influenced by this political and antireligious atmosphere, and being indoctrinated by his evil friends, Bartolo joined the satanic sect and soon aspired to the satanic priesthood. After a long preparation of studies, fastings and mortifications, he was "ordained" a priest by a bishop of the sect. Despite Bartolo's horrible experiences during ordination and the physical ailments he suffered as a result, it is said that "...he continued for some time to exercise the office of satanic priesthood by preaching, by officiating at the rites, and by publicly ridiculing the church, its priests and all matters relating to the Catholic religion."

It might be credited to the fervent prayers of the Longo family

73

that Bartolo experienced a conversion. Bad companions had brought him to Satan; a good friend brought him back to God. Vicente Pepe, a citizen of his hometown, was at the time living and teaching near Naples. With prayers, care and love, this good friend brought Bartolo back to the faith of his family and their devotion to the Mother of God. Vicente eventually succeeded in placing Bartolo in the care of a Dominican friar, Alberto Radente, who helped him in the final stages of withdrawal from the sect.

After Bartolo had confessed and received Holy Communion, the friar convinced him that he had to make reparation to the people for the scandal he had caused. The friar then introduced Bartolo to a group of pious people who cared for the poor, the sick and the needy. Among this group was a rich widow, Countess Mariana di Fusco, who owned a large tract of land near the ancient city of Pompeii, which had been destroyed by the eruption of Vesuvius in the year 79 A.D. and remained buried in ash for almost 2,000 years.

Surrounding this ancient, excavated city, which was visited by countless tourists, were fields where 300 people lived. Being an attorney, Bartolo was commissioned by Countess di Fusco to collect the rent from these poor farmers. Seeing the sad situation of the people, Bartolo began to devise means to help them. It was because of these charities that Bartolo became an apostle of Our Lady of the Holy Rosary. He wrote:

> One day in the fields around Pompeii called Arpaia...I recalled my former condition as a priest of Satan. Friar Alberto had told me repeatedly never again to think of, or reflect on, my former consecration as a priest of Satan, but I thought that perhaps as the priesthood of Christ is for eternity, so also the priesthood of Satan is for eternity. So, despite my repentance, I thought: I am still consecrated to Satan, and I am still his slave and property as he awaits me in Hell. As I pondered over my condition, I experienced a deep sense of despair and almost committed suicide. Then I heard an echo in my ear of the voice of Friar Alberto repeating the words of the Blessed Virgin Mary: "One who propagates my Rosary shall be saved." These words certainly brought an illumination to my soul. Falling to my knees, I exclaimed: "...If your words are true that he who propagates your Rosary will be saved, I shall reach salvation because I shall not leave this earth without propagating your Rosary." Like an

answer to my promise, the little bell of the parish church of Pompeii rang out inviting the people to pray the Angelus. This incident was like a signature to my firm decision.

Without delay, Bartolo organized a parish mission and invited a group of priests to speak about devotion to the Holy Rosary. To conclude this mission, Bartolo wanted to exhibit a painting of Our Lady. He found an appropriate picture in a Naples shop, but, unfortunately, he did not have enough money to purchase it. On his return home he shared his disappointment with Friar Alberto, who told him of a painting that a nun named Mother Concetta had in her convent. Since she was willing to part with it, Friar Alberto encouraged Bartolo to ask for it. When he saw the painting, Bartolo was extremely displeased by its pitiful condition. Since he declined to take it, the nun insisted with the words, "Take it with you; you will see that the Blessed Mother will use this painting to work many miracles." These words would prove to be prophetic.

Bartolo arranged for the painting's transport to Pompeii. When it arrived, it was wrapped in a sheet and was situated atop a load of manure which was being taken to the fields near Pompeii. The day of the painting's arrival was November 13, 1875. Every year on this date the faithful observe the anniversary with special prayers and observances.

As a fitting shrine for this painting, which was restored on three occasions to its former beauty, Bartolo arranged for the building of a magnificent church. Its construction was funded by the pennies of the poor and the substantial gifts of the rich. Situated high atop the main altar of this artistically enriched sanctuary, the painting has been the instrument through which many miracles of healing have taken place.

Visitors to the Sanctuary are attracted to this colorful painting which depicts the Blessed Mother seated upon a throne with twelve stars forming a halo around her head. On her knee is the Child Jesus, who is handing a Rosary to a Dominican friar, while the Blessed Mother is handing a Rosary to a Dominican nun. Pope Leo XIII once stated, "God had made use of this image to grant those favors which have moved the whole world."

While the Sanctuary was being constructed, Bartolo also turned his interest to helping orphans, writing books about the history of and devotion to the Rosary, and composing novenas and a prayer manual for use at the Sanctuary. While engaged in these activities Bartolo found time on April 1, 1885 to marry the widow, Countess Mariana di Fusco.

Together the couple spent their time and money in helping the many orphans who were entrusted to their care. They likewise helped candidates to the priesthood and religious life, Bartolo being credited with paying for the education of about 45 seminarians. In his letters to these seminarians he inquired about the progress they were making in their studies, and he always urged them to cultivate and propagate devotion to the Rosary.

Bartolo Longo, the former satanist, the devout convert, respected lawyer and champion of the orphaned, lived a long life of 85 years, dying on October 5, 1926. His tomb, as well as that of his wife, is found in the crypt of the Sanctuary.

Standing as a monument to the memory of Bartolo Longo is the magnificent Sanctuary of Pompeii. There is no doubt to whom this shrine is dedicated: a statue of the Virgin Mary holding the Child Jesus is situated high atop the church. A long Rosary falls from Our Lady's hand and the word "Pax" is inscribed beneath the statue. Across the facade of the Church are Latin words which boldly proclaim that the church is dedicated to the Virgin of the Holy Rosary.

Near the Church are buildings for the girl orphans, as well as other buildings for the boys. In addition to their usual studies, the children are taught skills and trades which will help them later in life.

It is estimated that 10,000 pilgrims visit the Sanctuary each day; but twice a year, on May 8 and the first Sunday of October, at least 100,000 pilgrims are present to join in the solemn prayers which Bartolo Longo composed.

The promise of the Blessed Mother that "One who propagates my Rosary shall be saved" was realized when Pope John Paul II affirmed the salvation of Bartolo Longo's soul at the ceremony of beatification which took place on October 26, 1980.

Above: A painting of Bl. Bartolo Longo, 1841-1926, who sets an example for anyone who desires spiritual conversion. As a young man studying for a law degree at the University of Naples, he became involved with satanism and was even "ordained" a priest of a satanic sect. The prayers of his family were answered when a good friend brought Bartolo back to the Catholic Church.

Below: A sculpture of Bl. Bartolo Longo surrounded by orphaned boys and girls. He and his wife devoted much time and money to helping orphans and paid for the education of about 45 seminarians.

A painting depicting Bl. Bartolo Longo and his wife, Countess Mariana de Fusco, offering Pope Leo XIII a model of a church they had built. *(Painting by Arzuffi.)*

Bl. Bartolo, "Father of Orphans," is captured in this painting which shows him toward the end of his long life. He died in 1926, at the age of 85. The magnificent Sanctuary of the Holy Rosary stands as a monument to his memory and is visited by many pilgrims. *(Painting by Antonini, 1950.)*

A photograph of the monument created by Domenico Ponzi of
Rome in honor of Bartolo Longo. It is located in the square at
Pompeii. The lower part of the monument is a statue of Bl. Bartolo Longo and orphans; the upper part shows Our Lady surrounded by angels.

80

Chapter 22

ST. BENEDICT JOSEPH LABRE

1748 - 1783

Jean-Baptiste Labre and Anne-Barbe Grandsire of Amettes, France, were the parents of 15 children; the eldest, born on March 26, 1748, was Benedict Joseph Labre. His father, a successful shopkeeper, was able to provide all his children with an education. Benedict Joseph's early training was received in his native village in a school conducted by the vicar of the parish. According to the life written by Benedict Joseph's confessor, Marconi, and the biography compiled from the official process of his beatification, Benedict Joseph is depicted as having exhibited in his youth a seriousness of thought and strong attraction to prayer and mortification.

This early piety seemed to indicate a calling to the holy priesthood, and for this reason, when Joseph was twelve years old, his parents placed him with his paternal uncle, Francois-Joseph Labre, the parish priest of Erin. Joseph was tutored in preliminary studies and made considerable progress in the study of Latin, history and other subjects. However, instead of the priesthood, Benedict Joseph felt called to a life of solitude and expressed a desire to become a Trappist monk. Because he was a minor, his uncle sent him to his parents for permission to enter this strict order, but they refused to give their consent. Once more Benedict Joseph took up residence in his uncle's rectory, redoubling his penances and acts of piety in preparation for the life to which he felt himself called.

After the holy death of his uncle during an epidemic in 1766, Benedict Joseph, who had dedicated himself during the scourge to the service of the sick and dying, returned to Amettes. Once again he spoke of his intention of becoming a religious at La Trappe. Fearing that further opposition would be against the will of God, his parents gave their reluctant consent. But Benedict Joseph's maternal uncle, the Abbe Vincent, suggested that instead of La Trappe, Benedict Joseph might apply to the Carthusians at Val-Saint-Aldegonde.

His application to that monastery was refused, but Benedict Joseph was directed to another monastery of the Order at Neuville. There he was told that, as he was not yet twenty, there was no hurry and that he must first learn plainchant and logic. During the next two years Benedict Joseph unsuccessfully applied twice to the monastery at La Trappe. He then returned to Neuville and spent six weeks there as a postulant with the Carthusians. Since he did not seem called to that order, he then obtained admission to the Cistercian Abbey of Sept-Fonts in November, 1769. During his stay there he endeared himself to the whole community by his humility and his exactness in religious observance. Unfortunately, his health suffered, and it was decided, after so many attempts to become a religious, that apparently his vocation lay elsewhere.

After recovering his health, Benedict Joseph crossed the Alps into Italy. At Chieri in Piedmont he wrote a touching letter to his parents—the last they ever received from him. In it he apologized for the uneasiness he had caused them and informed them of his intention to enter an Italian monastery. A short time after the letter was dispatched, he seems to have had an internal illumination which set aside all doubts concerning his vocation. He then understood that it was God's will that he abandon his country, his parents and the pleasures of the world to lead a penitential life, not in the wilderness or in a cloister, but in the midst of the world—devoutly visiting, as a pilgrim, the famous places of Christian devotion. During the rest of his life he never wavered in his belief that this was the will of God. He submitted this inspiration to the judgment of his confessor, who told him that he might safely follow it.

Benedict Joseph began his pilgrimage clad in an old coat, with a rosary about his neck, another between his fingers, and his arms folded over a crucifix which lay upon his breast. In a small bag he carried a copy of the New Testament, a breviary which he recited daily, and a copy of *The Imitation of Christ*. The only clothes that he had were the ones he wore. He slept on the bare ground, often in the open air. His food often consisted of leftovers which were either provided by charity or obtained from garbage. He never asked for alms, although the charity of others frequently pressed them upon him. After spending a small amount on his meager necessities, he gave the rest to the poor.

If Benedict Joseph was strict in his poverty, he was also strict in his behavior in that he rarely spoke unless to acknowledge or distribute alms. As he made his way along the roads in all kinds of weather, he remained absorbed in meditation. He spent whole days praying in church, and was so frequently lost in prayer that he was unaware of his surroundings. Once in his later years, when he was praying before a crucifix in church, an artist was able to paint the portrait which has preserved his likeness.

A penance which Benedict Joseph practiced to the extreme was that of remaining unwashed. It is a well-known fact that the Saint was infested with vermin, a condition which is said to be more galling than the wearing of a hairshirt. If he often attracted criticism for this condition, he was nevertheless regarded as saintly on account of his unaffected humility, his poverty and his spirit of perfect union with God.

During his first seven years as a pilgrim, Benedict Joseph visited the principal shrines of Europe including Loreto, Assisi, Naples, Bari, Fabriano in Italy, Einsiedeln in Switzerland, Compostela in Spain and Paray-le-Monial in France. The next six years that remained to him were spent in Rome, Benedict Joseph leaving the city only once a year to visit the Holy House of Loreto. While in Rome he slept in the Colosseum and spent his days in visiting the various churches of the city. He was particularly attracted to churches in which the Forty Hours Devotion was being observed. So often was he seen in adoration of the Eucharist during this devotion that the Romans nicknamed him, "The Saint of the Forty Hours." Many who were edified by his saintly conduct were brought to a greater appreciation of the Eucharist and experienced an increased attraction to prayer.

Eventually, because of his many infirmities, Benedict Joseph was obliged to accept night shelter in a hospice for poor men. The administrators were greatly impressed with the Saint's humility and piety and were aware that he always arrived last to receive his portion of soup, which he frequently gave to someone he thought was hungrier than himself.

At the beginning of Lent in 1783, the Saint contracted a severe cold, but he refused to abandon his pious practices. Finally, on the Wednesday in Holy Week, he attended Mass for the last time in his favorite church, St. Maria dei Monti. On the steps outside the church he was overcome with weakness. With a crowd of people milling around the Saint, a butcher stepped forward and took him to his own home.

After receiving the last Sacraments, Benedict Joseph Labre died peacefully about eight o'clock in the evening of April 16. Immediately word of his passing spread throughout the city, while youngsters in the street cried out, "The Saint is dead! The Saint is dead!" Burial was in the Church of St. Maria dei Monti, where he often had prayed before a favorite picture of the Madonna.

Benedict Joseph's remains are still kept beneath an altar in a side chapel of this church. The butcher's house where the Saint died has been converted into a chapel. A reclining statue depicting Benedict Joseph marks the place of his death.

In the life of the Saint written by his confessor, Marconi (an English version is dated 1785), mention is made of 136 certified miracles that occurred in less than two months following the Saint's death. These miracles were so extraordinary that they contributed to the conversion of John Thayer of Boston, who was in Rome at the time of the Saint's death. John Thayer later became a priest.

Benedict Joseph Labre, the "Beggar Saint of Rome," was canonized by Pope Leo XIII on December 8, 1881.

St. Benedict Joseph Labre as an artist painted him while he was in ecstasy before an image of the Blessed Virgin Mary. The eldest of 15 children, Benedict Joseph had difficulty in finding his vocation and finally settled on a pilgrim's life, in which he practiced severe self-mortification. *(Cavallucci, National Gallery, Rome.)*

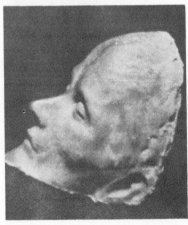

Above: St. Benedict Joseph Labre was devoted to this fresco, located at Santa Maria dei Monti, in Rome. It pictures Sts. Lawrence, Stephen, Francis and Augustine.

Left: The death mask of St. Benedict Joseph Labre, who died on April 17, 1783. When he died, children in the streets cried out, "The Saint is dead! The Saint is dead!" His funeral drew a tremendous crowd, and the military had to be summoned to the scene to restore order. The Saint was known for frequent divine favors such as ecstasy, levitation and bilocation.

A photograph of the room where St. Benedict Joseph Labre died. It is now a chapel, though at his death it was owned by a butcher. The two corner cupboards hold the Saint's prayerbook and other small belongings.

Above: A photograph of the statue of St. Benedict Joseph Labre which is located on the spot where he died.

Below: A close-up photograph of the statue of St. Benedict Joseph Labre.

Chapter 23

ST. BENEZET

d. 1184

Known as "Little Benedict the Bridge Builder" St. Benezet spent his pious youth in Savoy tending sheep for his mother until one day, during an eclipse of the sun, he heard a voice that addressed him three times out of the darkness. The voice instructed him to build a bridge over the river at Avignon.

During the Middle Ages the building of bridges at convenient locations was considered a work of mercy, since travelers had to journey out of their way, often enduring great hardships to reach places where they could cross rapid streams or rivers. Bridges were so necessary that rich men were often urged to make provision for them in their wills, and bishops often conferred indulgences on those who financially supported the building of a bridge or those who contributed their labor.

Disregarding his small stature, his complete ignorance of the mechanics of bridge-building and his total lack of funds, Benezet did as the voice had prompted him. He arrived at Avignon and presented himself to the Bishop. Through various means he gained the approval of the Bishop and began work on a stone bridge in the year 1177. For seven years he directed the operations, and when he died in 1184, the main difficulties of the enterprise had been overcome. He was buried upon the bridge itself, which was not completed until four years after his death.

The wonders that occurred from the moment the foundation was laid, as well as the miracles that occurred at the tomb, inspired the city officials to build a chapel on the bridge. In this chapel the body of the Saint was enshrined for almost 500 years.

Weakened from age and the constant pressures of the current, part of the bridge fell into ruin in 1669 and completely destroyed the chapel. Fortunately, the Saint's coffin was rescued—and when it was opened the following year, the body was found in a state of perfect preservation, although the iron bars about the coffin were badly damaged by rust due to excessive dampness. The body was again found in excellent condition in 1674 during its translation to the Church of the Celestines. During the French Revolution of 1789, a group of revolutionaries seized the incorrupt body and sacrilegiously destroyed it. Only a few bones survived, and these are kept in the parish Church of St. Didier in Avignon.

St. Benezet is regarded as the founder of the Order of Bridge-Building Brothers, whose constitution was approved in 1189, four years after the Saint's death. St. Benezet is also recognized as one of the patron saints of Avignon, and he is quite appropriately regarded as the patron of all bridge builders.

The statue of St. Benezet located in the Church of St. Didier, Avignon. The twelfth-century Saint is recognized as patron of bridge builders. When a youth, he heard a voice addressing him during the darkness of an eclipse, instructing him to build a bridge over the river at Avignon. Wonders occurred from the moment the foundation was laid, inspiring city officials to build a chapel on the bridge. There the body of the Saint was enshrined for almost 500 years.

Chapter 24

ST. BIBIANA

d. 363

The Church of Santa Bibiana in Rome stands on the site where once stood the home of the noble family of Flavian, a prefect of Rome, his wife Dafrosa, and his two daughters, Demetria and Bibiana (Viviana). All four suffered for the Faith in the year 363, during the persecution of Julian the Apostate. Flavian, a zealous Christian, was eventually apprehended. For refusing to renounce his faith, he was deposed from office and branded on the face. He was then banished to Aquapendente (as *The Roman Martyrology* states) and died a few days later. Dafrosa, being equally faithful to Christ, was confined to her home. Later she was carried outside the gates of the city and beheaded. Bibiana and her sister, Demetria, were deprived of all that they owned, suffering extreme poverty for five months—a time that was made meritorious by their prayers and fasting.

Brought before Governor Apronianus, Demetria made a generous confession of her faith. A biographer states that after this declaration she dropped dead before him. Apronianus then gave orders that Bibiana should be placed in the care of a wicked woman named Rufina, who was extremely successful in persuading young girls to indulge in sinful occupations. But when all Rufina's efforts failed, Apronianus became enraged at the courage and perseverance of the young girl and passed the sentence of death upon her. She was to be tied to a pillar and whipped with scourges loaded with lead. Bibiana died during this beating. Her body was left exposed in the open air so that scavenging dogs might feed on it, but after two days the untouched body was carried away by a priest named John and was buried at Bibiana's home beside the remains of her mother and sister.

In the year 465 a pious lady named Olympia built a church over the tomb. This church was consecrated by Pope Simplicius and was later repaired by Honorius III. When it was again repaired in 1628 by Bernini for Urban VIII, the relics of Bibiana, Demetria and Dafrosa were placed in an oriental alabaster shrine under the high altar.

Inside the Church of St. Bibiana is a statue of the Saint by Bernini, and at the back of the church, protected by an iron grille, is the column of red porphyry to which she was tied when she was scourged.

A seventeenth-century statue of St. Bibiana. The Saint was a fourth-century Christian martyr who was beaten to death during the persecution of Julian the Apostate. Her parents and sister also went to their deaths rather than renounce Christianity.

Chapter 25

ST. BLAESILLA

d. 383

Hardly anything would be known of the youthful widow, St. Blaesilla (Blesilla), had it not been for the letters of St. Jerome. Born in Rome, Blaesilla was one of St. Paula's four daughters. As the eldest, Blaesilla was married to Furius, a son of the devout Titiana. Soon after her marriage, Blaesilla seems to have grown indifferent to her religion and to have turned to the enjoyment of all that her wealth and position afforded her. But this was abruptly ended when she was widowed after only seven months of marriage. Upon the death of her husband, Blaesilla was attacked by a fever. Yielding to the promptings of grace, she determined to devote herself to the practices of devotion should she recover. After her sudden restoration to health she spent the rest of her short life in great austerity. Blaesilla died at Rome in the year 383 at the tender age of 20.

St. Jerome, in writing to Blaesilla's mother, St. Paula, conveyed in very high terms his opinion of Blaesilla's great sanctity. He further wrote to St. Paula expressing his sympathy at her loss and admonishing her for her prolonged grief. "Blaesilla," he wrote, "has received her crown, dying in the fervor of her resolution, in which she had purified her soul for near four months."

St. Jerome's translation of the Book of Ecclesiastes is said to have been undertaken at Blaesilla's request.

Chapter 26

ST. BLANDINA

d. 177

France may seem too distant from persecuted Rome to have produced second-century martyrs, but in those times Lyons and Vienne (located in what was then known as Gaul) had an organized community of Christians which has given us 48 heroes and heroines of the Faith. These are all known, but prominent among them is St. Blandina, a slave, who was a victim of the persecution under Marcus Aurelius. What we know of these martyrs is given to us in a letter which is preserved by Eusebius of Caesarea in Book V of his *Ecclesiastical History.* In this letter, which was addressed to the churches of Asia and Phrygia, the social ostracism and physical torments of these martyrs are carefully outlined.

The letter, which is described as one of the most precious documents of Christian antiquity, recounts that orders had been given for general arrests, and this included some of the servants who were not Christians. Afraid of being tortured, some of these captives falsely accused the Christians "of feeding on human flesh like Thyestes and of committing incest like Oedipus, as well as other abominations which it is unlawful for us even to think of, and which we can scarcely believe ever to have been perpetrated by men."

Although the charges were untrue, shame and torment afflicted the pious souls on hearing themselves charged with such disgraceful acts. Eusebius gives us some idea of the resulting public attitude toward the Christians:

> When these things were made public, all men were exasperated against us, including some who had formerly shown friendliness towards us. . .The fury of the mob, the governor and the soldiers fell most heavily upon Sanctus, a deacon from Vienne, on Maturus, newly baptized but a noble combatant, on Attalus, a native

of Pergamos, who had always been a pillar and support of the Church, and on Blandina, a slave.

At first the martyrs suffered general indignities including insults, stone throwing, blows and plundering—but gradually the non-Christians grew so furious at the crimes alleged against the Christians that more serious punishments were demanded. The Christians were then subjected to torture and were put to death in various ways.

St. Blandina was of such a delicate constitution that her mistress, who was also a victim of the persecution, "was in distress lest she [St. Blandina] should not be able, through the weakness of her body, to be bold enough even to make confession [of her faith]." But fortified with the grace of God, St. Blandina displayed so much courage and withstood so much abuse while imprisoned that Eusebius relates:

> They took turns in torturing her in every way from morning until evening, and they themselves confessed that they had nothing left to do to her and they marveled that she still remained alive, seeing that her whole body was broken and open, and they testified that any one of these tortures was sufficient to destroy life, even when they had not been magnified and multiplied.

Always mindful of the false charges leveled against the Christians, St. Blandina, in spite of her tortured body, repeatedly affirmed, "I am a Christian woman and nothing wicked happens among us." With three of her companions, St. Blandina was brought into the amphitheater to be subjected to wild beasts. St. Blandina, however, was the only one hung from a stake. Remaining there with her arms extended, she served as a symbol of the Crucifixion, giving courage to her friends. When none of the beasts would touch her, she was removed from the stake and taken back to the jail.

Eusebius records that,

> In addition to all this, on the last day of the gladiatorial sports Blandina was again brought in [to the amphitheater] with Ponticus, a boy of about 15 years, and they had been brought in every day to see the torture of the others, and efforts were made to force them to swear by the idols, and the mob was furious against them so that there was neither pity for the youth of the boy nor respect for the sex of the woman.

Ponticus, encouraged by the example of St. Blandina, endured many tortures before dying heroically. As for the blessed Blandina,

> After scourging, after the beasts, after the gridiron, she was at last put in a net and thrown to a bull. She was tossed about a long time by the beast, having no more feeling for what happened to her through her hope and hold on what had been trusted to her and her converse with Christ. And so she, too, was sacrificed and the heathens themselves confessed that never before among them had a woman suffered so much and so long.

The remains of the martyrs were not given the Christian burial they deserved, but were left exposed for six days. After being subjected to many indignities and outrageous acts, the bodies were at last burned and the ashes thrown into the Rhone River. The year of St. Blandina's death was 177.

Chapter 27

BL. BONAVITA

d. 1375

The little town of Lugo, situated fourteen miles west of Ravenna, Italy was the place of Bl. Bonavita's birth and death. Here he worked as a humble blacksmith, spending his time either at labor or in the performance of good works. It is recorded of him that whether working or at leisure, whether sitting or walking, indoors or out of doors, he was often so rapt in contemplation as to be unaware of all that was taking place around him. This was demonstrated the day a fire destroyed many of the houses in Lugo. When the whole population of the city was feverishly working to extinguish the fire, Bl. Bonavita passed by, totally unaware of what was taking place. When his attention was gained, he made the Sign of the Cross over the flames. From that moment the fire is said to have been totally extinguished.

As a Franciscan tertiary Bonavita had the true spirit of the Order and a love of poverty. His zeal for the poor was shown one bitter, wintry day when he found a poor man half frozen outside the Church of San Francesco. Bonavita immediately gave the man his own clothes. The little urchins of the town ran after the nearly naked blacksmith, throwing stones at him and shouting words of abuse. On another occasion Bonavita gave his newly mended shoes to a beggar. With the proceeds from his strenuous profession, it was his custom to feed the hungry, to visit prisons and to bury the dead.

Through his prayers, and with the Sign of the Cross, Bl. Bonavita worked many wonders. He died a holy death in the year 1375.

Chapter 28

ST. BONIFACE OF TARSUS

d. 306

Boniface is described as having been "a big fine figure of a man, with a heavy shock of hair." Prior to his conversion he was also described as having been fond of wine and "debauchery." By way of making less of these vices, one biographer promptly adds that he was extremely generous to the poor.

When Boniface became acquainted with a formerly dissolute Roman lady named Aglae, who had become converted, he was so impressed that he followed her example and was baptized.

By way of pleasing Aglae and doing penance for his past sins, Boniface journeyed from Rome to the East in search of certain relics. Upon reaching Tarsus, he saw a group of confessors being led to torture. He kissed their chains and attempted to defend them. For this he was condemned to death, and was subsequently beheaded.

Aglae eventually obtained the relics of Boniface. These she placed in an oratory fifty stadia from Rome. It is thought that this church was built by Algae specifically to enshrine the relics of Boniface. The church was rebuilt by Pope Honorius III, and in 1216 the bodies of St. Alexius and St. Boniface were discovered and placed under the high altar. These relics were last seen and identified in 1603. In this church are also kept the relics of Aglae. The church was first named for St. Alexius, but later was given a double patronage and is known as the Church of St. Alexius (Sant' Alessio) and St. Boniface.

Chapter 29

BL. BONIZELLA PICCOLOMINI

d. 1300

Due to a fire in the cathedral that destroyed a number of documents, few facts are available concerning Bl. Bonizella. It is known, however, that Bonizella was connected by birth with the old Umbrian nobility and married Naddo Piccolomini of Siena. She was apparently childless, and upon being left a widow she retired into the district of Belsederio, where she devoted herself and her possessions to the relief of the needy.

After her death in 1300, when her body was lying in its casket, an unusual phenomenon was observed: a number of bees alighted upon the hand that had distributed so much consolation to the afflicted. Some years later bees appeared again when they swarmed over Bonizella's tomb. This resulted in the discovery of her incorrupt body.

Because of this discovery, and the many spectacular miracles that occurred at her tomb, Bonizella is held in great veneration in the dioceses of Siena and Pienza.

It is reported that once, when the incorrupt body was placed on view, a thief removed a gold ring from the finger of Bl. Bonizella. He was punished for his crime by being struck blind, but his sight was immediately restored when the ring was returned.

Chapter 30

ST. BORIS AND ST. GLEB

d. 1015

Sts. Boris and Gleb were the sons of St. Vladimir, who is called the "Baptizer of Russia," and of his Christian wife, Anna. Due to St. Vladimir's previous marriages, Boris and Gleb had ten stepbrothers and two stepsisters. They claimed as their great-grandmother the great St. Olga, the first Russian noblewoman to receive Baptism and the first Russian woman to be canonized.

Before his death, St. Vladimir had divided his territories among his 12 sons, keeping Kiev, the capital, for the eldest son, Svyatopolk. Boris received as his territory the little city of Rostov; Gleb received the city of Murom.

From their childhood the two younger sons of St. Vladimir were especially close to one another. Boris could read and write and had studied the lives of the saints. In obedience to his father's wish, he was married at an early age and is known to have governed his territory with kindness and mercy.

The eldest brother, Svyatopolk, promptly earned the name "The Accursed." Married to a daughter of the King of Poland, he is known to have been driven by an unbridled ambition. While his father was alive, Svyatopolk plotted against him and refused to honor him. After his father's death, when Svyatopolk was regarded as the Grand Prince, he devised a scheme to gain control of the whole country by the systematic assassination of his brothers.

When Boris, who was then 20 years of age, learned of his stepbrother's intention to have him killed, he was confronted with the agonizing problem of how a Christian should react under the circumstances. He remembered passages from Scripture, particularly the one that cautioned, "If any man say, I love God, and hateth his brother, he is a liar." (*1 Jn.* 4:20). He likewise considered that since his father was dead, his eldest brother held the father's place,

102

and he could not raise his hand against either.

Throughout the night Boris experienced a painful interior struggle. He gained some comfort from reading the Psalms and the Gospels and gained courage from remembering that St. Wenceslas and St. Barbara both were killed by their relatives. He also considered the words of Ecclesiastes on the vanity of worldly power and riches and the value of good deeds and charity. After praying fervently that Our Lord would accept the sacrifice of his life, Boris dismissed his armed guards and kept only a servant with him.

Soon afterwards, the murderers made their way into his tent, which was pitched near the River Alta, and attacked the young prince "like wild beasts." Boris' faithful servant, a Hungarian, attempted to save his master by standing in front of him, but the servant was promptly killed. Boris was then wounded by thrusts from a lance. Before dying he spoke these words: "Make haste to complete your task, and may peace be with my brother Svyatopolk, and with you my brothers."

Prince Gleb, who was a few years younger than Boris and is thought to have been a mere boy at the time, was also marked for assassination. On a pretext, Svyatopolk invited Gleb to visit him at Kiev. While Gleb was traveling along the River Dnieper, not far from the city of Smolensk, the boat on which he was making his journey encountered the boat carrying the hired assassins. When Gleb realized the danger, he experienced a moment of weakness and begged for his life, but then he quickly regained his courage and accepted his destiny, saying, "I submit to you, my brothers, and to my brother, my prince." He acknowledged that to die meant being reborn to a new life and a better existence and that by dying in this manner he was "dying for Christ." We are told that the fatal stroke was given by Gleb's own cook, who crept up behind him and cut his throat, "like a butcher killing a sheep, a meek lamb bringing a clean sacrifice to the Lord." Gleb's body was carelessly discarded on the riverbank.

Svyatopolk the Accursed also saw to the assassination of another brother, Svyatoslav. But then, five years later, his brother Yaroslav of Novgorod appeared with a powerful army to avenge the deaths of his three brothers. Svyatopolk the Accursed was driven from his capital and fled to his father-in-law, the King of Poland, but the time of justice had apparently arrived. Having fled his capital in humiliation, he died while attempting to save his life.

The legitimate successor of the cruel Svyatopolk was Yaroslav, who became known as Yaroslav the Wise. He ruled Kiev, the capital of Russia, with justice and mercy and inaugurated a period known in history as the "Golden Age" of both the religious and secular cultures. In an effort to do honor to the memory of his two younger brothers, Boris and Gleb, he had their bodies tranferred to Vychgorod, near Kiev, where they were buried in the Church of St. Basil in the year 1020. Their tomb became a place of pilgrimage and was illustrious for many miracles. Finally bowing to Yaroslav's wishes, the ecclesiastical authorities started proceedings for the canonization of the two brothers.

Difficulties were soon faced by the Church authorities. Neither Boris nor Gleb had been killed for religious reasons, nor were they, in a true sense, martyrs like those of the early Church. Because they had died young, it could not be claimed that they had risen to the higher levels of holiness. They had performed no miracles during their lives, and were neither hermits nor missionaries. It was debatable whether their act of self-sacrifice could be considered an act of heroic virtue. Nevertheless, the people were profoundly impressed with the lives and deaths of their two princes, and they argued that just as Christ died an innocent Lamb, without resistance, so too did Boris and Gleb die in virtue and innocence.

After much debate and consideration, the two brothers were raised to the honors of the altar before the canonization of their great-grandmother, St. Olga, and their father, St. Vladimir. Thus the first four saints to be formally canonized by the Church in Russia were two young men, a father and a grandmother—all laymen. The canonization of the two brothers by the Church in Russia was confirmed by Pope Benedict XIII seven centuries later, in 1724. Their feastday was given as July 24.

The veneration accorded the two Saints is described as having been extraordinary. Their tomb at Vychgorod was considered one of the most important places of worship in the country. Also important was a chapel that was erected on the banks of the River Alta at the spot where Gleb met his death.

Even though the two brothers represent two different personalities and died at different times, their names have become inseparable. Churches are always dedicated to both of them, and Russian icons always represent them together.

Because the two Saints were held in such high regard, the Russian Orthodox Church used to celebrate—in what was considered an exceptional practice—the feast of Sts. Boris and Gleb six times a year.

Chapter 31

ST. CAESARIUS

d. 369

St. Caesarius was the younger of the two sons of Gregory the Elder of Nazianzus and St. Nonna. His sister was St. Gorgonia; his elder brother was St. Gregory, who was the bishop of Nazianzus and is now numbered among the Doctors of the Church.

After receiving careful training at home, Caesarius studied at Caesarea in Cappadocia, and then at the celebrated schools of Alexandria. There his favorite studies were geometry, astronomy and especially medicine, in which he surpassed his fellow students. St. Gregory of Nazianzus tells us that his brother Caesarius was respectful to his teachers, friendly to his comrades, avoided evil companionship and associated with men of high character and principles.

While practicing his trade in Byzantius, which was then the capital city of Europe, Caesarius gained such fame as a physician that public honors, a distinguished marriage and a seat in the Senate were offered him—all of which he declined.

At Constantinople Caesarius became the foremost physician of his Age and acquired a great reputation for his medical skills. This reputation found its way to the court of Constantius, where he occupied an exalted position as physician of the court. Later he exercised his skills at the court of Julian the Apostate, much to the regret of his virtuous family. Julian nominated him to be his first physician and excluded him in several edicts which he published against the Christians.

St. Gregory, in his oration at the funeral of Caesarius, related that during the time his brother spent at court "neither his [Caesarius'] fame nor the luxury surrounding him corrupted the nobility of his soul. Although he possessed many important honors, his own first claim to dignity consisted in being and being known as a Christian."

If Caesarius resisted all the privileges of the court, he also resisted all of Julian's efforts to make him renounce his faith. St. Gregory relates that "when Caesarius had foiled all of Julian's verbal subtleties and every hidden and open attempt, pushing them aside as child's play, he proclaimed in a loud and clear voice that he was a Christian and would so remain."

Finally Caesarius was persuaded by his father and brother to resign his posts at court and to retire, contrary to the wishes of Julian that he remain.

Later Caesarius made his home in Bithynia, with Emperor Valens, serving as controller of the imperial revenue and in charge of the treasury. When an earthquake occurred at Nicaea, Caesarius "was sheltered in unbelievable safety by the falling ruins and suffered almost no ill effects from his peril. Yet it was enough to make him take fear, as his teacher and guide to a more important salvation, and to devote himself entirely to his heavenly destiny."

Eventually the unmarried, 40-year-old Caesarius contracted an illness which proved fatal. His death occurred at the end of the year 368 or early in 369. His remains were sent to Nazianzus, where he was extolled and honored. Present at his funeral were his mother and father, as well as his brother St. Gregory of Nazianzus, who delivered the funeral oration.

In his will Caesarius directed that all his possessions should be distributed to the poor, an order which his servants unfortunately abused in their own interests.

Chapter 32

ST. CASIMIR

1458 — 1484

Of the 13 children born to Casimir IV, King of Poland and Princess Elizabeth of Austria, the third child was Casimir, who came into the world in October, 1458. Described as being devout from childhood, the boy benefited greatly from the instructions of his tutor, John Dlugosz, a man of extraordinary learning and piety. While all the princes of the family loved this holy man, Casimir profited most from his holy example and, as a result, advanced rapidly in the spiritual life.

Disliking the excesses of the court, Casimir wore plain clothes, frequently slept on the floor as a penance and often spent the night in prayer. He was especially devoted to the sufferings of Our Lord, to the Blessed Mother and to the Holy Sacrifice of the altar, during which he often appeared to be enraptured. He is said to have been invariably serene, cheerful and affable to all, especially the poor, to whom he gave all he possessed. He also encouraged the generosity of his father and his brother Wladislas, King of Bohemia.

When the nobles of Hungary became dissatisfied with their king, Matthias Corvinus, they begged the King of Poland to allow them to place his son, Casimir, on their throne. At the time, Casimir was a mere 15 years old and did not wish to accept their offer, but in obedience to his father he consented and went to the frontier at the head of an army of 20,000 men.

While Casimir was on his way to Hungary, King Matthias settled his differences with his nobles and assembled a large body of troops to confront those of Casimir. In the meantime, a great many of Casimir's men were leaving the ranks for lack of payment. On learning that King Matthias was in control and ready for combat, Casimir's officers advised him to abandon the plan and return to Poland. Word had also reached Casimir that Pope Sixtus IV was against the expedition. This influenced Casimir to accept the advice of his officers and to return to Poland.

Casimir's father was furious at the failure of his ambitious project and would not permit Casimir to return to Cracow, but relegated him to the castle of Dobzki, three miles from the city. The young prince meekly accepted his banishment and remained in confinement for three months, spending his time in penitential exercises. Convinced of the injustice of the war in which he had almost been engaged, Casimir resolved never again to take up arms; he refused to be persuaded when he was urged to do so on at least two occasions. He was likewise steadfast in refusing to renounce celibacy to comply with his father's plan that he marry the daughter of Emperor Frederick III of Germany.

When his brother Wladislas became ruler of Bohemia, Casimir became heir apparent to the Polish throne and ruled the country from 1479 to 1483 while his father was in Lithuania on affairs of state. During this brief administration, Casimir is known to have exercised conspicuous prudence and justice.

The last 12 years of his life were spent mainly in prayer and penance. Toward the end Casimir suffered from a lung disorder, which is now thought to have been consumption. While on an important mission in Lithuania, he became critically ill and predicted the last hour of his life. After receiving the Sacraments he died on March 4, 1484 at the age of 26. Burial was in the Church of St. Stanislaus (now the Cathedral) at Vilna (Lithuania), where his remains are still found.

Before his death, Casimir asked that a copy of the long hymn *Omni Die Dic Mariae* be placed in his hands before his burial. A copy of this hymn, which he had frequently recited, was accordingly buried with him. Part of this is familiar to us as the hymn "Daily, Daily Sing To Mary." Although Casimir is sometimes credited with being the composer, this hymn is known to have been popular years before his birth.

The many miracles wrought through his intercession immediately after his death caused Casimir to be venerated as a saint. Sigismund I, King of Poland, petitioned the Pope for Casimir's canonization, and Pope Leo X commissioned the Papal Legate to investigate the life and miracles of the future Saint. This inquiry was completed in 1520, and in 1522 Casimir was canonized by Adrian VI. Pope

Clement VIII designated March 4, the anniversary of Casimir's death, as the Saint's feastday, and Pope Paul V extended the observance to the entire Church. The feast is still celebrated on March 4.

It is reported that 120 years after Casimir's death, his body and all the rich robes in which it was wrapped were found intact, in spite of the moisture of the vault in which they were entombed.

St. Casimir is the Patron Saint of Poland and Lithuania and is recommended to young people as a pattern of holy purity.

In art the Saint is represented in a Polish costume, with insignias of royalty and a lily in his hand.

A painting of St. Casimir of Poland (1458-1484), Patron Saint of Poland and Lithuania. He is recommended to young people as a pattern of holy purity.

Chapter 33

ST. CASSIAN

d. 304

St. Cassian was a schoolmaster in the City of Imola, some 25 miles west of Ravenna, Italy. As a Catholic he conscientiously taught young boys to read and write and gave them a fine example by the Christian virtues which he practiced in the performance of his duties.

When a persecution against the Church reached Imola about the year 304, Cassian was interrogated by the governor of the province. Since he steadfastly affirmed his allegiance to the Christian Faith and repeatedly declined to sacrifice to the gods, the prefect condemned him to death and ordered that he should suffer in the place of his employment.

At that time it was the custom in schools to write upon wax that had been smoothed on a board of boxwood. The letters were formed in the wax with an iron stylus, or pen, which was sharp at one end for marking, but blunt at the other end for correcting and smoothing.

When the judgment was rendered, Cassian was brought to his classroom and was disrobed before 200 boys. It was then ordered that his death should be accomplished at the hands of his students, who were told to stab their teacher with their iron pens. Whether out of vengeance for past corrections, or whether they were forced to do so, it is said that the boys threw their tablets, pens and knives at the Saint's face and head and often broke them upon his body. Others cut his flesh or stabbed him with their pens, while others made sport of cutting letters out of his skin. Covered with blood and wounded in every part of his body, the Saint withstood the torment in an heroic fashion until death released him from his agony.

St. Cassian was buried by the Christians at Imola, where his relics were honored with a splendid shrine.

Prudentius, who poetically recorded the manner of the Saint's death in Peristephanon IX, tells that while on his way to Rome he visited and prayed before the martyr's tomb. He also mentions a picture over the altar depicting the martyrdom of the Saint.

Chapter 34

BL. CASTORA GABRIELLI

d. 1391

Described as being exceedingly beautiful and of a sweet, retiring disposition, Castora was a member of a prominent family of Gubbio, Italy. Her father was Count Petruccio Gabrielli; her mother was a sister of Paul Gabrielli, a bishop of Lucca.

In obedience to her parents, Castora married a man of her own rank, Gualterio Sanfaraneo, a doctor of laws, whose home was at St. Angelo in Vado. Soon after their marriage, her husband proved to be a man of violent temper and unbearable disposition. Castora had much to suffer, but she bore all her trials with true Christian patience. When her household chores were completed, she spent the remaining time in prayer, pleading for her husband's change of heart and begging for all the graces she needed in order to endure the unhappiness of her state.

Castora's only child, a son named Oddo, grew up to be an upright and pious man as the result of his mother's training and example.

After her husband's death, Castora became a tertiary in the Franciscan Third Order. With one of the ideals of the order being that of poverty, Castora decided to sell all her possessions and to give the proceeds to the poor. Her virtuous son agreed to the sale and joined in his mother's generosity.

Bl. Castora spent her days in prayer and penance until her death in 1391. She first was buried at Macerata, but through the efforts of her son, her relics were brought back to St. Angelo in Vado, where they were laid to rest in the Church of St. Francis—the church in which she had so often prayed for her husband during the days of her unhappy marriage.

Chapter 35

ST. CATHERINE OF GENOA

1447 - 1510

The Fieschi family of Italy distinguished itself in its long history by giving to the Church a cardinal and two popes, Innocent IV and Adrian V. Another member of the family, Jacopo Fieschi, who was the Viceroy of Naples for King Rene of Anjou, married Francesca di Negro. They were parents of five children; the last, born in 1447, was a daughter whom the Church recognizes as St. Catherine of Genoa.

The three sons and two daughters of the family were afforded all the advantages of their father's prestigious position and their mother's noble family. Despite the many privileges offered them, the two girls turned their wholehearted attention to the devout practices of their faith. Catherine's sister, Limbania, entered the religious life as a canoness regular, but when Catherine attempted to join her sister, her entrance was delayed because of her youth. The following year, 1461, Catherine's father died. Soon afterwards there began a political realignment between two of Italy's politically important families, the Guelph Fieschi family and that of the Ghibelline Adorno. The union of the two families was settled when, on January 13, 1463, at the age of 16, the pious Catherine Fieschi was married to Giuliano Adorno.

The two were different in temperament, character and ideals. Catherine, in addition to being physically beautiful, was intelligent, caring, modest, thrifty, sensitive to the needs of others, deeply religious and of an even temperament. Giuliano was pleasure-loving, self-indulgent, undisciplined, hot-tempered, a spendthrift and—by his own admission—an unfaithful husband. It is no wonder then, with the clash of these two personalities, that Catherine was unhappy. Since her husband was seldom at home, Catherine spent the first five years of her marriage in virtual solitude and sadness. During the next five years Catherine unsuccessfully attempted to relieve her inner depression and desperation by engaging in the gaieties and the recreations of the world. Throughout her unhappy state, Catherine never lost her trust in God, and she continued all the practices of her religion.

After enduring years of intense unhappiness, Catherine was rewarded by God with an experience that occurred on March 20, 1473. One contemporary biographer claims she was making her confession, another that she was kneeling before a priest for his blessing, when she was suddenly overcome by grace and an immense love of God. Lifted above her miseries, Catherine was thereafter radically changed. A few days later she was granted a vision of the Crucified. After making a general confession of her sins, she became a daily communicant, which was a rare practice at the time.

Almost simultaneously with the transformation in Catherine's life, her husband's life was also changed. After living for years in extravagance and self-indulgence, Guiliano's financial situation became so desperate that he was on the verge of bankruptcy. This misfortune, together with Catherine's prayers, resulted in his complete conversion. He agreed to a life of perpetual continence and joined the Franciscan Third Order. Although Catherine admired the Franciscans, she never seemed inclined to imitate her husband in this respect, but did join him in practicing one of the ideals of the order, that of poverty.

The couple moved from their palazzo into a small, humble house in a poorer section of the city and devoted themselves to the care of the poor of the area, as well as of the sick in the Hospital of Pammatone. For six years they continued in this situation, until they were invited to live in the hospital itself. From the year 1479, when the couple moved into the hospital, until 1490, Catherine worked as an ordinary nurse—but in 1490 she began serving as the hospital's administrator, and later she worked as its treasurer.

Catherine's sanctity and tireless heroism in the service of God's poor was exemplified during the plague of 1493, when it is estimated that 80 percent of the city's population perished. During this plague Catherine is said to have contracted the fever from a dying woman whom she had impulsively kissed. She recovered from the fever, but her overall health suffered from then on, making it necessary for her to resign as administrator of the hospital in 1496, after having served six years in that capacity.

The following year Giuliano died following a painful illness. Catherine reputedly said to a friend, "Messer Giuliano is gone, and as you know well, he was of a rather wayward nature, so that I suffered much interiorly. But my tender love assured me of his salvation before he had yet passed from this life." In his will Giuliano provided for his illegitimate daughter Thobia and her unnamed mother. In her charity and thoughtfulness, Catherine made herself responsible for seeing that Thobia should never be in want or neglected, and since she had no children of her own, Catherine became, as it were, Thobia's adopted mother.

During much of her life Catherine's spirituality developed solely under the influence of grace. But then, shortly after her husband's death, she benefited from the spiritual direction of the priest, Cattaneo Marabotto, to whom the Church is indebted for his writings on the Saint's spirit, doctrine, mystical experiences and interior life. Catherine was ever mindful of temporal necessities and continued nursing the sick and managing the details of her husband's estate. She was also quite busy advising and instructing the many people who were attracted by her spiritual teaching.

Catherine suffered for many years from various ailments until at length, in 1507, her health gave way completely. One of her physicians was the doctor of King Henry VII of England, but he and other physicians were unable to diagnose her condition. They eventually decided that her ailments had supernatural origins, since she lacked all the symptoms that they could recognize. Finally, on September 15, 1510, "This blessed soul gently breathed her last in great peace and tranquility and flew to her tender and much-desired Love."

Burial was in the hospital chapel. Eighteen months later, when the body was exhumed to be placed in a marble sepulchre, it was found perfectly preserved, in spite of excessive dampness. In response to popular demand, the body was exposed for eight days. Immediately cures attributed to Catherine's intercession began to take place, and veneration of the Saint began and continued from that time onward. Moved a number of times, the body was placed in a glass-sided shrine in the year 1694—the same reliquary in which it is still exposed. The incorrupt body was carefully examined by physicians in 1960. They recorded after their inspection that "The conservation is truly exceptional and surprising and deserves an analysis of the cause. The surprise of the faithful is justified when they attribute this to a supernatural cause." The relic in its glass-sided reliquary is now located high atop the main altar of the church built in St. Catherine's honor in Genoa, Italy.

The Saint's thoughts, sayings and spiritual insights are contained in two books, the *Treatise on Purgatory* and the *Spiritual Dialogue*. The Holy Office declared that these two works were enough to prove her sanctity.

Catherine was canonized by Pope Clement XII in 1737; she received that honor together with St. Vincent de Paul, St. Francis Regis and St. Giuliana Falconieri.

This painting of St. Catherine of Genoa is found at the Hospital of Pammatone, Genoa, Italy. During the plague of 1493, the Saint tirelessly nursed the poor while she also carried out her duties as administrator of the hospital.

A photograph of the glass reliquary which contains the incorrupt body of St. Catherine of Genoa. It is located high atop the main altar of the church built in the Saint's honor in Genoa, Italy. St. Catherine's unhappiness early in her marriage, a result of her husband's waywardness, was transformed when one day she was struck by grace and immense love of God. She was privileged with a vision of the Crucified Lord and became a daily communicant, which was quite unusual in 1473. Her husband eventually underwent a dramatic conversion and joined the Franciscan Third Order.

120

Chapter 36

ST. CEADWALLA

d. 689

Like many members of early English royalty who were forced into exile when another deprived them of their title and throne, Ceadwalla plotted a return and entertained ambitious plans for the increase of territories that he would claim as his kingdom. Unfortunately, his efforts in this regard produced what seems to have been unnecessary bloodshed, vengeful killings and the sufferings of innocent people who were forced to leave their homes.

In the year 685 the young Ceadwalla "began to contend for the kingdom" and collected a band of companions who fought with him for the restoration of his land. He "harried" Sussex and killed Aethelwalh, its king. Unfortunately, his bold adventure failed when two of the dead king's ealdormen drove him from the territory. Accepting this failure as a momentary setback, Ceadwalla marched again, this time into the West Saxon kingdom, and he claimed it as his own. He then formed the ambitious plan of adding all southeastern England to his kingdom. He also invaded the Isle of Wight and began the cruel and systematic extermination of its inhabitants so as to replace them with settlers from his own province.

To insure that his position would not be coveted by its rightful claimants, he sent retainers to search for the two boys who represented the Island's dynasty. These boys had fled into the Jutish country, where they thought they were well concealed—but when Ceadwalla's plot to kill them became known, a certain priest named Cynebert baptized them as a preparation for the inevitable. They were soon captured and killed according to Ceadwalla's orders.

Ceadwalla also made himself King of Sussex and vengefully killed one of the two ealdormen who had driven him from the country after his earlier invasion. He then invaded Kent in 686 and secured a partial recognition as its king. During his reign of over two years, he kept a firm and peaceful hold on his kingdom. As Albertson reports in his *Anglo-Saxon Saints and Heroes*, "With a bold heart he held his kingdom safe, either by the victorious edge of the sword or an indulgent treaty of peace."

What is curious about Ceadwalla, who was unbaptized, is that while killing, causing innocents to suffer and entertaining what might be called egotistical ambitions, he founded a Christian monastery at Hoos between the Thames and the Medway and was an associate and patron of churchmen. He gave a fourth of the Isle of Wight for church purposes and entrusted it to St. Wilfrid, who eventually converted many of its citizens.

Ceadwalla's mind was turned from conquest and ambition to his eternal destiny sometime after suffering a severe wound during his raid on the Isle of Wight. Stenton records in his *Anglo-Saxon England* that Ceadwalla, "who had led a life of incessant violence," was severely wounded during this raid and that he "was plainly conscious of approaching death." The King relinquished his control over the territories he had so violently captured, abandoned his crown and decided to journey to Rome to be baptized. The Venerable Bede reports that:

> King Ceadwalla, having most honorably governed his nation for two years, quitted his crown for the sake of Our Lord and His everlasting Kingdom and went to Rome, being desirous to obtain the peculiar honor of being baptized in the church of the blessed apostles...and he hoped at the same time that, laying down the flesh as soon as baptized, he should immediately pass to the eternal joys of Heaven.

Ceadwalla left England for Rome in the summer of 688, and upon reaching Samer near Calais, he made a sizable donation for the building of a church.

On Holy Saturday in 689 he was baptized at Rome in the presence of Pope Sergius, who received him into the Church and gave him the baptismal name of Peter. Ten days later, on April 20, Ceadwalla died while wearing the white clothes of the newly baptized. He was about 30 years old.

He was buried in St. Peter's, and on the Pope's command an epitaph was ordered for his tomb. The Archbishop of Milan is said to have composed a 28-line verse for this epitaph. When the great

St. Peter's Basilica was built, the remains of the Saint were removed to the crypt where English-speaking pilgrims and tourists can still read the epitaph, which ends with the words, "Sure wise was he to lay his sceptre down, and gain in Heaven above a lasting crown."

Chapter 37

ST. CECILIA

d. 177

Cecilia was a member of a distinguished Roman family. She outwardly complied with all that pertained to the customs and manner of dress that were expected of a young woman of her position, but, unknown to others, she fasted often and wore a coarse garment beneath her clothes.

Despite her desire to remain a virgin, she was given in marriage to Valerianus, a nobleman. The young Saint obediently participated in the marriage ceremony, but when she was alone with her bridegroom, Cecilia was successful in persuading him to respect her vow of virginity and converted him to the Faith. Following his Baptism, Valerianus was favored with a vision of Cecilia's guardian angel that greatly comforted him during his future trials.

Valerianus and his brother Tiburtius, who was also converted by Cecilia, were later martyred for the Faith. Then Cecilia was arrested for having buried their bodies; she was given the choice of sacrificing to heathen gods or being put to death. Cecilia chose to die for the Faith, as had Valerianus and Tiburtius.

Because Cecilia was a member of a distinguished and well-known family, Turcius Almachius, the Prefect of Rome, thought it best to execute her in private instead of in public, which might bring criticism from various quarters. For this reason it was decided that she should be placed in the bath (the *caldarium*) of her home, which was to be kept intensely heated until the suffocating atmosphere deprived her of life.

Cecilia entered the place of martyrdom and remained there the rest of the day and night without being harmed. Since this method of execution was not successful, she was ordered to be beheaded in the same place. Due to inexperience or lack of courage, the executioner failed to sever her head with the three blows prescribed by law. Cecilia lay dying on the pavement of her bath, fully conscious, with her head half severed, until she expired three days later. The position of her fingers, three extended on her right hand and one on the left, was accepted as her final profession of faith in the Holy Trinity.

Christians clothed Cecilia's body in rich robes of silk and gold and placed it in a cypress coffin in the same position in which she had died. She was first interred in the Catacomb of St. Callistus. In 822 Pope Pascal I had the body removed, with the relics of Valerianus and Tiburtius, to the Basilica of St. Cecilia.

An exhumation of the incorrupt body was made in 1599. A sculpture made by Stefano Maderno at this time represents the Saint in the exact posture of her body. The statue is now situated slightly below and in front of the high altar. The marble slab on this altar is the one on which the Saint was placed during the attempted suffocation, and it may be the one on which she died. The body of the Saint, together with the relics of Valerianus and Tiburtius, are interred in the crypt of the church.

Cecilia is often depicted in art with an organ to express what was often attributed to her in panegyrics and poems based on her *Acts,* that "...while the musicians played at her nuptials, she sang in her heart to God only." When the Academy of Music was founded in Rome in 1584, Cecilia was made its patroness, whereupon her veneration as patroness of Church music became universal.

Rotalfoto, Milan

This photograph shows a famous statue of St. Cecilia, who died in the year 177. Her body was still incorrupt at the last exhumation in 1599, at the time of which this statue was made, showing the exact position of her body when it was found at the exhumation and which is believed to be the position in which she died. Her body had the sword cut on her neck (visible in this picture) and her hands depict the mystery of the Trinity; the left hand has one finger extended to show the unity of God and her right hand has the thumb and two fingers extended, to depict the Three Divine Persons.

An artist's rendering of St. Cecilia, patroness of musicians and Church music, who chose to die for the Faith rather than sacrifice to heathen gods.

A terra-cotta bust of St. Cecilia, of whom it is often said that "while the musicians played at her nuptials, she sang in her heart to God alone."

A fresco depicting the heavenly crowning of St. Cecilia. The Saint wished to remain a virgin, but she nevertheless obeyed the wishes of her distinguished Roman family and married a nobleman named Valerianus. He respected her vow of virginity, and was converted to the Faith. Valerianus and his brother were also martyred. *(Fresco by Sebastiano Conca.)*

128

An early seventeenth-century fresco of St. Cecilia before the judge at her trial. *(Fresco by Domenichino.)*

129

Chapter 38

BL. CHARLES OF BLOIS

d. 1364

When Duke John III of Brittany died in 1341 without leaving an heir or a close blood relative, his dukedom in northwestern France was claimed by two rivals: a stepbrother, John de Montfort, and John's neice, Joan, who was married to Bl. Charles of Blois. The Parliament of Paris decided for Joan and her husband, but John de Montfort lost little time in deciding to settle the matter through open warfare. The conflict that developed between the two claimants occupied Bl. Charles for the rest of his life.

The virtuous Charles, while preferring to settle the claim peacefully, was prompted to engage in warfare with the support of the King of France. John de Montfort was encouraged and supported by England's Edward III. Although this struggle cannot be considered a war to defend the Faith, Charles nevertheless fought for what he and his countrymen felt was right and just.

Always concerned that the war would affect his subjects tragically, Charles tried to alleviate their fears by offering to settle the dispute by means of a single combat between his opponent and himself—a challenge that was not accepted by his rival.

After he captured the City of Nantes, Charles immediately provided for the poor and suffering. He also showed the same consideration at Rennes, Guingamp and elsewhere. Offering up suffrages for the repose of the souls of those who were slain, Charles founded religious houses, wore a hairshirt and recited the Office. He also prayed for the souls of the fallen during a pilgrimage he made to the shrine of St. Yves at Treguier.

When the Siege of Hennebon was delayed so that the troops could attend Mass, one of Charles' officers felt compelled to protest. Bl. Charles replied, "My Lord, we can always have towns and castles. If they are taken away from us, God will help us to get them back again. But we cannot afford to miss Mass." This incident, as well as Charles' general religious behavior, caused the less devout of his followers to observe that Charles seemed more fit to be a monk than a soldier.

For four years Bl. Charles resisted his rival, but after the fall of several cities he was defeated, captured and shipped to England. He was housed in the Tower of London, and his ransom was set at a hundred thousand gold florins. The money was sent for his release but, unfortunately, the ship that carried it sank in a storm. Like many of the prisoners of the Tower, Charles sanctified his time by prayer and patience. This and his holy demeanor merited the admiration of his fellow prisoners and his guards. The holy soldier finally regained his liberty after a confinement of nine years.

Bl. Charles promptly resumed his struggle and fought against John de Montfort for another nine years. The last engagement against his rival took place at Auray on September 29, 1364. Early that morning Bl. Charles received the Sacraments; he was later killed on the field of battle by an Englishman.

It is sad to consider that after so gallant a struggle, Bl. Charles' rival won the Dukedom of Brittany by default. Yet Butler *(Lives of the Saints),* in a stroke of belated justice, titles the holy warrior "Bl. Charles of Blois, Duke of Brittany."

Because of his care for the poor and suffering of the captured cities, as well as his founding of religious houses, the care with which he guarded the spiritual welfare of his troops, his laudable virtues and the many miracles worked at his tomb, the cultus of Bl. Charles of Blois was confirmed by Pope St. Pius X in 1904.

Chapter 39

BL. CHARLES THE GOOD

1083 - 1127

Charles was called "The Good" by his subjects because of his virtues and his wise and kindly rule as the Count of Flanders and Amiens. His father, St. Canute, King of Denmark, had been slain in St. Alban's Church in 1086.

Born about the year 1083, Charles was only three years old at the time of his father's death. Following this tragedy, his mother, Adela van Vlaanderen, took Charles to the court of her father, Robert de Frison (Fries), Count of Flanders. Charles' grandfather and an uncle, Robert II, greatly influenced him and trained him in all chivalrous exercises. In due time Charles earned the honor of being knighted.

When his uncle, Robert II, joined the Crusade to do battle against the infidels in Palestine, Charles went with him and distinguished himself in combat. Upon his return home, Charles again engaged in battle, this time against the English.

When Robert II died, he was succeeded by his son Baldwin who, having no children, designated his cousin Charles to succeed him. Baldwin was also instrumental in arranging Charles' marriage with Margaret, daughter of Renault, Count of Clermont, whose dowry consisted of the County of Amiens. Charles assisted his cousin Baldwin in the government of Flanders, so that when Baldwin died, the people, having become accustomed to Charles, received him happily.

Trouble was brewing, however, in the form of other claimants, and for several years Charles had to face a great deal of resentment and resistance to his authority. His most serious opponent was Countess Clemence of Burgundy, the widow of his uncle Robert. She supported her niece's husband, William de Loo, Viscount of Ypres. The Countess was successful in organizing an uprising among the Flemings of the seacoast, while the feudal nobles in her district of Furnes joined her troops, hoping to increase their power. They succeeded in taking the City of Audenarde and invaded West Flanders, but Charles' army soundly defeated them.

The reputation of Charles was such that he was offered the imperial dignity after the death of Henry V. He refused this honor, as well as an offer of the crown of Jerusalem. In humbly refusing these honors Charles expressed the intention of devoting himself entirely to the Flemish people. This, he thought, was more in keeping with the will of God.

When external problems were under control, Charles devoted himself to formulating laws, which he then strictly enforced. By his example, he brought his country to a high level of culture. Being simple and modest, he detested flattery. He observed the fasts of the Church and performed other penances. When he was criticized for defending the poor against the rich, he said, "It is because I know so well the needs of the poor and the pride of the rich." He detested blasphemy to such an extent that any member of his household who swore by God's name was punished by a fast of bread and water for 40 days.

The peace and security of the country seemed threatened when there was an eclipse of the sun in August, 1124, which the irreligious accepted as a sign of forthcoming troubles. Trouble did indeed visit the land, in the form of a famine which came a year later. The grain that sprang up was destroyed by winds and storms. The poor suffered greatly and were forced to beg at the strongholds of the great lords. But even though the poor were sick from disease and malnutrition, they failed to arouse the sympathy of those who could have helped them, and many died by the wayside.

Charles did all he could to relieve the victims of the disaster. Daily at Bruges, and at each of his castles, he fed a hundred poor men, and at Ypres he distributed 7,800 two-pound loaves in one day. He reprimanded certain nobles for allowing men to die at their gates, forbade the brewing of beer in order to save grain, set a fixed price for the sale of wine, and ordered the land to be sown in grain—and in peas or beans, which grow faster. When he was informed that certain nobles were hoarding grain to sell later at a higher price, Charles and his almoner, Tancmar, forced them to sell at once and at a reasonable price. This so infuriated these nobles that the chief of the profiteers, Lambert, and his brother Bertulphus, the dean of St. Donatian at Bruges, devised a plot to murder Charles. Also conspiring in this endeavor were Erembald, the chief magistrate of Bruges, together with his five sons, who resented Charles for having corrected their violent activities.

It was the custom of the holy Count to walk barefoot each morning to the Church of St. Donatian to attend Holy Mass. One morning, before starting on his walk, he was warned that there was a conspiracy against him. He replied, "We are always in the midst of dangers, but we belong to God. If it be His will, can we die in a better cause than that of justice and truth?" While he was reciting the Psalm *Miserere* before the altar of Our Lady in the church, the conspirators went into action. Wielding swords, his enemies cut off one of his arms; his head was slashed by Bertulphus' nephew, Borchard. Thus Bl. Charles died on March 2, 1127. He was about forty-four years old.

The relics of Bl. Charles the Good, who merited the martyr's crown, are kept in the Cathedral of Bruges (Sint-Salvatorskathedraal). Devotion to the holy martyr was approved and encouraged by Pope Leo XIII in 1882.

CHARLES LE BON. 13.^E CONTE.

Bl. Charles the Good, Count of Flanders (1083-1127), was murdered by conspirators at the altar of Our Lady in the Church of St. Donatian at Bruges, Belgium.

This painting shows Bl. Charles the Good's generosity to the poor.

Bl. Charles, son of St. Canute (King of Denmark), was called "the Good" by his subjects because of his virtues and his wise and kindly rule.

J. Petyt., Brugge

Again, these artworks recall Bl. Charles' murder at the altar, as well as his goodness to the poor. On the morning of his death, when warned of the conspiracy, Bl. Charles replied, "We are always in the midst of dangers, but we belong to God. If it be His will, can we die in a better cause than that of justice and truth?"

Bl. Charles the Good (1083-1127) is represented here wearing his garb as ruler of Flanders and Amiens. He maintained high standards of Christian living and greatly aided the poor. It is said that during the famine of 1125, he distributed 7,800 two-pound loaves to the poor in just one day. By ordering the nobles to sell grain at a reasonable price, rather than hoard it to sell later at a higher price, Bl. Charles angered a group of men, who then conspired to have him murdered.

Chapter 40

ST. CHARLES LWANGA AND COMPANIONS
(The 22 Martyrs of Uganda)

d. 1885 - 1887

It took considerable courage for 25-year-old Fr. Simon Lourdel of the White Fathers of Africa to venture into Uganda with his one companion, Brother Amans. The country was inhabited in 1879 by natives who pillaged, massacred and exercised all manner of debauchery. They occasionally offered human victims to the spirits and took natives from other tribes into captivity. There were also sorcerers who took pleasure in terrorizing the country.

Despite the dangers, the good priest and his companion made it safely in a small boat to the village of King Mutesa of Uganda. There they were cordially received and were later joined by their three companions, who had been left some distance away at the village of Kagweye.

Fr. Lourdel lost no time in speaking of the Christian Faith to the King, who seemed interested until he was told that he must keep only one wife and send all the others away. In his meetings with the King, Fr. Lourdel became aware of a dangerous enemy in the person of the King's chief assistant, Katikiro, who seemed to resent the white-robed missionaries. Other members of the court also seemed to mistrust the priests; wild rumors were spread about them, and sinister plots were said to be planned by them.

The priests, however, were able to teach the Gospel and were successful in baptizing a large number of natives. When Fr. Lourdel learned that others were planning on capturing the priests and putting them to death by fire, he and his companions prepared to leave. They gathered together the children they had ransomed and as many of the newly baptized as wanted to come with them. They set off by boat to the Village of Kagweye, where they arrived on January 4, 1883.

Almost two years later, the priests learned that King Mutesa, knowing that he was about to die, had called for the young Christian, Joseph Mukasa, the chief of the royal pages and one of the first to have been baptized by Fr. Lourdel.

After the King sent away his wives, Joseph Mukasa comforted the dying leader, but it is unknown if the King was baptized—although it is known that the King died in Joseph's arms on October 10, 1884.

Succeeding his father as leader of the tribe was King Mwanga, who was only 18 years old. He had always seemed to like "The Praying Ones" and sent word that the priests were once more welcome in Uganda. He even went so far as to send canoes to bring the missionaries and their belongings to his village.

The priests' return in July of 1885 was heartwarming. The natives were pleased to see them again, and the priests, for their part, were happy to learn that their convert, 26-year-old Joseph Mukasa, and the other Christians had instructed several hundred natives, who were now awaiting Baptism.

One who was not pleased to see the return of the priests was Katikiro, who had served the old King as his chief assistant. He remained in the same position of influence to assist the youthful King Mwanga. Since the young King looked favorably toward the "Praying Ones," Katikiro devised a plan to kill his master and to install as the new leader Mwanga's brother, who was more inclined to agree with him that the priests posed a great threat and should be banished from the country. But before this could be accomplished, three Christians learned of the planned assassination and warned King Mwanga. Katikiro was successful in pleading his ignorance of the plot but, from then on, his hatred of the Christians increased.

When Katikiro learned in November of 1885 that an Anglican bishop, the Rev. Hannington, and his assistants planned on passing through Uganda to the Lake Victoria area, Katikiro persuaded the King that the priests were sending for still more white men who would all plot to dethrone him. After learning of their plot to massacre the Anglican Bishop, Fr. Lourdel pleaded for their lives and begged the King to greet the new arrivals with respect and courtesy. The priest's efforts were futile, since Hannington was massacred, together with some of his companions.

Fr. Lourdel visited the King to learn the truth of the rumor that many of the Anglicans had been killed, but he received only silence for his questions. Joseph Mukasa also spoke to the King about the matter, but this was a grave mistake, since Katikiro was successful in persuading the King that Joseph Mukasa was not only against him, but was also planning some revenge for the killing of Hannington.

The King had other reasons for distrusting Joseph, since Joseph, as chief of the pages, customarily hid the boys when the King intended to entice them into committing sins of impurity.

The next morning, when Joseph Mukasa was returning from the Mission Chapel after receiving Holy Communion, he was apprehended on the King's orders. While his wrists were being securely tied, Joseph asked, "Come now, what are you doing? If I must die for my faith, do you think that I am going to try to escape? A Christian who dies for God does not fear death!" He was brought into the woods, where a fiery death awaited him. But Mukajanga, the chief of the executioners, displaying an uncommon compassion, refused to let him die by fire. Instead, Mukajanga drew his sword. Joseph then pronounced his final words, "Tell the King that I pardon him gladly for killing me without reason, but that I advise him to repent. If not, I shall be his accuser before the judgment seat of God."

Joseph then knelt in prayer and in a moment, with one strike of the blade, he was decapitated. His body was thrown on the fire, where it was devoured by flames. It was on November 15, 1885 that Joseph Mukasa became the first native of Uganda to die for the Faith.

The executioner reported to the King what had taken place and repeated the victim's final words, which were to prove troublesome to the superstitious King. Katikiro, for his part, was once more successful in turning the King against the Christians by claiming that Joseph would be only the first of many dangerous Christians to be killed. After all, what could be expected of those who do not sacrifice to the gods of the tribe, who neither pillage, massacre, or engage in war? What would happen to the Kingdom if most or all of the King's subjects became Christians?

The priests and their congregation drew new courage from the example of Joseph Mukasa and vowed to die bravely for the Faith if the King called for their assassination. Inspired by the martyrdom, many asked for instruction and begged for Baptism; in one week, there were more than one hundred Baptisms. One of those who was baptized at this time was Charles Lwanga, the strongest athlete of the court, "the most handsome man of the Kingdom of the Uganda."

He had previously worked under Joseph Mukasa and was now his replacement as the chief of the royal pages.

For almost six months, from October 1885 to March 1886, there was almost complete peace in the village. The King had retired to his summer home some distance from the village and was known to throw only occasional rages against the Christians. But one day after his return, when he called for his young servant, a 14-year-old boy name Mwafu, the son of the dreaded Katikiro, he learned that Mwafu was nowhere to be found. When Mwafu finally appeared before the King and offered as his excuse that Denis Sebuggwawo had been teaching him Catechism, the King flew into a rage.

Denis, who had been standing nearby, thinking that his friend was in danger, presented himself to the King's fury. Snatching a lance, the King brutally pierced it through Denis' throat and contemptuously left the 16-year-old boy where he lay on the ground. The boy died the next day, after a night spent in prayer and extreme pain. Denis Sebuggwawo thus became the second martyr of Uganda.

The King bitterly regretted the recall of the priests and became a staunch enemy of the Christians. Crazed with hatred, he gave orders that the gates of the compound should be closed and that guards should make certain no one left the village. He had a fire lit and had drums beaten all night as a signal for the assembly of executioners. The King knew that among his pages there were many Christians. These would be found out and killed as a punishment.

During the night, while the drums sounded, Charles Lwanga assembled the pages and other Christians. They prayed constantly that those who would die for the Faith would do so courageously in the name of Jesus Christ. Charles also baptized the boy pages, Mugagga, Mbaga, Gyavira and Kizito, all of whom had been longing to be received into the Church.

The next day, while the servants went about their duties, Charles Lwanga, as chief of the pages, was ordered to gather the boys before the hut of the King. When they approached the King, they prostrated themselves in the usual manner. Then the King ordered those who did not pray to stand to one side. Those who prayed should line up outside.

Charles was the first to leave. Kizito, a 12-year-old lad who had been baptized the night before, followed him, as did the newly baptized Mbaga, Gyavira and Mugagga. Athanasius Bazzekuketta also went outside, as did Ambrose Kibuka and Achilles Kiwanuka, who were cousins. When all had assembled, the King asked if they were all Christians and if they wished to remain so, even to death. When all had professed their faith and their willingness to die for it, the death sentence was passed and the executioners moved toward them. Mukajanga, the chief executioner, who had martyred Joseph Mukasa, also moved forward. When he did so, he noticed among the Christians and a few condemned Anglicans his own son, Mbaga Tuzinde. When Mbaga refused to recant, the executioner reluctantly accepted the inevitable.

The group then began to move slowly, but valiantly, toward the place of execution seventeen miles away, a wooded area known as Namugongo. None of the condemned uttered a cry, shed a tear or made a gesture of defense, but moved obediently under the eyes of several guards.

When the line passed the hut where James Buzabaliawo was imprisoned, the King ordered that this Christian should also join the line. James accepted his fate and humbly told the King, "In Heaven I will pray to God for you."

Standing nearby was Fr. Lourdel, who had been trying to approach the prisoners but had been prevented from doing so by the guards, who vehemently forbade the priest to even speak to them. The prisoners, however, smiled and motioned to him. Fr. Lourdel could do nothing but give them his blessing and his prayers.

Voluntarily joining the line was Bruno Serunkuma, one of the King's bodyguards who had secretly taken instructions at night. Also added to the line was Pontian Ngondwe, whom the Kabaka had at one time given the charge of growing bananas. When Pontian asked that he be martyred without delay, the guards were delighted to comply with his request. After knocking him down, one of the executioners raised his lance and ripped Pontian's body in several places before cutting off his head. Pontian was between 35 and 40 years of age.

While the line was still on its way, another young man tightly held by two executioners was added to the group of Christians. He was Mukasa Kiriwawanvu, a frequent visitor to the Mission. When Gyavira saw his friend he smiled broadly and moved toward him, saying, "I am glad to die with you for our Master Jesus Christ."

When the prisoners were near the Village of Mengo they were tied securely with ropes and were forced to lie on the ground. To make certain they would not move or escape, slave-yokes were placed on their necks. The slave-yoke consisted of a stick, the end of which branched into a V. When this fork was placed over the neck of the prisoner and shoved into the ground, it pressed against the throat, causing pain and preventing the prisoner from moving.

When the prisoners were being secured in this manner, two of the guards arrived with 20-year-old Athanasius Bazzekuketta, who previously had the task of guarding the King's treasures. Athanasius had tripped and fallen along the way. As a punishment, he was severely beaten. He was then taken to a place where ashes and pieces of bone littered a small area. The guards indicated that this was the place where Joseph Mukasa had been killed some six months earlier. This was also to be the place of martyrdom for Athanasius, whose chest was swiftly pierced by a lance. Afterward the executioner jumped repeatedly on his victim before the martyr's head, arms and legs were cut off and the body hacked to pieces.

The next morning, May 27, when the yokes on the prisoners were removed, Gonzaga Gonza stood up with great difficulty. The day before, with his shackles cutting into his flesh, Gonzaga had bled profusely during a five-mile walk. Because weakness and pain now made it impossible to walk, he fell to the ground. When one of the executioners saw that Gonzaga was unable to continue on the journey, he decided to finish him off where he lay and killed him with a thrust of a lance. Gonzaga died without making a sound.

Bruno Serunkuma, who had willingly surrendered, was suffering severely from the tight ropes, the ravages of a high fever and an unquenchable thirst. When the line of prisoners passed the hut of his brother, he called for his brother to bring him a little banana wine. But Bruno must have remembered the thirst of Our Lord on the Cross, because he refused the drink offered him and continued on.

Meanwhile another Christian arrived; it was Luke Banabakintu, who had taught Catechism to the young pages. He had been stopped at the same time as Matthias Mulumba, a 45-year-old Christian man who was the father of a family. Both were condemned to die with the pages, but Matthias stopped along the way and asked to be martyred where he stood, at a place known as Kampala. The executioner complied. Following the orders of Katikiro, Matthias was tortured with unbelievable cruelty.

While the flesh was being cut from his body, Matthias moaned and prayed, "Katonda! Katonda! (My God! My God!)." After sawing off his hands and feet, the executioner had the cruelty to tie up the severed arteries and veins in order to stop the bleeding and thus prolong his agony. Matthias was left to die, but two days later, when natives were cutting reeds nearby, they heard a voice moaning, "Water. Water." When they discovered the butchered and bleeding body, they ran away, terrified. Several days later they found that the body had been dried by the sun.

During this time, Katikiro sent armed men to find the Christian relatives of Matthias. They found and questioned the 35-year-old Noah Mawaggali, a maker of pipes and earthen pottery. When Noah acknowledged that he was a Christian and would not stop praying as they had asked him to, he was seized, stabbed and tied to a tree, with his arms extended to each side. Before he died, he endured the additional torture of having his flesh torn away, piece by piece.

His younger sister boldly surrendered, asking to be killed with the others, but she was only imprisoned. Manaku, who had changed her name to Matilda at her Baptism, became the first girl in Uganda to embrace virginity for the love of Jesus Christ.

Since the prisoners were to die by fire, a great many trees and branches had to be gathered into a large pyre. During the six days that the pyre was being prepared, the prisoners suffered from their shackles and slave-yokes. They did not spend the time idly, however, but in constant prayer and in exhorting one another to courage and trust in God.

On June 2, when the enormous pyre was ready, war drums were brought out and savage chants were sung throughout the night. The following morning, the group was marched to the pyre by the guards, who had painted themselves in a frightening manner with red clay.

Suddenly from the forest ran the young boy, Mbaga, the son of the chief executioner, Mukajanga. He had previously been removed from the group by his father, who had hoped to save his life. But the boy had escaped, and he ran happily to join his comrades.

On the way to the pyre, the condemned were tapped on the head with a long reed held by a chief executioner named Senkole. This tap on the head was a pagan rite to prevent the souls of those killed from returning to harass the King. If a tap was not given, the prisoner was reprieved. For reasons not known, three of the prisoners were spared. These were Denis Kamyuka, Simeon Sebuta and Charles

Werabe. To them we owe the details of what is known of the martyrdom of the Christians of Uganda.

According to a traditional procedure, the chief executioners had the right to reserve for themselves one of the condemned, whom they could torture as they pleased. Chosen for this special treatment was Charles Lwanga, who signaled to his comrades, "I shall see you very soon! Very shortly I shall join you in Heaven!" Charles was made to wait while the prisoners were placed on reed mats that had been prepared the night before. Each was then rolled on his mat until he was enclosed in a bundle of wood which was securely tied about him.

The three who had been spared then saw the distraught Mukajanga release his son from the bundle of wood and plead with the boy to renounce his faith. But Mbaga only asked to die with the others. In an effort to spare his son the torture of being burned alive, Mukajanga had one of the executioners beat his son on the head with a club. The boy was killed instantly by the blow. The body was then placed in the reed fencing and was brought to the pyre.

To the amazement of the guards and the executioners, the prisoners prayed aloud. "You can very well burn my body," Bruno Serunkama said, "but you cannot burn my soul, for it belongs to God." The pyre was then lit. After the fire consumed its victims, the attention of the executioners turned to Charles Lwanga.

When Charles saw that a special pyre was being prepared for him, he asked to be untied so that he could help in arranging the place of torture. In a peaceful and almost cheerful manner, Charles arranged the wood and sticks and then laid down upon them. When the executioner announced that Charles would be burned over a slow fire, Charles answered that he was very glad to be dying for the True Faith.

The fire was ignited. With the flames licking at his feet, Charles stiffened, but did not utter a single cry. The torture lasted a long time. Charles twisted under the pain, but remained ever faithful to his religion and was heard to moan repeatedly, "Katonda! (O my God!)."

On the way back to the village, Denis Kamyuka heard one of the executioners pronounce words to which the others agreed, "We have killed many men in our time, but never such as these! The others did nothing but moan and weep, but these prayed right to the end!"

A few days later, two Christians from a nearby village came secretly to the places of torture, collected a few charred bones and ashes and brought them to the Mission Chapel. These relics were deposited in a reliquary, where they are still kept, in the Church of St. Mary of Rubaga.

Katikiro, the hateful assistant at court and initiator of the whole drama, had remained at Namugongo, but he was far from satisfied with his vengeance and was alert for still more Christians. It was then that he remembered 30-year-old Andrew Kaggwa, an officer in the King's army. Not only had Andrew been a friend of Joseph Mukasa, the first martyr, but he had contributed his influence to the return of the missionaries.

Fortunately for Andrew, he had received Holy Communion the night before his capture and was thus fortified to accept what was planned for him. On May 26, 1886, after he denied many false charges, his arm was cut off and given to Katikiro, who had asked for this token. Andrew was then beheaded and his body cut into pieces.

Adolph Ludigo and Anatole Kiriggwajjo also died for the Faith, but the last of the martyrs was John Mary Muzeyi. He had been a page to the old King Mutesa. As a young man he had often ransomed slaves, whom he took to the mission; he had shown admirable courage in taking care of the sick during an epidemic of the plague.

John Mary was absent on the morning when the pages were condemned to death, but Katikiro remembered him and called for his arrest, which took place on January 27, 1887, while John Mary was walking along a path. His head was quickly cut off and his body thrown into muddy water. A woman who had known John Mary witnessed the execution and later told the details of his death.

The proud leaders of the tribe who had been instrumental in the martyrdom of the Christians all experienced horrible deaths. King Mwanga was first of all dethroned by a revolution which obliged him to flee. He was then captured by the English, who led him in chains to a prison where he soon died at the age of 34.

During the revolution, Katikiro was captured and killed by two of his servants. His body was left to be eaten by dogs.

Mukajanga, the executioner, was afflicted with a horrible skin disease which covered his entire body with infected sores. His chief assassin, Senkole, was snatched and devoured by a crocodile along the banks of a lake.

Built on the very spot where the royal hut of King Mwanga formerly stood is the Cathedral of Rubaga. The country of Uganda now has several dioceses, each one having its minor seminary, and there are three major seminaries for all the dioceses. The White Fathers, as well as other missionary priests and religious, continue to help in spreading the True Faith. Also assisting are many natives who became members of religious orders.

During the years following the persecution, news of the heroic deaths of the Ugandan martyrs became well-known due to the testimony of Denis Kamyuka, who had been saved from a fiery death. During an ecclesiastical inquiry, Denis repeated the details that had surrounded the death of the martyrs. Finally on June 6, 1920, Pope Benedict XV proclaimed the 22 martyrs "Blessed." Fourteen years later, Charles Lwanga, the chief of the pages, was designated the Patron of the African Youth of Catholic Action. The martyrs were canonized by Pope Paul VI on June 22, 1964.

Baray/Fleurus/Proost, Turnhout, Belg.

The Church of St. Mary of Rubaga replaced the palace of the pagan King which once stood on the same spot. The blood of St. Charles Lwanga and companions was apparently the seed of Christians, since by 1964 there were two million Christians in Uganda.

B. Baray/Ed. Fleurus/H. Proost & Co., Turnhout, Belgium

Much of what is known about St. Charles Lwanga and the other martyrs of Uganda (d. 1885-1887) comes from information supplied by Denis Kamyuka (pictured here), companion of the Ugandan martyrs, who testified at an ecclesiastical inquiry in 1920. The martyrs were canonized in 1964.

150

St. Charles Lwanga, who along with 21 companions was tortured and killed for the Christian Faith by a superstitious pagan king. When St. Charles Lwanga saw that a special pyre was being prepared for his execution, he asked to be untied so that he could arrange the sticks. When the executioner announced that Charles was to burn over a slow fire, the martyr responded that he was very glad to die for the True Faith.

Chapter 41

BL. CLARITUS

d. 1348

Bl. Claritus (or Chiarito) was the last male scion of the wealthy Voglia family. An Augustinian convent that he had founded in old Florence in the year 1342 was popularly known as Il Chiarito, although Claritus had dedicated it to Our Lady, the Queen of Heaven.

Claritus' wife, Nicolasia, eventually took the veil and became a member of this foundation. Claritus spent the rest of his life working at the convent as a general helper and servant to the nuns. He remained in this humble capacity until he died of the plague, which ravaged the city in 1348.

Bl. Claritus' relics were held in great veneration in the convent church. They exhibited the remarkable phenomenon of emitting a heavenly scent whenever one of the nuns was about to die.

Chapter 42

ST. CLOTILDE

474 - 545

Clotilde was born in Lyon, France about the year 474 to Chilperic, the ruler of the Burgundians of Lyon, and Caretana, a fervent Catholic. When Clotilde's father died, her mother took the 16-year-old girl and her sister Sendeleuba to Geneva. Sendeleuba eventually took the veil in the convent of St. Victor at Geneva, but Clotilde became the bride of Clovis, King of the Salian Franks, when she was about 18 years old.

The wedding took place at Soissons, which Clovis had made his new capital. Although Clovis was a pagan, he—like his father— maintained a friendly relationship with the bishops of the realm, especially with St. Remigius, Archbishop of Rheims. St. Remigius previously had sent Clovis a warm letter of congratulations when he had ascended the throne at the age of 15.

Clotilde exercised great influence over her husband and tried every means to convert him to the Faith. Although Clovis resisted and continued in his pagan beliefs, he did permit Clotilde to baptize their first child, a son named Ingomar, who died in infancy. He likewise permitted the Baptism of the other children: Clodomir, Childebert, Clotaire and a daughter who bore her mother's name.

Clovis' decision to become a Christian was made dramatically on the field of battle when he was in the process of losing to the Alemanni. When his troops were on the verge of yielding to the enemy, Clovis turned for help to Clotilde's God, promising to accept the Faith if he were victorious. The tide of the conflict took a miraculous turn; the battle was won, and on Christmas morning, 496, Clovis was baptized with great pomp by St. Remigius in Rheims Cathedral. His sister Abofledis and 3,000 of his Franks were also received into the Church at the same time.

Clovis was also successful in further conquests in Gaul. Clotilde

153

no doubt was happy with this accomplishment, which furnished fresh fields for extending the Catholic Faith. Together, Clovis and Clotilde founded in Paris the Church of the Apostles Peter and Paul, which was to serve them as a mausoleum and which was afterwards renamed for St. Genevieve. In this church Clotilde buried her husband, Clovis, when he died in 511. The couple had been married 19 years.

While the years previous to Clovis' death were relatively happy ones, Clotilde's widowhood was saddened by family feuds and the problems of her three sons and daughter.

The first problem involving Clotilde's children concerned her daughter, the princess Clotilde, whose husband—the Visigothic Amalaric—was abusing her. So cruel and inhuman was his behavior, as reported in the news that reached the rest of the family, that St. Clotilde's son Childebert was outraged. Rising to the defense of his sister, he gathered together an army, battled against Amalaric, defeated him and put him to death. Childebert was in the process of bringing his sister home when she died on the journey as a result of the harsh treatment she had endured at the hands of her husband. We can only imagine St. Clotilde's grief upon receiving the body of her only daughter.

Another difficulty involved Clotilde's son, Clodomir, who attacked his cousin St. Sigismund, captured him and mercilessly put him to death, together with his wife and children. Later Clodomir was himself killed in retaliation by St. Sigismund's brother Godomar in the battle of Vezeronce in the year 542.

Following the death of Clodomir, St. Clotilde adopted his three little sons, intending to raise them as her own children. Her two remaining sons, Clotaire and Childebert, decided to acquire undisputed possession of their deceased brother's inheritance, which they divided between themselves. Knowing that their three little nephews, who were the rightful heirs, presented a hindrance to their greed, the two brothers—under the pretense of wanting their nephews to visit them—persuaded St. Clotilde to send the children to them. No sooner had the children arrived than Clotaire, with his own hand, killed two of the children, who were 10 and seven years of age. The youngest child, Clodoald, escaped and afterwards became a monk near Paris, at the monastery of Nogent, which later was renamed St. Cloud in his honor.

Brokenhearted at the loss of her two grandsons, plus the knowledge that her two sons had plotted the murders and that one had actually performed the deed, St. Clotilde left Paris and moved to Tours. There she spent the rest of her life in helping the poor and suffering and in praying at the tomb of St. Martin, to whom she had a great devotion.

While at Tours, St. Clotilde learned that her two sons, Childebert and Clotaire, had been feuding and were on the verge of battle. In her anguish, St. Clotilde spent the whole night in prayer before St. Martin's shrine, begging God to put an end to the conflict. The Saint's prayers were answered the very next day, when the armies were facing each other on the field of battle. Before the conflict could begin, a storm arose with such turbulence that the troops scattered for safety.

A month later St. Clotilde was seized with a serious ailment; she died at the age of about 71, having been a widow for 34 years. The two sons who had caused their mother so much grief buried St. Clotilde beside her husband and children in the Church of the Apostles, which Clotilde and Clovis had built many years before. The church was later renamed after St. Genevieve, the Patroness of Paris.

Chapter 43

BL. CONTARDO FERRINI

1859 - 1902

Milan proudly claims as its native son Contardo Ferrini, who was born in that city on April 4, 1859 to a Christian couple. Little is recorded of his mother; his father was a teacher of mathematics and physics. Although his home life was pleasant, we are told that both Contardo and his father seem to have lived under the domination of Contardo's mother. This might account for Contardo's abnormally sensitive nature and his perception of the world as being hard and hostile. He was highly intelligent, and at the time of his First Holy Communion he was already greatly influenced by Holy Scripture and by St. Augustine's *Confessions*.

At school and at the university, Contardo impressed most of his classmates as being irritatingly self-sufficient and withdrawn. Inwardly, however, he was suffering for his refusal to approve or imitate the lifestyles of those around him, who took his high standards, especially concerning purity, as criticism of themselves. For this reason Contardo had few friends, but one who shared his high ideals and who understood him was Achille Ratti, who later became Pope Pius XI. Like the future pope, Contardo was an ardent mountaineer, and may have enjoyed the sport in the company of this good friend.

When Contardo's mother and her friends attempted to interest him in various marriageable young ladies, he made it clear that he was not called to the married state, nor did he feel that he had a religious vocation. He was to remain single all his life.

Having studied law at Borromeo College at Pavia, he received his doctorate in 1880; he later received his post-graduate education in Berlin. It is reported that Contardo was acquainted with a dozen languages, some of which helped him tremendously in his studies of the Scriptures. Specializing in Greek and Roman law, he was recognized as one of the outstanding authorities in this field. For this reason, the University of Pavia created a special chair for him in 1883. In 1887 he was made professor of Roman law at Messina, and in 1894 he returned to the University of Pavia. The following year he was elected to the Milan City Council, on which he served for a brief time.

Bl. Contardo was a profound scholar and an inspired and talented teacher who demanded much from his students. In turn, his students greatly admired and respected him. His colleagues, as well as his students, regarded him as a sterling example of one who lived a life of holiness in the midst of of intellectual pursuits.

Bl. Contardo not only engaged in scholarly and legal pursuits, but he also was active in social and charitable endeavors, having worked for the Society of St. Vincent de Paul in both Berlin and Milan. He was associated with the Ambrosian Library and helped found the St. Severinus Boethius Society for university students.

As a Franciscan tertiary, his interior life was distinguished by a great devotion to the Mass and by study of the Scriptures. Although his life was difficult, restricted and lonely, he accepted his lot with patience and virtuously observed the precepts of the Church.

Contardo died of typhoid fever in 1902. Soon after his death, Contardo was put forward as a candidate for canonization. Among the witnesses who testified to his virtues were his friends, his colleagues and Achille Ratti, the future Pope Pius XI.

Twenty-five years later, in 1927, the sanctity of Contardo Ferrini was given a glowing tribute by Cardinal Carlo Salotti during the funeral services the Cardinal conducted for Joseph Moscati, a physician and professor of medicine. During the funeral oration the Cardinal drew a parallel between Contardo, the professor of law, and Joseph Moscati, the professor of medicine. The Cardinal ended the oration by saying:

> I agree in thinking that we are in the presence of a new Contardo Ferrini. Two men of similar sentiments: two truly worthy scientists; two sterling characters: two devotees of fervent and sincere piety: two pure souls, who remained untouched by the filth of our times and by the lusts of the sense: two professors of lay universities, who have sanctified their chairs by the purity of their teaching: two apostles who have left their mark on this generation. Perhaps God wishes to glorify them together, so that they should be an example to our century, and so that there

should be some recognition of what science and a good Catholic laity is worth when placed at the service of a noble cause and the realization of the evangelical ideal.

Contardo Ferrini was beatified in 1947, only forty-five years after his death. Joseph Moscati, who died in 1927, was canonized in 1987.

Chapter 44

STS. COSMAS AND DAMIAN

d. 303

The Eastern Church venerates a small group of saints who are called "the moneyless ones" because they practiced their professions without accepting payment. The best-known of these saints are twin brothers Cosmas and Damian, who were born in the middle of the third century in Egea, a city in Cilicia which belonged to the Patriarchate of Antioch, in Asia Minor. They studied medicine in Syria and, as devout Christians, imitated the Divine Healer while traveling through the towns and villages of their native country. They cured countless infirmities without accepting payment and saved the souls of many by converting them to the True Faith.

In the year 303, during the persecution of the Christian Church by the Roman Emperor Diocletian, their charitable endeavors came to the attention of the authorities. They were arrested for being Christians and remained true to their faith under torture. The prefect Lisia, in his office as Governor of Syria and therefore the supreme magistrate of Rome, sentenced them to death, together with their brothers: Antimo, Leonzio and Euprepio. Various legendary accounts relate that they were miraculously preserved from death by fire, drowning, stoning, etc., although the sword finally claimed them when both were beheaded. Although their martyrdom is universally considered to have taken place in September of the year 303, there is controversy concerning the place. It is generally thought that they died in either Egea in Cilicia, their native city, or Ciro (Cyrrhus, Cyr) in Syria, where they were buried. Over their tombs a basilica was constructed, which was later enlarged by Constantine.

When Felix IV (526-530) was elected pope, there were already five churches in Rome dedicated to Cosmas and Damian. Pope Felix, who was particularly devoted to them, decided to erect in their honor a basilica which would be their principal sanctuary. The Roman Temple of Romulus and an adjacent room which had been the library of the Vespasian's Forum were converted into a church and dedicated to the two physicians. In this church Pope Felix placed an altar of peacock-streaked marble, which remains in its original location, although poor drainage has reduced it to crypt-level. In this crypt, which is really a lower church, the Holy Sacrifice is celebrated each Sunday. Originally consecrated by Pope Felix, the altar was reconsecrated by Pope Gregory the Great (590-604), who placed principal relics of the two Saints beneath the altar.

In the upper basilica, behind the high altar, is found the Monumental Mosaic on which construction was begun during the pontificate of Pope Felix. Sts. Cosmas and Damian are depicted holding their crowns of martyrdom. They are being led by the Apostles Peter and Paul to Christ, who is the central figure.

Sts. Cosmas and Damian are regarded as patrons of physicians, surgeons, druggists and dentists. The names of both Saints are mentioned in the Canon of the Mass and in the Litany of the Saints. They are particularly remembered each year on September 26, when their feastday is liturgically celebrated.

The ceiling of the Basilica of Sts. Cosmas and Damian. (*Painted by Marco Tullio Montagna.*)

A mosaic of the twin brothers Sts. Cosmas and Damian, who are regarded as patrons of physicians, surgeons, druggists and dentists. Born in the middle of the third century, these devout Christians traveled through the towns and villages of Asia Minor imitating the Divine Healer by curing countless infirmities without accepting payment, and by converting souls to the True Faith.

The mosaic pictured on these two pages is located behind the high altar of the Basilica of Sts. Cosmas and Damian in Rome. The Saints are depicted holding the crowns of martyrdom which they earned when they were executed under the persecution of the Roman Emperor Diocletian.

Chapter 45

ST. CUTHMAN

d. 900

Of Anglo-Saxon extraction, Cuthman was born in the south of England and seems to have led a worry-free life during his childhood and early manhood. His parents were careful to instruct him in the Faith, and he benefited from the pious atmosphere of their home. He is said never to have disobeyed his parents, and he was diligent in shepherding his father's flock of sheep. This employment gave him leisure to engage in lengthy prayer. It was noticed that he had an unusual influence over his sheep and that he always returned home from the fields at the appointed time.

Life became difficult for Cuthman and his invalid mother after his father's death. Because of his mother's delicate health, Cuthman spent all that he had and all that he could earn in supporting and caring for her. Finally he had to sell the family's livestock and property, since it became necessary for him to look elsewhere for work. Cuthman was obliged to take his mother with him whenever he went looking for work, and as a means of transporting her he built a "sort of carriage," or a "wheelbarrow," as one writer calls it. Traveling from place to place looking for work entailed serious hardships and austerities for both of them, but they accepted these cheerfully as a penance.

Upon the pair's reaching Steyning in Sussex, tradition says that a wheel fell off the cart, and this Cuthman accepted as a sign that God willed them to stay there. Cuthman built a little cottage of wood and thatch as a shelter for his mother; there they devoted themselves without distraction to fervent prayer. As soon as their simple little home was completed, Cuthman prepared the ground next to it for the foundation of a church, which he began to build himself. The people who lived in the area were so affected by his zeal that they contributed toward the completion of the work. Cuthman is said to have labored all day, while engaged at the same time in silent prayer.

When the church was completed, Cuthman spent part of his time in preaching and converting pagans to Christianity. Miracles are said to have been worked through his prayers—and after his death in the year 900, more wonders were worked at his tomb. His relics were later removed to Winchester Cathedral, which became the destination of many pilgrims.

Chapter 46

ST. DAGOBERT II

d. 679

St. Dagobert's father was the sainted King Sigebert, who ruled Austrasia for 18 years and died at the age of 26. When Sigebert died in 656, his son Dagobert was a small child. No mention is made of his mother, but it seems that Dagobert was left helpless against the influence of those around him. His guardian was Grimoald, a son of Bl. Pepin of Landen, who had served three monarchs with great virtue and distinction. But Grimoald was unlike his sainted father and actually schemed to take the kingdom away from the child Dagobert and award it to his own son Childebert.

To achieve this end, Grimoald arranged for the child Dagobert to be kidnapped and taken out of the territory. Dido, the Bishop of Poitiers, was eventually given custody of Dagobert and took him to safety in Ireland. There Dagobert is said to have been educated at the court of the High King.

When he was old enough, Dagobert traveled throughout England. There he became friends with St. Wilfrid of York. Also in England, he met and married an English princess, by whom he had several children. Two of these, Irmina and Adela, are also venerated as saints.

When Childebert, who sat unworthily on the throne of Austrasia, was murdered in 675, Dagobert was repatriated through the efforts of St. Wilfrid and recovered his kingdom. Dagobert's exile had lasted 20 years.

When St. Wilfrid was on his way to Rome, he visited Dagobert's court at Metz. King Dagobert wished to reward St. Wilfrid's services by naming him to the vacant see of Strasburg, but St. Wilfrid graciously refused, claiming that the will of God lay elsewhere. Dagobert then entrusted the see to the Irish St. Florentius, whom Dagobert had helped in the founding of a number of monasteries.

St. Wilfrid's enemy—and Dagobert's as well—was Ebroin, the

Mayor of the Palace of Neustria. Dagobert was forced into a war with Theodericus III by the political maneuverings of Ebroin, who is described as having been an unscrupulous minister and a tyrant. Dagobert survived the war, but his death—which occurred while he was hunting in the forest of Woevre in Lorraine on December 23, 679—was attributed to the treachery of Ebroin.

St. Dagobert was first buried at Stenay, but his remains were taken at a later time to the cathedral at Rouen. The relics were subsequently translated back to the Church of Stenay. His founding of monasteries and his zeal for religion and the good of his people led to his cultus as a saint.

Chapter 47

ST. DAVINUS

d. 1051

Endeavoring to follow the counsels of perfection in the most literal sense, Davinus gave away his possessions to the poor, left his family and country and embraced the life of a pilgrim. The pious and formerly wealthy young Armenian practiced continual fasting and mortification while journeying to the holy places in Jerusalem. After visiting the tombs of the Apostles in Rome he intended to make his way to the famous shrine of St. James at Compostella, but being extremely weary from his travels he could go no further than Lucca. While accepting the hospitality of a pious lady named Atha, he became gravely ill. He died in the year 1051, on the day and at the hour he had predicted.

Great respect was given his mortal remains, which were first buried in a cemetery, and afterwards in the Church of San Michele. In 1547 his body was found to be incorrupt.

St. Davinus is believed to have been canonized in the thirteenth century.

Chapter 48

ST. DOMINIC SAVIO

1842 - 1857

St. Don Bosco said of this saint, "In the life of Dominic Savio you see innate virtue cultivated up to heroism during his whole life." Dominic was to achieve this heroic virtue during a lifetime consisting of only 14 years.

Dominic's exceptional life began on April 2, 1842, in Castelnuova, Italy; he was the second in a family of 10 children. His parents, Charles and Brigid Savio, were hard-working peasants who moved to Riva and then to Murialdo, where Charles found more profitable work as a blacksmith. Dominic's sanctity can be credited to the early training given him by his parents, whose faith and devotion served as examples for their children to imitate.

At the age of five, Dominic was already attending daily Mass. If he arrived early, before the doors were opened, he would kneel on the steps in prayer. When he was old enough, he served Mass almost daily. Although the usual age for receiving First Communion was twelve, the pastor decided that since Dominic was not only well-prepared but also had an intense desire for the Sacrament, the boy should be permitted to communicate at the age of seven.

The day before he received his First Holy Communion, Dominic begged his mother's and father's pardon for all that he might have done to displease them, and he promised to practice virtue with the help of God.

On the day Dominic was to communicate for the first time, he composed resolutions which were to be his rule for life. He wrote them in a little book and often read them. They were as follows: "I will go to confession and Communion as often as my confessor allows. I will keep holy the feast days. My friends shall be Jesus and Mary. Death—but not sin."

At Murialdo, Dominic finished his primary studies and was then

169

sent to Castelnuova for further study. Since it was necessary for him to walk to school, return for lunch, walk back to school and then return at the end of the day, the walk amounted to eight miles, in all kinds of weather. The boy never complained, and when asked if he was not afraid to walk alone, especially in bad weather, he replied that his guardian angel was with him.

As an example of how Dominic avoided the least influence of sin, we are told that once when he was swimming with a group of boys, they began to make vulgar remarks and to laugh at improper gestures. Dominic immediately left the water, dressed and went home.

Eventually his father's work forced the family to move to Mondonio, where Dominic resumed his studies. One day, while the teacher was absent from the room, two boys stuffed snow and trash into the iron stove that was heating the room. When the teacher returned he became extremely angry. The two guilty boys were so frightened that they falsely accused Dominic of the deed. He remained silent about the matter while he was being scolded before the entire class. When he was later vindicated and asked why he did not defend himself, Dominic replied that Our Lord has also been accused falsely and had remained silent.

Eventually Fr. Cugliero, his teacher, recommended Dominic to St. John Bosco (Don Bosco). The two Saints met in 1854. Don Bosco immediately recognized the beauty of the boy's soul, and it was agreed that Dominic should attend Don Bosco's school, the Oratory of St. Francis de Sales. There he became the delight of his teachers, who used his politeness and studious manners as an influence on other boys. Dominic is known to have prevented fights and to have spoken out against tardiness and absence from school.

Once when St. John Bosco preached a sermon on being a saint, Dominic adopted mortifications and penances that were too strict and unsuitable for his age. On learning of these, Don Bosco ordered him to abandon them and instead to observe the following simple suggestions, which can be adopted by all children: to fulfill the duties of his state, that of being a schoolboy; to do good to companions who by nature are displeasing; to forgive those who are vulgar or rude; to consume all food or drink at meals and not to waste anything; to study all subjects at school, even those that are not appealing; to be humble when others are chosen before you for favorite tasks or privileges; never to complain about the weather, but rather to thank God for it; to be bright and cheerful when inclined to be otherwise; and to take advantage of every opportunity to show love for Jesus Christ. Don Bosco concluded by reminding the future saint that "Obedience is your greatest possible sacrifice."

When Don Bosco was displeased with the small number of boys approaching the Communion railing, Dominic and some of his friends formed the Immaculate Conception Sodality. Their goal was not only to increase the frequency of reception of Holy Communion, but also to promote devotion to the Blessed Sacrament and the Blessed Virgin.

Dominic's life of grace was soon marked by ecstasies before the tabernacle, prophetic dreams and mystical knowledge of souls in need of the Last Sacraments and of the sick who were in need of prayers. It is told of Dominic that once while at school he begged permission to return home. There he found his mother close to death during a difficult childbirth. Dominic placed a green scapular on her breast and then returned to school, knowing she would be safely delivered—as indeed she was.

Never in robust health, Dominic became ill and was sent home for a rest; he knew he would never return to the Oratory. At home his condition worsened. He was diagnosed as having inflammation of the lungs, the customary cure being bleeding. This was performed so often that Dominic was soon reduced to a dying state. After reciting prayers for a happy death and receiving the Last Sacraments, Dominic expired on March 9th, 1857, when only 14 years of age. His last words were, "What a beautiful thing I see."

In 1876 Dominic, accompanied by many holy souls, appeared to Don Bosco in a vision and revealed that he was in Heaven. The young Saint was canonized in 1954 by Pope Pius XII. He is considered a true model for the youth of our times, since he lived a simple life of virtue—a type of life that can be imitated by youths of all ages.

A painting of St. Dominic Savio (1842-1857), whose devout life ended following an illness when he was only 14 years old. St. Dominic Savio appeared to St. John Bosco in a vision in 1876, accompanied by many holy souls, and revealed that he was in Heaven.

1857 S. DOMENICO SAVIO 1957

LABORARE EST ORARE

Opere Don Bosco, Torino/Gros Monti & C., Torino

This painting calls to mind St. Dominic Savio's exemplary conduct and favorable influence on his schoolmates.

St. Dominic Savio looks heavenward in this painting, illustrating the boy's life of grace, which was marked by ecstasies before the tabernacle, prophetic dreams and mystical knowledge of souls.

Chapter 49

ST. DOROTHEA OF MONTAU

1347 - 1394

From the age of 17 until she was 35 years of age, this saint suffered prolonged grief and unhappiness. Born in 1347 of poor parents at Montau (Marienburg), Germany, Dorothea was married at the age of 17 to Albert, a swordsmith of Danzig, by whom she had nine children. The youngest child, a daughter, eventually became a Benedictine nun, but the rest all died during their childhood. The grief that Dorothea experienced at the loss of her children was alleviated only by the grace and comforts of her faith. Her husband offered her little or no consolation; in fact, while their children were sick and dying, she had much to suffer from Albert, who was ill-tempered and overbearing. For most of her married life Dorothea had much to endure on this account.

Eventually, however, her gentleness and patience affected his disposition to such an extent that in 1382, after almost 20 years of married life, Albert agreed to accompany his pious wife on a pilgrimage to Aachen. The change in Albert was so dramatic that he began to share his wife's spiritual life and readily agreed to accompany her on other pilgrimages. Together the couple prayed at a number of shrines, including Einsiedeln and Cologne. They were planning a journey to Rome when Albert became ill, but at his insistence Dorothea went alone. Upon her return, she learned that her husband had just died.

Widowed at the age of 43, Dorothea moved to Marienwerder, and in 1393, with the approval of her confessor, she took up residence in a cell by the church of the Teutonic Knights. She was there only a year, but during that time she gained a great reputation for holiness. Many were the visitors who came to her asking for advice in temporal and spiritual matters, and many were those who came to her hoping for a physical cure. We are told by her spiritual director,

175

who wrote her Life, that Dorothea had a very intense devotion to the Blessed Sacrament and was often supernaturally enabled to look upon it.

Dorothea was greatly revered by the people who knew her; they acclaimed her a saint immediately after her death in 1394.

Devotion to St. Dorothea spread to Poland, Lithuania, Bohemia and elsewhere. Unfortunately, the church at Marienwerder where Dorothea was buried was seized by the Lutherans. Since then her relics have not been found.

Chapter 50

ST. DROGO

d. 1186

Drogo's father died shortly before he was born, and his mother died during childbirth. When he was ten years old, Drogo (or Druon) learned that his mother's life had been sacrificed to save his. He went into a depression, during which he accused himself bitterly for having been the cause of her death. But, thankfully, he learned to trust in the wisdom of God and accepted his mother's death as the will of the Almighty.

Always inclined to prayer and good works, Drogo was 18 when he decided to follow Our Lord's example of complete poverty. He decided to abandon his home, his country and his inheritance to embark on the penitential life of a pilgrim. He journeyed through several countries, visiting the holy places along the way and being inspired by the Saints whose shrines he visited. Having received many spiritual blessings and having advanced in the interior life, Drogo felt the need to settle down; he did so at Sebourg, near Valenciennes.

At Sebourg he was hired as a shepherd by a kindly woman named Elizabeth de la Haire. While he was engaged in this humble occupation his virtue became well-known, and he was regarded as a saint by his employer and the people of the district. Many noticed that while he was tending his flocks in the fields, Drogo was often seen at the same time attending Holy Mass in the village church. This gift of bilocation gave rise to a local saying: "Not being St. Drogo, I cannot be in two places at the same time."

After tending sheep for six years, Drogo resumed his pilgrimages, returning from time to time to visit his patroness. It is said that he made nine visits to Rome before his travels ended in a pathetic manner.

The physical condition that made it impossible for Drogo to continue traveling has been described as a "peculiarly repulsive hernia

177

which could not be hidden.'' He was then at Sebourg, where he had spent several years tending sheep. In an effort to shield himself from his neighbors, so as not to offend them by his appearance, he retired to a cell that had been built against the church. Through a small window he was able to assist at Holy Mass without entering the body of the church, and he was fed through the generosity of those who admired his virtue and pitied his condition. He never left this small room beside the church and spent 40 years praying, fasting and suffering greatly from his affliction.

When he died in 1186, at the age of 84, Drogo was popularly honored as a saint, and his tomb became a favorite place of pilgrimage. He is regarded as the patron of shepherds and is invoked by those who suffer from hernia.

Chapter 51

ST. DYMPHNA

d. 650

Dymphna was the only child of a pagan king and a Christian queen who ruled a section of Ireland in the seventh century. Dymphna bore a striking resemblance to her beautiful mother, an attribute that was to threaten her purity and caused the loss of her life.

After the death of the Queen, the inconsolable King, on the verge of mental collapse, consented to the court's entreaties that he distract his thoughts from his beloved wife by marrying a second time. The King's only requirement was that the new wife should resemble his first. Since no one in the country could compare except the daughter, she was suggested as the replacement for her deceased mother. The emotional turmoil of the King allowed this sinful suggestion to seem plausible.

When the illicit marriage was proposed, Dymphna confided the news to her confessor, a pious priest named Gerebern, by whom her mother and other members of the family had been instructed in the Faith. He advised Dymphna to explain to her father the sinful and horrible nature of his proposal, and to pray to God that he would change his mind and ask God for forgiveness for ever having considered such a union. Dymphna obeyed her confessor, but the King was deaf to all her arguments. He appointed a certain day on which the ceremony should take place. Knowing too well the obstinate and vindictive nature of the pagan King, and realizing that it was useless to attempt to change his plans, Gerebern decided that flight was the only means of preserving Dymphna's purity.

Secret plans were made for Gerebern, as well as the court jester and his wife, to accompany Dymphna in her escape from the country. After crossing the sea to the coast of Belgium, they traveled inland and settled 25 miles from Antwerp in the village of Gheel, near the shrine dedicated to St. Martin of Tours. With Gerebern instructing them and offering the Sacrifice of the Mass, the group led virtuous lives, spending time in devotions and in acts of penance.

The King made a diligent search for his daughter, and followed her as far as Antwerp. From there he sent spies, who discovered the refuge of the fugitives. The clue by which they were traced was their use of strange coins—similar to those which the spies themselves offered in payment.

When the King finally confronted Dymphna, he at first tried to persuade her to return home with him—but he became enraged when he was again unsuccessful in his marriage proposal. When both Dymphna and her confessor attempted to explain the sinfulness of such a marriage, the King indignantly accused the priest of being the cause of Dymphna's disobedience—and ordered his immediate decapitation.

Deprived of the priest's support, Dymphna still remained steadfast. In a fury, her father ordered her execution. When his soldiers hesitated, the King himself severed his daughter's head with his own sword. Dymphna was barely 15 years of age.

The two bodies were left exposed on the ground for days, since everyone was afraid to approach them because of the King. The bodies were eventually buried, in a humble manner, by the villagers.

The maiden was soon regarded as a saint, a martyr of purity and a champion over the wiles of the devil, who had brought her father to madness. In due time those afflicted with lunacy sought her intercession and journeyed to her tomb in pilgrimage.

On account of the growing number of pilgrims, it was decided to give her body and that of her confessor worthier tombs inside the chapel. In digging for the remains, workmen were surprised to find the bodies in two coffins of white stone, of a kind unknown in the neighborhood of Gheel. This gave rise to the legend that the bodies had been reburied by angels after the original interment, since no one could remember their burial in white coffins. When the remains were exhumed, a red stone identifying the maiden was found on the breast of Dymphna.

During the Middle Ages, those who visited Gheel to invoke the Saint were encouraged to make a novena of nine days at the shrine, while many afflicted persons participated in seven ceremonies called "penances." Among other practices, they were to attend Mass daily and recite prayers intended to exorcize the demons who were thought to have caused their illness. Until the 18th century the same prayers were said in Gheel for all the sick, without distinction between those believed devil-ridden and the mentally ill. During these prayers the red stone found on the remains of St. Dymphna was hung around the necks of the afflicted.

The relics of the Saint are kept in a silver reliquary in a church that bears her name in Gheel, near Antwerp, Belgium. The church is believed to be situated over the Saint's original burial place.

Today St. Dymphna is invoked worldwide for restoration of mental stability, as well as of religious fervor. She is the patroness of those suffering from mental and nervous disorders.

A statue of St. Dymphna.

An artist's conception of the youthful martyr St. Dymphna, patroness of those afflicted with mental and nervous disorders. She is a consolation to those who request her intercession. The Saint was executed in the year 650 by her own father after the 15-year-old girl refused to marry him. This pagan Irish king had become inconsolable after the death of St. Dymphna's mother. Soon after Dymphna's death, the maiden was regarded as a saint, a martyr of purity and a champion over the wiles of the devil.

182

Chapter 52

ST. EDGAR, KING OF ENGLAND

d. 944 - 975

Upon the death of King Eadwig in 959, his brother Edgar was chosen to replace him. Little change was seen in the personnel of the government in this transfer of power, but the effect upon the Church was said to be momentous. One of the first acts of the new King was to order the return of St. Dunstan, who had been exiled for denouncing the vices of Edgar's predecessor. With St. Dunstan and other capable men assisting him, Edgar had a reign that was prosperous and peaceful—so much so that he was given the name, "the Peaceable."

Edgar's personal life, on the other hand, was scarred with a few difficulties. Ethelfleda the Duck, so named because of her pale complexion, was Edgar's first wife. Born of this marriage was a son, the future St. Edward, who followed his father to the throne of England. Upon Ethelfleda's death soon after childbirth, Edgar married Elfrida, a widow who was the daughter of Ordgar, the Earl of Devon. This marriage produced two sons, one of whom died in childhood.

Historians believe that a curious situation took place before Edgar's first marriage. According to Stenton in his book, *Anglo-Saxon England,* "The first event of his time which made a strong impression upon his contemporaries was his long-deferred coronation, which took place at Bath on Whitsunday 973."

By way of explaining the delay, or perhaps in an effort to conceal the real reason, Stenton continues, "Up to this time there had been no fixed order for the coronation of an English king...he had deliberately to postpone his [own] coronation until he felt that he had come to full maturity of mind and conduct."

However, according to Butler, who relied upon a biography of Edgar as written by William of Malmesbury in 1125, the coronation was

183

delayed for seven years by St. Dunstan as punishment for Edgar's rape of Wulfrida, a woman who lived in Wilton Abbey. Butler writes:

> More certain it is that Edgar in his youth ravished St. Wul-
> frida from her convent, so becoming the father of St. Edith of
> Wilton; for this sacrilegious rape St. Dunstan imposed the pub-
> lic penance that Edgar should not wear his crown for seven years,
> and in fact he was not crowned in Bath abbey church until two
> years before his death.
>
> This horrid episode is not without its edifying side: for it shows
> that if the men of the past were not afraid to commit atrocious
> sins, neither were they ashamed to submit to religious authority
> and perform humiliating penances.

Another writer, in giving the history of the Benedictine convent known as Wilton Abbey, mentions that the abbey

> ...is best known as the home of St. Edith, the child of a "hand-
> fast" union between Edgar, King of the English, and Wulfrida,
> a lady wearing the veil though not a nun, whom he carried off
> from Wilton probably in 961. After Edith's birth, Wulfrida re-
> fused to enter into a permanent marriage with Edgar and retired
> with her child to Wilton. Edith received the veil while a
> child...and at the age of fifteen refused the abbacy of three
> houses offered by her father...She built the Church of St. Denis
> at Wilton, which was consecrated by St. Dunstan, and died shortly
> afterwards, in 984, at the age of 23.

Although St. Dunstan delayed Edgar's coronation for seven years, Edgar himself seems to have added additional years to his penance. We can only imagine the humiliation this entailed—a king deprived of a crown, the sign of his pre-eminence and authority. We can also imagine that the whole kingdom knew of the reason for the delay, and the whispering that took place as a result. The delay might also explain Stenton's statement that Edgar "had deliberately to post-pone his coronation until he felt that he had come to full maturity of mind and conduct."

The humiliation caused by the delay apparently did not alter the admiration in which Edgar was held by his nobles. As proof of this, his eight sub-kings (tributary princes), after his coronation, rowed Edgar along the River Dee in an impressive procession from his pal-ace at Chester to the Monastery of St. John the Baptist. These eight kings represented Scotland, Cumberland, and the Isles, and five were from Wales. They were accompanied by a fleet of boats carrying Edgar's nobles.

Butler writes that "Edgar's public life was more in accordance with that popular reputation which attributed sanctity to him." The great achievement of his reign was the revival of religious life and ecclesiastical observance. Assisted by St. Dunstan, St. Ethewold of Winchester and St. Oswald of Worcester, Edgar restored the secular clergy, which had grown lax, to the proper observance of their priestly calling. They were urged not only to fulfill their spiritual duties, but to care for the material and intellectual well-being of their parishioners. In several cathedrals and collegiate churches the chapters were replaced by Benedictine monks; other religious were encouraged to live in community and according to a rule.

In addition to achieving ecclesiastical reform and promoting spiritual revival among the clergy and in monastic institutions, Edgar was successful in keeping England secure against foreign enemies. At the time of Edgar's death, a writer in the *Chronicle,* in referring to the security of England during Edgar's reign, comments that "No fleet was so proud, nor host so strong that it could prey on England while that noble king held the throne." Edgar is also credited with maintaining a standard of political order which set a pattern for later generations.

Edgar died quite suddenly at the age of 31, having officially reigned as King of England for only two years. He was buried at the Abbey of Glastonbury, and as a result of various miracles attributed to his intercession, his relics were later enshrined above the high altar of the chapel.

The cult to St. Edgar has not been officially approved by the Holy See.

A painting of St. Edgar, King of England (944-975), with Our Lord. The artwork is located in the British Museum. Even though St. Edgar's reign was so peaceful and prosperous that it won him the name, "the Peaceable," his personal life was scarred with difficulties such as the death of his first wife and the scandal that resulted after he raped a woman who lived in Wilton Abbey. The latter incident caused a seven-year delay of his coronation. Even so, St. Edgar achieved ecclesiastical reform and promoted spiritual revival among the clergy. *(Br. Museum.)*

Chapter 53

ST. EDMUND, KING OF EAST ANGLIA

d. 870

Although he was almost 15 years old at the time he was crowned King of East Anglia in the year 855, Edmund proved to be a model ruler from the first. He was eager to treat all with equal justice, and he performed his duties in a kind and Christian manner. He is said to have been as talented and successful a ruler as he was virtuous.

Edmund's character is well illustrated by Lydgate the Benedictine, who wrote in the fifteenth century that Edmund was "in his estate most godly and benign, heavenly of cheer, of counsel provident, showing of grace full many a blessed sign. . ." In his eagerness to advance spiritually, Edmund retired for a year to his royal tower at Hunstanton and is said to have learned the whole Psalter by heart so that he might recite it regularly.

During the ninth century, the Northmen (or Danes) began to raid the coasts of England with greater frequency than they had formerly. The largest Danish invasion that ever took place occurred in the year 866 and began in Northumbria. When the invaders reached East Anglia, Edmund at first tried to resist by negotiating with the enemy. The *Anglo-Saxon Chronicle* states that "in the year 867 a great army [of Danes] came to the land of the Angle race and took up winter quarters among the East Angles, and there they were provided with horses. And the East Angles made peace with them." The invaders then crossed the Humber and took York. Next they marched south into Mercia as far as Nottingham, plundering and burning as they went.

The preceding account of what took place is the earliest record available, but the traditional account of what took place is given by other historians, and in particular by St. Abbo of Fleury in his *Passio Sancti Eadmundi*. These reports are summarized by Butler in this manner:

187

The barbarians poured down upon St. Edmund's dominions [in 870], burning Thetford, which they took by surprise, and laying waste all before them. The king [St. Edmund] raised what forces he could, met a part of the Danes' army near Thetford, and discomfited them. But seeing them soon after reinforced with fresh numbers, against which his small body of soldiers was not able to make any stand, he retired towards his castle of Framlingham in Suffolk. The barbarian leader, Hinguar, had sent him proposals which were inconsistent both with religion and with the justice which he owed to his people. These the saint rejected, being resolved rather to die a victim of his faith and duty to God than to do anything against his conscience. In his flight he was overtaken and surrounded at Hoxne, upon the Waveney. . .Terms were again offered him prejudicial to religion and to his people, which he refused, declaring that religion was dearer to him than his life, which he would never purchase by offending God.

After restraining him with chains, Edmund's captors conducted him to Hinguar. When the party arrived there the same demands were made of Edmund, but these he again rejected, declaring that his religion was dearer to him than his life. This refusal was preliminary to a most cruel martyrdom.

After beating him with cudgels (short heavy clubs), the Danes tied him to a tree and cruelly tore his flesh with whips.

During these tortures Edmund called upon the name of Jesus. Exasperated by his conduct, his enemies began to shoot arrows at him. This continued until his body is said to have taken on the appearance of a porcupine. When the enemy grew tired of this activity, Hinguar commanded his men to decapitate their victim. At the time of his death, Edmund was approximately 30 years old.

Edmund's first burial place was at Hoxne, but his relics were removed in the tenth century to the City of Beodriesworth, which was renamed St. Edmundsbury, or Bury St. Edmund. During another conflict with the Danes, the relics were taken to London, but were brought back to St. Edmundsbury three years later. During the reign of King Canute (d. 1035), the great Benedictine abbey of St. Edmundsbury was founded. The body of St. Edmund was the principal relic in the abbey church, which was the destination of many pilgrims—including King Canute and Henry VI. In 1465 a fire in the Abbey caused substantial damage—from which it never fully recovered. The Abbey was finally dissolved by Henry VIII in 1539. The disposition of the Saint's relics is a matter of dispute.

In art St. Edmund is depicted with a sword and arrow, the instruments of his torture.

Chapter 54

ST. EDWARD, THE BOY KING

d. 979

St. Edward was the son of St. Edgar the Peaceful (d. 975), the sovereign King of all England, and of Edgar's first wife, the beautiful Ethelfleda, who died soon after her son's birth. Edward was baptized by St. Dunstan, the Archbishop of Canterbury, who took a great interest in his upbringing and his advancement in virtue.

When Edward's father died, the whole country is said to have been thrown into a state of confusion since neither of his two surviving sons was old enough to rule. At his father's death, Edward was only 13 years old. At once the deceased King's second wife, Elfrida, opposed Edward's ascension, even though King Edgar had nominated Edward as his successor. Elfrida wanted the throne for her own son, Ethelred (Aethelred), who was then only seven years old. We might surmise two main reasons for Elfrida's choice: one could have been pride in wanting her own son to succeed to the throne of England; the other was perhaps that Edward had offended many important persons. According to Stenton in his book, *Anglo-Saxon England,* Edward was given to "intolerable violence of speech and behavior...his outbursts of rage had alarmed all who knew him, and especially the members of his own household."

It may have been for this reason that a large number of nobles sided with Elfrida in opposing Edward and promoting the election of Ethelred, the younger brother. However, St. Dunstan, the clergy and most of the nobles rejected the effort and elected Edward in accordance with his father's will.

Under the guidance of St. Dunstan, the young King's temper was brought under control, and he advanced in wisdom and charity while developing into a young man of great promise and virtue.

Historians and biographers all agree that Edward was murdered in a most despicable manner. The details of the crime are given by

190

William of Malmesbury in his eleventh-century biography of Edward. The facts are also mentioned in the early biographies of St. Oswald and St. Dunstan.

St. Edward's untimely death occurred in this manner: On the evening of March 18, 979, after hunting in the forests of Dorsetshire, King Edward was feeling tired; he decided to visit his stepmother, Elfrida, at Corfe Castle, which was nearby. From all appearances, his relationship with Elfrida and his stepbrother Ethelred had grown friendly since his coronation. But in spite of this appearance, William of Malmesbury informs us that since the time of the coronation, Elfrida had developed a hatred of Edward and waited for an opportunity to have him killed. The earliest accounts of the murder state that as Edward approached the castle, Elfrida and several servants went out to meet him with every sign of welcome and respect. Before Edward dismounted, though, the servants surrounded him, seized his hands and stabbed him.

Another report adds other details: that as Edward approached, Elfrida was informed that he had ridden well ahead of his company and was alone. Elfrida pretended pleasure at seeing him and ordered a cup of mead to be brought to him at the castle gate. While he was still mounted and drinking from the cup, Elfrida made a sign to one of her servants, who stabbed the young King in the abdomen with a dagger. Edward immediately set spurs to his horse and tried to ride out to meet his attendants, but being weak from the wound and loss of blood, he slipped from the saddle. His leg caught in the stirrup, and he was dragged until he died.

Elfrida had Edward's body thrown into a marsh, thinking to be rid of it altogether. However, a beam of light is said to have caused its discovery. The body was taken up and buried without ceremony in the Church of Our Lady at Wareham. A few years later, Aelfhere of Mercia removed Edward's body to the convent at Shaftesbury Abbey, where miracles soon multiplied. As a result of these reports, Edward was soon regarded as a saint and a martyr. Butler, while admitting that devotion to the Saint was widespread and strong, nevertheless states that "Edward's claim to martyrdom is of the slenderest." However, having won the affection of the people, and having been regarded as a defender of the Church and a model of virtue, Edward is recognized by the title of Martyr in all the old English calendars on March 18. He is also regarded as such in the *Roman*

Martyrology.

Elfrida reportedly was overwhelmed with remorse for her crime and, in reparation, built the monasteries of Ambresburg and Wherwell. She retired to the monastery at Wherwell and died there after practicing austere penances.

Ethelred was crowned King of England a month after Edward's murder, but he was unable to escape the results of the murder. He reigned in an atmosphere of skepticism which diminished the prestige of the crown. Even though he was too young to have been an accomplice in his brother's murder, the crime had been committed for his sake—and he was never able to escape its memory. Public opinion was still strong against him 30 years after the murder, when Ethelred ordered the general observance of his brother's festival. His reign was troubled with unrest, and it was his fate to be regarded as a weak king. It was never forgotten that, as Stenton puts it, "He had come to power through what his subjects regarded as the worst crime committed among the English peoples since their first coming to Britain."

It is reported that no one was punished for taking part in the murder of the 17-year-old king who had reigned for only three and a half years.

A statue of St. Edward, the Boy King of England (d. 979), which is located in the Church of St. Edward, Corfe Castle. He died at age 17 after a reign of only 3-1/2 years. The Saint here wears the robe of an adult king, which is obviously too long. The son of St. Edgar the Peaceful and Ethel-fleda, St. Edward the Boy King was murdered by his stepmother, Elfrida, because she wanted her son to become king. Elfrida was later overwhelmed with remorse.

Chapter 55

BL. EDWARD COLEMAN

d. 1678

Born in Suffolk, England, Edward was the son of an Anglican minister who provided for his son's education at the University of Cambridge. Afterwards, Edward became a zealous convert to the Catholic Faith and secretary to the Duchess of York.

A contemporary Protestant chronicler refers to him as "a great bigot in his religion and of a busy head." But Edward Coleman was a man of talent and a dedicated Roman Catholic in a land which rejected the Pope and instead professed King Charles II as the head of the Church of England.

Edward's downfall came because of his friendly correspondence for many years with Père la Chaise, the French King's confessor, and his correspondence with other foreign friends. At this time, what became known as the "Popish Plot," or the "Oates Plot," appeared on the English scene. This was named for Titus Oates, a notorious informer, who intended to advance his own prestige and selfish interests by discovering alleged schemes of Roman Catholics to assassinate the King and restore the Pope's influence in England.

When Edward Coleman's foreign correspondence was discovered, he was arrested as a participator in the "Popish Plot" and brought to trial at the Old Bailey on November 28, 1678. Edward was additionally charged with a plot to assassinate the King with the assistance of a foreign power. Although Edward engaged in a vigorous defense, proving that this charge and others were false, he was nevertheless convicted and sentenced.

On December 3, 1678, Edward Coleman was brought to the place of execution. His dying statement was recorded as follows:

> It is now expected I should speak and make some discovery of a very great plot. I know not whether I shall have the good

194

fortune to be believed better now than formerly; if so, I do solemnly declare, upon the words of a dying man, I know nothing of it. And as for the raising of sedition, subverting the government, stirring up the people to rebellion, altering the known laws, and contriving the death of the king, I am wholly ignorant of it...I am, as I said, a Roman Catholic, and have been so for many years, yet I renounce that doctrine which some wrongfully say that the Romish Church doth usher in to promote their interests: that kings may be murdered, and the like; I say, I abominate it.

After making other statements in which he continued to proclaim his innocence and to profess his allegiance to the Catholic Faith, Edward Coleman recited some private prayers. The sentence was then executed. "He was hanged by the neck, cut down alive, his bowels burnt, and himself quartered."

Blessed Edward Coleman was beatified in 1929.

Chapter 56

ST. EDWARD THE CONFESSOR

d. 1066

Beginning in the eighth century and continuing for over 200 years, the Danes invaded, sacked and troubled England in an attempt to colonize it. Eventually three Danes succeeded each other to the throne of England; and all three, in one way or another, were related to the English St. Edward the Confessor, who was to succeed them.

Although various skirmishes are noted during the reign of St. Edward, he is said to have restored relative peace to the land; his personal life, on the other hand, was disturbed by family difficulties and intrigues which one could hardly expect or imagine from one's mother, father-in-law and brothers-in-law.

King Ethelred the Unready was Edward's father; his mother was Emma, a Norman. When the Danes were causing a disturbance in the year 1013, Edward, then ten years old, was sent with his brother Alfred to the safety of Normandy. Three years later, in 1016, three important events are recorded in the history of the English nation: Edward's father, King Ethelred, died and was succeeded by Ethelred's illegitimate son, Edmund Ironside—who reigned only a few months before dying at the age of 27; and, during the year of her husband's death, the widow Emma married the Danish Canute, who succeeded Edmund Ironside to the throne of England.

One would have expected Ethelred's son Edward to succeed him to the throne, but the ambitious Emma seems to have influenced the succession and maintained her noble prestige by marrying Canute, who at the time of his marriage to Emma already had an illegitimate son, Harold Harefoot. Of her marriage to Canute, Emma had a son, Hardecanute. After reigning for 19 years, Canute died at the age of 40. The year was 1035. After the reign of three Danish kings, those who wanted a return to English supremacy persuaded Edward's brother Alfred to return to England to claim the throne.

It seems unbelievable that Emma would "be privy" to a plot to have her own son murdered and denied his legitimate claim to the throne. Nevertheless, she is accused by some of engineering such a plot when Alfred, her son by Ethelred, returned to England at the persuasion of the English nobles. Soon after he arrived in England Alfred was seized, blinded, mutilated and murdered by the retainers of Harold Harefoot. Emma seems to have preferred the sons of Canute over her sons by Ethelred, as witnessed by the succession of Canute's illegitimate son, Harold Harefoot, who then seized the crown of England; however, he wore it for only five years. After his death he was succeeded by Emma's son by Canute, Hardecanute, who reigned only two years and then died quite suddenly in 1042 "as he stood at his drink" at the wedding feast of his father's retainer, Tovi the Proud.

Except for the year 1035, when Edward returned briefly to England with his brother Alfred, he had remained in prayerful exile in Normandy. But then, with the death of his stepbrother Hardecanute, Edward was elected king by popular acclamation in London before Hardecanute was even buried. As difficult as it is to imagine, Edward's mother Emma did not support her son's election, but rather forwarded the claim of Magnus of Norway, who claimed—by some previous agreement with Hardecanute—that he should succeed him. However, Edward's election stood.

Thus Edward returned to England in 1042 to reign as King of England; he was crowned at Winchester on Easter Sunday, 1043, becoming King Edward III. He was then 40 years of age. History claims that after the neglect, quarreling and oppression experienced during the reigns of Harold Harefoot and Hardecanute, the people of England welcomed Edward, who represented the old English line of kings; and "All men took him, as was his right."

After his coronation, Edward took severe measures to restrain his mother. In the autumn of the year 1043, Edward rode with three of his earls to Winchester, where his mother was living, took possession of all her property and confiscated her lands. This was done to discourage an invasion by Magnus of Norway. Emma, it seems, was accused of inviting Magnus to invade England for the purpose of dethroning her son and of placing her treasure at Magnus' disposal. Since all writers speak of Edward's kindly and pious nature, this action of his mother must have wounded him grievously.

Other steps were taken to ensure Edward's peaceful occupancy of the throne, but having spent almost 30 years in Normandy, Edward was understandably more Norman than English. Although many of Canute's appointees remained at court and the Anglo-Danish influence remained, Edward displeased many by bringing to his English court a number of Normans, while learned and saintly Norman priests were brought in to occupy vacant bishoprics and to serve in the King's chapel. Since Edward was a virtuous man, his Norman friends must have had similar ideals, so that the appointments were probably not harmful. Nevertheless, some have claimed that the Norman Conquest began, not at the battle of Hastings, but at the accession of St. Edward.

One who was violently opposed to the Norman influence at court was the ambitious, powerful and troublesome Earl Godwin, who was Edward's chief minister. Perhaps it was to appease Earl Godwin, or to reassure him and strengthen his influence against the many Normans in the court, that Edward took as his wife and queen Earl Godwin's daughter Edith, although it has been mentioned by many that Edward had little inclination for matrimony.

According to the biographies of the Saint written from a religious perspective, Edward lived with his wife in perfect continence for the love of God and with an aim to greater perfection. Although the continency of the King and Queen was "notorious," William of Malmesbury, in writing a hundred years later, adds, "I have not been able to discover whether he acted thus from dislike of her family or out of pure regard for chastity." Roger of Wendover, the chronicler, relates the same fact, but adds that Edward was certainly unwilling "to beget successors of a traitor stock." Another theory is presented below which might substantiate the claim that his marriage was contracted more in the interests of maintaining peace than out of affection, and that his observance of chastity was due to his lack of husbandly love for his wife.

With the enforced submission of his mother, Edward now had to contend with the many difficulties created by his father-in-law, Earl Godwin, and his family. With the accession of King Edward, Earl Godwin's position at court had become stronger, and his elder sons were naturally promoted to earldoms.

Swein, Godwin's eldest son, after only three years of noble respectability severely damaged his reputation by seducing an abbess.

He then abandoned his earldom when he was not allowed to marry her. When Edward refused to reconcile with him, given the gravity of his sin, Swein visited his cousin Earl Beorn, who was in command of a royal warship off Pevensey, and asked him to act as his friend at court. The two earls were on their way to the King when, for unexplained reasons, Earl Beorn was persuaded to first visit Swein's ship. There Earl Beorn was seized by Swein's men and afterward killed. When the news reached King Edward, he summoned the whole army at Sandwich. All of these men solemnly declared Swein to be "nithing," that is, a man without honor, which made him an outcast in any part of the realm.

Later, Harold, another of Godwin's sons, joined his father and his brother Swein in the dastardly act of assembling a great army to war against Edward for the release of prisoners who had been taken after a skirmish with Edward's men. The King assembled his men to deal with Godwin, but the King was surprised by the attack. Edward was saved from humiliation by two of his earls, who came with forces and surrounded Godwin and his men. Upon seeing their king among the opposing warriors, Godwin's men refused to fight. The deadlock was settled with an exchange of hostages and an agreement that Godwin and his sons should appear in London before the witan to answer the charges which the King would bring against them. Since Godwin had failed to impose his will on his son-in-law by force, he accused Edward of humiliating and disillusioning his followers.

After various appearances before the witan, Godwin's holdings were confiscated and he was given five days in which to leave the country. Godwin and his wife, with three of their sons and a daughter-in-law, made their way to Bosham in Sussex, while Harold sailed for Ireland with a younger brother, Leofwine.

Stenton, in his *Anglo-Saxon England,* relates that "The king completed his deliverance by sending his wife away from court to live in retirement at Wherwell Abbey." If Edward had any affection for his wife, it seems that sending her away was a harsh thing to do. However, this virtual banishment might indicate that since Edward did not trust the members of her family, he probably did not trust the influence they might have over her—which might produce further difficulties. On the other hand, this sending her away into virtual exile might support the theory that Edward had little or no affection for his wife.

If Edward expected peace from his exiled father-in-law, he was mistaken. A year after he was banished from the kingdom, Godwin came back into power. Instead of relying upon thegns and free landowners who refused to fight their king, Godwin assembled a force of seamen who were less scrupulous. After making friends with the enemies of England, he was provided with a great many ships which were to war against King Edward's fleet of 50 ships. After Godwin's ships surrounded the King's small fleet, peace was agreed upon when Bishop Stigand of Winchester mediated a settlement in which, among other concessions, noble titles were given and lands were awarded to Godwin's sons. Stenton says it is doubtful if King Edward ever recovered completely from this humiliating experience.

Of Edward himself, William of Malmesbury tells us that he "was a man by choice devoted to God, living the life of an angel in the administration of his kingdom, and therefore directed by Him...He was so gentle that he would not say a word of reproach to the meanest person." Edward was loved by the common people for his holiness and his wise laws, and especially for abolishing the "Dane gelt," a hated tax. It is said that "He was the first English king to touch scrofulous swellings and sores for the purpose of healing them."

Butler says:

> He was generous to the poor and strangers, especially if they were from abroad, and a great encourager of monks. His favorite diversions were hunting and hawking, at which he would go out for days on end, but even then never omitted to be present at Mass every morning. In appearance he was tall, of regal bearing and well-built, with a ruddy face and white hair and beard...
>
> Even during his lifetime his people regarded him as a saint, crediting him with the powers of healing and forward sight into the hidden mysteries of the future. A contemporary poet writes of him as being noble, chaste and mild, guarding his people until death came and the angels bore his soul into the Light of Heaven. Despite his austerity, he was an ardent sportsman and addicted to all such manly activities. He would spend hours in prayer, and then go off happily to the chase. It was Edward's piety that gave him the name "The Confessor."

During his early exile in Normandy, Edward made a vow to undertake a pilgrimage to St. Peter's Tomb at Rome if God would be pleased to answer certain prayers. This vow, of course, was made prior to his marriage. When he was settled on the throne he revealed this obligation to his council members, who declared that the country could not survive in peace without him. Pope St. Leo IX, therefore, dispensed Edward from his vow upon the condition that he give to the poor the amount of money he would have spent on the journey and, additionally, that he build or repair a monastery in honor of St. Peter.

King Edward selected an abbey in London which dated back to at least 785. He repaired and endowed it out of his own patrimony. Because of its location, the church of this abbey (St. Peter's Abbey) became known as Westminster to distinguish it from the minster (abbey church) of St. Paul in the eastern part of the city. The new abbey was to house 70 monks, but five centuries later Queen Elizabeth dissolved it and designated the church a "collegiate" church to be served by secular priests.

The last years of St. Edward's life were disturbed by many difficulties, including troubles between the Northumbrians and their earl, Tostig Godwinsson, and a rebellion by Harold, Edward's brother-in-law.

When the nobles of the realm were gathered at the royal court for the feast of Christmas, the new choir of Westminster Abbey was consecrated. St. Edward was ill before the ceremony began and died a week later, on January 5, 1066. He was then about 62 years old.

His tomb in Westminster Abbey was hardly sealed when his brother-in-law Harold, who had intrigued in an attempt to win the throne from Edward, quickly seized the vacant throne of England and was hastily crowned on the very day of Edward's burial. But Harold's victory was short-lived. He was defeated within the year by William the Conqueror at the Battle of Hastings.

King Edward was canonized in 1161. Two years later, St. Thomas Becket had the incorrupt body of the Saint translated to a shrine in the magnificent choir of Westminster Abbey. Another translation was conducted during the thirteenth century, when the body was placed in a shrine behind the high altar. The relics of the Confessor are said to be the only relics of a saint remaining *"in situ"* after the violence of the Protestant Reformation.

This portion of the Bayeux Tapestry depicts St. Edward the Confessor (d. 1066) sitting in state. While St. Edward restored relative peace to his country, his personal life was exceptionally turbulent.

A sketch of the shrine of St. Edward the Confessor at Westminster Abbey. The Saint's relics are said to be the only relics of a saint remaining "*in situ*" after the violence of the Protestant Reformation.

Chapter 57

ST. EDWIN

d. 633

An unhappy, unstable childhood characterized the early years of St. Edwin, who was deprived of his patrimony and obliged to wander from one temporary home to another. Additionally, he survived a number of threats and plots against his life.

It all began in the year 588 with the death of Edwin's father, Aella, King of Deira, England. At that time Ethelfrid, King of the Bernicians, seized Aella's kingdom and united all the Northumbrians into one monarchy. To secure his position over the territory that was to fall to Edwin, Ethelfrid placed the life of the three-year-old Edwin in jeopardy, making it necessary for the child to be quickly and secretly removed from the area. Edwin was moved from one friendly prince to another, his life being in continual danger from Ethelfrid's persistent efforts to destroy him. Eventually, when Edwin was a young man, he was accepted into the household of King Redwald of East Anglia.

When Ethelfrid learned the whereabouts of the exiled Edwin, he sent messengers to offer King Redwald a great sum of money to murder Edwin, but this was refused. Ethelfrid sent messengers a second and a third time, but Redwald continued to refuse until Ethelfrid threatened to invade his kingdom. According to the Venerable Bede,

> Redwald, either terrified by his threats or gained by his gifts, complied with his request and promised either to kill Edwin, or to deliver him up to the ambassadors. This being observed by a trusty friend of his [Edwin's], he went into Edwin's chamber, where he was going to bed, for it was the first hour of the night; and calling him out, discovered what the king had promised to do with him, adding, "If, therefore, you think fit, I will this very hour conduct you to a place where neither Redwald nor Ethelfrid shall ever find you."

Edwin thanked his friend but declined the offer, saying that Redwald had always proved to be a friend, and that "If I must die, let it rather be by his hand than by that of any other person." An unusual incident then took place. After his friend left him, Edwin remained outside, brooding over his misfortunes—when, as Bede reports, Edwin

> on a sudden, in the dead of night, saw approaching a person whose face and habit were equally strange, at which unexpected sight he was not a little frightened. The stranger coming close up, saluted him and asked him why he sat there alone and melancholy on a stone at that time, when all others were taking their rest, and were fast asleep?

The stranger then told him that he knew who Edwin was, why he grieved, and the evils which Edwin thought would happen to him at the hands of Redwald. The stranger then promised to deliver Edwin out of his anguish, to restore his kingdom to him and to persuade Redwald to preserve his safety if Edwin would promise to follow the directions of someone who would teach him the way to salvation. After Edwin promised to comply, the stranger placed his hand upon Edwin's head and said, "When this sign shall be given you, remember this present discourse that has passed between us and do not delay the performance of what you now promise." The stranger then vanished. The Venerable Bede suggests that the stranger might have been an angel.

As the stranger had promised, Redwald "was diverted from his treacherous intention by the persuasion of his wife" and prepared to do battle to restore to Edwin his rightful claim to the throne. Redwald assembled a large army and marched against Ethelfrid, who was unprepared. During this battle, which took palce in 616, Ethelfrid was killed on the field of combat. In an ironic development, Edwin, then about 29 years old, was invited to reign as king—not only that portion of the kingdom which was bequeathed to him by his father, but also of the whole of Northumbria, over which his enemy had previously ruled. Edwin received the title of "bretwalda" and had a certain lordship over the other English kings.

We are told nothing of Edwin's first wife, but the Venerable Bede tells us that upon her death in 625, Edwin asked for the hand of Ethelburga, sister of Eadbald, the Christian King of Kent. The proposal met with some resistance, and Edwin was told that "It is not lawful to marry a Christian maiden to a pagan husband." The objection was overcome when Edwin gave his assurance that his wife would be free to practice her religion and that he would consider converting to her religion. Knowing that the word of the King was trustworthy, Ethelburga journeyed to Northumbria with her confessor, St. Paulinus, one of St. Augustine's fellow missionaries and the man who would be the celebrant at the royal wedding.

It seems that no king of that era, no matter how respected and beloved he might be, could relax his vigilance or be certain of a secure and peaceful reign. Edwin was no exception. One year after his marriage his life was again threatened, this time by Cuichelm, King of the West Saxons. Cuichelm sent an assassin named Eumer to stab King Edwin with a dagger which had been dipped in poison, "to the end that if the wound were not sufficient to kill the king, it might be performed by the venom." Eumer would certainly have killed Edwin if Lilla, Edwin's favorite minister, had not stepped between them to protect his monarch. In so doing, Lilla saved the king's life with the loss of his own.

During the same night, that of the attempted assassination, Queen Ethelburga gave birth to a daughter. King Edwin gave thanks to his idols for her safe delivery, but St. Paulinus told him that it was not the false gods that were responsible for the queen's easy and safe delivery, but rather it was the true God, whose Son was Jesus Christ. The King considered the matter and gave his consent for his newborn daughter to be consecrated to God. She was baptized on Whitsunday and was named Eanfleda.

Following the Baptism, Edwin promised Paulinus that if God made him victorious over Cuichelm, who had ordered his assassination, and those who had conspired against his life, that he would himself become a Christian. He assembled his army and marched against Cuichelm, King of the West Saxons. Once again Edwin found cause to rejoice: his enemy was killed on the field of battle. Moreover, his army either killed or took as prisoners all those who had plotted against him. After this decisive victory Edwin abandoned the worship of idols and listened to the instructions of St. Paulinus. St. Bede reports that Edwin, a man of unusual wisdom, "sat much alone by himself, silent of tongue, deliberating in his heart how he should act and to which religion he should adhere."

Pope Boniface V, aware of Edwin's struggle in the matter, sent him an encouraging letter and a silver looking-glass. For the Queen, the Pope sent an ivory comb and a letter in which he asked her to use her powers of persuasion to influence the King in his decision.

St. Paulinus continued to instruct the King, but without any sign that Edwin would honor his pledge to convert if he were victorious over his enemy. But one day, while praying for Edwin, Paulinus approached him and placed his hand upon his head, asking him if he remembered the sign. Edwin suddenly recalled the stranger from the past who had also placed a hand on his head, telling him to remember the incident. Overcome with emotion and trembling, Edwin fell to his knees; but Paulinus, raising him up, told him kindly, "You see that God has delivered you from your enemies; and He offers you His everlasting Kingdom. Take care on your side to perform your promise by receiving His Faith and keeping His Commandments."

After overcoming the emotion of the moment, Edwin still had a spark of resistance; he told Paulinus that he would assemble his nobles and councilors to ask their advice—and that if they agreed, they too might join him in accepting the new Faith. During this meeting Coifi, the chief priest, declared with amazing candor that, by experience, it was manifest that their gods had no power: "No one has worshipped them more diligently than I, but others are more preferred and more prosperous than I am. If our gods were any good they would favor me, who have been more careful to serve them!" Another said that the short moment of this life is of little consequence if it is put in the balance with eternity. Others also spoke negatively of their gods and favorably of the new beliefs. Paulinus then addressed the assembly, after which Coifi applauded his words and asked the King to destroy the idols and to set fire to the pagan temples.

The promises Edwin had made, first to the stranger and then to Paulinus, were honored on Easter Sunday in the year 627 with his Baptism in the wooden church of St. Peter. He had previously arranged for the building of this church; it has since been replaced by the present York Minster.

Following his Baptism, Edwin became zealous for the conversion of his people, and to these he was an example of a devout and sincere convert. So many of Edwin's subjects now asked for Baptism that the Venerable Bede tells how the King and Queen entertained Paulinus for five weeks at their royal Villa of Yeverin in Northumberland, with the Saint being occupied from morning to night in instructing and baptizing the crowds that flocked to him. Of the King's family members, Paulinus baptized four sons, one daughter and one grandson.

Under Edwin the laws of the kingdom were much respected. As proof of this we are told that St. Edwin, concerned for the welfare of travelers, provided brass cups at springs which were located near frequently used roads. It is said that no man would dare touch these cups for any reason except for the purpose for which they were provided. As another example, Venerable Bede tells that "A woman with her newborn babe might walk throughout the island, from sea to sea, without receiving any harm."

For Edwin, peace did not last long. Once again an enemy threatened his life, this being the Welsh Chief Cadwallon, who marched against him with Penda, the pagan King of Mercia. King Edwin faced the enemy on the field of battle. During the conflict he was killed, together with his son Osfrid. The day was October 12, 633. Edwin was 47 years of age.

Since Edwin had died during a conflict with the enemies of the Faith, he was regarded as a martyr and as such was allowed by Pope Gregory XIII to be depicted in the English College Church at Rome. His relics at York Minster and at Whitby were held in great veneration.

Chapter 58

ST. ELIZABETH OF HUNGARY

1207 - 1231

Elizabeth was born in the year 1207 to Andrew II of Hungary and his wife, Gertrude of Andechs-Meran. To obtain a favorable political alliance, Elizabeth was promised in marriage to Louis (Ludwig), the eldest son of Landgrave Herman of Thuringia and Hesse (now Germany). At the age of four she was taken to the Thuringian Castle of the Wartburg, near Eisenach, there to be groomed as the wife of the future Landgrave.

During her maidenhood, Elizabeth is said to have been "perfect in body, handsome, of a dark complexion; serious in her ways, modest, of kindly speech, fervent in prayer, and always full of goodness and divine love." Yet with all these attributes she did not meet with approval or affection from her new family. Instead, her humble and retiring habits annoyed Louis' sister Agnes, who often told her that she was fit only to be a servant. The other young girls of the court, who saw that Elizabeth no longer participated in their games, dances and frivolous life, were accustomed to repeat what Agnes said and would openly mock her. Even influential officers of the court, disregarding the respect that was due Elizabeth, would publicly insult her, saying that in nothing did she resemble a princess.

As Elizabeth approached marriageable age, her prayerful life instigated a general explosion of persecutions and insults. All members of the court declared themselves against her marriage to Louis, while Sophia, his mother, even attempted to persuade Elizabeth to take the veil in a convent. Sophia asserted that her son should have a spouse who was noble, rich, well-connected and of truly royal manners.

Louis, far from sharing their opinions, once told Lord Gauthier, while the two were resting during a hunt:

Dost thou see that mountain before us? Well, if it were of pure gold, from its base to its summit, and that all should be given to me on the condition of sending away my Elizabeth, I would never do it. Let them think or say of her what they please; I say this—that I love her, and love nothing better in this world: I will have my Elizabeth; she is dearer to me for her virtue and piety than all the kingdoms and riches of the earth.

When Landgrave Herman died in 1216, his heir was his eldest son, the sixteen-year-old Louis. Five years later Louis announced his intention to marry Elizabeth and imposed silence on all who were inclined to speak against her. When Louis was 21 years of age and Elizabeth was 14, they were married at a High Mass in the presence of many nobles. The wedding celebration lasted three days, with splendid banquets, dances and tournaments.

To Louis' credit it must be stated that throughout his life, when criticism of his wife's generosity was made to him, he always upheld and approved her charitable and religious endeavors. His love for Elizabeth increased each day, and as often as he saw her despised by others on account of her virtues, the more did he love and defend her.

The wedded life of Elizabeth and Louis has been called by one chronicler, "an idyll of enthralling fondness, of mystic ardor, of almost childish happiness, the like of which I do not remember in all I have read of romance or of human experience." We are told of many instances in which Louis demonstrated his tender affection for his wife. One of her ladies-in-waiting revealed that "My lady would get up at night to pray, and my lord would implore her to spare herself and come back to rest, all the while holding her hand in his for fear she should come to some harm. She would tell her maids to wake her gently when he was asleep—and sometimes, when they thought him sleeping, he was only pretending."

We are also told that when Louis had visited a city he would always bring back a present for her—a knife or a bag or gloves or a coral rosary. "When it was time for him to be back she would run out to meet him, and he would take her lovingly on his arm and give her what he had brought."

The holy couple had three children: Herman, who was born in 1222 and died when he was 19; Sophia, who was named for her grandmother, became Duchess of Brabant and lived to the age of

60; and Gertrude, who became the Abbess of the Convent of Altenburg and is now venerated as Blessed.

During the year 1221, Elizabeth founded a convent of Franciscans near her church, in her capital city of Eisenach. In her contact with members of this order she heard of St. Francis of Assisi, who was still living; also, she learned of the existence of the Franciscan Third Order, an organization for lay people, which was flourishing in Italy and in other countries. She was struck by the advantages which affiliation to the Third Order would afford a fervent Christian, and she humbly begged Louis for permission to be enrolled as a member. Having obtained his consent, she was the first in Germany to be associated with the Third Order. After her death Elizabeth would become patroness of the female members of the Franciscan Third Order. During her lifetime St. Francis learned of her membership and often spoke kindly of her.

Louis, we know, put no obstacles in the way of his wife's charity, her simple life or her long prayers. In 1225, when Germany was experiencing famine, the Saint nearly exhausted the store of grain through distribution to the needy during her husband's absence. On Louis' return, the officers of his household complained to him of Elizabeth's generosity to the poor. To this Louis replied, "As for her charities, they will bring upon us a divine blessing. We shall not want, so long as we let her relieve the poor as she does."

We have been told that once, when Elizabeth was on an errand of mercy, her husband approached her and inquired about what she was concealing in her apron. On opening the apron, instead of loaves of bread, miraculous roses were revealed. Similar stories are also told of Bl. Paola Gambara-Costa, St. Germaine Cousin, St. Dorothy and St. Isabel of Aragon.

Since the Castle of the Wartburg was built on a steep rock, the infirm and weak were unable to climb up to it. To relieve these unfortunates, St. Elizabeth built a hospital at the foot of the rock for their reception. There she often fed the poor with her own hands, made their beds and attended them even in the heat of summer when the place became stifling. The Saint founded another hospital in which 28 people could be attended. She also fed 900 daily at her gate, besides countless others in different parts of the country. While the amount expended on the poor seemed at times to be excessive, the Saint's charity was tempered with discretion. She would not tolerate idleness among the poor who were able to work, employing them at tasks that were suited to their strength.

When the Fifth Crusade was being launched, Louis of Thuringia joined the endeavor. On the feast of St. John the Baptist, in the year 1227, he parted from Elizabeth and went to join Emperor Frederick II in Apulia. On September 11 of the same year, he was dead of the plague at Otranto.

The news of Louis' death did not reach Germany until October, just after the birth of Elizabeth's second daughter. When told of her husband's death Elizabeth cried, "The world is dead to me, and all that was joyous in the world." It is said that she ran to and fro about the castle, shrieking like one crazed.

The harsh opinion that Agnes and Sophia had for Elizabeth was softened somewhat by the sharing of grief, but the same opinion of her which was shared by Louis' brothers, Conrad and Henry, was intensified. According to the testimony of Elizabeth's lady-in-waiting, Isentrude, Henry, who was acting as regent for Elizabeth's son and who had pledged to defend the little family, devised a scheme to seize power for himself. Only a few months after Louis' death, while Elizabeth was deep in mourning for her husband, she had to endure the humiliation of hearing Henry falsely accuse her, before witnesses, of having ruined the country, of having wasted and exhausted the state treasury, and of having deceived and dishonored her husband. Satisfied that the allegations were enough to justify his next action, Henry declared that as punishment Elizabeth would be dispossessed of all that she had previously considered her own.

Elizabeth and her children, together with two attendants, were forced to leave the castle immediately. The fierce winter cold in which they were obliged to travel without proper provisions inflicted extreme discomfort on the banished group.

Upon reaching the city of Eisenach, which had often benefited from Elizabeth's charity, the exiles faced a new and painful trial. Henry had caused a proclamation to be made in the city that whoever would receive Elizabeth or her children would experience his displeasure. All the inhabitants of Eisenach are said to have obeyed the order—all, that is, except one tavern owner, who offered Elizabeth a humble shack where he kept kitchen utensils and where swine were lodged. These he displaced to make room for the visitors.

While staying in this humble situation, Elizabeth is said to have prayed, "O Lord, may Thy will be done. Yesterday I was a duchess with strong castles and rich domains; today I am a mendicant, and no one would give me asylum." Having been reduced to absolute poverty, Elizabeth anguished for her poor children, who were weeping from cold and hunger. She who had fed thousands was now obliged to beg food for her children and attendants.

Elizabeth then sought refuge with her Aunt Matilda, who was the Abbess of Kitzingen. Next she visited her Uncle Eckembert, Bishop of Bamberg, who put his Castle of Pottenstein at her disposal. Having left little Sophia with the nuns of Kitzingen, Elizabeth brought her son Herman and the baby to the castle provided by her uncle. Bishop Eckembert asked Elizabeth to consider the practical benefits to be derived from a second marriage, but she refused to listen to his plans, saying that she and her husband had exchanged promises never to marry again.

Early in 1228, the body of Louis was solemnly brought home. Accompanied by her faithful servants, Isentrude and Guda, Elizabeth was conducted to the place where the coffin lay. The coffin was opened, and Elizabeth was permitted to look upon the remains of her husband. "Then what her heart felt of grief and love none could know but Him who reads the secrets of the hearts of the children of men." All the afflictions Elizabeth had first experienced on learning of her husband's death were renewed in her soul as she threw herself on the bones and fervently kissed them. So abundant were her tears, and so violent was her agitation, that the Bishop and the nobles attempted to console her and to lead her away. With his family present, Louis was buried in the abbey church at Reinhardsbrunn (Reynhartsbrunn), a church which he had previously chosen as his burial place.

Following the burial, at the prompting of various nobles, a reconciliation was arranged between Elizabeth and Louis' family. Sophia and her son Conrad were present when Henry was brought before Elizabeth. He begged forgiveness for the injuries he had caused her, stating that he regretted them sincerely and that he would make ample atonement. Elizabeth answered by weeping as she tenderly embraced him. With the softening of hearts, a financial provision was then made for Elizabeth and her children, which greatly relieved Elizabeth's mind concerning the children's welfare.

From the year 1225 until the time of her death, Elizabeth had

had for her confessor Master Conrad of Marburg, a priest who has often been criticized for being domineering, brutal, severe and quite unsuitable to be her director. Yet others have asserted that it was because of his offensive and scrupulous methods that Elizabeth overcame nature and attained sainthood.

After her children had been provided for, Elizabeth went to live in Marburg. Next to her small cottage she built a hospice where she provided for the sick, the aged and the poor. Master Conrad is said to have acted as a necessary brake on her enthusiasm since he prevented her from begging from door to door; he also prevented her from risking infection by caring for people with leprosy and other diseases. But Isentrude, Elizabeth's attendant, reports that:

> Master Conrad tried her constancy in many ways, striving to break her will in all things. That he might afflict her still more he deprived her of those of her household who were particularly dear to her, including me, Isentrude, whom she loved; she sent me away in great distress and with many tears. Last of all he turned off Guda, my companion, who had been with her from her childhood, and whom she loved with a special love. With tears and sighs the blessed Elizabeth saw her go. Master Conrad did this with good intentions, lest we should talk to her of past greatness and she be tempted to regret. Moreover, he thus took away from her any comfort she might have had in us because he wished her to cling to God alone.

For her companions he substituted two "harsh females," who reported to him on Elizabeth's words and actions when these opposed his detailed commands. He punished Elizabeth with slaps on the face and blows with a "long, thick rod" which left marks that remained for weeks. Before Isentrude left her side, Elizabeth is known to have remarked to her, "If I am so afraid of a mortal man, how awe-inspiring must be the Lord and Judge of the world!"

Having already endured the false accusations of Henry, who had declared her wasteful and foolish, Elizabeth was also tried by some who now inflicted another cross. Various suspicions were hinted at as to the nature of her connection with Master Conrad. It was claimed that this priest had seduced the widow of Louis and carried her away to Marburg, there to enjoy her property and riches. The rumors appeared sufficiently serious to prompt Lord Rodolph de Varila to investigate the situation. After declaring the rumors to be unquestionably false, he reportedly told Elizabeth, "I beg, then, of my dear lady to watch over your renown, for your familiarity with Master Conrad has given rise to false notions and unjust suspicions in the minds of the vulgar and ignoble herd." On learning of the rumors for the first time, Elizabeth is said to have offered this humiliation to God by praying:

> Blessed in all things be our most dear and merciful Lord Jesus Christ, Who deigns to receive from me this little offering. For His love I devoted myself to His service; I forgot my noble birth; I despised my riches and possessions; I permitted my youth and beauty to fade away; I renounced my father, my country, my children, and, with them, all the consolations of life; I became the poorest of the poor. One only treasure did I retain—my womanly honor and reputation: but now, from what I learn, it seems that He requires that also; as He accepts, as a special sacrifice, my fair fame, I must strive to endure for His sake this ignominy. I consent to be looked upon as a dishonored woman; but oh, my dear Lord, remember my poor children; they are innocent; deign to preserve them from any shame that might fall upon them on my account.

Elizabeth lived in great austerity and worked continually in her hospice and in the homes of the poor. Even when she herself was sick, she would try to spin or card wool. After only two years at Marburg, her health deteriorated. During the evening of November 17, 1231, Elizabeth died, being then only 24 years old.

For three days her body lay in state in the chapel of the hospice, where she was to be buried, and where many miracles would take place through her intercession. Master Conrad began collecting depositions to be considered for her canonization, but he did not live to see her raised to the honors of the altar.

Pope Gregory IX canonized Elizabeth in 1235. During the following year her relics were translated to the Church of St. Elizabeth at Marburg, which was built in her honor by her brother-in-law Conrad. This translation took place in the presence of Emperor Frederick II, and of "so great a concourse of divers nations, peoples and tongues as in these German lands scarcely ever was gathered before or will ever be again." There the relics of St. Elizabeth of Hungary rested, an object of pilgrimage to all Germany and beyond.

But in the year 1539 a Protestant landgrave of Hesse, Philip the Magnanimous, a descendant of the Saint, wanting to abolish her cult, removed the relics to a place unknown. However, the Church of St. Elizabeth in Marburg is still a place of pilgrimage and is of great interest to pilgrims and tourists. There can be seen the Saint's tomb and many works of art depicting the life of the Saint.

All that we know of St. Elizabeth has come to us from her two handmaidens, Isentrude and Guda, as well as the two "harsh females," the letters of Conrad to the Pope, and other documents sent to Rome in view of her canonization.

A statue of the lovely St. Elizabeth of Hungary (1207-1231), wife of Louis of Thuringia. Married in 1221 at age 14, Elizabeth was deeply in love with her husband, who loved her ardently in return. The couple had three children. Louis died from the plague in 1227 while fighting in the Crusades. When she heard the news, Elizabeth cried out, "The world is dead to me, and all that was joyous in the world!"

A painting which depicts a ward in one of the hospitals built through St. Elizabeth of Hungary's generosity. She cared for the sick and poor with her own hands, made their beds and otherwise attended them. At one point St. Elizabeth was feeding 900 people daily at her gate. Elizabeth's humility and generosity to the poor gained her much ill-will from her in-laws, even though her husband supported her actions.

The "Elizabeth Window" at St. Elizabeth's Church in Marburg.

St. Elizabeth of Hungary lived in great austerity and worked continually in the hospice she had built and in the homes of the poor.

Statues on the High Altar of St. Elizabeth's Church are of the Blessed Virgin Mary and the Christ Child *(left)* and St. Elizabeth *(right)*. St. Elizabeth of Hungary and her children were reduced to absolute poverty for several months following Louis' death, due to the injustice of Elizabeth's in-laws. A reconciliation was later achieved.

221

St. Elizabeth's tomb at St. Elizabeth's Church in Marburg.

This relief on St. Elizabeth's mausoleum depicts the death of the Saint.

The ornate shrine of St. Elizabeth, also located at the cathedral in Marburg.

St. Elizabeth of Hungary (1207-1231), from a stained-glass window in St. Elizabeth's Church. Though the Saint's relics are no longer at the church, the cathedral is still a place of pilgrimage where visitors view St. Elizabeth's tomb and the artwork depicting her life.

225

Chapter 59

ST. ELIZABETH, QUEEN OF PORTUGAL

1271 - 1336

Elizabeth (or Isabel) was born in 1271 to Peter III, King of Aragon, Spain, and Constantia, daughter of Manfred, King of Sicily. Her grandfather was Emperor Frederick II; her great-aunt was none other than the great St. Elizabeth of Hungary, who had been canonized by Pope Gregory IX in 1235, only 35 years before the birth of her namesake.

The young princess was of a sweet disposition, and from her early years she was attracted to prayer and virtue. At the age of eight she began to fast and to practice self-denial, although those who cared for her cautioned against such practices for fear that her health would be jeopardized.

At the tender age of 12 she was married to Denis, King of Portugal, who admired her beauty and personality. Although he did not feel inclined to imitate Elizabeth's devotions, he allowed her full liberty to spend her time and income as she pleased. Given this freedom, she arranged her time with great care and rarely interrupted her schedule except for extraordinary reasons. She rose very early every morning and recited Matins, Lauds and Prime before she attended Holy Mass. Certain hours during the day were allotted to her domestic affairs, public business and charities. In the afternoon she again spent time in prayer before the recitation of Vespers. Her food was simple, her dress was modest, and her conversation was humble and pleasant.

Elizabeth was particularly attracted to relieving the poor, and she gave orders that all pilgrims and poor strangers should be given shelter and necessities. She visited and served the sick and founded in different parts of the kingdom many charitable establishments, particularly a hospital near her own palace at Coimbra. She established a house for penitent women at Torres Novas, as well as a refuge for foundlings. She also provided marriage dowries for girls who were poor. Although busy with many projects, she did not neglect her immediate duties, and she gave her husband respect, love and obedience.

Whether Denis lost interest in his wife because of her multiple devotions and works of charity, or whether he would have turned away from her regardless, we do not know for certain. But we are informed that while he was a good ruler and was devoted to his realm, in private he was selfish, sinful and dissolute.

The Saint tried every means to reclaim her husband and she grieved deeply for the scandal that he gave to the people. She never ceased praying for him or asking the prayers of others for his conversion. She showed great courtesy and patience during this trial and lovingly cared for Denis' illegitimate children, providing for their present and future welfare. When the ladies of the court reproached her for treating her husband's faults too leniently, the Saint replied, "If the King sins, am I to lose patience and thus add my transgressions to his? I love better to confide my sorrows to God and His holy Saints and to strive to win back my husband by gentleness."

A story is told of an incident which, if it actually happened, probably contributed to the King's conversion. The Queen had a page who faithfully and secretly distributed her donations to the poor when she was unable to do so herself. Another page, envious that he was not given this assignment, reported to the King that the Queen had an excessive fondness for this fellow page and that he performed secret functions for her.

Denis believed the report, and because of his jealousy, arranged with the lime-burner that on a certain day he should throw into the kiln the first page who should arrive with a royal message. On the day appointed, Denis sent the Queen's page to the lime-kiln, but when the page passed a church, he stopped to attend Holy Mass, as was his custom. This delay saved him. The King then sent the informer to verify the outcome of the plan. He arrived first and was burned to death. The Queen's page, after finishing his prayers, passed the lime-kiln and brought back word to the King that his order had been fulfilled. The King saw in this twist of events that God, because of the Holy Mass, had vindicated the honor of the Queen.

St. Elizabeth had two children, Alfonso, who afterward succeeded his father, and a daughter, Constantia. Alfonso showed a very rebellious spirit when he grew up, due in part to the favor in which his father held his illegitimate sons. In 1323, Alfonso declared war against his illegitimate brothers and the King. Queen Elizabeth re-established peace and a reconciliation after finding it necessary to ride out on horseback between the opposing forces. Pope John XXII wrote in praise of her efforts, but many suggested to the King that Elizabeth secretly favored her own son—and for a time she was banished from the court.

When Denis became seriously ill, Elizabeth never left him except for her attendance at church services. She served and attended him with great patience and devotion during his long and tedious illness and had many Masses offered for his complete repentance. The Queen's prayers were answered when Denis expressed sincere sorrow for the errors of his life and died a holy death.

Elizabeth made a pilgrimage to Compostella to pray for her husband's soul and then spent a period of mourning at the convent of the Poor Clares which she had founded at Coimbra. She herself never joined the community, but she was professed in the Third Order of St. Francis. She lived in a house which she built near the convent and often visited the nuns, frequently serving them at table. One of her companions during this time was her daughter-in-law, Queen Beatrice.

Always devoted to maintaining peace, St. Elizabeth once averted a war between Ferdinand IV of Castile and his cousin, who had laid claim to the crown. She again acted as peacemaker when the same prince challenged her own brother, James II of Aragon. Unfortunately, her efforts to save the lives of countless men ironically caused her own death.

In 1336 Elizabeth's son, now Alfonso IV, set out on an expedition against his son-in-law, the King of Castile, who had married Alfonso's daughter Maria and had neglected and abused her. Elizabeth prepared to meet and reconcile the two kings—against the advice of her servants, who cautioned her to postpone her journey on account of the heat. But stating that she could find no better way to risk her health than by seeking to prevent the miseries of war, Elizabeth left for Estremoz, where her son was camped.

Although very ill and knowing that her death was not far off, Elizabeth was successful in reconciling the two sovereigns. Shortly thereafter she confessed and received Holy Viaticum and the Last Rites of the Church. Calling upon the most holy Mother of God, she died peacefully in the presence of her son and daughter-in-law. She was buried in the church of the Poor Clare monastery at Coimbra, which she honored after her death with many miracles.

Queen Elizabeth of Portugal was canonized by Pope Urban VIII in 1625.

Ed. Conf. Rainha S. Isabel, Coimbra

The new sarcophagus of St. Elizabeth of Portugal (1271-1336), grand-niece of St. Elizabeth of Hungary. The Saint's body is incorrupt. (In Portugal she is known as "Isabel!")

Teófilo Rego/Centro N.S. do Perp. Soc., Porto

A statue of St. Elizabeth of Portugal, who married King Denis of Portugal when she was only twelve years old. As a young wife, she spent her carefully scheduled days in prayer and good works.

Ed. Conf. Rainha S. Isabel, Coimbra

Above: St. Elizabeth of Portugal's statue at Coimbra, the city where she exercised great generosity to the poor.
Below: The former tomb of St. Elizabeth. She was buried in the church of the Poor Clare Monastery at Coimbra and after her death honored the church with many miracles.

Ed. Conf. Rainha S. Isabel, Coimbra

231

Chapter 60

ST. ELZEAR AND BL. DELPHINA

d. 1323 / d. 1358

Soon after Elzear was born, his mother took him in her arms and offered him to God with great fervor. She begged that he might never offend His Divine Majesty, but might rather die in his infancy than live to commit a serious sin. His mother's prayers were answered, since later in life St. Elzear acknowledged that he had never committed a mortal sin. The lessons in virtue which he had received from his mother were perfected by his uncle, William of Sabran, Abbot of St. Victor's at Marseille. It was in that monastery that Elzear was educated.

Having been born in Provence, France, in the year 1285, Elzear was still a child when Charles II, King of Sicily, arranged Elzear's engagement to Delphina, daughter and heiress to the Lord of Puy-Michel. Delphina was an orphan. Like her intended, who was educated by an uncle who was an abbot, Delphina was educated by her aunt who was an abbess. When Elzear and Delphina were both about 15 years old, their marriage took place at Chateau-Pont-Michel.

It is claimed by at least one biographer that the couple decided, on their wedding night, to live as brother and sister. And it is known that in 1315, in the chapel of their castle, after they received Holy Communion, they stood at the foot of the altar and publicly pronounced their vows of perpetual continence. This is claimed by some to indicate that both were inclined toward a religious vocation, but entered into the marriage state under obedience to the advice of their elders.

Elzear was 23 years old when he inherited his father's honors and estates. He became the Baron of Ansouis in Provence and Count of Ariano in the kingdom of Naples. When Elzear had to journey to Italy to take possession of the lordship of Ariano, he found the Italians poorly disposed toward him as a Frenchman. Then, when a rebellion was threatened, Elzear's cousin, the Prince of Taranto, advised him to subdue the rebels with executions and force of arms—a course of action which Elzear refused to take. Instead of pursuing a confrontation, Elzear spent three years in opposing the rebellion with tact, gentleness, meekness and patience. His friends reproachfully accused him of being indolent and cowardly, but in the end the rebels abandoned their effort. With submission and respect, they invited the Saint to take possession of his territory.

In explaining why he bore the insults, injuries and difficulties with patience, Elzear explained, "If I receive any affront or feel impatience begin to arise in my breast, I turn all my thoughts toward Jesus Christ crucified and say to myself: Can what I suffer bear any comparison with what Jesus Christ was pleased to undergo for me?"

Elzear once again countered insults with patience and forgiveness when he was going through papers that had been left by his father. Several letters were found that had been written by a certain gentleman who suggested that Elzear should be disinherited because he was more of a monk than a soldier. When Delphina read the insults and criticisms that were also mentioned in the letter, she expressed the hope that her husband would deal with the writer as he deserved. But Elzear reminded her that Christ commands us not to seek revenge but to forgive injuries and to overcome hatred with charity. He destroyed the letters and never spoke of them again. When the gentleman came to him, not knowing that Elzear had read his letters, Elzear greeted him affectionately and won his friendship.

The gentleman was wrong in his opinion of Elzear. While the Saint had the virtues and demeanor of a monk, he was also a soldier, having taken up arms in Italy on behalf of the Guelf party. With his followers he helped to drive Emperor Henry VII from Rome in 1312.

Elzear exercised charity in a number of areas. He visited prisoners who were condemned to death, converted many with tender words and secretly aided widows, orphans and the poor. He recited the Divine Office every day and communicated almost as often. He once said to Delphina, "I do not think that any man on earth can enjoy a happiness equal to that which I have in Holy Communion." In one of his letters to her he wrote, "You want to hear often of me. Go then and visit our loving Lord Jesus in the Blessed Sacrament, and enter in spirit into His Sacred Heart. You will always find me there.''

While Elzear was devout and spent much time in prayer, he did not neglect the temporal concerns of his position. Diligent in the care of his household, he drew up the following regulations:

> Everyone in my family shall daily hear Mass, whatever business he may have. If God be well served, nothing will be wanting...Let no persons be idle. In the morning a little time shall be allowed for meditation, but away with those who are perpetually in the church to avoid doing their work. This they do, not because they love contemplation, but because they want to have their work done for them...When a difference or quarrel arises, let the scriptural precept be observed that it be composed before the sun goes down. I know the impossibility of living among men and not having something to suffer. Scarcely a man is in tune with himself one whole day; but not to be willing to bear with or pardon others is diabolical, and to love enemies and to render good for evil is the touchstone of the sons of God...I strictly command that no officer or servant under my jurisdiction or authority injure any man in goods, honor or reputation, or oppress any poor person, or damage anyone under color of doing my business. I do not want my castle to be a cloister or my people hermits. Let them be merry, and enjoy recreation at the right times, but not with a bad conscience or with danger of transgressing against God.

St. Elzear himself set the example in everything that he prescribed to others, and Bl. Delphina concurred with her husband in all his views and was perfectly obedient to him. Although strictly observing their vow of chastity, they were nevertheless perfectly suited to one another. They were warm, affectionate and caring, while harmony and peace held sway in their dealings with one another and in their household.

When King Robert of Naples sent St. Elzear to Paris to ask for the hand of Mary of Valois for King Robert's son, Bl. Delphina was concerned for her husband amid the dangers of the Parisian court. Elzear observed that since, by the grace of God, he had kept his virtue in Naples, he was not likely to come to any harm in Paris.

But a danger of another kind did await Elzear in Paris in the form of a sickness that proved to be fatal. While he awaited death, he made a general confession and continued to confess almost every day of his illness, even though he is said never to have offended God by mortal sin. The history of Christ's Passion was read to him every day, and in this he found great comfort in spite of his pains. After receiving the Holy Eucharist for the last time, Elzear said with great joy, "This is my hope; in this I desire to die." On September 27, 1323 Elzear died in the arms of Fr. Francis Mayronis, a Franciscan friar who had been his confessor. In accord with Elzear's orders, his body was carried to Apt and there interred in the Church of the Franciscans.

Fourteen years earlier, about the year 1309, St. Elzear had assisted as godfather at the Baptism of William of Grimoard, son of the Sieur de Grisac. William was a sickly child whose restoration to health was credited to the prayers of his godfather. Fifty-three years later this William became Pope Urban V, and in 1369 he signed the decree of canonization of his godfather, Elzear, whose name is listed in the *Roman Martyrology* on September 27, the day of his death.

Bl. Delphina survived her husband by 35 years. She remained at the Neapolitan court until the death of Queen Sanchia, who had entered the Order of the Poor Clares. Delphina then returned to France and led the life of a recluse, first at Cabrieres and then at Apt. She distributed the proceeds of her estates to the poor, and during her last years she was afflicted with a painful illness, which she bore with admirable patience until her death. She was buried beside her husband in Apt.

Both St. Elzear and Bl. Delphina were members of the Third Order of St. Francis, and for this reason they are particularly venerated by the Franciscans.

Chapter 61

ST. EPIPODIUS AND ST. ALEXANDER

d. 178

One year after the martyrdom of Sts. Blandina and Pothin in Lyons, France, the persecution of Marcus Aurelius continued to claim other victims. Among them were two young men, St. Epipodius and St. Alexander, who likewise suffered and died in Lyons. Epipodius was a native of that city, while Alexander was a Greek by birth. From their first studies together in the same school, they had become friends and together advanced in virtue. Both were Christians of good position and unmarried.

Betrayed by a servant who denounced them as Christians, Epipodius and Alexander became fearful. They had been friends of Blandina and Pothin, and knew of their sufferings and cruel death. They feared similar treatment when they learned of their own betrayal and impending capture. For this reason they journeyed to a neighboring town, where they hid themselves in the house of a poor widow. We are not certain exactly how long they were able to avoid detection, but eventually they were arrested. Still hoping to avoid a cruel death, Epipodius attempted to escape. In the process he lost a shoe, which was later treasured as a relic.

We are not told exactly what prompted a change, but after a three-day imprisonment Epipodius and Alexander showed exemplary courage by boldly professing their faith when questioned by the Governor. The two were then separated. Epipodius, the younger, was considered the weaker of the two and the one who might be more easily perverted. He was treated kindly at first, but when he refused to deny his faith he was struck soundly on the mouth. With bleeding lips, Epipodius continued to profess his faith. He was then stretched on the rack while his sides were torn with iron claws. To satisfy the people, who were clamoring for his death, the Governor ordered Epipodius to be beheaded.

Two days later Alexander expressed a fervent desire to join his friend, and he prayed fervently that Epipodius' brave martyrdom would encourage him in his trials. While stretched on a rack, he withstood a scourging by three executioners. With profound courage Alexander continued to profess his faith. His steadfastness so infuriated those who were inflicting the pain that he was sentenced to the ultimate punishment—crucifixion. Due to his extremely weakened condition, the martyr died the moment his mutilated limbs were fastened to the cross.

The triumph of these two martyrs is believed to have taken place in the month of April, in the year 178. Christians privately carried off their bodies and buried them upon a hill. There miraculous cures took place during a pestilence which afflicted the city of Lyons. The author of their *Acts,* Ruinart, attests to these miracles.

Unusual relics of these two Saints included dust taken from their tombs—something which St. Eucherius, Bishop of Lyons, first mentioned in his panegyric of the two martyrs. St. Gregory of Tours also attested to the benefits derived from this dust on behalf of the sick. In the sixth century, the bodies of the two martyrs were deposited with the body of St. Irenaeus under the altar of the Church of St. John. This church was later renamed for St. Irenaeus. The relics of St. Epipodius and St. Alexander were said to have been discovered, identified and solemnly translated in 1410. However, at the present time the Church of St. Irenaeus has neither a reliquary, tomb or statue in their honor.

Chapter 62

ST. ETHELBERT

d. 793

St. Ethelbert was the son of Ethelred, King of the East Angles and Leofrana, a lady of Mercia. Because he was taught to practice virtue, St. Ethelbert became a man of singular devotion and humility, and he ruled wisely when he became king.

To secure the peace of his country by providing it with an heir, he planned to propose marriage to Alfreda, who was the daughter of King Offa of the Mercians and his wife Cynethryth. Hoping to make arrangements for the wedding, Ethelbert journeyed to Villa Australis, where the royal family was then staying. He was afforded all the courtesies of the Mercian court—but behind all the pleasant formalities, his hosts were plotting his death. At the instigation of King Offa's wife, who thought to acquire Ethelbert's territory, arrangements were made with a certain Grimbert to murder their guest while he was on his way for an interview with King Offa. Thus it happened that Grimbert seized St. Ethelbert, bound him securely and then beheaded him.

The body of St. Ethelbert, together with the head, was first buried in secret on the banks of the Lugg. During the night of the burial a great beam of light rose from the grave to Heaven. On the third night after the burial the Saint appeared to a holy man, the nobleman Brithfrid. Ethelbert indicated the place of burial and asked Brithfrid to convey the relics to Stratus-way. During the journey the head fell out of the cart and healed a man who had been blind for 11 years. The body was finally entombed at Fernley, the present Hereford, which soon became famous for miracles and a place of pilgrimage.

Seemingly as a stroke of justice, the fortunes of the royal Mercian trio were drastically changed. Cynethryth died miserably within three months of Ethelbert's murder; her daughter Alfreda, the intended bride, retired to live a solitary life at Croyland. Offa, filled with shame for his part in the crime, built a great tomb over the grave of Ethelbert and gave a tenth of his wealth to enrich the church, which later became a cathedral. He also gave land to the church of Hereford and founded St. Albans and other monasteries; in addition, he made a penitential pilgrimage to Rome.

Later, at the Cathedral of Hereford, the name of Ethelbert was joined with that of the Blessed Virgin as titular saint, so that the cathedral became known as the Church of St. Mary and St. Ethelbert. The shrine was destroyed by the Welsh in 1055, but it was restored after the Norman Conquest. Thirteen English churches besides the Cathedral at Hereford are named for St. Ethelbert, and one of the gateways of Norwich Cathedral bears his name.

Hereford Cathedral Library

St. Ethelbert, King of the East Angles (d.794), is depicted here with his head severed. It is said that the Saint appeared after his death to the holy nobleman Brithfrid and asked that his relics be conveyed to Stratus-way. On the journey, the head rolled out of the cart and restored sight to a man who had been blind for 11 years.

A statue of St. Ethelbert. This eighth-century king was murdered by beheading while he was making arrangements to marry. The mother of his bride-to-be had instigated his death in hopes of acquiring his territory. St. Ethelbert's body and head were secretly buried on a riverbank, but were removed after a great beam of light arose from his gravesite during the night.

Chapter 63

ST. EULALIA OF MERIDA

d. 304

A hymn written by Prudentius at the end of the fourth century, along with St. Eulalia's *Acta* of a much later date, give us the particulars of the martyrdom of St. Eulalia, the most celebrated virgin martyr of Spain.

When the edicts of Diocletian were issued, by which it was ordered that all should offer sacrifice to the gods of the empire, Eulalia was a mere 12 years of age. The courage with which the martyrs rejected the edicts and died for the Faith so inspired the young girl that she too wanted to offer her life for her Christian faith. This desire for martyrdom troubled Eulalia's mother to such an extent that she took her daughter into the country. But during the night Eulalia left without telling her mother, arriving at Merida at daybreak.

When Dacian, the judge, entered the court to begin the daily session, Eulalia presented herself before him and declared that he should not attempt to destroy souls by making them renounce the only true God. Dacian was at first amused with the actions of the young girl and attempted to flatter and bribe her into withdrawing her words and observing the edicts. When she firmly renounced this tactic, Dacian then changed his attitude and showed her the instruments of torture, saying, "These you shall escape if you will but touch a little salt and incense with the tip of your finger."

What next transpired startled those in the courtroom. Eulalia at once threw down the image of the false god, trampled on the cake which had been laid for the sacrifice and spat at the judge. The sentence of the girl was quickly pronounced.

Two executioners seized her and took her to a place of torture, where they began to tear her body with iron hooks. As an added punishment for her actions, lighted torches were applied to her wounds. Quite unexpectedly, the fire from the torches caught Eulalia's hair, surrounding her head in flames. Stifled by the smoke and flames, Eulalia died. In his poem, Prudentius tells us that a white dove seemed to come out of her mouth and fly upward. Seeing this, the executioners became so terrified that they fled.

Eulalia's body was entombed by Christians near the place of her martyrdom. Later a church was built over the spot. Of this place Prudentius wrote in his hymn, "Pilgrims come to venerate her bones, and she, near the throne of God, beholds them and protects those that sing hymns to her."

The relics of the 12-year-old martyr are now found in the Cathedral of Oviedo in a seventeenth-century chapel dedicated to her.

Chapter 64

ST. FABIOLA

d. 399

Fabiola was a patrician Roman lady who is described as being lively, passionate and headstrong. When her married life became impossible because of the activities of her unfaithful husband, she obtained a divorce under the Roman law. St. Jerome, who later became her teacher and spiritual adviser, described the situation in this manner:

> We are told that her husband was a man of such heinous vices that even a prostitute or a common slave could not have put up with them. If I describe them I shall mar the heroism of the woman, who preferred to bear the blame of separation rather than to expose the shame of the man and thus reveal the stains upon his character.

St. Jerome continues:

> Fabiola, as men say, put away a vicious husband; she put away a man who was guilty of this and that crime; she put him away because—I almost mentioned the scandal which the whole neighborhood proclaimed but which his wife alone refused to reveal.

Contrary to the teaching of the Church, Fabiola married again while her first husband was still living. We are not certain how long this alliance lasted, but when this second husband died, she realized the sinfulness of the union. Following the man's death she appeared before the gates of the Lateran basilica dressed in penitential garb and did public penance for her sin, an act which made a great impression upon the Christian population of Rome. With some formality she was readmitted to the Sacraments by Pope St. Siricius.

While repenting for her sinful union, Fabiola gave large sums of money to churches and communities in Italy. She also founded a hospital for the sick whom she gathered from the streets and alleys

243

of Rome. This hospital is considered to have been the first Christian public hospital in the West. In this hospital Fabiola personally is known to have aided the sick and ministered to those with repulsive ailments.

In the year 395 Fabiola went to visit St. Jerome in Bethlehem; there she lived in the hospice directed by St. Paula. Under the direction of St. Jerome, she applied herself with the greatest zeal to the study and contemplation of the Scriptures and to ascetic exercises.

When the Huns invaded the eastern provinces of the empire and a dispute developed between St. Jerome and Bishop John of Jerusalem regarding the teachings of Origen, Fabiola found it advisable to leave Bethlehem for Rome. She continued a correspondence with St. Jerome, who wrote, at her request, a treatise on the priesthood of Aaron and the priestly dress.

At Rome, Fabiola joined the former senator, Pammachius, in erecting a large hospice for the poor and sick. Fabiola continued her personal labors among these unfortunates until her death in the year 400. On learning of her passing, St. Jerome sent a letter to Oceanus, one of her relatives. In this letter (No. LXXVII) he wrote:

> Fabiola, the glory of the Christians, the wonder of the Gentiles...whatever point I take first pales in comparison with what is to come. Shall I tell of her fastings? Her alms are greater still. Shall I praise her humility? It is outstripped by the ardor of her faith. Shall I mention her studied squalor, her plebeian dress, and the slave's garb she chose in condemnation of silken robes?

St. Jerome went to great lengths to tell of Fabiola's generosity to the poor and sick; he wrote, "Let others praise her piety, her humility, her faith. I will rather extol the ardor of her soul."

It is recorded that the whole of Rome attended the funeral of their beloved benefactress Fabiola. Not only Rome, but the Holy Land also felt the loss, as St. Jerome says: "This only do I grieve for, that we in the Holy Land lost in her a most precious jewel."

Chapter 65

ST. FELICITAS AND HER SEVEN SONS

d. Second Century

Felicitas was a Christian woman of social importance who lived in Rome and served God in her widowhood by applying herself to prayer, fasting and works of charity. Through her prayers and edifying example she and her whole family were instrumental in turning many away from the adoration of false gods, leading them instead to adore the true God through joining the Christian Faith.

Their success in this endeavor angered the pagan priests, who reported the matter to Emperor Antoninus, claiming that if Felicitas was not forced to venerate the gods, the gods would be so irritated that it would be impossible to appease them. To satisfy the priests, the Emperor sent an order to Publius, the prefect of Rome, to have the mother and her sons apprehended and brought to him.

Taking Felicitas aside, the Emperor attempted to persuade her to sacrifice to the gods—but when kind words did not impress her, he tried to frighten her with threats of bodily harm to herself and her sons if she did not comply.

Felicitas stood firm and refused to offend the true God by such an act. As her sons were being brought before the Emperor, the brave widow exhorted them to remain firm in their faith. All seven refused to cooperate and were severely whipped. The Emperor then ordered that they be sent to different judges, who would order punishments as they deemed proper.

Januarius, the eldest son, was eventually scourged to death; Felix and Philip were beaten with clubs; Silvanus was thrown down from a steep rock; Alexander, Vitalis and Martial were beheaded, as was their mother, last of all.

Concerning the death of St. Felicitas, St. Augustine wrote:

Wonderful is the sight set before the eyes of our faith. We have heard with our ears and seen with our minds a mother choosing for her children to finish their course before herself, contrary to the movement of human instincts. For all men would rather leave this world before their children, but she chose to die after them...It was not enough that she had to look on; we are yet more astonished that she encouraged them...seeing them contend, she contended, and in the victory of each one she was victorious.

St. Gregory the Great also appreciated the sacrifice of the heroic mother. On the festival of St. Felicitas, November 23, in the church built over her tomb on the Via Salaria, he said that the Saint,

having seven children, was as much afraid of leaving them behind here on earth as other mothers are of surviving theirs. She was more than a martyr, for seeing her seven children martyred before her eyes, she was in some sort a martyr in each of them. She was the eighth in order of time, but was from the first to the last in anguish, beginning her martyrdom in the eldest and finishing it in her own death...Seeing them in torments she remained constant, feeling their agony by nature as their mother, but rejoicing for them in her heart by hope.

St. Gregory contrasts our faith against the heroic faith of this martyr and instructs us in the following manner:

Let us be covered with shame and confusion that we should fall so far short of the virtue of this martyr...Often one word spoken against us disturbs our minds; at the least breath of contradiction we are discouraged or provoked; but neither torture nor death was able to shake her courageous soul. We weep without ceasing when God requires of us the children He hath lent us; and she bewailed her children when they did not die for Christ, and rejoiced when she saw them die.

Alban Butler, the hagiographer, adds this counsel:

Parents daily meet with trouble from disorders into which their children fall through their own bad example or neglect. Let them imitate the earnestness of St. Felicitas by forming to virtue the souls which God has committed to their charge, and with this saint they will have the greatest of all comforts in them, and will by His grace count as many saints in their family as they are blessed with children.

St. Felicitas was buried in the catacomb of Maximus on the Via Salaria, beside her son Silvanus. The crypt where Felicitas was laid to rest was later enlarged into a subterranean chapel, which was rediscovered in 1885. Still visible on the rear wall of this chapel is a seventh-century fresco which depicts St. Felicitas and her seven sons. Overhead is a figure of Christ bestowing on them the crown of eternal life. The relics are now found in the Church of Santa Susanna ("The Church of American Catholics" in Rome). Toward the end of the eighth century, the relics of the Saint and her son Silenus were placed in the crypt of this church, which is decorated with frescoes depicting scenes in the life of this holy mother and her courageous sons.

Chapter 66

BL. FERDINAND OF PORTUGAL

1402 - 1443

Bl. Ferdinand, Prince of Portugal, was born at Santarem on September 29, 1402. He was one of five sons born to King John I of Portugal and Philippa, daughter of John of Gaunt, Duke of Lancaster. Ferdinand suffered throughout his life from various sicknesses, but bodily weakness did not hinder his spiritual growth.

While still a young boy he showed a remarkable attraction to prayer and for the devotions and ceremonies of the Church. At the age of 14 he was reciting the canonical hours and fasting on Saturdays and the vigils of feasts. Ferdinand was frugal in his diet, solicitous for the sick and the poor and careful in overseeing the spiritual well-being of his servants. Much to the admiration of the court, he remained untouched by the temptations and frivolities around him. His generosity to the Church was occasioned by his desire to participate in its prayers and good works, and for a similar reason he had himself enrolled in all the pious congregations of the kingdom.

Upon the King's death in 1433, Ferdinand's brother Edward ascended the throne. Ferdinand's inheritance was so small that Edward conferred on him the Grand Mastership of the Knights of Aviz, a religious military order. Since Ferdinand was not a cleric, a special papal dispensation was necessary before he could assume the office. When this dispensation was obtained, Ferdinand accepted only because he did not wish to be a burden to his family.

Bl. Ferdinand never married and seems never to have been drawn to the clerical state. However, he was eager to participate in a crusade against the enemies of the Church. It was largely at Ferdinand's prompting and in opposition to the advice of Pope Eugenius IV, that King Edward planned an expedition against the Moors in Africa. Leading the expedition were the King's two brothers, Henry the Navigator and Bl. Ferdinand. They set sail on August 22, 1437. During the voyage of four days Ferdinand became dangerously ill due to an abscess and fever, which he had concealed before his departure in order to prevent a delay.

After the group arrived at Ceuta (a Spanish military post in Morocco, opposite Gibralter), a grave mistake was discovered. The Portuguese found that through some mismanagement they numbered only 6,000 men, instead of 14,000 as ordered by the King. They were advised to wait for reinforcements, but the two princes, eager to do battle against the heathen, decided to advance toward Tangier.

The Portuguese fought bravely against an overwhelming number of Moors, but the result was disastrous. The Moors cut off their communication with the fleet, their only source of supplies. Faced with starvation or surrender, the Portuguese were finally compelled to negotiate humiliating terms: the surrender of the City of Ceuta and its fortress, in return for safe passage to their vessels.

When the Moors demanded that one of the princes be left with them to insure the delivery of the city, Ferdinand bravely offered himself as hostage. With him remained 12 attendants, including Joao Alvarez—his secretary, and later his biographer. The Moorish emir, Sala ben Sala, brought Ferdinand to Arsilla, where the holy prince continued all his devotions and showed great charity to his fellow captives, in spite of lingering sickness and suffering.

Developments then took a strange course. With his brother held prisoner, Henry the Navigator changed his mind about surrendering Ceuta and its fortress. He offered instead to release the son of Sala ben Sala, who was a prisoner of the Portuguese. The exchange of hostages was scornfully rejected. Sala ben Sala insisted on the recovery of Ceuta, which would restore to him his former seat of government. Once more Henry refused to surrender Ceuta. He left for Portugal to devise other means to win Ferdinand's release.

Ceuta was left in the command of the Portuguese Cortes, who answered the threats of the Moors with repeated refusals to surrender the fortress—which had been captured at the cost of many lives and whose location would serve as a point of departure for future conquests.

Various attempts were made to free the Prince, but all were rejected and only served to make the Moors more resentful toward him. On May 25, 1438, Ferdinand and his companions were taken to Fez, where he was handed over to the cruel Lazurac. He was placed in a dark dungeon and, after many months of imprisonment, was made to work like a slave in the gardens and stables. In spite of the Prince's harsh treatment, abuse, insults and misery, we are told by his companion and biographer, Joao Alvarez, that he never lost patience, never complained, nor did he ever speak a harsh word against the Moors. Ferdinand refused to attempt an escape—which would have meant leaving his loyal companions to worse treatment.

Although it is said that Bl. Ferdinand's brothers made great efforts to release him, they still refused to surrender Ceuta. Apparently abandoned by his brothers, Bl. Ferdinand spent the last 15 months of his life confined in a dark dungeon. He spent most of his time in prayer and in preparation for death, which he knew was near at hand. He was finally stricken with a fatal disease.

While Bl. Ferdinand was still detained in the dungeon, his captors permitted a physician and a few faithful friends to visit him. The day before he died, he confided to his confessor that he had been greatly consoled by a vision of the Blessed Virgin, who was accompanied by St. John and the Archangel Michael. The next day, June 5, 1443, after making a general confession and a profession of faith, the saintly prince died peacefully after having endured six years of imprisonment.

After the death of his holy prisoner, the cruel Lazurac had still other indignities to inflict upon him. He ordered the body of the Prince to be opened and the vital organs removed. He then had the body suspended head downward for four days on the wall of the City of Fez.

Of Ferdinand's companions, four soon followed him to the grave, one joined the ranks of the Moors, and the others regained their liberty after Lazurac's death. Joao Alvarez carried Ferdinand's heart to Portugal in 1451.

Prince Ferdinand was held in great veneration by the Portuguese because of his saintly life and devotion to country. Miracles were reported through his intercession, and in 1470 he was beatified by Pope Paul II. In 1473 his remains were brought back to his native soil. Amid special ceremonies they were deposited in the monastic Church of Our Lady at Batalha, in the diocese of Leira.

Chapter 67

ST. FERDINAND III OF CASTILE

d. 1253

The father of St. Ferdinand III was Alphonso IX, King of Leon; his mother was Berengaria, the elder daughter of Alphonso III, King of Castile. In addition to Ferdinand, there were two daughters and one other son in the royal family.

When Berengaria's brother Henry died in 1217, Berengaria became heiress to the throne of Castile—but she resigned her rights in favor of her 18-year-old son Ferdinand, who was proclaimed King in Palencia, Valladolid and Burgos. Some disturbance and opposition was experienced, but these were dismissed by the young monarch, who displayed remarkable prudence and clemency.

Ferdinand was greatly assisted in the administration of his duties by the wise advice of his mother, whom he consulted and obeyed until the day of her death. It was on his mother's advice that in 1219 he married the accomplished and virtuous Princess Beatrice, daughter of Philip of Suabia, King of Germany. This happy and blessed union produced seven sons and three daughters. It is reported that this marriage "was never clouded by the least discordance."

Butler reports that St. Ferdinand was severe in the administration of justice but readily pardoned all personal injuries, and no sooner were rebellions crushed than he granted general amnesties. Ferdinand selected his governors, magistrates and generals wisely, and he devised a court system that was an improvement over the previous arrangement. He also saw to the compilation of a code of laws, which continued to be in use until modern times. He founded several bishoprics and contributed to the building or repairing of cathedrals, churches, monasteries and hospitals. No necessity could make him impose heavy taxes on his subjects; and when it was suggested that he should raise a subsidy for his struggles against the Moors, he rejected the proposal, saying that God would provide other means and that he feared the curse of one poor old woman more than the whole army of the Moors.

Although Ferdinand's rule up to this time was, for the most part, peaceful and orderly, one situation developed that grievously troubled him. This occurred when his own father, the King of Leon, laid claim to Ferdinand's dominions and invaded them. Ferdinand attempted to give his father all reasonable satisfaction, and he finally established peace with him. Later Ferdinand lent him his own forces to fight against the Moors.

Ferdinand had long ago resolved never to wage war against any but the enemies of the Christian Faith. When the infidels grew bolder and a confrontation to check their advances was imperative, Ferdinand opened his first campaign in 1225 and continued battling Islam until his death. By the year 1230 he had taken some 20 strongholds. Totally devoid of personal ambition, he was far more interested in rescuing Christians and Christian property from the hands of the unbelievers. He was known to have prayed, "Thou, O Lord, Who searchest the heart of man: Thou knowest that I desire Thy glory and the increase of Thy Faith and holy religion."

For his soldiers, Ferdinand set an example of devotion by fasting, praying, spending whole nights in pious exercises, especially before an engagement, and giving to God the glory of his victories. A large picture of Our Lady was carried before him into battle, while a small one was attached to his saddle. As for the spoils of war, he kept nothing for himself, but richly endowed the Cathedral of Toledo, which he had founded.

Ferdinand's father had apparently married a second time, since at his death in 1230 he left his Kingdom of Leon to the two daughters of this marriage. However, the clergy and the people wanted Ferdinand as their monarch. It took two to three years for Ferdinand to resolve the matter and to settle the affairs of his new kingdom, which from that time became united with Castile.

In 1234 Ferdinand resumed his wars against the Moors. The City of Cordova, which had been in the hands of the Mussulmans for 520 years, was conquered after a long siege. Ferdinand entered the city on the Feast of Sts. Peter and Paul in the year 1236. The chief mosque of the city was converted into a church, and the great bells which had been taken from Compostela by the labor of Christian slaves were returned to their proper home, this time transported by the Moors.

During the year of the conquest of Cordova, 1236, Ferdinand's wife, Queen Beatrice, died. She was deeply mourned by her husband and by her subjects. After a respectable length of time, Ferdinand married Jane of Ponthieu, who bore him two sons and one daughter, Eleanor, the future wife of Edward I of England.

After the victory of Cordova, Ferdinand laid siege to Seville, the largest, strongest and most densely populated city in Spain. After 16 months (some claim 26 months) the Moors surrendered. Axataf, the governor general of the Moors in Seville, looked from the top of a hill at the city for the last time and declared with tears that only one specially favored by God could have taken so strong a city with so few men. In thanksgiving for his victory, which completed the downfall of Mohammedanism in Spain, St. Ferdinand rebuilt the Cathedral of Seville, which became one of the most magnificent churches in all of Christendom.

In addition to founding and aiding many places of worship, including the Cathedral of Burgos, St. Ferdinand is acknowledged as the founder of the University of Salamanca.

During the last three years of his life, Ferdinand remained in Seville to regulate the affairs of the city. He was preparing an expedition against the Moors in Africa when he contracted his final illness. Realizing that his death was approaching, he prepared himself by a devout confession, and after receiving the Last Sacraments he died on May 30, at the age of 53. He had reigned in Castile for 35 years. In accord with his wishes his body was clothed in the habit of the Third Order of St. Francis, a secular order which he had joined many years before. His body was buried in the Cathedral of Seville, where it is still venerated. St. Ferdinand was canonized in the year 1671 by Pope Clement X.

Chapter 68

ST. FLORA AND ST. MARY

d. 851

All that we know of these two virgin martyrs was recorded by St. Eulogius of Cordova, Spain. Like the two women, he also suffered imprisonment and martyrdom during a persecution by the Moslems of North Africa, who had invaded Spain.

Flora was a Mohammedan in her early years by virtue of her father, but her mother secretly instructed the child in the Christian Faith. After her Baptism her own brother, a Moslem, vengefully betrayed her before the judge of the city. The magistrate had her scourged and beaten on the head until, in some parts, her skull was exposed.

Eulogius wrote, "I, wicked sinner that I am, knew her from the beginning of her sufferings; these hands of mine have touched the scars made by the whip on that lovely and noble head, from which the hair was torn out."

After these sufferings, Flora was released into the custody of her brother in the hope that he could persuade her to renounce the Christian Faith. A short time later she escaped over a high wall and took shelter with a sister who lived in Ossaria. After a time the Moslems were not only persecuting Christians, but were also inflicting punishments on those who concealed them. Flora's sister and her household were fearful that the poor girl would be betrayed and that they would suffer as a result. For this reason Flora was asked to leave. She then returned to Cordova and entered the Church of St. Acisclus to pray for guidance.

There she met the virtuous Mary, the sister of the deacon St. Valabonsus, who had died for the Faith a few days earlier. After much prayer and consideration, Flora and Mary realized that their arrest was inevitable and decided to make a courageous profession of their faith to the magistrate of the city. This they did. They were subsequently confined in a dungeon where no one had access to them except some wicked women who were sent to corrupt them. Of this effort Eulogius, who was in prison at the time, wrote to them,

> They threaten to sell you into a shameful slavery, but do not be afraid: no harm can come to your souls, whatever infamy they inflict on your bodies. Cowardly Christians will tell you that churches are empty and without the Sacrifice because of your obstinacy, and that if you will only yield for a time all will be well. But you may be certain that for you a contrite and humble heart is the sacrifice that pleases God most: you cannot now draw back and renounce the faith you have confessed.

Every effort was made to induce the girls to renounce their faith. Somehow Eulogius was able to visit the prisoners; he wrote, "I encouraged her [Flora] as best I could, bringing to mind the crown she had earned. Bowing low before her, I asked her prayers; and then, new heart put into me by all she had said, I left her angelic presence and went back to my dungeon."

During the afternoon of November 24, 851, Flora and Mary were beheaded after making the Sign of the Cross and bowing their heads to the sword.

During St. Eulogius' last visit with the two martyrs, they told him that they would intercede in Heaven for his release and the release of his brethren. Five days after the virgin martyrs' execution, Eulogius was given his freedom. In *The Memorial of the Saints,* St. Eulogius attributes his deliverance to the intercession of the two Saints. By means of his preaching, writings and example, he strengthened the Spanish Christians, especially when the persecution was intensified in 853. Six years later St. Eulogius was himself beheaded.

Chapter 69

ST. GENESIUS

d. c. 300

Considered to be the favorite comedian of his day, Genesius was the leader of a theatrical troupe that performed one day at Rome before the emperor and a large audience. A professed heathen, Genesius performed a comedy routine that day which consisted of ridiculing the ceremonies of the Christian Church. He intended to amuse the emperor by mocking the Sacrament of Baptism by performing a little skit in which he supposedly received the Sacrament.

While Genesius acted the part of a dying Christian, a fellow actor, impersonating the character of a priest, approached Genesius and asked, "Well, my child, why hast thou sent for me?" There was a momentary pause—during which Genesius suddenly received the grace of conversion. Then, in all seriousness, Genesius replied, "I desire to receive the grace of Jesus Christ and to be relieved from the weight of my sins, which oppress me." The actor who pretended to be a priest continued the performance by pouring water over the comedian's head.

During this time Genesius is said to have had a vision of an angel who was surrounded by a heavenly light. Holding in his hand a book in which the sins of Genesius had been written, the angel immersed the book in the baptismal water and then showed it to Genesius. The sins had all been removed, and the book was perfectly white.

As the play progressed, Genesius was clothed in the white robe of the neophytes, after which certain players representing soldiers came to seize him and present him to the emperor as a Christian. But when he was brought before the emperor, he was no longer a comedian playing a part, but a true believer in Jesus Christ. He described for the emperor the vision he had experienced and professed himself to be a Christian. At first the emperor was greatly amused, thinking the profession of faith to be a part of the play, but when he realized the seriousness of the situation, he became so irritated that he ordered Genesius to be severely beaten with clubs. After the beating Genesius was handed over to Plautian, Prefect of the Praetorium, who was to inflict torture in an effort to make Genesius renounce the Faith.

On Plautian's orders, Genesius was stretched upon the rack, torn with iron hooks and burned with torches. During these sufferings Genesius declared, "All possible tortures shall never take Jesus Christ from my heart or from my lips. My only grief is that I have so long persecuted His holy name, and have learned to adore Him so late." Genesius was then beheaded.

It should be mentioned that Genesius did not properly receive the Sacrament of Baptism during the performance, but he seems to have received Baptism of desire, or at least Baptism of blood at his martyrdom.

Genesius was venerated at Rome in the fourth century. A church built in his honor was repaired and embellished by Gregory III in 741. In the Roman Church of Santa Susanna the relics of St. Genesius are found in the Chapel of St. Lawrence, which was added in 1585 by Pope Sixtus V (d. 1590).

The Church historian and theologian Ruinart (d. 1709) gives information on St. Genesius (who died between the years 285 and 303) in his monumental work on the lives of the martyrs which he called *Acta Primorum Martyrum Sincera et Selecta.* Based on authentic documents, it is said that "Taken as a whole the collection is not surpassed even today."

Chapter 70

ST. GENGULPHUS

d. 760

Gengulphus (or Gengoul) was a Burgundian knight who was especially admired for his bravery, his accomplishments for the Frankish kingdom and his upright and virtuous life. He was also held in the highest regard by Pepin the Short, Mayor of the Palace of the whole Frankish kingdom and later the King of the Franks. Gengulphus was so likeable and even-tempered that he and Pepin were often found side by side.

Gengulphus eventually married a woman of rank whom he deeply loved and trusted, but soon after their marriage she proved to be scandalously unfaithful to him and unbearably ill-tempered. When corrections and appeals proved useless, the peace-loving Gengulphus made provisions for her care and withdrew to his castle in Burgundy. During his retirement from public life he led the life of a recluse, spending his time in penitential exercises and in supplying alms to the needy.

According to historical accounts, Gelgulphus was killed by his wife's paramour who, at her instigation, broke into his chamber one night and murdered him as he lay in bed.

Another man who suffered much from trials presented by his wife was St. Gummarus, who served at about the same time under Pepin the Short.

After the wide distribution of his relics, Gengulphus was honored in Holland, Belgium and Savoy.

Since he suffered great humiliation and heartache as the result of his wife's infidelity, Gengulphus is regarded as the patron saint of those who are unhappily married.

Chapter 71

ST. GERALD OF AURILLAC

d. 909

During a lingering illness that kept him confined to his chambers, Gerald occupied the time in studies, prayer and meditation. He derived so much satisfaction from these that he never again participated in the pleasures and comforts of the world. Following the death of his parents, he became the Count of Aurillac (France), and he distributed among the poor most of the income he derived from his noble position.

Despite what others might expect from one who was titled, Gerald dressed in a manner consistent with the austere life he led. He ate simple foods and awakened every morning at 2 o'clock for the recitation of the Divine Office. He then heard Holy Mass and divided his day between his secular duties and his life of prayer and penance.

Following a pilgrimage to Rome, Gerald founded at Aurillac, a church which he dedicated to St. Peter. In the year 898, Benedictine monks from Vabres occupied the abbey which the Saint had added to the church. St. Gerald considered entering the abbey himself, but he was persuaded by St. Gausbert, Bishop of Cahors, to remain in the world. The future saint was assured that he could accomplish more for the Church and his neighbors by fulfilling the duties of his royal state.

For the last seven years of his life Gerald patiently endured the hardships of blindness. In the year 909, when he was 54 years of age, he died at Cezenac, but he was buried at Aurillac in the abbey which he had founded. This abbey later became celebrated as a center of literary and scientific studies. It is thought to have been governed for a time by St. Odo, Abbot of Cluny, who was one of St. Gerald's first biographers.

Chapter 72

BL. GERARD OF MONZA

d. 1207

Grieved in his early youth by the death of his parents, Gerard clung to the consolations of his faith throughout his formative years. Upon reaching manhood, Gerard spent his entire inheritance in building a hospital for the poor. During the rest of his life he worked in the hospital as both administrator and nurse, rendering to the poor whatever services were needed, no matter how revolting or menial they might be. To make certain that the forgotten sick were not neglected, it was his practice to wander through the city in search of them and to carry them on his shoulders to the hospital. Lepers he washed with his own hands, and he greeted each newcomer with the kiss of peace. After years of practicing this charity, Gerard advanced rapidly in virtue. Soon many of the patients he tended were being unaccountably cured, until he was credited with miraculous powers of healing.

After a time Gerard placed the institution under the protection of the cathedral canons and composed a rule which has been preserved. Later, however, the staff consisted almost entirely of Franciscan tertiaries.

The holy man's charities always included the poor, and no beggar who asked for help was ever turned away. Once, during a famine, the Saint distributed so much of the hospital's grain that the supply was nearly exhausted. In desperation, the steward turned to Gerard for a remedy. The holy man encouraged him to place his trust and confidence in God; he then retired to pray. When next the steward entered the storerooms, he found so much corn that he could scarcely open the door. The cellar is also said to have experienced an unexplained increase in its supply of wine.

Another miracle attributed to Bl. Gerard accounts for the cluster of cherries with which he is often depicted in art. One winter's night he asked permission to spend the night in prayer in the Church of St. John the Baptist. The doorkeepers at first resisted, but then they told Bl. Gerard that he could stay if he could do the impossible by supplying them the following day with cherries—which were definitely out of season. Bl. Gerard humbly accepted the condition, and the following day, we are told, he brought the doorkeepers bowls of fresh, ripe cherries.

Following his most holy death on June 6, 1207, Gerard was buried in the Church of St. Ambrose, which later adopted his name.

More than 350 years after Gerard's death, his cultus, which had languished, was revived by St. Charles Borromeo (d. 1584) of Milan. St. Charles wrote Gerard's biography and promoted his cause. Due to this saintly Cardinal's efforts, Gerard's cultus was confirmed in 1582.

Bl. Gerard is considered the principal patron of Monza, his native city, and is honored throughout the dioceses of Milan and Como.

Chapter 73

ST. GERMAINE COUSIN

1579 - 1601

In the apostolic brief that placed the pious shepherdess St. Germaine Cousin among the Blessed, she is described as "a simple maiden, humble, and of lowly birth, but so greatly enlightened by the gifts of divine wisdom and understanding, and so remarkable for her transcendent virtues, that she shone like a star, not only in her native France, but also throughout the Catholic Church."

Germaine was born at Pibrac, a village ten miles from Toulouse, France. She was the daughter of Laurent Cousin, a poor agricultural laborer, and Marie Laroche, who died when her daughter was scarcely out of the cradle. Germaine was born with a right hand that was crippled and powerless. Always a sickly child, she soon developed a scrofulous condition of the neck glands that deformed her appearance with huge swellings.

In addition to her physical ailments, the child had to endure a father who had no affection for her, while his second wife actively disliked her. After taking charge of the household, the stepmother treated Germaine harshly—and after the birth of her own children she pretended a desire to spare her children from the contagion of scrofula and convinced the father that Germaine should be isolated from the family. Thus in all kinds of weather the child was made to sleep in the stable or under the stairs. For her food she was given scraps of bread and leftovers, and as soon as she was old enough, Germaine was sent to tend the sheep in the pastures. She was destined to remain a shepherdess for the rest of her life.

With perfect resignation and simplicity of heart, Germaine accepted the treatment she received—and this God used to lead her to higher spirituality. While tending the flocks in the quiet of the fields, she communed with her divine Creator. She was devoted to the recitation of the Holy Rosary, which she recited with great care.

When the church bell signalled the Angelus, she would kneel down and pray, regardless of the mud or snow.

Germaine attended Holy Mass every day. If she was in the fields when it was time for the Holy Sacrifice, she would plant her crook in the ground and commend her flock to her guardian angel before hurrying to the church. On her return, she never once found any of the sheep missing—this despite the fact that wolves lurked in the neighboring forest waiting to attack unattended animals. Germaine received Holy Communion as often as it was then allowed. She never engaged in the social life of the peasants or mixed with girls of her own age, but she did take pleasure in instructing children in the truths of the Catholic Faith and encouraging them in the love of God.

Because of the treatment given her by her parents, Germaine was likewise treated by neighbors with intolerance—but they began to change their attitude when strange reports started circulating about her. They became aware of her daily attendance at Mass and her prayerful attitude. Then one day, when the stream she had to cross to attend Mass was so swollen with rain that others would not dare attempt a crossing, two villagers solemnly swore that when Germaine approached the stream, the waters separated to permit a safe and dry passage—just as the Red Sea had parted for the Israelites at the time of Moses.

Although given little food for her meals, Germaine somehow shared her meager rations with the poor. One winter day her stepmother ran after her with a stick, loudly claiming that Germaine was holding stolen bread in her apron. When Germaine was ordered to open her folded apron, there fell out only fragrant flowers of a variety unknown to the region. The witnesses to this event, Pierre Pailles and Jeanne Salaires, gave sworn testimony concerning the miracle.

The villagers soon began to treat Germaine with courtesy, claiming that the young girl was a saint. Her father and stepmother even relented toward her and offered to take her into the house, but Germaine declined their offer, preferring to live as before.

Quite unexpectedly, Germaine was found one morning lying dead on her straw mat under the stairs. She was 22 years of age.

In view of her saintly conduct and the miracles witnessed by the villagers, the body of the poor shepherdess was buried in the Church of Pibrac, where she had so often attended Holy Mass. In 1644, 43 years after her death, two church workers, Gaillard Barous and

Nicholas Case, opened the vault to make room for another burial. Upon lifting the flagstone covering the tomb, the workmen were amazed to find the body of a beautiful young girl lying in a perfect state of preservation.

A tool which one of the men had used to remove the stone had slipped, injuring the nose of the body and causing it to bleed. Villagers flocked to the church to see the wonder for themselves. The older members identified Germaine by the withered arm and the wounds which the scrofulous condition had left on her neck. Her body was removed and placed in a lead casket, which was kept in the sacristy for many years.

Miracles of healing became so numerous that a petition was filed in the year 1700 for the beatification of the shepherdess. During the same year, a medical examination by experts revealed that the body had not been embalmed. Other tests showed that the preservation was not due to any property inherent in the soil. After remaining incorrupt for almost 200 years, the body was destroyed in 1795 during the French Revolution by a revolutionary tinsmith named Toulza, who threw quicklime and water on the body.

Because the cause of beatification was interrupted by the Revolution, it was resumed in 1850. Documents presented at the time attested to more than 400 miracles or extraordinary graces, and 30 postulatory letters from Archbishops and Bishops asked the Pope for Germaine's beatification. The miracles that were presented during the consideration of the petition included those of every kind of healing. One extraordinary miracle involved the multiplication of food for the distressed community of the Good Shepherd at Bourges in 1845.

Pope Pius IX proclaimed Germaine's beatification on May 7, 1854 and on June 29, 1867 he canonized her, placing her name on the list of virgin saints.

The little shepherdess, so abused and neglected during her lifetime, has been greatly loved and venerated throughout the world, but especially in Pibrac. There, on her feast day, June 15, huge pilgrimages wend their way to the church, where special ceremonies are observed in her honor. There Germaine's relics are kept in a splendid reliquary resembling a small church. Atop this reliquary is a miniature statue of the kneeling Germaine, who is holding her shepherd's crook. Behind her, several sheep seem to be grazing.

In addition to the church where Germaine attended Mass and where she is now buried, pilgrims to Pibrac may also visit the Cousin home with its attached barn, where Germaine slept every night and where she died.

In art, Germaine is represented with a shepherd's crook or with a distaff, with a watchdog or a sheep, or with flowers in her apron.

The house of the pious shepherdess St. Germaine Cousin of Pibrac, France (1579-1601). As a child she was isolated from her family and was fed only bread scraps and leftovers. As soon as she was old enough, she was sent to the pastures to tend sheep. There she communed with God, leaving the fields to attend daily Mass. It is said that the waters of a rain-swollen stream once miraculously parted to allow Germaine to cross over and attend Mass.

A statue of St. Germaine. The Saint suffered from poor health—scrofula and a paralyzed right hand—as well as the ill-treatment of her stepmother. When she grew older, St. Germaine became well-known for her piety and supernatural experiences.

The beautiful last resting place of St. Germaine recalls that her body remained incorrupt until it was destroyed in 1795 during the French Revolution.

Chapter 74

ST. GODELIEVE

c. 1049 - 1070

The persecution and cruelty suffered by this holy saint at the hands of her husband and mother-in-law would seem almost unbelievable had it not been recorded by a contemporary priest by the name of Drogo. From his pen, as well as others, we learn the following fantastic history of St. Godelieve.

Born about the year 1049 in the castle of Londesvoorde in the County of Boulogne, Belgium, Godelieve was the youngest of the three children born to Hemfried, Lord of Wierre-Effroy, and his wife Ogeva. During her childhood Godelieve was accustomed to perform exercises of piety and was soon distinguished for her extraordinary virtues. The poor who flocked to her always found a generous friend, but Godelieve's efforts to help them often placed her in difficulties with her father and her father's steward.

By the time Godelieve had reached her 18th year, the fame of her beauty and admirable qualities had spread throughout the district. Many suitors presented themselves, but all were rejected in favor of the resolution she had made of renouncing the world for the cloister. However, one suitor, Bertolf of Gistel, would not be put off. Apparently driven by an egotistical necessity to win where others had failed, he appealed to her father's suzerain, Eustache II, Count of Boulogne, whose influence proved successful in persuading Godelieve to marry.

Following the wedding ceremony, Bertolf and his bride journeyed to Gistel. There the young bride found a bitter and unrelenting enemy in Bertolf's mother, who influenced her son to abandon his new wife on the very day of their arrival. Godelieve was given over to the care of her mother-in-law, who was not content with petty persecutions, but treated her with "fanatic brutality." Apparently the mother had other plans for her son and was furious that he had disregarded them in favor of this girl from Boulogne. Godelieve's mother-in-law not only heaped abuse on her, but she also placed her in a narrow cell with barely enough nourishment to support life. It was apparent that the mother-in-law wanted to be rid of her, but she dared not kill Godelieve directly. As though her sufferings, both mental and physical, were not enough, Godelieve's husband, under the influence of his mother, would not go near his bride, and he spread scandalous stories about her.

After a time, Godelieve succeeded in escaping to her father's house. Her unexpected return, together with her poor physical condition, alarmed Hemfried. He ordered Godelieve, under obedience, to confide to him the conditions under which she had been living. Although Godelieve wanted to spare her husband, she was nevertheless forced under obedience and respect for her father to tell all that had occurred at her husband's home. After Godelieve had revealed the cruelty of her existence there, her father was so outraged that he reported the matter to the Bishop of Tournai, as well as to the Count of Flanders. These threatened Bertolf with the terrors of the Church and State. It was ruled that Bertolf should reconcile with his wife and in the future treat her with respect.

Seemingly repentant, Bertolf promised to restore his wife to her rightful position in his household and to treat her with gentleness. But Godelieve's return to Gistel was met with renewed persecution in a vain attempt to ruin her health and finish her life.

Bertolf resorted to more direct action in the year 1070. He pretended a complete change of heart and a desire for reconciliation—this with the intention of averting the suspicion of the crime he was contemplating. Then, after instructing two servants on what they were to do, Bertolf left for the City of Bruges. While he was gone, Godelieve was tricked one dark night into stepping outside her home by a back door. Once she was outside, the two servants seized her; placing a thong tightly around her neck, they took her to a nearby pond, where they held her head beneath the water until she was dead. Intending the death to appear to have been from natural causes, they placed Godelieve's body back in her bed, but the marks about her neck revealed the criminal cause of her death. Since her husband was far away at the time, Godelieve's father could not place a claim against him.

Bertolf soon married for a second time, but the daughter of this marriage, Edith, was born blind. A miraculous recovery of sight took place when her eyes were bathed in the water taken from the pool where Godelieve had died. This miracle so affected Bertolf that he experienced a true conversion. He journeyed to Rome to obtain absolution for the murder of Godelieve, finally entering the monastery of St. Winoc at Bruges, where he expiated his sins by a life of severe penance.

At Bertolf's request, his daughter Edith erected a Benedictine Abbey at Gistel. This abbey experienced various damages and repairs throughout the centuries. In 1953 important alterations were made. When these were completed, the Abbey St. Godelieve was solemnly consecrated on June 26 of that year. The Abbey, which is still in the care of the Benedictine nuns, is also known as the Abbey Ten Putte, the "Abbey by the Well," since a well is maintained there which has the same water as that found in the pool in which Godelieve died. The well is at the place where Edith received her sight.

Following Godelieve's death, God confirmed her virtues by so many miracles that her body was exhumed in 1084 by the Bishop of Tournai for enshrinement in the church. A copy of the formal verification of the Saint's relics made at that time, 14 years after Godelieve's death, has been preserved. This verification of the relics was found when the shrine was solemnly visited and examined in 1907. The Saint's relics, recognized at various times by ecclesiastical authority, are to be found in various cities of Belgium, but important relics of the Saint are still kept in the church of the Abbey.

At the place where Godelieve was murdered there stands a statue of the Saint which has been revered by pilgrims for centuries. Also of interest to pilgrims is the Little Cellar, or Prison of Godelieve, which is found in the basement of the Abbey's south wing. This is the place where Godelieve withstood abuse and neglect—so heroically that she has been regarded as "the most blessed woman in Flanders."

St. Godelieve has always been depicted with four crowns, a unique iconographical feature. These crowns are the symbols of her virginity, her marriage, her repudiation (which is regarded as the equivalent to widowhood) and her martyrdom.

The Saint is invoked at the Abbey during the whole year, but especially during the annual solemnities which take place between July 6 and July 30. Her intercession is particularly sought in cases of eye or throat disorders and for maintaining or re-establishing peace in families.

The eleventh-century Belgian girl St. Godelieve was cruelly treated by her mother-in-law and was murdered by servants at the instigation of her husband, Bertolf. He soon re-married, but the daughter of this marriage was born blind. Many miracles followed Godelieve's death. When sight was restored to Bertolf's daughter through Godelieve's intercession, Bertolf was converted to a life of penance. St. Godelieve is usually depicted with four crowns representing her virginity, her marriage, her repudiation by her husband and her martyrdom.

271

Chapter 75

ST. GORGONIA

d. 374

St. Gregory Nazianzus the Elder and his wife St. Nonna had three children: St. Gregory Nazianzen, the great Doctor of the Church; St. Caesarius, a physician by profession; and St. Gorgonia, who was the eldest. Gorgonia married a man from Iconium named Vitalian; they had three children, whom Gorgonia brought up with the same care that she had received from her parents.

What we know of St. Gorgonia is given to us by her brother St. Gregory Nazianzen in the funeral oration he delivered at the time of her death. This eulogy, still extant, is very lengthy in praise of her virtuous life. St. Gregory begins the eulogy in this way:

> In praising my sister, I shall be honoring my own family. Yet while she is a member of my family I shall not on that account praise her falsely, but because what is true is for that reason praiseworthy. Moreover, this truth is not only well-founded, but also well-known.

After speaking of her many virtues, St. Gregory tells the following about Gorgonia's exemplary marriage:

> Though she was linked in carnal union, she was not on that account separated from the Spirit, nor because she had her husband as her head did she ignore her first Head. When she had served the world and nature a little, to the extent that the law of the flesh willed it, or, rather, He who imposed this law on the flesh, she consecrated herself wholly to God. And what is most excellent and honorable, she also won over her husband and gained, instead of an unreasonable master, a good fellow servant. Not only that, she also made the fruit of her body, her children and her children's children, the fruit of her spirit, and dedicated to God, instead of her single soul, her whole family

and household. And she rendered marriage itself laudable by her pleasing and acceptable life in wedlock and by the fair fruit of her union. And she exhibited herself, as long as she lived, as an exemplar of every excellence to her children.

St. Gregory Nazianzen speaks of the Saint's great humility and modesty and gives a lesson to those who are overly fond of outward appearances:

> She was never adorned with gold fashioned by art into sur-passing beauty, or with fair tresses fully or partly exposed, or with spiral curls, or with the ingenious arrangements of those who disgracefully turn the noble head into a showpiece. Hers were no costly, flowing, diaphanous robes, hers no brilliant and beautiful gems, flashing color round about and causing the fig-ure to glow with light...But while she was familiar with the many and various external ornaments of women, she recognized none as more precious than her own character and the splendor which lies within. The only red that pleased her was the blush of modesty, and the only pallor, that which comes from absti-nence. But pigments and makeup and living pictures and flow-ing beauty of form she left to the women of the stage and the public squares, and to all for whom it is a disgrace and a re-proach to feel ashamed.

We are told that St. Gorgonia "was known as a counselor not only of her family...but also of all those about her, who regarded her suggestions and recommendations as law." She also gave a courte-ous and generous welcome to all who came to her in God's name, particularly travelers, the blind, the lame, widows and orphans. "Her house," we are told, "was a common hospice for all her needy rela-tives, and her goods were as common to all the needy as their own personal belongings." We are also informed that she frequently fasted and spent many evenings in fervent prayer.

To demonstrate his sister's great confidence in God, St. Gregory Nazianzen tells us of an incident in the life of the Saint: It was well-known by her neighbors that she was riding one day in her carriage when the mules pulling it went out of control. During the chase the carriage overturned and

> she was dragged along horribly and suffered serious injuries...Al-though crushed and mangled internally and externally in bone

and limb, she would have no physician save Him who had permitted the accident...Nor from anyone else but Him did she obtain her restoration...Although her suffering was human, her recovery was supernatural, and she gave to posterity a compelling argument for the display of faith in affliction and patient endurance in misfortune.

When the accident first occurred, Gorgonia's neighbors were scandalized that such a terrible thing should happen to someone who was so virtuous. But they were amazed at her unexpected recovery, and "They believed that the tragedy had happened for the very reason that she might be glorified by her sufferings."

Another time the Saint became seriously ill with a strange ailment that St. Gregory said did not seem human. "Nor did the skill of physicians who carefully examined the case, both singly and in consultation, prove of any avail." The disease seems to have presented itself at frequent intervals with a fever, coma, pallor and a paralysis of mind and body. When Gorgonia realized that the physicians could not help her, she visited the church (when the disease had somewhat abated) and prostrated herself with faith at the altar. Then she performed what St. Gregory calls "an act of pious and noble impudence." She placed her head on the altar "and pouring abundant tears upon it, as she who had once watered the feet of Christ, she vowed that she would not loose her hold until she obtained her recovery." After receiving the Body and Blood of Our Lord, she felt herself completely recovered, and "went away relieved in body and soul and mind..."

When the time for her death approached, St. Gorgonia "enjoined on her husband, her children and her friends such precepts as befitted one so full of love...and she discoursed beautifully on the future life, making her last day a day of solemn festival." St. Gorgonia's holy passing, in the arms of her mother, St. Nonna, greatly edified all who gathered about her bed. St. Gorgonia died in the year 374. Her feast day was formerly observed on December 9.

Chapter 76

ST. GOTTESCHALC

d. 1066

Gotteschalc, an Abotrite prince, was a student at the Abbey of St. Michael in Luneberg, Germany when he learned that his father, Uto, had been murdered by a Saxon. The young man felt the loss of his father so acutely and so bitterly that he left the Abbey about the year 1030, and even renounced the Christian Faith.

In an attempt to avenge his father's death, Gotteschalc gathered together a group of his tribesmen and joined with two other Wendish princes and their forces to do battle. They harassed the territories of the Saxons and carried their devastations as far as Hamburg and Holstein until Gotteschalc was captured by Duke Bernard of Saxony, who kept him in close confinement for a considerable time.

When he was finally released, Gotteschalc found that his father's territories had been seized by a powerful chieftain named Ratibor. Since he saw no prospect of regaining his patrimony, he went to Denmark with a number of his tribesmen and offered his services to King Canute, whose daughter he eventually married.

After distinguishing himself in the wars with Norway, Gotteschalc was sent on a number of expeditions to England. In the year 1043 he returned to his own country, where the Abotrites welcomed him as their chief. In time he gained control over other tribes, until Adam of Bremen claimed that Gotteschalc was the most powerful prince who had ever ruled the Slavs.

It is uncertain when Gotteschalc returned to the Christian Faith, but the zeal which he had devoted to avenging his father's death he now redoubled in favor of making amends for his mistake in rejecting the True Faith. During a reign of about 20 years, he worked hard at correcting whatever wrong he had done, seeing to the conversion and civilization of his subjects. With the help of Adalbert, Archbishop of Hamburg, Gotteschalc introduced priests into all parts of

275

his principality. One of the missionaries, a Scotsman named John, is said to have baptized several thousand catechumens. Gotteschalc frequently assisted the priests by translating sermons and instructions into the Slavonic language.

So great was Gotteschalc's zeal for the Faith that he founded monasteries in several cities; in Madgeburg he established three of them. He likewise worked hard to spread the Faith among distant tribes.

After the death of Emperor Henry III, who had maintained peace between the Slavs, Bohemians and Hungarians—and after the death of Duke Bernard, who had ruled Saxony for 40 years—trouble once more arose.

A strong anti-Christian reaction began, and it claimed Gotteschalc as one of its first victims. He was attacked and killed in the City of Lenzen on June 7, 1066, during a violent persecution that also claimed the lives of many other Christians and a number of ecclesiastics.

The anti-Christian persecution continued under Gotteschalc's successor, but he was succeeded by Gotteschalc's son Henry, under whom the Faith was reinstated throughout the land.

Chapter 77

ST. GUDULE

d. 712

Surrounded by holiness among her family members, St. Gudule (Goule, Goelen) was the daughter of St. Amalberga. She was a sister of St. Reinelda and St. Emembertus, and a niece and godchild of St. Gertrude of Nivelles, under whose care she was educated in the ways of holiness.

After St. Gertrude's death in 664, Gudule consecrated her virginity to God and led an austere life of prayer and fasting at home, in the company of her saintly family. Although her home was two miles from the Church of St. Saviour at Morzelle, she went there every morning before dawn with her maid, who carried a lantern before her. The light once went out and is said to have been miraculously lighted again at Gudule's prayers. For this reason St. Gudule is usually pictured holding a lantern or a candle.

St. Gudule died on January 8, 712. She was buried at Ham, near Villevord; but in the reign of Charlemagne, her body was removed to the church in which she had so often prayed, that of St. Saviour at Morzelle, where she was entombed behind the high altar. Charlemagne, out of veneration for her memory, is said to have visited her tomb and to have founded a convent nearby, which adopted her name. Unfortunately, this convent was destroyed during the invasions of the Normans.

The relics of St. Gudule, while in the care of Charles, Duke of Lorraine, were translated to Brussels between the year 977 and 988, with their final resting place (1047) being the great collegiate Church of St. Michael, which was later renamed to include the name of St. Gudule. (The name has since—in 1962—been changed back to that of its original patron, though the Church is still sometimes called the Cathedral of St. Gudule.) This collegiate church was pillaged and vandalized on June 6, 1579 by the heretics, who disinterred the

Saint's bones and scattered them.

St. Michael is regarded as the patron of Brussels with St. Gudule as its patroness.

Chapter 78

ST. GUMMARUS

d. 774

As the son of the Lord of Emblehem, Belgium, Gummarus served in the court of Pepin the Short, where he demonstrated the results of his youthful training in the Faith by being humble, honest, exact in his duties and fervent in all the exercises of devotion. Although Pepin was occupied with ambitious endeavors, he greatly admired the virtues of his courtier and raised him to a high position with added responsibilities.

Presumably as a reward for his faithfulness, Pepin proposed a match between Gummarus and a lady of noble birth named Gwinmarie. Both parties consented and the marriage was solemnized. However, soon after the wedding Gwinmarie displayed her true temperament. According to the description handed down to us, she was extravagant, proud, capricious, impatient, incorrigible, unteachable and had a tiresome and frightful disposition.

The devout and patient Gummarus suffered terribly from the trials which his wife continually presented. With heroic virtue, Gummarus attempted for several years to encourage his wife toward more controlled behavior—but without result. Finally, Gummarus was granted a reprieve of sorts when he was asked by King Pepin to accompany him in his wars: first in Lombardy, then in Saxony and again in Aquitaine. Gummarus was absent for eight years. Upon his return home he found that his wife had created complete disorder and confusion in his household, and that almost all of his servants, vassals and tenants had suffered from her overbearing oppression. Losing no time, Gummarus corrected his affairs and made restitution to all who had suffered.

Eventually, Gummarus' patience and kindness seemed to correct his wife's disposition. She seemed sincerely ashamed of her past conduct, and for a time she appeared to be truly penitent. This was only temporary, however, since she reverted to her old faults—which seemed to be even more serious than before. Gummarus tried once more to influence her, but at length he had to admit that this was impossible. By mutual consent the two separated.

Gummarus lived for a time in a cell near their home, but later he set off on a pilgrimage to Rome. He got no further than Nives-donck; there he built himself a hermitage and lived alone for some years, until his holy death about the year 774. Afterwards, his hermitage became a place of pilgrimage. St. Gummarus is venerated at Lier, which is near the village of his birth.

Chapter 79

ST. GUNTRAMNUS

d. 592

When King Clotaire I was on his deathbed, he divided the French Kingdom among his four sons. Sigebert received the territory of Austrasia; Charibert received Neustria; Chilperic received Soissons; and Guntramnus (or Gontran) became King of Burgundy and sovereign over part of Aquitaine. He was 36 years old at the time, and according to Butler, Guntramnus "lived a somewhat dissipated life, which afterwards caused him remorse." What especially pricked his conscience in later life was his divorce from his wife, Mercatrude. Additionally, he reproached himself for having ordered the execution of Queen Austrechild's physicians because they had failed to cure her.

It would be difficult to find a family in which brothers and their wives were more at odds, often with unholy intrigues and tragic results.

The problems seem to have flowered when the eldest brother, Charibert, died in 567 without leaving a male heir. It was Guntramnus who suggested that a council be held in Paris to decide upon a friendly division of Charibert's property. The council was held, but only Guntramnus observed the terms which had been decided upon. Even though the others had agreed to the terms, the division of Charibert's estate produced quarrels between Chilperic and Sigebert, who were already at odds because of their wives.

Sigebert, it seems, had married the beautiful Brunehilda, daughter of Athanagild, King of the Visigoths. Chilperic had married Brunehilda's sister Galeswinta; but when Chilperic's mistress, Fredegonda, became jealous, Chilperic had Galeswintha assassinated and placed Fredegonda upon the throne. Brunehilda's determination to avenge the death of her sister involved bitter quarrels not only between the two women, but also between their husbands.

In 575 Sigebert took to the field, determined to bring matters to a conclusion. Chilperic, already banished from his kingdom, had taken refuge behind the walls of Tournai; this manuever provided safety, but no hope for escape. Just when defeat for Chilperic seemed imminent and victory for Sigebert was anticipated, Sigebert was killed by an assassin sent by Chilperic's wife, Fredegonda. Brunehilda was briefly imprisoned while her bitter enemies, Chilperic and Fredegonda, reveled in their victory. Nine years later, justice seems to have been served when Chilperic was himself killed by an assassin.

The difficulties which King Guntramnus had to contend with during this time were awesome. He continually attempted to make peace between his two brothers and their wives, while at the same time he was also defending part of his territory from the Visigoths, as well as defending himself against the intrigues of Gondowald, his illegitimate brother, who wanted the throne for himself.

After the deaths of his two brothers, Chilperic and Sigebert, Guntramnus served as a father to their children. Toward his two fierce sisters-in-law, Fredegunda and Brunehilda, Guntramnus was singularly patient and forbearing, although Fredegunda on several occasions attempted to take his life. Brunehilda was likewise devious and untrustworthy. Following Guntramnus' death, Brunehilda became very influential through the reigns of her son and grandsons—but she grievously offended so many nobles, and so many of the citizenry, that she was punished by means of a frightful death. She suffered the humiliation of being tied to the tail of a wild horse and trampled to death.

Although Guntramnus is described as having led "a dissipated life" in his youth, he was admirably virtuous during his maturity. Throughout his reign he would not permit his people to be oppressed. While serving as regent of the lands of his deceased brother Chilperic, he abolished fines and returned to the people properties that had been unjustly taken from them by his brother.

It is said that few kings were as popular with their subjects as was Guntramnus. He often visited his people in their homes and sat at their tables. When Guntramnus entered a town, the citizens would rush out to meet him, crying, "Noel, Noel! Long live the King!"

Although Guntramnus held the Church and her clergy in the highest veneration, he was convinced that some of the most serious evils of the time arose from the lack of proper ecclesiastical discipline and from the bishops taking undue interest in secular affairs. He arranged for important synods, at which regulations were enacted to correct disorders. Guntramnus also founded or endowed many churches and monasteries, and he encouraged a better observance of Sundays and festivals.

A dear friend of Guntramnus was St. Gregory of Tours (d. 594). St. Gregory aided the King in many of his endeavors involving the Church, and he wrote nearly all we know of Guntramnus.

After reigning for 31 years, Guntramnus died at the age of 68 and was immediately regarded as a saint by his subjects. He was buried at the Abbey of Baume les Dames, which had been founded in the fifth century. Unfortunately, during the Revolution the church of this abbey was leveled.

Chapter 80

ST. GUY OR GUIDO

d. 1012

Commonly known as the Poor Man of Anderlecht, St. Guy was born in the country near Brussels of poor, hard-working parents. Unable to provide him with a formal education, his parents diligently instructed him in the principles of the Faith and in the practices of holy religion. St. Guy prayed that he would always bear its hardships with joy and in a spirit of penance. This he did with admirable virtue, giving to his poor neighbors his humble possessions and feeding them while he himself fasted.

When St. Guy was old enough to leave home, he wandered about for a time until one day, while he was visiting the Church of Our Lady at Laeken, near Brussels, a priest offered him the position of sacristan. St. Guy accepted with pleasure, declaring it a great privilege to work for the church. Under his direction the good order and cleanliness of the church was scrupulously maintained, to the admiration of all who came there to pray. St. Guy's conduct and recollection while engaged in his chores gave a silent lesson that the dwelling place of God should be visited with prayerful reverence.

Eventually a merchant of Brussels, on learning of St. Guy's generosity, offered him a partnership in his business, arguing that St. Guy could make considerable money with which to relieve the poor. St. Guy, considering his meager efforts to help the poor and the larger amount of good he could accomplish with the earnings promised him, consented to leave his duties in the church and join the merchant aboard ship.

Upon the vessel's leaving the harbor, disaster struck. The ship sank, and all the merchandise on board was lost. St. Guy survived, but he was left destitute since the position of sacristan had been filled during his brief absence. It was then that he realized the mistake he had made in following his own plans instead of remaining in the humble and secure employment in which Providence had placed him.

In reparation for this mistake and to avoid those who were beginning to admire his virtue, St. Guy journeyed on foot to Rome and then made his way to Jerusalem, where he visited most of the celebrated shrines. On his return to Rome he met Windulf, Dean of the Church of Anderlecht, which is situated a short distance from Brussels. Since Windulf and his companions were then preparing to journey to the Holy Land, St. Guy was prevailed upon to act as their guide, since he had previously told them of his visit to that country and of his familiarity with the holy shrines. Once again St. Guy made the long journey to Jerusalem, this time in the company of his countrymen. After the completion of their tour, just as they were about to set sail for Europe, the Dean and his friends contracted the plague. St. Guy helped them during their sickness, and then arranged for their funerals.

After an absence of seven years, St. Guy returned to Belgium. He made for Anderlecht, and there he reported to the chapter all that pertained to the deaths of the Dean and those who had traveled with him. Exhausted from the journey and ill from the many hardships he had experienced along the way, St. Guy remained in Anderlecht. He was soon accepted into the hospital of Anderlecht, where he peacefully died in the year 1012. He was first buried in the cemetery of the canons; then, after miracles took place at his tomb, his body was translated to a shrine.

St. Guy or Guido (d. 1012), known as the Poor Man of Anderlecht. This statue stands before the crypt where he was first buried in Anderlecht, Belgium. His body was translated to a shrine after miracles took place at his tomb.

Born of poor, hard-working parents, Guy gave up a secure position as church sacristan to enter into a business venture in hopes of earning considerable money with which to help the poor. The venture was ill-fated, though, and he was left destitute. This statue is at the Church of St. Guido in Anderlecht.

As an act of reparation and in order to avoid people who were beginning to admire his virtue, St. Guy walked to Rome and then traveled to Jerusalem as a pilgrim.

Above: One of the first shrines of St. Guy, decorated with paintings depicting scenes from his life.

Below: St. Guy's tombstone in the crypt where he was buried. Approximately the last seven years of his life were spent making or guiding others on pilgrimages.

Chapter 81

ST. HALLVARD

d. 1043

Because their father, Vebjorn, was a landowner and a merchant, Hallvard Vebjornsson and his brother Orm were considered persons of rank and honor. Thorny, Hallvard's mother, was related to St. Olav's mother. The family lived quite comfortably on their large estate, which was located on the side of the Drammenfjord which is approximately 15 miles from Olso, Norway.

Hallvard was a Christian from childhood. Neighbors said that he was chaste, honest, religious, obedient to his parents and kindly to everyone. When the brothers were old enough, their father began to take them on his merchant travels. Hallvard was about 13 years old at the time of his first voyage. It is not too surprising, then, since Hallvard was introduced so early to traveling abroad, that he was permitted to travel alone on matters of business while he was still an adolescent.

Accounts of two incidents that took place during this time have come down to us. We are told that once, when Hallvard's ship lay off the coast of Gothland, a rich young man came by to speak with the visitors from the North. Upon seeing Hallvard, he inquired as to who the young boy might be, since there was something remarkable about him. The rich young man told Hallvard, "I am certain that you are destined to do great things in your time." He invited Hallvard and all his companions to his home for a banquet and gave Hallvard rich gifts. We are told that this young nobleman of Gothland died as a martyr 30 years later. He is known as St. Botvid, the Apostle of Sodermanland.

The second incident that occurred during St. Hallvard's adolescence resulted in his early death.

First we must consider the punishment given in those days for stealing, which was considered a lamentable and despicable offense—so much so that no one had pity for a thief. A freeborn woman who had stolen was exiled; a bondwoman who had stolen suffered the loss of her ear for the first offense, the other ear for the second offense, and for the third offense her nose was cut off. The grim humor of the law allowed that "after that she can sniff and steal as much as she likes."

Hallvard's meeting with a strange woman came about one day when he left home to cross the Drammenfjord to transact business in the district on the other side. He was stepping into his boat when a woman came running toward him. She was terribly frightened and begged Hallvard to take her with him in the boat and row her to the opposite shore as quickly as possible. Hallvard helped her on board and had rowed only a short distance when three men came running to the shore from the same direction from which the woman had come. They boarded another boat and frantically rowed after Hallvard and the woman. In answer to Hallvard's question the woman acknowledged that she knew the men, but she explained that they accused her of stealing—a crime which she had not committed. Hallvard asked her if she were willing to prove her innocence through the ordeal by fire. She answered that she would do so, if only the men would spare her life.

When the boat gained on them the men asked Hallvard to surrender the woman, whom they wished to kill for the crime of breaking into the house of their brother. They claimed that she had "wrenched the bolt away which holds fast the boom across the door."

Having noticed that the woman was pregnant, Hallvard argued that it would require a man of considerable strength to do what they claimed she had done to gain entrance. With the poor woman huddled in the front of the rocking boat, Hallvard tried as best he could to defend her by presenting the inconsistencies of the accusation and by appealing to the men's sense of charity. But they were quickly losing patience.

Suddenly one of the men drew his bow and shot an arrow that struck Hallvard in the throat. They killed the woman also and buried her on the shore. Hallvard's body was thrown into the fjord with a millstone around the neck. Legend says that the body floated up, in spite of the millstone, and was buried in the church at Husaby.

Immediately, signs and miracles took place at Hallvard's grave, and he was acknowledged a martyr who had given his life in the defense of one of God's unfortunates.

Hallvard died in the year 1043. Years later his body was laid in a shrine and was moved to the new Christ Church in Oslo. The Catholic Church set May 15 as his feast day. Later, when Oslo became a bishopric, St. Hallvard was named patron saint of the diocese. It is said that his image has been incorporated in the arms of the city ever since. In art, the Saint is pictured as a handsome youth holding a millstone.

Chapter 82

ST. HEDWIG

d. 1243

St. Hedwig was one of eight children born at the Castle of Andechs to Count Berthold IV. The vocations of the Saint's brothers and sisters indicate the religious atmosphere in which the family was raised. Of Hedwig's four brothers, two became bishops: Ekbert of Bambert and Berthold of Aquileia. Of her sisters, Gertrude married and became the mother of the great St. Elizabeth of Hungary, while another sister, Mechtilde, became Abbess of the convent at Kitzingen. Hedwig herself became a canonized saint.

Hedwig was educated in the convent of Kitzingen, and according to an old biography, she was 12 years old in 1186 when she married Henry I of Silesia, Poland. At the time of the marriage, Henry was 18 years old. When Henry succeeded his father as Duke of Silesia in 1202, Hedwig began to play a prominent part in her husband's administration. Her prudence and piety greatly influenced the government of the land, and she was successful in maintaining peace among the nobles within her area of influence. She gave her support to new monastic foundations and assisted those already in existence.

It was chiefly through the monasteries that German civilization was spread in Silesia. Together, Henry and Hedwig founded several religious houses and invited the Cistercians, Dominicans and Franciscans into their territory. Henry founded the Hospital of the Holy Ghost at Breslau, and Hedwig tended leper women in the hospital at Newmarkt. The first religious house for women in Silesia was founded by Henry in 1202, this being a convent for Cistercian nuns at Trebnitz (Trzebnica).

For some years after her marriage, Hedwig resided chiefly at Breslau. There she gave birth to seven children. Hedwig suffered one of the most painful afflictions that can befall a mother when three of her children died in early childhood. Another three died as adults during the Saint's lifetime.

After the birth of their last child, Hedwig and her husband pronounced a vow of chastity before the Bishop of Breslau. Their marriage continued for another 30 years, during which Duke Henry never wore gold, silver or purple and never shaved his beard. Because of this he was surnamed Henry the Bearded.

The couple's two sons, Henry and Conrad, were the occasion of a good deal of trouble. In 1212 Duke Henry divided his duchies between them, but on terms which were not pleasing to Conrad. Hedwig supported the cause of Henry, who was the elder. The two brothers, notwithstanding their mother's efforts to reconcile them, went into battle; Henry won decisively over his younger brother, who fled the territory. Henry eventually succeeded to his father's title. Conrad died while still a young man, as a result of a fall from his horse while hunting.

Besides the deaths of her children, Hedwig had other trials which greatly afflicted her. In the year 1227 her husband was wounded when he was treacherously set upon by the Duke of Pomerania. Hedwig immediately hastened to Gonsawa, where the bloody deed had taken place, to care for her severely wounded husband. As a result of this deed, war broke out in 1229 between Henry and Conrad of Masovia over the possession of Cracow. Conrad was defeated, but he succeeded in surprising and capturing Henry in a church while he was attending divine services. When Hedwig learned of her husband's imprisonment, she went immediately to seek his release. Her gentle manner and appearance made such an impression on Conrad of Masovia that he made peace with Henry and released him, although Conrad did ask for and obtain certain concessions.

Following the death of her husband in 1238, St. Hedwig moved to the Convent of Trebnitz. Hedwig's biographers state emphatically that she did not become a member of the order, but lived there as a lay woman. She had two reasons for moving into the convent: so that she might live in a state of poverty while practicing mortification and acts of piety, and so that she could direct her vast revenues into works of charity. She is known to have attained a high degree of prayer and perfection in the convent.

A situation which developed at this time clearly indicates Hedwig's virtue and patience. The Saint became acquainted with a poor old washerwoman who did not know the Our Father. Since the woman was very slow at learning the prayer, Hedwig continued instructing her for ten weeks, and even had the woman sleep in her room, so that at every spare moment they might attempt to recite it together. As a result of Hedwig's patience the old woman not only learned the prayer, but understood it as well.

Hedwig suffered yet another loss and was deeply grieved when her son Duke Henry II died at Wahlstatt in 1241 in a battle against the Tartars. Hedwig is said to have known of her son's death three days before the news reached her. She concealed her grief and controlled her tears while she consoled Henry's wife Anne, his children and his sister Gertrude.

St. Hedwig's faith and high degree of perfection were honored by God with the gift of miracles. A nun of Trebnitz who was blind recovered her sight by the blessing of the Saint, and Hedwig's biographer gives an account of several other miraculous cures obtained through her prayers. She made several predictions, in particular, one concerning her death. During her last illness, St. Hedwig insisted on being anointed before others could be convinced of the seriousness of her condition.

Hedwig was deeply loved by her people and was regarded as a saint after her death at the age of 69, in October, 1243. She was interred in the church attached to the convent. Her grave is situated to the side of the high altar; the tomb of her husband, Duke Henry I, is found in front of the altar.

Hedwig's daughter-in-law testified concerning the raptures with which Hedwig was sometimes favored, as did Herbold, her confessor, and other observers. As a result of these testimonials and considerations regarding her holiness, Hedwig was canonized by Clement IV in 1267, only 24 years after her death. In 1706 her feast was added to the general calendar of the Latin rite; Hedwig is honored as the patroness of Silesia.

Chapter 83

ST. HEDWIG, QUEEN OF POLAND

d. 1399

The life of St. Hedwig contains all the tragic elements that could sustain the theme of a present-day novel. The hardships she endured during her 28 years of life have been carefully noted by contemporary writers and documented in the history of Poland.

Hedwig was born in 1371, the youngest of the daughters of King Louis, who was the nephew and successor to Casimir the Great. When King Louis died, he left the Kingdom of Poland in a very disturbed state. Additionally, the country suffered from what amounted to a civil war over the question of who should succeed Louis to the throne since he did not have a male heir. After two years of the kingdom's instability, those who had the authority to do so agreed to accept Princess Hedwig (Jadwiga) as their sovereign. She was then only 13 years old. She was accepted on one important condition: that the choice of her husband would meet with the authorities' approval.

According to the unanimous testimony of contemporaries, Hedwig was extraordinarily beautiful, intelligent, gentle—and above all, devout. Many were the suitors who were attracted to her attributes and her prestigious position. The attentions of these aspirants must have been very tiresome and frustrating for Hedwig, since her father had engaged her when she was four years old to William, Duke of Austria. During the nine years that followed her engagement, Hedwig had learned "to regard him as her future husband, giving him all the affection of her childish heart."

Influenced by political considerations, the Polish Diet would not approve Hedwig's marriage to William. Numerous confrontations took place between the nobles, with many continuing to plead the cause of Hedwig and William. When a final refusal was made, William disregarded all the personal dangers involved and made the romantic decision to find his promised bride and carry her off. This attempt failed; we are not told why. Hedwig could have renounced the throne in favor of her marriage to William, but given Hedwig's character it is not surprising that she sacrificed personal interests for the sake of duty.

At about this time an alliance that was politically satisfactory was presented to Hedwig as a religious duty. She was asked to marry the still-pagan Jagiello, the Grand Prince of Lithuania; he promised to become a Christian before the marriage and also pledged that all his people would receive Baptism as well. He also promised to unite his Lithuanian and Russian lands with the Polish Crown and to recover at his own expense the territory which had been taken from Poland. He further promised to pay Duke William of Austria, who had been promised Hedwig's hand, an indemnity of 200,000 gulden.

Even though of tender age, Hedwig demonstrated special maturity by acting according to her conscience. She accepted this marriage that would benefit both her country and her Church.

Nevertheless, a tremendous struggle was involved for Hedwig in agreeing to set aside William, her true love, for a loveless marriage to Jagiello, whom she did not know. This is demonstrated by the historical notation that after her decision she covered herself with a thick black veil and proceeded on foot to the Cathedral of Cracow. Entering a side chapel, she fell to her knees and prayed for the next three hours for a detached heart and for perfect resignation to the will of God. She offered to Our Lord the sacrifice of her earthly happiness and all the sorrows that would purchase the salvation of so many souls. Before leaving the chapel, she spread her black veil over the crucifix to signify her sacrifice and the union of her sorrows with those of her Saviour. It is said that the crucifix is still kept and is known as the Crucifix of Hedwig.

Jagiello kept his word. He was baptized in 1383 (or 1386) and received the new name of Wladislaus. Following the marriage he was crowned King of Poland on the strength of being the consort of Queen Hedwig. Soon after the close of the coronation festivities at Cracow, a large body of ecclesiastics from Poland crossed into Lithuania, where they overcame a small resistance on the part of the heathen priests and baptized the people who gathered there in large numbers. As the result of this union between Poland and Lithuania, a mighty Christian kingdom arose in Eastern Europe, and Lithuania was for the first time brought into immediate contact with Western civilization.

During the years that followed, Hedwig governed wisely and justly. She eliminated laws that were a hindrance to the poor and won the love of her subjects by her charity, gentleness and concern. For the newly converted people, she encouraged learning, which exerted a civilizing influence.

As for her association with Wladislaus, she seems to have exercised a moderating influence upon his headstrong and impetuous nature and to have defended herself adequately against his irrational outbursts of jealousy. We are told that she was conscientious in all her wifely duties and that her husband regarded her with deep affection. He also admired her quiet and efficient management of the Kingdom and their household, as well as her spiritual qualities and her pleasant disposition.

After some time Wladislaus was overjoyed upon learning that his virtuous wife was expecting a child. He is said to have been extravagant in the preparations he made for the grand event, and he wrote from the frontier where he was conducting a campaign that he was providing jewels and rich draperies. Hedwig wrote in reply:

> Seeing that I have so long renounced the pomps of this world, it is not on that treacherous couch—to so many the bed of death—that I would willingly be surrounded by their glitter. It is not by the help of gold or gems that I hope to render myself acceptable to the Almighty Father, who has mercifully removed from me the reproach of barrenness, but rather by resignation to His will and a sense of my own nothingness.

Although wise in the administration of the Kingdom and her household, Hedwig is described as having been unwise in the practice of penance—which is thought to have injured her health.

On the anniversary of her great renunciation, Hedwig went unattended to the cathedral to make a vigil before the veiled crucifix. Hours later she was found unconscious by her ladies-in-waiting. Soon afterward the Queen went into labor and she died during childbirth. This tragedy was worsened when the baby daughter survived her mother by only a few days.

St. Hedwig was only 28 years old at the time of her death in 1399. Many who had benefited from her charities and her kindness also benefited after her death by answers to prayers through her intercession and by miracles that occurred at her tomb.

Chapter 84

BL. HELEN DEI CAVALCANTI

1396 - 1458

Bl. Helen was a member of the Valentini family of Udine, Italy, and was given in marriage at the age of 15 to a knight named Antonio dei Cavalcanti. During 25 years of happy wedded life, Bl. Helen appears to have led a normal existence as the mother of a large family of children.

The unexpected death of her husband came as a great shock to Bl. Helen. Realizing that the grief and difficulties of widowhood lay ahead of her and that her future would be devoted to God alone, she cut off her beautiful hair and laid it on her husband's bier, together with her jewelled headdress. "For love of you alone have I worn these," she said. "Take them down into the earth with you."

As the result of conferences given by the learned theologian Angelo of St. Severino, Bl. Helen decided to become a tertiary of his order, the Hermits of St. Augustine. From that moment on she devoted herself to works of charity, to prayer and to mortification. Her costly dresses were made into vestments, while her jewels were sold for the benefit of the poor for whom she labored. One of her many mortifications consisted in abstaining from meat, eggs and milk and living almost entirely on roots, bread and water.

With the consent of her director, Bl. Helen took a vow of perpetual silence, which she observed all year 'round except on Christmas night. It is clear, however, that this obligation did not extend to speaking to the members of her household, which included servants and her sister Perfecta. It is from them that details of her holy life are derived.

Bl. Helen was subject to many trials, especially in that she was terrified by loud noises and suffered temptations to commit suicide. She was apparently tormented by the devil, since she was once discovered lying bruised upon the ground and was twice found with a broken leg. Once as she was crossing a bridge on her way to church, Bl. Helen was thrown into the river. She scrambled out and attended Holy Mass as usual, despite her dripping clothes.

Helen was one of many who was cured during a pilgrimage to the tomb of St. Peter Parenzo at Orvieto.

In later years she left the house only to attend the Church of St. Lucy. There she spent many hours in prayer. Although she was tried by many temptations, she was also consoled by spiritual joys and ecstasies. Bl. Helen seems to have had the gift of healing, since many sick persons were cured through her prayers.

During the last three years of her life Bl. Helen was unable to rise from her bed, but she insisted upon maintaining her bed of stones and chaff.

Bl. Helen died on April 23, 1458 at the age of 62. Her cultus was confirmed in 1848.

Chapter 85

BL. HELEN DUGLIOLI

d. 1520

When Prosper Lambertini was Archbishop of Bologna (afterwards Pope Benedict XIV), he wrote about one of the citizens of that city, a housewife, Helen Duglioli. The Archbishop's biography and those biographies written by others mention nothing about noble parents, wealth or position. Rather, Bl. Helen seems to have been an ordinary young lady who pleased her mother by marrying against her own inclinations.

When she was 20 years of age Helen took as her husband Benedict dal'Oglio. Their wedded life, which endured for 30 years, was distinguished by peace, happiness and a mutual love of the Church and the practice of virtue.

When Benedict died, Helen devoted herself completely to works of charity—so much so that she endeared herself to all those with whom she came in contact, as well as to those who heard of her gracious care of the less fortunate.

Helen soon followed her husband to the grave, and those who had already revered her as a saint during her lifetime continued to venerate her as such after her death.

In the Archbishop's account of the Saint, he mentions the tributes paid to Bl. Helen immediately after her death, and he refers to the local publications which bore witness to the devotion of the citizens.

A contemporary of Bl. Helen, Piertos Aretino, wrote in his *Ragionamenti* about the large number of candles, pictures and *ex votos* that were deposited at the tomb of Bl. Helen.

The spontaneous cultus which developed after Helen's death in 1520 was confirmed in 1828 by Pope Leo XII.

Chapter 86

ST. HELEN (ELIN) OF SKÖFDE

d. c. 1160

The Bishop of Skara, Sweden, St. Brynolph, wrote that Helen (Elin) was a member of a distinguished family and a favored daughter of her country.

When her husband died, Helen remained a widow and spent the rest of her life in works of charity and piety. The gates of her home are said to have always remained open to the needy, and the Church of Sköfde was built almost entirely at her expense.

Helen's humble life would probably have remained hidden and unknown to us had it not been for the circumstances surrounding the death of her daughter's husband. He is described as having been so unreasonable and cruel that his own servants killed him. Soon after his death, Helen left on a previously arranged pilgrimage. During her absence, the dead man's family, wanting to avenge their relative's death, began to question the servants. Under the pressure of the questioning they admitted the crime—but they placed the blame on Helen, whom they said had planned the attack and then left on pilgrimage to divert suspicion from herself. The relatives believed the story, and as soon as the innocent and unsuspecting Helen returned from her journey, the dead man's family attacked and killed her. This took place at Gothene about the year 1160.

Helen's body was brought to Sköfde for burial, and many wonderful cures took place during that time. A catalog of these miracles was sent by Stephen, the Archbishop of Upsala, to Pope Alexander III. In 1164 Helen's name was inscribed in the list of canonized saints.

The veneration paid to Helen and her relics was so great that it vigorously survived the Protestant Reformation when it came to Sweden, centuries later.

At that time much attention was given to a holy well near her church, which was known as St. Lene Kild. At various times the

Lutheran authorities criticized the attention given the well as being a remnant of what they called popish and anti-Christian superstition. Eventually all the wells in the area, whether they contained mineral or pure water, were filled with stones and rubbish. However, another holy well, that at the Church of Tiburke, known as St. Elin's, attracted pilgrimages. These came every summer, bringing cripples and the sick in great numbers. It was customary for the pilgrims to remain all night at the place and then leave their crutches and make votive offerings as a token of gratitude.

Although she did not die for the Faith, St. Helen is listed as a martyr—possibly because she died innocent of the charge made against her.

Chapter 87

ST. HELENA

d. 330

Almost as though the events had been written as the plot for a romantic novel, the early life of St. Helena began with her humble birth in the city of Drepanum, about the year 250. She was the daughter of an inn-keeper. Visiting the inn one day was the dashing Roman General Constantius Chlorus, whose future was bright with the prospect of a position in high office. Constantius was apparently attracted to Helena from the start and eventually married her, taking her from the drudgery of her work at the inn to a place of honor and position. One son was born to the couple—Constantine—who would later be known as "Constantine the Great."

Unfortunately, when Constantius Chlorus was made Caesar (emperor) by Diocletian, he was persuaded to divorce the humbly born Helena and to marry a woman whose gentle breeding rendered her more suited to be the wife of a Caesar. Constantius Chlorus gave in to the suggestion, divorced Helena and married Theodora, the stepdaughter of the Emperor Maximian.

Constantius Chlorus lived only 14 years after his rejection of St. Helena. When Constantius died in the year 306, Helena's son Constantine was proclaimed Caesar by his troops at York. Eighteen months later, Constantine officially became Emperor.

Having the highest regard for his mother, Constantine lost little time in redeeming her from her life of veritable disgrace and humiliation, which had been caused by the well-known rejection by her husband. This loving son restored his mother to a place of respect by naming her the Empress of the World and Mistress of the Empire. Additionally, he honored his mother by renaming the city of her birth Helenopolis and having coins struck with her image.

St. Helena was converted when she was about 63 years old, according to the Church historian Eusebius (260-340). Constantine himself was a catechumen until shortly before his death.

"She became such a devout servant of God that one might believe her to have been a disciple of the Saviour of mankind from her very childhood." Butler claims that even though ". . . she was so advanced in years before she knew Christ, her fervor and zeal were such as to make her retrieve the time lost in ignorance; and God prolonged her life many years to edify by her example the Church which her son labored to exalt by his authority."

Rufinus calls her faith and holy zeal incomparable, and St. Helena kindled the same fire in the hearts of the Roman people. She dressed simply when she assisted in the churches amid the people, and she humbly participated in the Divine Office, which was her greatest delight. St. Helena made use of the treasures of the Empire for the relief of the poor and distressed. She built a number of churches and enriched them with precious vessels and ornaments. After her son's victory over Licinius in 423, in which he became master of the East, the noble lady went to Palestine to venerate the places made sacred by the bodily presence of Our Lord.

About this time Constantine wrote to Macarius, Bishop of Jerusalem, requesting that a church be built over the holy sepulchre, "worthy of the most marvelous place in the world." St. Helena, then almost 80 years old, took charge to make certain the work was completed. She also erected the church in Bethlehem near the Grotto of the Nativity, and the church on the Mount of the Ascension near Jerusalem. She likewise restored older churches and set out to find precious relics—in particular, the Cross on which the Saviour died.

There is some controversy regarding St. Helena being credited with the discovery of the True Cross. It must be noted that neither the pilgrim Aetheria, who visited Jerusalem about the year 395, nor St. Cyril of Jerusalem, writing in 351, nor Eusebius mention the finding of the Cross or directly connect its discovery with the name of St. Helena. Nevertheless, tradition gives credit to the Saint for finding three crosses and for discovering which of the three was the one on which Our Lord was slain.

St. Ambrose, in his sermon on Theodosius, is perhaps the first to credit St. Helena with the finding. St. Ambrose claims that St. Helena identified the True Cross by the title that was still attached to it. He also states that St. Helena found the nails of the Crucifixion. One of the nails found its way to the Church of Santa Croce in Jerusalem, where it is still kept in a precious reliquary. Another nail was attached to the bridle of Constantine's horse, which is thought to fulfill what was written by the Prophet Zacharias: "In that day that which is upon the bridle of the horse shall be holy to the Lord." (*Zach.* 14:20). The other nail, according to St. Ambrose, was made into a crown.

Whether or not St. Helena actually took part in the finding of the Cross, it is beyond dispute that her last days were spent in Palestine. Eusebius wrote about her humility and charity in this manner:

> In the sight of all she continually resorted to church appearing humbly dressed among the praying women...She was kind and charitable to all, but especially to religious persons; to these she showed such respect as to serve them at table as if she had been a servant, set the dishes before them, poured them out drink, held them water to wash their hands, and though Empress of the World and Mistress of the Empire she looked upon herself as servant and handmaid of Christ.

Butler adds that "Whilst she traveled over the East with royal pomp and magnificence she heaped all kinds of favors both on cities and private persons, particularly on soldiers, the poor and those who were condemned to the mines; distributing money and garments, and freeing many from oppression, chains and banishment."

The last coins made by order of her son bore her full name, Flavia Julia Helena, and were minted in the year 330, which is considered to be the year of her death. St. Helena was about 83 years old at the time. The Byzantines refer to Constantine and St. Helena as "the holy, illustrious and great emperors, crowned by God and equal with the Apostles."

The Empress St. Helena (d. 330) and her son, the Emperor Constantine, are represented holding the True Cross of Christ in this Cappadocian fresco. An old tradition gives St. Helena credit for finding three crosses and discovering which one was that of Our Lord.

The ancient coin pictured (*at top*), greatly enlarged, appears to read, HELE NANP. (*Staatliches Münzkabinett, Berlin*). The bronze medallion (*at bottom*), also greatly enlarged, says FLAVIA HELENA AUGUSTA. (*British Museum*).

Chapter 88

ST. HENRY II

d. 1024

The saint who was to bear the awesome responsibilities of being the King of Germany and Italy, and Emperor of the Holy Roman Empire, was born in 973 to Henry, Duke of Bavaria and Gisella of Burgundy. Seemingly destined for the priesthood, Henry became acquainted with ecclesiastical interests at an early age through his education at the Cathedral School in Hildesheim, and later from Bishop Wolfgang of Regensburg. His early interest in the clerical state was abandoned when he married the virtuous Cunegunda, who belonged to the noble Luxembourg family. Because the marriage was childless, some have speculated that a vow of continence was involved, while many others claim that there is no foundation for this assumption.

In 995 Henry succeeded his father in the Duchy of Bavaria. Upon the untimely death of his cousin Otto III in 1002, Henry, as the last male survivor of the Imperial House of Saxony, inherited the claim to the royal crown of Emperor of the Holy Roman Empire. Soon afterward he was crowned King of Germany, and two years later King of Italy. Realizing the danger to his soul from the honor and prosperity attendant upon these noble positions, Henry cultivated a spirit of humility and holy fear, realizing that God intended him to use his position to promote His glory, the welfare of the Church and the peace and happiness of the people.

Despite his prayer for peace, Henry was obliged to engage in numerous wars and suppress many revolts and rivals in the defense and consolidation of the Empire. He engaged in ecclesiastical and monastic reforms, restored and created dioceses, built and repaired places of worship, appointed bishops and opened synods. He endowed so many monasteries, and made so many foundations for the relief of the poor, that his brother-in-law, the Duke of Bavaria, and other relatives complained that he employed his patrimony wastefully. Either

309

to prevent further endowments or as a result of jealousy, the Duke of Bavaria recruited others of the family to take up arms against Henry. After defeating them on the field of battle, as an act of Christian charity Henry pardoned all who had engaged in the revolt.

Another difficulty with the family arose when disturbances became prevalent in the northwest part of the Empire. Behind the difficulty were Henry's brothers-in-law, the Counts of Luxembourg: Adalbero, who had made himself Bishop of Trier by "uncanonical methods" and Theodoric, who had had himself elected Bishop of Metz. True to his duty, Henry would not tolerate any selfish family policy at the expense of the empire, and he judiciously corrected the situation.

After an expedition in Italy against the Greeks, Henry became seriously ill at Monte Cassino, but he is said to have been miraculously cured at the intercession of St. Benedict. At this time he somehow contracted a lameness which endured for the rest of his life. Neither this difficulty nor his uncertain health restricted Henry from his restless activity in the management of his realm.

A story is told that Henry, wanting to become a monk, promised obedience to the Abbot of St. Vanne at Verdun—but the Abbot placed him under obedience to continue the administration of the Empire.

Henry is regarded as the most important ruler in Europe at the beginning of the eleventh century and one of the greatest rulers of the Holy Roman Empire. He died in the year 1024 and was canonized by Pope Eugenius III in 1146. He is greatly venerated at the Cathedral of Bamberg, where he is buried beside his wife, St. Cunegunda, who was canonized in 1200.

Coins bearing the likeness of St. Henry II (d. 1024), King of Germany and Italy and Emperor of the Holy Roman Empire. His wife was St. Cunegunda.

Emperor Henry II, from an eleventh century missal (*Royal Library, Munich*). Henry spent so much money helping the poor and endowing monasteries that his relatives complained he was wasting his patrimony. Henry also made ecclesiastical and monastic reforms, restored and created dioceses, built and repaired churches, appointed bishops and opened synods.

Chapter 89

BL. HENRY THE SHOEMAKER

d. 1666

Henry the Good, as he was often called, was born near the end of the sixteenth century to a poor couple of the working class at Arlon in Luxembourg. His life provides an instance of heroic virtue practiced amid the toil and poverty of a laboring man's daily life. From his youth Henry combined the trade of a shoemaker with the zealous practice of virtue, being mindful of his own sanctification and that of his neighbors. His chief concern was to lead others to the knowledge and love of God, and it grieved him to see the sinfulness and indifference of many of his fellow workmen. For them he fasted and did penance, and for those who were receptive to leading a spiritual life Henry formed a pious society, which he placed under the patronage of St. Crispin and St. Crispinianus.

When he opened a shop in Paris in 1645, Henry formed there a similar association for shoemakers which became known as *Freres Cordonniers*. Baron de Renti took a special interest in Henry and his religious organization and made certain that the members did not lack the necessities of life. He obtained for Henry the rights of citizenship and recognition as a master shoemaker so that he could accept apprentices and journeymen who wished to follow his rule. This rule, which the Baron helped Henry to draft, was a strict one. The members rose at five a.m., had prayer in common at stated hours, attended Mass daily, visited prisons and hospitals and made an annual retreat.

The association grew and prospered. Branches were started in other cities, and the tailors established a society for themselves along similar lines.

It has been stated that the good influence which Bl. Henry exerted over his fellow tradesmen, and all the people who knew of him, cannot be overestimated.

Henry the Good died in Paris on June 9, 1666 after contracting pneumonia. He was buried in the cemetery attached to the Hospital of St. Gervais, where he had often waited upon the patients.

The earliest biography written about him is dated 1670, four years after his death, and is entitled *L'Artisan Chretien, ou la Vie du bon Henry* (The Christian Artisan, or the Life of Good Henry).

Chapter 90

BL. HENRY OF TREVISO
(Bl. Henry of Bolzano)

d. 1315

Because of his impoverished childhood, Henry was unable to attend school and never learned to read or write. Having been born in Bolzano, Italy, he was forced to seek employment at Treviso, where he supported himself as a day laborer.

Bl. Henry's spiritual life was commendable. He gave to the poor whatever he could spare from his meager wages and never missed an opportunity to serve God or his fellow man. He heard Mass daily and received Holy Communion as frequently as was customary at the time. He went frequently to confession as a means of preserving his purity of conscience and never failed to attend sermons and instructions. When not employed in physical labor, Bl. Henry spent his time in prayer.

It has been noted that while Bl. Henry's soul was endowed with the beauty of grace, his physical appearance was somewhat unattractive. He was a thick-set little man with sunken eyes, a long nose and a crooked mouth. Not helping his appearance were the shabby clothes he wore. He was frequently mocked and ridiculed by both children and wicked adults, but he was never heard to utter a word of complaint, even when severely provoked. He seemed never to resent the treatment he received, and many marveled at his serenity under stress and his friendliness with everyone he met.

When Henry could no longer work, a charitable citizen named James Castagnolis gave him a room in his house. Henry's food, and the alms he received from his neighbors, were shared with beggars. Nothing was held over from one day to the next.

Even when Henry suffered from advanced age and bodily weakness, he continued to visit neighboring churches until the time of his death on June 10, 1315.

As soon as Henry's passing was announced, his little room was thronged with visitors who regarded him as a saint. Many who proclaimed his sanctity were those who had formerly ridiculed his appearance. Relics were sought after by eager devotees, who obtained fragments of his hairshirt, a wooden log which had been his pillow, and twigs, cords and straw that had served as his bed. The crowds were so enthusiastic that the body was finally removed to the cathedral, but when the doors were closed for the night, the people broke in. When the Bishop was roused from his sleep and informed of the disturbance, he and his associates found it necessary to have a barricade constructed about the body to control the people who wished to express their admiration of Henry's virtues and to be the recipients of miracles that were being reported.

When the number of these miracles increased, the magistrates of the town appointed notaries to keep a record of them. Within a few days of Bl. Henry's death, no fewer than 276 miracles were recorded. These were later set forth by the Bollandists in the *Acta Sanctorum,* in which they occupy 32 closely printed columns. The Bollandists also printed a Life of Bl. Henry that had been written by his contemporary, Bishop Pierdomenico de Baone.

The penitential instruments used by Bl. Henry were preserved after his death in the Cathedral of Bolzano. In Italy, Bl. Henry is known as San Rigo.

A painting of Bl. Henry of Treviso (d. 1315), a laborer of great sanctity. Because of his homely appearance, he was often mocked and mistreated, yet he was always serene and friendly. When he died, eager devotees sought after relics and even broke into the cathedral where his body had been taken. Within a few days 276 miracles were recorded.

Chapter 91

ST. HERMENGILD

d. 585

Leovigild, the Arian King of the Spanish Visigoths, fathered two sons, Recared and Hermengild, by his first wife, Princess Theodosia. She saw to it that both sons were instructed in the Arian heresy, which their father also professed. Upon the death of Theodosia, Leovigild took as his second wife Goswintha, a fanatical Arian. This heresy denied the divinity of Christ and is considered to have been the most devastating of the early heresies. Eventually the heretics established their own hierarchies and churches.

In the year 576, Hermengild married the princess Indegundis, a zealous Christian. This marriage produced a clash in the family, with Goswintha resenting her daughter-in-law to the extent that physical violence was used in an attempt to make Indegundis abandon her Christian faith. The young princess, however, stood firm. Because of the patience his wife exercised with her mother-in-law and also due to her prayers—and the instructions from St. Leander, Archbishop of Seville—Hermengild waited until his father's absence and then publicly renounced the heresy. He was welcomed into the Christian Faith, receiving the imposition of hands and the anointing with chrism upon his forehead.

Leovigild, who had already been influenced against his son by Goswintha, was furious when he heard of his son's open profession of the Christian Faith. He immediately deprived Hermengild of his title and called upon him to resign all his dignities and possessions. This Hermengild refused to do.

With the support of the Christians, Hermengild raised the standard of a holy war against the Arians. This endeavor was poorly planned, ill-equipped and lacking in manpower. The attempt proved to be a tragic mistake.

Because the Arians were powerful in Visigothic Spain, Hermengild sent St. Leander to Constantinople to obtain support and assistance. But the emperor to whom the appeal was made died soon afterward, and his successor was obliged to use all available troops in an effort to resist an invasion of the Persians.

Disappointed with the unavailability of additional forces, Hermengild turned in desperation to the Roman generals who still ruled a strip of Spanish land along the Mediterranean Coast. They took his wife and infant son as hostages and made promises to Hermengild which they failed to keep. For over a year Hermengild was besieged in Seville by his father's troops, and when he could hold out no longer he fled to the Roman camp, only to be warned that those he had thought were his friends had been bribed by Leovigild to betray him.

Hermengild next made his way to the fortified town of Osseto, which he defended with 300 men, until the royalist soldiers captured the town and burned it.

In desperation Hermengild entered a church and fell at the foot of the altar. Leovigild did not violate the sanctuary, but he permitted his younger son Recared, who was still an Arian, to go to his brother with an offer of forgiveness, if he would submit and ask for pardon. Hermengild had no other recourse but to accept his father's offer. A reconciliation took place, and for the moment Leovigild waxed sentimental and restored to his son some of his former dignities.

Hermengild's stepmother, Goswintha, in the meantime had lost none of her former antagonism for Christians. As soon as the Arian father and his Christian son returned home, she was successful in estranging them once more. Hermengild was subsequently stripped of his royal robes, loaded with chains and imprisoned in the tower of Seville. (Another source claims he was imprisoned in Tarragona.) He was accused of treason and was offered his liberty if he would renounce his Christian faith. His reply was: "I am ready to lose sceptre and life rather than forsake the divine truth." For this statement he was transferred to a filthy dungeon, where he was subjected to various forms of torture. Praying fervently that God would sustain him in his sufferings, Hermengild added voluntary mortifications to what he already suffered at the hands of his persecutors.

St. Gregory the Great in *The Dialogues* (Book III, Chapter XXXI) tells what occurred next:

When the solemn feast of Easter was come, his wicked father sent unto him in the dead of the night an Arian bishop to give him the communion of a sacrilegious consecration, that he might thereby again recover his father's grace and favor; but the man of God, as he ought, sharply reprehended that Arian Bishop which came unto him, and giving him such entertainement as his deserts required, utterly rejected him; for albeit outwardly he lay there in bands, yet inwardly to himself he stood secure in the height of his own soul.

The father, at the return of the Arian prelate, understanding this news, fell into such a rage that forthwith he sent his officers of execution to put to death that most constant confessor in the very prison where he lay, which unnatural and bloody commandement was performed accordingly: for as soon as they came into the prison, they clave his brains with a hatchet, and so bereaved him of mortal life, having only power to take that from him which the holy martyr made small account of.

St. Gregory the Great continues by telling that as soon as the death of Hermengild was made known, miracles from Heaven occurred. "For in the night time singing was heard at his body, some also reported that in the night burning lamps were seen in the place by reason whereof his body, as of him that was a martyr, was worthily worshipped by all Christian people."

St. Gregory also relates that the father was grief-stricken for having murdered his own son, but he never actually renounced Arianism. Yet, when he was on his deathbed, he recommended his son Recared to St. Leander, with the hope that the Saint would convert his remaining son to the Christian Faith. St. Gregory relates that

Recared the king, not following the steps of his wicked father, but his brother the martyr, utterly renounced Arianism, and labored so earnestly for the restoring of the Christian religion that he brought the whole nation of the Visigoths to the True Faith of Christ, and would not suffer any that was a heretic in his country to bear arms and serve in the wars. And it is to be admired that he became thus to be a preacher of the True Faith, being he was the brother of a martyr whose merits did help him to bring so many into the lap of God's Church, wherein we have to consider that he could never have effected all this if Hermengild had not died for the testimony of true religion.

After her husband's death, Indegundis fled with her son to Africa, where she died. Her son was then given to the custody of his grandmother Brunhilde.

Hermengild was venerated as a martyr soon after his death. Sixtus V, acting on the suggestion of King Philip II, extended the celebration of the martyr's feast, April 13, throughout the whole of Spain.

Chapter 92

ST. HOMOBONUS

d. 1197

Commerce frequently encourages an attachment to material things and provides opportunities for many vices, including lying and defrauding. But St. Homobonus brought to his business many virtues—including those of honesty and integrity.

Born in Cremona, Italy, this saint was given his name at Baptism—Homobonus, meaning Good Man. His father owned a mercantile business in which he trained his son at an early age. It was from his father that Homobonus was inspired to continue the trade with fairness. To this he added economy, care and hard work. He looked upon his business as an employment given him by God, and he found in the profession many opportunities for exercising virtue. It is said by Butler that "Homobonus was a saint by acquitting himself diligently and uprightly, for supernatural motives, of all the obligations of his profession."

After a time the Saint married. His wife was a prudent and faithful assistant who seems to have been almost as virtuous as her husband.

Upon the death of his father, the Saint inherited a considerable stock in trade, as well as a house in town and another in the country. Although it appears that Homobonus had the means to live a carefree life and to accumulate every possession and convenience that he might have desired, an attachment to material possessions had no part in his character. Not content with merely tithing, he distributed considerable amounts of money to unfortunates. He sought out the poor in their homes, where he supplied their necessities and tenderly encouraged them to repentance and a good life. We are told by the author of his biography that God often recognized the Saint's charity by miracles worked in favor of many whom he helped.

St. Homobonus was a man of considerable devotion to the Blessed Sacrament. It was his custom every night to go to the Church of

St. Giles a little before midnight to assist at Matins, and frequently he did not leave the church until after Holy Mass the next morning. He always consecrated Sundays and holy days entirely to devotion. Prayer sanctified all his actions, and it was during prayer before the Holy Eucharist that he died.

On November 13, 1197, after attending Matins, Homobonus remained kneeling before the crucifix until Mass began. At the *Gloria in Excelsis,* he stretched out his arms in the figure of a cross and fell on his face to the ground. Those who saw him thought he did so out of devotion, but when he neglected to rise they discovered that he was dead.

Since the virtues of the saintly merchant were well-known to Sicard, the Bishop of Cremona, this prelate went himself to Rome to solicit the canonization. Less than two years after the merchant's death, Homobonus was canonized by Pope Innocent III. He was soon recognized as the patron of tailors and clothworkers, and as such was venerated throughout Italy, as well as in France and Germany.

The Saint's body was removed in 1357 to the cathedral, although his head remains at the Church of St. Giles, where he was originally buried.

St. Homobonus (d. 1197), a saintly merchant, patron of tailors and clothworkers, who practiced exemplary generosity to the poor. God often recognized his charity by miracles. St. Homobonus fell on his face and died during the *Gloria in Excelsis* at Mass. He was canonized two years after his death. This sculpture is on the facade of San Omobono, Cremona, Italy.

Chapter 93

LITTLE ST. HUGH OF LINCOLN

d. 1255

Little St. Hugh was an abducted child, the son of a widow, who suffered a cruel death at the age of nine.

On the occasion of a Jewish gathering in Lincoln on July 31, 1255, a man named Koppin (some biographies name him Jopin) lured the child into his house, where the little Saint was kept for almost a month. It is difficult to imagine that men could be so cruel to an innocent child, but on August 27 Koppin and some fellow Jews, who hated Christians, wanted to denounce Jesus Christ. They expressed their hatred for the Saviour by torturing and scourging the innocent child. They crowned him with thorns and even crucified him. When they attempted to dispose of the little body, the earth refused to cover it. The body was then thrown down a well.

During Hugh's absence, his frantic mother and her neighbors were searching for him. Finally, Hugh's schoolmates directed suspicion to the home of the Jew, Koppin, who was promptly arrested—together with 92 other Jews of the city. To the outrage of all who heard about the crime, Koppin confessed the murder and denounced his accomplices.

By order of King Henry III and his parliament, Koppin was punished by being tied to a horse and dragged to death. Eighteen accomplices who were named by Koppin were hanged at Lincoln. The remainder of the Jews were imprisoned in London, but were set at liberty after paying large fines. These were suspected of having been charged as the result of an over-enthusiastic sweep of arrests.

When Hugh's body was recovered from the well, a blind woman received her sight after touching it. Other miracles soon followed. Finally the chapter of Lincoln solemnly translated the relics from their parish church to the cathedral, where they were entombed next to the vault of Robert Grosseteste, Bishop of Lincoln (1175-1253), who was regarded in England as a saint. Unfortunately, there is now only slight evidence of St. Hugh's shrine in the south choir wall of Lincoln Cathedral.

The account of Little St. Hugh is mentioned in "The Prioress's Tale" of Chaucer's *Canterbury Tales*. Both St. Hugh and St. William of Norwich, who was 12 years old when he suffered a similar death, were subjects of favorite ballads. (Little St. Hugh is not to be confused with the Cistercian St. Hugh of Lincoln, who lived from 1140-1200.)

Chapter 94

ST. HUNNA

d. 679

St. Hunna (or Huva) belonged to the reigning ducal family of Alsace and was married to a wealthy nobleman, Huno, who was from the village of Hunemeyer, which is located in the northeastern part of France. Although a member of a distinguished family who could provide her with convenience, leisure and luxury, she was known for her tireless efforts in helping the poor and sick. In addition to the alms she generously distributed, she was inclined to help the unfortunate in a more personal fashion, and despite her social status, she undertook the most menial tasks for their relief. Eventually she became known by her contemporaries as "The Holy Washerwoman."

St. Hunna's family seems to have been greatly influenced by Deodatus (St. Die), Bishop of Nevers, since St. Hunna's son, who was his namesake, was baptized by him and subsequently entered the monastery which he had founded at Ebersheim.

St. Hunna's death occurred in the year 679. Because of her great humility and other virtues, as well as her extraordinary help to the poor, she was canonized in 1520 by Pope Leo X.

Chapter 95

ST. HYACINTH AND ST. PROTUS

d. c. 257

Pope Damasus (d. 384) wrote an epitaph in honor of these two martyrs in which he calls Protus and Hyacinth brothers. They are also believed to have been slaves. The two martyrs were burned alive during the persecution of Valerian, in which St. Eugenia also perished.

The relics of Sts. Hyacinth and Protus which were saved from the flames were wrapped in a precious cloth and buried in the catacomb of St. Hermes on the ancient Salarian Way. During the fourth century, when access to the burial chamber became impossible, Pope Damasus had a staircase built and the place cleared so that devotees of the martyrs could easily reach the tombs. Centuries later the remains of St. Protus were transported to Rome; however, those of St. Hyacinth were not touched because the condition of the surrounding masonry niche indicated a hazardous situation. In 1845, though, Fr. Marachi discovered this niche intact. On the marble slab was the inscription: *D P III IDUS SEPTEBR. YACINTHUS MARTYR*. When the tomb was opened, only ashes and gold thread were found, along with what appeared to be parts of the charred bones of St. Hyacinth. It is said that a subtle perfume of roses arose from the bones upon their discovery.

The relics of the two Saints are now found beneath the high altar of San Giovanni dei Fiorentini in Rome.

The facts mentioned above are all that we know for certain about these two martyrs. The various simple biographies which have come down to us are said to be fictitious. Since other authentic facts are not available, all we know is that these two brothers of lowly estate suffered and gave their lives for the Faith and were honorably buried in consecrated ground, apparently by those who were edified by their bravery and love for Christ and His teachings.

Chapter 96

BL. IDA OF BOULOGNE

d. 1113

Ida is called the Mother of Monarchs because two of her sons, Godfrey and Baldwin, became kings of Jerusalem and her granddaughter became Queen Consort of England. Not only is her progeny titled, but her ancestors are as well, since both of her parents were descended from Charlemagne. Her father was Godfrey IV, Duke of Lorraine, and her husband was Eustace II, Count of Boulogne.

Married at the age of 17, Bl. Ida seems to have had a happy marriage; both husband and wife were equally dedicated to good works—especially to the restoration and building of churches. As a mother, Bl. Ida was careful in the education of her three sons, considering it her prime duty to train them in the ways of holiness and to teach them by her example all the good that can be achieved through generous almsgiving to the needy.

At the death of Count Eustace, his widow was left in control of valuable holdings. Ida had previously inherited from her father various estates in Lorraine and Germany. These holdings she arranged to sell, and the greater part of the money she derived from these sales was given to relieve the poor and in the construction of monasteries. Among the monasteries which Bl. Ida either built or restored are counted St. Villemar at Boulogne; St. Vaast, which accepted the religious who were sent from Cluny; the monastery of Samer; Our Lady of the Chapel, Calais; St. Bertin Abbey; and the abbeys of Bouillon and Afflighem.

Bl. Ida regarded it a blessing of the highest order that she had as her spiritual director one of the greatest men of the Age, St. Anselm, Abbot of Bec in Normandy, who was afterward the Archbishop of Canterbury. Some of his letters to Bl. Ada have been preserved; these indicate the generosity which she lavished on his abbey and the monies she donated for the relief of pilgrims traveling to it. In one of these letters St. Anselm expressed his gratitude in this manner:

> You have bestowed so many and so great kindnesses upon men, whatever their order, coming to our monastery or traveling from it, that it would be wearisome to you if we were to send you messages or letters of thanks for them all; nor have we anything with which to reward you as you deserve. So we commend you to God, we make Him our agent between you and us. All that you do is done for Him; so may He reward you for us, for Him, you do so much.

Many hours were spent by Bl. Ida in praying for the success of the Crusade, and it is recorded that while she was making fervent intercession for the safety of her son Godfrey, it was revealed to her that he was at that very moment making his victorious entry into Jerusalem. From him she received various relics from the Holy Land, which she distributed among several foundations.

As Ida grew older, she retired from the world. Although she had the highest regard for monastic life, she never showed an inclination to enter a convent. She preferred to express her love for God by being a dutiful wife, a loving mother and a generous benefactress of the poor.

Bl. Ida died when she was over 70 years old, after a long and painful illness. She was first buried in the church of the Monastery of St. Vaast. The first biography of Bl. Ida was written at this monastery by a monk, a contemporary, who compared Ida to Queen Esther in the Old Testament. One chronicler suggests that Ida can also be compared to the valiant, prudent wife in Proverbs (31:10-31).

After several translations, Bl. Ida's relics finally came to rest at Bayeux.

Chapter 97

ST. IDA OF HERZFELD

d. 813

Because her father, Duke Theodericus, was held in great esteem by Charlemagne, Ida had the advantage of being educated at the Emperor's court. She was also fortunate for the holy example of her mother. The conversations they shared on religious topics made a deep impression on Ida during her formative years. Ida's mother eventually became the Abbess of Soisson, much to her daughter's edification. Ida was additionally blessed by her association with two uncles, St. Adelhard and St. Wala, both of whom were monks.

Charlemagne gave Ida in marriage to a lord of his court named Egbert and bestowed upon her a great fortune in money and property—not only, it is said, because of her merit, but also in recompense for her father's services. The couple lived in perfect harmony while sharing a mutual love of the Faith and the practice of virtue.

Unfortunately, Ida was left a widow while she was still very young.

Upon the death of her husband, Ida redoubled her prayers and penances; with the revenues of her estates she increased her generosity to the poor. She advanced rapidly in the spiritual life, always endeavoring to conceal the heavenly favors she received during prayer.

After her son Warin left to become a monk at Corvey, St. Ida changed her residence to Herzfeld, where she spent the remainder of her life in the performance of good works. It is claimed that, to remind her of her earthly end and her need to help God's poor, she had a stone coffin made which was filled each day with food for the needy.

Her last years were spent in offering to God the penance of a painful illness, which she endured with admirable patience.

St. Ida died in the year 813 and was buried at Herzfeld in the cemetery of the convent she had founded there.

Chapter 98

BL. ISABELLA OF FRANCE

1225 - 1270

France celebrated the birth of Princess Isabella in March of 1225. Her father was Louis VIII, King of France; her mother was Blanche of Castile. A year later the family welcomed a son, Louis, who was to become St. Louis IX, King of France.

While still a child at court, Isabella (or Elizabeth) responded to her mother's pious care and showed an extraordinary devotion to prayer and pious exercises. Pope Innocent IV recognized her virtues by allowing her to retain Franciscan friars as her special confessors. She was also blessed with exceptional qualities of mind; she studied natural history, medicine, logic and Eastern languages. She also added Latin to her studies so that she might read the liturgy of the Church and the writings of the Fathers.

When the court of France was held at Saint-Germain, Isabella fell so sick as a result of her mortifications that all thought she would die. Public prayers were offered for her recovery, and in desperation her mother brought to her bedside a certain holy woman from Nanterre who predicted that Isabella would recover her health but would remain dead to the world.

She did recover. And when her personal beauty and gentleness drew the attention of suitors, Isabella declined their offers of marriage. She refused Count Hugo of Austria, and then Conrad, King of Jerusalem, who was the son of the German Emperor Frederick II. Pope Innocent IV sent her a letter urging her to accept Conrad for the good of the country and the Church, but Isabella answered the Pope so humbly and wisely that he did not hesitate to praise her fixed determination to remain a virgin for the sake of Christ.

Throughout her life Isabella was never heard to speak impatiently, and she prayed so fervently as to gain the admiration of many. She rose for prayer long before dawn and continued her devotions until midday. Every day before her dinner she would admit a number of poor people, whom she personally served. After her meal she customarily went out to visit the sick and poor. In addition to her charities in France, she paid the expenses of ten knights in the Holy Land as her share in the Crusade. She suffered several long illnesses, which she bore with admirable patience. She also suffered greatly when the Crusade failed and her brother, St. Louis IX, was captured and held prisoner.

When Isabella wanted to establish a convent of the Order of St. Clare, her saintly brother began in 1255 to acquire the necessary land at Longchamps, which was approximately two leagues from Paris. A year later the first stone of the convent church was laid, and three years later the building was completed. It was dedicated with the name, the Convent of the Humility of the Blessed Virgin. Pope Alexander IV gave his sanction to the new rule which Isabella had compiled. When nuns from the Poor Clare convent at Rheims took up residence in the new convent, St. Louis—in accordance with a special provision of the rule—entered the chapter house with a few chosen attendants and gave a little address to the nuns. Although the rule was not as strict as was the rule of St. Clare, it proved a hardship to some and was later mitigated by Pope Urban IV.

Isabella herself never entered the cloister. She continued to wear secular clothing, though she followed most of the rule in her own home, which was nearby. The reason she did not enter the order was that her bodily sufferings would not permit her to keep the rule completely. Moreover, by keeping part of her property she could help to support the house and continue her charities to the poor. In her house at Longchamps she kept the fasts of the order as much as she could and maintained an almost constant silence. Before receiving Communion she would always kneel and beg the pardon of her servants. She lived in this manner for ten years.

During the last few days of her life, Isabella spent several whole nights in contemplation and experienced ecstasies which were witnessed by her confessor and Sister Agnes de Harcourt, the Abbess of Longchamps, who afterward wrote Isabella's biography.

Isabella died at the age of 45, on February 23, 1270, and was buried in the convent church. In 1521 Pope Leo X allowed the Abbey of Longchamp to celebrate her feast with a special office. At first celebrated on August 31, Bl. Isabella's feast is now observed in some places on February 26, in others on February 22.

The convent founded by Bl. Isabella and St. Louis had an unhappy ending. It was closed during the French Revolution, and in 1794 the empty and damaged building was offered for sale. Since no one wished to purchase it, it was destroyed. In 1857 the walls were pulled down, except one tower, and the grounds were added to the Bois de Boulogne.

Chapter 99

ST. ISIDORE THE FARMER

d. 1130

High above the main altar of the Cathedral of Madrid is found an ornate reliquary containing the incorrupt body of St. Isidore the Farmer, a man who began life amid tragically poor circumstances.

Isidore was born toward the end of the eleventh century to very devout parents who instilled in his tender heart a love of his religion and a dread of sin. But because of their extreme poverty, they were unable to support the young Isidore. For this reason, they sent him at an early age to a wealthy landowner of Madrid, John de Vergas, for whom he was to work for the rest of his life.

After a time Isidore married a virtuous girl, Maria Torribia, and became the father of a son. But this child died unexpectedly. The grief of the parents inclined them to accept their son's death as a sign from God. Thereafter, they agreed to observe perfect continence; they continued to live exemplary lives while suffering the trials and hardships of their poor situation.

It was Isidore's custom to attend Holy Mass each morning, and because of this, he was frequently late in reporting to the fields. When news of this reached John de Vergas, he decided to hide one morning to test the truth of these accusations and to gather sufficient evidence for Isidore's dismissal. To John de Vergas' amazement, he observed that while Isidore did report late for work after lingering in church, his plowing was nevertheless carried out as usual—accomplished by unseen hands which guided snow-white oxen across the fields. On another occasion angels were seen plowing on either side of Isidore, so that three times as much work was accomplished. Sometimes heavenly beings performed his work while he was rapt in prayer. After John de Vergas and his employees realized what was taking place, they began to view Isidore as a chosen soul and thereafter accorded him the greatest respect.

A miracle was witnessed by Isidore's fellow workers when he used half of a sack of grain to feed a flock of starving birds one wintry day. When the men reached the mill, the sack proved to be filled to capacity—and after being processed, it produced double the usual amount of flour.

The Saint's generosity to the poor was evidenced in that he frequently shared his meals with them. On one occasion, when he had been invited to a confraternity dinner, Isidore brought with him a large group of beggars. His host complained that he had reserved a portion for Isidore, but that he could not possibly feed all the people Isidore had brought with him. St. Isidore replied that there would be quite enough for Christ's poor. When the food was brought out, there was enough for all, and a great quantity of food was left over.

Isidore died on May 15, 1130 (some sources claim 1170 or 1172), when he was approximately 60 years of age. At his bedside was his wife, who survived him by several years. In Spain she is venerated as Santa Maria de la Cabeza, because the relic of her head *(cabeza)* is often carried in procession in times of drought. First buried in the cemetery of St. Andrew's Church, Isidore's body, found incorrupt, was transferred 40 years later to a more honorable shrine within the church.

Two important miracles of St. Isidore have been carefully recorded. The first occurred in the year 1211, when King Alphonsus of Castille was engaged in fighting the Moors in the Pass of Navas de Tolosa. St. Isidore is said to have appeared in a vision and to have shown the King an unknown path—by means of which he was then able to surprise and defeat the enemy. The other miracle occurred more than 400 years later, when King Philip III became seriously ill at Casaribios de Monte. When physicians despaired of saving his life, the shrine of St. Isidore was removed from the Church of St. Andrew for the journey to the Monarch's bedside. At the hour the relic was removed from the church, the fever left the King—and when the relic was brought into his presence, he recovered completely.

Because of these miracles, the royal family of Spain petitioned the Pope for the canonization of the holy farmer. In March of 1622 Isidore was canonized, together with four well-known saints: St. Ignatius, St. Francis Xavier, St. Teresa of Avila and St. Philip Neri.

The body of St. Isidore has been transferred, over the centuries, to six different locations. Each time, it was placed in a different sepulchre. In May of 1969, the City of Madrid observed the bicentennial celebration marking the last translation of the body, that to the Cathedral of Madrid. During this observance the body of the Saint was exposed for ten days to great throngs of people who passed in solemn files to view the 800-year-old relic.

St. Isidore is venerated as the patron of peasants, farmers and day laborers. He is also honored as the patron of Madrid, Leon, Saragossa and Seville.

Chapter 100

BL. IVETTA OF HUY

1158 - 1228

At the tender age of 13 years, Ivetta (Jutta) was forced by her wealthy father to marry, contrary to her natural inclinations. Then, after only five years of married life, during which Ivetta bore three children, the unexpected death of her husband left her a widow at the early age of 18.

After a time, Ivetta's good looks attracted the interest of many suitors, who annoyed her with their attentions. Since her family was one of means, it is unclear whether she had servants who assumed the care of the children or whether she waited until they were grown; but it is suggested that it was to avoid the attentions of these gentlemen that she devoted herself to nursing lepers in the lazar house. Ten years were spent in this occupation, at which time Ivetta felt inclined to become a recluse. She accordingly retreated to a small chamber, where she lived and had mystical experiences which have been recorded in detail in a contemporary Latin biography. She had the gift of reading the hearts of others, as well as having knowledge of distant events. It is claimed that on three occasions she received Holy Communion miraculously.

By her prayers Ivetta converted her father and one of her sons, who had fallen into sinful ways. Another of Ivetta's sons joined the Cistercian Order and later became the Abbot of Orval.

While living the life of a recluse, Ivetta did not forget her neighbors, but helped many souls who came to ask her advice.

Having been born in Huy near Leyden, the Netherlands, in 1158, Blessed Ivetta died there on January 13, 1228, when almost 70 years of age.

Chapter 101

BL. JACOBA

d. c. 1273

Lady Jacoba di Settesoli belonged to the highest Roman nobility and was the mother of two children when she became acquainted with St. Francis of Assisi about the year 1212. When the Saint was in Rome, he was often a visitor in her home, and once while visiting there he ate an excellent cream concoction called "mortairol," which is composed principally of almonds, cream and sugar. In gratitude for Jacoba's hospitality and kindly attentions, St. Francis gave her a lamb as a gift. St. Bonaventure once claimed that the lamb seemed to have been educated by the Poverello, St. Francis, since it followed its mistress to church and remained with her while she was praying. When it was time for Jacoba's morning devotions, the lamb would awaken her by gently bumping her or bleating in her ear.

After the death of her husband, Gratian Frangipini, Jacoba was inclined to enter the religious life. However, she was prevented from doing so by the responsibility of protecting the inheritance of her two young sons, who still depended upon her care. Being unable to enter the convent, she became a member of the Franciscan Third Order.

A few days before his death, St. Francis had one of his friars write to Jacoba to tell her, "Set out as soon as possible if you wish to see me once more. Bring with you what is necessary for my burial, and some of the good things which you gave me to eat when I was sick in Rome."

Jacoba lost little time in journeying to the hut near the Portiuncula chapel where St. Francis lay in his final illness. With her were her two sons and a great retinue, all of whom wanted to bid the Saint a final farewell. Jacoba also brought with her all that was needed for the Saint's burial, including a veil to cover his face, a cushion for his head, a cloth to cover his body and all the wax candles needed for the funeral. She is also said to have brought the creamy almond dessert that he liked, but he could no more than taste it because of his condition.

When Jacoba arrived at the little hut that served as an infirmary, there was a great stir when she entered and approached the dying Saint. It was strictly forbidden for women to enter the friary, but St. Francis made an exception in tender gratitude to this Roman noblewoman who had been such a special benefactress of his order. Having previously been named "Brother Jacoba" by Saint Francis on account of her fortitude, she was permitted to remain in the Saint's room until his holy death.

Among Jacoba's many sufferings was the grief of witnessing the death of her two sons and of surviving her grandchildren.

Lady Jacoba apparently remained a close friend and benefactress of the Friars Minor, as verified by the insertion of her name in *The Little Flowers of St. Francis,* a book which was written a century after the death of the Poverello. Jacoba is mentioned as having visited Brother Giles in Perugia. She spent her last days at Assisi in order to be near those who knew the holy Founder.

Jacoba died about the year 1273 and is buried in the Basilica of St. Francis in Assisi. Her tomb is inscribed with the words, *Hic Requiescat Jacoba Sancta Nobilisque Romana* ("Here lies Jacoba, a noble and saintly Roman lady").

Chapter 102

BL. JAMES BIRD

d. 1593

Two years after the death of Ven. Laurence Mumphrey, who was martyred at the age of 19, James Bird died for the same cause, in the same manner, at the same age and in the same place.

James Bird was born in Winchester, England after Henry VIII had separated England from the Church of Rome. As the son of Protestant parents, James was reared as a Protestant, but on becoming convinced that the Catholic Church was the only true church, he received instructions and was baptized. He continued his studies at Douai College, but upon his return to England his zeal for his new faith caused him to come under scrutiny. He was soon apprehended and imprisoned. His charge was the same as that of Ven. Laurence: high treason. This accusation was made because James asserted that the Pope was the head of the Church on earth. James pleaded guilty to this charge and to the charge of being reconciled with the Church of Rome. His freedom was offered him if he would attend just one Protestant service. He steadfastly refused to compromise his conscience. When his father entreated him to make this one concession for the sake of his liberty, James replied that as he had always obeyed his father in the past, he would do so now—if by so doing he would not offend God.

After enduring the trials of his imprisonment, James was brought to the place of execution; there he was hanged, drawn and quartered. That is, he was hanged for a short time, then cut down alive and disemboweled, then his body was cut in four pieces. His head, like that of Ven. Laurence, was set on a pole atop one of the city gates.

Bishop Challoner, in his *Lives of Missionary Priests,* reports that one day while James' head was still upon the pole his father passed by, and while viewing the head of his son, he thought the head seemed to bow as though in reverence. The father then cried out, "Ah! my son Jemmy, who not only living wast ever obedient and dutiful, but now also, when dead, payest reverence to thy father! How far from thy heart was all affection or will for treason, or any other wickedness!''

When James calmly met his martyrdom in 1593 he was only 19 years of age.

Chapter 103

BL. JAMES DUCKETT

d. 1602

After receiving his education in Protestant schools, James Duckett was apprenticed in London, where he was given a book entitled *The Foundation of the Catholic Religion*. This book so shattered his belief in the reformed religion that he stopped attending the Protestant services in which he had been a regular participant.

Those with whom James lived noticed the change, found the book and carried it to Mr. Goodaker, the minister of St. Edmunds. He sent for James and asked him why he no longer attended (Protestant) services. James answered that he would continue to stay away from church until he had heard more convincing arguments in favor of the Protestant church than those he had previously heard. For this answer he was committed to Bridewell Prison. From there he was set free through his master's efforts, but he was soon accused again of not attending services. This time he was sent to Compter Prison. His master once again obtained his liberty, but being afraid of his association with James, his master released him from his apprenticeship.

Being free of this commitment, James was instructed in the Catholic Faith and within two months was received into the Church by the venerable priest, Fr. Weeks, who was then a prisoner in the Gatehouse. From then on, James Duckett's life is described as having been virtuous and exemplary in all respects.

After living two or three years as a single gentleman, James married a good Catholic widow, Anne Hart, whom he supported by publishing and dealing in Catholic books. He did this not only for their own instruction and edification, but also for the assistance of their neighbors' souls. This occupation exposed James to many dangers and persecutions. He was apprehended and imprisoned so often that in his 12 years of married life, he passed nine of them in prison.

James Duckett had one son, who afterward became the Prior of the Carthusians at Newport. Attributed to the son are the following details of James Duckett's last confinement:

> Peter Bullock, a bookbinder, after he had been condemned a twelvemonth, in hope, as many imagined, of obtaining his pardon, informed Lord Chief Justice Popham that James Duckett had had 25 of Father Southwell's *Supplications to the Queen,* and had published them. Upon this his house was searched at midnight but no such book found, nor sign thereof; yet they found the whole impression of *Mount Calvary* and some other Catholic books. However, James Duckett was apprehended and carried to Newgate, it being the 4th of March...Then evidence being called in, the same Peter Bullock accused James Duckett that he had some of Father Southwell's *Supplications to the Queen,* which he denied, having none of them. Bullock also avouched that he had bound for him divers Catholic books, and, amongst the rest, Bristowe's *Motives* which James acknowledged.

When the jury was asked to deliberate a verdict on the evidence given by only one witness, they found James not guilty. But Judge Popham stood up and told them to reconsider that Duckett had had Bristowe's *Motives* bound for him—a book that was controversial and contrary to the teaching of the new Anglican religion. The jury again deliberated, and this time found James guilty of a felony. The sentence of death was pronounced.

We are given a glimpse of the heartache suffered by James' wife on the day of his death, as described by their son:

> On Monday morning, the day designed for his death, his wife came to speak to him, which she could not without tears. He bid her be of good comfort, and said his death was no more to him than to drink off the caudle which stood there ready for him. "If I were made the Queen's secretary or treasurer you would not weep. Do but keep yourself God's servant, and in the unity of God's Church, and I shall be able to do you more good, being now to go to the King of kings."

Peter Bullock, the bookbinder who had accused James Duckett in the hope of obtaining his own pardon, was not successful in this attempt. Rather, he found himself in the uncomfortable position of being in the same cart with James as they were both led to the place of execution. Concerning this situation, James Duckett's son continued:

> As he [James] was carried towards the place of execution, in the way his wife called for a pint of wine to drink to him. He drank, and desired her to drink to Peter Bullock, and freely to forgive him; for he, after all his hopes, was, in the self-same cart, carried also to execution. Being come to the place, and both he and Peter standing up in the cart, "Peter," saith he, "the cause of my coming hither, God and thyself knowest, for which I, from my heart, forgive thee, and that the world and all here may witness that I die in charity with thee," he kissed him, both having the ropes about their necks. Then he said to him, "Thy life and mine are not long. Wilt thou promise me one thing? If thou wilt, speak: wilt thou die, as I die, a Catholic?" Bullock replied, he would die as a Christian should do. And so the cart was drawn from under them.

Thus Bl. James Duckett died at Tyburn, on April 19, 1602.

Chapter 104

ST. JAMES INTERCISUS

d. 421

During a great persecution of Christians in Persia, St. James served as a military officer and enjoyed considerable influence with King Ysdegerd I. To maintain this favor he renounced his Christian faith. Both his mother and wife, devout and steadfast Christians, were extremely grieved on learning what James had done for earthly influence. Upon the death of King Ysdegerd they wrote to James in the following thought-provoking words:

> We were told long ago that for the sake of the king's favor and for riches you have forsaken the love of the immortal God. Think where that king now lies, on whose favour you set so high a value. He has returned to the dust, which is the fate of all mortals, and you cannot hope to receive the least help from him, much less protection from eternal torment. If you persevere in your crime, you yourself by the divine justice will receive the same punishment as your friend the king. As for us, we will have no more to do with you.

The letter so affected James that he repented, avoided the court, renounced the honors that had occasioned his fall and openly affirmed his faith in Jesus Christ.

His words were soon reported to the new king, who was very annoyed. Realizing he would never be successful in persuading the Saint to renounce his faith, the King threatened him with a lingering death.

After consultation with the council, it was decided that the criminal should be hung up and his limbs severed, one after another. When the dreadful sentence was made public, the city flocked to see this new form of punishment, while the Christians offered prayers for James' perseverance.

On reaching the place of martyrdom, James spent a moment in

prayer and then offered his body to the executioners. At first they cut off his right thumb. When he did not abandon his faith, but continued his prayers, they cut off every finger, and then his toes. His limbs were then hacked off, joint by joint, and his thighs were torn from the hips. Lying a naked trunk, in indescribable agony, James continued his prayers until at last his head was struck from his body.

When the Christians secretly obtained the relics of the Saint, they discovered that the body had been cut into 28 different pieces. The author of the Saint's *Acts,* who claims to have been an eyewitness, adds that following the heroic death, "We all implored the intercession of the blessed James."

The family name of St. James has been lost to us, but on account of the manner of his death, the name "Intercisus" was appended to that of St. James—"intercisus" meaning "chopped-to-pieces."

Chapter 105

BL. JEANNE MARIE DE MAILLE

1332 - 1414

At Roche Ste. Quentin in Touraine, France, on April 14, 1332, a daughter was born to Baron Hardouin VI of Maille, France and his wife, Jeanne de Montbazon. The infant received the name Jeanne at her Baptism, and at her Confirmation that of Marie.

Jeanne Marie's father died during her adolescence, and she became the sole heir to a considerable fortune. Her grandfather, who was her guardian, judged it prudent for her to marry a young man who had been her childhood companion. He was Robert, the heir of the Baron of Sille. Although Jeanne Marie had decided to vow her virginity to God, she obeyed her grandfather and married Robert.

Previous to this, Jeanne and Robert had decided that they would live in continence. It was well-known that during their childhood they were particularly fond of each other, and at the time of their marriage there was a deep love between them. Christian virtue, order and piety distinguished their home, which became famous as a place of relief for the poor and afflicted. While engaged in their works of charity, they came to know three orphans, whom they adopted and educated.

Their peaceful and holy situation was disturbed by war when Robert followed King John into battle in defense of his country against the English. In the disastrous Battle of Poitiers, he was seriously wounded and left for dead. When King John was captured and imprisoned, Touraine was left to the mercy of the enemy troops, who overran the land and pillaged the Chateau of Sille. Robert was imprisoned, and the sum demanded for his ransom was 3,000 florins. Since the generosity of the holy couple had drastically reduced their holdings, Jeanne Marie found it necessary to sell her jewels and horses and to borrow what was additionally needed to win her husband's freedom.

The harshness that Robert experienced during his confinement made him sensitive to the needs of prisoners, so that, upon his release, he and Jeanne Marie made many donations for the ransom of captives. They continued this and other charities while living a holy life which was characterized by self-denial until Robert died in 1362, after 16 years of marriage.

The grief that Jeanne Marie experienced at her loss was intensified by the unkindness of Robert's family, who criticized her bitterly for impoverishing the estate through her charities. They went so far as to deny Jeanne Marie her rightful share of the estate and actually forced her from her home. With nowhere to go, Jeanne Marie took refuge with an old servant, who received her grudgingly and treated her with contempt when she learned that Jeanne Marie was without funds and was in need of charity.

Eventually Jeanne Marie journeyed to Tours, where she lived in a small house next to the Church of St. Martin. There she devoted herself to prayer, to the devotions held in the church and to the care of the poor and sick, especially lepers. She was particularly untiring in her efforts to win back to virtue women who were living an immoral life.

Having become a Franciscan tertiary, Jeanne Marie wore a distinctive dress which caused her to be insulted and mocked as she made her way on her errands of mercy. Once a madwoman threw a stone at Jeanne Marie, which struck her back so severely that she carried the mark of the blow until her death. Not only did she suffer throughout her life from the injury caused by this blow, but to this penance she added others, including the wearing of a hairshirt.

When her husband's family restored the Chateau des Roches to her, Jeanne Marie resolved to continue a life of poverty and gave the chateau and everything else she had to the Carthusians of Liget. She also made a declaration wherein she renounced any property which might be given to her in the future. In so doing, she alienated her own relatives, who considered her a disgrace to the family.

When Jeanne Marie became completely destitute, no one would house her. She was obliged to beg from door to door and to sleep in hovels and dog kennels. For a time she worked among the servants of the hospital of St. Martin, performing the most menial chores. But there her holiness was not appreciated and she came to be humiliated, ridiculed and eventually expelled. Jeanne Marie accepted all these trials with meekness and was rewarded with visions and special graces which allowed her to understand some of the mysteries of our faith.

When she was 57 years old, Jeanne Marie began living in a tiny room near the Minorite church at Tours. Some of the people who lived nearby considered her a madwoman or a witch, but many others recognized her as a saint.

Jeanne Marie eventually came to the attention of Louis, Duke of Anjou and Mary of Brittany, who chose her to be the godmother of their infant son. She taught the little prince about God and Heaven and likewise instructed the little children in her neighborhood. These would flock around her and chant the words she had taught them, "Blessed be God and Our Lord Jesus Christ." It is said that she also taught the words to a magpie which she had tamed.

In addition to her other mystical gifts, Jeanne Marie was also given the gift of prophecy. She felt compelled to share some of the prophecies with the King, and she was once detained at court for seven days by Queen Isabel of Bavaria.

Bl. Jeanne Marie converted and healed many. She redeemed numerous men from prison and was so highly regarded by the King that he once granted her request and liberated all the prisoners in Tours.

Bl. Jeanne Marie was denied her wish to suffer martyrdom, and instead died in her poor room on March 28, 1414. She was buried in the Minorite church where she had spent so many hours in prayer.

Chapter 106

BL. JOAN OF AZA

d. c. 1190

Bl. Joan (Jane, Joanna), the mother of the great St. Dominic, was born in the castle of Aza, near Aranda in Old Castile. Though nothing is known for certain of her childhood, it is thought that she married at an early age, according to the custom of the time and country. Her husband was Don Felix de Guzman, who was the royal warden of the small town of Calaroga in the province of Burgos. His character, we are told, rendered him in every way worthy to become her husband, and the household over which they ruled was remarkable for its piety and good order.

Bl. Joan is described as having been a person of beauty, charm and intelligence. She was likewise pious, and she possessed great energy in the practice of good works, particularly in visiting the poor and sick in their humble dwellings. Although she was a woman of rank who had attendants to help her, she diligently applied herself to the discharge of all that was required of her state. Following the completion of her domestic duties, Bl. Joan spent the remainder of the day in prayer and frequently spent the whole night in devotional exercises.

Of this truly Christian marriage, four children were born. Anthony, the eldest, became a secular priest. He was so attracted to holy poverty that he distributed his patrimony to the poor and retired to a hospital, where he spent the remainder of his days humbly ministering to the sick. Mannes, the second son, also became a priest. In due time he became one of the first Friar Preachers and has received the honor of being beatified. A daughter was also born to the holy couple. Although her name is not given, she is known to have had at least two sons who became preaching friars.

With their two sons dedicated to the Church, Don Felix and Bl. Joan were hopeful of having another son, one who would carry on the succession of their family. For this reason Bl. Joan journeyed to the shrine of St. Dominic of Silos, a saint renowned throughout Spain for his numerous miracles. With the permission of the abbot of the monastery, Joan began a novena to the Saint, spending her days and many of the nights in the monastery church absorbed in fervent prayer. On the seventh day of the novena, St. Dominic of Silos appeared to her and declared that her prayers were heard and that she would become the mother of a son who would be the light of the Church and the terror of heretics. In gratitude, Bl. Joan offered to St. Dominic of Silos the child who was to be given her through his intercession, and she promised that the child would bear the name of Dominic in honor of this favor.

Before the birth of her son, Bl. Joan beheld him in a vision, or dream; he was represented by the figure of a black and white dog holding in its mouth a torch which illuminated the whole world. This dog became a symbol of the Dominican Order and later gave rise to the pun *"Domini Canes,"* "the watchdogs of the Lord."

Sometime before Dominic's birth, Bl. Joan, in her usual generosity, distributed to the poor the entire contents of a cask of excellent wine. Realizing that her husband might become annoyed on finding the cask empty, Bl. Joan knelt down in the cellar and offered the following prayer: "O Lord Jesus, though I do not deserve to be heard, I beseech Thee, nevertheless, to take pity upon me in the name of Thy servant, and the dear little child whom I bear in my womb and whom I have consecrated to Thee." At the completion of her prayer the cask was found to be miraculously filled with wine.

At the time of Dominic's Baptism, either his godmother or Bl. Joan had a vision in which there appeared on the baby's forehead a star which enlightened the whole world. Because of this vision St. Dominic is often depicted in art with a star on his forehead.

When Dominic was only a few weeks old, Bl. Joan and Don Felix brought him to the shrine of St. Dominic of Silos and offered him to the service of God. Bl. Joan also carried the infant to the tomb of his great-uncle, Blessed Peter of Ucles, who founded the Order of the Knights of St. James of the Sword. Joan seems to have visited this place frequently; a hermitage there still bears her name.

When Dominic reached the age of seven, Bl. Joan entrusted him to the care of her brother, the archpriest of the neighboring town of Gumiel d'Izan. Another of her brothers, the Abbot of La Vid, seems also to have shared in the education of the future founder of the Dominican Order.

Bl. Joan is believed to have died sometime between the years 1185 and 1194. She was buried in the parish church of Calaroga, but her remains underwent two transferals: first to the Guzman family burial place at Gumiel d'Izan; later, in 1350, to the Dominican Church at Penafiel by Prince John Emmanuel, who had a great devotion to Bl. Joan.

Butler states that it has not been given to many mothers of saints to be themselves beatified, but that Joan achieved this distinction by her own virtues and not by those of her children. He further states that the beauty of Joan's soul was shared with the greatest of her sons.

At the request of King Ferdinand VII, Joan of Aza was beatified by Pope Leo XII in 1828.

Chapter 107

BL. JOAN OF SIGNA

c. 1245 - 1307

The small village of Signa, on the Arno River near Florence, is recognized as the birthplace of Bl. Joan, who was born there about the year 1245.

Her parents were very poor peasants who found it necessary to send the young Joan into the fields to tend the sheep and goats. While her flocks were grazing, she would collect her fellow herdsmen around her and give them simple instructions in the true Faith. She urged them to live as Christians, and by her example they learned to live a prayerful and charitable life.

Possibly inspired by the tales she had heard of St. Veridiana of Castelfiorentino, who had died about the time Joan was born, she became a solitary in a cell on the banks of Arno, not far from her native village. There she lived in great holiness and mortification for 40 years, having entered upon this life at the age of 23. Her reputation for miracles was great, and people came from all parts to consult her and bring their sick and afflicted.

Immediately after her death on November 9, 1307, a cultus sprang up which was greatly enhanced in 1348 when an epidemic was suddenly halted through her intercession. This cultus was confirmed by Pope Pius VI in 1798.

Blessed Joan of Signa is particularly venerated by the Franciscans as a tertiary of their order.

Chapter 108

STS. JOHN, ANTHONY AND EUSTACE

d. c. 1342

Known also by their Lithuanian names of Kumets, Kruglets and Nezilo, these three kinsmen of rank were employed as chamberlains in the household of Duke Olgierd, who ruled Lithuania from 1345 to 1377.

For a time they belonged to a sect of fire-worshippers, but after receiving instruction from a priest named Nestorius, they were baptized and became sincere Christians. They were conscientious in the performance of their religious duties, especially those regarding fasting and abstinence. Eventually they were cast into prison for their refusal to comply with the practices of paganism. After enduring many trials, they were condemned to death.

Anthony was hanged on January 14, and John, the eldest, was hanged on April 14. Eustace, the youngest, had to endure other tortures. He was beaten with clubs, his legs were broken, and the hair of his head was violently torn off because of his refusal to allow his hair to be shaved according to the custom prevailing among the pagans of the region. Eustace suffered and died at Vilna on December 13.

All three saints died about the year 1342 and were buried in the Church of the Holy Trinity at Vilna, of which they have been regarded as the patrons since the time they were martyred. They are honored in the *Roman Martyrology* and also in that of the Russians.

Chapter 109

BL. JOHN SLADE AND BL. JOHN BODEY

d. 1583

In the *Stow Chronicle* of 1583 and in other works, mention is made of two men who were tried and condemned at the same time and for the same cause.

"John Slade, schoolmaster and John Bodey, Master of Arts, being both condemned of high treason for maintaining of Roman power, were drawn, hanged, bowelled and quartered," stated the *Stow Chronicle*. However, the two men neither suffered at the same place nor on the same day.

Bl. John Slade was born in Dorsetshire, England, and after receiving his education at New College, Oxford, he became a schoolmaster. His zeal in practicing his religion attracted the attention of the Protestants, who caused his arrest. He and Bl. John Bodey were arraigned together at Winchester and were there tried and condemned. Their case is different from many others who suffered for the same cause because they were tried twice and sentenced to death both times upon the same indictment. The reason for the death sentence was that they denied the Queen's spiritual supremacy and maintained that of the Pope.

Bl. John Slade was hanged, drawn and quartered at Winchester on October 30, 1583. He suffered and died for the Faith with great courage and virtue.

*　　　　　*　　　　　*

Bl. John Bodey was born in the city of Wells, in Somersetshire, in 1549. His father was a wealthy farmer and merchant of Wells. Like Bl. John Slade, John Bodey was educated at New College, Oxford, where he earned the degree of Master of Arts. For a time he also studied canon and civil law.

On May 1, 1577 he arrived at Douay College in France, which

served during that time as a refuge for those leaving England for the Catholic cause. Upon his return to England, his religious devotions and zeal for the Faith were noticed by the enemies of the Faith. He was apprehended in 1580 and, with Bl. John Slade, was first tried in the spring of 1583 for refusing to recognize the Church of England. Since the first trial was declared to have been unjust and illegal, the two were retried in August of the same year. They were again found guilty and were sentenced to the usual punishment— that of being hanged, drawn and quartered.

After the second trial, John Bodey wrote to Dr. Humphrey Ely on September 16 expressing the patience and constancy of himself and his fellow prisoners and asking "the good prayers of you all for our strength, our joy and our perseverance unto the end."

Some have suspected that John Bodey was married, because Bl. William Hart (d. 1583), also of Wells, in writing to his own mother mentioned that John Bodey was in prison with him and then asked to be recommended to "Mrs. Bodey and all the rest."

Challoner relates that, as John Bodey was being taken to the gallows at Andover on the day of his death, November 2, 1583, "as he was drawn along the streets on a hurdle, his head being in danger of being hurt by the stones, an honest old man, pitying him, offered him his cap, in part to save his head; which Mr. Bodey with thanks refused, adding withal, that he was just now going to give his head, life, and all for his Saviour's sake."

Cardinal Allen informs us that when John Bodey was at the gallows, Mr. Kingsmell told him to confess the crime for which he was condemned so that the people would know the reason for which he was about to die. John Bodey then professed his obedience and fidelity to the Queen in all civil matters and added, "Be it known to all of you that are here present, that I suffer death this day because I deny the Queen to be the supreme head of the Church of Christ in England. I never committed any other treason, unless they will have hearing Mass or saying the Hail Mary to be treason."

It is said that John Bodey's mother, on hearing afterward about her son's death, made a great feast to which she invited her neighbors, rejoicing all the time that by his martyrdom her son's soul "was happily and eternally espoused to the Lamb."

Both John Slade and John Bodey were beatified in 1929.

Chapter 110

BL. JOHN FELTON

d. 1570

John Felton was from an ancient and wealthy Norfolk family and was related by marriage to the family of Anne Boleyn. His wife had been lady-in-waiting to Mary Tudor, the first daughter of Henry VIII, and was a personal friend of Elizabeth I, the King's second daughter. This was an unusual set of circumstances considering that all three—Anne, Mary and Elizabeth—were the principals during a turbulent time in English history.

On February 25, 1570, Pope St. Pius V issued the bull *Regnans in excelsis,* directed against Queen Elizabeth, who was at the time ostensibly a Catholic. By this bull she was declared excommunicate. Because she claimed to be the head of the Church of England, the Pope also declared that she should be deprived of the kingdom which she claimed and deprived of her subjects' allegiance. The Pope likewise accused her of sheltering heretics, oppressing and persecuting Catholics, and coercing her subjects into heresy and rejection of the Holy See, all of which was contrary to her coronation oath.

Early on the morning of May 25, the Feast of Corpus Christi, the citizens of London discovered that a copy of this bull of excommunication was fastened to the door of the house belonging to the Anglican Bishop of London. It had been put there during the night by Mr. John Felton, who lived in Southwark at a mansion built on the site of the former Cluniac Abbey of Bermondsey.

What we know of this incident was written in 1627 by G. Farrar, a priest known as a notary apostolic, who obtained his information from Felton's married daughter, Frances Salisbury. She tells us that,

the danger of such an employment, which my father took for an act of virtue, daunted him no whit. Whereupon promising his best endeavors in that behalf, he had the bull delivered him

358

at Calais, and after the receipt thereof came presently to London, where being assisted with one Lawrence Webb, doctor of the civil and canon laws, he fastened it to the bishop's door.

Fearful of the punishment he would receive for such an audacious act, Dr. Webb at once left the country—but Mr. Felton would not think of leaving and calmly awaited the result of his action.

A great disturbance followed the discovery of the document, and searchers were sent to discover the culprit. When the chamber of a well-known Catholic attorney in Lincoln's Inn was being inspected, a copy of the bull was found. The attorney was arrested, and while being racked he confessed that he had received it from John Felton.

The next day the Mayor of London, the Lord Chief Justice, the two sheriffs of London and other officers presented themselves at the house of John Felton to arrest him. When Felton heard the knockings at his gate, he went to a window, and seeing the group ready to break down the gate, he called to them to have patience, saying he knew they had come for him. Felton's wife, who joined her husband at the window, fell down in a swoon at the sight of the officers.

Although John Felton admitted to what he had done, he was not brought to trial for three months. He was kept in the prison of Newgate and in the Tower and was three times racked in the hope that he would confess to a political intrigue with the Spaniards. But there had been no such intrigue. Felton had simply done what he thought was right and just and what he had to do to satisfy his conscience and principles; he had published the bull because it was a legitimate censure by the Pope for the Queen's religious offenses.

When he was finally brought to trial at the Guildhall on August 4, 1570, John pleaded guilty, forthrightly declaring the supremacy of the Holy See. By virtue of this confession and statement he was dragged four days later to St. Paul's churchyard, where a scaffold had been set up opposite the door on which the bull had been posted. Overcoming his great fear at seeing the instruments of his execution, John pointed at the bishop's door, saying, "The Supreme Pontiff's letters against the pretended Queen were by me exhibited there. Now I am ready to die for the Catholic Faith."

As a token of good will, he removed a valuable diamond ring from his finger and entrusted it to the Earl of Sussex for delivery to the Queen. This ring was of particular interest to the Lord Chief

Justice, who had thought to claim it from the dead body.

After reciting the Miserere and commending his soul to God, John was hanged. The executioner would have let him hang until he was dead, but the Sheriff ordered that he be cut down alive. As John's heart was being torn from his body, his daughter Mrs. Salisbury heard him twice utter the name of Jesus.

John Felton was beatified with other English martyrs by Pope Leo XIII in 1886.

Eighteen years after the death of John Felton, his son Thomas Felton, who had been two years old at John's death, followed his father to martyrdom. Thomas, a Minim friar, refused under torture to reveal the names of priests; he was hanged at age 20 and was beatified in 1929.

Chapter 111

ST. JOHN RIGBY

c. 1570 - 1600

John Rigby was the son of a Lancashire gentleman who had suffered a reversal of his wealth and holdings. Because of his father's situation John Rigby was forced to seek whatever employment he could find, and he finally accepted a domestic position in the home of Sir Edmund Huddleston. His position in the household was awkward in that he was a Catholic living in a household whose members conformed to the Protestant religion. Because of the penal laws of the time, he occasionally attended Protestant services—a weakness which he afterward deeply regretted.

After a time John confessed to a priest who was in the Clink Prison and was reconciled to the Catholic Church. Thereafter he led an irreproachable life and was successful in winning back several lapsed Catholics to the good graces of the Church.

John Rigby came under the focus of the authorities through his employment. His employer, Sir Edmund, had a daughter, Mrs. Fortescue, who was summoned to appear in court on the charge of having been reconciled to the Catholic Faith. Because she was ill at the time, John Rigby was sent to the Sessions House of the Old Bailey to notify the court that she could not attend. While the judge was questioning him about Mrs. Fortescue, he turned his attention to John Rigby and inquired about his own religion. John Rigby frankly acknowledged that he was a Catholic and that he would not go to the church of which the Queen claimed headship. For this bold statement he was committed to Newgate Prison.

On June 19, 1600, during one of John Rigby's court appearances, an incident took place which many regarded as being miraculous. When John Rigby was standing before the bar, the judge saw that the prisoner had no irons on his legs; he sharply rebuked the keeper, who quickly brought a pair to the prisoner. John Rigby, taking them in his hands, kissed them, made the Sign of the Cross and gave them to the keeper. They were securely fastened on his legs and remained in place until John's appearance in court the next day. On that day while John Rigby was standing in the Sessions House, the irons inexplicably fell off his legs. The keeper once again fastened them to the prisoner's legs, but after a short time they again fell off. The man who had twice secured them to the prisoner's legs was so amazed that they had fallen off a second time that he refused to put them on again.

It was then that John Rigby remembered that a Catholic maid called Mercy had told him that morning about a dream she had in which his irons had fallen off his legs. On being asked what he thought of the irons falling off his legs, which most thought to be miraculous, John Rigby answered that he hoped it was a token that the bands of his mortality would soon be loosed.

Two days later, when he was told that he would die that day, he answered, "It is the best tidings that ever was brought me since I was born." After bidding farewell to his fellow Catholics and asking for their prayers, John Rigby went to the yard, knelt down, made the Sign of the Cross, stood up, and with a smile he boarded the cart that would take him to the place of execution. On the way to St. Thomas' Watering, the place of execution, he was met by the Earl of Rutland and Captain Whitlock, who were on horseback. Stopping the cart, they asked him his name and other questions, which he answered in this manner: "My name is John Rigby, a poor gentleman of the house of Harrock, in Lancashire; my age about thirty years; and my judgment and condemnation to this death is only and merely for that I answered the judge that I was reconciled [to the Catholic Faith], and for that I refused to go to [the Protestant] church."

The captain asked him to acknowledge the Queen as the head of the Church of England and thus save himself. This he would not do. After conferring with the sheriff's deputy about the matter in the hope of saving Rigby's life, the captain rode back to the cart and asked the prisoner, "Are you a married man or a bachelor?" "Sir," said John Rigby, "I am a bachelor, and more than that, I am a maid." After a few more words, the captain asked for John's prayers and then permitted the cart to move on to the appointed place.

Challoner, in his *Memoirs of Missionary Priests,* reports the brutality of John Rigby's death. After he had been hanged,

> The deputy commanded the hangman to cut him down, which was done so soon that he stood upright on his feet like to a man a little amazed, till the butchers threw him down. Then coming perfectly to himself, he said aloud and distinctly, "God forgive you. Jesus receive my soul." And immediately another cruel fellow standing by, who was no officer, but a common porter, set his foot upon Mr. Rigby's throat, and so held him down that he could speak no more. Others held his arms and legs whilst the executioner dismembered and bowelled him. And when he felt them pulling out his heart, he was yet so strong that he thrust the men from him who held his arms. At last they cut off his head and quartered him, and disposed of his head and quarters in several places in and about Southwark. The people, going away, complained very much of the barbarity of the execution; and generally all sorts bewailed his death.

John Rigby was canonized in 1970. He is one of the Forty Martyrs of England and Wales.

Chapter 112

BL. JOHN STOREY

c. 1504 - 1571

John Storey's life as an attorney was one of many difficulties; he struggled in one way or another during the terms of two kings, Henry VIII and Edward VI, as well as during the reigns of two queens, Mary I and Elizabeth.

At first, though, his career went very well. Sometime after receiving his law degree from Oxford University, John Storey was selected by King Henry VIII's commissioners to fill one of the recently founded lectureships. He was chosen for this position because he was regarded as "the most noted civilian and canonist of his time." In accepting this post he became Oxford's first Regius Professor of Civil Law. He also served two years as the Principal of Broadgates Hall, now Pembroke College. This position he resigned in 1537 to be admitted to Doctors' Commons and to practice as an advocate.

After his marriage, John Storey entered Parliament, where his eloquence soon drew attention. He had taken the Oath of Supremacy in the reign of Henry VIII, but in the first parliament of Edward VI, Henry's son, who was less than 16 years old, John Storey boldly opposed the Act of Uniformity. In an impassioned speech he exclaimed "Woe to thee, O Land, whose king is a child." The House of Commons was so greatly incensed at his opposition to the Act and his bold statement that John Storey was committed to the Tower for three months. Soon after his release, he retired with his family to Louvain, Belgium, where he freely practiced his Catholic faith.

While staying in Louvain he appears to have spent a great deal of time in devotional exercises with the Carthusians; but when Queen Mary ascended the throne, he returned to his native country. Highly respected by Queen Mary and the court, John Storey was made Chancellor of the dioceses of Oxford and London and Dean of the Arches. He also served as the Queen's proctor at Cramner's trial. Regarding

John Storey Delaney states, "Despite some historians' claims that he was the most active of Mary's agents in bringing heretics to trial, it is now known that he helped save many of the victims."

When Elizabeth began her reign, John Storey was still in England; he was the foremost opponent of the Bill of Supremacy in the new Parliament. For refusing to acknowledge Queen Elizabeth as the head of the Church, he was arrested and suffered imprisonment, first in the Fleet and then in the Marshalsea. He defeated the authorities' further plans for him when he made his escape the night before his trial.

Once more he made for Louvain, where he and his dependents were so impoverished that he was forced to become a pensioner of the King of Spain. Unable to practice his profession while in exile, he accepted a position as a searcher of heretical books and other contraband in English ships that were stationed in Antwerp. In this capacity John Storey was recognized as a Catholic by agents of the British government, who devised a plan with a skipper and others to capture him. The plan was a simple one in which John Storey was enticed into a ship secretly bound for England. As soon as he was in the hold examining the cargo, the hatches were closed, the anchor was raised and he found himself trapped and on his way to certain punishment for refusing to deny his faith in favor of the Church of England.

At Yarmouth he was delivered to the authorities and was charged with treason. During his trial in 1571, he refused to plead and was condemned to death. Before his execution he undoubtedly prayed for his wife and the family he had left in Louvain. It is said that he was executed at Tyburn with greater barbarity than was usual, remaining to the end a loyal son of the Catholic Church.

Chapter 113

ST. JOSEPH MOSCATI

1880 - 1927

Joseph Moscati was the only layman beatified by Pope Paul VI during the Holy Year of 1975, and he was the only layman canonized by Pope John Paul II during the Marian Year of 1987-1988.

This physician, professor and researcher, whom Pope John Paul II described as "the concrete realization of the ideal of the lay Christian," began life in Benevento, Italy, on July 25, 1880. He was the seventh of the nine children born to his pious parents. His father was a magistrate, who was later to become the President of the Court of Assize in Naples. In the serene environment of their devout Catholic family, Joseph and his brothers and sisters grew to be testimonials to their parents' mutual love. The children were docile and obedient to their parents' guidance and were nourished by prayer and good example.

Having received his earliest education at home, Joseph was enrolled in the school of Victor Emmanuel in 1889 and was prepared for his First Holy Communion by Monsignor Henry Manrano. This first reception of Our Lord took place on December 27, 1890, when Joseph was 10 years old.

During the years of his primary and secondary education, Joseph was described as being friendly to all, but somehow unwilling to associate much with others. He was, nevertheless, well-liked by his companions and earned the esteem of his teachers. Said to be "a little outspoken," he was "of a gentle and kindly disposition, deeply sincere and serene." Because of his "all-embracing intellect and uprightness of character," as well as his practice of virtue and prayer, Joseph was frequently presented by his professors as an example to his companions.

He was blessed with a quick mind and a keen desire for advancement in his studies. In grammar school his high marks were such that he was given a yearly scholarship. At the age of 17, after brilliantly completing his studies in the higher grades, Joseph received a first-class Classical Diploma and began considering the choice of a career. He would not study law, as had his father, but after praying for guidance he finally decided upon a career in medicine and entered the University of Naples.

Joseph followed the same pattern as in previous years: always dedicated to duty, he avoided frivolous amusements and applied himself to his studies after having dedicated his day to God by daily Mass and fervent prayer.

During his first year at the University, Joseph suffered the loss of his beloved father, who died a holy death. Although he himself was intensely grieved, Joseph consoled his mother and family; he later wrote to a friend who was suffering a similar loss, "God takes the place of those whom He has taken to Himself."

Joseph's application to his lessons was rewarded in 1898, during the first year of his medical studies, when he won the annual prize for the best results in zoology. During the second year he frequented hospitals, laboratories and clinics during his studies in anatomy, physiology and pathology. He is said to have been so absorbed in his studies that he failed to notice the activity around him. Professor Bevacqua related that while Joseph was under his instruction in the medical clinic he was impressed not only by Joseph's serious, composed and attentive attitude, but also by the ease and spontaneity with which he answered all the questions, even the most difficult, which even the more experienced pupils were unable to answer. These answers were given in a low voice, which the professor interpreted as Joseph's way of preventing the humiliation of these older students.

Joseph was awarded his degree in Medicine and Surgery, with the highest honors, on August 14, 1903, when he was 23 years old. He next entered a contest to prove his suitability for the post of Coadjutor Extraordinary in the United Hospitals; he won this "with such ease as to dumbfound both his examiners and his companions." He then began his terms of service in the infirmaries and casualty departments of the hospitals.

Joseph's concern for the welfare of his patients was demonstrated in April of 1906, during a time when Mt. Vesuvius was beginning to show renewed activity. Dr. Moscati became alarmed and quickly left for Torre del Greco, where elderly invalids were being tended at a branch of the United Hospitals. Journeying through a thick rain of ash, he helped to evacuate the inmates while encouraging and comforting them. Hardly had Joseph and the last patient left the hospital when the roof collapsed with a terrible roar. Joseph is said to have been a true instrument of Providence in this evacuation.

His charity was again demonstrated during another calamity, when cholera struck in 1911. By his self-sacrifice and devotion to duty, Joseph helped to curb the spread of the disease in the overcrowded slums of Naples.

The year of the epidemic proved to be a particularly busy one for Dr. Moscati. He completed his final studies and scientific preparation, and in June he brilliantly passed the extremely difficult examinations for Medical Coadjutor of the United Hospitals. In July of the same year he was chosen as holder of the Naples University Chair in Chemical Physiology and began lecturing on laboratory research as it applied to clinical medicine. Professor Piazza noted that:

> There was no development in medicine that he did not know thoroughly because there was not the slightest detail of research with which he was not familiar. He followed in the journals of various countries the new developments in science. As he had lived for many years in scientific institutes and in the wards of the Hospital for Incurables, dedicated to the study of science and invalids, everyone was astonished at this young man of only 36 who in so short a time was reaching the head of the whole medical world of Southern Italy.

Having attained these successes and advancements, Dr. Moscati considered for a time whether or not to marry. After many vigils and fervent prayer, about the year 1912 or 1913 he consecrated himself to a life of celibacy. Having made this decision, he thought that he was called to the religious life as a member of the Company of Jesus. But the Jesuit Fathers themselves discouraged him, since they felt that the will of God for him was to remain in the world in the practice of the medical profession.

During the year 1914, which marked the start of World War I, Dr. Moscati suffered the loss of his mother. The following year, when Italy declared war against Austria, Dr. Moscati volunteered for military service and received the rank of major. While caring for the wounded Italian soldiers he gave them the most prompt and scrupulous treatment, but his consolation lay not only in seeing the soldiers profiting from his medical assistance, but also in seeing them become good and devout Catholics, assisting at Mass and receiving the Sacraments.

Dr. Moscati's policy was to save souls by caring for the body. His deep conviction was that the health of the body depends upon the soul remaining in the state of grace. Everyone noticed the spiritual care he took of all those whom he approached, and it was extraordinary that what relatives and friends had been unable to bring about by lengthy arguments, he obtained by a few words whispered in the ears of sufferers.

An example of this occurred one day in the Hospital for Incurables, where an elderly patient was dying from cancer of the stomach. The patient absolutely refused to listen to any suggestion that he receive the Sacraments. The man's sister, realizing her helplessness, turned to Dr. Moscati. He approached the dying man and spoke a few words to him. The dying man listened attentively, and then, to the astonishment of his family, he asked for the Sacraments and received them with devotion.

Many incidents are told of sinners returning to the Sacraments through the influence of this good doctor, and many are the times that he refused payment for his services. Once at Amalfi, after having examined all the patients who were presented to him, he refused payment from all of them—and to those who asked why, he replied, "These are working folk. What have we that has not been given us by Our Lord? Woe to us if we do not make good use of God's gifts!"

Another time he was called to visit a railwayman who lived in a squalid lodging. The saintly doctor carefully examined the man and then explained to his relatives the serious nature of the ailment. He prescribed remedies and encouraged them to have confidence that the man would be cured. He then advised them to call the parish priest at once, "Because," he said, "one must attend first to the salvation of the soul and only then to that of the body." While this was taking place the patient's friends were donating their hard-earned money for the prescription. When Dr. Moscati saw what they were doing, he too contributed to the fund, saying that he wished to associate himself with their humanitarian actions. The workmen are said to have been so surprised by the doctor's generosity and kindness that they fell at his feet and attempted to kiss his hands, "but he escaped and left the hovel hastily."

Often, in an effort to help poor people whom he treated free of charge, he would leave them money—doing this secretly, however, to avoid embarrassing them. Of the many incidents in which this occurred, we are told that one poor woman found 50 lire folded in her prescription; another found 500 lire under her pillow; and another poor person was cared for in the hospital at the doctor's expense. Dr. Moscati's favorite patients were the poor, the homeless, religious and priests—and from them he would never accept a fee.

When his patients became frightened, he was always ready to quiet their fears and to provide spiritual advice and consolation. To a nun who said that she did not want to die of suffocation, Dr. Moscati replied, "A religious should never talk thus, for even an ordinary Christian must be ready to die that death which God wills for him." To another religious, who complained of a rather rigid diet, the doctor said, "God makes us suffer here in order to reward us in the heavenly Kingdom; by resigning ourselves to dietary restrictions, and suffering, we shall have greater merit in the eyes of the Almighty."

At times the doctor seems to have been divinely inspired. Once after carefully examining a priest, he sat down at his desk to write a prescription, but then wrote nothing. Instead, he picked up a copy of *The Imitation of Christ* and read, "In thy cell thou shalt find that which thou mightest lose outside. The cell, when continually dwelt in, becomes sweet, and when it is ill-cared for engenders afflictions." The priest understood the message and made the necessary adjustments in his manner of living.

Another time Fr. Cibarelli witnessed evidence of the doctor's advanced spiritual life and what appeared to have been his divinely inspired treatment of his patients. Concerning a visit to a poor female patient, Fr. Cibarelli wrote, "He made the palpations and tappings with great concentration, his eyes half-closed and his head on one side as if he were not visiting a patient, but listening to voices from above." Dr. Marzo wrote, "It seemed at times that his diagnostic foresight, permeated with inward knowledge, was inspired by supernatural beings." Prof. Landolfi added, "His diagnoses sometimes appeared to border on the miraculous, and occasionally it seemed that angels came to the aid of one who was so near to them."

His field of action included not only the sick, but also students at the University of Naples. There he became the center of attraction for scholars, who were amazed by his bewildering mastery of the sciences, his imposing moral uprightness, and his rare spiritual greatness. Students, colleagues and young graduates greatly admired him—while the doctor, for his part, enjoyed his work with them. We are told of his happiness when his pupils accompanied him to Holy Mass, stayed to pray with him and afterward went home with him. One of his pupils wrote, "In contact with him we were overcome by the irresistible fascination of his goodness, and not only did we drink of the inexhaustible fountain of his doctrine, but we were drunk with the sweet perfume of gentleness and goodness which emanated from his pure candid soul."

To someone who asked one day how he managed to cope with such a busy and demanding schedule, the Saint replied in the words of St. Paul, "I can do all things in Him who strengthens me." The doctor always maintained that it was the daily reception of Jesus in the Sacrament of the Holy Eucharist that sustained him in his daily work. At the foot of the altar he would remain motionless, as if in ecstasy, kneeling on the stone floor while contemplating the Most Blessed Sacrament.

The doctor's second source of strength was his deep and heartfelt devotion to Our Lady, especially under the title of the Immaculate Conception. Members of his family tell that he always carried a rosary in his pocket and that before making a serious decision he would take the rosary in his hand and kiss it. It is said that never a day passed that he did not remain at the foot of Our Lady's altar in the attitude of a truly devoted son.

As a result of his devotion to the Eucharist and to Our Lady there came, as a natural consequence, the most outstanding virtues, one of which was purity, a virtue which he maintained by vigilance and continual mortification. Dr. Moscati limited his hours of sleep, observed all the fasts and abstinences imposed by the Church, avoided amusements and worldly friendships, and denied himself the comforts and advantages which his social and economic position would have permitted him.

In his charity Dr. Moscati refused to speak of others' defects or faults. He declined, with delicate care, to cover up the mistakes of his colleagues, and he made heroic efforts to overlook the jealousy, envy and animosity that were sometimes directed against him. The doctor also practiced profound humility and was frequently seen performing the most menial services for his poor patients.

The Saint had many times predicted that his life would not be a lengthy one. On April 12, 1927, he rose at the normal time for his meditation and went to St. Clare's Church, where he served Mass and received Holy Communion. He returned home and advised his sister, with whom he lived, to arrange for a priest to hear the confession of a colleague, a lapsed Catholic, who was a patient in the hospital. The doctor is said then to have visited a poor, sick woman in her home and to have made his usual rounds in the hospital. Returning home, he began examining the many patients who were awaiting him. At three o'clock he felt ill. He stopped work and retired to his room. Dr. Moscati sat in his chair, crossed his arms, and died a peaceful death. He was 46 years old.

The news of Dr. Moscati's death spread quickly, arousing grief and deep regrets. His body soon was visited by many students, colleagues, the poor, religious and outstanding members of the government. Among the first visitors was His Eminence Cardinal Ascalesi, who said to those present, "The doctor belonged to the Church. It was not those whose bodies he had cured, but those whose souls he had saved who were waiting to greet him when he left this earth."

The funeral two days later was an imposing and moving ceremony during which Dr. Moscati's colleagues made speeches which were full of regret, grief, admiration and the highest praise for the virtues of the departed. The local paper, *Il Mattino*, reported, "Rarely indeed has Naples witnessed such an impressive spectacle of infinite sadness." The doctor's sister once wrote, "They speak of me as the sister of the Saint," while Prof. Morisani closed his letter of condolence to Dr. Moscati's brother thusly: "...every family which had the good fortune to know your brother, today remembers and venerates him as a saint."

Dr. Moscati's interest in the care of the sick continues from Heaven, as indicated by the cures that have continued to take place through his intercession. A biographer of the Saint reported:

> During his lifetime, Dr. Moscati's physical presence at the bedside of his patients gave them comfort and an interior consolation and peace. After his death, sufferers have frequently obtained graces and cures through him, usually seeing him beside them

with a power for good which God communicates to him in the world of the blessed, a thousand times more effective than during his lifetime. Many moving episodes which have no human explanation confirm this.

In 1973 two miracles obtained through Dr. Joseph Moscati's intercession were approved by the Sacred Congregation for the Causes of Saints. On November 16, 1975 he was solemnly beatified by Pope Paul VI, who cited the doctor's career as an example of harmony between science and faith. Pope Paul VI fixed November 16 as Bl. Joseph Moscati's feastday. At the doctor's canonization on October 25, 1987, many people from Naples were among the crowd of 80,000 who attended the Mass, which was concelebrated by 25 bishops and two cardinals.

The body of St. Joseph Moscati is kept in an artistically decorated sarcophagus which is situated under the main altar of the Church of the Gesu Nuovo in Naples.

St. Joseph Moscati (1880-1927), a medical doctor, dedicated his life to saving souls by caring for the body, at times effecting dramatic conversions by whispering a few words to his suffering patients. His favorite patients were the poor, the homeless, and religious—and from all of these he would never accept a fee. The Saint maintained that the daily reception of the Holy Eucharist sustained him in his daily work, and that he was strengthened by his devotion to Our Lady.

Chapter 114

ST. JOSEPH OF PALESTINE
(Count Joseph)

d. c. 356

When Rabbi Hillel was on his deathbed, he was touched by grace and requested Baptism. Since the Rabbi did not want his fellow Jews to know of his conversion, a Christian Bishop, disguised as a physician, was secretly brought to him. A tub of water was ordered under the pretext that it would be used during a medical treatment, but in reality it was used for the Baptism of the converted Jew, who died soon afterward.

Witnessing the Baptism was St. Joseph of Palestine, one of Rabbi Hillel's assistants. Since he had been a longtime confidant of the Rabbi, Joseph was given the care of the Rabbi's son, Judas, and some of the Rabbi's possessions, which included a number of Christian books. Joseph read some of these works and was impressed by them, but he was not yet ready to convert.

Sometime later, his ward Judas failed in an attempt to seduce a Christian girl. Judas even resorted to magic, but the virtuous maiden refused his advances. Joseph was much impressed by the refusal of the Christian girl and once again considered the virtues of Christianity.

One night, while Joseph was sleeping, he seemed to see Christ and to hear the words, "I am Jesus whom thy fathers crucified; believe in Me." Yet Joseph was still not fully convinced that he should reject the faith in which he had been reared and acknowledge Christianity as the only true faith.

Joseph accepted the appointment to the office of ruler of the synagogue at Tarsus, but was very unhappy in this position. In time he aroused the suspicions of the Jews, who became dissatisfied with his conduct. Finally, when they found him reading the Gospels, they became so enraged that they beat him and threw him into the River Cnydus. This bit of persecution opened his heart to grace and resulted in his Baptism.

When Constantine the Great became master of the East in 324, he gave Joseph the title of "comes," or count, with the authority to build churches throughout Galilee, wherever he thought they were needed. Joseph set about building churches in Tiberias, Diocaesarea, Nazareth, Capharnaum and Bethsan. These were built with many difficulties, since the Jews worked hard to obstruct Joseph's plans. It is claimed that when the Jews stopped his limekilns from burning, Joseph made the Sign of the Cross upon a vessel of water and, invoking the name of Jesus, poured it on the kilns, which were immediately fired.

Not only the Jews, but the Arians also conspired against him. Arianism is now considered to have been one of the most devastating of the early heresies. Arians' denial of the divinity of Christ was condemned by the Council of Nicaea I in 325. The Arians established their own churches and hierarchies, and for a reason not given, Joseph was afraid that they would seize him and attempt to ordain him forcibly to their priesthood. It is believed that it was for this reason that Joseph, a widower, married a second time, thus making himself ineligible for Holy Orders.

When Constantius began to persecute the orthodox priests, St. Joseph retired from Tiberias to the neighboring Scythopolis, where in 355 he lodged St. Eusebius of Vercelli, who had been banished by the Arians. Since his was the only Catholic house in the city, St. Joseph harbored many other priests, including St. Epiphanius, who wrote of Joseph's efforts to help the Church and its ministers.

St. Joseph of Palestine died about the year 356, at the age of 70.

Chapter 115

BL. JOSEFA NAVAL GIRBES

1820 - 1893

The city of Algemesi, located approximately twenty miles south of Valencia, Spain, is the birthplace of the newly beatified Josefa Naval Girbes, who was born there in 1820. Her early education was limited to embroidery and the rudiments of reading, but she soon became well informed concerning the doctrines of the Catholic Faith.

Known throughout her lifetime as Señora Pepa or simply Pepa, she received spiritual guidance from her parish priest. These instructions, together with her extraordinary virtues, enabled her to grow deeply in the love of God. By the time she was 30 years old, she was well advanced in the spiritual life, and by the time she was 55 she had reached the state of mystical union with God.

When Pepa was still a young woman she felt called to share with others all that she had learned about her faith. With the approval of the parish priest, she began to teach the art of embroidery to the young women of the city. These free lessons were accompanied by spiritual readings and wholesome conversations. Pepa's house continued to become a popular place for young women to practice needlework and to learn the practice of virtue until it was said that, under Señora Pepa's guidance, her pupils became experts at both.

Her curriculum of study gradually developed from basic catechism to instruction on the highest stages of prayer. She also involved her students in the activities of the parish and, moreover, prepared them for vocations as spouses and mothers or as members of religious orders. She also became active in preparing children for their First Holy Communion.

Since more room was needed to accommodate Pepa's many pupils, a family friend gave her an orange grove known as the Huerto de la Torreta, the "Orchard of the Little Tower." In 1877 many of her pupils began to gather there. Eventually Pepa's house and the Huerto became known as a pre-novitiate for Christian mothers.

Since her spiritual life was shaped by the Discalced Carmelite Order, Pepa's life was marked by a great devotion to Our Lady of Mount Carmel, St. Teresa of Avila and St. John of the Cross.

When Pepa was 71 years old she began to suffer from a heart condition in addition to the other infirmities of her age. Two years later she peacefully died on February 24, 1893.

Having been a tertiary of the Discalced Carmelite Third Order for many years, Pepa was buried in the Carmelite habit, as she had requested.

This teacher of embroidery and of sanctity was beatified by Pope John Paul II on September 25, 1988.

Chapter 116

ST. JULIA

Fifth Century

When the City of Carthage was taken by Genseric in 439, a noble maiden of the city named Julia was captured and sold as a slave to Eusebius, a pagan merchant of Syria. Setting aside her life of ease and privilege, Julia accepted her fate as the will of God and lived an exemplary life as a humble servant. She became so valuable to her master that he took her with him on a journey to Gaul, where he engaged in his profession as an importer of eastern goods. Having reached the northern part of Corsica, at a place now known as Cape Corse, their ship anchored. Eusebius went ashore to take part in a local pagan festival, while Julia remained on board, refusing to participate in the superstitious ceremonies, which she openly rejected.

When Felix, the Governor of the island, was notified that Julia had dared to insult the gods by refusing to join in their festival, he confronted her owner, Eusebius, with this allegation. Eusebius admitted that Julia was his Christian slave, but he said that he overlooked her Christianity because she was a faithful, cheerful and conscientious servant whom he trusted with all he had. The Governor was so impressed with all that Eusebius claimed of his servant that he offered four of his best female slaves in exchange for her. To this offer Eusebius replied, "If you were to offer me all your possessions, they could not equal the value of her services!"

Later that night, while Eusebius was in a drunken slumber, the Governor took it upon himself to encourage Julia to sacrifice to the gods. As an inducement, he even offered her her freedom from slavery if she would comply. Julia emphatically declined his proposal, saying that the only freedom she desired was to continue serving her Lord Jesus Christ.

Unaccustomed to such a bold reply by one in such a lowly position, the Governor viciously gave orders that she should be beaten on the face and that her hair should be torn out. After she underwent these sufferings, Julia was finally crucified.

We are told that monks from the Island of Giraglia rescued her body, which was later translated to different places. In the year 763 the body was removed to Brescia by the Lombard King Desiderius. The relic was placed by the Benedictine nuns in their church, which was consecrated the same year by Pope Paul I.

Julia is the Patroness of Corsica, which now claims some of her relics.

Chapter 117

ST. JULIAN THE HOSPITALLER

dates unknown

According to Caxton's version of the *Golden Legend*, Julian was of noble birth. As a young man he left home without giving notice and went forth to seek adventure. He eventually made the acquaintance of a noble prince, with whom he traveled. In the service of this prince he proved himself so well in battle and was so well-received in the palace that the King made him a knight. As a reward for his gallant services he was given a rich widow as his bride, and for her dower he received her castle.

When Julian first left home, his mother and father went in search of him. They traveled about the country, and at length came to his castle. Julian's wife, on seeing them approach, went out to meet them; upon learning who they were and the reason for their journey, she welcomed them with the utmost charity. Because Julian was on a journey, his wife gave the weary travelers her own bed on which to rest.

The next morning, while Julian's wife was attending services in church, Julian returned and entered his chamber. Intending to awaken his wife, he saw two figures in his bed. He at once thought that

a man had lain with his wife, so he slew them both with his sword. And after that he went out and saw his wife coming from the church. Then was he much abashed and demanded of his wife who they were that lay in his bed. Then she said that they were his father and mother, who had long sought him, and she had them to lie in his bed. Then he swooned and was almost dead, and began to weep bitterly and to cry aloud, "What shall I do that have slain my father and my mother."

In great torment Julian decided to leave, saying to his wife, "Adieu and farewell, my right dear love; I shall never rest till I have knowledge if God will pardon and forgive me for what I have done and that I shall have worthy penance."

To this his dutiful wife replied, "Right dear love, God forbid that ye should go without me; like as I have had joy with you, so will I have pain and heaviness."

Together Julian and his wife journeyed to a great river over which many people were ferried. They built a hospital nearby and helped travelers who were ill or weary from their journeys. Julian also helped in ferrying men back and forth across the river.

After a time, during a particularly cold winter's day, Julian discovered a man who was almost dead from the cold. Julian placed the man in his bed and covered him warmly, while overlooking the fact that the man appeared to be a leper. When Julian's charitable concerns were satisfied, the man suddenly became animated and said, "Julian, Our Lord hath sent me to thee, and sendeth thee word that He hath accepted thy penance."

The pious couple continued their charities. Eventually both rendered their souls to God.

Many hospitals were dedicated to St. Julian, especially in the Netherlands. He is also depicted in a stained-glass window in Rouen Cathedral. This window seems to have been sponsored by a guild of ferrymen.

St. Julian is considered the patron of innkeepers, travelers and boatmen. In art he is often represented as a ferryman with a boat.

Chapter 118

ST. JULITTA AND ST. CYRICUS

d. 304

When the edicts of Diocletian were being strictly enforced against Christians, St. Julitta, a pious widow of Iconium, decided to seek safety in a more secluded location. Taking her three-year-old son Cyricus (Quiricus) and two maidservants, she went to Isauria, where she found the persecution raging under Alexander, the Governor. From there the little party traveled to Tarsus, where Julitta was promptly recognized and imprisoned.

When she was called to trial, St. Julitta appeared, leading her child by the hand. As a woman of distinction, she owned property and many possessions—but when asked about these, she answered only that she was a Christian. For her refusal to cooperate, she was condemned to be racked and scourged.

While preparations were being made to rack Julitta, the child Cyricus was taken from her. The separation caused him to cry pitifully for his mother. In an effort to comfort him, the Governor took the beautiful child on his knee, but the boy would not be consoled. While his mother was being racked, he held out his arms to her and in a small voice kept repeating, "I am a Christian too." In a desperate struggle to be near his mother the child kicked Alexander and scratched his face. Furious at this behavior, the Governor seized Cyricus by the foot and threw him down, fracturing his skull. The boy died almost immediately from his injury.

Overcoming her distress at seeing her child killed before her eyes, St. Julitta prayed instead of giving in to grief; she thanked God for granting her child the crown of martyrdom. The Governor, still furious at the child and angry with the attitude of the mother, ordered that her sides be torn with hooks. After this was done, he ordered that she be beheaded and that her child's body should be cast out of the city with the bodies of criminals.

Following St. Julitta's execution in 304, her body and that of St. Cyricus were rescued by her two servants, who buried them in a field near the city. When peace was finally restored through the efforts of Constantine, the maids revealed the location of the graves, to the satisfaction of many Christians who came to venerate the two martyrs.

The feastday of Sts. Julitta and Cyricus was formerly observed on June 16. They are also mentioned in the calendars and menologies of the Greek and other oriental churches. Veneration of the two martyrs was common in the West at an early date, as is proved by the chapel dedicated to them in the Church of Santa Maria Antiqua at Rome. In France St. Cyricus is known as St. Cyr.

Chapter 119

ST. JULITTA

d. 303

St. Julitta was a wealthy woman of Caesarea in Cappadocia who owned many farms, cattle and slaves. A dishonest but powerful man of the area, through intrigue, managed to acquire a considerable portion of her estate. When the matter could not be resolved amicably, Julitta found it necessary to seek protection under the law. When the man was brought to court, a decision in St. Julitta's favor seemed inevitable since the man could not produce a title to the holdings. In a desperate attempt to gain favor with the judge and thereby secure a right to the property, he denounced Julitta as being a Christian.

To test the charge, the judge ordered fire and incense to be brought into the court and commanded St. Julitta to offer sacrifice to Zeus. To this the Saint bravely responded, "May my estates be ruined or given to strangers, may I lose my life, and may my body be cut into pieces, rather than that by the least impious word I should offend God. If you take from me a little portion of this earth, I shall gain Heaven for it."

With these words Julitta pronounced judgment on herself and the matter at hand, since earlier the same year the Emperor Diocletian had issued edicts against the Christians. In these edicts he declared them impious and debarred them from all protection of the law and from the privileges of citizenship. In compliance with the edict of Diocletian and in retaliation for the audacity of her declaration of faith, the judge promptly gave the usurper full title to the lands he had maliciously claimed as his own, and condemned Julitta to death by fire.

Had St. Julitta denied her faith in Jesus Christ, her property would probably have been restored to her; instead, she smiled at her loss in such an edifying manner that the pagans were amazed to see a woman of her rank, age and fortune renounce everything for the sake of her faith.

Turning her back on that which the world holds dear, Julitta walked bravely into the fire and died after inhaling stifling smoke. Her body, which was untouched by the flames, was buried by fellow Christians.

What we know of St. Julitta, who died in 303, is given to us by St. Basil in a homily written about the year 375. Of the Saint's body he says,

> It enriches with blessings both the place and those who come to it...the earth which received the body of this blessed woman sent forth a spring of most pleasant water, whereas all the neighboring waters are brackish and salt. The water preserves health and relieves the sick.

The feastday of St. Julitta was formerly observed on July 30.

Chapter 120

ST. JUSTUS AND ST. PASTOR

d. 304

A town formerly called Complutum, now Alcala de Henares, Spain, was the birthplace of these two young saints, who were brothers. Their parents were persons of rank and were Christians who carefully instructed their children in the Christian Faith. They were also taught all the things that children of their age generally learn, and thus they attended school every day.

During the Roman occupation of Spain, when the Emperor ordered that all Christians should be persecuted, the Roman Governor of Spain, Dacian, who hated Christians, went about from town to town seeking those of the Faith and killing those he found. When he arrived at Alcala de Henares, he issued a proclamation that was read in the marketplace, commanding everyone, under pain of death, to offer sacrifice to the gods who were the supposed protectors of the Roman Empire.

The proclamation caused the Christians to be terrified. Justus, who was then seven years old, and Pastor, who was nine, were at school when a messenger approached the teacher to report the news of the Governor's proclamation. While some of the students took no notice and continued to work at their lessons, Justus and Pastor listened keenly to the message. They were immediately struck with a supernatural grace and, full of courage, they threw down their books, left school and ran to the place where the Governor was interrogating a group of citizens.

The two boys pleaded for his attention and professed that they were Christians. At first the Governor avoided them but when they persisted, he marveled that they had come of their own free will to profess a thing that might result in their death. Instead of being mindful of their tender age, Dacian ordered them to be whipped, hoping that this would soon bring them to their senses.

As the two brothers were being led away, they encouraged each other to be unafraid. The officers who heard what they said were amazed that little children could be so willing to suffer for their beliefs.

The children suffered with constancy, and the officers reported the matter to the Governor. Dacian was unimpressed by the report or by their youth, but he was concerned about what others might think if he killed them publicly. He then ordered that Justus and Pastor be beheaded secretly in a place where none of the people could see them. They were accordingly led out into a field and were beheaded against a great rock.

The Christians of Alcala de Henares discovered their bodies and buried them at the place where they had died. Later, a chapel was built there, and still later their relics were enshrined under the high altar of the collegiate church at Alcala de Henares.

Although it might seem that the story of the two young martyrs is unworthy of belief, it is said that there can be no question as to the genuineness and antiquity of the cultus of these two Saints. St. Paulinus of Nola (d. 431) was so impressed with the supernatural courage of the martyrs that when his own son died at a tender age, he had the child buried close beside the two young Saints.

In the breviary of Toledo there is a beautiful and ancient hymn that was written in honor of Sts. Justus and Pastor, preserving all the details of their martyrdom.

Chapter 121

BL. KATERI TEKAKWITHA

1656 - 1680

Kateri's mother was a Christian who had been converted in southeast Canada by French missionaries; her father was a young Mohawk chief. While living with the tribe near the Mohawk River, at a place known as Ossernenon (Auriesville, New York), they became the parents of a beautiful daughter in the year 1656. A year or two later a baby boy joined the family. Neither of the children was baptized. The Indian women of the village would permit only a Blackrobe (Catholic priest) to perform this sacred function for their children, and it was to be years before one found his way to the village. Kateri's mother nevertheless prayed for her children and bequeathed her faith to them through her good example.

The family was a happy one until the year 1660, when tragedy struck in the form of a smallpox epidemic that claimed a third of the Ossernenon population. Kateri, her mother, father and brother all contracted the disease; four-year-old Kateri was the family's only survivor. She was to retain a reminder of the disease in the form of badly pitted skin on her formerly beautiful face and a weakness of vision, her eyes having become particularly sensitive to light. Bright sunshine or the glare of water or snow were a source of pain to her throughout her life. As long as she was in the dim longhouse all went well—but once outside, if the weather was bright and clear, Kateri found it necessary to shield her eyes and grope her way to where she intended to go. She was finally given the name "Tekakwitha," which translates: "She-who-feels-her-way-along," or "She-who-pushes-with-her-hands."

It was a custom among the Indians to move their settlement following floods, epidemics or similar catastrophies. For this reason, the Mohawks of Ossernenon moved after the disease to the top of a hill about a mile to the west of the old village. This new village was given the name "Ganawage." Here the little orphan was adopted by her uncle, the chief of the Turtle clan. He took her into his long-house and placed her under the care of her aunts.

Although Kateri was still very young, her aging aunts began to prepare her for a future marriage which would bring another provider into the family. From a social standpoint, since she had been taken into the household as a needy orphan, it seemed a moral duty for Kateri to repay her benefactors by adding to the family a man who would assist with the hard work, as well as the hunting and fishing.

During the summer of 1667 the village was visited by three Jesuit missionaries, Frs. Pierre Cholenec, Jacques Bruyas and Jean Pierron. They were lodged in Kateri's longhouse, which seems a loving forethought of Divine Providence. Kateri, who was then 11 years old, was entrusted with the care of the visitors, who, for their part, were struck with the modesty and sweetness with which she acquitted herself of this duty. On the other hand, the affable manners of the guests, as well as their regularity in prayer and religious exercises, so impressed the young girl that she would have asked then for Baptism, we are told, if the missionaries had remained longer in her village. When they left after a three-day visit, they unknowingly left in the heart of Kateri the desire to become a Christian.

While Kateri was growing up, her poor eyesight prevented her from fully participating in the activities of the other girls; however, she busied herself with family chores and cooking. While sitting in the shadows she worked hard and became adept at beadwork, needlework and weaving corn husks into mats, aprons and slippers. She was also skilled at cooking, sewing animal skins and adorning shirts and moccasins with the flattened quills of porcupines or elk's hair. She prepared ribbons of eelskin, and she mastered the art of dyeing cloth a deep red with sturgeon glue. On cloudy days she helped her aunts weed the crops and sow corn. During late summer, she took part in gathering acorns, sweet chestnuts and hazelnuts, as well as helping with the harvesting of Indian corn.

When Kateri approached a marriageable age, her conviction that she was not meant for the married state greatly concerned her adopted family, who thought that her skills and sweet disposition would be welcomed by a husband. In fact, we are told that Kateri's attitude toward marriage violently clashed with that of her family, who even attempted to trick her into marriage. When Kateri refused to give attention to a young brave they had selected for her, one biographer tells us she voluntarily left the longhouse for a time—although another biographer claims that she was expelled by her angered family.

When Kateri was 18 years old, she overcame her shyness to ask Fr. Jacques de Lamberville for Baptism. She attended the Father's instructions that were given in the "wigwam of prayer," and was baptized on Easter Sunday, April 5, 1676. It was then that she was given the name of "Kateri," Catherine in English, in honor of St. Catherine of Alexandria.

The joy that Kateri felt at her Baptism was soon met with persecution. Her uncle resented her conversion, and new trials presented themselves when Kateri refused to work in the fields on Sundays. In retaliation, her aunts accused her of idleness and refused to give Kateri food on the days she did not work. Although Kateri already performed most of the housework, her aunts pressured her with commands throughout the day in an effort to break her will. When the strain of physical labor had caused Kateri to become extremely weak, her duties were relaxed—but her uncle and aunts decided to try another tactic, that of criticizing and frightening the convert into abandoning the Faith.

Scoldings and mockery had proved successful with other converts, who had given in under the strain, but Kateri bore the persecution with humility and remained steadfast. As if the persecution at home were not enough, the villagers and even children pointed a finger and cruelly taunted her for being a Christian. This ill treatment is said to have lasted a year and a half. Father de Lamberville wrote that even during this difficult time, the young convert never relaxed from her initial fervor, nor complained of the harsh treatment.

Finally, the priest advised Kateri to move to the Mission of St. Francis Xavier at Kahnawake, which was on the south bank of the St. Lawrence River, facing Montreal. Many converts and their families had already tranferred to this village of prayer where conditions provided them with complete freedom to express their devotion and exercise their faith. Kateri decided to take the priest's advice.

Because of the animosity of her family, Kateri did not notify them of her plan to move. She patiently remained until the time that God seemed to arrange her departure. During the autumn of 1677, when Kateri's uncle left for Fort Oranje on a trading expedition, Kateri seized her chance and left during the night. Fr. de Lamberville had given her a note for Fr. Jacques Fremin, superior of the Mission of St. Francis Xavier. In the note he had written, "I am sending you a treasure; guard it well!" When her uncle returned to the village and learned of Kateri's departure, he became furious and attempted to follow her; but fortunately he turned back.

At the Mission, Kateri was profoundly happy to join the other converts. Their deep fervor delighted her. She already knew some of the women and two of the three Jesuits stationed there: Fr. Jacques Fremin; Fr. Pierre Cholenec, who was to be her spiritual director; and the third priest, Fr. Claude Chauchetiere, who was to become Kateri's first biographer.

It was the custom of the missionaries to test the faith of their converts by postponing the reception of Holy Communion for several years. But when Kateri's spiritual director became better acquainted with her spiritual progress, an exception was made. It was decided that she should receive her First Holy Communion on Christmas Day, 1677, this being about 20 months after her Baptism. From that time on Kateri is said to have advanced rapidly on the road to holiness. Her motto was, "Who will teach me what is most agreeable to God so that I may do it?"

In the humble bark church of the Mission, Kateri began her morning prayers at four o'clock in the morning. She attended the first Mass at dawn and another at sunrise. Several times during the day, she visited the church to pray before the Blessed Sacrament. She never missed evening prayers with the congregation, and she lingered after everyone else had left. At the end of each week she examined her conscience, went to confession and did penance for her failings.

What seemed like a pleasant and ideal situation for the young convert was soon changed when Kateri was falsely accused of an indiscretion with a married brave. The situation that prompted the accusation occurred during the hunting season when one of the men, who had been hunting elk all day, returned to the hut and wearily sat on a bench next to Kateri. An innocent comment was made, to which the young girl responded with a smile. The brave, a sincere Christian, unfortunately had an envious and suspicious wife. When the wife noticed that Kateri went out every afternoon during the time of rest, at the same time that the men were hunting, she suspected that Kateri was secretly meeting her husband somewhere in the forest. The wife did not know that Kateri had constructed a little shrine in the woods, where she went each day to pray.

Some days later, the wife felt that her apprehensions were confirmed when her husband mentioned that he had constructed a canoe in the woods and needed help to pull it to the clearing. "Kateri will come to help," he said, since he knew how charitable she was in offering her services to all who were in need. The Indian squaw told Fr. Fremin of her suspicions, and he, in turn, confronted Kateri, who steadfastly denied the charges against her. Unfortunately, the squaw confided the matter to friends, who betrayed her trust and told many others of Kateri's supposed indiscretion.

Kateri suffered greatly from this accusation, since many persisted for a long time in their belief of her guilt. But eventually they became fully convinced of her innocence and reverted to their former opinion that Kateri was indeed an "angel in the flesh."

While on a trip to Montreal, where she visited the Hospital of Hotel Dieu which was conducted by the Daughters of St. Joseph, Kateri was impressed with these religious, who had consecrated themselves to God by the vow of chastity. On returning to the Mission, she thought of founding a monastery for Indian nuns, but Fr. Fremin objected since Kateri knew little about such a life. She nevertheless expressed a desire to dedicate her chastity to God by means of a vow. Fr. Cholenec, her spiritual director, wrote:

> The thing [the vow of chastity] was so unusual...and appeared so incompatible with the life of the Indians, that I thought it best not to precipitate matters, so as to give her plenty of time to weigh a matter of such consequence. I tried her, therefore, for some time, and after I had noted the great progress she made in every kind of virtue, and above all with what profusion God communed with His Servant, it seemed to me that Kateri's design could come from no other source than from Him. Thereupon, I at last gave her permission to carry it out...

On the Feast of the Annunciation, March 25, 1679, at eight o'clock in the morning, after Kateri received Holy Communion, she renounced marriage forever by making a vow of perpetual virginity. Her spiritual director wrote,

> With a heart aglow with love, she implored Him to be her only spouse and to accept her as His bride. She prayed to Our

Lady, for whom she had a tender devotion, to present her to her Divine Son; then, wishing to make a double consecration in one single act, she offered herself entirely to Mary at the same time that she dedicated herself to Jesus Christ, earnestly begging her to be her mother and to accept her as her daughter.

After making this solemn vow, Kateri lived a penitential life. She observed a complete fast on Wednesdays and Fridays and increased her devotions.

During the summer of the same year she contracted a serious illness that almost claimed her life. After recovering, she resumed her devotions and works of charity, especially those attentions she gave to the sick and the elderly. During the winter she again suffered from headaches, a fever, painful stomach cramps and frequent vomiting. To these sufferings Kateri added other penances which greatly reduced her strength. During Lent of the following year, the fever and pain returned with such intensity that Kateri was forced to remain in bed. During Holy Week, when everyone despaired of her recovery, Kateri received the Last Sacraments and quietly died at three o'clock in the afternoon, on April 17, 1680. She was not quite 24 years old.

Immediately after her death a mysterious event occurred that was witnessed by the priests and all who were present. Within the space of a few minutes, the eyewitnesses saw the ravages of sickness disappear, to give way to a fresh, smiling and radiant countenance. Even the pockmarks that had disfigured Kateri's face from childhood could no longer be seen. Fr. Cholenec was greatly surprised, and gasps of wonder and awe were heard. Later, many testified to this marvel under oath.

Two French tradesmen who had come from LaPrairie to take part in the Holy Week ceremonies were so overwhelmed with wonder and reverence at the beautiful and radiant change in Kateri, whom they had known, that they offered to make a coffin for her. According to Iroquois custom, Indians were usually buried on a bier of bark and covered only with a blanket. The priests consented to having Kateri buried in a special wooden casket. (This circumstance made it possible to identify her remains beyond any doubt when they were exhumed in 1684.) Kateri was buried on Holy Thursday, April 18, the day after her death.

Countless reports of unusual favors, cures and blessings have been reported since that time, resulting in a petition for her beatification. Kateri was eventually proclaimed Venerable in 1941 by Pope Pius XII and was beatified on June 22, 1980 by Pope John Paul II.

Kateri's remains are kept in a marble sarcophagus in the Church of St. Francis Xavier in Kahnawake, Quebec, which continues to be a place of devotion for thousands of pilgrims. Also visited by pilgrims is Kateri's original grave, which was situated on the crest of the riverbank three miles east of Kahnawake. The site is marked by a cross 20 feet high and a monument in the shape of a sarcophagus.

Photo Armour Landry

The marble sarcophagus which contains the remains of Bl. Kateri Tekakwitha (1656-1680) in the Church of St. Francis Xavier in Kahnawake, Quebec. Thousands of pilgrims visit the site.

Emile Brunet, S.C.

Photo Armour Landry, Montreal

Above: Rev. Michael K. Jacobs, S.J., the first Iroquois priest, and Iroquois altar boy Collin Phillips at Bl. Kateri's sarcophagus.

Left: A statue of Bl. Kateri Tekakwitha, the orphaned daughter of a Christian mother and a Mohawk chief. The visit of three Jesuit missionaries to Kateri's village when she was 11 years old left her with the desire to become a Catholic. She was baptized on Easter Sunday, 1676, and as a result soon met with persecution by some in her community. She eventually attached herself to the mission of St. Francis Xavier at Kahnawake on the St. Lawrence River. Kateri wanted to become a nun; this was not possible, but she did make a vow of chastity and practiced many penances. Bl. Kateri's body, ravaged by sickness, underwent a marvelous transformation within minutes following her death at age 24.

Chapter 122

ST. LADISLAS

1040 - 1095

The laws, discipline and organization established by the virtuous St. Stephen, King of Hungary, were maintained and strengthened by St. Ladislas. Considered the equal of Stephen in virtue, Ladislas followed Stephen in being regarded as one of Hungary's national Christian heroes and as one of the greatest saints Hungary has produced. Ladislas was also a capable administrator. He extended the borders of his country, kept its enemies subdued, established it as a great nation, spread the Faith throughout his dominions and gave them a legacy of peace.

Born in 1040, only two years after the death of St. Stephen, Ladislas was the son of Duke Bela I and the Polish Princess Richeza. Ladislas and his elder brother Geyza were born in Poland, where their Hungarian father was then living in exile. Ladislas was seven years old when his father was recalled to Hungary by Bela's brother King Andrew I.

A family situation that was to cause Ladislas difficulties almost to the time of his death occurred in this manner: Ladislas' uncle, Andrew I, had a son, Solomon, who was the son of King Andrew's old age. Upon King Andrew's death, his brother Bela succeeded him to the throne. Upon Bela's death confusion developed concerning the succession; the lines of contention that were drawn included, on one side, those who supported Solomon, the son of King Andrew, and on the other, those who supported his cousin, Geyza (the elder son of King Bela and Ladislas' elder brother).

Since the Hungarian succession depended upon election more than on a family's line of succession, the Magyar nobles, infuriated with Solomon's jealousy and intrigues, refused to acknowledge him as their king. The matter could not be settled peaceably and resulted in a dispute on the field of battle at Mogyorod. Solomon suffered a bitter wound to his pride and ambition when the victors proclaimed their new king to be Geyza, Ladislas' elder brother.

Geyza, however, ruled for only three years. At his death a council of clergy, nobles and city magistrates again rejected Solomon's claim and elected Ladislas to succeed his brother.

Ladislas proved to be an ideal king. Having already proved himself to be an impressive warrior, he was a symbol of able leadership in the affairs of both Church and state. His dealings with his subjects were distinguished by his fairness, courtesy and pleasant disposition; his dealings with his Creator were marked by his faithful fulfillment of his religious duties, his zeal for the Faith, his high moral values and the simplicity and virtue of his life.

Devoid of political ambition, Ladislas suggested that half of his kingdom could be assigned to the leadership of his cousin, the brooding and jealous Solomon, who was still smarting from his failure to win the throne of Hungary. As the Magyar nobles refused this arrangement, the Magyars and Solomon negotiated a settlement of the issue. It was finally decided that Solomon would forever abandon his claim to the crown in exchange for a liberal pension. For the signing of this agreement, Solomon invited Ladislas to meet with him in a certain area on the River Moschotz.

Ladislas was on his way to meet with Solomon when he discovered that Solomon was preparing to make an attempt on his life. Solomon was arrested and placed under guard in the fortress of Visegrad.

At this time, when St. Stephen was about to be canonized, Ladislas was preparing to remove the relics of the Saint to a more honorable shrine. Remembering that Stephen had forgiven and released his kinsmen who had made an attempt on his life, Ladislas believed that it would displease St. Stephen if he were to continue the confinement of his kinsmen Solomon, who had been charged with a similar crime. During the solemnities connected with the translation of Stephen's relics, Ladislas forgave and released Solomon, who had spent only a short time in prison.

Ladislas was to suffer still more because of the frustrated Solomon. Soon after his release, Solomon enlisted foreign aid and returned at the head of a horde of Kumanian barbarians. But once again he was defeated. After the battle, he disappeared into the forest. Although it is not mentioned in history books what happened to him after that, tradition claims that he died as a penitent in a cave at Pola on the Adriatic.

Ladislas is known to have married Adelaide, the daughter of Duke Welf of Bavaria, but little is told of their life together.

Although Ladislas left a legacy of peace, during his lifetime he had to face repeated invasions from the Kumans, the Russians and other barbaric tribes. Despite these difficulties, he was successful in spreading the Christian Faith, in eradicating pagan customs, building many churches, establishing bishoprics, and promulgating a code of laws for the regulation of the religious and civil affairs of the country.

To support the claim that Ladislas was devoid of political ambition, it is told that Ladislas refused the German imperial crown because he wished to be nothing else but a Hungarian.

The leadership abilities and the virtuous reputation of Ladislas were recognized by the kings of France, England and Spain when Ladislas was chosen to be the commander-in-chief of allied crusading armies who were intent on delivering the Holy Land from the Saracens. Ladislas was preparing to accept this responsibility when he contracted a mortal illness. He died at Neutra on July 30, 1095.

His body was conveyed with great solemnity to Grosswardein for burial in the cathedral which he had built. From the moment of his death he was regarded as a saint and was venerated by the Hungarian people, whose mourning is said to have endured for three years. In the year 1192 he was canonized by Pope Celestine III.

Foto Horvai Jozsef/Nyomda, Budapest

St. Ladislas (1040-1095), a Hungarian king who exhibited admirable qualities of leadership in matters of Church and State. Fairness ruled his actions toward his subjects; zeal for the Faith and a virtuous life characterized the way in which St. Ladislas carried out his religious duties. Despite many difficulties, he did much to spread Catholicism and to eradicate pagan customs. It is said that the Hungarian people mourned their sovereign for three years, regarding him as a saint from the moment of his death.

401

Chapter 123

BL. LAURENCE HUMPHREY

1572 - 1591

Laurence was born in Hampshire, England to parents who were Protestant. He was a studious youth who became so familiar with Holy Scripture and religious works that he often disputed with Catholics on the meaning of various passages. At the age of 18 he entered into a discussion with Fr. Stanney, and after several meetings he was converted to the Catholic Faith. He became a very virtuous and charitable person who delighted in visiting prisoners and sick persons, in instructing the ignorant and in exercising the corporal and spiritual works of mercy.

In 1591, when he was 19 years old, Laurence became seriously ill, and in a delirious state he allegedly called Queen Elizabeth a heretic. He was quickly reported to the authorities by Protestants who supposedly had overheard his words. Before he was quite recovered, he was taken from his sickbed and cast into the prison at Winchester. His charge was that of treason.

When Laurence was brought to court, the judge showed him the rosary beads that had been taken from him at the time of his arrest. Laurence asked to see them and when they were handed to him, he reverently kissed them and blessed himself with the crucifix. The judge asked him, "Do you take that for your God?" Laurence answered, "Not so, my lord, but for a remembrance of the death which my Saviour suffered for me."

During his trial Laurence solemnly testified that he could not remember ever having said that the Queen was a heretic, but the Protestants testified that he did indeed speak such words. Laurence would not dispute the evidence of the witnesses who had allegedly overheard him. He testified that he was willing to suffer for his words, though he was not conscious of having said them.

In consequence of this testimony the judge passed sentence. Laurence was to be returned to prison. Later, he was to be taken to the place of execution, there to be half-hanged, so that while still living he could be cut down and disemboweled. His head was to be cut off, his body quartered, his head to be set on a pole and his limbs to be hung on the four gates of the city. "And all this," said Laurence, "is but one thing." "What thing?" asked the judge. Laurence answered calmly, "One death."

After being returned to prison, Laurence spent almost all his time in prayer while lying prostrate on the ground. When the time came for his execution, he approached the gallows and made the Sign of the Cross. At this the hangman sneered, saying, "You hold with the Pope, but see to what this allegiance has brought you." Laurence remained silent and smiled. Seeing this, the hangman gave him a blow under the ear, saying, "What! Do you laugh me to scorn?" Laurence quietly answered, "Why do you strike me? I have given you no such occasion." The words were scarcely spoken when the hangman performed his duty.

For words supposedly spoken in delirium, Laurence gained the crown of martyrdom in 1591, being at the time almost 20 years of age. He was beatified in 1929.

Chapter 124

ST. LEONIDAS

d. 202

Among the saints who died in Egypt for the Faith, one of the best-known is St. Leonidas, a learned Christian philosopher. He was a married man and the father of seven sons, of which the eldest, Origen, became known as a great Christian scholar. In fact, the fame of the son eclipsed that of his father, causing Leonidas to be sometimes identified simply as "the father of Origen." But it was due to the father that the son was able to reach such a reputation for learning, since Leonidas, aware of his child's many talents and keen intellect, gave Origen the primary education upon which his Greek literary studies depended. Leonidas likewise helped Origen in his studies of Holy Scripture. He no doubt had his son memorize what they studied together, since as an adult Origen knew the Bible so well that he could recite extended passages at will and could associate verses throughout the Bible on the basis of key words. Leonidas also provided his sons with a wholesome family life in which family prayer, the practices of their faith and the love of God held the greatest importance.

When the persecution was at its height at Alexandria, Leonidas—who was an illustrious citizen of the city—was apprehended and imprisoned on the order of Laetus, the Governor of Egypt. When it seemed a certainty that his father would be martyred, Origen, then 17 years old, was so eager to join his father in dying for the Faith that his mother locked up all his clothes to keep him at home.

While Leonidas was in prison, Origen wrote a touching letter to him, encouraging him to accept with courage and joy the crown that was offered him. Origen added, "Take heed, sir, that you do not, for our sakes, change your mind."

Leonidas stood firm in his faith and was beheaded in the year 202. The Saint no doubt felt great regret at leaving his family, but we might surmise that he felt satisfied that his properties would adequately support them. However, the state, having put him to death, confiscated Leonidas' property and possessions, which reduced his wife and children to extreme poverty.

Chapter 125

ST. LEOPOLD

1073 - 1136

St. Leopold III, the Margrave of Austria, was affectionately known as "Leopold the Good." He was born at Melk in 1073 and was brought up under the influence of the reforming bishop St. Altmann of Passau. When he was 23 years old, he succeeded his father. In 1106, when he was 33 years of age, he married Agnes, the daughter of Emperor Henry.

Agnes was a widow who had borne two sons by her first husband. During her marriage to Leopold, 18 more children were added to the family. Eleven of these survived childhood. One of them was Otto, who was to become the Cistercian Abbot of Marimond in Burgundy. It would be at Otto's request that St. Leopold would found the Abbey of Heiligenkreuz (Holy Cross) in Wienerwald in the year 1135.

Another great foundation made by St. Leopold was Klosterneuburg, near Vienna, for Augustinian canons. Still another foundation was the Benedictine Monastery of Mariazell in Styria, Austria, whose church is now a popular place of pilgrimage. By virtue of these important monasteries, Leopold did a great service to the Church, by making it possible for the True Faith to be spread throughout Austria.

Leopold's lands were twice invaded by the Magyars, but on each occasion he defeated them in the field; the second time he and his men dispatched nearly all of the enemy's forces.

When his brother-in-law Henry V died in 1125, the Bavarians wanted Leopold to claim the imperial crown, but Leopold refused to be nominated. He became a staunch adherent of Lothaire II.

After serving 40 years as Margrave of Austria, St. Leopold died in 1136, at the age of 63. He was buried at the Augustinian abbey of Klosterneuburg, which he had founded.

On January 6, 1485, 350 years after Leopold's death, Pope Innocent VIII proclaimed his canonization. It was the only canonization ceremony performed by this pope. Leopold was declared the national patron of Austria in 1663, with his feast being observed as a national holiday. The Saint is usually pictured in a suit of armor, with a flag and a model of a church.

Chapter 126

BL. LODOVICA ALBERTONI

1473 - 1533

In the holy City of Rome in the year 1473, Bl. Lodovica was born into a distinguished family of ancient lineage, her father being Stefano Albertoni and her mother, Lucrezia Tebaldi. While she was still an infant, Lodovica lost her father. Her mother married again, but for reasons not known, Lodovica was raised not by her mother, but by her grandmother—and then by two of her aunts.

Perhaps it was because Lodovica had an unstable childhood, having been a member of four different households, that her family wanted a more stable situation for her. It might have been for this reason that they pressured her to marry Giacomo de Cithara, a young man of noble family and great wealth, who could undoubtedly provide her with a home she could finally consider her own. And in fact Lodovica did marry Giacomo. She became the mother of three daughters and lived with her husband in harmony and affection until his death in 1506.

After Lodovica was widowed, she began to spend more time in prayer and penance and was received into the Franciscan Third Order. The time that remained after her household duties were completed was spent in the service of the sick and the poor and in visiting the seven great basilicas of Rome.

Lodovica was somewhat original in her acts of charity, as, for example, when she baked bread for the poor and slipped gold and silver coins into the loaves. She prayed that those most in need would receive the loaves which contained the coins of greater value. After a time Lodovica lost her fortune because of her excessive generosity. Her relatives supplied her with food, but even this she shared with the needy.

During the last years of her life, Lodovica was frequently in ecstasy and experienced a number of bodily levitations during prayer.

She went to her eternal reward on January 31, 1533 after repeating the dying words of Our Lord, "Father, into Thy hands I commend my spirit."

Miracles were reported while Lodovica's body lay in the church awaiting burial, and many occurred later at her tomb. The veneration paid to Lodovica was confirmed by Pope Clement X in 1671.

Chapter 127

ST. LOUIS IX, KING OF FRANCE

1215 - 1270

Located in the central region of France is the little town of Poissy, which boasts of being the place where St. Louis was born on April 25, 1215. The Church of Notre Dame is similarly proud of its baptismal font, since it was there that the future Saint was received into the Catholic Church.

As the son of Louis VIII and Blanche of Castile, Louis was heir to the French throne and was crowned at the age of 11, shortly after his father's death. His mother served as regent until he came of age, and it was she who was most responsible for forming the character of the young King. She was particularly careful "to instill into his soul the highest regard and awe for everything that pertained to divine worship, religion and virtue." The Saint was deeply impressed in his youth when his mother told him, "I love you, my dear son, as much as a mother can love her child; but I would rather see you dead at my feet than that you should ever commit a mortal sin."

It was unprecedented that a woman should rule France, but Louis' mother, Queen Blanche, governed wisely and prevented several feudal lords from taking advantage of the youthful king.

Louis greatly admired his mother, and even though she was difficult at times, he showed her the greatest respect and exercised remarkable patience with her shortcomings. Joinville, the Saint's companion and biographer, could not conceal his dislike for the Queen Mother; she is described by him—and by others—as being headstrong, strong-willed and domineering.

The possessive nature of the Saint's mother has been carefully recorded. We are told that the King, in later life, recalled how his mother had accompanied him to the woods and the river when he wished to play—this in a situation when attendants at the castle would normally have been entrusted with his safety.

At the age of 19 Louis married Margaret, the daughter of Raymund Berenger, Count of Provence. The marriage was celebrated on May 27, 1234. In due time 11 children were born to the couple: five sons and six daughters. This union produced descendants who were kings of France for over 500 years—until January 21, 1793, when Louis XVI was guillotined. Of Louis' children, Isabella was considered his favorite, but the Saint also had a close relationship with his eldest son, Louis, who unfortunately died at the age of 16. It is said that the King grieved hard and long following his child's death.

Although King Louis was able to control the affairs of his kingdom and settle numerous disputes, he apparently found it difficult to alter a troubling condition within his own family. The problem involved the jealousy and animosity that the Queen Mother demonstrated toward Louis' young wife. The King's biographer, Joinville, did not care for the Queen Mother and disapproved of her harshness toward Margaret. He especially did not like the fact that:

> the Queen Mother arranged, early in the marriage of her son, to separate the couple by having her apartment beneath that of her son, and above that of his wife. The young couple, however, devised a plan to thwart the Queen Mother's plans to separate them and managed to meet by stealth during the day, despite Blanche's watchful eye. The young couple worked out a plan that they could talk together on a spiral staircase which led down from one floor to the other; and had so laid their plans that when the doorkeepers saw the Queen Mother coming to the apartments of her son, they would rap on the doors with their rods; and the King would come running into his rooms, so that his mother might not catch him; and the ushers of Queen Margaret's apartment did the same when Queen Blanche was on her way thither, so that she might find Queen Margaret there.

While this may seem somewhat amusing and romantic, the following is not, and it shows the excess of Queen Blanche's desire to separate the couple, even when the King was properly at the side of his seriously ill wife. Joinville again tells us that:

> The queen dowager would not suffer her son to accompany his lady, and so prevented it as much as lay in her power. When the King traveled through his lands with the twain, Queen Blanche

had him separated from his queen, and they were never lodged
in the same house. It happened one day while the court lingered
at Pontoise that the King was lodged in the storey above the
apartments of his queen. He had given orders to the ushers of
his chamber that whenever he should go to lie with his queen,
and his mother was seen coming to his chambers or the Queen's,
to beat the dogs until they cried out and thus gave warning.
Now one day Queen Blanche went to the Queen's chamber,
whither her son had gone to comfort his lady—for she was in
danger of death from a bad delivery. His mother, perceiving him,
took him by the hand and said,

"Come along—you will do no good here."

Queen Margaret, seeing that she was to be separated from
her husband, cried aloud: "Alas, will you not allow me to be
with my lord, neither when I am alive nor if I am dying?"

We are not told the King's reaction to his mother's jealousy, but
it would seem that the Saint, although having the greatest respect
for his mother, would nevertheless have remained with his wife to
offer her whatever relief his presence would afford.

When Queen Blanche's death was made known to Queen Margaret, she began to weep bitterly. This puzzled Joinville, and he asked
her why she was crying for a woman who had caused her so much
bitterness. Queen Margaret explained that her tears were not so much
for her mother-in-law as they were for her husband, whom she knew
would sorrow bitterly.

Joseph Dahmus, in his *Seven Medieval Kings,* tells us that in later
life the King was "correct without being warm" toward his wife and
most of his children, and that Margaret would undoubtedly have
preferred a more demonstrative husband. What seems to have caused
the difficulty, Dahmus reports, is that, with the Queen Mother gone,
Margaret cultivated a "fondness for political meddling. Margaret had
a passionate and ambitious nature and often permitted her emotions
to urge policies upon Louis which he considered unwise."

Margaret's favorite sister was Eleanor, wife of Henry III of England;
therefore, Margaret was inclined to intrigue on behalf of the English.
Margaret's other sister, Beatrice, was the wife of St. Louis' brother,
Charles of Anjou, with whom she was forever at political odds.

The couple's oldest son, Louis, was a favorite of the King. Because
of the close relationship between the boy and his father, we are told

that Margaret never attempted to gain her son's confidence. But as soon as Louis was dead at the age of 16, Margaret turned her attentions to cultivating the confidence of the next eldest, Philip, who would succeed his father. Dahmus tells us that Philip, who was then 15, was persuaded, at the instigation of his mother, to make several sacred oaths: that he would remain under her tutelage until he was 30; that he would never make an alliance with his uncle, Charles of Anjou; that he would accept as counselors only those persons of whom she would approve; and that he would make known any hostile acts involving her. He was also, of course, to keep his oaths a secret. But somehow King Louis heard of them, and much to his credit he took decisive action and immediately petitioned Rome for a papal bull dispensing the boy from his oaths.

Dahmus tells us that the King had already issued orders which limited the expenditures of the Queen and prohibited her from issuing instructions to any of the crown officials. He even forbade her to take into her service anyone without first securing his approval.

Despite ill health, countless responsibilities and the troubling situations that are encountered by all monarchs, St. Louis held fast to his faith and religious practices, properly corrected his wife, maintained the leadership of the family and was an example of all that was good and just.

Among the Saint's many good traits was his outstanding generosity to the poor. Whereas it was usually expected, both before and after the time of St. Louis, for kings to be adding to their personal wealth, St. Louis seemed to have been bent on diminishing his. The King was not wealthy; his principle source of income was the revenues from his estates, which were not large. Nevertheless, he gave generously of what he had. Joinville, who had been the Saint's companion for more than 22 years, tells us that "From his childhood up, Louis was compassionate toward the poor and suffering; and it was the custom that, wherever he went, six score poor should always be replenished in his house with bread and wine and meat or fish every day."

We are also told that his manner of giving was personal. The Saint customarily waited upon the poor as they sat about his table. He would cut the meat for those who were unable to do so, and he gave them coins when they left. He also kept lists of needy people whom he regularly relieved in every province of his realm. According to Joinville, "The hospitality of his palace was so courteous, generous and plentiful that nothing like it had been known for a long time past at the courts of his predecessors."

In addition to helping religious orders, St. Louis provided dowries to needy girls who wished to be married. He was likewise concerned for the many homeless women who roamed the city, and for these he established a house near Paris. He founded the House of the Filles-Dieu for reformed prostitutes and also constructed several hospitals.

Louis is known to have visited these hospitals, where he would perform the most menial services for the sick. Because he wanted to keep his acts of kindness a secret, he delighted in helping the blind, since they were unable to recognize their benefactor. Much to the admiration of his contemporaries, he also ministered to lepers, who were considered the most wretched members of medieval society. One in particular seems to have been favored, a leprous monk of the Abbey of Royaumont. When Louis learned of the hideous appearance of the monk—his face being greatly disfigured by the disease—Louis paid him many visits, during which he patiently fed the monk and performed other services for him.

The Saint once asked Joinville, his companion, if he would rather be a leper or a person who had committed a mortal sin. Joinville promptly replied that he would rather have committed 30 deadly sins than be a leper. Louis seemed unhappy with the answer and replied:

> There is no leprosy so foul as deadly sin, seeing that a soul in deadly sin is in the image of the devil. And truly when a man dies, he is healed of the leprosy of the body, but when a man dies that has committed a deadly sin, great fear must he needs have lest such leprosy should endure so long as God shall be in Heaven.

Although the King often ministered to the sick, he was not a well man himself—yet he gave no evidence that his frail constitution ever prevented him from undertaking any of his responsibilities. In addition to the malarial infection which he contracted in 1242 and from which he never entirely recovered, he suffered occasional attacks of erysipelas (a feverish and acute disease often attacking the face, producing an intense reddish inflammation of the skin and underlying tissues).

Although the Saint was a man who loved peace, when the need arose to redeem Christian lands from the heathen oppressors he did not shrink from battle and was a courageous participant.

For a description of St. Louis the soldier, and for a report of his gallantry, we turn again to his companion Joinville, who tells of what they both experienced while engaged in a Crusade against the Saracens. In describing the arrival of the King at a place of battle in Egypt, Joinville recorded:

> He came up with all his attendants in a clamor of trumpets. He halted on a rise of ground to say something to his men-at-arms, and I assure you, I never beheld so handsome a man under arms. He towered shoulder high above his company, and his gilded helm was crested with two fleur-de-lys, and in his hand he bore a long German sword. At the sight of him my knights and I, all wounded as we were, became impatient to join the battle again with him. An esquire brought up one of my Flemish war horses, and I was soon mounted and at the side of the King, whom I found attended by that experienced man, Sir John de Valeri. Sir John advised him—seeing that the King desired to enter the midst of the fighting...
>
> You must believe me when I say that the good King performed that day the most gallant deeds that I ever saw in any battle. Whenever he saw his men distressed he forced himself in and gave such blows with battle ax and sword, it was wonderful to behold.

St. Louis participated in this Crusade after a seemingly miraculous recovery from an illness that had caused him to be seriously feverish and comatose. Even though his French soldiers were supported by German troops and thousands of English knights, they faced an unexpected enemy. These formidable opponents were the summer heat, disease and famine. With sickness rendering many of the soldiers incapable of battle, Louis' brother Alphonse provided reinforcements of men and supplies. Another brother, Robert, also arrived on the scene.

When a difference of opinion arose as to the most advantageous route to attack, Louis decided to follow Robert's advice to attack Mansurah. This proved to be a tragic mistake. Upon arriving at the city, Robert disregarded Louis' orders to wait until his troops were reinforced. Thinking that he could surprise the enemy, Robert ordered his troops to enter the narrow streets of the city, where they were soon rendered helpless. Almost all of the 500 men were systematically cut down. St. Louis grieved over the rashness of his dead brother, which had cost the lives of so many valiant men.

The Crusade was now destined to failure. Although the campaign, for the most part, had been well-planned, with participants who were able and heroic, they had no defense against famine and disease. Thousands are said to have died in the fighting, thousands more from dysentery, and still more thousands of the sick were slain by the Egyptians.

Louis was forced to surrender and was taken prisoner. Butler relates:

> To the insults that were sometimes offered him, he opposed an air of majesty and authority which kept his guards in awe. When he was asked and refused to give up the captured castles in Syria, he was threatened with the most ignominious treatment and with torture—to which he coolly replied that they were masters of his body and might do with it what they please, the most important part, his soul, being the possession of God.

During his confinement he endured harshness, sickness, insults, frequent interrogations and chains. Yet, the Saint did not permit prison conditions to diminish his religious fervor, and he continued the recitation of his usual prayers and practiced his customary devotions.

At least one historian claims that if it were not for the ransom that St. Louis was eventually able to produce, not one man would have lived to return to France.

Few saints, it is said, have made two mistakes on so grand a scale or so costly to human life as was this first Crusade of St. Louis and the one that followed 20 years later. Joinville claims that those persons "committed a deadly sin who encouraged his going on the second Crusade." Dahmus, in his biography of the Saint, reflects that, because of his frail health, the Saint was "imprudent in attempting his first Crusade, and suicidal in undertaking the second."

Nevertheless, the King once again went forth to free Christian lands from the heathen and was well-prepared with men and arms to do battle. After landing at Sardinia, rather than proceeding to Egypt, as his advisers had recommended, he was persuaded instead to sail for Tunis. Historians have given different reasons for this change in the King's plans. It is thought that the King was somehow tricked by the enemy into believing that the Moslem emir of Tunis was ready for conversion and that he would then join forces with the King to help in his lofty endeavors.

The Saint was grievously betrayed. Upon arriving at Carthage, the King found that the emir had deserted the city. From Carthage he crossed hot sands toward Tunis, as the emir had hoped he would. The emir saw no point in opposing the Christian troops, since the heat would do battle for him. Arriving as they did after a famine, the King's troops were met with insufficient water and food, unrelenting heat and various diseases. The King's son, John-Tristan, who was just approaching manhood, fell victim to the disease. Having been born at the time of the first Crusade, he died during the second Crusade, a victim of the same afflictions that troubled his companions. The Saint's grief on the death of his son was abbreviated by his own overwhelming sickness.

Before he died, the Saint prayed for his troops: "God have mercy on these, Thy people...lead them to safety in their own land..." He received the Last Sacraments and died at three in the afternoon of August 25, 1270.

It has never been said that St. Louis died a martyr, but since the Saint was attempting to free Christian lands from the occupation of the heathen, he nevertheless can be said to have sacrificed his life in defense of the Faith.

After a time his bones were taken by his son Philip to the Abbey Church of St. Denis in France. Unfortunately, the relics were later scattered during the Revolution.

Philip had also participated in the Crusade and had fallen ill with disease. But he recovered from his illness, and on the day of his father's death he was named to succeed to the throne of France. He was known as Philip the Hardy, and also as Philip the Bold.

The two Crusades in which St. Louis took part were perhaps the only major failures he encountered; he was admirably successful in settling other skirmishes and disputes and in maintaining peace in his realm. Perhaps his greatest accomplishment was winning the respect, admiration and love of his people.

Considered a saint during his lifetime, King Louis was canonized by Pope Boniface VIII in 1297. The feast day of St. Louis is observed each year on the anniversary of his death, August 25. This day is particularly observed by tertiaries of the Franciscan Third Order since he, along with St. Elizabeth of Hungary, is the patron saint of that lay institute.

Left: The young St. Louis IX (1215-1270), King of France, crowned at age 11, learned early of the sufferings of the poor. *(V. H. Lesur.)*

Right: Seated at the center of this painting is St. Louis' mother, Blanche of Castile, who told him in his youth, "I love you, my dear son, as much as a mother can love her child; but I would rather see you dead at my feet than that you should ever commit a mortal sin." Louis made this attitude his own; he stated to his companion Joinville (who disagreed with him) that leprosy was preferable to committing a mortal sin. *(A. Cabanel.)*

Left: This painting depicts St. Louis when he was engaged in the Crusades in Palestine. During the second campaign in which he fought, both he and one of his sons (Louis had 11 children) fell to illnesses contracted from the hardships of unrelenting heat, disease, and lack of food and water. *(A. Cabanel.)*

Right: St. Louis ruled his subjects ably and settled numerous disputes among them. His many virtues included outstanding generosity to the poor. He even went so far as to wait upon the needy at his own table, cutting the meat for those unable to do so and giving his guests money when they left. He particularly delighted in helping the blind, since they could not recognize their benefactor, and he even personally cared for lepers, the most wretched members of medieval society. *(A. Cabanel.)*

419

An enlarged detail of a statuette of St. Louis IX, King of France. Louis was considered a saint in his own lifetime and was canonized 27 years after his death. St. Louis' relics were scattered during the French Revolution.

Chapter 128

BL. LOUIS MORBIOLI

1433 - 1495

From the biography of this beatus written by a Carmelite Friar, Fr. Baptist, only a few years after Louis' death, we learn that Louis Morbioli was born to a bourgeois family of Bologna, Italy in 1433. He is said to have been a handsome young man who married at an early age. But even though married, he led a careless and, at times, a sinful life. Fr. Baptist recorded that Louis was given to avarice, ambition and sensuality. Another biographer tells that as a young man, Louis "was notorious for his loose living, even after he had contracted marriage." He was regarded as a scandal by his neighbors and all who knew him.

In 1462, while he was visiting the monastery of the canons regular of St. Saviour at Venice, Louis became so seriously ill that his life was threatened. During his convalescence, the counsels given him by the monks led to Louis' complete conversion. This interior change was immediately noticed by the people of Bologna. Formerly a man of fashion, Louis now wore the same plain garments summer and winter, and he no longer curled and trimmed his hair.

After Louis had made arrangements to provide for his wife, she agreed to a separation so that he could perform penances for his past sins and minister to the poor and sick. He then began to go from place to place, preaching the word of God. He begged alms for the poor and taught Christian doctrine to the young and un-schooled. During his leisure time, Louis carved religious figures out of bone and wood.

During the last years of his life, Louis lived below the staircase of a mansion in Bologna. When he took seriously ill, he refused the attentions of a physician and asked instead for the Holy Sacra-ments, which he received with the greatest devotion.

Louis died on November 9, 1495. Burial was in the cemetery of the cathedral, but because of the number of miracles attributed to his intercession, his body was transferred to a tomb within the cathedral. Unfortunately, 100 years later, during alterations and the rebuilding of the cathedral, his grave was lost and has never been recovered.

His cultus was confirmed by Pope Gregory XVI in 1842. The Carmelites claim that Louis became a tertiary of their order after his conversion. Bl. Louis Morbioli is still venerated by this order and the people of the Diocese of Bologna.

Chapter 129

BL. LOUIS OF THURINGIA

1200 - 1227

When Louis of Thuringia was 11 years old, he was betrothed to Elizabeth of Hungary, the daughter of King Andrew II. Elizabeth at the time was four years old, and according to the custom among ruling families, the child was taken to the castle of her intended husband to be educated in the traditions and culture of her adopted land. Louis was 16 years of age when he succeeded his father, Landgrave Hermann I. Five years later, in 1221, his marriage to Elizabeth was ratified. Louis was 21 years old and Elizabeth 14. The arranged marriage had been one of political expediency, but it proved to be also a marriage of virtuous souls and one of the happiest marriages recorded in the annals of the Saints. The couple became the parents of three children, one of whom was Bl. Gertrude of Altenburg.

In his biography of St. Elizabeth, Count de Montalembert gives us a description of Bl. Louis:

> The nobility and purity of his soul were manifested in his exterior. His manly beauty was celebrated by his contemporaries. All boast of the perfect proportion of his figure, the freshness of his complexion, his long fair hair, and the serene, benevolent expression of his countenance. Many imagined they saw in him a striking resemblance to the portrait which tradition has preserved of the Son of God made man. The charm of his smile was irresistible. His deportment was noble and dignified—the tone of his voice extremely sweet. No one could see him without loving him. What particularly distinguished him was an unstained purity of soul.

This purity was tested on two occasions, which contemporary writers have related in some detail. The first incident occurred when a certain knight wanted to put Louis' innocence to the test and found

423

in the neighboring village a young girl of remarkable beauty. He brought her to Louis' chamber in the castle; Louis, after answering the knock at his door, was bewildered when the girl entered. When Louis asked the purpose of her visit, the knight replied that he had brought her so that Louis might do with her what he pleased. At these words Louis took the knight aside, ordered him to restore the girl to her family and warned that if any harm came to her, the knight would be hanged. The narrator of this incident stated that he concealed the name of this false knight to avoid giving scandal.

At another time Louis was standing at a window, looking down upon a square where the people were dancing. An attendant pointed out to him the wife of one of the citizens, who was remarkable for her beauty and grace. The attendant offered to make her available to Louis. Upon hearing this proposal, Louis was so shocked that he turned to the servant and said, "Be silent. If ever again thou darest to sully my ears by such language, I will drive thee from my court!"

Holy Mass was celebrated every day in the presence of Louis and his family, and it was with exemplary devotion that he assisted. He was a zealous defender of the rights of the Church, the monasteries and the poor. As an example of this, we are told about some Thuringian citizens who were robbed and beaten in Poland. Louis demanded reparation, but when none was forthcoming he led his troops into Poland and gained satisfaction by force of battle. The same crime then occurred at Wurtzburg. Once again Louis marched, this time to recover stock that had been stolen from a trader. It is claimed that "no sovereign of his time surpassed him in courage, nor even in physical strength and agility in the exercises of the body." He had what was called a "vehement passion for justice" and is known to have sufficiently punished violators of the law. He banished from his court those who were unkind to the poor and those who brought him false and malicious tales. Blasphemers and those who spoke "impure words" were condemned to wear a mark of shame in public. He is also known to have been cheerful and kind to his subjects and never to have offended anyone by pride or coldness.

In his association with his wife he was most loving and thoughtful, displaying, even in the presence of others, a tenderness which was well-recorded by contemporary writers. (See the chapter on St. Elizabeth of Hungary.) Louis in every way approved of, and encouraged, the charity and devotions of his wife. Once he found in his bed a leper who had asked for relief at the door of the castle. For a moment Louis was tempted to anger, but then he saw not the leper, but the crucified Son of God. As a result of this episode, he paid for the building of a lazar house on the slope of the Wartburg.

At the request of the Emperor, Louis spent several months at court assisting the Emperor in restoring peace between Bologna and the cities of Lombardy. Friar Berthold tells that when Louis returned home, Elizabeth, "a thousand times and more, kissed him with her heart and with her mouth." When Louis inquired how his people had fared during his long absence, Elizabeth replied, "I gave to God what was His, and God has kept for us what was ours." To a complaining treasurer, Louis replied, "Let her do good and give to God whatever she will, so long as she leaves me Wartburg and Neuenburg."

During the following year Louis volunteered to follow Emperor Frederick II on the Sixth Crusade. He made his brother Henry regent and turned his energies to enlisting crusaders. To arouse men's hearts to this endeavor he had a Passion Play presented in the streets of Eisenach, and he visited the monasteries of his domain asking for prayers. On the Feast of St. John the Baptist he parted from Elizabeth and set out toward the Holy Sepulchre. When the troops reached Otranto, Louis contracted the plague (or malarial fever) and became so seriously ill that the Last Sacraments were administered. The illness was to be mortal. Before Louis died it seemed to him that the cabin in which he lay was full of doves. "I must fly away with those white doves," he said, and then died. The year was 1227. He was only 27 years of age. When news of his death reached Elizabeth, she cried, "The world is dead to me, and all that was pleasant in it!"

Bl. Louis' final resting place was in the Benedictine Abbey of Reinhardsbrunn, which he had often visited, and where he is popularly called "St. Ludwig."

The character and life of Bl. Louis are summed up in the noble motto which he had chosen from his earliest years: "Piety, chastity, justice towards all."

Chapter 130

ST. LUCHESIUS

d. 1260

As a young man, Luchesius took little interest in religion; rather he was wholly occupied in worldly interests—especially money-making and politics. He made himself so unpopular by his violent partisanship of the Guelph cause in the long drawn-out dispute between the Guelph and Ghibelline parties that he found it advisable to take his family and leave Gaggiano, his native place, and to settle at Poggibonsi. There he carried on a lucrative business as a greedy merchant and grain speculator.

For some time all seemed well in the new location for Luchesius and for his wife, Buona (Bonadonna) dei Segni, and their little children. But when Luchesius was between 30 and 40 years old, he underwent great sorrow when his children died. Touched by divine grace during his period of mourning, Luchesius completely changed his life. He became deeply committed to his faith, engaged in works of mercy, visited the sick and aided prisoners. He felt that he could no longer enrich himself, as he had done in the past, by buying corn and other food items when they were cheap in order to sell them at a great profit in times of scarcity and need. His business now seemed to him to be incompatible with the lessons in Holy Scripture. To become more observant of Our Lord's teachings, Luchesius and his wife gave to the poor all their possessions, except a piece of land that Luchesius wanted to cultivate by his own labor.

When St. Francis of Assisi visited Poggibonsi in the year 1221, great crowds gathered to hear his words. Among the group were Luchesius and his wife. St. Francis had either just formed his Third Order for laymen, or was in the process of forming it, when both Luchesius and his wife were accepted as members. It is a matter of dispute whether or not they were the very first members of the Franciscan Third Order. This is an organization formed for those desiring to live a spiritual life in the world under the influence of the Franciscan Order.

After becoming Franciscan tertiaries, the pious couple surrendered themselves to a most penitential and charitable life. Sometimes Luchesius would distribute to the poor every scrap of food that was in the house. Because they were already impoverished, Buona would gently speak against such extreme generosity since she was not then her husband's equal in his perfect trust in Divine Providence. But experience taught her that God supplies His faithful with all their necessities.

By virtue of his fasting, almsgiving and prayers, Luchesius attained to great sanctity and was rewarded with ecstasies, levitations and the gift of healing. When it became evident that he had not long to live, his wife begged him to wait a little so that she, who had shared his sufferings, might also share in his joy. Buona's prayers were answered. She died shortly before her husband; some believe they died on the same day, April 28, 1260.

St. Luchesius first gained papal attention when Gregory X approved his cult in 1273 during a visit to Poggibonsi; Buona's cult was confirmed in 1694. A basilica that was built over the tomb of St. Luchesius about the year 1300 was almost completely destroyed by Allied bombing in 1944, but it has since been rebuilt.

Chapter 131

STS. LUCIAN AND MARCIAN

d. c. 250

The history of these martyrs is preserved to us in both Latin and in Syriac; the Greek text, which is probably the original, has been lost.

We are told that both Lucian and Marcian applied themselves to the study and practice of black magic. When they attempted to effect their charms on a Christian maiden, the evil spirits were defeated by the Sign of the Cross. This inability to apply their black magic is said to have converted them. Having received the gift of faith, they publicly burned their books of black magic and devilish materials in the City of Nicomedia.

After receiving Baptism, Lucian and Marcian distributed their possessions among the poor and retired into solitude to practice mortification and prayer. Later they made frequent journeys to preach Christ to the Gentiles in order to gain souls for the Kingdom of Heaven. But after the edicts of Decius against the Christians were published in 250, the two were apprehended and brought before the Proconsul Sabinus, who asked Lucian by what authority he presumed to preach Jesus Christ. Lucian replied, "Every man does well to endeavor to draw his brother out of a dangerous error." When Marcian concurred in this statement, the judge commanded that Lucian and Marcian be cruelly tortured. To this they remarked that while they had worshiped idols and had committed many crimes and had made open profession of practicing black magic without incurring any difficulty, they were being punished for being good Christian citizens. At this, Sabinus condemned them to be burned alive.

The two went joyfully to the place of execution, singing hymns of praise and thanksgiving to God. "We are ready to suffer," they said, "but we will not renounce the true God, lest we be cast into a fire which will never be quenched." Lucian and Marcian were martyred in Nicomedia around the year 250.

Chapter 132

ST. LUDMILA

c. 860 - 921

Ludmila was the daughter of a Slavic prince. She was also the wife of Borivoj, Duke of Bohemia. When her husband was baptized in 871 by St. Methodius, the Apostle of the Slavs, Ludmila also became a Christian. Together she and her husband built the first Christian church in Bohemia, at Levy Hradec, to the north of Prague, where Borivoj had a castle.

The two Christians met with considerable displeasure from the leading families of the area, who were opposed to Christianity. Borivoj tried to remedy the situation by forcing Christianity on his subjects, but this led to an uprising which forced him and Ludmila to seek protection in Moravia; there they remained until the leader of the rebels was assassinated.

Borivoj died when he was only 35 and was succeeded within a few years by his Christian sons, Sphytihnev and Ratislav. Ratislav had married a Slavic princess, Drahomira, who was a Christian in name only. When a son, Wenceslas, was born to Ratislav and Drahomira, the widowed Ludmila—then living in retirement at Prague—was entrusted with his upbringing. She was then about 50 years old, a woman of great virtue and learning.

It was to Ludmila's great care and instructions in the Faith that Wenceslas owed the foundation of his sanctity. Joining her in the instruction of Wenceslas was Ludmila's chaplain, Paul, who had been a disciple of St. Methodius. By the time he was ready to attend college at Budec, Wenceslas "understood Latin books as if he were a bishop and read Slavonic with ease."

The early death of the boy's father placed his mother, Drahomira, in the office of regent and made it necessary to remove Wenceslas from Ludmila's immediate charge. Drahomira sympathized with the anti-Christian party in Bohemia and was a forceful and ambitious

429

woman. Upon learning of her son's Baptism in the Christian Faith and the great influence exerted over Wenceslas by Ludmila and the Catholic priest Paul, Drahomira became exceedingly angry and envious of her mother-in-law.

Afraid that Wenceslas might seize the government before his time and promote the spread of Christianity in Bohemia, Drahomira and the anti-Christians made every effort to keep Wenceslas away from his grandmother's influence. To make certain of this, it is said that Drahomira sent two noblemen to the holy Ludmila; they strangled her with her own veil on September 15, 921.

Ludmila's body was buried in the Church of St. Michael at Tetin, but three years later, St. Wenceslas removed it with great ceremony to St. George's Church at Prague. There St. Ludmila is greatly venerated, as she is throughout Czechoslovakia.

Ludmila's death was not the only crime placed against her daughter-in-law Drahomira, since Drahomira later instigated the death of her own son Wenceslas. The murderer was Drahomira's other son, Boleslas, who hacked his brother's body to pieces.

Wenceslas is the subject of the popular Christmas carol, *"Good King Wenceslas."*

Chapter 133

ST. LUFTHILD

d. c. 850

The few facts given us about the life of St. Lufthild reveal that in her youth she suffered grievously at the hands of a very cruel stepmother, who was often enraged by the child's generosity and love of the poor. Eventually Lufthild left home, or was driven from it by her stepmother. The future Saint lived as best she could on her own and eventually became a recluse, consecrating all her time to God in contemplation and the practice of penance.

After Lufthild's death, devotion to her was immediately enkindled by virtue of the many miracles worked at her tomb. In the years 1623 and again in 1901, her tomb in Cologne was opened for recognition of the relics.

In the *Acta Sanctorum,* under January 23, the Bollandists record that Lufthild inspired considerable devotion, which is evidenced by the many places named in her honor.

Chapter 134

ST. LYDWINE OF SCHIEDAM

1380 - 1433

The only girl in a family of nine children, Lydwine was born in the Netherlands, at Schiedam, near The Hague, in the year 1380. Her father, Pierre, was the town watchman by trade; her mother, Petronille, came from Ketel, a village in the neighborhood of Schiedam. Both parents were exemplary Christians who were faithful to their religious duties.

Unaware that she was soon to deliver, Lydwine's mother was attending High Mass one Palm Sunday when the pains of childbirth came upon her so quickly that she was forced to hurry home. It is said that her only daughter was born at the moment when the Passion of Our Saviour was being read in the church.

At her Baptism, the child was given the name Lydwine, which has various spellings, all of which are derived from the Flemish word "lyden," meaning to suffer. One of her biographers, the lay brother of the Observants, John Brugman, claims that the name signifies "great patience" in the German tongue. The Saint's early biographers, Thomas à Kempis, John Gerlac and John Brugman, all of whom were her contemporaries, observe that both her name and the moment of the day on which she was born were prophetic, since her life was one of sufferings in union with the Passion of the Saviour.

At the age of seven, Lydwine assisted her mother with the housework—which was considerable in a household of eleven people. As Lydwine grew older, she became a clever housekeeper, and at the age of 12 she was a serious girl who cared little for the games or amusements of her friends and neighbors. At the age of 15 there seems to have been nothing to distinguish Lydwine from other lively, healthy and pretty girls of her age, except that she was unusually pious. Since she had taken a vow of chastity, she was obliged to reject several offers of marriage.

Toward the end of her fifteenth year, while recovering from an illness, Lydwine was persuaded by friends to join them in skating the canals that had frozen hard in the bitter winter of 1395-1396. Although she offered the poor state of her health as an excuse, they insisted that the exercise and fresh air would be beneficial. When her father agreed with them and gave his consent, Lydwine relented.

On reaching the canal near her home, Lydwine and her companions were just beginning to skate when a friend, who was late, hurried to overtake them. She fell against Lydwine, causing the future Saint to fall against a piece of ice with such force that one of the ribs on her right side was broken.

The accident became known throughout the town, bringing many who offered advice on how to heal the fracture and reduce the pain. In spite of the family's poverty, renowned physicians of the Low Countries were called in. Their prescribed medicines may only have worsened the condition. A hard abscess soon developed, and as the physicians and others could not cure Lydwine's infirmities, they gradually abandoned her.

Lydwine's pain was so intolerable that she could find no relief either lying, sitting or standing. One day when she could bear the pain no longer, she threw herself from her couch and fell upon the knees of her father, who had been weeping as he sat by her side. This fall broke the abscess; but instead of releasing the infection externally, the abscess opened internally, forcing the infected matter to pour from Lydwine's mouth. These vomitings shook her whole body and so quickly filled the vessels used to catch the outpourings that those who attended Lydwine had little time to empty them before they were filled once more.

Finally, being unable to stand, yet feeling a constant urge to change her position, Lydwine undertook to drag herself around on her knees—a practice that she continued for three years. When Lydwine became unable to move even in this fashion, she was confined to bed for what would be the rest of her life.

The wound under the rib gradually swelled and developed a gangrenous condition. Horrible as it is to consider, the putrefaction bred worms that developed in three large ulcers. Various remedies were attempted, but these only caused the patient additional discomfort. A tumor then appeared on St. Lydwine's shoulder; this too putrefied, causing almost unbearable neuritis. (This affliction is thought to have been the dreaded "plague" of the Middle Ages.) The disease also affected Lydwine's right arm, consuming the flesh to the bone. From this time onward the arm was useless and prevented the Saint from turning on her side. Violent neuralgic pains then began, along with a pounding noise in her head.

The once-beautiful girl, who had attracted many potential suitors, was now becoming a pitiful sight. Her forehead became cleft from the hairline to the center of the nose. Her chin dropped under the lower lip and her mouth swelled. Her right eye became blind and the other became extremely sensitive to light. She suffered violent toothaches, which raged sometimes for weeks. A severe inflammation of the throat nearly suffocated her and caused bleeding from the nose, mouth and ears. St. Lydwine's nose was then invaded by sores, her lungs and liver decayed, and a cancer devoured her flesh. When the pestilence ravaged Holland, Lydwine was one of the first victims, becoming afflicted with two additional abscesses.

St. Lydwine's sad condition would have been life-threatening in the extreme, had not God supported her whom He had chosen as a victim soul. At the beginning of her sufferings the Saint complained of her condition—until she came to realize, with the help of her confessor, John Pot, and others, that her sufferings were not only intended to expiate the sins of others, living and dead, but would also draw down great benefits for the Church. She then accepted her trials willingly and patiently, and even said that if a single Hail Mary could gain her recovery, she would not utter it.

Added to these ailments was that of dropsy, with its swelling of the body—which gradually developed so alarmingly that Lydwine's stomach ruptured and had to be held together with wrappings. A cushion placed atop her stomach was required in order to press back her organs. Each time the position of the Saint was changed, it was necessary to bind her firmly with napkins and cloths—otherwise her body would literally have fallen to pieces.

The supernatural origin of the Saint's condition is proved by her extraordinary fast and her sleep patterns. During the last 19 years of her life, St. Lydwine underwent a complete fast. According to the sworn deposition of witnesses, this fast was only interrupted for the reception of the Holy Eucharist. During the 11 years preceding this complete fast, the Saint ate only as much as a healthy person consumed in three days. Those who attended St. Lydwine also testified that during the last seven years of her life she experienced a perpetual insomnia, and that in the entire 23 years previous to this seven-year period, the Saint had slept the equivalent of only three good nights.

Because of this lack of nourishment and sleep, the Saint became an object of curiosity and was visited and questioned by countless people—a situation that only added to her trials.

St. Lydwine was spared one trial, however. She was never misunderstood or neglected by her family. Fortunately, in their simple piety, they recognized her sanctity. The poor body of the invalid, so invaded by disease, infection, sores and revolting openings, did not disgust them. In fact, they were aware, as were all others who came near Lydwine, that a sweet perfume came from these sickened areas.

Certain mystical phenomena became evident during her lifetime: she began to heal the sick, to see events at a distance, and she could describe places she had never visited. She began to prophesy, to bilocate and to read hearts. About the year 1407, St. Lydwine began to be favored with ecstasies and visions of angels, the Blessed Mother, the Holy Child, various saints—including St. Paul and St. Francis of Assisi—and the suffering Saviour. Finally she received the stigmata, a phenomenon which she prayed would be hidden. "Marvelous to relate," says Michel d'Esne, Bishop of Tournai, "a little skin immediately covered these wounds, but the pain and bruise remained." In accordance with her prayer, the pain of these divine wounds lasted to the end of her life.

The Saint was subject to fits of epilepsy and apoplexy in her final years. Violent toothaches never left her, and a new ulcer developed in the breast. Finally she suffered nerve contractions that contorted her limbs.

From the time of her first injury on the ice until the day of her death, the sufferings endured by the victim soul lasted for 38 years.

The Saint died on Easter Tuesday in the year 1433, at about three in the afternoon. Soon after her death, the body of St. Lydwine was miraculously transformed. Her wounds were healed, the cleft in the forehead that had so long disfigured her disappeared, and she seemed as lovely as a girl of 17 who was smiling in her sleep. Around the body wafted a heavenly scent that was detected by many who came to pay their respects.

In the special office for her feast, St. Lydwine is described as "a prodigy of human misery and of heroic patience." Benedict XIV also recognized the Saint's extraordinary sufferings in his Decree of Beatification when he wrote, "It seemed as if a whole army of diseases had invaded her body." He likened Lydwine to Lazarus, Job and Tobias, "the models of patience God has set before the sick and afflicted of all times."

St. Alphonsus Liguori, in one of his spiritual treatises, refers to the Saint in this way:

> Let it, then, be your endeavor, during the remainder of your life, to love and have confidence in Him; and do not become sad when you find yourself in afflictions and tribulations; for this is a sign, not of His hatred, but of the love which God bears toward you. And therefore, in reference to this point, I will here cite for you the example of the virgin St. Lydwine; and I know not whether there is to be met with among the annals of the Saints an instance of any other soul suffering so great affliction and desolation as did this holy virgin.

In Schiedam there are many places that remind one of the city's Patron Saint. A street, a square and a school bear her name. There is St. Lydwine's Chapel, and the parish church at the Singel bears her name. There is also at Schiedam the St. Lydwine Committee, which receives and answers correspondence from around the world from those who request more information about the Saint.

The feast day of St. Lydwine is observed in the Netherlands on June 14.

Steens N.V., Schiedam

St. Lydwine of Schiedam (1380-1433) broke a rib when ice skating with friends when she was 15 years old. For the rest of her life, the Saint was "a prodigy of human misery and heroic patience." She lived a life of mystical suffering and expiation as a victim soul. *(Drawing by H. Levigne.)*

St. Lydwine, who was remembered by St. Alphonsus Liguori in these words: "I know not whether there is to be met with among the annals of the Saints an instance of any other soul suffering so great affliction and desolation as did this holy virgin." Lydwine's body underwent such ruptures, cancer, infection, decay, abscesses, sores and openings that it was necessary to bind her members with cloths when her position was changed, lest her body literally fall to pieces. Yet a sweet fragrance came from her afflicted members. (*Statue by P. M. Kersten.*)

437

SINT
LIDUINA

BID
VOOR
ONS

A prayer card from the Netherlands pictures St. Lydwine, who for 38 years endured bodily torment of unparalleled proportions. For 19 years she ate nothing but the Holy Eucharist; for her last seven years she suffered perpetual insomnia. She received the stigmata and other mystical favors. After her death her body healed, leaving her as lovely as a girl of 17 years.

Chapter 135

ST. MACRINA THE ELDER

d. c. 340

When Maximian was waging a fierce persecution against the Christians, Macrina and her husband were forced to leave their home. For a period of seven years they endured many privations while hiding in the forests of Pontus, near the Black Sea. After the danger passed, they returned to their home—but when another persecution erupted, they again suffered when their revenues, vast landholdings and personal possessions were confiscated. We can well imagine that St. Macrina accepted her sacrifice and loss of property with a good heart, willingly offering her privations in union with those suffered by her Saviour.

St. Macrina advanced rapidly in the spiritual life through her friendship with St. Gregory Thaumaturgus, who was the first bishop of her native town, Neocaesarea. She was the mother of at least one son, who became the father of four children who are now Saints of the Church: Basil, who was later to be known as St. Basil the Great (329-379), Father and Doctor of the Church; St. Gregory of Nyssa, who was the Bishop of Nyssa and Archbishop of Sebaste, and who is also regarded as a Father of the Church; St. Peter, who also served as Bishop of Sebaste; and St. Macrina the Younger, who was the superior of one of the earliest communities of women ascetics.

It is from the writings of St. Basil that we learn something of the virtues of the saintly grandmother who implanted in the minds of these children the seeds of piety and the desire for Christian perfection which was later to raise them to the glory of sainthood. In one of his many letters, St. Basil honors and praises his grandmother in this manner:

> What clearer proof of our faith could there be than that we
> were brought up by our grandmother, a blessed mother, who

came from among you? I have reference to the illustrious Macrina, by whom we were taught the words of the most blessed Gregory [Thaumaturgus], which, having been preserved until her time by uninterrupted tradition, she also guarded, and she formed and molded me, still a child, to the doctrines of piety.

St. Basil is apparently paying tribute to the fact that the religious instruction he received from his grandmother was so sound that he never afterward had to modify it. With reference to this he wrote:

> ...For, even if other matters are deserving of our groans, yet of this one thing at least I dare to boast in the Lord, that never have I held false opinions concerning God, nor did I, thinking otherwise than now, learn differently later. But the concept of God which in childhood I received from my blessed mother and from grandmother Macrina, this unfolding more completely, I have held within me, for on arriving at full reason I did not exchange one teaching for another, but confirmed those principles which they had handed over to me.

St. Macrina survived her husband, but the exact date of her death is not recorded; she is thought to have died about the year 340.

Chapter 136

ST. MAMMAS

d. 275

When the Christian couple, Theodotus and Rufina, were in prison awaiting martyrdom, Rufina gave birth to the future St. Mammas. After the heroic couple's execution, a Christian widow named Amya was favored with a vision of an angel who suggested to her that she should take care of an orphaned infant, who would be found in prison. The good woman found the child Mammas, arranged for legal possession, and raised the boy as her own, instilling in him a great love for the Christian Faith. Her efforts were rewarded when Mammas was 12 years old. At that early age he zealously began to make converts to the Faith. Meanwhile Amya died, leaving Mammas heir to certain monies, which he quickly distributed among the poor.

The success of Mammas in winning many converts to the Faith was brought to the attention of Democritus, the governor of the territory. In consideration of Mammas' youth, the governor asked him to sacrifice at the temple of Jove, promising that if he did so, "I will not fail to use my interest with the emperor for your advancement." The Saint strenuously resisted. Seeing that he could not weaken Mammas by reasoning, Democritus presented the matter to Emperor Aurelian, who commanded that Mammas be brought to him. While standing before Aurelian, the Saint was tempted by the Emperor with these words: "I wish, my son, to employ you at court, but you must therefore abandon the Christian Faith. Choose, then, a happy life at my palace or an ignominious death upon the scaffold."

To this St. Mammas replied:

> The choice, O prince, is already made. You propose to me a death which shall render me forever happy, or a short life that must make me eternally miserable. Your gods, which are but deaf and blind statues, can confer no favor upon me. I adore

the one only true God, and for Him I am most willing to lay down my life.

This profession of faith so infuriated the Emperor that he commanded that the Saint's flesh be torn with scourges. Mammas endured this torment with commendable patience. The Emperor, who appeared moved by the horrible injuries inflicted upon the tender body of the youth, said in a tone of entreaty, "Mammas, merely say with your mouth that you will sacrifice." But Mammas replied, "It would displease my God were I to deny Him. Continue to torture me as long as it pleases you. . ." The refusal so exasperated Aurelian that he commanded guards to burn the Saint with torches. When the guards attempted to apply the fire, they were themselves burned, while the Saint remained unhurt.

Aurelian then ordered that Mammas should be thrown into the sea. The hagiography of the Saint tells that while he was being led to the water an angel appeared and put the guards to flight. Mammas took refuge on a mountain in the neighborhood of Caesarea and lived in solitude for 40 days.

A new governor was appointed in the meantime. When he learned that a Christian, condemned by the Emperor, was living on the mountain, he sent a troop of soldiers to seize him. When Mammas was brought before the Governor, the latter said to the Saint, "You are a rash person, opposing, as you do, the edicts of the Emperor; but torments shall alter you." Mammas was subsequently stretched on the rack, but when he displayed considerable fortitude the governor ordered him to be burned alive. The fire, however, is said to have touched not a hair of his head, but merely to have burned the ropes that bound him. St. Mammas was at last put to the sword. Though still a youth, he nevertheless died a martyr's death, as had his parents.

During the reign of Constantine, a church was built over the tomb of St. Mammas in Caesarea. Although some sources claim that the Saint was of noble birth, St. Gregory Nazianzen, relying on other sources, concluded one of his sermons with an allusion to the Saint in which he called him "the renowned Mammas, a shepherd and a martyr." St. Basil too mentioned the humble beginnings of the Saint in a homily which was intended to illustrate that poverty and humility constitute real glory.

Chapter 137

BL. MARCEL CALLO

1921 - 1945

On the feast of the Immaculate Conception, December 8, 1921, Marcel Callo, who was two days old, was baptized in the church of Notre-Dame de Bonne Nouvelle at Rennes, France.

Marcel's father was an employee of the Bridge and Streets Department of the city, but because of the responsibilities of raising nine children, it was difficult at times for Marcel's parents to provide all that was necessary for them.

While Marcel was still a child he was described as having been a leader, always happy, frank and open. He liked to organize and to express and defend his ideas, but when he was not pleased he would show his displeasure by a movement of the shoulder. Something of a perfectionist, Marcel liked everything to be in order, but he understood that he had to make concessions since he was not always correct.

As an older child of the family, Marcel was expected to help in the care and management of the household. He willingly helped his mother by washing the dishes, straightening the house, and by helping to wash and dress his younger brothers and sisters. Everything was easy for him, and he did his chores with care and in good spirits.

Marcel attended St. Anne School at Rennes and received a certificate after completing his primary studies. At the age of almost 13 he was apprenticed to a printer. He was proud not only to support himself, but also to help in the support of his family. Like all the young people in the area, he gave all his salary to his mother, who in turn gave him what he needed for his expenses. He loved his trade and was proud to work with his hands. He once wrote that, "Work assures us of the necessities of our existence and is for us a source of merit for the other life."

At least one difficulty arose during his apprenticeship, that of his

443

fellow workers telling improper stories and using vulgar language. For this reason Marcel preferred the company of his comrades in an organization known as the JOC, *Jeunesse Ouvriere Chretienne* (Young Christian Workers). His friends in this organization corresponded more to his ideals and behavior. Under the inspiration of Pere Cardijn and Pere Guerin, who were its founders, the JOC provided instruction in the Catholic Faith, good fellowship and wholesome activities.

His friends in the JOC later described Marcel as having been "dynamic, very cheerful...he knew how to laugh and how to make people laugh. He was an excellent friend." Another friend said, "Marcel possessed a joyful character, always happy and always very Christian." Another reported, "I always thought he had a good sense of humor. He was alive, dynamic and had the stuff of a leader." These friends also revealed that Marcel liked to wrestle, play football, ping pong, cards and bridge.

In 1941, when Marcel was 20 years old, he met and fell in love with Marguerite Derniaux. Unlike his fellow workers who tended to degrade women, Marcel preferred the ideal behavior of his JOC friends. As he once said,

> I am not one to amuse myself with the heart of a lady, since my love is pure and noble. If I have waited until I was 20 years old to go out with a young lady, it is because I knew that I wanted to find real love. One must master his heart before he can give it to the one that is chosen for him by Christ.

It was almost a year later, in August of 1942, that Marcel declared his love, and it was four months later that he "suffered the embarrassment" of their first kiss. As his fiancée later wrote, "That day I was celebrating the completion of the training for my work. After Mass he kissed me for the first time. He had wanted to delay this gesture in order to thank God that we knew each other."

Four months later, they imposed on one another a rule for the spiritual life. This included the recitation of the same prayers, the frequent assistance at Holy Mass and the reception of the Holy Eucharist.

Marcel's orderly life of work and prayer was interrupted on March 8, 1943, when World War II touched the City of Rennes. On that day the city suffered a terrible bombardment. The train station and the streets around it were destroyed. Since Marcel worked close by, he and his worker friends went about helping those who were injured. When he noticed that the place where his sister, Madeleine, worked was leveled, Marcel dug under the debris and eventually discovered her body. It is reported that he fought the pain of his sorrow to tell his parents and family the terrible news.

What he feared for a long time eventually presented itself in the form of an order to report to the S.T.O., *Service du Travail Obligatoire* (Service of Obligatory Work) in Germany. With France occupied by the Germans, young men were forced to report for work in Germany. Failure to do so would result in the arrest of a man's family.

Because of the recent death of his sister, Marcel delayed in telling his family of his imminent departure. An aunt to whom he confided his secret told him that she knew he would greatly benefit his friends. To this Marcel responded, "Yes, Aunt, I will do everything possible to do well because you know that it is not as a worker that I leave, but as a missionary."

Eleven days after his sister's death, Marcel left on a five-day trip to Zella-Mehlis, Germany. There he reported to a factory that made rockets which would be used against the French people. Although Marcel lived in a barracks and was forced to work, he and his companions were not considered to be prisoners. They had the freedom to come and go, and could participate in various activities.

Being far from his family, Marcel missed the first Mass of his newly ordained brother and the First Holy Communion of his little sister. Probably as a result of homesickness, Marcel suffered for three months from discouragement and had to fight against a terrible depression. During this time Marcel wrote that in Zella-Mehlis there was no Catholic church, but he was able to find a room where Holy Mass was offered on Sundays. This, he said, was a great comfort to him. In writing to his family he described his feelings and his need for consolation, and reported that, "Finally Christ reacted. He made me to understand that the depression was not good. I had to keep busy with my friends and then joy and relief would come back to me."

Marcel began almost at once to restore good morale and hope among his deported friends. He organized a team of his Christian workers and had matches of bridge, cards, sports and other activities. He also organized a theatrical group which performed small plays. Around this time he wrote, "I believe I am still in Rennes in full activity. I give much and I receive much in return. When I do good things for others I am satisfied."

He continued to organize these activities with a holy deliberation despite suffering from painful boils, headaches and infected teeth which he said often transformed his head into a balloon. He also endured these sufferings while working more than 11 hours a day.

For his French comrades, Marcel was able to arrange for a solemn Holy Mass to be celebrated in their language. In a letter home, Marcel wrote,

> We had our first French Mass this morning. The result is that I am happy...it was a successful beginning. What enthusiasm!...We sang with one voice and we chanted the Credo. For us it was magnificent...At the end I addressed a few words, then we prayed for all the ones we left in France and for all our friends working in Germany. All the people were very pleased...They came to congratulate us and asked us for a French Mass every month. I am very happy to arrive at that result.

Eventually, Marcel's religious activities were brought to the attention of the German officials. This prompted Marcel's arrest on April 19, 1944. While Marcel was being taken away, Joel Poutrel, one of Marcel's friends, demanded a reason for the arrest. The agent of the Gestapo responded, *"Monsieur est beaucoup trop catholique"*— "Monsieur is too much of a Catholic." Marcel appealed to his friend: "Please write to my parents and to my fiancée that I am arrested for Catholic action."

During his interrogation, Marcel admitted that he was engaged in Catholic activities and that he knew this was forbidden in Germany. He was taken to the prison in Gotha, where he continued his life of prayer and his concern for his companions. It is believed that Marcel received his last Holy Communion during his stay at Gotha. Consecrated Hosts were secretly brought into the prison and were confided to a JOC friend, Henri Choteau, who kept them in a box for distribution. In a small journal that Marcel kept in prison he wrote, "16 July...Communion...immense joy."

After he was officially accused of participating in Catholic activities among his French friends, an activity regarded as harmful to the German people, Marcel was moved on October 24 to the prison at Mathausen. He was to suffer there for five months. In spite of sickness, he inquired about the needs of his companions, and encouraged them by saying, "It is in prayer that we find our strength."

Marcel suffered from general weakness, fever, swelling, bronchitis, malnutrition and dysentery. It is said that he never complained and that he "expired softly like a lamb." He died on the feast of St. Joseph, March 19, 1945, exactly two years from the day he left France for Germany.

Before Marcel left France his fiancée had told him, "You will be a martyr." Marcel Callo had replied, "I will never be good enough for that." But apparently the Catholic Church thought otherwise, since Marcel was beatified by Pope John Paul II on October 4, 1987. Beatified during the same ceremony were two Italian martyrs, Antonio Mesina, who died in 1935, and Pierina Morosini, who died in 1957.

Bl. Marcel Callo (1921-1945), *bottom right,* and his friends in the JOC, or *Jeunesse Ouvriere Chretienne* (Young Christian Workers) at Rennes, France, in 1941-42. One fellow member said, "Marcel possessed a joyful character, always happy and always very Christian." Another said, "He was alive, dynamic, and had the stuff of a leader." It was at this time that Marcel fell in love with Marguerite Derniaux; he had waited until age 20 to go out with anyone "because I knew that I wanted to find real love. One must master his heart before he can give it to the one that is chosen for him by Christ."

This illustration of Bl. Marcel Callo is from a French postcard (*by artist Pierre Gilles*). The insignia of the JOC organization appears in the upper left corner; bottom left is a scene from Marcel's life at Rennes. At the right is a representation of his imprisonment by the Gestapo because of his Catholic activities which he carried out despite painful boils, headaches and infected teeth which "transformed his head into a balloon." Bl. Marcel fell ill and died in prison.

A photograph of Bl. Marcel Callo. He was beatified in 1987.
Before the devout young man left France for obligatory labor
in Germany (where he was forced to work in a factory that
made rockets to be used against the French people), his fiancée had said to him, "You will be a martyr."

Chapter 138

ST. MARCELLUS

d. 298

St. Marcellus was one of the martyrs who suffered before the outbreak of the great persecution of Diocletian in the year 303. The particulars of his passion are preserved in existing documents. A translation of Marcellus' *Acts* reads as follows:

> In the city of Tangier, during the administration of Fortunatus as governor, the time came for the birthday of the Emperor. When everyone was feasting and sacrificing, a certain Marcellus, one of the centurions of the Trajan legion, considering the banquet to be heathen, cast away his soldier's belt in front of the standards of the legion which were then in camp, and testified in a loud voice, saying: "I serve Jesus Christ, the Eternal King." He likewise cast away his vine switch [the distinctive badge of a centurion] and his weapons, adding, "Henceforward I cease to serve your emperors, and I scorn to worship your gods of wood and stone, which are deaf and dumb. If such be the terms of service, that men are forced to offer sacrifice to gods and emperors, behold, I cast away my vine switch and belt, and I renounce the standards and refuse to serve."
>
> Everyone was bewildered at hearing such things; they laid hold of him and reported the matter to Anastasius Fortunatus, the Commander of the legion, who ordered him to be cast into prison. When the feasting was over, he gave orders, sitting in council, that the centurion Marcellus should be brought in.

Fortunatus questioned Marcellus, but the Saint only replied that he rejected the gods and served only Jesus Christ, the Son of God. To this Fortunatus replied that he could not overlook such rash conduct, and he referred the matter to Aurelius Agricolan, Deputy for the Prefects of the Guard.

On October 30 at Tangier, Marcellus was brought into court before

Agricolan. The charges against him were outlined in a letter from Fortunatus, which was read aloud:

> From Fortunatus to you, my lord. This soldier, having cast away his soldier's belt, and having testified that he is a Christian, spoke in the presence of all the people many blasphemous things against the gods and against Caesar. We have therefore sent him on to you, that you may order such action to be taken as Your Eminence may ordain in regard to the same.

Agricolan then questioned Marcellus about his rank as centurion and his actions the night of the celebration. Assured that the charges against him were accurate, Agricolan gave his verdict:

> The actions of Marcellus are such as must be visited with disciplinary punishment. Marcellus, who held the rank of centurion of the first class, having admitted that he has degraded himself by openly throwing off his allegiance, and having besides put on record, as appears in the official report of the Governor, other insane expressions, it is our pleasure that he be put to death by the sword.

After begging for God's blessing upon Agricolan, Marcellus was subsequently beheaded. The year was 298.

Chapter 139

ST. MARGARET THE BAREFOOTED

1325 - 1395

The Italian City of Cesolo has as its patroness a saint who was especially dedicated to relieving the misfortunes of the poor. Known affectionately as *"la scalza,"* "the barefoot," Margaret was born at Cesolo in the year 1325. Throughout her childhood she was admired for her modesty, piety, obedience, devotion to her family and her love for God and the poor.

When she was 15 years old, she accepted the suggestion that she marry. Her future husband was a gentleman of the city who greatly respected her virtues. After her marriage, Margaret continued all her devotions and prayers and inflicted upon her body various penances for the love of God and the salvation of the world.

Margaret's love of the poor eventually inspired her to go barefoot during the performance of her charities, in this way imitating many whose extreme poverty forced them to walk about without shoes. When her own situation prevented her from giving bread to the poor, she gave generously of her energies and begged from door to door on behalf of those whose health prevented them from doing so.

Her husband, it is said, was understandably annoyed by this practice and was especially indignant when Margaret became known as *"la scalza."* He was no doubt embarrassed and shamed before his neighbors, and we can imagine the difficulties this must have caused in the couple's relationship. It would seem that the Saint would have wanted to spare her husband by being mindful of his feelings and that she would have worn shoes despite her inclination to go without them. We may well find it difficult to understand the reasoning of this saint. She is said to have endured her husband's ill-treatment with admirable patience.

After her husband's death, Margaret continued her charities until the time of her own death at the age of 70. She passed to her eternal reward on August 5, 1395 and was buried in the Church of St. Dominic. The veneration paid to the Saint immediately after her death has continued uninterruptedly to the present day. Pope Boniface IX encouraged devotion to the Saint by conceding indulgences to those who visited her tomb in the Church of St. Dominic. In the year 1920, the remains of the Saint were transferred to the church at Cesolo, where St. Margaret is said to be "constantly" venerated. The relics are kept in a reclining statue of the Saint, which is seen in a glass-sided reliquary above the main altar of the church.

St. Margaret the Barefooted (1325-1395), whose love for the poor inspired her to go barefoot during the performance of her charities—much to the indignation of her husband, who was a gentleman of the city of Cesolo. This painting is above the altar of the church at Cesolo.

The relics of St. Margaret the Barefooted in the church at Cesolo, where they are kept in a reclining statue in a glass-sided reliquary above the main altar of the church.

Chapter 140

BL. MARGARET OF CASTELLO
(Bl. Margaret of Metola)

d. 1320

Bl. Margaret of Castello was blind, hunchbacked, dwarfed and lame. Her right leg was much shorter than the left, which was malformed, and she is described quite candidly as "ugly." We know of this and other details of her life from the biography written by her contemporary, the Franciscan, Hubert of Casale, and that of a canon regular of the Cathedral of Castello, who wrote in 1345, only 25 years after Margaret's death.

Margaret's father was Parisio, the Captain of the People, a fearless and capable soldier whose military capture of the mountaintop castle of Metola made him a national hero. As a reward for his victorious leadership he was given the castle, together with the extensive estate of which it was a part. To this mountain stronghold Parisio brought his young bride, Emilia (Margaret's mother). Medieval biographers fail to give us their family names; also omitted is a description of the noble lord and his lady. However, it is confirmed by Hubert of Casale, who knew Margaret well, that she came "from a noble and wealthy family."

The joyfully anticipated birth of their first child was turned into a veritable tragedy when the newborn was examined. Immediately, Margaret's parents were overwhelmed with disappointment, anger and loathing. They seem to have felt shamefully disgraced that they, the two most important personages of the district, had been inflicted with a malformed infant. All efforts were then made to keep the infant and her deformities a secret. Since the parents wanted nothing to do with their misshapen baby, a trusted servant was given charge of the child, and it was this servant who saw to Margaret's Baptism and the choice of a name.

Apparently Margaret was given at an early age to prayer and visits to the castle's chapel. It was during one of these visits to the chapel that her identity was almost discovered. Fearing that they would become known as the parents of the deformed child, Parisio and his wife decided that because of the child's devotion to prayer, they would make of her a recluse. Inspired by those holy solitaries who lived in cells adjoining churches, Parisio decided to imprison the child in a similar manner. In a little church in the forest, about a quarter of a mile away from the castle, was the Church of St. Mary of the Fortress of Metola. Against the wall of this church Parisio had a mason build a room with a window opening into the chapel, through which the child could assist at Holy Mass. Another small window, opening to the outside, was so arranged that food could be passed without anyone seeing the occupant. The child was unceremoniously thrust into the prison and the mason walled up the doorway. Margaret was six years old at the time. She was never to know parental love, to play with other children or to enjoy the company of people. She was condemned, however, to suffer loneliness, extreme cold in the winter and suffocating heat in the summer.

It was soon learned by the chaplain that the blind girl's mind was "luminous." Margaret grew in grace and knowledge of her faith under the priest's instructions, so much so that years later she astonished the Dominican friars at Citta di Castello with the extent and depth of her theological knowledge.

As though the sufferings of her bodily deformities were not enough, Margaret, at the age of seven, bound herself to a strict monastic fast—a fast extending from the middle of September (the Feast of the Holy Cross) to the following Easter. For the rest of the year Margaret fasted four days a week. On all Fridays of the year her only nourishment consisted of a little bread and water.

During the thirteenth year of her imprisonment, when Parisio's territory was threatened with invasion, Lady Emilia and her attendant left the castle and took Margaret with them to the safety of Mercatello. As soon as they arrived, Margaret was led to an underground vault, where she was once more imprisoned. In this place Margaret suffered more intensely than before. At Metola she had been sustained by the benefits of her religion: Holy Mass, the Sacraments of Penance and the Holy Eucharist and the visits of the chaplain. At Mercatello she was deprived of all consolations.

In August of the year 1307, when Margaret was twenty years old, five pilgrims from Rome brought news of the wonderful cures taking place in the city of Castello at the tomb of a Franciscan tertiary, Fra Giacomo. When peace was restored in September, Parisio and Emilia, after hearing details of various cures, took Margaret to the tomb of Fra Giacomo. Because there were many crippled and sick pilgrims who were vying for positions about the tomb, Margaret was placed among them while the parents withdrew to make room.

Throughout the day Margaret prayed fervently for a cure. After several hours, when the parents saw with disappointment that Margaret was not cured, the nobleman and his wife did the unbelievable— they abandoned their blind daughter in the church and returned to Metola.

Left without funds in a strange city, the blind and lame girl was obliged to sleep in doorways and to stumble along the streets until she was befriended by two beggars, Roberto and Elena. Always hoping that her parents would return for her, Margaret finally realized, at the inn where Parisio and Emilia had stayed, that her parents had indeed purposely abandoned her. Margaret must have been deeply grieved on learning the truth, but it is known that never, throughout her lifetime, did she accuse them or speak unkindly of the rejection or the harsh treatment she had endured at their hands. Instead, she often made excuses for them and always professed her love for them.

In addition to Roberto and Elena, Margaret also was befriended by others. Whole families of the poorer class assisted Margaret by taking her into their homes. When one family felt an economic strain, another would house her. For several years Margaret passed from one house to another.

When news of her extraordinary piety reached the cloistered nuns of St. Margaret's Monastery, Margaret was invited to join them. Margaret accepted the invitation with great joy and anticipated a lifetime of prayer and work in the monastic environment. The sisters were happy to receive her and were amazed when Margaret quickly learned the different parts of the convent. They were even more astonished to discover that, despite her blindness and afflictions, she was able to clean rooms, help in the preparation of meals and perform other household chores.

In joining the community, Margaret bound herself to live according to the rule of the order. Unfortunately, with the passage of time and the death of the foundress, the rule was not observed according to its high ideals. Instead, there were many relaxations—which were justified with various explanations. After a time, when Margaret continued to observe the rule strictly, the consciences of the sisters became greatly troubled. To ease their discomfort, Margaret was asked to leave. Once again the little cripple suffered rejection by those she loved.

Not only was Margaret saddened when she was forced to leave the religious life, but she suffered as well from public ridicule and contempt. Word had spread that she had been expelled from the convent because she could not adjust herself to community life, that she had peculiar ideas about the religious life, and that her conduct had become eccentric, so that she upset the whole community. Many decided that she was no saint, after all, and that the discipline of the convent had revealed her hidden faults. Even the children, who heard their parents gossip about the matter, began to persecute Margaret with cruel remarks. It is said that even in church she was the object of sneering words. Through it all, Margaret defended the sisters and spoke of their kindness and patience.

Little by little the true nature of the situation was revealed. The reputation of the convent diminished, while Margaret's reputation rose to a great degree. During this time Margaret attended the *Chiesa della Carita*, the Church of Charity, which was conducted by the Dominican friars. This was also the headquarters of the Mantellate, a religious organization that eventually developed into the present Third Order of St. Dominic. Women who wished to live a more religious life, but who for any reason were unable to enter a convent, could affiliate themselves with the Dominican Order by joining the Third Order. These secular women continued to live at home, but they bound themselves to a more religious schedule of life, and at all times, both at home and abroad, they wore the Dominican religious habit. This consisted of a white tunic, a leather belt and a long white veil. They also wore a black cloak or mantella, and it is for this reason that they became popularly known as the Mantellate.

Knowing of Margaret's desire to join a religious order, members of the Mantellate invited her to join them. Since only widows and mature women were then accepted into the Mantellate, this is the first recorded instance of a young, unmarried woman joining the order.

After her investiture, which was conducted by the prior himself, Margaret attended weekly discourses and soon had a complete understanding of the Dominican system of spirituality, in which study, prayer and penance are foremost.

In addition to the prayers prescribed by the rule, Margaret daily recited the 150 Psalms of David, the Office of the Blessed Virgin and the Office of the Holy Cross. All these she said from memory. Her medieval biographer states—without giving details—that the blind Mantellata learned these prayers in a miraculous fashion. It was soon learned that Margaret passed quickly from meditation to contemplation. Then, after hearing of the penances practiced by St. Dominic, Margaret applied herself to practicing similar mortifications. Additionally, she often spent whole nights in prayer and attended Holy Mass every morning. It is recorded that Margaret observed this remarkable program of mortification until her final illness.

Margaret also embarked on a life of charity to the sick and dying. It is said that "No sick person was too far away for her to limp to; no hour of the day or night was ever too inconvenient for her to hasten to those in agony." She would do all in her power to provide needed food and medicine for the sickly poor who were unable to secure these necessities for themselves. The dying also benefited from her attentions, and many a hardened sinner converted because of her.

Although devotion to St. Joseph was then uncommon, Margaret's medieval biographer remarks, with a bit of humor, that she would talk about St. Joseph as long as anyone remained to listen. It is suggested that Margaret was one of the pioneers of devotion to St. Joseph.

After living for several years in the homes of the poor, she was invited to live with a wealthy family named Offrenduccio. Also living in the same house were the lady Ysachina and an only daughter, Francesca. Margaret's prediction that Ysachina and Francesca would eventually join the Mantellate was realized.

We do not know how long Margaret lived with the Offrenduccio family, nor why she left, but it is known that the blind girl ultimately went to live with the Venturino family. Having been born into wealth and position, Margaret was now destined to pass the last years of her life in the palace of a wealthy nobleman. Declining the sumptuous room she was offered as her own, Margaret decided upon the garret, which was small and open to the elements.

Soon after Margaret moved into this home, she overheard a conversation in which the frightful conditions of the local prison were described. Upon learning that the prisoners were kept in underground cells without fresh air or light and that many slept on the damp stones—that they needed clothing and were sometimes starving and dying without medical care—Margaret began her ministry among these unfortunates and invited some of the Mantellate to join her. Every day they were seen entering the prison, their arms laden with bundles of clothing, food and medicine.

Many were the prisoners Margaret brought back to the good graces of the Church, but one obstinately resisted her entreaties. One day, while one of the Mantellate was bathing his skin ulcers, Margaret bowed her head in prayer. When the prisoners next looked in Margaret's direction, she was elevated twenty inches from the ground. With her hands joined in the attitude of prayer and her head now thrown back as if looking heavenward, Margaret remained in deep prayer before slowly descending to the ground. It is said that the prisoner, formerly known for his blasphemous language, now said in a choked voice, "Little Margaret, please pray for me."

Many other phenomena are related by her contemporary biographers. It is recorded that Margaret, although completely blind, could nevertheless "see" Our Lord. She is known to have confided to her confessor that from the Consecration of the Mass until the Communion she did not see the priest, the crucifix, the missal or anything else, only her Saviour.

Once when her godchild, a niece of Lady Gregoria, was dying, Margaret did not join the family members at the bedside but remained in the hall, where she knelt in prayer for a lengthy period of time. When a nearby church bell rang, the sick girl awoke and announced that she had been cured through the prayers of her godmother, Margaret.

One wintry day a fire broke out on the ground floor of the Venturino home. With servants and volunteers frantically attempting to fight the fire, which quickly increased in intensity, the whole house was declared doomed. It was then realized that Margaret was upstairs in the garret. In answer to the shouts of the crowd, Margaret was seen to appear at the head of the stairs. Although choking from the smoke, and without the least sign of alarm, she removed her black mantle, rolled it into a bundle and threw it down the stairs. The medieval biographer tells us what happened next: "In the sight of the crowd of men who had rushed to Venturino's house to fight the blaze, when the cloak of Margaret was thrown into the flames, the raging fire was instantly extinguished."

The healing power of her prayers was used in favor of Sister Venturella, one of the Mantellate. Afflicted with a tumor of the eye which threatened to blind her, Sister Venturella was grieved that she did not have enough money to pay for her medical treatments. When Sister Venturella complained to poor Margaret, who had never experienced sight, that she did not want to be blind, Margaret told her to accept the prospect of blindness as a penance and as a means of growing more in virtue. But when Sister Venturella declared that God was asking too much of her, Margaret saw the futility of further arguments. She stretched out her right hand and asked Venturella to place it over her eye. We are told that, "The instant Margaret's hand touched the diseased eye, the tumor disappeared and Venturella's sight became perfect."

The medieval biographer mentions that there were many other miracles for which Margaret became celebrated throughout the land, but few details are given concerning them. He also adds that "many other things concerning her sanctity should be truthfully told." He apparently felt that it was unnecessary to relate those extraordinary deeds, about which the people were well informed.

At the beginning of the year 1320, Margaret's closest friends realized that she would soon claim her heavenly reward. After receiving the Blessed Sacrament and the comforts of the Church, with the friars and the Mantellate reciting the prayers for the dying, Margaret peacefully died. It was the Second Sunday after Easter, April 13, 1320. Margaret was thirty-three years old.

According to the Dominican custom of the time, the bodies of their members were buried without a coffin, in accordance with holy poverty. For this reason Margaret's body was exposed on a wooden frame. After the funeral services in the church, the friars prepared to carry the body outside to the church cemetery. It was then that a violent argument took place, instigated by those who claimed that the Saint should be placed in a coffin and buried in the church. Described as "a stupendous uproar," the argument continued until a man and his wife brought their crippled daughter into the church. Suffering from an acute curvature of the spine, the child was unable to walk and was mute as well. Pushing their way through the crowd, they placed the child beside Margaret's body. Touched with pity, the crowd began praying with the parents for the child's cure. Suddenly, all stared in amazement as the left arm of the body began to rise. Reaching over, it touched the young crippled girl. A moment later the girl, who had never been able to walk, rose unaided and spoke for the first time, declaring that she had been cured through Margaret's prayers.

The cure settled the dispute as to Margaret's burial place. The prior provided a coffin, and the city council decided that they would pay the expense of having the body embalmed. In the Middle Ages no preservative chemicals were used; a delay in decomposition was attempted by simply removing the viscera and the heart and placing spices in their place. Corruption was expected to take place within a week or two. Following this primitive procedure, Margaret's body was entombed in one of the chapels of the Dominican Church.

News of Margaret's final miracle, as well as the other wonders worked throughout her life, became well-known, so that many soon flocked to pray beside her tomb. Soon more than two hundred affidavits were received testifying to permanent cures received through her intercession.

Margaret was eventually beatified by Pope Paul V on October 19, 1609, with April 13 being assigned as her feast day.

Dressed in the black and white habit of the Mantellate, the marvelously incorrupt body of Blessed Margaret is now seen in a glass sarcophagus in the chapel of the School for the Blind in Citta di Castello, Italy.

Bl. Margaret of Castello, Italy (d. 1320), who was blind, hunchbacked, dwarfed and lame. At age six Bl. Margaret was walled up in a room next to a chapel; she was abandoned by her parents at age 20. She worked many miracles during her life and after her death. The incorrupt body of Bl. Margaret is kept in a glass sarcophagus in the chapel of the School for the Blind in Citta di Castello, Italy. *(Statue by Tony Moroder of Moroder International, Milwaukee; located in Bl. Margaret's shrine, St. Louis Bertrand Church, Louisville, Ky.)*

Chapter 141

ST. MARGARET CLITHEROW
(St. Margaret of York)

1556-1586

Considered to be the first woman to have died under the religious suppression of Queen Elizabeth, Margaret was born in 1556 and lived all her life in the City of York. She was the daughter of Thomas Middleton, a wax-chandler (maker and seller of candles). He was a man of means and of some importance in the community, since he held various civic positions and for a time was a member of the Common Council. Five months after his death his widow married Henry May, who took up residence with the family at the Middleton house in Davygate.

Margaret lived with her mother and stepfather for four years, until the age of 15. Then she married John Clitherow, a grazier and butcher who, as her father had been, was wealthy and held a number of civic positions. There is every indication that Margaret's early married life was happy. Three children joined the family: two boys, Henry and William, and one daughter, Anne.

Margaret had been raised a Protestant. In the manner of girls of her class, she was taught from childhood how to run a household, but not how to read and write. Two or three years after her marriage she became a Catholic, because, as her confessor wrote of her, she "found no substance, truth nor Christian comfort in the ministers of the new church, nor in their doctrine itself, and hearing also many priests and lay people to suffer for the defense of the ancient Catholic Faith." Margaret's husband did not object to his wife's conversion, but he himself remained a faithful member of the new religion of which Queen Elizabeth professed leadership.

At first, Margaret freely practiced her faith and worked toward reconciling many to the Catholic Church. She became more cautious, though, when laws against Catholics were enacted and strictly enforced. Fines were initially imposed upon Mr. Clitherow for his wife's continued absence from Protestant services; later, for her continued absence from these services, she was imprisoned in York Castle. Between the years 1577 and 1584 Margaret was imprisoned several times. The second time she was seized and imprisoned, she was released because she was expecting a child. In 1584 she was imprisoned for 18 months.

The conditions in the prison were unbearable. Records from that time reveal that the cells were dark, damp and infested with vermin, so that many died during their confinement. Margaret made the best of her condition by regarding her imprisonment as a time of prayerful retreat. She also used the time in learning how to read, and she returned to her home with habits of prayer and devotion which had been unfamiliar to her from her Protestant upbringing. She also began to fast four times a week, a practice she continued after her release. Her devoted husband once stated that he found but two faults in his good wife: she would not accompany him to the Protestant church, and she fasted too much.

During this time, Cardinal Allen had been conducting a seminary at Douai, France for the purpose of training young priests who would return to their native England to minister to those who had remained loyal to the Catholic Faith. When these priests returned from Douai, Catholic life began to revive in the city and the shires. Finally a law passed in 1585 made it high treason for any Englishman who was ordained a priest since the first year of Elizabeth's reign to remain in the Kingdom; and it was a felony for any person to harbor or relieve a Catholic priest. By these statutes it was only necessary to prove that a man was a Catholic priest, whether English or not, in order to condemn him to a cruel death—and a similar punishment was reserved for those who aided him.

We are not certain when Margaret began to conceal priests in her home, but when warned of the great risk she was inviting by accepting all the priests who came to her for sanctuary, she replied, "By God's grace all priests shall be more welcome to me than ever they were, and I will do what I can to set forward God's Catholic service." Margaret had in her home a secret hiding place with a passageway through which priests could hide or escape to the outside of the building. Here Frs. Thompson, Hart, Thirkill, Ingleby and many others took refuge. The place was apparently cramped and uncomfortable, since we are told that the entrance was "painful to him that was not acquainted with the door, by reason of the straitness thereof, and yet large enough for a boy."

Whenever a priest was visiting, Margaret arranged for the Catholics of the area to attend Holy Mass. Fr. John Mush, her confessor and first biographer, wrote of Margaret that,

> She had prepared two chambers, the one adjoining to her own house, whereunto she might have resort any time, without sight and knowledge of any neighbours...The other was a little distant from her own house, secret and unknown to any but to such as she knew to be both faithful and discreet...This place she prepared for more troublesome storms, that God might yet be served there when her own house was not thought so safe, though she could not have access to it every day as she desired.

Accounts of her contemporaries reveal that Margaret was witty, happy and charming. Neighbors commented on her pleasing appearance. They noted that she spoke always in a low voice and enjoyed a simple diet of rye bread, milk, pottage and butter. Like a true Yorkshire woman she was careful about the neatness and cleanliness of her home, which was located in an area called The Shambles. Being a woman of some means, she had a number of servants. These she treated kindly, but she did not hesitate to correct them when their work was not properly completed—and she often worked beside them to show them how to execute their chores properly.

Margaret was also a capable businesswoman, who often helped in her husband's butcher shop located near their home. She was careful that the prices she asked for her husband's wares were fair and just. "In buying and selling her wares she was very wary to have the worth of them, as her neighbors sold the like, as also to satisfy her husband, who committed all to her trust and discretion." Mindful of her husband's many responsibilities, she often urged him to close the shop with its many concerns and instead to sell only on the wholesale level, which was less troublesome.

Everyone loved Margaret, we are told. Rev. Mush recorded that her friends "would run to her for help, comfort and counsel" and he told how "with all courtesy and friendship she would relieve them." Her neighbors respected her, and even though many were of the Protestant faith, they shielded her activities and warned her of danger.

Her servants, who also knew of her illegal harboring of priests, loved her and were careful to guard her secret.

She was consistent in the practice of her faith, beginning every day with an hour and a half devoted to private prayer and meditation. If a priest was available, Holy Mass followed. Margaret regularly confessed, and although she was not an educated woman, she had learned to read during her imprisonments and often read the Holy Scriptures, the works of Thomas à Kempis and Perrin's *Exercise*. She had also learned, probably during her imprisonment, the whole of the Little Office of Our Lady.

When her son Henry came of age, Margaret obtained the permission of her husband to send him to Douai so that he might receive a Catholic education in the seminary that had been established to train missionary priests.

Sending a son or daughter outside the Kingdom to receive a Catholic education was considered a crime, and as soon as the Council learned of it, John Clitherow was ordered to appear before them for questioning. Since the Clitherow house had been marked as a rendezvous for missionary priests who ministered to the Catholic inhabitants of the city, and because the authorities had learned of the Clitherows' son's absence from the Kingdom, a retaliation of some sort was expected.

On March 12, 1586, while John Clitherow was testifying before the Council and Margaret was busy with her household concerns, two sheriffs of the City, accompanied by other men, entered the Clitherow house to search it. Nothing suspicious was found at first, but on opening the door to a remote room, the men found some children of the neighborhood who were being taught by a schoolmaster named Stapleton, whom they mistook for a priest. In the confusion that developed, Stapleton escaped through the secret room. Another account tells that Fr. Mush, Margaret's confessor, and Fr. Ingleby were also in the house at the time—but if so, they too escaped.

An 11-year-old boy who was then living with the family was terrorized into revealing the secret hiding place. No one was found in the secret place, but in a nearby cupboard the authorities found church vessels, books and vestments that had been used during Holy Mass. The articles were taken as evidence and Margaret was arrested, together with all who were found in the house. The others were soon released, but Margaret was taken to the Common Hall for questioning and was then imprisoned in the Castle. After being reassured that family members had been released and were safe, her good spirits returned and she promptly began to help the 35 women who were imprisoned with her.

During Margaret's next court appearance, the charges against her were revealed. These included the claim that she harbored and maintained priests who were working in opposition to the Queen's new religion. When the judge asked her whether or not she was guilty, Margaret replied that she had never harbored enemies of the Queen. Then, following the procedure of the court, Judge John Clinch asked her how she wished to be tried. Instead of the accepted reply, "By God and the country," Margaret replied, "Having made no offense, I need no trial." The vestments that had been found in her home during the raid were presented in evidence, but still Margaret refused to agree to a trial. Judge Clinch made every effort to get her to plead. At the same time his fellow judge, Francis Rhodes, who later had a part in the condemnation of Mary Queen of Scots, began to insult Margaret. "It is not for religion that thou harbourest priests," he called at her, "but for harlotries."

Knowing that she would die regardless of her answer, Margaret was also aware that during a trial, her children, servants and friends would be called as witnesses and would either lie to save her and commit perjury and sin, or if they testified truthfully, would bear the burden of having caused her death. She therefore repeatedly rejected a trial and steadfastly refused to acknowledge the Protestant church of Queen Elizabeth. The Council was then forced to pronounce the sentence which English law decreed for anyone who refused to plead and be tried by a jury: *peine forte et dure*, that is, that she should be pressed to death. Margaret accepted the sentence calmly and thanked God that she would suffer for the sake of the Catholic Faith.

When John Clitherow heard of the sentence passed on his wife, "He fared like a man out of his wits and wept so violently that blood gushed out of his nose in great quantity." He reportedly said, "Let them take all I have and save my wife, for she is the best wife in all England and the best Catholic, also."

Margaret was then confined in John Trew's house, where she found no peace because of the various people who visited her, trying in vain to make her acknowledge the new religion and thus gain her liberty. Even her stepfather, Henry May, who had been elected Mayor of York, tried to win her over. She was not allowed to see her children and only once saw her husband, and then in the presence of a guard.

The date set for her punishment was March 25, which was also Lady Day (the Feast of the Annunciation). The evening before she was to suffer Margaret sewed her own shroud, and during the night she prayed. She had already sent her hat to her husband, "in sign of her loving duty to him as head of the family," and she had dispatched her shoes and stockings to her twelve-year-old daughter, Anne, "signifying that she should serve God and follow in her mother's steps."

At eight the next morning, March 25, 1586, female attendants helped to robe Margaret in the linen garment she had made. Surrounded by the officers of the law and by her executioners, she was then led to the place of martyrdom, only a few yards from where she had been imprisoned. To reach this place she passed through a large crowd of people who had congregated to see the strange sight of a woman led to slaughter. "All marveled to see her joyful, smiling countenance." Arriving at the place, she knelt down and with a strong voice she prayed for the Pope, cardinals, clergy, Christian princes, and especially for Queen Elizabeth, that God would return her to the Faith and save her soul.

After Margaret lay down upon the ground, a sharp stone was placed under her back—and when she had extended her arms in the form of a cross, her hands were bound to posts on either side. A slab of wood the size of a door was laid over her, and weights were dropped upon it. With her bones breaking at every additional weight placed upon her, Margaret did not cry out in pain. Instead, her last words as the weight was increased were, "*Jesu, Jesu, Jesu,* have mercy upon me." Her torment lasted approximately a quarter of an hour. We are told that her body remained in the press for six hours. At the time of her death, Margaret was 30 years of age.

Margaret's crumpled body was taken by the executioners to a secret burial place. Later, when her remains were found by her Catholic friends, they were given a proper burial, although the place is now unknown. One of her hands was kept, and this is found in a crystal vessel at Bar Convent, York, which is now a museum.

The martyr's daughter, Anne, inspired by the life and death of her mother, became a nun at Louvain; her two sons, Henry and William, both became priests.

Nearly 400 years after her death, on October 25, 1970, Margaret was declared a saint by Pope Paul VI before a crowd estimated at fifty thousand in St. Peter's Basilica, Rome.

In the City of York there are many reminders of St. Margaret Clitherow. Beautifully maintained and appearing as it did in the sixteenth century is the street called The Shambles, where the Clitherow butcher shop was located. The home of the Saint, at No. 35 The Shambles, is now a chapel in her honor. There a service is held every Saturday. A stone memorial is located at the place of Margaret's execution, and Catholic services are still performed in the Church of St. Martin-le-Grand, where the Saint was baptized and married.

Gatehouse Prints

A sketch of St. Margaret Clitherow (d. 1586), who was crushed to death for having hidden Jesuit priests in her house at No. 35 The Shambles.

THE SHAMBLES
YORK

BRIAN LEWIS

Gatehouse Prints, Whitby

A sketch of The Shambles in York—the street where St. Margaret Clitherow and her husband lived and maintained a butcher shop. The house where St. Margaret lived with her family is now a chapel in her honor.

472

DRG J. Arthur Dixon

Above: This photograph of The Shambles shows that the neighborhood retains its medieval character. It is one of the most famous streets in England.

Following page: A statue of St. Margaret Clitherow (St. Margaret of York). The night before she was executed, the Saint sewed her own shroud and prayed. She had already sent her hat to her husband as a sign of her loving duty to him. When he first heard the terrible sentence he was like a man out of his wits; he wept violently and exclaimed, "Let them take all I have and save my wife, for she is the best wife in all England and the best Catholic also!" Margaret died at age 30; she was canonized in 1970.

ST. MARGARET CLITHEROW

Chapter 142

ST. MARGARET OF CORTONA

1247 - 1297

Margaret was the daughter of a farmer whose property was located in Laviano, Italy. When she was only seven years of age, Margaret lost her good mother, who had trained her with tenderness and affection. Two years later her father brought home a stepmother who was a harsh and demanding woman without much interest in the high-spirited little girl.

When Margaret grew to be a beautiful young lady who thirsted for affection, she was seduced by a young cavalier from Montepulciano who took her to his castle with a promise of love, luxury and marriage. For nine years Margaret lived openly as his mistress, causing great scandal—especially when she flaunted her situation by dressing splendidly and riding a beautiful horse through the streets of the city. The cavalier never married Margaret, in spite of her frequent entreaties and the eventual birth of a son. Although seemingly happy and pleased with her casual lifestyle and the luxuries that surrounded her, Margaret at times realized the sinfulness of her life.

One day the cavalier left to visit one of his estates, but he failed to return home. Throughout the night and the next day Margaret waited anxiously for his return. Finally, the dog that had accompanied him returned home alone and tugged at her dress, indicating that she should follow him. After Margaret went running with the dog through the woods, he stopped at the foot of an oak tree and began to scratch among the leaves. With horror Margaret saw the mangled body of her lover, who had been assassinated and then hastily buried. Suddenly she began to suffer from an overwhelming sense of guilt and from a feeling of dread regarding the condition of her lover's soul.

Losing no time, Margaret surrendered all her possessions to the dead man's relatives, and wearing the robe of a penitent and holding her little son by the hand, she returned to her father's house to ask for forgiveness and shelter. But prompted by Margaret's stepmother, her father refused to receive her. While suffering from this painful rejection, Margaret was suddenly inspired to journey to Cortona to ask the help of the Friars Minor, whose gentleness with sinners was well-known.

When Margaret entered the city, her profound misery attracted two noble ladies, Marinana and Raneria, who heard her sad story and welcomed Margaret and her son into their home. They introduced her to the Franciscans, who became her Fathers in Christ.

For three years Margaret struggled against temptation, since, as Butler states, "The flesh was not yet subdued to the spirit." When her confessor, Fr. Giunta Bevegnati, tried to moderate her excessive austerities, Margaret replied, "Father, do not ask me to come to terms with this body of mine, for I cannot afford it. Between me and my body there must needs be a struggle till death."

Fr. Giunta and Fr. Giovanni de Castiglione carefully guided Margaret through periods of alternating exaltation and feelings of despair. Her desire to do penance for her sins and to correct the scandal she had given was overwhelming and had to be frequently corrected by her Franciscan confessors. One Sunday she went to Mass at Laviano, her birthplace. With a cord around her neck she asked pardon of everyone for her past scandals. She also had intended to have herself led like a criminal through the streets of Montepulciano with a rope around her neck, but Fr. Giunta forbade this as being unseemly for a young woman and conducive to spiritual pride. He did permit her to go to the church there one Sunday, though, to ask the pardon of the congregation.

Later Margaret began to earn a living by serving as midwife to the ladies of the city. Then she turned her attentions to serving the sick and the poor. She left the home of the two ladies who had befriended her and began to live in a small cottage; there she subsisted on alms and food given her by those who were attracted to her work and who were in sympathy with her situation. The better portions of the food given her, and the donations, were in turn surrendered to the more needy.

At the end of three years Margaret experienced relief from her interior sufferings and reached a higher level of spirituality. The granting of her desire to become a member of the Third Order of St.

Francis was delayed until her confessors were satisfied with her sincerity. At about the same time that she was admitted as a tertiary of the Third Order, her son was sent to school at Arezzo, where he remained until he entered the Franciscan Order.

From the time she became a tertiary, Margaret advanced rapidly in prayer and was drawn into very direct communion with her Saviour. Fr. Giunta gives the details of her life, describing some of her visions and ecstasies, in the *Legend,* which is also referred to as the Saint's *Vita,* or *Life.*

In the year 1286, the Bishop granted a charter which enabled Margaret to work for the sick on a permanent basis. At first she nursed them in her own cottage. After a time she was helped by several women, one of whom gave her a house to use as a hospital. When more space was needed, Margaret implored the city council to assist her in starting a hospital. Margaret's dream became a reality when the new structure was named the Spedale di Santa Maria della Misericordia. The nurses who helped her were her fellow tertiaries, who eventually formed a congregation known as the Poverelle. Margaret founded the Confraternity of Our Lady of Mercy, whose members were pledged to support the hospital and to search out and assist the poor.

Margaret's life of penance was never interrupted. Her nights were spent almost without sleep, in prayer and contemplation. When she did lie down to rest, her bed was the bare ground and her pillow a stone or a block of wood. Her food consisted of a little bread and raw herbs, and water was her only drink. To these penances, which she practiced with the consent of her confessors, other sufferings, which proved more painful, were exacted by certain people who, from the beginning of her repentance, had doubted her sincerity and the validity of her conversion.

These sufferings were caused by false rumors regarding her association with the Franciscan friars, especially with Fr. Giunta. The rumors were augmented when, by Divine command, Margaret retired to a cottage at some distance from the friars' church. According to Fr. Giunta, the friars were satisfied with this arrangement because they realized that Margaret's health was broken and they worried that they might lose custody of her body after her death. The rumors, added to the memory of Margaret's former life of sin, prompted many to look upon her with contempt and to regard her as a madwoman and a hypocrite. What pained Margaret was not the ill-will that she accepted humbly, as a means of gaining grace; but rather, the general indignation suffered by the friars on her account. Restrictions were placed on Fr. Giunta's contacts with her, and in 1289 he was transferred to Siena, where he remained for seven years, until shortly before Margaret's death. All these trials Margaret bore quietly and meekly, giving herself more to prayer and rising higher in the spiritual life.

During the last years of her life, Our Lord said to her: "Show now that you are converted; cry out and call others to repentance...The graces I have bestowed on you are not meant for you alone." Obedient to this command, Margaret began a more active life of converting sinners. With a holy eagerness and with wonderful success, Margaret brought many back to the Sacraments. Sinners were brought to repentance, and feuds were ended. In his Life of St. Margaret, Fr. Giunta writes that the fame of these conversions soon spread, and hardened sinners flocked to Cortona to listen to the Saint's exhortations. Penitents came not only from all of Italy, but also from France and Spain. Miracles of healing took place, and those who had spread rumors and condemned her, now turned to Margaret in their difficulties.

Margaret received the Sacraments from Fr. Giunta and died on February 22, 1297 at the age of 50, after having spent 23 years in penance. On the day of her death she was publicly acclaimed a saint, and the citizens of Cortona accorded her a magnificent funeral. A church was soon built in her honor, and even before she was canonized in 1728 by Pope Benedict XIII, a yearly festival was held in her memory.

The incorrupt body of the Saint is now enshrined behind a sheet of crystal under the altar of the Basilica of Cortona. The red velvet background of the reliquary is studded with precious gems and valuable ornaments donated by her grateful clients.

St. Margaret of Cortona (1247-1297), a member of the Third Order of St. Francis. The Saint spent her life in penitential works to make reparation for the nine years she had spent as mistress to a young cavalier. *(Painting by della Quercia, the Vatican.)*

Below: Wax image of St. Margaret of Cortona. Margaret earned a living by serving as a midwife. Later she began to nurse the sick in her own cottage, supported by alms. This work developed into a hospital. Our Lord told Margaret to bring others to repentance; thus her last years were spent converting many sinners.

Above: St. Margaret's conversion came suddenly one day when her lover's dog came home without him. When the dog led Margaret to the mangled body of her companion, who had been murdered and hastily buried in the woods, she was overwhelmed by a sense of guilt and a feeling of dread over the condition of his soul. She journeyed to Cortona and embarked on a life of penance and charity under the guidance of the Franciscan Friars.

480

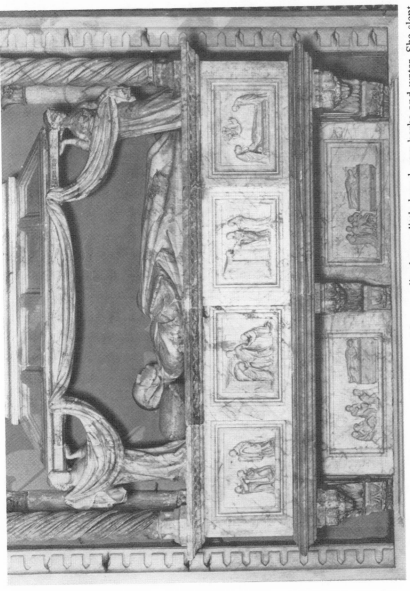

The sarcophagus of St. Margaret of Cortona. Margaret lived on a little bread, raw herbs and water. She slept on the bare ground with a stone or block of wood for a pillow. She spent 23 years in penance.

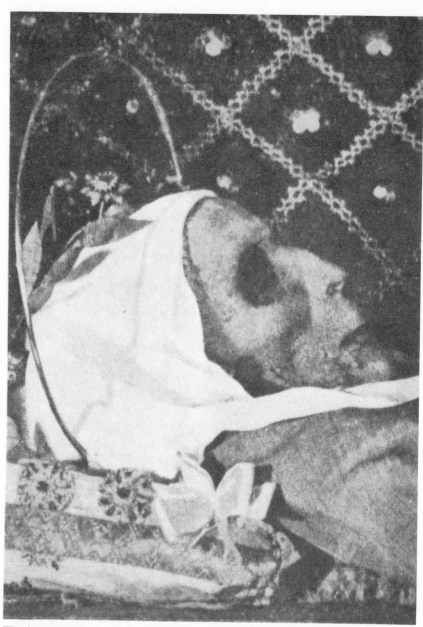

The incorrupt body of St. Margaret of Cortona is enshrined behind a sheet of crystal under the altar of the Basilica of Cortona. In the last years of her life Margaret became famous for bringing souls back to the Sacraments. Even hardened sinners listened to her, and penitents flocked to Cortona from Italy, France and Spain. Miracles of healing also took place. Margaret was acclaimed a saint on the day of her death.

Chapter 143

BL. MARGARET FONTANA

d. 1513

The people of Modena, Italy, who had known Margaret Fontana during her lifetime, told what they knew of her many virtues to her biographer, the Dominican Desiderio Paloni. In materials written about her some 70 years after her death, we are told that Margaret turned her back on the comforts of the world to lead a life of simplicity, austerity and recollection. She seemed destined for the cloister, but though she made a vow of perpetual virginity, she remained in the world, joining the Dominican Third Order and spending her time in aiding the sick and the poor. Margaret was so charitable that her family had to caution her to be more discreet in giving away what was theirs, since they might soon be in need of relief themselves.

Although Margaret endeavored to keep her pious practices secret, everyone seems to have known something of her intense interior life. She would pass whole nights lying on the ground in prayer. Because she shared a room with her mother, she was always careful to wait until her mother was asleep before beginning her prayers. When Margaret was reproached for her austerities, she would answer, "It is not for a servant of God to be fastidious, but crucified and mortified for Christ."

Margaret's biographer, Desiderio Paloni, wrote of her:

> The Church Militant on earth has made known with what fair decorum, with what holiness of life she wore the habit of St. Dominic, how in her own religious state she lived in recollection, and what has been the sweet fragrance of her fame. She passed all her days with never a quarrel, however just it might have been; her life was ever blameless, she was dear to all, praised by all, known to all and honored by all as a saint. She was meek and gentle as a lamb, full of love and pity, honorable and straightforward, simple and pure as a dove, sparing of her words,

wise and direct in her replies, kind in her dealings and venerated for her every act.

Bl. Margaret Fontana was also frequently visited by demons, but she drove them away with a Sign of the Cross. After her death in the year 1513, Bl. Margaret was invoked by those afflicted with demonic possession. Also, because of her miraculous powers of healing, she was invoked by women suffering in childbirth.

Bl. Margaret Fontana (d. 1513), a Dominican tertiary, turned her back on the comforts of the world to lead a life of simplicity, austerity and recollection. She spent whole nights lying on the ground in prayer. She was frequently visited by demons, but drove them away with the Sign of the Cross. She has been invoked by those suffering from demonic possession and, because of her miraculous powers of healing, by women suffering in childbirth.

485

Chapter 144

BL. MARGARET OF LOUVAIN

1207 - 1225

In his *Dialogue on Miracles,* Caesarius of Heisterbach tells the story of the martyr Margaret of Louvain, who was 18 years old at the time of her death. She was born at Louvain into humble circumstances in the year 1207. When she was old enough, she was employed as a waitress and domestic helper in the inn owned by a relative named Aubert. He was a good and pious man who frequently housed needy travelers without payment. Margaret, a virtuous girl, was pleased to help in these works of mercy. She labored hard and was a blessing to her employer, even though she had problems in the exercise of her chores. Because of the recollected and worthy manner in which she performed her work and because she was indifferent to the attentions and comments of men, she was called "the proud Margaret."

In the year 1225 Aubert and his wife decided to sell their business and enter religious life. During their last night at home, some evil men visited them under the pretext of wanting to offer the couple their best wishes for the future. The men were actually interested in the money the pious couple had received for their business—money that was to be given to the religious houses to which they were going. Soon after the arrival of the men, Aubert asked Margaret to fetch some wine for their guests. As soon as Margaret left the house, the men made their evil intentions known. When the pious couple refused to relinquish the money, the men murdered them. The ruthless thieves located the money and were about to make off with it when Margaret returned with the wine.

Because Margaret had come upon the scene and discovered what had taken place, the robbers carried her to a lonely spot near the River Dyle, where they decided to kill her. But in an attempt to spare Margaret's life, one of the men offered to release her if she would make a vow to keep silent about the crime. When Margaret steadfastly refused to cooperate, she herself was murdered. Her throat was slashed and her side was stabbed.

The virginal body of the young girl was then carelessly thrown into the river. However, a supernatural light and the sounds of angelic voices aided in its discovery. The clergy of St. Peter's Collegiate Church at Louvain claimed the body and carried it in a solemn procession to their churchyard for burial. Here miracles soon were reported.

The Cistercian monk, Caesarius, asks in his *Dialogue on Miracles,* "What would you say was the cause of martyrdom in the case of this girl?" The answer was,

> Simplicity and an innocent life...There are different kinds of martyrdom, namely, innocence, as in Abel; uprightness, as in the Prophets and St. John the Baptist; love of the Law, as in the Machabees; confession of the Faith, as in the Apostles. For all these different causes Christ the Lamb is said to have been "slain from the beginning of the world."

To this Butler adds, "All Christian virtues, being protestations of our faith and proofs of our fidelity to God, are a true motive of martyrdom."

The veneration paid to the virgin martyr was approved in 1905 by Pope St. Pius X. It is said that devotion to Bl. Margaret of Louvain has been active from the time of her death in 1225 to the present.

Chapter 145

BL. MARGARET POLE

1471 - 1541

Margaret Plantagenet Pole was the niece of two English kings, Edward IV and Richard III. Their brother, George Plantagenet, the Duke of Clarence, was her father; her mother was Isabel, the eldest daughter of the Earl of Warwick. Henry VII, whose wife was Margaret's cousin, gave Margaret in marriage to Sir Reginald Pole, a Buckinghampshire gentleman. The marriage, contracted in 1491, produced five children; it ended after 19 years, in 1510, with Reginald's death. Of Margaret's five children, the fourth, Reginald, was to become Cardinal and Archbishop of Canterbury. He was also to be the indirect cause of his mother's martyrdom.

When Henry VIII ascended the throne of England, he conferred on Margaret Pole the title of Countess of Salisbury and described her as the saintliest woman in England. He also passed an Act of Restitution by which Margaret came into possession of her ancestral domains, which had been forfeited by attainder during the previous reign.

When Princess Mary was born to Henry VIII and Catherine of Aragon, the sponsor chosen for the royal infant was Margaret Pole, who was also appointed governess of the princess and head of her household. In time, Henry became attracted to Anne Boleyn, whom he wanted to marry—but first there was the matter of his marriage to Catherine. The King tried every means to have the Pope annul the marriage, but when the Pope refused to do this, that is, to grant an annulment, Henry himself declared the marriage invalid.

When the King married Anne Boleyn, Princess Mary was still in Margaret's care. However, Margaret was promptly removed from her post, even though she begged to remain and serve her royal charge.

After Anne Boleyn's fall, Margaret returned to court; but when her son Reginald wrote his treatise *Pro Ecclesiasticae Unitatis Defensione*

(In Defense of the Unity of the Church), which was a work against the royal claim to ecclesiastical supremacy, and refused to return to England from his self-imposed exile, Henry VIII became so incensed that he expressed the desire to rid himself of Margaret's entire family.

In November of 1538, two of Margaret's sons and others of their family were arrested on a charge of treason and were committed to the Tower. With the exception of Geoffrey Pole, they were executed in January. Ten days after the apprehension of her sons, Margaret was also arrested and was examined by Fitzwilliam, Earl of Southampton, and Goodrich, Bishop of Ely. They reported to Cromwell that although they had "travailed with her" for many hours, she would "nothing utter." They concluded that either she did not share in her sons' treason, or else she was "the most arrant traitress that ever lived." Butler comments, "They had to own that the tall, dignified woman had the brains as well as the stature of a man." She was, nevertheless, taken into custody and committed to Lord Southampton's house in Cowdray Park.

Cromwell introduced a Bill of Attainder against Bl. Margaret, and from one of her coffers he produced a white silk tunic which was embroidered on the back with intricate designs. Somehow Cromwell interpreted some of the designs as representing the Five Holy Wounds. He claimed that this connected her with Sir Henry Neville's and Bl. Thomas Percy's uprising in the North and the conspiracy connected with it, since the banner of their troops had borne symbols of the Holy Wounds. For this false charge Parliament condemned her to death without a trial. Other charges were pressed against her, to which she was never permitted to reply.

Following her conviction, Bl. Margaret was removed to the Tower where, for nearly two years, she suffered from the cold and from insufficient clothing.

On May 28, 1541, Bl. Margaret was told that she would die within the hour. Declaring that she was not guilty of the crimes lodged against her, she nevertheless walked calmly from her cell to the East Smithfield Green, within the precincts of the Tower, where a low wooden block had been prepared for her beheading. The regular executioner being absent, his understudy performed the deed and clumsily hacked at her neck. Margaret Pole was 70 years of age.

Margaret was beatified in 1886, together with other English martyrs.

Remembering the kindness that Henry VIII had extended to Bl.

Margaret Pole at the beginning of his reign, it is ironic that she is considered to have been the first woman martyred under his Act of Supression and his persecution of Catholics.

Chapter 146

ST. MARGARET OF SCOTLAND

1045 - 1093

When St. Edward the Confessor died without an heir to the throne of England, his nephew, Edgar Aetheling, was nominated to succeed him. Unfortunately, Edgar Aetheling was still very young and soon demonstrated his inability to defend his claim against his rival, Harold, St. Edward's brother-in-law, who seized the throne for himself.

Because Edgar Aetheling was considered the true successor, his position in England was rendered a very precarious one—and for this reason he, his mother and sisters decided to retreat to Hungary. They boarded a ship, but it met with contrary winds and was driven by storms to the Scottish coast.

There the royal family was warmly received by Scotland's King Malcolm III. By this hospitality Malcolm returned the favor which England had afforded him years earlier, following the murder of Malcolm's father, King Duncan. At that time, Malcolm had been forced to leave Scotland and had taken refuge in England. Edward the Confessor had then afforded him every courtesy, even helping him to regain his kingdom.

While Edgar Aetheling, together with his mother and his sisters, were in the Scottish court, King Malcolm—a widower—became captivated by the charms of Edgar's sister, Princess Margaret, who was as beautiful as she was accomplished. Although her natural inclination would have led her to prefer the cloister, Margaret realized that her duty lay elsewhere; she yielded to the wishes of her mother and the Scottish King.

Margaret's wedding to King Malcolm, which was celebrated amid national rejoicing, took place at the Castle of Dunfermline in the year 1070, when Margaret was 25 years old. The marriage was to bring great blessings upon Malcolm and Scotland. In great part because of Margaret's virtues, the union proved to be a very happy one.

Soon after the wedding, Margaret's mother and sister returned to England, where they entered religious life—one at Winchester and the other at Romsey Abbey in Hampshire. They left Margaret in a foreign land with a husband who was rough, uncultured, could neither read nor write and who, as a warrior, had led raids in England, dragging into captivity multitudes of fair-haired Saxons. But, in spite of all his faults, Malcolm had a willingness to amend his shortcomings and a great desire to please his new bride. Through the great influence she acquired over him, Margaret softened his temper, polished his manners and rendered him one of the most virtuous kings who has ever occupied the Scottish throne. Soon the couple's chief objective in life became to maintain justice, make their subjects happy and establish religion. One of the Saint's early biographers wrote, "She incited the King to works of justice, mercy, charity and other virtues, in all which by divine grace she induced him to carry out her pious wishes. For he, perceiving that Christ dwelt in the heart of his queen, was always ready to follow her advice."

The change which Margaret produced in her husband was extended to her adopted country. She promoted civilization and encouraged education for her subjects. She criticized the long delays in the courts of justice, and she asked that the suits of the poor be given preference over those of others. She urged her husband to correct his soldiers and to forbid them to pillage the homes of the Scottish people. She settled quarrels and ransomed many of the Saxon slaves whom Malcolm had brought to Scotland.

Marriage laws, as well as the observance of Lent and Easter, were regulated, and trading on Sundays was rendered unlawful—although this reform met with stubborn resistance. Margaret defended her case with arguments taken from Holy Scripture, and she was so convincing in doing so that all opposition ceased. Margaret also stressed that thanksgiving to God should be given after every meal—a prayer that became known as St. Margaret's Blessing. With her husband, St. Margaret founded several churches, notably that of the Holy Trinity at Dunfermline.

To correct many grave abuses among priests and the people, she instigated synods, whose rules were helpful in correcting various evils. Perhaps St. Margaret's principal success lay in bringing the Church in Scotland into union with the Roman Church. She made it her constant effort to obtain priests who were eminent for their learning and virtue, and she implored her husband to give them positions of influence.

Margaret's confessor, Bishop Turgot, wrote a beautiful biography of the Saint in which he gave an inspiring picture of the influence she exercised over the rude Scottish court. Among the ladies of the court, St. Margaret formed an embroidery guild to provide vestments and altar linens. In referring to the guild and the care St. Margaret took to regulate the behavior of the ladies while they were performing a service for the Church, Bishop Turgot wrote:

> These works were entrusted to certain women of noble birth and approved gravity of manners who were thought worthy of a part in the Queen's service. No men were admitted among them, with the sole exception of such as she permitted to enter along with herself when she paid the women an occasional visit. There was no giddy pertness among them, no light familiarity between them and the men; for the Queen united so much strictness with her sweetness of temper, so pleasant was she even in her severity, that all who waited upon her, men as well as women, loved her while they feared her, and in fearing loved her.

Bishop Turgot goes on to describe Margaret's disposition and holy conduct:

> While she was present no one ventured to utter even an unseemly word, much less to do aught that was objectionable. There was a gravity in her very joy, and something stately in her anger. With her, mirth never expressed itself in fits of laughter, nor did displeasure kindle into fury. Sometimes she chided the faults of others—her own always—with that commendable severity tempered with justice which the Psalmist directs us unceasingly to employ, when he says, "Be ye angry and sin not." Every action of her life was regulated by the balance of the nicest discretion, which impressed its own distinctive character upon each single virtue. When she spoke, her conversation was seasoned with the salt of wisdom; when she was silent, her silence was filled with good thoughts. So thoroughly did her outward bearing correspond with the staidness of her character that it seemed as if she had been born the pattern of a virtuous life. I may say, in short, every word that she uttered, every act that she performed, showed that she was meditating on the things of Heaven.

Margaret's private life was most austere: she ate sparingly, and in order to obtain time for her devotions she permitted herself only a minimum amount of sleep. Every year she kept two Lents: the one at the usual season, and the other before Christmas. During these penitential times she always rose at midnight and went to church for Matins. The King often shared her vigils. She also had scheduled times during the day for prayer and spiritual reading. We are told that although Malcolm could not read he loved to handle his wife's books of devotion and would often take them secretly to have them illuminated or ornamented with gold and precious stones. One of the most prized of these books was a copy of the Gospels which the Queen took with her on her travels. On one occasion it was accidently dropped by a servant into a stream which they were crossing. When it was finally removed from the water, the book was found unharmed except for a small watermark on the cover. The book is now preserved among the treasures of the Bodleian Library at Oxford.

Perhaps St. Margaret's most outstanding virtue was her love of the poor. She often visited hospitals, in which she tended the patients with her own hands. She erected hostels for strangers and ransomed many captives—especially those of English nationality. When she appeared outside her palace she invariably was surrounded by beggars, none of whom went away unaided.

The royal couple was blessed with eight children, six sons: Edward, Edmund, Edgar, Ethelred, Alexander and David; and two daughters: Matilda (Maud) and Mary. With the utmost care, Margaret instructed them in the Christian Faith and supervised their other studies. When the princesses were old enough, Margaret made them the companions of her spiritual exercises and works of mercy.

Matilda married Henry I of England and came to be known universally as the Good Queen Maud. On her tomb was written in golden letters, "A day would not suffice to tell of all her goodness and uprightness of character." Mary became the wife of Count Eustace of Boulogne and the mother of Matilda, who gave birth to Stephen, the English king. Three sons, Edgar, Alexander and David, successively occupied the Scottish throne and proved capable and pious rulers; in fact, David reigned for 29 years and is commonly regarded as one of the best and noblest of the Scottish kings. Ethelred became the Abbot of Dunkeld and Earl of Fife. Edmund, after a careless and wandering life, repented and became a monk. The eldest son,

Edward, joined his father in the following ill-fated expedition.

In the year 1093, William Rufus, who had succeeded to the English throne, surprised and captured Alnwick Castle. King Malcolm demanded restitution of the fortress, which had previously belonged to Scotland; and when it was refused, he laid siege to the castle. The English defenders, after suffering greatly from the situation, offered to surrender if Malcolm would come in person to receive the keys. Malcolm rode out to meet them. He leaned forward to accept the keys, which were presented to him on the point of a spear. As his fingers were about to touch the keys, the soldier who was holding the spear thrust the weapon through the King's eye, killing him.

Margaret's son, Edward, carried on the siege to avenge his father, but advanced too recklessly and was slain as well. With both leaders dead, the Scots abandoned the siege and relinquished rights to the castle.

During the last six months of her life, St. Margaret was confined to her bed. The day her husband was killed she seemed exceptionally sad and restless, and she said to her attendants, "Perhaps this day a greater evil hath befallen Scotland than any this long time." When her son Edgar arrived back from Alnwick, she asked how his father and brother were. Afraid that the sad news might weaken his mother, he replied that they were well. She looked at him and exclaimed, "I know how it is!" Then raising her hands toward Heaven she said, "I thank Thee, Almighty God, that in sending me so great an affliction in the last hour of my life, Thou wouldst purify me from my sins, as I hope, by Thy mercy."

On November 16, 1093, St. Margaret died. This took place four days after her husband's death, when she was 47 years of age. She was buried at Dunfermline before the high altar where years earlier she had become the bride of the Scottish King. The Abbey Church of Dunfermline was largely destroyed in 1560 by the Protestant Reformers.

St. Margaret was canonized by Pope Innocent IV in 1250. Her feast is observed on November 16, the anniversary of her death.

Chapter 147

ST. MARGARET WARD
and Bl. John Roche

d. 1588

Margaret Ward is referred to in her biographies as "Mrs. Ward," but nothing is told of her husband, family or early life. We are simply informed that she was born at Congleton, in Cheshire, of a gentleman's family and "was in the service" of a lady of distinction, Mrs. Whitall, in London.

Margaret's history actually begins with the priest, Richard Watson, a virtuous and zealous missionary, who had labored hard and successfully in the Lord's service. Under the edicts of Henry VIII, priests were considered traitors whose activities were punishable by death.

The Rev. Watson was eventually apprehended. Having suffered torture, insupportable labors, the intense miseries of his confinement and human frailty, Rev. Watson unfortunately agreed to attend a Protestant service and thereby gain his freedom. But when he was free, his conscience troubled him so much that he visited one of the prisons where his fellow priests were suffering. He confessed his sin and was absolved. To correct the bad example he had given and to relieve his conscience, he visited the same Protestant church, stood in the middle of the congregation and declared in a loud voice that he had made a mistake in attending their services, which "you untruly call the service of God, for it is indeed the service of the devil." He was immediately apprehended and dragged to prison, where he was placed in a small cell in the dungeon. For a whole month he was given only a little bread and water. He was then transferred "to a lodging at the top of the place," where his condition was made even worse by threats, harrassments and insults. The priest's sufferings were at length made known to the Catholic community, but no one dared to visit or help him for fear of being apprehended.

Only Mrs. Ward had the courage to step forward.

To obtain permission to visit Rev. Watson, Margaret first became acquainted with the jailer's wife. She finally obtained permission to make occasional visits to the priest, provided that the jailers were permitted to examine her basket of provisions both before and after her visits. These examinations were meant to prevent letters from being given to the priest or sent out by means of his visitor. Gradually the guards began to trust Mrs. Ward and admitted her without examination.

Rev. Watson then devised a plan by which he could escape—provided he had a rope. Mrs. Ward obtained a rope and smuggled it in under the bread and other food in her basket. Arrangements were made for two Catholic watermen to anchor their boat near Bridewell Prison between two and three in the morning. Almost at the last moment, one of the boatmen refused to participate in the plan. Mrs. Ward confided her difficulty to her young Irish servant John Roche, alias Neale, who decided to help her.

At the appointed time, Rev. Watson, misjudging the distance between the top of the building and the ground, doubled the rope and let himself down. On reaching the end of the rope, about halfway down the building, he could do nothing else but fall the rest of the way. He did so, landing on top of a shed whose roof gave in with a loud noise. The priest was not only stunned in the fall, but also broke an arm and a leg in the process. Helped by the watermen, the priest exchanged clothes with John Roche and was making his escape when he remembered the rope. He asked one of the men to fetch it, saying that if they did not retrieve it the woman who had brought it to him would suffer for having helped him to escape. But since the noise had alerted the guards, there was no time to return for the rope. The priest made his escape, but the guards, on seeing the rope, immediately suspected that Mrs. Ward had been instrumental in providing it to the prisoner. John Roche was soon captured because the priest's clothing, which he wore, betrayed his part in the plot.

The following morning, justices and constables went to Mrs. Ward's home, rushed in, apprehended her and carried her to prison, where she was put in chains. She remained in that state for eight days. She was then hung by the hands, with her toes barely reaching the floor. She remained in this situation for so long a time that she became crippled and paralyzed. When she was brought to the court, she was asked by the judges if she "was guilty of that treachery to the Queen, and to the laws of the realm, by furnishing the means by which a traitor had escaped from justice." With a cheerful countenance Mrs. Ward answered that "she had never in her life done anything of which she less repented than the delivering of that innocent lamb from the hands of those bloody wolves." She repeatedly refused to attend the church of which Queen Elizabeth professed head, or to ask pardon of the Queen, or to do anything that was contrary to her conscience and her allegiance to the Catholic Faith.

Margaret Ward was sentenced to be hanged, drawn and quartered. Challoner reports that "she was executed at Tyburn, August 30, 1588, shewing to the end a wonderful constancy and alacrity, by which the spectators were much moved and greatly edified." Bl. John Roche was also hanged, drawn and quartered at Tyburn on August 30, 1588.

As for the Rev. Watson, after his injuries were healed he was one day walking down a street when he met his former jailer, who recognized him. After he was apprehended, he confessed the details of his escape and was subsequently martyred.

St. Margaret Ward was canonized by Pope Paul VI in 1970.

Chapter 148

BL. MARIA BARTOLOMEA BAGNESI

1514 - 1577

Soon after her birth to a wealthy Florentine family, Maria was placed in the care of her foster mother. Unknown to Maria's mother, who assumed that her infant was receiving adequate care and proper nutrition, the foster mother actually subjected the infant to an inadequate diet which proved to be so detrimental that Maria was never able in later life to eat a normal meal.

When Maria's elder sisters entered the religious life, Maria, too, wanted to join them but she was prevented from doing so due to the death of her mother. Maria, who was then almost 18 years old, was obliged to assume the supervision of her father's household. She conscientiously discharged her duties, with a view to eventually entering a Carmelite convent. When her father unexpectedly arranged a marriage for her, Maria was so shocked and grieved that she suffered a complete breakdown of her health. She was left a bedridden invalid, and the mysterious illness that claimed her body affected her eyes, ears, head, stomach and viscera, causing temporary blindness and deafness and often preventing her from eating or sleeping. Her situation became even more complicated after she submitted, with unfailing resignation, to the revolting and painful remedies prescribed for her by the physicians and charlatans employed by her father. Her condition became so critical that on eight occasions she received the Last Sacraments.

When Maria was 32, her father finally abandoned hope for her health and eventual happiness in a married vocation. He suggested that she join the Third Order of St. Dominic. For a short time thereafter, Maria regained enough strength to rise and attend Mass at the Basilica of St. Mary Novella, to which she was bound as a Dominican tertiary. Her return to relatively good health was only temporary. Her previous afflictions returned with such intensity that she once more took to her bed. Although suffering intensely, Maria was never heard to utter a complaint, and she continued to exercise a wonderful influence on a great many people who came to her seeking advice on spiritual matters. Divinely enabled to read the hearts of her visitors, Maria was also granted a share in heavenly knowledge and was blessed with the gift of advanced prayer. Because of Maria's close union with God, enemies were reconciled, the grief-stricken were consoled, sinners were converted and many of the sick were healed.

When the family's fortune became strained, a new form of penance was inflicted on the helpless invalid—a tyrannical servant, who afflicted Maria with various forms of abuse. Maria patiently endured this persecution for 24 years.

During her sickness, Maria was sustained by the spiritual direction of two holy Dominican priests, who led her to the very heights of perfection. She also maintained a close friendship with the Carmelite sisters of St. Mary of the Angels, who were to be enormously blessed at a later date by the presence of St. Mary Magdalene de' Pazzi.

When Maria died in 1577 at the age of 63, she had been an invalid for 45 years. The Carmelites, who had been unable to accept Maria Bagnesi as a member because of her poor health, wished at least to retain her body after her death. And so it happened that after Maria Bagnesi's departure from this world, her body was first borne by the Dominican Friars through crowds of people to the Dominican Church of St. Mary Novella. The body was then carried to the Carmelite convent, where it was entombed beneath the high altar.

Several years later, the coffin was transferred to the cloister. It was then that the incorrupt condition of the body was discovered.

Of the many miracles of healing performed by Bl. Maria Bagnesi, the most noteworthy was the one performed in favor of St. Mary Magdalene de' Pazzi (d. 1607), who was at the time only 18 years of age. On June 16, 1584, when St. Mary Magdalene had spent three and a half painful months in the convent infirmary, she asked to be taken to the shrine of the Venerable Maria Bagnesi to pray for a cure. The Saint was immediately cured, and upon visiting the shrine later that same day, she beheld the Venerable Maria Bagnesi in the glorious company of Our Lord and His Mother.

Maria Bartholomea Bagnesi was solemnly beatified in 1804 by Pope Pius VII.

The still incorrupt body of Bl. Maria Bagnesi is now seen in the chapel of Carmelo di S. Maria Magdalena de' Pazzi in Florence. There also is found the incorrupt body of St. Magdalen de' Pazzi.

Chapter 149

BL. MARIA CHRISTINA OF SAVOY

1812 - 1836

Descended from a long line of kings and queens, Maria Christina was the daughter of Victor Emmanuel I, King of Sardinia, and Maria Theresa of Austria, who was the niece of Emperor Joseph II. Born at Cagliari, Sardinia on November 14, 1812, she was known throughout her life for her kind, charitable and pious traits. When Maria Christina's father died in 1824, his successor to the throne of Sardinia, Charles Albert, waited until Maria Christina was 20 years old to arrange a politically motivated marriage. Bowing to pressure and a keen sense of duty to her country, the young woman abandoned her plans for religious life and married Ferdinand II, King of Naples.

While fulfilling the obligations of her state in the Bourbon Court of Naples, Maria Christina continued her religious practices and exercised an exemplary influence both on her husband and all who were about her. The people of Naples referred to her as a saint, even though they were unaware of the full extent of her good deeds.

At Naples, on January 31, 1836, when Maria Christina was 23 years old, she gave birth to her only child, who became Francis II, the last Bourbon King of Naples. Much to the distress of her subjects, Maria Christina died 15 days after the delivery.

Because her virtues and good deeds were so well-known during her brief life and because the graces obtained by her intercession after her death were so numerous, the Italian episcopate and many Catholic sovereigns petitioned Pope Pius IX for Queen Maria Christina's canonization. The decree introducing her cause was issued in 1859, and the decree approving the heroic nature of her virtues was issued in 1937.

Chapter 150

ST. MARIA GORETTI

1890 - 1902

Poverty dominated the life of the Goretti family from the very beginning. Maria's mother, Assunta, was an orphan who had never learned to read or write. Maria's father, Luigi, after finishing his tour of military service, returned to Corinaldo, Italy, married Assunta and began to farm for a living. The third child of this marriage was our saint, who was born on October 16, 1890. She was baptized the day after her birth and received the names of Maria and Teresa.

Although Luigi worked hard, his small piece of land could not support his growing family. Eventually, when Maria was six years old, the family's situation became so critical that Assunta and Luigi made plans to move from Corinaldo, a place where they had lived in peace and happiness despite their poverty. The Goretti family settled at Colle Gianturco near Rome, where they stayed for two years farming a piece of land with the help of the Cimarelli family. In later years Assunta revealed that their condition there was no better than it had been before, since they were forced most of the time to "live off chestnut flour pudding and maize bread."

After becoming acquainted with the Serenelli family, which consisted of the father, Giovanni, and his son, Alessandro, all three families journeyed to Ferriere di Conca, a place near Nettuno. Here the Serenelli and Goretti families shared a farmhouse called "la Cascina Antica," while the Cimarelli family lodged in a newer house nearby. Arrangements had been made for all three families to work the land of Count Mazzoleni. Unfortunately, malaria was rampant in that area of the countryside and as a result many died. One year and three months after he and his family arrived there, Luigi contracted the disease and succumbed to it. He was only 41 years old. His widow, who was only 35, was left with six children. The eldest child was 12 years old; the youngest was three months.

After the death of her husband, Assunta was forced to take his place in the fields. Maria, who was then nine and a half years old, willingly and generously assumed the duties of the household and the care of the children. She also assumed the household chores of the Serenellis. She went each day to fetch water from the fountain; she did the washing in the river, and the mending; and she frequently went to the Village of Conca to buy household provisions. From time to time she would go to Nettuno to sell eggs and chickens, and with what she got for them she would buy what the family needed, according to the orders of her mother. Normally she walked to Nettuno with the Cimarellis. The journey was scorching in the summer, and the road was often muddy in the winter. While in Nettuno, they would visit the shrine of Our Lady of Graces to confess, attend Holy Mass and receive Holy Communion.

Assunta revealed that Maria was always obedient because she was of a meek and loving disposition. She also possessed a spirit of mortification, suffering in silence the shortage and sometimes the absence of food. When neighbors gave her sweets, she would always bring them home to share with the other children. We are told that on one occasion, when Maria was doing her customary marketing, a merchant gave her an apple and a sugar cookie, which she slipped into her bag. When the merchant asked why she was saving them, Maria replied that they were for her brothers and sisters.

Maria remained uneducated, her diet was meager and her responsibilities went far beyond what was considered bearable for one her age. Yet Assunta could not relieve her little family of their squalid and harsh situation, since Giovanni Serenelli kept most of the profits from their hard work.

In spite of the difficulties she had to endure, Maria was a cheerful child who by habit was prompt and obedient, regardless of what was asked of her. In addition to her inherent goodness, Maria was also a beautiful child with light chestnut hair. Her intelligence was also obvious to everyone, as was a certain refinement and a delicacy of personality which seemed out of place in the drabness of the Marshes.

While poor in worldly goods, Maria was nevertheless wealthy in the love of the Catholic Faith. It has often been indicated that Maria's sanctity can be attributed to the care with which her mother taught her the basics of the Faith and trained her in the way of virtue.

In addition to lessons from her mother, Maria derived great benefit from the sermons of the parish priest at Sunday Mass and from the training she received prior to her First Holy Communion, which was received on June 29, 1901. For this occasion her clothing and accessories were provided by caring neighbors. According to custom, Maria had already received the Sacrament of Confirmation at an earlier time.

In later years, Assunta described the prayer-life of the little family:

> At home we would close the day by reciting the holy Rosary, except during summer when sometimes we couldn't manage it as there was so much work to do. Little Maria never missed it; and after her father's death, when we had already gone to bed, she would recite another five Mysteries for the repose of his soul. She did this in addition because she knew that I couldn't have Masses celebrated because I didn't have enough money.

While the Goretti family, headed by the widowed mother, stayed faithful to the practice of virtue, the Serenelli family was very different. In their part of the house the father sought relief from his poverty through alcohol, and both the father and son amused themselves with pornographic magazines. Tragedy was soon to follow, when the youth took the life of young Maria.

About a month before the murder, twenty-year-old Alessandro Serenelli started to give Maria difficult chores to perform and always complained that they were not completed according to his orders. Sometimes Maria was reduced to tears, but she continued to do what was assigned to her. Unknown to Assunta, Alessandro then began to make improper advances to the future saint. Not wanting to burden her mother with another problem, Maria never spoke of it.

On the morning of July 5, 1902, Alessandro ordered Maria to mend one of his shirts. While her mother was busy threshing, Maria sat at the top of the stairs along the outside of the house. Maria placed her little sister, Theresa, on a quilt beside her while she began to do the mending. After a while Alessandro, who had been working with Assunta, excused himself and left for the house. After climbing the stairs he grabbed Maria, pulled her into the kitchen, produced a knife and demanded that she submit to him. Protesting that it would be a sin against the law of God to do so and that if he did he would go to Hell, Maria refused to yield. In a rage, Alessandro stabbed her 14 times, each in vital areas: the heart, lungs and intestines.

When little Theresa awoke and began to cry, Assunta sent her son Mariano to quiet the baby and to find Maria. Alessandro's father, who was standing in the shade at the bottom of the stairs, joined Mariano—and together they found Maria, mortally wounded, on the floor of the kitchen. Alessandro was in his room, pretending to be asleep.

At the hospital in Nettuno, surgeons Bartoli, Perotti and Onesti marveled that Maria was still alive; they operated on the victim for two hours without administering an anaesthetic. Because of her serious condition she was not given the water she asked for, but she did receive Holy Communion, the Last Rites and was made a Child of Mary. For 20 hours Maria lay in excruciating pain, a model of perfect patience and forgiveness. With her virginity preserved, she spent her last hours on earth praying and forgiving Alessandro for what he had done. "Do you forgive your murderer with all your heart?" she was asked. Maria replied, "Yes, for the love of Jesus I forgive him...and I want him to be with me in Paradise."

During her final hours of life, Maria often turned her gaze toward an image of Our Lady, and at the prompting of the chaplain she recited ejaculatory prayers. Just before she breathed her last, she called, "Theresa," as though she had suddenly remembered the child she had left on the landing of the stairs. After this she calmly breathed her last. It was three o'clock on the sixth of July, 1902. Maria was eleven years, nine months and twenty days old.

Maria was buried in the cemetery at Nettuno, but later her remains were removed to the Shrine of Our Lady of Graces, where she had so often prayed and received the Sacraments.

Alessandro was tried for the murder and received a prison sentence of 30 years. For a time he remained unrepentant, but he at last experienced conversion during a vision of Maria, who appeared to him in his prison cell. During this vision a garden appeared before him, while a young girl with dark, golden hair and dressed in white went about gathering lilies. She drew near him with a smile and encouraged him to accept an armful of the flowers. After he accepted them, each lily was transformed into a still, white flame. Maria then disappeared.

Upon his release from prison, the now-repentant Alessandro first sought forgiveness from the Saint's mother and then found employment as a gardener in a Capuchin monastery, where he worked until his death. He testified to Maria's sanctity during the Cause of Beatification, as did 30 other witnesses who had known her.

Maria was beatified on April 27, 1947, 45 years after her death. She was canonized on June 24 during the Holy Year of 1950. Because of the unprecedented crowd attending the ceremony, Pope Pius XII performed the canonization outdoors, the first such ceremony to be held outside St. Peter's Basilica. Present were Maria's brothers and sister and her mother, Assunta, who had the distinction of being the first mother to witness the canonization of her child.

During the time of the beatification and canonization, a wax figure of the Saint, which enclosed her bones, was taken to Rome in a glass-sided reliquary; there it was displayed to countless visitors in the Church of Sts. John and Paul. Later the relics were returned to Nettuno.

Among the pilgrims who have visited these relics is Pope John Paul II, who traveled the 40 miles from Rome to Nettuno in September of 1979. While in Nettuno, the Holy Father exhorted young people to look upon Maria Goretti as an example of purity to be emulated in this permissive society. The Holy Father also visited a 70-year-old Franciscan Missionary nun, Sister Theresa, the sister of the Saint.

The Cascina Antica, the house where Maria Goretti lived for three years, is often visited by pilgrims. It remains as it was during the Saint's lifetime. In the middle of the house on the upper floor is the kitchen where Maria was mortally wounded. A marble plaque indicates the exact place where she was found. Also seen here is a bronze bas-relief, the gift of Pope Pius XII, which vividly recalls the Saint's martyrdom. On the exterior of the house the pilgrim can see the steps where Maria was mending Alessandro's shirt shortly before the martyrdom. Pointed out are the bedroom where she had slept in innocence, the threshing-floor where she had played with her brothers and sister, the fountain where she had gone for water and the exact location along the river where she had washed clothes.

Maria Goretti, a poor, unschooled child who died when not quite 12 years old, is the pride of modern Italy and a model for the youth of the world.

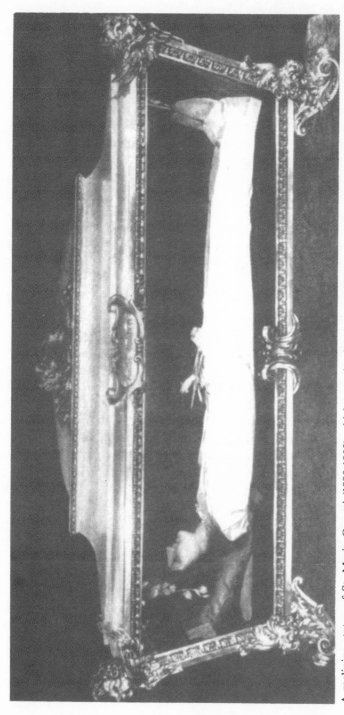

A reclining statue of St. Maria Goretti (1890-1902) which contains her bones. While poor in worldly goods, Maria was blessed with a great piety and love of the Catholic Faith. The Martyr of Purity died at age 11 from knife wounds inflicted by a young man who desired to rob her of her virginity. Before she died she forgave the 20-year-old murderer, Alessandro Serenelli.

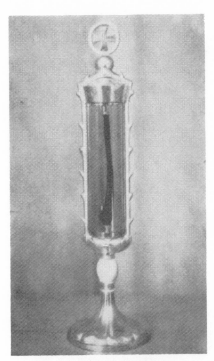

A relic of St. Maria Goretti's arm which is kept in her crypt at Corinaldo. During her short life Maria did the washing, cooking and cleaning for the family and cared for her baby sister while her widowed mother worked in the fields to support the family.

Assunta Goretti, Maria's mother, and Alessandro. After years in prison, Alessandro was converted after a dream in which Maria offered him some lilies. Assunta forgave Alessandro; he testified during Maria's beatification cause.

St. Maria Goretti is the pride of modern Italy and a model for the youth of the world.

Chapter 151

ST. MARINO
(St. Marinus)

Fourth Century

One of the smallest and most ancient states in the world is the independent Republic of San Marino. Situated south of Rimini between the Italian Provinces of Forli, Pesaro and Urbino, it comprises an area of 38 to 40 square miles. Its capital, San Marino, is situated on the slopes of Monte Titano, the highest mountain of a rugged sandstone ridge. Throughout its history the republic served as the refuge for many who fled oppression, especially those seeking safety during World War II.

The Republic takes its name from St. Marino, who was born in the fourth century and was a stonemason by trade. On learning that the walls and town of Rimini were being rebuilt, he and another mason, St. Leo, went there to find work. Both were employed at squaring and working stone in the quarries of Monte Titano. Although the Republic in later years proved to be a safe haven for many, in the fourth century a number of Christians had been sentenced to labor in the quarries because of their loyalty to the Christian Faith. There Marino and Leo discovered a new outlet for their charities and helped their fellow workmen in their labors and encouraged them to persevere. They were also successful in converting many to the Faith.

After three years, St. Leo was ordained a priest and left the area. St. Marino was made a deacon and continued his work in the quarries so that he could be near his converts and could continue his ministry among the captive Christians. Marino worked for 12 years on an aqueduct and was known as a skilled and tireless mason, a good man and a model Christian workman.

According to a history of the independent State of San Marino, the Republic originated with the foundation of a hermitage by a pious mason named Marino. The Bollandists give the following report of how the mason became a hermit, although the story is doubted by some authorities. It seems that while Marino was working, a Dalmatian woman saw him and falsely claimed that he was the husband who had deserted her many years earlier. On hearing her accusation, Marino panicked and barricaded himself in a cave on Monte Titano. The woman eventually gave up her claim.

Disregarding this questionable story, it is thought that St. Marino, wearied from years of strenuous work, decided to spend the rest of his life as a hermit in prayerful solitude. In 1586 the reputed relics of the Saint were found. They are now located atop the high altar in the Basilica of St. Marinus. In the nearby Church of St. Peter are found two niches hewn in the rock, which are pointed out as having been used as beds by St. Marino and his companion, St. Leo.

Chapter 152

ST. MARY OF EGYPT

c. 430

We learn the story of Mary of Egypt from a holy monk, St. Zosimus. After living for 53 years in the same monastery in Palestine, he was divinely directed to a monastery near the Jordan. It was the practice at this monastery on the first Sunday in Lent for the members to disperse in the desert, where they were to live penitentially until Palm Sunday.

Many years later, during the Lenten season, Zosimus found himself 20 days' distance from the monastery. While he was resting and reading his Office, he was distracted by the movement of a white-haired, sun-tanned figure which he took to be a hermit. The figure moved away, but when Zosimus approached for a blessing, he was told, "Abbot Zosimus, I am a woman. Throw your mantle to cover me that you may come near me." Surprised that the woman knew his name, Zosimus gave her his mantle, and after praying together they entered into conversation. In answer to his questions, she revealed her identity, and with shame and remorse she disclosed the sinfulness of her early life.

"My country," she said, "is Egypt. At the age of twelve, while my father and mother were still living, I went without their consent to Alexandria. I cannot think without trembling of the first steps by which I fell into sin or of the excesses which followed." She then revealed that for 17 years she led the life of a public prostitute. At the end of that time she had joined a group of Libyans who were on a pilgrimage to Jerusalem for the Feast of the Exaltation of the Holy Cross. She had gone on the pilgrimage, not out of devotion, but with the intention of gratifying an insatiable lust. She told St. Zosimus, "I embarked with them to seduce them, and I seduced them all to the last one." Upon arriving in Jerusalem she had continued her sinful activities.

513

On the day of the feast, she joined the crowd on the way to the church where the relic of the True Cross was to be exposed for veneration. But again, as the biographer states, she went with the crowd only to seek out new victims whom she might lure into sin. When she reached the church door, she suddenly felt herself blocked by an invisible barrier. She attempted to enter four times, but was always held back. Finally, she retreated to a corner of the churchyard to consider the unusual situation. In a rush of remorse she came to realize that she was excluded from the church because of her wicked life. Upon seeing a statue of the Blessed Mother, she began to weep bitterly. With the deepest humility she implored Our Lady for help and for permission to enter the church, where she might express sorrow for her sins before the sacred wood on which Jesus had suffered. Mary promised that if she were permitted to do this, she would then renounce the world and its ways and do penance the rest of her life. Relying upon the help of the Mother of God, Mary once more approached the door of the church, and this time succeeded in entering without difficulty.

After venerating the Holy Cross, Mary returned to the statue of the Blessed Mother to express her gratitude, and while praying there for guidance she seemed to hear a voice from afar telling her to "cross the Jordan and you will find peace." That same evening Mary reached the Jordan, confessed her sins and received Holy Communion in a church dedicated to St. John the Baptist. The following day she crossed the river and wandered into the wilderness; there she lived completely alone for 47 years, eating herbs and dates, enduring bitter winter cold and intense summer heat. She revealed to the holy monk that she had been severely tempted on many occasions, but she had always implored the intercession of the Blessed Virgin, who never failed to help her.

At Mary's request Zosimus promised not to reveal what she had said to him until after her death. He also promised to meet her again on Maundy Thursday of the following year to give her Holy Communion.

The next Lent, Zosimus made his way to the place where he had encountered Mary the previous year, but on the way he saw Mary standing on the opposite bank of the Jordan. After she made the Sign of the Cross, she proceeded to walk upon the surface of the water until she reached dry ground on the opposite side. She then met the monk and received the Blessed Eucharist with deep devotion. After they had prayed together, Zosimus offered Mary a little basket of dates, figs, and lentils. She accepted only three lentils, and thanked him for his kindness. After commending herself to his prayers, she asked him to return the following year to the place where they had first met.

The next year, when Zosimus went back into the desert to keep this second appointment, he found Mary's dead body stretched out upon the ground. Beside the body these words were traced in the sand: "Abbot Zosimus, bury the corpse of lowly Mary." We are told that the monk, having no spade with which to prepare a grave, was assisted by a lion who helped to dig the grave with his claws.

The monk returned to his monastery where, for the first time, he recounted all that he knew concerning Mary, the penitent. Zosimus lived for many more years until he died a saintly death at the age of one hundred.

Mary's Life was written not long after her death by one who learned the details from the monks of the monastery to which Zosimus had belonged. The Bollandists give good reasons for believing that the Life was written before the year 500.

This Life was instrumental in converting Bl. John Colombini (d. 1367), whose early life was marred by his ambition, avarice and a tendency toward outbursts of anger. After reading the life of St. Mary of Egypt he corrected his faults and began a ministry among the sick and poor. After providing for his wife, he founded the Congregation of Jesuati and died a holy death.

St. Mary of Egypt (c. 430) was miraculously converted from the life of sin she had led since age 12 and spent 47 years alone in the desert, where she endured bitter winter cold and intense summer heat. It is said that a lion used his claws to assist the monk who buried the Saint's body after her death.

516

Chapter 153

ST. MATILDA

895 - 968

At a time when it was customary for girls of gentle birth to be educated in convents, Matilda was confided to the care of her paternal grandmother, the abbess of the Convent of Erfurt. Born about the year 895, Matilda was the daughter of Dietrich, a powerful Westphalian count and Reinhild of the royal Danish house. When Matilda reached womanhood, news of her beauty, piety and learning reached Duke Otto of Saxony; he was seeking a suitable wife for his son, Henry, who had recently obtained an annulment of his marriage to a woman named Hathburg. Following the dissolution of their marriage, Hathburg retired into a convent. It was only then that Henry journeyed to Erfurt to win the hand of the beautiful Matilda.

It is said that Henry fell in love with Matilda at first sight. She was sitting in the oratory, psalter in hand and absorbed in devotion when Henry first saw her. It is speculated that Matilda was as captivated by the charms of her admirer as he was of her. Henry was then 33 years old. He was tall, handsome and had "flashing and penetrating eyes...he was joyous in festivities, but without diminishing his dignity. In war he was loved and feared." Henry is said to have been "overmuch addicted to hunting," and engaged too often in hawking, a sport which was then very popular. This sport won for him the nickname of "the Fowler," a name that followed him through history.

The marriage was celebrated with great festivities in 909 at Wellhausen. The union was well-received and proved to be an exceptionally happy one, Matilda bringing to her husband a wholesome, virtuous influence. Three years after their wedding, Matilda gave birth to her first son, Otto, and soon thereafter Henry succeeded to his father's dukedom. Then, at the beginning of the year 919, when King Conrad died without an heir, Henry was raised to the German throne. In

517

this capacity it became necessary for him to lead his soldiers into warfare. Matilda feared for her husband's safety while he fought with great success against the Danes, the Bohemians, the Hungarians and other aggressors.

While Henry was victorious in these endeavors, part of his success was attributed to the prayers of Matilda, who was known as an exceptionally good and pious queen. It is said that throughout her life she retained the humility which had distinguished her as a girl and that she lived a simple life, although surrounded by the trappings of the royal palace. To her servants she seemed a loving mother; to the distressed, someone who always relieved their sufferings; to her subjects she lightened their burden of taxation and increased their prosperity. If Matilda was a generous queen and a loving wife and mother, Henry was a benevolent king and a thoughtful and kind husband. Together with her husband, Matilda planned good and just laws and worked hard for the advancement of the Church. Although his wife was liberal in almsgiving, Henry never complained, nor did he show irritation at her pious practices. He trusted her in all things and depended upon her good advice and prayers.

Their happy marriage was blessed with five children: Otto, who became the Emperor of the Holy Roman Empire; Henry the Quarrelsome, who became the Duke of Bavaria; St. Bruno, who became Archbishop of Cologne; Gerberga, who married Louis IV, King of France; and Hedwig, who became the mother of Hugh Capet.

When King Henry suffered a serious apoplectic seizure, Matilda rushed to church to pray for his recovery; but while she was at the foot of the altar, word was brought of Henry's death. She at once arranged for a priest to offer Holy Mass for the repose of his soul and, in the fullness of her grief, she removed the jewels she was wearing and gave them to the priest as a pledge that she renounced, from that moment onward, all the pleasures of the world. The holy couple had been married for 23 years.

King Henry had expressed a wish that his eldest son, Otto, should succeed him, but Matilda favored her son Henry, and persuaded a few nobles to vote for him. In the end, Otto was chosen and crowned. Matilda is said to have "expiated her unjust partiality by severe afflictions and in the end by voluntary penance." The matter, however, did not end with Otto's coronation, since his brother, Henry, unwilling to give up his claim, raised a rebellion against him. After discovering that he could not win, Otto pardoned his brother and made him Duke of Bavaria.

Matilda continued living in the palace, but her life was one of penance, prayer and works of charity. She wore the simplest clothes and was frugal in her food and drink. All her jewelry was given over for the benefit of the poor, and her generosity was such as even to arouse criticism. Her son Otto finally accused her of having a secret treasury and of wasting the crown revenues. He forced upon his mother the indignity of having her give an accounting of all she spent, and he even sent spies to watch her movements and to check the amount of her donations. As if this were not enough of a humiliation, she was sorrowed upon learning that her favorite son, Henry, was aiding and siding with his brother against her. With humility and patience she bore her trial, once remarking with what is called "a touch of pathetic humor" that it was a consolation to know that her sons were united, even though it was only to persecute her.

To satisfy them, Matilda resigned the inheritance and gave up the properties left her by her husband and retired to the country residence where she had been born. But as soon as she left, Duke Henry became ill and one misfortune after another fell upon the Kingdom. Since it was felt that this was a punishment for the treatment given the Queen by her sons, Otto's wife, Edith, persuaded her husband to recall his mother, to ask her forgiveness and to restore all he had taken from her. Matilda freely forgave her sons and returned to court, where she resumed her charities. These included nursing the sick, feeding the hungry, bathing those whose afflictions prevented them from doing this for themselves and paying the fines of those who were imprisoned for debt.

St. Matilda had fires lighted in public places to relieve the sufferings of the homeless during the winter months, and she distributed lanterns so that they would not lose their way in the dark.

The trials St. Matilda suffered because of the disagreements of her two sons once again fell to her when the unhappy Henry began another revolt against Otto. Afterwards, he punished a rebellion in his own Bavaria with incredible cruelty, sparing not even the clergy. It seems that the nickname "the Quarrelsome" was appropriately annexed to his name by historians. St. Matilda was deeply saddened by his conduct, and when in 955 she saw him for the last time she prophesied his approaching death and pleaded with him to be reconciled with the Church. When the news of his death reached her, she was prostrated with grief. In his memory she established a number of convents and monasteries.

Otto apparently reconciled completely with his mother and showed his leniency with her charitable activities by leaving the Kingdom in her charge while he journeyed to Rome to be crowned Emperor of the Holy Roman Empire.

Matilda had the pleasure of a family reunion at Cologne on Easter of 965. With all her surviving children around her she was treated with an outpouring of love and honor. It was her great consolation that one of her sons, Bruno, became a priest and afterward Archbishop of Cologne. Following this gathering of the family, Matilda retired from the world, spending her time in visiting her foundations.

At Quedlinburg she contracted a fever which developed into a terminal situation. Realizing that her death was approaching, she sent for Richburga, the Abbess of Nordhausen, who had formerly been her lady-in-waiting and had assisted her in all her charities. According to the traditional story, the Queen proceeded to give away everything in her room until she was told that only her burial linen remained. She instructed them to give it to her grandson, Bishop William of Mainz, who died very suddenly 12 days before his grandmother's death.

The Saint died a most humble death in the year 968 after receiving the Last Rites. Her body was buried beside that of her husband in the church of the Convent of St. Servatius and Dionysius at Quedlinburg, East Germany. Matilda was regarded as a saint immediately after her death.

Chapter 154

VEN. MATTHEW TALBOT

1856 - 1925

The groom was Charles Talbot, a man of thirty years who was distinguished by his uncommonly small stature and somewhat aggressive bearing. His bride was Elizabeth Bagnall, a girl not quite twenty years old who is described, almost unkindly, as being rather "plain-looking." This marriage, which was blessed by the parish priest, took place in 1853 in the small seaside village of Clontarf, which was located two miles from Dublin, Ireland.

While Charles worked as a dock laborer, Elizabeth settled down to prepare for a family. Their first child, John Joseph, was born in 1854; their second son, Matthew, was born on May 2, 1856. During 21 years of marriage, Elizabeth gave birth to 12 children—three girls and nine boys—three of whom died young.

When Matthew was eleven years old, he was enrolled at the Christian Brothers' School. At this time in Irish history, when children started to work at an early age and compulsory school attendance was unthought of, the Christian Brothers labored to help the children of poor families who were able to spend only a short time in school. For this reason Matt Talbot was placed in a "special" class and taught the basics of reading and writing. He was also taught his prayers and the truths of the Faith in preparation for his reception of the Sacraments.

When Matt left school in the summer of 1868, after only one year of schooling, he began working in Dublin as a messenger boy for a wine merchant. His sister, Mrs. Mary Andrews, reported in 1931 that while Matt worked at this job,

> He learned to take alcoholic drink to excess. Our father saw this, gave him a severe thrashing and found a new situation for him as a messenger boy in the Port and Docks Board Office.

But Matt continued to drink notwithstanding all my father did to cure him. Matt left his job after three years so as not to bring disgrace on his father, who was also employed by the Port and Docks Board. Matt then became a bricklayer's laborer, but continued his drinking habits; though he always worked very hard, all his wages went in drink—he even pawned his boots to buy drink. He often missed his Easter duty in those years, but was always careful about Sunday Mass...he had no women or girl friends and there was never anything against his moral character.

It is well-known that Matt's father, Charles, was himself an alcoholic. According to Pat Doyle, a close friend of the family, "Matt and all of them (Matt's brothers) had the liking for drink from the father." The only exception was John, the eldest.

Another of Matt's sisters, Mrs. Susan Fylan, gives us other details of her brother's activities:

He told me himself that he sold his boots and shirt to get drink, and he used to get drink on credit, often having his wages spent in advance. He was quiet most of the time when drunk, but used to curse and swear; he used to come home and lie down; drunkenness [was] his only vice; he was hot-tempered and when drunk used to have rows and fights, but ordinarily he was quiet and was not cross with us at home...I heard him say (after his conversion) that even when drinking he was devout in his mind to the Blessed Virgin and used to say an odd Hail Mary, and he attributed his conversion to this.

Although Matt was given to heavy drinking, he remained a good and steady workman. While employed as a hodman for a bricklayer, he is known to have accomplished more in half-an-hour than the rest managed to perform in an hour. The Master Builder customarily placed him in front to make the rest of the men keep up with him. For this reason Matt became known as "the best hodman in Dublin."

Since his capacity for drink far exceeded the amount of his income, Matt sometimes supplemented his wages by collecting and selling empty bottles. When his thirst still persisted, he often went outside Carolan's Pub to collect tips for holding horses.

One of Matt's nieces, Mrs. Annie Johnson, said in 1948 that Matt and his brothers had such a craving for whiskey that they once stole a violin from a fiddler and sold it for drink. From his early teens until his late twenties, Matt remained an alcoholic who carelessly lost his self-respect, refused to listen to the appeals of his mother and drank not only his earnings, but any money he and his companions could come by honestly or otherwise.

Matt's sister, Mrs. Andrews, gives some of the details preceding Matt's conversion. Matt, it seems, had missed work for several days because of his drunken condition. He was without money and was waiting at the corner of William Street and North Strand for his friends. Since they were leaving work with their wages, Matt expected them to invite him for a drink. When all of them passed by him without the expected offer, Matt turned for home. Matt's sisters tell that upon entering the house,

> Mother said, "You're home early, Matt, and you are sober!" Matt replied, "Yes, Mother, I am." After dinner he remained in the house, which was not usual, and finally remarked to Mother, "I'm going to take the pledge." She smiled and said, "Go, in God's name, but don't take it unless you are going to keep it." As he was going out, Mother said, "May God give you strength to keep it."

Matt went straight to Clonliffe College, where he made his confession and took the pledge for three months. The following morning, a Sunday, Matt received the Holy Eucharist for the first time in years. Afterwards, he was a changed man. He worked regularly, avoided his former companions and spent more time in church. Although there remained a constant inclination to return to his former habits, he struggled to keep the pledge, and when the three months expired, he renewed the pledge for life.

Matt's conversion is said to have occurred in the year 1884, when he was about 28 years old.

After taking the pledge Matt was a changed man, who was never heard to swear again. It has been said that "His workmates were astonished when they heard of Matt taking the pledge; and they were still more astonished when he kept it."

The same energy and determination that Matt devoted to his labors were the same traits that he brought to the service of God. Still working as a hodman, fetching mortar and bricks for the trained workers, he spent every free moment in prayer. His sister, Mrs. Mary Andrews, tells us that after his day's work until ten at night, Matt was seldom off his knees. He observed fasts and slept on a broad plank with a solid lump of wood for a pillow. He attended Holy Mass daily, and on October 18, 1891, Matt joined the Franciscan Third Order. Since his income was no longer being squandered on alcohol, he gave freely to his mother, the poor and religious organizations, especially the missions.

Eventually Matt left home because his brothers continued to drink, despite his efforts to reform them.

Several witnesses testified that Matt went weekly to Confession in Clonliffe and that he was engaged for a long time in paying back the debts he had accumulated during the earlier years. He even spent years in searching through the poorhouses of Dublin for the fiddler whose violin he had stolen, so that he could reimburse him for the price of the instrument. When this effort was unsuccessful, Matt invested the money in Masses for the welfare of the fiddler's soul.

During the early years of his conversion, Matt began to collect books on religious topics. Remembering that his early education was meager, Matt must have labored over reading these books until he gained some proficiency. It is said that his selection of books clearly indicates that he was under the direction of some zealous and unusually perceptive priest who was, himself, a man of great spirituality and deep prayer. All of these books, which bear many of Matt's notes, are carefully kept today in the Archbishop's house in Dublin.

Among these books is a pocket-sized copy of the New Testament which is thought to have been carried by Matt for a long period of time. As a result of reading various biographies, Matt developed a great devotion to St. Teresa of Avila, St. Therese of Lisieux and St. Catherine of Siena.

In one of his books, which he gave to a friend, John O'Callaghan, Matt had written on the fly-leaf these thoughtful words: "Three things I cannot escape: the eye of God, the voice of conscience, the stroke of death. In company guard your tongue. In your family guard your temper. When alone guard your thoughts."

In another book he wrote, "In prayer we speak to God, in spiritual reading and sermons God speaks to us."

When the new Matt had firmly replaced the old, he is described as being always in a good humor and friendly with everyone. His usual greeting was "God be with you," and he was frequently heard singing hymns. His room was free of luxuries and was quite bare except for his plank bed, a chair, a table, a crucifix and some holy pictures. Throughout his life, Matt wore only old clothes that had been given to him. According to Raphael O'Callaghan, who knew Matt well,

> There was nothing striking or impressive in Matt Talbot's appearance. To meet him on his daily rounds he was a very commonplace type of working-man, poorly clad, but clean. He was somewhat below middle height, of slight and wiry build. He walked rapidly, with long strides and loose, swinging gait. His bearing indicated recollection, rather than preoccupation.

In spite of Matt's short stature and his neat but well-worn attire, it is known that about the year 1892 he attracted the attention of a pious Catholic girl who worked as a cook for a Protestant clergyman. Seeing his regular habits and his respect for the women with whom he came in contact, she decided to make his acquaintance and finally suggested marriage. She informed him that she had considerable savings and was in a position to furnish a home in a proper fashion. Matt considered the proposal, but declined the offer after completing a novena for guidance. He later told a confidant that "the Blessed Virgin told me not to marry."

As the years passed and Matt's spirituality deepened, his pious practices likewise increased. The late Sean T. O'Ceallaigh, a former President of Ireland, once testified that as an altar boy, he came to know Matt Talbot personally.

> I came to know him during the time I served Mass at St. Joseph's Church. I knew him from 1890 to 1897 and I spoke to him occasionally. Sometimes I used to open the door for the 7 a.m. Mass, and on such occasions I used to see him waiting on the steps of the church before the door was opened...We altar boys called him Mr. Talbot. Sometimes the boys referred to him as "holy Joe"...In the mornings he used to wait, kneeling on the steps of the church, praying, with his rosary beads in his hand. He usually received Holy Communion...I also saw him in church at the evening devotions and I saw him making the Stations of the Cross after these devotions...He used to pray very fervently and seemed to have a great esteem for prayer...He often prayed with outstretched arms, with his eyes raised to the crucifix, and seemed oblivious of everyone...I would say that he was the nearest I could imagine to one in ecstasy.

> It was before Our Blessed Lady's altar that he was always to be found; he showed special devotion to her...On Sundays he heard several Masses.

Although Matt's free time from work was devoted to prayer and recollection, he was still very much interested in the welfare of those he met. Mr. O'Ceallaigh added:

> He often spoke to myself and some of the other boys. He would ask us if we said the Rosary and if we were fond of doing so; he recommended us to say it. He often asked us a question in Catechism and gave us good advice...He was friendly and kind to us, and we were not afraid to approach him; on the contrary, we used to go to him frequently and talk with him. He was very affable.

Soon after his conversion, Matt gave away his pipe and tobacco, and never smoked again. Added to his ever-present craving for alcohol, Matt suffered the penance of additionally depriving himself of nicotine. Mr. O'Callaghan reveals that Matt once confided to him that it cost him more to give up tobacco than to give up alcohol. John Robbins, who knew Matt Talbot for about 30 years, tells us that "Matt made what I considered a heroic sacrifice in giving up smoking, for he had been a very heavy smoker, using seven ounces of tobacco in the week. When he decided to give it up he went to his confessor in Clonliffe to take a pledge against it."

A number of years after his conversion, Matt began working as a laborer for the timber merchants, T. & C. Martin. The change seems to have been made solely because his working hours enabled him to attend the 6:15 a.m. Mass, and provided more time before work for his prayers and devotions.

Matt was known at the lumberyard as being a most conscientious workman who would not waste a moment of his time. His fellow workmen noticed that during his free time and lunch period, he either read a devotional book or prayed in a secluded area of the lumberyard so as to avoid notice. His noontime meals were so frugal as to draw the attention of many who wondered how he could perform his strenuous work on such little nourishment. Matt avoided all ostentation, and he was always in good humor. He was much respected as being a holy man, and he was liked by his fellow workers, even though he reprimanded them for using foul language.

After Matt's father died in March of 1899, Matt accepted the responsibility of taking care of his mother, since his hard-drinking brothers had moved elsewhere. Undoubtedly Elizabeth was greatly pleased in her old age to be in the company of her devout son and to be able to benefit from the help given by a daughter who lived at home and married late in life.

Matt's mother was soon aware that, in addition to his other penances, Matt undertook frequent fasts besides those observed for Advent, Lent, Ember Days and certain vigils. He ate sparingly at other times and slept but four hours nightly, devoting his waking hours to prayer. He is known to have been under the guidance of a spiritual director who knew of these penances and apparently approved of them. Yet another penance, and one that was also undertaken with the consent of his spiritual director, consisted in the wearing of chains under his clothing. These were so arranged about his body that a constriction and discomfort existed at every movement, yet no one was aware of his difficulty or even suspected that he was performing this unusual form of penance.

Some of Matt's other activities included joining several religious organizations which he financially supported and whose meetings he faithfully attended. Among these groups were the Men's Sodality of the Immaculate Conception, the Pioneer Total Abstinence Association of the Sacred Heart, the Apostleship of Prayer, the Living Rosary and the Confraternity of St. Michael the Archangel. For 35 years, until his death, Matt was a faithful member of the Third Order of St. Francis, having been admitted to profession by Rev. Fr. P. J. Cleary, O.F.M. on October 18, 1891.

In the year 1913, when the Big Strike in Dublin was called, Matt Talbot also went on strike with his fellow workmen. There was no bitterness in this action, and he was never asked to picket or attend meetings like the others; but his belief was the same as theirs, that a workingman deserved a fair wage. He was greatly pleased that those who undeniably had been underpaid received a decent wage as a result, and he was likewise pleased that his own earnings were increased since he could contribute more to charity and the missions.

Matt's mother died in 1915. One of her granddaughters told how kind and devoted Matt was to his mother, and how she often woke at night to see her son kneeling by his bedside praying. Elizabeth was known in the family as a woman of wisdom who did not comment on his unusually long devotions, and there is no record of her having gossiped to neighbors about his pious activities.

During the last years of his life, Matt suffered from kidney and heart ailments. During the year 1923, two years before his death, Matt was admitted twice to the Mater Misericordiae Hospital. While Matt was under the care of the Sisters of Mercy, they considered his condition so grave on the first occasion that he was administered the Last Rites. After his release from the hospital, his condition was one of great discomfort, with shortness of breath and difficulty in breathing.

During Matt's second visit to the hospital, Sr. Veronica remarked that he spent every moment he could in the chapel. One of Matt's roommates has given other details and stated that he had seen Matt

> praying during the night with arms outstretched and holding his rosary in his hand. He used to lead the recitation of the Rosary in the ward. He was very grateful for anything done for him; his disease could cause considerable suffering when he got the attacks, but Matt did not complain and he ate whatever he got. As far as I can recall, Matt spent all his free time visiting the Blessed Sacrament.

Before Matt's second discharge from the hospital, Dr. Moore warned him of the possibility that he might die suddenly of heart disease.

During the last months of his life, Matt confided that he suffered a great deal from pain in his heart and that he frequently experienced great weakness. But somehow his condition improved, so that he was able to return to light duty at work. It is known that he continued to work, and that he did so the day before his death.

At 9:45 on Trinity Sunday, June 7, 1925, while Matt Talbot was walking to Mass on Granby Lane, he paused and then fell to the ground. A number of people rushed to him, while one of them ran to summon a priest. When the priest arrived, it was obvious that Matt Talbot, the reformed alcoholic, was dead. While the 20 people who were present knelt beside the body, Fr. Walsh recited prayers for the dying.

At the time of his death, Matt Talbot was 69 years old. Forty-one of these years had been spent in penance and prayer.

When Matt's body was being prepared for burial, the penitential chains were discovered and removed. One of the chains, it was noticed, had been placed below one knee, immediately below the kneecap, "so placed that it must have caused pain when kneeling." The attendants reported that the chains were not imbedded in the flesh, but that they had apparently been worn for a long time, since grooves had been worn into the skin. The chains were removed and were later placed beside the body in the casket.

Although Mattt died on a Sunday, his burial in Glasnevin Cemetery did not take place until the following Thursday. The humble casket was accompanied by many of the poor who had previously benefited from his generosity.

Matt Talbot's reputation for holiness soon became widespread, and it was everywhere speculated that he would eventually be awarded the honors of the altar. In 1931, six years after his death, the first Enquiry into his life and virtues was begun. Six years later a Papal Decree was signed which introduced his Cause. Another Enquiry took place in 1948. During these two Enquiries, 68 persons who had known Matt Talbot gave depositions concerning his former alcoholic dependency, his courageous reform and his virtuous and penitential life of 41 years.

As part of the procedure toward beatification, Matt Talbot's remains were exhumed in 1952. One of those present at this ceremony was the former altar boy, Sean T. O'Ceallaigh, who served his country as the President of Ireland.

In February of 1962, the remains of Matt Talbot were removed to the Church of Our Lady of Lourdes on Gloucester Street, the parish church of the area where Matt had lived for many years. The tomb has a glass panel which reveals the coffin, and it bears a plaque inscribed, "The Servant of God, Matthew Talbot, 1856-1925."

Another plaque is situated on a wall on Granby Lane and reads,

> The mark opposite this plaque indicates the spot where the Servant of God, Matt Talbot, collapsed and died on Trinity Sunday June 7, 1925. His cause of beatification and canonization was introduced in Rome May 3, 1947. Erected by the Dublin Matt Talbot Committee Nov. 5, 1972."

A simple cross, chiseled into the sidewalk on Granby Lane, indicates the spot where Matt Talbot died.

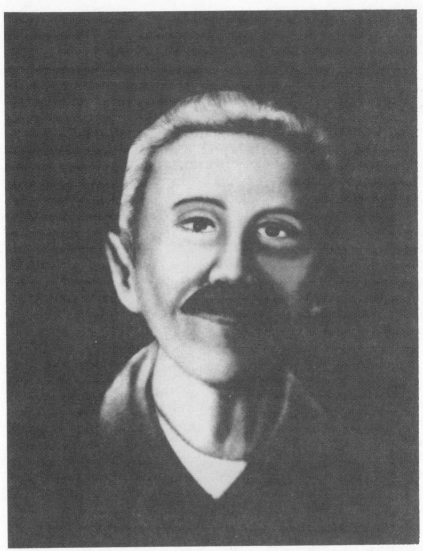

Ven. Matt Talbot (1856-1925), the saintly alcoholic. Matt began drinking to excess around age 12 and swore off alcohol forever around age 28. He spent the rest of his life in prayer, fasting, great penance, physical labor and charity. After his death, penitential chains were found on his body. This photograph of Matt Talbot was taken from a group photo made when he worked at a furniture factory. The original was not clear, but the picture has been enhanced through modern techniques. It is the only photograph of Matt Talbot known to exist.

Chapter 155

BL. MICHELINA OF PESARO
(Bl. Michelina Metelli)

d. 1356

When Michelina was 12 years old, her wealthy and distinguished parents contracted a marriage for her with a member of the ducal Malatesta family of Rimini. The union was quite a happy one—yet, when the death of her husband left her a widow at the age of 20, with one little son, "she seems to have been by no means disconsolate." She had always been fond of pleasure, and she continued her carefree and worldly life as before, apparently giving little or no thought to religion.

Staying in Pesaro was a certain Franciscan tertiary by the name of Syriaca, who spent most of her time in prayer and who lived on the alms and the hospitality of the charitable. Michelina was one of those who opened their doors to the holy woman. Under Syriaca's virtuous influence, Michelina experienced a complete conversion of her life, and when her son died during childhood she renounced the world and its pleasures. On Syriaca's advice Michelina became a Franciscan tertiary. She distributed her possessions to the poor and begged for her food. The change in her life was drastic and difficult for one who had been accustomed to comfort and plenty.

Once, in the early days of Michelina's new life, she confided to a former associate that she longed for a taste of freshly roasted pork. Eager to give her this small gratification, her friend promptly invited Michelina to dinner. But when the meat was served, Michelina suddenly recollected herself. Refusing to sit at the table, she withdrew to do penance for this weakness in deviating from her resolution to mortify herself by eating only rejected scraps obtained by begging.

Michelina's relatives were at a loss to understand her new way of life. Her poverty, which was self-imposed as a result of the distribution of her wealth to the poor, was considered an act of mental derangement. Added to the confusion and embarrassment experienced by her relatives was Michelina's habit of begging and living without a permanent residence. All of this made them decide that she was mentally disturbed. To correct Michelina's supposed mental condition, they went to the extreme of actually shutting her up as a lunatic. Throughout her ordeal, Michelina was so patient and gentle that her relatives finally concluded that, although deluded, Michelina was quite harmless and could be released. Michelina promptly continued her life of poverty, mortification and good works. She nursed lepers and others afflicted with repulsive diseases, performing for them the most menial chores.

Toward the close of her life, Bl. Michelina made a pilgrimage to Rome, where on one occasion, when she was absorbed in prayer, she was allowed a mystical participation in the sufferings of Our Lord. She died on Trinity Sunday in 1356, at the age of 56. From the moment of her death Bl. Michelina was venerated by her fellow citizens, who kept a candle burning day and night before her tomb in the Franciscan church. In 1580 the house she had once occupied at Pesaro was converted into a church, and in 1737 her cultus was solemnly approved.

Married at age 12 and widowed at age 20, Bl. Michelina of Pesaro (d. 1356) continued her worldly life of pleasure after her husband's death. But then a holy woman inspired her to give away her wealth and become a Franciscan tertiary, to devote herself to prayer and good works. Michelina lived by begging and had no permanent home. She carried out her self-imposed poverty to such an extent that at one point her relatives had her shut away as a lunatic. Nevertheless, she was venerated as a saint upon her death. *(Painting by Federico Barocci.)*

Chapter 156

ST. MONICA

331 - 387

St. Monica was born of Christian parents in North Africa, probably at Tagaste, sixty miles from Carthage. Her early training was entrusted to a faithful retainer who had been a nurse to other young members of the family, including Monica's father. This servant was wise in her treatment of her young charge, but somewhat strict. One of her regulations was that of never drinking between meals. This led to one of the few incidents recorded of Monica's early life. What we know of this and other details of her life were given to us by her son, St. Augustine, in his *Confessions*. In Book IX, Chapter VIII, he tells that the servant strictly enforced this regulation, "preventing thereby a naughty custom." St. Augustine records the servant as having said, "Now ye drink water because ye are not suffered to have wine; but when once you come to be married, and be made mistress of butteries and cellars, you will scorn water then, but the custom of drinking will prevail upon you."

By virtue of this teaching the servant "brought the girl's thirst to so honest a moderation, as that now they cared not for what was not comely."

But, as St. Augustine relates:

> There stole upon her a lickerish inclination toward wine. For when, as the manner was, she, being thought to be a sober maiden, was bidden by her parents sometimes to draw wine out of the hogshead, she, holding the pot under the tap, would at the mouth of it, before she poured the wine into the flagon, wet her lips as it were with a little sip of it...And thus unto that daily little every day adding a little more (for whoever contemneth small things, fall by little and little), fell she at last to get such a custom, that she would greedily take off her cups brimful almost of wine.

534

St. Augustine relates that his mother's attraction for wine was checked by a servant who, in a physical manner, made the future saint realize the seriousness of her actions.

> For a maid which she used to go withal into the cellar, falling to words, as it happened, hand to hand with her little mistress, hit her in the teeth in a most bitter insulting manner, calling her "wine-bibber" with which taunt she being struck to the quick, reflected upon the foulness of her fault, yea, and instantly condemned it to herself, leaving it quite.

Following this confrontation with her maid, Monica never again gave way to temptation, and following her Baptism, which occurred soon afterward, she lived an exemplary life in every detail.

As soon as she reached a suitable age, her parents gave her in marriage to Patricius, a pagan and a citizen of Tagaste. Unfortunately, Patricius was violent-tempered and dissolute. St. Augustine tells us that, "She so discreetly endured his wronging of her bed, that she never had any jealous quarrel with her husband for that matter. Because she still expected Thy mercy upon him, that believing in Thee, he might turn chaster."

St. Augustine describes his father as being "of a passing good nature, also very hot and irritable." Patricius never physically abused his wife, although it seemed the custom for the women of that area to have on their bodies and faces the bruises of their domestic difficulties. They were amazed that Monica never displayed signs of ill-treatment from a husband whom they knew was difficult and verbally abusive. One day Monica confided to the women her method of handling an annoyed husband: "Guard your tongue when your husband is angry." St. Augustine tells that "Those wives that observed it, finding the good, gave her thanks for it; those that did not were kept under and afflicted."

In addition to having a difficult husband, Monica also had a difficult mother-in-law whose presence, as a permanent resident of the house, added considerably to the younger woman's difficulties. Afterwards, when the mother-in-law came to realize that it was the gossiping of the servants that sparked her dislike of Monica, she had the servants severely reprimanded. In addition, she promised a harsh punishment for anyone who would again speak against her daughter-in-law. St. Augustine adds, "They lived ever after with a most memorable sweetness of mutual courtesies.''

Patricius and Monica had at least three surviving children: a daughter, Perpetua; a son, Navigius, who was to be his mother's support during many difficulties; and Augustine (354-430), whose love of pleasure and carefree attitude was to cause his mother many years of anxiety.

During their years of marriage, Monica's goodness influenced her husband to learn more of the True Faith. He was eventually enrolled among the catechumens and later was baptized. Thereafter, the relationship of the couple developed into a warm spiritual devotion, which was heightened by their mutual love of the Church. Only one year after his Baptism, Patricius became ill and suffered acutely for several months. With Monica in devoted attendance, she attempted by every means to alleviate his pain. He died in the peace and joy of his faith, with his saintly wife beside him.

At the time of his father's death, Augustine was a 17-year-old catechumen, awaiting Baptism. He was also a student in Carthage, devoting himself especially to rhetoric. Monica was soon to learn, to her great unhappiness, that Augustine was indulging in all the vices of a carefree and self-indulgent young man. Although Monica pleaded with him to abandon his sinful life, Augustine ignored her efforts. While studying science and philosophy, he joined a group that prided itself with being against the established order. During this time he became infatuated with a young woman, and for the next 15 years he lived with her in an unmarried state. She gave birth to a son, who was named Adeodatus. Sometime during these 15 years he publicly renounced the Catholic Faith and declared that he was aligned with the Manichaean heresy. Once when Augustine attempted to visit his mother, Monica forcibly demonstrated her displeasure with her son's activities by refusing to let him stay in her house or eat at her table.

A prophetic vision was given Monica about this time. She seemed to be standing on a wooden beam, while weeping over her son's sinful life, when a celestial being inquired about the cause of her grief. He then told her to dry her eyes, adding, ''Your son is with you.'' Looking toward the spot he indicated, she saw Augustine standing on the beam beside her. When she told Augustine about the dream, he sarcastically remarked that they might easily be together if Monica would reject her faith. She promptly replied, ''He did not say that I was with you; he said you were with me." Monica's ready reply made a deep impression upon her son. This occurred about the end of the year 377, almost nine years before Augustine's conversion.

Monica prayed and fasted to effect her son's conversion. Once, while asking the advice of a wise bishop who had formerly been a Manichaean himself, he reassured her with words that have since become famous: "Go now, it is not possible that the son of so many tears should perish."

When Augustine was 29 years old and planned on teaching rhetoric in Rome, Monica opposed the plan, thinking that this would delay his conversion. On learning that his mother intended to accompany him, he deceived her into thinking that he was going to the docks to bid farewell to a friend, whereas he actually set sail without notifying her. Although grieved at this trickery, she followed Augustine to Rome only to learn that he had continued on to Milan. There he came under the influence of the great bishop St. Ambrose. By the time Monica finally joined her son she was greeted with the pleasant news that he was no longer a Manichaean, although not yet a baptized Catholic. To St. Ambrose she expressed heartfelt gratitude. The holy bishop, for his part, had the highest opinion of St. Monica and never tired of praising her to her son.

For some time, Monica had been trying to arrange a suitable marriage for her son; but in August of 386, Augustine told her what she had been waiting and praying for—that he completely accepted the Catholic Faith. Moreover, he declared that he would, from then on, live a celibate life. Before Augustine's Baptism, Monica joined him and his friends in pious conversations, some of which are recorded in the *Confessions*. During these discussions, Monica displayed remarkable insight and judgment and showed herself to be exceptionally well-versed in the Holy Scriptures. At Easter in the year 387, St. Ambrose baptized St. Augustine and some of his friends.

On its way back to Africa during the same year, the group reached Ostia, where it became necessary for them to await the arrival of their ship. During their stay, Monica contracted her final illness. Before she died she expressed her appreciation to Almighty God for having fulfilled all her hopes. The greatest of these were Augustine's conversion and consecration into the service of the Church. On being asked if she would not be afraid to die and be buried so far from home, the Saint replied, "Nothing is far from God, neither am I afraid that God will not find my body to raise it with the rest." After a five-day coma, Monica regained consciousness and said to her sons, "Here you will bury your mother." Navigius expressed the hope that she would recover and return home with them, but she repeated her request and added, "The one thing that I ask of you both is that you should remember me at the altar of the Lord, wherever you may happen to be." After an agony of several days, Monica died peacefully. St. Augustine records that the Saint died in the "six and fiftieth year of her age, and the three and thirtieth of mine."

Augustine considered it unbecoming to cry at the funeral of one who had died a holy death, but when he was alone he wept bitterly while considering what she had endured for his sake. His love for his mother and the bitter grief he experienced at her passing are recorded at length in his *Confessions.*

St. Monica was first buried at Ostia, but her relics are now kept in the Church of St. Augustine in Rome. They can be found under the altar of the Blessed Sacrament at the end of the left aisle.

St. Augustine went on to become the Bishop of Hippo. By virtue of his strong and lasting influence on Christian theology and philosophy, he is now recognized as a Doctor of the Church.

Successive generations of the faithful have venerated St. Monica as a special patroness of married women, and a pattern for all Christian mothers, especially mothers of wayward children. Having prayed for St. Augustine's conversion for 17 years, she is a worthy example and a source of encouragement for mothers who might at times become discouraged by the resistance of their children to reform their lives. These mothers may take courage in the fact that, in praying so diligently for her son, this mother not only produced a saint for the Church, but in the process also attained sainthood herself.

St. Monica's feast day is observed on August 27; St. Augustine's is celebrated the following day, August 28.

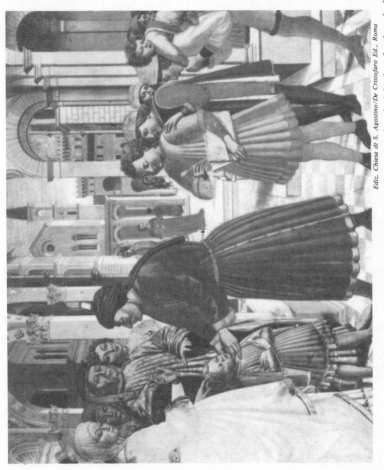

St. Monica (331-387) is depicted *(at left)* with her son, St. Augustine, at school. Much of what is known of St. Monica is learned from the writings of her son in his book, *Confessions*. Because by her continual prayers she obtained the conversion of St. Augustine, who had spent years in licentiousness and heresy, St. Monica is considered a model for Christian mothers.

St. Monica witnesses the Baptism of her son, St. Augustine. Thus began to be accomplished those famous words of a wise bishop who had assured St. Monica that "the son of so many tears" would not perish. St. Augustine went on to become a priest, bishop, and Doctor of the Church.

The death of St. Monica. Before she died, the Saint thanked God for having fulfilled all her hopes. Following St. Monica's funeral, St. Augustine grieved bitterly over what his mother had endured for his sake.

St. Augustine *(left)* and St. Monica. Having prayed for St. Augustine's conversion for 17 years, St. Monica is an inspiration for mothers who are discouraged by their children's resistance to reforming their lives.

A fifteenth-century image of St. Monica. Possessed of an attraction for wine as a girl, St. Monica overcame this fault after a maidservant called her a "wine-bibber." After she married, Monica patiently endured the hardships that resulted from a hot-tempered and wayward husband, as well as a difficult mother-in-law. St. Monica is the Patroness of Married Women.

Chapter 157

ST. NICARETE

Fifth Century

Although three historical sources mention her, very little is known of St. Nicarete. Church historian Sosomen briefly refers to her, while the *Roman Martyrology* describes her as a maiden of Constantinople who "flourished in holiness during the reign of the Emperor Arcadius." St. Chrysostom refers to her in his fourth letter to Olympias, in which he describes Nicarete as "a lady skillful in the healing arts." She is said to have successfully nursed the Saint back to health when he was seriously ill.

St. Nicarete belonged to a pious family of Nicomedia and left home to live in Constantinople, where she devoted herself to good works. Knowing of her virtues and prayerful life, St. Chrysostom suggested that St. Nicarete become a deaconess and supervise the consecrated virgins of the city. However, St. Nicarete would undertake neither office, feeling herself called to serve the Church in more humble and less responsible occupations. She steadfastly upheld and defended the Bishop against his adversaries and, because of this, she suffered persecution early in the fifth century, with St. Olympias and others of the faithful.

Chapter 158

ST. NICHOLAS OF FLÜE

1417 - 1487

Although he is not recognized as the Patron Saint of Switzerland, St. Nicholas occupies a unique place with his countrymen and is perhaps Switzerland's best-known religious figure. His history is interesting in that, during his lifetime, he was a farmer, soldier, magistrate, judge, councillor, father of 10 children and a hermit.

Nicholas was born in 1417 of a relatively wealthy and much respected farming family. His father was Henry von Flüe, who held a civil post in the cantonal service, in addition to his farming duties. Nicholas' mother, Emma Robert, was a devout woman whose two sons, Nicholas and Peter, joined her in a religious organization known as *Gottesfreunde*, or Friends of God. The members of this society tried, by a life of strictness and devotions, to adhere loyally to the practices of the Catholic Church, with an aim at a close relationship with God. Nicholas was especially responsive to his mother's good example and the training he received; he was remarkable from childhood for his piety, his love of peace and his sound judgment.

At the age of 22, this peace-loving man was drafted into the army and fought in the war with Zurich. A fellow soldier recorded that Nicholas "did but little harm to the enemy, but rather always went to one side, prayed, and protected the defeated enemy as best he could."

Sometime after this campaign, Nicholas married a religious-minded girl named Dorothea Wissling, with whom he lived happily; but in 1460 he was again drafted into the army during the Thurgau War. This time he was the captain of a company consisting of 100 men. In this responsible position he maintained strict discipline, restraining his soldiers from all excesses, and succeeded in saving the Dominican convent of St. Catherine at Diesenhofen, which others wanted to burn because it was suspected of being a refuge of the enemy.

Upon his return from the war, Nicholas' countrymen appointed him magistrate and judge and sent him to councils and meetings where his clear-sighted wisdom was highly respected. By his own admission, he had considerable authority as a judge and councillor, but he also said that he did not remember ever having been unjust or having acted in consideration of a person's social position. Despite his obvious talents, he despised temporal honors and repeatedly refused the highest post of all, that of landamman, or governor. A contemporary has said of him,

> A noble simplicity ruled his speech. He displayed such balance of judgment in the cases brought before him that his decision immediately convinced everyone as being right. His spirit of justice and impartiality, as well as his reputation for piety and mercy, had gained for him widespread confidence, and he was often chosen arbiter in serious controversies.

Another contemporary has told that, "He was a friend of peace, a defender of widows and orphans; he was merciful and exhorted the others to show mercy."

Throughout the years of his married life, the holy man continued the devout practices of his youth, and his 10 children were all educated in the Faith. The youngest son, Nicholas, developed a vocation to the priesthood and studied at the University of Bale, where he earned a doctorate degree in theology. For many years he served as the parish priest of Sachseln. John, the eldest son, became landamman during his father's lifetime; he testified to his father's virtue as follows: "My father always retired to rest at the same time as his children and servants; but every night I saw him rise again and heard him praying in his chamber until morning. Often, too, he would go in the silence of the night to the old church of St. Nicholas or to other holy places."

At times Nicholas would also retire into solitude in the valley of the Melch, but when he was about 50 years old he felt irresistibly drawn to abandon the world altogether and to spend his days in the contemplative life of a solitary. He revealed this new vocation to his wife, who recognized the will of God and did not oppose her husband. Nicholas resigned his offices, placed his affairs in order and took leave of his wife, his father, and all his children on October 16, 1467, just three and a half months after the birth of his last child. Nicholas must have amply provided for his family's financial future, because the family never seems to have suffered in a material fashion from the loss of its provider.

At the time of his leaving, Nicholas went barefoot and bareheaded, wearing simple clothes and carrying in his hands his rosary and his staff. His destination appears to have been Strasbourg, but before crossing the frontier, he received the hospitality of a peasant, a Friend of God, who persuaded him to remain in his own country. The next morning, when a fierce thunderstorm produced lightning in the direction in which he meant to travel, Nicholas accepted this as a sign from God and retraced his steps.

It is recorded that one evening during the homeward journey, as he lay under a tree, Nicholas was seized with such violent gastric spasms that he thought his last hour had come. The pain passed, but from that time on he lost all desire for ordinary food or drink and maintained a perpetual fast. According to his own description of what took place, he said that, "A light from heaven seemed to surround me, and I felt in my intestines a violent pain, as if someone had first probed them with a sharp knife and then cut them out. From that instant, I have never felt the need of human food or drink, and have never used them."

Months later, hunters discovered Nicholas in a pasture, where he had made himself a shelter of boughs and moss. When word was brought to his brother Peter and his friends, they went to caution him that he might die of exposure. They successfully persuaded Nicholas to move to Ranft, another part of the valley, where the people of Obwalden built him a little cell with an attached chapel.

In this place Nicholas spent 19 peaceful years. His days were carefully planned, with the morning hours being spent in prayer. Having received from God the gift of counsel, Nicholas spent the afternoon and evening hours interviewing pilgrims, churchmen and politicians who came to ask for his advice on spiritual or temporal matters. His perpetual fast attracted many of the curious, who were given the reply, "God knows" when they asked about it. The truth concerning his perpetual fast was verified by the cantonal magistrates, the physician of Archduke Sigismund and envoys of Emperor Frederick III. Once a year Nicholas took part in the great procession in Lucerne, but otherwise he only left his retreat to attend divine service in a nearby church, and he occasionally visited the Blessed Mother's shrine at Einsiedeln.

The faithful added a room to Nicholas' chapel in his later years. This room served as the residence of a priest, who offered daily Mass for the Saint. The wife and children of Nicholas frequently attended Mass here and were at times among the pilgrims who listened to his words of spiritual counsel. When the need arose, his wife and children did not hesitate to ask his advice in their personal difficulties or concerning the affairs of the household.

When the cantons came together at the Diet of Stans to negotiate a settlement of their opposing positions, which threatened a civil war, their fierce arguments obstructed a resolution of the matter. When they were at the point of returning home to settle matters by arms, the parish priest of Stans stood up and suggested that they should ask the opinion of Blessed Nicholas on how best to settle their differences. The cantons gave their consent, and sent the priest and perhaps others to the cell of the holy man. Some have suggested that the charter known as the Edict of Stans was drafted in the presence of Nicholas at his retreat, while the chronicler Diebold Schilling tells that the priest Imgrund arrived back in Stans to relay the solution given him by Nicholas. Schilling does not record the words of the message, but he informs us that within an hour, the Council had arrived at a unanimous agreement. The date was December 22, 1481.

That Christmas, with a war averted, the whole of Switzerland celebrated joyously, and the Stans Council expressed, in laudatory terms, its gratitude to Nicholas for his wise recommendations. Letters of thanks from Berne and Soleure to the holy man are still extant, as well as a letter written on his behalf by his son John, thanking Berne for a gift of money which would be expended upon the Church.

One of the Saint's visitors, Albert von Vonstetten, dean of the monastery of Einsiedeln, gives us a description of the Saint. He was described as being tall, brown and wrinkled, with thin grizzled locks, a short beard, bright eyes, white teeth and a shapely nose. The dean adds, "He praises and recommends obedience and peace. As he exhorted the Confederates to maintain peace, so does he exhort all who come to him to do the same."

Six years after the Council of Stans, Nicholas was seized with his last illness, which lasted eight days and caused him extreme suffering. He bore his affliction with perfect resignation and died peacefully in his cell, on his birthday, having reached the age of 70. Immediately after his death he was honored in all Switzerland as a patriot and as a saint, but his cultus was not formally sanctioned until 1669.

His remains are found in a shrine under a black marble canopied altar of the present church of Sachseln. The clothes formerly worn by the Saint are said to be kept in a cupboard of the church, but his rosary was broken in pieces for distribution among members of his family.

In 1917, the fifth centenary of the birth of "Bruder Klaus" was celebrated throughout Switzerland with remarkable enthusiasm. Thirty years later, his name was added to the list of saints, when he was canonized in 1947 by Pope Pius XII.

Foto Reinhard, Sachseln

The hermitage cell and chapel of St. Nicholas of Flüe (1417-1487), known affectionately as "Bruder Klaus." Perhaps Switzerland's best-known religious figure, he was, during his lifetime, a farmer, soldier, magistrate, judge, councillor, father of ten children and a hermit.

St. Nicholas of Flüe, who was irresistibly drawn at the age of 50 to the contemplative life of a solitary. When he departed from his family (with his wife's consent),
St. Nicholas went barefoot and bareheaded, wearing simple clothes and carrying
in his hands his rosary and his staff. He ended up in a little cell with an attached
chapel, where he spent 19 years. St. Nicholas lost all desire for human food or
drink and maintained a perpetual fast.

Foto Reinhard, Sachseln

The "meditation cloth" of St. Nicholas of Flüe, kept in the parish church of Sachseln. During his life the Saint was widely sought after for political advice and spiritual counsel. On one occasion a civil war was averted after representatives of the various cantons sought Nicholas' advice. As soon as Nicholas died he was honored as a patriot and a saint.

Chapter 159

VEN. NICHOLAS HORNER

d. 1590

During the reign of Queen Elizabeth, when priests were considered traitors and those who hid or aided them were liable to be severely punished, there lived in London a tailor, Nicholas Horner, who is said to have been a "good and perfect Catholic, a man of plain and just dealing."

Nicholas was apprehended for harboring priests and was imprisoned in a place of detention known as Newgate. According to their usual custom, the jailors clamped irons on both the prisoner's legs, even though one of his legs was seriously injured. The iron aggravated the condition to such an extent that amputation of the leg was inevitable. Afraid that he would give scandal to his fellow Catholics in the prison by impatience or cries of pain during the amputation, Nicholas prayed fervently to Almighty God. As Nicholas reported later, he received comfort from a certain good priest who was in prison called "Mr. Hewett," who was later martyred. This priest consoled the patient by "holding the head of Nicholas betwixt his hands whilst it was adoing (the amputation)...and by means of a certain meditation, which he purposely used at the beginning of the pain, which was of Christ bearing His Cross to the Mount of Calvary. Of all these things many other Catholics were also eye and ear witnesses."

Pollen, in his *Acts of English Martyrs,* continues:

> But afterwards when it was cut off it pleased God to give Nicholas such patience that he not only comforted the other Catholics that were there prisoners, but also drove the surgeons and other strangers that beheld the same into admiration. For whilst it was in cutting off, he being made to sit on a form neither bound nor holden by any violence, neither offered to stir nor used any impatient screech or cries, but wringing his

553

hands in very good order, often said, "Jesus, increase my pains
and increase my patience."

Because the wound of the amputation was slow in healing, Ven.
Nicholas endured almost 12 months of intense pain. Many outside
the prison, on learning of his condition, petitioned for his release.
When he was set at liberty, he found lodging in Smithfield, but soon
thereafter was apprehended again and taken to the prison named
Bridewell. There he was interrogated as to the number and names
of priests who had found lodging in his home. He refused to reveal
this information and was hanged by the wrists until he was almost
dead.

During his next court appearance, Ven. Nicholas was condemned
and sentenced to die because, as two witnesses testified, he had once
made a jerkin for a priest by the name of Rev. Christopher Bales,
who was martyred at a later time.

When the date for his execution was set, Nicholas told certain
of his fellow prisoners of a strange sight he had witnessed one night
that would comfort them, assuring them that if he knew he would
live, he would most certainly keep the incident to himself. The story
of this vision was told by Nicholas to a friend, who in turn transmit-
ted it by letter to Fr. Robert Southwell, S.J. (d. 1590). It is reported
by Pollen in this manner:

> After his condemnation one night, as he was in his close room
> alone, saying his prayers, happening to look aside, he did see
> about the head of his shadow against the wall, in proportion
> of a half circle, a far brighter light than that of the candle, even
> as bright as the light of the sun; and thinking that his sight
> failed him, did rub his eyes and looked again, and seeing the
> said light to continue, took off his kercher from his head to
> see whether it happened of any accident thereof; but notwith-
> standing the light continued all one a good space after. So that
> at last he began to think with himself, that it was a sign given
> him from God to signify a crown unto him. Therefore he im-
> mediately said, "O Lord, Thy will be my will," or to that effect,
> and so within a while it vanished away.

Within a few days Nicholas suffered martyrdom, having a title
set above his head on the gibbet. His body was afterward drawn
and quartered because he had relieved and assisted the priest

Christopher Bales.

Having been born at Grantley, Yorkshire, England, the date unknown, Ven. Nicholas Horner died at Smithfield on the fourth of March, 1590.

Chapter 160

ST. NICHOLAS PEREGRINUS
(St. Nicholas the Pilgrim)

d. 1094

Facts concerning the early life of St. Nicholas are untrustworthy, but it is definitely known that he was a pious and simple-minded Greek who journeyed to Italy. He remained in Otranto for a time and then traveled about in the District of Apulia.

Clad in a single garment that reached to his knees, Nicholas went about carrying a cross in his right hand, while crying aloud wherever he went: "Kyrie eleison." In a pouch he carried apples and other articles, which he gave to the children who flocked around him, echoing his chant.

Often St. Nicholas was roughly handled as a vagrant or a madman, but after his death in Trani, he was soon venerated as a saint because of the miracles believed to have occurred through his intercession. On the strength of the many cures that occurred at his grave, he was canonized by Pope Urban II.

The Archbishop of Trani built a great church in his honor, to which his relics were transferred in 1143. To revive interest in the Saint, which had diminished through the centuries, a second translation of his relics was made in 1616, and a fraternity for boys was organized and placed under his patronage.

St. Nicholas Peregrinus, or St. Nicholas the Pilgrim (d. 1094), who wandered from town to town in southern Italy.

A statue of St. Nicholas the Pilgrim. He was canonized in 1098, only four years after his death, when many miracles were reported at his grave.

Foto Tonino Zito, Trani

A painting depicting St. Nicholas Peregrinus and an angel. Though the Saint was roughly treated during his lifetime, often being considered a vagrant or a madman, he attracted large crowds and after his death was venerated as a saint.

559

Chapter 161

ST. NONNA

d. 374

Nonna was raised a Christian, but she married Gregory, the Magistrate of Nazianzus, who was a member of a sect called the Hypsistarians. This "mixed marriage" eventually resulted in the conversion of the husband, and the birth of three children, all of whom are saints of the Church. St. Nonna is credited with producing for the Church one of the most famous, brilliant and saintly families of Christian history. The eldest child was St. Gregory of Nazianzus the Divine, who served as the Bishop of Nazianzus and became one of the greatest of the Doctors of the Church. His funeral orations for his sister, brother, father and mother are extant and give us wonderful details concerning the virtuous life of his family. The next child was St. Gorgonia, who married and had three children. The third was St. Caesarius, a physician by profession who chose to live in virtuous poverty while tending the ailments of the poor.

St. Nonna suffered the pangs of grief in witnessing the death of two of her children. Gorgonia died in her arms, and she heard the eulogy preached for her son, Caesarius, by her eldest son, St. Gregory of Nazianzus. In this eulogy St. Gregory gave credit to his holy parents for the many virtues of his brother and praised his parents in this way:

> This good shepherd [his father] was the product of his wife's prayers and guidance, and it was she who taught him the ideal of a good shepherd's conduct. He nobly fled from his idols, and later put demons to flight...They have been one in honor, one in mind, one in soul, and their bond no less a union of virtue and intimacy with God than of the flesh. They are equal in length of life and gray hairs, equal in prudence and splendor...they have despised this world and preferred the world beyond. They have cast aside riches, yet they abound in riches

through their noble traffic, since they scorn the goods of this world and deal rather with those of the next...I will add still one more word about them. They have been fairly and justly apportioned to the two sexes. He is the ornament of men, she of women, and not only an ornament but also a pattern of virtue.

Again, St. Gregory is effusive in his praise of his mother:

It is impossible to mention anyone who was more fortunate than my father. I believe that if anyone, from the ends of the earth and from all human stocks, had endeavored to arrange the best possible marriage, a better or more harmonious union than this could not be found. For the best in men and women was so united that their marriage was more a union of virtue than of bodies. While beauty, natural as well as artificial, is wont to be a source of pride and glory to other women, she is one who has ever recognized only one beauty, that of the soul...She rejected paint and other artificial means of adornment befitting women of the stage. She recognized only one true nobility, that of piety, and the knowledge of our origin and final destiny. The only wealth she considered secure was to strip one's self of wealth for God and the poor, and especially for kinsfolk whose fortunes had declined.

As though presenting her as a model for homemakers, St. Gregory tells of her efficiency in the execution of her household duties:

While some women excel in the management of their households and others in piety—for it is difficult to achieve both—she nevertheless surpassed all in both, because she was pre-eminent in each and because she alone combined the two. She increased the resources of her household by her care and practical foresight according to the standards and norms laid down by Solomon for the valiant woman. She devoted herself to God and divine things as though she were completely removed from household cares. In no wise, however, did she neglect one duty in fulfilling the other; rather, she performed both more effectively by making one support the other.

St. Gregory also mentions that St. Nonna "subdued her flesh by fastings and watchings," cared for widows and orphans, and relieved the misfortunes of the distressed.

Nonna survived her husband by a few months and died in church while participating in the Holy Sacrifice. She is thought to have been of a considerable age when she died in 374. St. Nonna is named in the *Roman Martyrology* and her feast is kept by the Greek monks of Grottaferrata, near Rome.

Chapter 162

ST. NOTBURGA

c. 1264 - 1313

The Church has designated two women as patrons of servants: St. Zita of Lucca, Italy, who died at the age of 60 and was named the patroness of domestic workers on September 26, 1953; and St. Notburga of Rattenberg, Austria, who died at the age of 48, and was named patroness of poor peasants and hired servants in 1862.

Notburga was born while St. Zita was still working as a servant in Lucca. When St. Zita died, Notburga was 13 years of age. Like her Italian counterpart, Notburga was of humble origins and, being unskilled, was obliged to work as a servant. At the age of 18 Notburga entered the service of Count Henry of Rothenburg, Germany. She was consigned to the kitchen, where she made it a practice to give all the edible leftover food to the poor who waited for her outside the castle's kitchen door. The less appetizing food she gave to the swine, as was customary. Not content with giving the leftover food to the poor, Notburga reduced her own portion of food to increase the amount she was able to give them.

With the death of Count Henry's mother, who looked favorably on the generosity of her servant, the count's wife, Ottilia, begrudged Notburga's generosity and ordered that all the food that was left after the meals should be put into the pig-buckets and fed to the swine. For a time Notburga did as she was ordered, but later she began to save the better food, and when the swine seemed content with the amount of the inferior food that she had given them, Notburga secretly distributed the better food among the needy. One day her master discovered what she was doing and dismissed her from his service.

After Countess Ottilia died, the poor, who were then receiving nothing from the castle's kitchen, claimed, in a bit of wishful thinking, that the ghost of the deceased Countess haunted the pigsties of Rattenberg Castle. Eventually, the rumors became so widespread that the Count found it necessary to have the place exorcised.

Notburga was next hired as a field worker by a farmer at Eben. During this time an incident occurred which is said to be known even by the children of the region. One Saturday afternoon during harvest time, Notburga was reaping when the church bell rang for Vespers. She immediately stopped working and prepared to attend church services. Her employer, however, ordered her to continue working. She refused, saying that Sunday began with Saturday Vespers and that all good Christians do not reap on Sunday in fine weather. The farmer argued that the weather might change and ruin his crops. "Very well, let this decide it," she replied, and picking up her sickle she threw it into the air, where it remained suspended.

During the time that Notburga was absent from Rothenburg, Count Henry was suffering various misfortunes because of the disputes between the Count of Tirol and the Duke of Bavaria. St. Notburga's biographer claims that the Count attributed all his misfortunes to his deceased wife, who stopped the charity of the kitchen, and was instrumental in Notburga's dismissal.

When the Count remarried and someone was needed to manage the household, Notburga was installed as housekeeper. She lived the rest of her days faithfully fulfilling her duties and helping the needy—with the approval of the Count and his new wife.

When Notburga was on her deathbed, she asked her master to continue relieving the poor. She also asked that they lay her dead body on a farm wagon, and that the oxen be permitted to roam at will. Her body was to be buried at the place where the oxen stopped. This was done, and the poor who came to witness her passage are said to have experienced miraculous occurrences. The oxen stopped before the door of the Church of St. Rupert at Eben. Here Notburga was buried, and in 1718 her relics were enshrined above the high altar.

Chapter 163

BL. NOVELLONE

d. 1280

Until the age of 24, Bl. Novellone lived a remarkably simple and carefree life. A shoemaker by trade, he was a native of Faenza, Italy. Butler tells that, "He did not grow up in the fear of the Lord, and his godless life was in no way altered when he received the Sacrament of Matrimony." But, at the age of 24, serious illness made him think of religion, in much the same way that the prospect of death has brought many a wayward soul to repentance and the practice of the Faith. While on his sickbed he pledged to amend his life, and to help him in this regard he became a tertiary in the Franciscan Third Order.

Novellone began to practice penance and gave liberally to the poor. He went as a penitent to Rome and then walked barefooted to the tomb of St. James the Apostle at Compostela, Spain. He visited this famous shrine ten times. It is said that he had much to suffer from his wife, but it is not surprising that she grew annoyed at his lengthy absences from home, and particularly of his generosity to the poor; neither is it surprising that she would strenuously complain about it. It might be allowed, however, that his wife might have engaged in this criticism to excess. Her attitude abruptly changed one day when a beggar came to her door asking for food. When he left, she found her storeroom well stocked with food, whereas a few minutes earlier it had been quite empty.

After the death of his wife, Novellone gave all that he had to the poor and determined to become a recluse so that he could spend his time in mortification and prayer. To attain this end he lived in a hut near the cell of Brother Lawrence, who was a Camaldolese monk. This was his only connection with that order. Some have incorrectly stated that he joined this order; however, he remained a layman until his death in 1280.

For 56 years Novellone had given his fellow citizens an example of a life well spent for Our Lord. At the end of his holy life, his sanctity was acknowledged by the people and the clergy when he was buried in the Cathedral of Faenza. The veneration paid to Bl. Novellone was approved by Pope Pius VII in 1817.

Chapter 164

ST. NUNILO AND ST. ALODIA

d. 851

The moorish caliph, Abderrahman II, terrorized Spain in the middle of the ninth century and produced for the Church many saints who defended their faith with their lives. Among these martyrs were two sisters, Nunilo and Alodia, who lived in the City of Huesca in northeastern Spain.

The early life of the two sisters was disturbed by the death of their father, a Mohammedan, and the remarriage of their Christian mother to another Mohammedan. Since the two girls had been raised in the Christian Faith, they suffered much in the exercise of their faith because of the brutality of their stepfather. After making vows of virginity, they were additionally troubled when suitors began to visit their home. To avoid these young men and to be enabled to practice their religion without the criticism and restrictions of their stepfather, they obtained permission to live in the house of a Christian aunt. Here they were free to practice their devotions and to spend all their time in prayer, except for the times when they were engaged in necessary duties.

Eventually the laws of Abderrahman were published, and countless Christians suffered as a result. The piety and faith of the two girls being well-known, it was inevitable that they were among the first who were arrested. They appeared before the cadi with Christian joy and resisted the flattery that was intended to induce them to renounce their faith. Promises and special favors were likewise rejected. When all failed, threats were made until finally they were placed in the hands of wicked women who were instructed to lead them into sin. Nunilo and Alodia were divinely enlightened and protected, and after many trials the women of sin had to admit that they could not conquer their resolution. Infuriated, the cadi ordered that they be beheaded in prison, which took place in the year 851.

Chapter 165

ST. OLAF II

995 - 1030

Known in history as "the perpetual King of Norway," Olaf II was a reckless youth who later corresponded to grace to become a defender of his people, a champion of his faith and a saint of the Church.

He was born in 995, and is known as Olaf Haraldsson, the son of Harold Grenske, King of Norway. Aasta, Olaf's mother, was the daughter of a prominent man in the Uplands. When Olaf's father died at a young age, his mother married a local king, Sigurd Syr, who became Olaf's stepfather.

One historian tells that in his childhood Olaf "was a contentious and self-willed boy" who was always supported by his mother, but who despised his stepfather. King Sigurd was a peace-loving man and a successful farmer, who would be called in our day a leader in agricultural reforms. Olaf, as a ten-year-old, was not impressed with his stepfather's innovations. A story is told that King Sigurd once asked Olaf to saddle a horse for him. Olaf came back leading the largest he-goat on the estate, which he had saddled with the King's harness. Olaf then insulted the King by saying that he thought this animal was as suitable for the King as horses were for other riders. The reason for Olaf's dislike of his stepfather is not given in historical accounts, but it seems that later they became good friends, with King Sigurd using his influence to forward his stepson's cause.

It is thought by some historians that Olaf was baptized during his infancy. Others tell that Olaf was an older child when he was baptized at Rouen by archbishop Robert.

Olaf was a minstrel in his childhood and was a clever carver in wood. His craftsmanship and talent were such that he could do almost any kind of work and that he was qualified to judge that which was done by others.

At a time when men matured early, Olaf was sent to sea when he was about 12 years old. He was to become a Viking as a matter of course, much the same as young men of today are sent to college or military school so that they might carry on the tradition of the family. For several years Olaf helped to ravage the shores of the Baltic, Jutland, Holland and Frisia. Olaf himself admitted that his men had nothing but what they stole, and many a time they spilled innocent blood and risked their own lives and souls for loot. He is regarded as the last great Viking chief.

In 1013 Olaf sailed to England and successfully assisted King Ethelred in his wars against the Danes. During the years he spent in England, he gained military experience, wealth and knowledge of the European systems of government. Although he had been baptized earlier, it was only during his stay in England that Christian principles began to influence Olaf's life. He became reacquainted with the Christian Faith and embraced it wholeheartedly, later becoming, as it were, a missionary. Olaf then decided to Christianize his native country, but he came to realize that the establishment of Christianity depended upon a united national kingdom and that the two developments would either fail or succeed together.

In 1015, when Olaf was 20 years old, he claimed the throne of Norway at a time when some of his kingdom was partitioned between the Danes and Swedes. He was fully conscious that, according to the law, this divided section of Norway was part of his realm. With 120 followers, he ventured out to subjugate the inhabitants and to build a united Norwegian kingdom. Before winter set in, he controlled a realm which, according to an old Skaldic poem, "had hitherto been held by five kings." Now that the whole of Norway was under his control, he turned his attentions to the complete conversion of the realm to Christianity.

The conversion of Norway had been started earlier by Haakon the Good and Olav Tryggoesson, but little progress had been made. To accomplish the conversion of his country, Olaf turned to England, the country he had helped in war, for the assistance he needed in this more peaceable endeavor. Olaf was successful in persuading a number of pious and learned priests and monks to work for the conversion of his country. One of these missionaries was Grinkel, who was chosen bishop of Nidaros, Olaf's capital. Olaf relied on the advice of this prelate, and on his recommendation he published many good laws and eliminated those ancient practices and customs that were contrary to the Gospel. In order to thoroughly abolish idolatry, he traveled in person from town to town, exhorting his subjects to open the eyes of their souls to the light of faith. A company of zealous preachers attended him, and in many places they demolished places of pagan worship.

In the next 12 years, during which Olaf reigned in peace, he established the first national government Norway had ever had. In the Uplands he showed keen insight into conditions in the country and inaugurated policies which he and subsequent kings were to follow for over a century.

But Olaf was not content with just encouraging his people to convert. His zeal at times overcame his better judgment and he often forced Baptism upon the unwilling, and he enacted civil legislation which was not approved everywhere. While remnants of heathenism continued to be found for centuries, Norway may be considered a truly Christian country from the time of St. Olaf.

In 1024, St. Olaf called a large meeting at Mostar to enact laws in which fundamental Christian principles were to replace the old heathen beliefs. Regulations were also introduced which were to remind each individual that he was now a Christian and that he lived in a Christian land. Tradition calls this code of laws, "The Laws as Given by Olaf the Saint." This meeting was in reality the birth of the Church of Norway. As a result of this meeting, the Bishops were given authority over the churches. They were to appoint priests and provide for church services. The people were to build churches, keep the holy days and provide financial support for the clergy. Missionaries arrived from Germany, but the English clergy continued to be the most numerous and to exert the greatest influence on the Norwegian church.

St. Olaf's time was not entirely spent in matters concerning the State and Church. Some of his time was spent on more personal pursuits, especially in wooing a Swedish princess named Ingejerd. Although their love seemed to be mutual, this was a time when parents had the last word on whom their daughters should marry. In this respect Olaf had some difficulty. Despite his prestige, wealth, friends and his position as the King of Norway, Ingejerd's family rejected Olaf as a future husband for their daughter and gave Ingejerd to the Russian Prince Jaroslav, who was considered a better match. Ingejerd is said to have continued to love Olaf, and Olaf, for his part, appears to have loved her very deeply, even to expressing this love in a song which he composed. Later, when Sweden experienced peace, Olaf was permitted to marry Ingejerd's sister, Princess Astrid.

After 12 years of tireless effort in organizing the Kingdom and establishing the Church, Olaf's peaceful reign came to an abrupt end. Canute, who ruled both England and Denmark, wanted to add Norway to his empire and gained the support of some Norwegians who resented the way the new faith had been thrust upon them. Others, knowing of Canute's power, decided to align themselves with the stronger force and sided with the enemy. In 1028, when Canute approached the nation with a large army, only a small number of Norwegians stood in support of Olaf, who could do nothing but withdraw before Canute's superior force. After Olaf's retreat, Canute was elected King of Norway.

Crossing into Sweden, St. Olaf spent several quiet months in prayer. His development as a Christian, according to the old accounts, reached its full stature in these last two years before his death while he was in exile in Sweden. Incidents during this time have been related concerning the King's power of prayer, which even cured the sick. A story is told of his dedication to the laws he had enacted: One Sunday evening, Olaf was busily carving a piece of wood—a skill he had learned in his youth. A page reminded him that it was a day when manual labor was forbidden by saying, "Tomorrow is Monday, my Lord." When he realized that the day was Sunday, Olaf asked to be given a lighted torch. He swept the chips together into his hand and lighted them, letting them burn in the palm of his hand. In this way the King showed his desire to practice, himself, the laws which he had imposed on others.

In the spring of 1030, St. Olaf organized an army for an attempt at regaining his kingdom. To prepare for the conflict and to beg God's assistance, he prayed and fasted for two days just before the battle. He went to Confession and Holy Communion the day before and invited his men to do the same. Realizing that the battle would be the last for many of his men, Olaf arranged for Masses to be said for those who would fall in battle.

At Stiklestad, on July 29, 1030, Olaf met his rebellious subjects and his enemy, whose army was twice the size of his own. No one on the battlefield that day realized that in two years' time they would turn to Olaf as their intercessor in Heaven. The struggle was heroic, but the opposing numbers were too great. St. Olaf is said to have been wounded by an axe-blow to his knee, and while he was supporting himself against a stone, Tore Hund drove his spear through the injured King.

While he was dying, St. Olaf was given one more blow to his throat. In the end, most of his men fell with him. Tore Hund, who had speared him during the battle, came afterward to his dead enemy, straightened out his body and dried the blood from his face. The warrior had received a deep wound in his hand, but when the King's blood touched it, it was immediately healed. Tore Hund was the first to tell the chieftains, who had fought against King Olaf, that he was convinced the dead King was a holy man.

St. Olaf was first buried in a steep sandbank by the River Nid, at the place where he had fallen in battle. Near the grave a spring gushed out, the water of which was credited with healing powers. So numerous were the reports of cures that Bishop Grimkel ordered that Olaf be venerated as a martyred saint and that a chapel be built over the place where he had fallen in battle. The large stone against which St. Olaf rested when he was wounded is thought to have been built into the altar. Later, the body of the Saint was carried with somber ceremonies to Nidaros, where it was placed above the high altar of St. Clement's Church.

With the death of Olaf, who had reigned for 16 years, the faith he had established in his country strengthened. Many regretted his passing, particularly since he had been the opponent of Canute, who laid heavy burdens on all Norwegians—the humble as well as those who held places of importance alike.

When St. Olaf's son, Magnus, came to power, the veneration of St. Olaf became widespread. In 1075 the chapel was replaced by a bishop's church, which in time became the great metropolitan Cathedral of Nidaros. During the Middle Ages the cultus of St. Olaf spread to Sweden, Denmark, the British Isles and beyond.

St. Olaf was the last western Saint to receive recognition in Constantinople. He is still regarded by all Norwegians as their patron and national hero. Few countries have produced a national saint who holds such an unusual place in both the political and religious development of a country as does St. Olaf, who is regarded as the

"Eternal King of Norway." He was also the patron of Norwegian bonder guilds, of Norwegian seamen and of homesteads and fields. Many were the pilgrims from afar who streamed to his shrine at Nidaros for the observance of St. Olaf's Day on July 29. According to an early chronicler, "All the nations of the northern seas, Norwegians, Swedes, Goths, Cimbrians, Danes and Slavs flocked on this day to Olaf's tomb in the church at Nidaros, where the Saint's reliquary rested near the altar."

The church at Nidaros, whose altar supported the casket of St. Olaf, unfortunately suffered three disastrous fires: in 1328, 1432 and 1531. Six years after the church's restoration, the casket of St. Olaf was removed. As a result of the Protestant Reformation, the valuable reliquary was sent to Copenhagen and was melted down. The body was buried in a place which is now unknown.

Chapter 166

ST. OLGA (HELGA)

d. 969

Probably of Slavic descent, Olga was considered a peasant when she married Igor, the Varangian Grand Duke of Kiev, Russia. During a campaign against the Drevlianians in the year 945, Igor was assassinated. Since the couple's son, Svyatoslav, was too young to rule, Olga served as regent and eventually effected revenge against the Drevlianians for her husband's death. The details of this effort are described in the *Chronicle of Nestor.*

Olga is given high praise for her courage and ability as a ruler, and for instituting administrative and fiscal reforms throughout the realm. She additionally hastened her country's recovery from the destructive wars that had devastated the land during her husband's reign.

Historians differ in the details of Olga's visit to Constantinople in the year 957. According to a Greek source, she had already been a Christian for several years when she visited the court of Emperor Constantine Porphyrogenitus to renew previously concluded treaties. According to another source, she went to Constantinople to be instructed in the Faith and to be baptized. Constantine Porphyrogenitus is said to have been her godfather. When he became enamored of her beauty and charm—and since he also wanted to align Olga's territory to his own—he proposed marriage. Olga readily recognized his true motive and wisely extricated herself from the situation by referring to Canon Law, which stated that a godfather could not marry his godchild.

Olga's Baptism, which is acknowledged by some to have taken place shortly after the death of her husband, was not followed by the conversion of the nation, since the pagans rallied around her son, Svyatoslav, who resisted all the efforts of his mother to instruct him in the Faith.

Olga's visit to Constantinople was followed by a letter to Emperor Otto I of Germany, asking that missionaries be sent into "the land of Kiev." St. Adalbert was sent, but unfortunately his mission was unsuccessful, some say because he and his associates did not use the Slavonic language.

After Svyatoslav came of age in 964, Olga again served as regent in Kiev while he was engaged in various wars.

Upon Olga's death in 969, her pagan son honored her request and gave her a Christian burial. She was soon regarded as a saint and is honored in the Russian and Ukrainian Churches. Because her conversion took place before the schism, she is also regarded as a saint of the universal Church. She is also recognized as the first Russian ruler (actually a regent) to be officially baptized. Olga did not live to see the conversion of Russia, but has the distinction of being the grandmother of St. Vladimir, who effected the Christianization of his people.

St. Olga

St. Olga (d. 969), the first Russian ruler to be officially baptized. St. Olga desired to convert her Russian countrymen to Christianity. This goal was accomplished by her grandson Vladimir.

This artwork commemorates 1,000 years of Christianity in the Ukraine. St. Vladimir *(left)* and St. Olga are portrayed holding crosses to symbolize the part they played in Christianizing Russia and the Ukraine. There were many Christians in the Ukraine even from the time of the Apostles, but in 988 St. Vladimir made the Ukraine a Christian nation.

Chapter 167

ST. OSWIN

Seventh Century

When St. Oswin's father, Osric, King of Deira, was killed by Cadwalla in 634, the young Oswin was taken for safety to Wessex, where he was baptized and educated. After the death of St. Oswald in 642, Oswin returned to the north to take possession of his kingdom. The Venerable Bede, in his *Ecclesiastical History of the English Nation,* recorded that St. Oswin was "a man of wonderful piety and devotion, who governed the Province of the Deiri seven years in very great prosperity, and was himself beloved by all men."

Bede continues with a description of St. Oswin, telling that he:

> was of a graceful aspect, and tall of stature, affable in discourse, and courteous in behaviour; and most bountiful, as well to the ignoble as the noble; so that he was beloved by all men for his qualities of body and mind, and persons of the first rank came from almost all provinces to serve him. Among other virtues and rare endowments, if I may so express it, humility is said to have been the greatest, which it will suffice to prove by one example. . .

Bede tells that St. Oswin gave an extraordinarily fine horse to Bishop Aidan, who ordinarily traveled on foot. It was the Saint's intention that the horse would relieve the Bishop during lengthy journeys and help him in crossing rivers. A short time later the Bishop met a poor man who asked for alms. The Bishop immediately dismounted and gave the beggar the horse, together with its royal harness and saddle. This charity was reported to St. Oswin before he went to dinner with the Bishop. Joining the Bishop, the King asked him, "Why would you, my lord Bishop, give the poor man that royal horse, which was necessary for your use? Had not we many other horses of less value, and of other sorts, which would have been good enough to give to the poor, and not to give that horse, which I had particularly chosen for yourself?''

The Bishop immediately answered, "What is it you say, O King? Is that foal of a mare more dear to you than the Son of God?''

On entering the dining hall, the Bishop took his accustomed seat, but the King, who had just returned from hunting, stood warming himself at the fire with his attendants. In a thoughtful manner, St. Oswin removed his sword, handed it to a servant, and fell down at the Bishop's feet. Begging for forgiveness, the saintly King declared, "From this time forward I will never speak any more of this, nor will I judge of what, or how much of our money you shall give to the sons of God.''

The Bishop was moved at the sight, and helped the King to his feet, saying he would be entirely reconciled to him, if he would sit down to his meat and lay aside all sorrow. At the Bishop's request, the King relaxed and became cheerful—but the Bishop grew so melancholy that he shed tears. One of his priests asked him in the Scottish language, which the King and his attendants did not know, why he cried so pitifully. The Bishop replied, "I know that the King will not live long; for I never before saw so humble a king; whence I conclude that he will soon be snatched out of this life, because this nation is not worthy of such a ruler.''

The Bishop's prediction was soon realized. St. Oswin's cousin Oswy, King of Bernicia, who it seems was insatiably jealous of his virtuous relative, declared open war against him. St. Oswin, seeing that his men were greatly outnumbered and wanting to spare the shedding of human blood in a useless confrontation, dismissed his forces at a place called Wilfaresdon. Attended by one faithful companion, Oswin retired to a town called Gilling. There he sought refuge at an estate he had earlier given to his friend Earl Hunwald. St. Oswin prayed that Oswy would content himself with possessing his kingdom and would permit him and his subjects to live in peace. Oswy, however, felt that as long as St. Oswin was alive, he would not be secure in his possession of Oswin's kingdom. Oswy, therefore, ordered one of his men, Ethelwin, with a group of soldiers, to search for the holy King and kill him.

St. Oswin resided in what he thought was a secure position with his friend, Earl Hunwald, to whom he had given the estate. But Hunwald was not the good friend the Saint supposed him to be and treacherously betrayed his guest. When Oswin saw the castle surrounded by soldiers, he prepared himself for death and entreated the enemy to spare the life of his faithful servant. Disregarding the appeal, the enemy ruthlessly killed St. Oswin and his servant and then buried them.

Queen Eanfleda, the wife of the envious King Oswy, obtained her husband's permission to establish at Gilling a monastery "in which continual prayers should be offered up for the eternal health of the Kings, both of him that had been slain, and of him that caused it to be done." The monastery was later destroyed by the Danes, but before their invasion the remains of St. Oswin were removed to Tynemouth. During another invasion they were hidden for safety, but in the year 1065 a monk of Tynemouth named Edmund discovered the relics as a result of a vision, and they were again enshrined in the year 1100.

Chapter 168

ST. PANTALEON

d. 305

According to the testimony of Theodoret and other early writers, St. Pantaleon was born in Nicomedia, Turkey. His father was Eustorgius, a pagan senator; his mother, a Christian, was Eubula. When he began studying medicine, Pantaleon proved to be so intelligent and competent that he was permitted to practice his trade before the completion of his formal studies. His reputation was such that he eventually became physician to Emperor Galerius Maximian. Although raised a Christian, Pantaleon became influenced by the activities and "false wisdom" of the court and, unhappily, fell into apostasy. A zealous Christian named Hermolaos awakened Pantaleon's conscience by prudent admonitions, and brought him again to the practice of virtue.

When Diocletian's persecution began in Nicomedia, Pantaleon distributed to poor Christians the wealth he had inherited upon the death of his father. For this act of charity he was betrayed by envious fellow physicians. The Emperor, whom he had medically treated, urged him to apostatize to escape certain martyrdom, but Pantaleon refused and was arrested, together with Hermolaos and two others. After bitter suffering his companions were beheaded, but Pantaleon's ordeal lasted one day longer. He was reportedly subjected to six different attempts on his life by burning, molten lead, drowning, wild beasts, the wheel and the sword. He was finally beheaded. St. Pantaleon is one of the Fourteen Holy Helpers, since he regularly treated the poor without receiving payment.

St. Pantaleon's cultus was firmly established 300 years after his death. His relics were diffused to many parts of Italy and France, but the greater portion of these are found in the church of Lucca, where they were officially recognized in 1715.

According to the practice prevalent in the times of the early persecutions, the blood of martyrs was collected by those who held the heroes of faith in high regard. So it was that a pious lady of Nicomedia gathered the blood of Pantaleon and kept it in her home. Apparently the blood displayed some unusual activity, since merchants of Amalfi, Italy heard of it and journeyed to Nicomedia to obtain it. The blood relic was brought to Ravella, Italy, 22 miles from Naples, where records of the year 1112 reveal that the blood was there in the cathedral consecrated to St. Pantaleon. The blood in its ancient flask is known to liquefy on various feast days, as does the blood of St. Januarius in Naples.

A famous visitor to this relic, and an observer of the miracle, was Cardinal Newman, then a newly ordained priest, who wrote from Naples to Henry Wilberforce in August, 1846. In his letter the Cardinal wrote:

> But the most strange phenomenon is what happens at Ravello, a village or town above Amalfi. There is the blood of St. Pantaleon. It is in a vessel amid the stonework of the altar—it is not touched—but on his feast in July it liquefies. And more, there is a prohibition against those who bring portions of the True Cross into the church. A person I know, not knowing the prohibition, brought in a portion—and the priest who showed the blood suddenly said, "Who has got the Holy Cross about him?" I tell you what was told me by a grave and religious man!

The unusual aspects of the miracle have been carefully documented since 1577, although the liquefaction occurred during the centuries previous to this date. It is indeed extraordinary that this sample of the martyr's blood and its unusual activity have endured for over 18 centuries.

Together with St. Luke and Sts. Cosmas and Damian, St. Pantaleon is regarded as the patron of physicians.

---

1. For a detailed description of the blood relic and the facts concerning its extraordinary liquefaction, consult the book *Relics* by this author.

B. N. Marconi, Genova

This painting of St. Pantaleon (d. 305), a physician, is located above his shrine at the altar of the church at Lucca, Italy. The Saint is one of the Fourteen Holy Helpers, since he regularly treated the poor without receiving payment.

These statues recall the healing practices of St. Pantaleon, who was beheaded under the religious persecution of Diocletian. The Saint suffered attempts on his life by burning, molten lead, drowning, wild beasts, the wheel and the sword. A blood relic of St. Pantaleon liquefies on various feast days.

Chapter 169

BL. PAOLA GAMBARA-COSTA

1473 - 1515

When Paola was only 12 years of age, a marriage was planned for her and a young nobleman, Lodovicantonio Costa. When the child showed reluctance to the plan, the famous Franciscan, Bl. Angelo da Chiavasso, was consulted for his opinion of the matter. In spite of Paola's wishes to postpone the marriage to a later time, Bl. Angelo pronounced that "the Lord had called His servant to the married state." Undoubtedly heartsick at the decision, Paola could do nothing but offer the sacrifice of her life to the will of the Almighty. Having been born in Brescia on March 3, 1473, Paola was married at the age of 12, with all the pomp and celebration suited to the high rank of both families.

During the early days of her marriage and in the years thereafter, Paola lived a virtuous live—in acute contrast to the laxity of the age in which she lived. Soon after her marriage, the young bride's virtue was demonstrated when she composed the rule which she meant to follow for the rest of her life. This she submitted to Bl. Angelo, her spiritual director, for his approval. The rule stated that she was to rise every morning at dawn to recite morning prayers and the Rosary in the chapel of the castle. Later she was to visit the Franciscan church in the neighborhood and attend Holy Mass. In the afternoon she was to recite the Office of Our Lady, and at bedtime she was to say another Rosary and her night prayers. And her duties to her husband were not overlooked in her rule, since the following clause was included: "I will always obey my husband, and take a kindly view of his failings, and I will do all I can to prevent their coming to the knowledge of anyone."

Three years after her marriage, when Paola was a mere 15 years old, her eldest son was born. Other children are also known to have joined the family.

Paola's biographers point out her extravagant generosity to the poor, which seems to have awakened her husband's resentment. As long as food was plentiful, her generosity did not annoy him—but in seasons of scarcity beggars swarmed to the castle to reap the benefits of her charity. Biographers point out, however, that in the case of grain, oil and wine, a supernatural multiplication seems to have taken place in proportion to Paola's generosity, so that her household was actually richer for her charities.

Eventually the young wife was confronted with a terrible trial, in the form of her husband's infidelity. Her husband became so bold in his immoral activities that he actually introduced into the castle a young woman of dubious character. She served him as a spy and became the actual mistress of the household. Paola suffered great humiliation from this ordeal and was concerned about the soul of her husband and his immoral friend. When her husband's mistress fell ill, Paola demonstrated her extraordinary charity by devotedly nursing her. Paola was successful in winning the woman's conversion by having her confess her sins to a priest before she died.

Still another trial confronted Paola, when she was accused of having poisoned her rival as an act of revenge. It was noted that the woman's body was found swollen, and the illness had terminated more quickly than would have been expected. But because of Paola's patience, charity and virtue, she was able to prove her innocence and regain her husband's affection. He returned to the Sacraments and the practice of his faith and allowed his wife to engage in her devotions and works of charity. The rest of Bl. Paola's life is said to have been passed in self-imposed penances and in peaceful wedlock.

Bl. Paola died on January 24, 1515, when she was 42 years old. After her death she was honored as a saint by all who knew her. She eventually was beatified by Gregory XVI in 1845.

Chapter 170

VEN. PAULINE JARICOT

1799 - 1862

The thirteenth child of a poor shepherd, Antoine Jaricot escaped poverty by his wit, intelligence, courage and hard work to become one of the leading silk merchants of Lyons, France. His marriage in 1782 to Jeanne Lattier produced seven children, the youngest being Pauline Marie, who was born on July 22, 1799.

Born into wealth and privilege, Pauline matured into a young woman of great beauty, charm and grace, so that she attracted the attention and admiration of many. Pauline is described by her contemporaries as being slightly above medium height, with a slender figure, dark eyes and dark curls that framed her oval face. She had a coquettish manner and was an excellent dancer. She was also the object of male attention and female envy. Pauline tells us that, "I dressed myself in all my finery, believing myself worthy of universal admiration and preening myself with the conceit of a peacock. Self-love made itself forcefully into my heart." As a result of wearing exquisite dresses and expensive adornments, she received all the admiration she expected. Pauline wrote, "I would have had to be made of ice not to enjoy the flattery, compliments and gentle words of praise I received."

Of all the young men who sought her attention, one succeeded in winning her heart, and for a time she was secretly engaged. In the year 1814, when the City of Lyons celebrated the Bourbon return to the French throne, Pauline was appointed a Lady-in-Waiting to the Duchess of Angouleme. Proud and delighted over her designation, she and her fiancé attended all the royal festivities with great pride and satisfaction.

Pauline's carefree life of pleasure and amusements was greatly altered as the result of a household accident. In October of 1814, Pauline stretched for a box on top of her wardrobe. She lost her footing

587

and fell from the stool on which she was standing. Even though Pauline was in great pain, the doctors were unable to find any broken bones and knew of no remedy that would alleviate her suffering— except for bleeding, which was then a popular medical procedure. Unfortunately, instead of improving the condition, the bleeding caused anemia, weakness and a general physical deterioration.

One symptom followed another as convulsions, chest pains and body spasms added to both Pauline's loss of weight and her power of speech. Embarrassed by her pitiful condition, Pauline finally sent word to her fiancé that she no longer wished to see him.

In compliance with the suggestion of the family doctor, her doting father arranged for Pauline to be sent to the Jaricot country home at Tassin, which was located outside Lyons. Here Pauline's mother, Jeanne, nursed the invalid herself, until the strain affected her health and she was returned to Lyons. When Jeanne died, no one mentioned the loss to Pauline, fearful that the news might cause Pauline additional suffering.

While Pauline was still at her family's country estate at Tassin, the parish priest visited the patient and suggested that she confess and receive Holy Communion. After a brief hesitation, Pauline received the Sacraments. Slowly she regained her health.

Within eight months of her arrival at Tassin, she was well enough to return to Lyons. Fully restored to health, Pauline once more participated in social events. Her creative manner of dress, her graceful bearing, her friendly and coquettish ways once more drew attention and admiration; but a mysterious uneasiness soon developed. Unable to understand why she sometimes felt like crying after attending a social function, Pauline found the solution to her problem one day when she attended a Holy Mass celebrated by Fr. Wendel Wurtz at the Church of St. Nizier.

On that occasion Pauline was wearing a sumptuous outfit which consisted of a pale blue silk dress, blue silk shoes and a hat trimmed with roses. In the church, which was located in what was considered to be the most fashionable part of Lyons, others were similarly well-dressed for Holy Mass. But the complacency and self-satisfaction of the wealthy citizens were soon disturbed, when Fr. Wurtz delivered a scorching homily against vanity. Feeling that the priest was looking directly at her when he spoke, Pauline went into the sacristy after Mass and asked the priest to explain a little more what he meant by the sin of vanity. She was greatly impressed when the priest mentioned that, for some people, vanity consists in the love of attention and those things which hold the heart captive when God is asking a person to rise to higher things. Pauline confessed her sins of pride and decided to renounce herself and worldly pleasures and, instead, to serve God alone.

Complying with the advice given by Fr. Wurtz, who served as her director, Pauline visited the poor in their homes and in the hospitals. She sold her jewelry and other valuables and distributed the money to the needy. As a sign of her final break with her past, she gave away her beautiful dresses and clothed herself in a plain, purple dress which she disliked. Naturally shocked by this drastic change, the family cautioned Pauline to be more discreet and restrained. But Pauline tells us that, "I took such extreme measures because, if I had not broken off all at once, I would not have done it at all. For the first several months, every time I met one of my girl friends dressed in the latest fashion I suffered bitterly...I suffered terribly during my first few months of conversion...I would never have been able to cure myself of vanity if I had not guarded myself carefully. Death seemed to me more preferable than renouncing all the vanities of the world."

While serving the poor, Pauline attended daily Mass and advanced rapidly in virtue. During Christmas week, in the year 1816, Pauline visited the Marian shrine at Fourviere, and while kneeling before the statue of the Blessed Mother, she pledged perpetual chastity.

Endowed with an ability to inspire others, the 18-year-old Pauline helped desolate and wayward girls of her own age and found work for them in her brother's silk factory. To enable them to advance spiritually, Pauline organized these girls into an association known as the Penitents or the Reparatrices (Women of Reparation). The members followed a simple rule of life and held regular meetings, at which they made plans to assist those poor or sick whom they knew to be in need of help.

In 1818, the French Foreign Missionary Society arranged a system whereby laymen assisted the missions with their contributions and prayers. Pauline joined the Society, but later she devised a system which proved more far-reaching and much more successful. She was encouraged in this endeavor by her brother Philèas, a priest who shared her concerns for the Asian missions.

In the beginning, Pauline begged pennies from the 200 Reparatrices at the factory. Within two years she had completed her plan for a system of collections which Fr. Wurtz claimed must have been inspired by God. The organization was established in 1822 and consisted of collectors, each of whom was to ask for pennies every week from ten contributors. The collectors would then give the money to a director, who would be in charge of many collectors. The director would finally forward the funds to a general committee. Known as the Society for the Propagation of the Faith, the organization finally became a worldwide agency which now contributes millions of dollars to foreign missions.

At first the success of the Propagation of the Faith drew criticism from Church leaders who felt that Pauline was meddling in Church business. Other organizations, which endeavored to raise funds for a similar cause, proved to be envious of her accomplishments. Two years after founding the Propagation of the Faith, Pauline finally quieted the vicious remarks and judgments against her by relinquishing the leadership of the organization to a board of directors which was composed of leading Catholic laymen of Lyons.

A few years later, in 1822, Pauline became seriously ill with what doctors diagnosed as a congested liver, an infected lung and a bad heart. The prognosis was that Pauline would probably be an invalid for the rest of her life. Nevertheless, Pauline was gradually restored to health.

Pauline's great organizational talents could not remain idle for long. Satisfied that the Propagation of the Faith remained a successful endeavor, she turned her attention elsewhere, to what was dear to her heart—prayer.

The year 1826 saw the beginning of what would become another worldwide organization, a system of prayer known as the Association of the Living Rosary. Members of this organization were divided into groups of 15, with each member being designated a particular Mystery of the Rosary whose decade was to be recited daily. In this way, the group would collectively pray an entire Rosary every day. The Rosaries were recited for those who had lost their faith—that their faith would be restored, and that faith would be given those who had never had the privilege of membership in the Catholic Church.

A second objective of the new foundation was the spread of good books and articles of piety. Twelve years after the founding of the Association of the Living Rosary, Pauline was able to inform Pope Gregory XVI that more than a million members were enrolled in the organization.

Once again criticism was leveled at Pauline by those who envied her success. In spite of the well-known fact that Pauline's wealthy father financially supported all her charitable endeavors, it was widely rumored that the money collected by Pauline was being used for her own selfish purposes.

To validate her leadership and maintain her integrity, Pauline appealed to Pope Gregory XVI for his approval of the Association of the Living Rosary and the Good Book Society. The Pope responded by forwarding a certificate of approval, but clerical opponents in France intercepted the document, which Pauline did not receive for many years.

Pauline's talent for organization was again demonstrated when, in August, 1832, she purchased a home at Fourviere and called it Lorette, after the shrine of Our Lady of Loreto in Italy. The lay women who lived there became known as the Daughters of Mary. The community consisted of working girls who labored with Pauline in assisting the poor. A frequent visitor to Lorette was the Rev. Jean Marie Vianney, the famous Curé of Ars, who walked the nine miles to Lyons to seek money and clothing for his orphanage at Ars. Pauline and the Curé of Ars shared not only an interest in the poor, but also a great devotion to the Roman martyr, St. Philomena.

Because the document sent by Pope Gregory XVI which authorized the continuance of the Living Rosary was still in the possession of the clergy, Pauline attempted to discourage critics by journeying to Rome to personally request the proper authorization from the Pope. The journey was a particularly difficult one since Pauline's health was very poor. In addition to a heart condition, her doctor diagnosed a growth on her lung. Because of Pauline's very weakened condition during the journey, her two companions thought she would die when they reached the snow-covered Alpine passes. But Pauline would not hear of returning home and continued to Rome, where they accepted the hospitality of the saintly Mother Madeleine Sophie Barat, the foundress of the Society of the Sacred Heart of Jesus.

When Pope Gregory XVI learned of Pauline's illness and her inability, because of weakness, to go to him for an audience, the Pope honored Pauline by visiting with her at the Convent of the Sacred Heart. In addition to the details concerning the Living Rosary, they discussed matters relating to the Propagation of the Faith and the proposal made by Pauline that the headquarters of the worldwide organization be moved to Rome.

As the Pope was leaving, Pauline overheard him telling Mother Barat that he thought he would never see Pauline again, since it seemed as though she were dying. Pauline responded by telling the holy Pontiff that she intended to visit the shrine of the martyr Philomena to ask for a cure. The Holy Father agreed to proceed with the final inquiry into the Cause of Philomena's sainthood, if, as Pauline bargained, she would return on foot to visit him.

A few weeks later, still sick and weak, Pauline and her companions left Rome by carriage for the shrine of the early martyr, Philomena, in Mugnano, near Naples. While attending Benediction at the shrine, the 35-year-old Pauline felt a surge of health. She stood up and walked unaided from the church. A few days later she stood in full health before the Pope, who was amazed that she had experienced a complete cure. As he had promised, the pontiff initiated a study into the Cause of Philomena's sainthood.

Pauline left Rome in May of 1836 and returned to the Lorette, where the members of the community marveled at her complete restoration of health. The cure was considered so phenomenal that the Curé of Ars walked to Lyons to see for himself the wonders performed by his patroness, the youthful Roman martyr, Philomena.

After her miraculous cure, Pauline turned her attention once more to the poor—and especially to working men who were being denied an honest wage. For them Pauline outlined a plan that would provide factory workers with better working conditions, education for their children, a Christian atmosphere in the workplace and at home, and a fair wage for their labors. Her dream was to establish a model factory town, whose organization and principles would inspire and result in many other ideal factory towns.

With the approval of the Curé of Ars, Pauline enlisted the financial help of prosperous businessmen, who invested in the plan. The funds they invested were deposited in what she called the "Bank of Heaven." When enough money was on deposit, Pauline bought a property called Rustrel, which was deemed perfect for the factory community.

In an attempt to silence the critics who had formerly accused her of personally benefiting from moneys collected, Pauline hired a financial adviser, Monsieur Jean-Pierre Allioud. At his suggestion, she also hired Monsieur Gustave Perre. Monsieur Allioud had advised Pauline in financial matters on previous occasions, and she had every reason to trust him implicitly. And Monsieur Perre came with a letter of endorsement from a priest at Apt.

But in May of 1846, Pauline discovered that both men had embezzled money from the Bank of Heaven. Perre, she learned, had paid off personal debts and had maintained a luxurious lifestyle. Pauline was held accountable to the investors for the purchase price of Rustrel, the interest on that amount since the day of purchase and debts contracted by Perre. She was to spend the rest of her life in trying to fulfill her promise to repay the full amount of the debts.

The Jaricot family, as well as many businessmen, advised Pauline to file for bankruptcy, after which she would be legally required to repay only a part of each debt, but Pauline would not hear of it and vowed to repay all the money that had been loaned to her.

While the rich benefactors were insisting on repayment, Pauline was asking for donations from wealthy families, but they usually refused to help her. The poor, it seemed, were her greatest comfort. They donated all they could spare, and several French bishops permitted her to collect alms in their dioceses. With a companion, Pauline begged from city to city. Only a few outstanding members of society helped her with generous donations, including John Henry Newman of England and Frederick Wilhelm of Prussia.

As Pauline struggled to collect pennies, many French clergymen and lay people viciously claimed that Pauline was receiving precisely what she deserved for meddling in Church business. Some people even seemed to enjoy the unusual turn of events, while some claimed that the Rustrel venture was a project devised for her personal benefit.

In 1852 Pauline sold the Rustrel property at a great financial loss. After the sale, she still owed a great deal of money and was forced to apply for a pauper's certificate. City authorities issued the certificate, which stated, "Pauline Marie Jaricot, living on the hill of Barthelemy, is in need and is receiving relief."

After she had exhausted every other means of raising money, her advisers insisted that Pauline ask for assistance from the Propagation of the Faith, based on her role as foundress. But the Council responded, "You never laid claim to the title of foundress of this movement until you found yourself in financial difficulty...Our money is for the missions, not for you."

Even Pope Pius IX considered it only proper for the Propagation to pay her debts, in consideration of all Pauline had done for the Church. The Pontiff even sent his Cardinal Vicar to the Archbishop of Lyons, asking him to give orders to the Propagation that they help Pauline in her difficulties. Despite papal intervention, the Council still refused to help and responded to the Pontiff, "The Propagation does not owe its existence to Mademoiselle Jaricot. Even if it did, it would not be entitled to divert any of its funds to this purpose, since her debts were incurred, not in a work of charity, but in an industrial and commercial enterprise."

Pauline suffered greatly during this time from insults and harassment, as well as from letters of complaint and crude remarks from those she passed on the streets. During her ordeal, Pauline was comforted by her staunch friend, the Curé of Ars, who gave her a small wooden cross on which was written, "God is my witness, Jesus Christ is my model, Mary is my support. I ask nothing but love and sacrifice."

In spite of poor health, 61-year-old Pauline continued her begging tours until her heart and lung conditions made it impossible for her to continue. She also suffered from an increase in body fluids which made her body grow larger and heavier. Her condition was so grave that her doctor held no hope for her recovery. Her companions at Lorette lovingly cared for her, and the poor whom she had helped in earlier times provided her with nourishing food and sweets.

The once wealthy and beautiful young girl who had danced so gaily at parties was now a woman reduced to abject poverty, poor health and humiliation. On January 9, 1862, she begged pardon of her companions for her faults and cried out, "Mary, my Mother, I am all yours!" These were her last words. Two days after her death she was buried in the family crypt at Lyons, with many priests, religious and the poor attending her funeral.

Cardinal Villecourt said of her, "Perhaps in Heaven she will obtain the conversion of those who were her oppressors and who made her undergo a long period of dying."

After Pauline's death, the family sold the property at Lorette and satisfied all her debts.

Pope Pius XI, on June 18, 1930, signed the official decree opening the cause of the beatification of Pauline Jaricot. Five years later, Church authorities exhumed and examined the remains of Pauline Jaricot as part of the beatification process.

In official documents, Pauline Marie Jaricot is recognized as the foundress of both the Propagation of the Faith and the Association of the Living Rosary.

Those wishing to join the Association of the Living Rosary may contact: The Living Rosary, P.O. Box 1303, Dickinson, Texas 77539.

Ven. Pauline Marie Jaricot (1799-1862). As a young girl, daughter of a wealthy and privileged family, Pauline attracted much admiration with her beauty, grace and charm. She lived a life of worldly amusement, following the latest fashions and preening herself, as she admitted later, "with the conceit of a peacock." But at age 16 a fall and a mysterious illness led to her conversion. Realizing that half-measures would never succeed in tearing her from worldly vanities, Pauline sold her jewelry, gave away her beautiful clothes, and clothed herself in a homely and unfashionable dress of purple, a color she very much disliked. For months she cringed interiorly whenever she was seen in this garb by one of her fashionably dressed girlfriends.

Embarking on a life of prayer and good works, at age 18 Pauline began to use her wonderful abilities to found religious organizations—which would grow to remarkable proportions in a few short years. Pauline founded the Society for the Propagation of the Faith and the Association of the Living Rosary. It was Pauline Jaricot who was instrumental in getting the Holy Father to raise St. Philomena to the honors of the altar; this came about after a miraculous cure which Pauline received through St. Philomena when Pauline was near death at age 35.

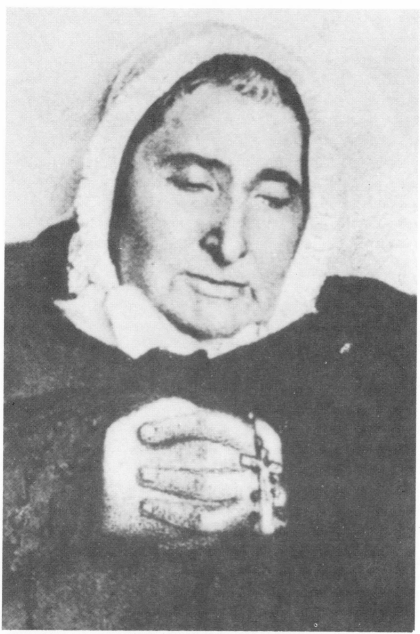

Pauline's last years were spent in illness and abject poverty. She scrimped and saved to make small payments on a huge debt incurred when her plans for a model Christian factory town fell through due to the dishonesty of collaborators. Edema caused Pauline's face and body to swell. During her sufferings Pauline was encouraged by her staunch friend, the Curé of Ars. She died peacefully in 1862.

Above: Fr. Phineas, Pauline's brother, who encouraged and assisted Pauline in gathering prayers and contributions for the missions.

Below: Pope Gregory XVI, who encouraged Pauline in spreading the Association of the Living Rosary, defended her against detractors, and whose astonishment at Pauline's remarkable cure through St. Philomena led to his raising St. Philomena to the honors of the altar in 1837.

Chapter 171

ST. PELAGIUS

d. 925

No details are given about the parents of Pelagius or about why, when he was a boy, he was in the care of his cousin, Hermoygius, the Bishop of Tuy. What is known is that the boy and his guardian were captured during a battle between the Moors and the Christians of Spain and were taken with other prisoners to Cordoba. Bishop Hermoygius soon grew tired of his confinement, his narrow cell and heavy chains and was eventually successful in persuading his captors to exchange him for Moorish prisoners who were held in Galicia. Bishop Hermoygius, upon his release, was to arrange for the exchange. By way of hostage, the Bishop left his young cousin, Pelagius, who was then a mere 10 years of age.

During the next three years, Pelagius grew into a handsome youth whose high ideals, religious fervor and intelligence merited the respect of his fellow prisoners. He soon came to the attention of Abdur-Rahman, who sent for the boy. Although furious that the Bishop had not fulfilled his part of the bargain by winning the release of the Moorish prisoners, Abdur-Rahman looked kindly upon Pelagius. The boy was offered his liberty, together with horses to ride, fine clothes, money and honor for himself and his parents—but on the condition that he deny his faith. Unimpressed by this offer of worldly goods and a life of privilege, the child of 13 displayed a maturity and strength of character rarely witnessed in one his age. Pelagius stood firm and is believed to have said,

> All that means nothing to me. A Christian I have been, a Christian I am and a Christian I shall continue to be. These things are transitory and will come to an end, but Christ, whom I serve, has neither beginning nor end; with the Father and the Holy Spirit He is the one true God, who created us from nothing and sustains all things.

When further promises and arguments, and even threats, did not change the youth's mind, he was condemned to death. He was suspended from the gallows, where he was dismembered—his limbs being thrown into the River Guadalquivir.

Pelagius' heroic death in 925 greatly edified the faithful who rescued his remains. His body was honorably buried, but was then taken to Cordoba in 967. Later, the remains were removed to Leon, but when the Moors again threatened in 985, his relics were taken to Oviedo. King Ferdinand of Aragon, in 1023, acknowledged his devotion to St. Pelagius by having the remains placed in a new silver sarcophagus.

The ordeal of the young martyr was sufficiently well-known to attract the attention of the celebrated nun-poetess, Hrotswitha (930-1002), Abbess of Gandersheim, who wrote of him in the year 962, 37 years after the boy's death. Her poem praising Pelagius consists of 414 verses.

Many churches throughout Spain were dedicated to the youthful martyr, who is represented in art with pincers, the instruments thought to have been used during his dismemberment.

Chapter 172

BL. PEPIN OF LANDEN

d. 646

Pepin of Landen, the Duke of Brabant, had the distinction of being the husband of Blessed Itta (Itte, Iduburga) and the father of Grimoald and two sainted daughters, St. Gertrude of Nivelles and St. Begga.

Considered to have been the wisest statesman of his time, he was mayor of the palace for three monarchs: King Clotaire II, King Dagobert I and the youthful King, St. Sigebert.

When King Dagobert succumbed to a sinful life, Pepin boldly rebuked him and continued to show his disapproval until the King repented. But when Bishop St. Amandus also attempted to convert Dagobert from his dissolute life, Dagobert banished the Bishop from the realm. Somehow, even though Pepin's disapproval was just as severe and unrelenting as was the Bishop's, Pepin seemed indispensible to the King, and he remained securely at court.

King Dagobert held Pepin in such high regard that he placed his son, St. Sigebert, in Pepin's care when Sigebert was only three years old. When the doting father crowned the child King of Austrasia, Pepin was entrusted with the education and care of the youth. Just before Dagobert died in 638, he demonstrated the trust he placed in Pepin's honesty by appointing Pepin to serve as administrator of the Kingdom for his successor, the eight-year-old King Sigebert. A man of lesser worth might have taken advantage of the situation to enhance his own fortune and position, but the trust Dagobert had in Bl. Pepin was well-placed.

While serving in the capacity of administrator of the Kingdom, Pepin relied upon the advice of two holy bishops, Arnulph of Metz and Cunibert of Cologne—and though a faithful minister to the King, he placed his foremost duty to the King of kings.

Pepin considered himself the humble servant of the people. He protected Christian communities of the north against the war-like invasions of the Slavs; he worked hard for the spread of the Christian Faith; and he appointed the most virtuous and learned men to serve as bishops.

Pepin was described as "a lover of peace, the constant defender of truth and justice, a true friend of all the servants of God, the terror of the wicked, the father of his country, the zealous and humble defender of religion." He was also a wise and virtuous man who cared for young Sigebert as though he were his own son. Under Pepin's guidance, Sigebert became a saint and is regarded as one of the most blessed among the French kings.

Even with all the official duties that fell to him, Pepin did not neglect his family. He and his wife, Bl. Itta, trained their children in virtue and instilled in them a love of all that was holy. The eldest of their three children, St. Begga, married Ansigisilus and became the mother of Pepin of Herstal, who grew up to become founder of the Carolingian dynasty. St. Gertrude (d. 659) served as the first abbess of the monastery founded by her mother at Nivelles and was regarded as a saint immediately after her death.

Blessed Pepin died in 646 and was buried at Landen, but his body was later translated to the monastery founded by his wife at Nivelles, where it lies in the same tomb as that of St. Itta and close to the altar of his daughter, St. Gertrude of Nivelles.

A reliquary of Bl. Pepin of Landen (d. 646), the wisest statesman of his time and the father of two sainted daughters. His wife was Bl. Itta.

Bl. Pepin advised three monarchs and worked for the spread of Christianity. He is especially remembered for his positive influence on St. Sigebert, one of the most blessed among French kings, who at the age of three years was placed under Pepin's care. This statue of Bl. Pepin is located in the church of St. Gertrude of Nivelles and stands opposite a statue of Pepin's wife.

Chapter 173

ST. PERPETUA AND ST. FELICITAS

d. 203

The names of these two saints are united in the Canon of the Mass and in biographies because they died together on the same day, only moments apart. For this reason they also share a common feast day in the calendar of saints. The major distinction between the two is that 22-year-old St. Perpetua was a woman of considerable wealth, while St. Felicitas was a slave. At the time of their arrest, Perpetua was the mother of an infant, and Felicitas was an expectant mother.

The record of the passion of St. Perpetua, St. Felicitas and their companions is one of the greatest hagiological treasures that has come down to us. In the fourth century these *Acts* were publicly read in the churches of Africa and were so highly esteemed that St. Augustine found it necessary to issue a protest against their being placed on a level with the Holy Scriptures.

It was in Carthage, in the year 203, during the persecution initiated by Emperor Severus, that five catechumens were arrested because of their faith. Among the five were our two saints. At first the prisoners seem to have been held under house arrest; but in a small diary which she kept, St. Perpetua wrote:

> A few days later we were lodged in prison, and I was greatly frightened because I had never known such darkness. What a day of horror! Terrible heat, owing to the crowds! Rough treatment by the soldiers! To crown all I was tormented with anxiety for my baby. Then Tertius and Pomponius, those blessed deacons who ministered to us, paid for us to be removed for a few hours to a better part of the prison and obtain some relief. Then all went out of the prison and we were left to ourselves.
>
> My baby was brought to me and I suckled him, for he was already faint for want of food...I suffered for many days, but

I obtained leave to have my baby to remain in the prison with me and, being relieved of my trouble and anxiety for him, I at once recovered my health and my prison suddenly became a palace to me and I would rather have been there than anywhere else.

Inevitably the infant was taken from her and was given to the care of its grandfather. While suffering the loss of her child, St. Perpetua was at least comforted that, "God granted that he no longer needed the breast, and that I was not to be tormented with my milk."

In an effort to have her renounce her faith in Jesus Christ and save her life, the Saint's father, who was a pagan, visited her in prison before she was to be questioned and plaintively asked her to "Have pity on your child." The President, Hilarian, joined with the father and said, "Spare your father's white hairs. Spare the tender years of your child. Offer a sacrifice for the prosperity of the emperors." It would have been an easy matter for St. Perpetua to renounce her faith and to reclaim her child and the family she loved, but when asked once again, "Are you a Christian?" she readily accepted the sacrifice of separation and replied, "Yes, I am."

One of St. Perpetua's fellow Christians in prison was St. Felicitas, who had been arrested with her. As an expectant mother, Felicitas knew that a woman in her condition would not be martyred until after the child's birth. Not wanting to be separated from her companions—but wanting to die with them—she and her companions prayed that her baby would be born one month earlier than expected, otherwise Felicitas would be scheduled to die with common criminals.

The prayers of the pious souls were answered. Three days before the date set for their martyrdom, Felicitas began her labor. During her difficult delivery a jailer scoffed at her, "You are groaning now. What will you do when you are thrown to the beasts, which you did not care about when you refused to sacrifice?" Felicitas answered, "Now I myself suffer what I am suffering; but then there will be another in me who will suffer for me, because I am to suffer for Him."

Assisted by St. Perpetua, Felicitas was delivered of a healthy daughter. But soon after the baby was born Felicitas had to part with it. She gave up the child joyfully for Jesus' sake, and committed it to the charge of her sister, a Christian, who promised to raise it with care.

When the day arrived for the martyrdom, the guards wanted to dress the men as priests of Saturn and the women as priestesses of Ceres; but the martyrs refused, saying, "We are come here of our own free will...We have sacrificed our lives to avoid doing such things. This was our agreement with you." The guards relented and permitted them to wear their regular clothes into the arena.

St. Perpetua and St. Felicitas, together with their Christian companions, first were cruelly scourged. They were stripped almost naked and were made to pass before a long line of the officers of the Amphitheater, each of whom struck them with whips that were fortified with balls of lead or iron. When the martyrs reached the end of the line their bodies were torn and bleeding. Afterward they were brought before the crowd to be killed by wild beasts.

Clothed in light garments, Sts. Perpetua and Felicitas were presented to a mad heifer, which tossed St. Perpetua first. She fell on her side, but she soon came to herself—and seeing that her dress was torn, she modestly arranged the garment and adjusted her hair. Upon noticing that St. Felicitas had also been tossed by the animal and was lying bruised, St. Perpetua helped her up. The spectators, now feeling pity for the two women, would not allow them again to be exposed to the animal. The two were accordingly led away to the gate called the *Sana Vivaria.* On seeing her brother along the way, as well as Rusticus, a catechuman who was a great friend of hers, St. Perpetua told them, "Stand firm in the Faith, love one another, and do not be frightened at our sufferings."

Those who survived the attacks of wild animals in the Amphitheater were generally dispatched by the sword. After she gave Perpetua the kiss of peace, St. Felicitas stepped forward first, suffered the blow and expired in silence. St. Perpetua happened to fall victim to an unskilled executioner, who wounded her in the neck without killing her. She at first cried out in pain, but then recovered and calmly guided the man's trembling hand. She received the fatal thrust of the blade and expired.

The martyrdom of St. Perpetua and St. Felicitas took place in the year 203, on the seventh of March—the day on which the Church continues to celebrate their feast day.

Chapter 174

BL. PETER TECELANO
(Bl. Peter of Siena)

d. 1289

The City of Siena, Italy boasts two Eucharistic miracles. One occurred in 1330, when a Consecrated Host stained a breviary page with blood. The other, starting in 1730, resulted in consecrated Hosts remaining perfectly preserved for over 250 years. Siena is likewise proud of its noteworthy native children: St. Catherine of Siena, St. Bernardine of Siena and Bl. Peter Tecelano, who is also known as Bl. Peter of Siena.

Engaged in the trade of comb-making, Peter lived happily for many years with his wife. But at her death, being childless, Peter experienced a great void and loneliness in his life. To alleviate this, he joined the Third Order of St. Francis and gave to his neighbors the money he had previously required for his household. He led a simple life and reached a high degree of sanctity. He worked hard and for long hours, and at night would go to a church to pray.

As Peter felt a longing to live more closely to St. Francis' followers, the guardian of the Friars Minor gave him permission to occupy a small room adjoining their infirmary, where he lived and carried on his business almost until the end of his life. He frequently visited the sick in the Hospital of Our Lady Della Scala and while realizing his duty to his neighbor, he likewise acknowledged his duty to his country. Once when he had been deliberately passed over in the collection of a war tax, he assessed himself and insisted on paying what seemed to him to be a fair amount.

Peter attained such a high degree of contemplative prayer and received so many spiritual graces that he was unable to hide his privileges and became well-known as an extremely holy man. Many asked for his opinions and advice, including priests, theologians, lay brothers and fellow workmen. With all the attention given him he remained a very humble person. In his own opinion, he listed talkativeness among his chief faults. It is said that it took him 14 years of hard work to control his tongue and build up the habit of silence.

Peter lived to an advanced age, and as he lay dying, he predicted the calamities that were soon to fall on Pistoia and Florence, as well as Siena. Peter Tecelano died in the year 1289 and was buried in a Franciscan church, where pilgrims journeyed from all over Italy to pray at his tomb. His cultus was approved in 1802 by Pope Pius VII.

Bl. Peter Tecelano (d. 1289), a comb-maker of Siena, Italy, is pictured with his finger on his mouth to depict his 14-year effort to control what he considered one of his worst faults—talkativeness. Bl. Peter is one of three saintly natives of Siena, the other two being St. Catherine of Siena and St. Bernardine of Siena.

1. Peter Tecelano, pictured in three of these panels, tried to alleviate the great feeling of loss he experienced at the death of his wife by joining the Third Order of St. Francis and giving away the money he had previously required for his household. He became known in his lifetime as an extremely holy man whose advice was widely sought, even by priests and theologians. Nonetheless, Peter remained very humble. On one occasion, when he was deliberately passed over in the collection of a war tax, he assessed himself and insisted on paying an amount he considered fair.

609

Bl. Peter Tecelano lived to an advanced age. As he lay dying he predicted calamities soon to fall on Pistoia, Florence and Siena. After his death pilgrims journeyed from all over Italy to visit his tomb in a Franciscan church.

Chapter 175

ST. PHARAILDIS

d. 740

A virtuous maiden who had secretly consecrated her virginity to God, Pharaildis was forced by her parents to marry a wealthy suitor. Having obeyed her parents by participating in the marriage ceremony, she resolutely determined to keep her vow and steadfastly refused to live with her new husband in the married state. Rejected and refused marital privileges, the new husband brutally mistreated his young wife. We are not told how long the marriage endured, but at length the husband died, leaving Pharaildis a widow—with her virginity intact.

Little else is recorded of this saint, except that she died about the year 740. There were reports of various translations of her relics and numerous miracles worked through her intercession. She became a very popular saint in Flanders and is known by different variations of her name: Varelde, Verylde or Veerle.

In art St. Pharaildis is sometimes pictured with a goose or loaves of bread. The goose may be connected with the city of Ghent, or Gand, where the Saint was born and where her relics repose. The bread is connected to a miracle which is said to have been worked beside her tomb. The miracle involves a beggar who was praying at the tomb; kneeling close by was a woman who was holding bread in her apron. When the beggar noticed the bread and asked for a piece, the woman hid the loaves and declared that she had nothing to give him. She later discovered that the loaves had been turned into stones.

St. Pharaildis is said to have caused a fountain of fresh water to spring out of the ground at Bruay, near Valenciennes, to relieve the thirst of harvesters. The water of this spring is thought to relieve children's disorders. St. Pharaildis is invoked by mothers who are anxious about the health of their children.

Chapter 176

ST. PHILEMON AND ST. APOLLONIUS

d. 305

During the persecution of Diocletian, it was the obligation of each citizen to honor the gods by offering sacrifice to them. Realizing that refusal to do this would result in their imprisonment and possible death, many frightened Christians occasionally hired pagans to offer this sacrifice in their stead. Certificates stating that they had complied with their obligation were to be brought back to them by the pagans who had taken their places. According to Butler, the Church did not necessarily regard these Christians as apostates and merely compelled these *"libellatici"* to do penance for this cowardly act.

Apollonius was well aware of the sufferings endured by many Christians who refused to deny their faith by sacrificing to the false gods. To avoid a similar end, he planned to escape detection as a Christian by hiring someone to take his place at a pagan ceremony. A well-known piper and dancer named Philemon was willing to do this favor for the price of four gold coins. To prepare himself, Philemon asked that he be given some of Apollonius' clothes and a cape with a hood so that he could conceal his face. While disguised in this manner, he went before the judge for questioning and to perform the rite. But when it came time to offer sacrifice, Philemon was suddenly converted by the Holy Spirit. He declared his belief in Jesus Christ and refused to acknowledge the idols.

When Philemon's true identity was made known, all who were present accepted the incident as a jest, thinking that the piper-dancer was also capable of impersonations. When the laughter was over and Philemon was asked in all seriousness to comply with the Emperor's edicts, the Saint, who had received Baptism by desire, stoutly refused to do so.

Apollonius was arrested during this time. Ashamed of his cowardice, he courageously proclaimed his belief in Jesus Christ, and to make amends for his weakness he persistently refused to recant, although there existed the possibility of torture.

The two Saints were eventually martyred in the year 305 by being sewn up in sacks and cast into the sea.

Chapter 177

ST. PHILIP HOWARD

1557 - 1595

A distinguished group stood around the gold baptismal font in the Chapel Royal at Whitehall, including Mary Tudor and her court; Philip II, the Catholic monarch of Spain who was godfather; and Thomas Howard, the fourth Duke of Norfolk, who was the father of the three-day-old infant, Philip Howard. The baptismal service was conducted by Nicholas Heath, the Chancellor of England and the last Catholic Archbishop of York. The date was July 2, 1557. The infant, who inherited the title of Earl of Surrey, was the future heir to other titles and property: the dukedom of Norfolk, the earldom of Arundel and the baronies of Fitzalan, Clun, Oswaldestry, Maltravers, Mowbray and Seagrave.

Philip's mother, who had taken seriously ill after his birth, never rallied and died less than two months later. His father, Thomas Howard, a Protestant, remarried soon afterward. Of this marriage two sons and a daughter were born. After the death of his second wife, Thomas Howard once again married—this time to Elizabeth Dacre, a widow, who brought one son and three daughters with her.

To his extensive properties in Norfolk, Thomas Howard added others through his three marriages and was by far the richest man in England. Anxious to keep the estates in his family, Thomas Howard decided that his own children should marry the Dacre children. By his first two marriages he had three sons and one daughter; the Dacres included three daughters and one son. Such a perfect pairing must have seemed to him a proof of a divine endorsement. Thus it came about that at the age of 12, Philip Howard, the future Saint, was publicly and willingly betrothed to his stepsister Anne.

After the death of his third wife, Thomas Howard, filled with family pride, contemplated marriage with Mary, Queen of Scots, who was then in captivity. His intentions were construed as a plot to dethrone Elizabeth, to assassinate her and re-establish Catholicism in the realm. Throughout the trial that resulted, Thomas Howard pleaded his innocence—but he inevitably was found guilty of high treason. On September 24, 1571, from his cell in the Tower, he wrote to the 14-year-old Philip the following advice:

> Serve and fear God above all things...Love and make much of your wife...Strengthen your young and raw years with good counsel. Make your abode at Cambridge, which is the fittest place for you to promote your learning in. Beware of the court, except it be to do your prince service, and that, as near as you can in the lowest degree, for that place has no certainty.

Thomas Howard was beheaded on June 2, 1572. Because he died a supposed traitor, his son, Philip, was not permitted to succeed to the dukedom of Norfolk. Philip did become the Earl of Arundel and Surrey, though, by virtue of his mother's family.

Philip followed his father's advice and attended Cambridge University, where he excelled in his studies. His memory was exceptional. Once he tested it by memorizing all the house signs on the left side of the street from St. Paul's to Temple Bar. On reaching home, he called a servant and dictated them in order. He then sent another servant to check the list. He had not missed a single sign and all were in the correct order. His powers of recall were such that he could recite perfectly a page of English, Latin or Italian which he had read through only once.

While at Cambridge it was noted that "he was tall of stature, yet ever very straight, long-visaged and of comely countenance...His memory was excellent, his wit more than ordinary. He was naturally eloquent and of a ready speech."

During the ceremony in which he received his degree, he professed that the Queen was the Supreme Governor of the Church. About this time he married Anne, who also conformed outwardly to the new religion.

By virtue of his titles, Philip was welcomed at the court of Queen Elizabeth. Dazzled by the new life that now opened up to him, Philip vied with other courtiers to win the special favor of the Queen, who only a few years earlier had signed his father's death warrant. He completely disregarded his father's advice to serve in the "lowest degree," and instead drew ever more extravagantly on his vast fortune in order to cultivate the favor of the Queen.

When Queen Elizabeth dined at Howard House on her return to London, Philip was solidly established in the royal favor. The court Chronicle for these years lists his frequent gifts to Elizabeth and the plays in which he took part for her diversion.

Once again Philip conveniently forgot his father's advice to "Love and make much of your wife." Instead, his young wife was deeply unhappy and shamelessly neglected, since there was no place for wives in the court of Elizabeth I. Despised and abandoned while Philip squandered both his and her fortunes, Anne was deeply hurt when rumors reached her that Philip was casting doubts on the validity of their marriage. This prompted her to make a desperate appeal to win him back. When her offer of a reconciliation was rejected, she went to live with Philip's grandfather, the Earl of Arundel, who accepted Anne as his own daughter.

In addition to the extended amounts of time Philip stayed at court and the costly gifts he gave to the Queen, Anne had other reasons for leaving her husband. Philip, it seems, was living a dissipated life. One biographer claims that, "There can be little doubt that at this time he was unfaithful to his wife." In a manuscript text now at Arundel, it is recorded that "he patronized corrupted, immodest women with which the court in those times did too much abound."

Upon the death of his maternal grandfather, Henry Fitzalan, the Earl of Arundel, with whom Anne had lived during her husband's time at court, Philip inherited the title and more property. He was then 23 years old and had the prestige of being considered the premier earl of England. After the Earl's death, Anne felt homeless and returned to Howard House where Philip, at first, resented her presence. But while he was still frolicking at court, Philip weakened under Anne's gentleness and gradually grew kinder and closer to her.

At this time Anne was contemplating a complete return to Catholicism. Previously she had conformed outwardly to the new religion, but maintained a secret love for the faith of her childhood. In time she was secretly restored to the good graces of the Catholic Faith. Philip approved of his wife's brave decision, which he himself was not prepared to make.

Meanwhile the Queen, always quick to notice any cooling of enthusiasm in her courtiers, observed Philip's changing mood. It wounded her vanity to see him giving less attention to her and more to his wife. Philip was then enduring various conflicts. He thought seriously of returning to the Faith after hearing the recently captured St. Edmund Campion (1540-1587) defend the Faith against a group of Protestants. But there was also the certain possibility of his being imprisoned and martyred should his return to the Faith become known.

After Anne gave birth to her first child, a daughter, Philip thought to please the Queen by baptizing the child in the Protestant church and naming her Elizabeth. But sometime in the year 1584, Philip was reconciled to the Catholic Faith. There is a tradition that he paced up and down in his torment. His first biographer wrote that after his return to the Faith, Philip "lived in such a manner as he seemed to be changed into another man, having great care and vigilance over all his actions and addicting himself to piety and devotions."

While staying at the Charterhouse in London, Philip "kept a priest by whom he could frequently receive the Holy Sacraments and daily have the comfort to be present at the Holy Sacrifice, whereto with great humility and reverence he himself in person would many times serve."

During the time of his conversion and until the time of his death, Philip was particularly penitent for the way he had treated his faithful and admirable wife during his frivolous time at court. In a letter to St. Robert Southwell he wrote, "I call Our Lord to witness that no sin grieves me anything so much as my offences to that party. He that knows all things knows that which is past is a nail in my conscience and burden the greatest I feel there; my will is to make satisfaction, if my ability were able."

Parliamentary records show that during the winter of 1584 Philip attended regular meetings of the Lords and took his turn at court ceremonies. He knew that he would eventually come under suspicion for the obvious change in the manner of his conduct. Realizing that he and his wife were in danger, Philip consulted the only Jesuit free in England, Fr. William Weston. Philip then decided to leave England. Before he left with his family, Philip wrote a long letter to the Queen, explaining that he had come to realize that if he remained in England, he "must consent either to the certain destruction of his body or the endangering of his soul." He proposed to leave his native country, but "not his loyal affection for her Majesty." Before the letter was delivered, he boarded a ship, but having been betrayed by one of his domestics (some believe that a letter to Cardinal Allen had been intercepted), he was seized at sea and brought back to London, where he was committed to the Tower (1585).

When a charge of treason could not be substantiated, he was arraigned on three other charges: reconciliation with the Catholic Church, attempted flight from the Kingdom without the Queen's permission, and correspondence with Cardinal Allen. He was sentenced to a term of imprisonment to be determined at the Queen's pleasure.

Sometime after Philip's imprisonment, Anne gave birth to their second child, a son, but news of the birth was deliberately kept from Philip as a punishment. When the birth could no longer be concealed, his jailers were instructed to torment him with the false information that it was another daughter. His greatest trial during this time is said to have been his separation from Anne.

Philip had spent 11 years at court; he was to pass 10 years in prison. But he was not without the consolations of the Church, since he corresponded frequently with St. Robert Southwell. Also imprisoned was a priest named William Bennett, who secretly celebrated Holy Mass, which was usually served by Philip.

When England was on the alert for the approach of the Spanish Armada, the prisoners considered that many Catholics would be slaughtered after the landing, and they began to pray earnestly for the safety, or at least the salvation, of those who would be killed. Following the defeat of the Spanish Armada, someone falsely reported that Philip had prayed for the defeat of England and for the success of the Spanish invasion. Because of this report, Philip was brought to trial before his peers and was falsely charged with high treason for having prayed for the success of the Spanish invasion, for having harbored priests and for having corresponded with Mary, Queen of Scots. Philip was convicted of the charges, based on the testimony of false witnesses. On April 14, 1589 he was sentenced to death.

The execution never took place. As the Bishop of Tarrasona wrote,

> Tis true he was not executed, but permitted to die a lingering death under a tedious confinement, being kept a close prisoner for 10 years. . .during which time he gave himself up to a strict and penitential course of life and to continual prayer and contemplation, to the great edification of all that knew him.

During the whole of his imprisonment, Philip was denied visits from his wife and family members, but he was permitted to correspond with them. He also wrote verses and papers on religious topics, and spent time in translating a number of devotional books.

What was surprising during this long and solitary confinement was his cheerfulness. He had great confidence in the mercy of God and wrote to a friend:

> I assure you, I prepare myself as much as my weakness and frailty will permit, and I had rather perform more than come short of what I promise, especially wherein my frailty and unworthiness and infinite sins may justly make me doubt of the performance. But I know God's mercy is above all, and I am sure He will never suffer me to be tempted above my strength; and upon this I build with all assurances and comfort.

During his imprisonment, Philip chipped an inscription into the wall, above the fireplace in his cell: "The more suffering we endure in this world, the greater our glory in the next." It was signed "Arundell" and was dated June 22, 1587. Beneath the name, a later prisoner added the words: *"Gloria et honore coronasti eum, domine."* ("With glory and honor you have crowned him, Lord." *Ps.* 8:6). On another wall of his cell Philip carved a small crucifix, about three inches high. Both the inscription and the crucifix are now protected behind glass and can be seen in the Beauchamp Tower.

Philip's last prayer was to see his wife, his daughter and the son who was born after his arrest. This was refused, except on condition of his attendance at a Protestant church. His freedom likewise rested on this condition.

Having entered prison in robust health at the age of 28, Philip Howard endured 10 years of confinement before dying a gaunt and wasted figure at the age of 38 on October 19, 1595. Philip was first buried in the same grave in the Tower church that had received the remains of his father.

In his will Philip left a portion of money to be distributed among "the lame and poor of London within three months of my death." In the event that the Catholic religion would be restored in England, he provided that both Howard House and his house in Norwich should be given to religious communities, and that all the religious lands in his possession should be restored to the Church. He had intended also, in such an event, to build a family chantry and was resolved, in case he outlived his lady, to leave the world and become a monk.

In 1624 Anne transferred his remains to West Horsley in Surrey, and then to a family vault in Arundel.

After Queen Elizabeth's death, Anne was held in high regard by all who knew her. Her days were devoted to prayer, nursing the sick, and rescuing orphans. When she died at the age of 73, she was buried next to the remains of her husband.

In 1874, when the cause of canonization of the English martyrs was first introduced at Westminster, Philip was included with those who had died on the scaffold. With them he was beatified by Pope Pius XI in 1929. In October 1970, with Edmund Campion, Robert Southwell and 37 others, he was canonized by Pope Paul VI.

A year following his canonization, Philip's remains were brought from the Fitzalan Chapel and were enshrined in Arundel Cathedral. In 1973 the dedication of the Cathedral was changed from "Our Lady and St. Philip Neri," to "Our Lady and St. Philip Howard." St. Philip Howard is the patron saint of the diocese of Arundel and Brighton.

When Philip died, his son Thomas was ten years old. He succumbed to the glamour of the court and apostatized, but before his death he returned to the Faith. His son, and Philip Howard's grandson, was Bl. William Howard (Viscount Stafford), who died for the Catholic Faith at the time of the Oates Plot. He was the last martyr of the English Reformation.

St. Philip Howard (1557-1595) as a child. *(From a portrait at Arundel Castle.)* Mary Tudor was present at Philip's Baptism; also present was his godfather, Philip II of Spain, after whom he was named. For a time young Philip was tutored by the brilliant Gregory Martin, who would later be the principal translator of the Douay Bible.

St. Philip Howard was dazzled by the world as he courted the favor of Queen Elizabeth. (Philip's father had been the richest man in England.) Philip spent money freely on the Queen, putting on sumptuous dinners and lavish entertainments, while neglecting—and probably being unfaithful to—his wife. But around age 27, St. Philip reformed his life and following the lead of his wife, returned to the Catholic Faith. He was imprisoned in the Tower; he was to spend ten years there and eventually die there, never being allowed to see his wife or set eyes on his son, born after his arrest. Toward the end, Elizabeth agreed to grant these requests, plus restore Philip's freedom and property, if he would once attend her church; sorrowfully, Philip had to refuse this condition.

Caraman/Catholic Truth Society

Left: St. Philip carved a small crucifix (shown approximately actual size) on his cell wall. He spent hours every day in prayer.

Below: This 1821 engraving shows the austerity of St. Philip's prison room in the Beauchamp Tower. He chipped these words in the wall: "The more suffering we endure in this world, the greater our glory in the next!" St. Philip died at age 38.

Caraman/Catholic Truth Society

J. Arthur Dixon. Photo by Michael Maclaren.

The Shrine of St. Philip Howard at Arundel Cathedral. Philip had spent his years from 28 to 38 in the Tower, losing his health, his property, his position and, in effect, his family for the Catholic Faith.

Chapter 178

BL. PIERINA MOROSINI

1931 - 1957

The family of Rocco and Sara Morosini included nine sons and Pierina, who was the only daughter and the oldest of the children. Born on January 7, 1931, Pierina lived a peaceful and prayerful life with her family on a small farm in Fiobbio, which is located in the Diocese of Bergamo in northern Italy.

Always a pious child, Pierina received the Sacraments according to the custom of the time. She was quick of mind and proved to be a willing assistant to her mother by helping with her brothers and performing chores, both inside the house and outside in the fields.

After finishing elementary school, Pierina enrolled in a sewing class and learned how to make clothes for the entire family. In addition to all the help she gave her family, Pierina wanted to assist them financially, and for this reason, when she was only 15 years old, she began working at a cotton mill in nearby Albino.

Separating the small town of Fiobbio and Albino was a hilly, forested area through which Pierina had to walk twice a day. She always recited her morning prayers on the path, received Holy Communion in the Church of Albino and then began her work at six in the morning with the Sign of the Cross. Her co-workers remember her as being cheerful, but not very talkative. They also claimed that she seemed to work while in a profound union with God.

After returning from a hard day's work, Pierina helped with the chores of the household. She was also an active member of an organization for young people known as Catholic Action. At the age of 16, she was named parish director of members in her age group. Pierina also distinguished herself among her townspeople by her devoted work on behalf of missionaries and the diocesan seminary. She also assisted in the cleaning of the church and endeared herself to all because of her sweet disposition and humble demeanor. Her many works of charity are said to be the result of her deep prayer life, which was woven throughout the various parts of her day.

Pierina had a profound attraction to the religious life and wanted to do missionary work among the lepers. Her aunt, who was a nun, recalls that when Pierina was a child she told her aunt in all confidence, "I want to be a nun and belong to Jesus."

Since the needs of her family prevented Pierina from leaving, she accepted the family's decision as being the will of God and never spoke of her great disappointment. Realizing that Pierina might never be able to join the religious life, her spiritual director permitted her to make private vows of chastity, poverty and obedience. To help herself maintain these vows as perfectly as possible, she wrote a twelve-point rule, which she observed for the rest of her life. In addition, she joined the Apostolate of Reparation, offering in a spirit of faith the many difficulties she encountered each day.

Pierina spent all of her life in Fiobbio and Albino, and never left except for a trip she made to Rome with members of Catholic Action. This took place in April, 1947, for the beatification of Maria Goretti, the little Saint who had died in the defense of purity. During the journey, the life of Maria Goretti understandably was the frequent topic of conversation. When Pierina was asked what she would do if she were confronted by an assailant, Pierina quickly replied that she would willingly imitate Maria Goretti by dying in the defense of purity. On another occasion she again stated that she would rather die than commit a sin.

Sometime after this trip to Rome, Pierina seems to have had a premonition that she would suffer martyrdom. Ten years later, this premonition was realized. On April 4, 1957, while she was on her way home from work, Pierina was confronted on the wooded path by a young man. Judging from the condition in which she was found and the many bloodied handprints in the area, Pierina had fought vigorously against the rapist and even attempted to crawl away. Found in the weeds nearby was a rock that was covered with blood and bits of flesh. This rock was in the shape of a hammer, and it was apparent that the man had used it to repeatedly strike Pierina in the head.

One of Pierina's brothers reported that on the day of Pierina's assault, he had a premonition that something would happen to her and was very agitated concerning her welfare. It was for this reason that he went along the wooded path to meet her after her work shift to accompany her home. Instead, he found his dying sister on the ground with her clothes in disarray and her long hair matted with blood. When her brother drew nearer, Pierina slowly moved her hand to her head, but did not speak or open her eyes. He reported that her face was bloody and her breathing was slow and labored. When he touched the left side of her face, which was covered by her hair, his hand was immediately covered with blood and pieces of flesh. It was obvious that a huge and ugly wound covered the left side of her face and head. The brother ran for help and returned with various relatives, who were shocked by what they discovered. It was then noted that the assailant had neatly arranged beside his victim her shoes, socks, purse, rosary and a photograph taken of her with three of her friends.

Pierina was removed to a hospital, where she was treated for her injuries; but she lapsed into a deep coma and died two days later, before she could describe or identify her assailant. Pierina was 26 years old. Her doctors reported that she was a victim of sexual aggression, to which one of the doctors added, "We have here a new Maria Goretti." The Vatican newspaper *L'Osservatore Romano* (October 5, 1987) reported that, "Her skull was broken and she was raped." Pierina is nevertheless designated as "virgin" as well as "martyr."

The funeral of the virtuous Pierina was attended by most of the people of Fiobbio and Albino. The crime committed against her so outraged the people that it quickly became well-known throughout the district. For this reason an article on the front page of the newspaper of Bergamo told of her life and death and was accompanied by a picture of the huge crowd that attended the funeral.

A memorial marker and a stone which recorded the heroism of Pierina were soon erected at the wooded place where she had been found mortally wounded. A larger memorial stone, which is topped with a marble bust resembling Pierina, is found in the piazza of the Church of Fiobbio.

During the ecclesiastical examination into the life of Pierina conducted in preparation for her beatification, the casket containing her remains was removed from her tomb on April 9, 1983. It was then carried in an impressive procession to the parish church of Fiobbio, where her relics are now entombed. This shrine attracts many of her devotees, who pray fervently for her intercession. It is customary for many to walk in procession to the place of martyrdom.

Pierina Morosini was beatified on October 4, 1987. Sara Morosini, Pierina's mother, had already met Pope John Paul II in 1981, but was privileged to meet him once again shortly after the beatification ceremony, while he was still seated upon the papal throne. While Sara Morosini knelt before him, the Pope placed his hands upon her head and spoke words of comfort. After the ceremony, the Pope again spoke privately with her and then met with Pierina's brothers and other members of the family.

Kept as a treasured relic is Pierina's copy of a biography of St. Maria Goretti. It is said that this book was Pierina's favorite and that she read it so often, she almost knew it from memory.

Pierina has been recommended as a model for working girls and as a model for holy purity.

Bl. Pierina Morosini (1931-1957), martyr of purity. At the age of 26, Pierina was brutally assaulted and murdered when walking home from work. She had spent her whole life close to home, except for a trip to Rome for the beatification of St. Maria Goretti in 1947. At that time, in reply to a question, Pierina had stated that she would willingly imitate Maria Goretti by dying in defense of purity. (Her favorite book, which she almost knew from memory, was a biography of St. Maria Goretti.) On another occasion, Pierina said she would rather die than commit a sin. Pierina was beatified in 1987.

Pierina had wanted "to be a nun and belong to Jesus," and to be a missionary to the lepers. But since family obligations stood in the way, her confessor allowed her to make private vows of chastity, poverty and obedience. To help her family (she was the eldest of ten children, though the only daughter) she went to work in a cotton mill at age 15. This memorial to Bl. Pierina Morosini is located in the piazza of the Church of Fiobbio, Italy.

Pierina walked to Mass and Communion daily before beginning work at six a.m. She was cheerful but not very talkative. Pierina had a deep prayer life, woven throughout the day, and she performed many works of charity, while being also a leader in Catholic Action. Her sweet disposition and humble demeanor endeared her to all. Most of her fellow townspeople attended the funeral of Bl. Pierina Morosini, whose relics are now entombed at the parish church of Fiobbio. Many devotees pray for Pierina's intercession.

Chapter 179

ST. POLLIO

d. 304

Butler tells us that, "There can be no doubt about the historical existence of St. Pollio," who served as lector in the ancient episcopal city of Cibales.

After the martyrdom of Bishop Eusebius, Pollio became the leader of those Christians in the diocese who remained true to the Faith and ignored the edicts of Diocletian.

Finally brought before Governor Probus, St. Pollio boldly confessed that he was not only a Christian, but he was also the chief of all the lectors in the city. When Probus asked, "Of what lectors?" Pollio answered, "Of those who read the Word of God to the people." When Pollio refused to sacrifice to the gods, Probus ordered the decapitation of the Saint. But when Pollio responded that he would be happy to suffer for Jesus Christ, Probus became so enraged that he changed his order from the swift death of decapitation to that of having Pollio burned alive.

When Pollio was led to the place of execution, he offered himself as a sacrifice to God and suffered courageously on the 28th of April, in the year 304.

Chapter 180

ST. POLYEUCTUS

Fourth Century

St. Polyeuctus was a wealthy Roman officer of Greek parentage. While still a pagan he made friends with a Christian named Nearchus, who eventually converted him to the Faith. When news of the persecution ordered by the Emperor reached Armenia, where Polyeuctus lived, he prepared to affirm his faith, should he be asked concerning it. Polyeuctus bravely announced his Christianity when the time came and declared that he was eager to die for the Faith. He was promptly apprehended and condemned to cruel tortures. After the executioners grew weary of tormenting him, they tried to persuade him with arguments to renounce his faith.

As if imprisonment, torture and arguing were not enough to discourage the Saint, his wife, Pauline, his children and his father-in-law visited him in prison and by means of tears and entreaties tried to convince him to renounce Christianity and return home with them. But the Saint withstood this heartrending offer and became more resolute in his faith. He steadfastly continued his profession of faith in Jesus Christ, and, as a result, he was condemned to death.

On the road to the place of execution, Polyeuctus exhorted the bystanders to renounce their idols and spoke so convincingly that many were converted. After he was beheaded, the Christians buried his body in the city.

Nearchus, who had converted him, gathered the Saint's blood in a cloth, and later wrote his *Acts*.

A church is known to have been dedicated to St. Polyeuctus before the year 377 at Melitene in Armenia. As a Roman officer, Polyeuctus had been stationed in this city with his troops. It is also the city where the Saint suffered and died.

Chapter 181

ST. POTAMIANA

d. 202

St. Potamiana was a young, pious and extremely beautiful slave whose master offered to free her at the expense of her chastity. Eventually, her steadfast refusals made him realize that he would probably never win her consent. Determined to try another tactic, he applied to the Prefect of Egypt, promising him a large sum of money if he could persuade the virgin to yield to him. If Potamiana still refused, the Prefect was asked to put her to death as a Christian.

The Prefect summoned Potamiana and showed her all the instruments of torture and used all his wiles to induce her to obey her master. At his constant urgings, the Saint at last replied, "How is it possible that there can be found a judge so unjust as to condemn me because I will not satisfy the inordinate desires of a lewd person?" When the Saint remained firm, she was condemned to be stripped and cast into a cauldron of boiling pitch.

Upon hearing the sentence, Potamiana said to the judge, "I beg of you, by the life of the Emperor whom you honor, not to oblige me to appear unclothed; rather suffer me to be slowly lowered into the cauldron fully dressed that you may see the patience which Jesus Christ, whom you know not, bestows upon those who trust Him."

The Prefect granted her request. A guard named Basilides, who was charged with leading her to the place of execution, treated the slave with the utmost respect and protected her from the insults and pressure of the crowd. Potamiana thanked him for his courtesy and told him that after her death she would pray to God for his salvation.

Upon reaching the place of martyrdom, Potamiana was lowered feet first into the cauldron of boiling pitch until the liquid covered her head. Her pious mother, Marcella, was martyred at the same time, in the year 202.

After witnessing the modesty and courage of Potamiana, Basilides surprised his fellow soldiers by refusing to take an oath when called upon to do so. He acknowledged himself a Christian and was consigned to prison. To fellow prisoners he revealed that Potamiana had appeared to him the third or fourth night after her martyrdom and had placed on his head a crown which she said she had won for him by her prayers. He received Baptism in prison, and after professing his faith, he was beheaded.

Chapter 182

ST. PRAXEDES

Second Century

Near the great basilica of Santa Maria Maggiore, on the Esquiline Hill in Rome, stands the Church of Santa Prassede (St. Praxedes), which was built on the site where the house of the Saint once stood. Mentioned in documents of the year 490, the church was restored and enhanced by various popes throughout the centuries. St. Charles Borromeo also figures in its history, having prayed there on many occasions and having supervised the restoration of the facade and the door.

The Saint for whom the church is dedicated was a Roman maiden of the second century who may, or may not, have been the sister of St. Pudentiana, with whom she is often mentioned. When Emperor Marcus Antoninus was searching for Christians to punish, Praxedes was also looking for Christians—but for other reasons: to relieve them with money, comfort and every charitable care. Some she hid in her house, others she encouraged to keep firm in the Faith, and for those who were martyred, she reverently buried their bodies.

Sometime during the second century, Praxedes was called to her heavenly reward. A priest named Pastor buried her in the tomb of her father and near that of St. Pudentiana in the Cemetery of Priscilla on the Salarian Way. She was at first venerated as a martyr, although it is unclear whether she actually died for the Faith.

During the restoration of the church by Pope Pascal I (817-824), the Pope had the bodies of St. Praxedes and St. Pudentiana removed to the Church of Santa Prassede, where they are now found in the confessio.

The Church of Santa Prassede has a number of interesting mosaics; one, located above the altar, depicts the Virgin and the Child Jesus between the figures of St. Praxedes and St. Pudentiana. In the nave of the church is a porphyry disc which seals the well of the original house, and in a side chapel is an oriental jasper column—said to be part of the original in Jerusalem, which is regarded as the column at which Christ was scourged. When he was in Rome, St. Charles Borromeo celebrated Mass every morning in the Chapel of the Column and sometimes passed the night in prayer in the crypt under the high altar. At the foot of the left aisle of the church is a marble slab on which St. Praxedes is said to have slept.

Chapter 183

ST. PROSPER OF AQUITAINE

d. 455

The scholarly training received by this saint seems typical of one who was preparing for the priesthood, but Prosper was never ordained. Rather, his vocation was to serve God in the married state. He received thorough literary, theological and philosophical training and was highly regarded by his friend, Hilary, who once described Prosper as a man distinguished *"tum moribus, tum eloquio et studio"* (for morals, eloquence and zeal). Prosper spent some time with the monks at Marseilles and later wrote to St. Augustine, describing the opposition of the monks to Augustine's doctrine on grace. St. Augustine responded with two treatises.

With Hilary as his companion, St. Prosper journeyed to Rome in 431 to obtain a favorable judgment of St. Augustine's doctrine from Pope Celestine I. After the year 440, Prosper was associated with Pope Leo I and aided the Pope with his correspondence and theological writings against the Nestorians.

St. Prosper was a strong opponent of Semi-Pelagianism, which caused a great disturbance at the time, and was an admirer and staunch defender of St. Augustine.

Prosper was a prolific writer whose works in both prose and poetry were devoted mostly to philosophical and theological themes. Among his many writings was the 1,102 hexameter, *"De Ingratis"* ("On Those Without Grace") and a poem written for his wife which was entitled, *"Poema Conjugis Ad Uxorem."*

Both the year of his birth and that of his death are uncertain. Nevertheless, it is estimated that St. Prosper of Aquitaine was about 65 years old at the time of his death, sometime around the year 455.

Chapter 184

ST. PULCHERIA

399 - 453

Unlike many nobles who were trained for years to accept the duties and cares of imperial office, St. Pulcheria assumed the burdens of governing the Byzantine Roman Empire when she was declared Empress at the tender age of 15 years.

Pulcheria was born on January 19, 399; her grandfather was Emperor Theodosius the Great, who ruled the ancient Roman Empire. Having two sons, he divided the Empire between them, giving the western part to Emperor Honorius and the eastern, Byzantine half, to Emperor Arcadius, who was Pulcheria's father. Unfortunately, Pulcheria was placed in an orphanage at the young age of nine, when her father died. Her mother had died four years earlier.

After the death of Pulcheria's father, the family's only son, seven-year-old Theodosius II, assumed the throne according to the right of succession. Because of his age, Theodosius was placed under the guardianship of Anthimus, who was considered to be one of the wisest men of the Empire and a good friend of St. John Chrysostom. But after only a few years, Anthimus died. Since Theodosius was then only about the age of 13, Pulcheria, as the eldest of the three surviving daughters, was named "Augusta" and was acknowledged to be her brother's partner in imperial dignity.

Theodosius was never suited to his exalted post. He was mild-mannered and had no interest in diplomacy or the affairs of government, being more inclined to hunting and especially painting and writing, which earned for him the nickname, "the calligrapher."

This lack of interest in his office is demonstrated by a story in which Pulcheria put him to the test. When Theodosius was older and should have shown more interest in what was transpiring in the Empire, Pulcheria composed a decree containing her own death sentence. Theodosius casually signed the document without reading it.

Pulcheria, however, was just the opposite of her brother, having a natural administrative ability—to which were added keen intelligence, a quick mind and a pleasant, and yet efficient, manner of dealing with people, all of which supplemented her lack of experience.

Many historians acknowledge this claim, including Edward Gibbon in his *Decline and Fall of the Roman Empire* (Chapter 32). Gibbon wrote:

> Pulcheria alone, among all the descendants of the great Theodosius I, appears to have inherited any share of his manly spirit and abilities...Her deliberations were maturely weighed; her actions were prompt and decisive; and, while she moved without noise or ostentation the wheel of government, she discreetly attributed to the genius of the Emperor the long tranquility of his reign...Praise may be due to the mildness and prosperity of the administration of Pulcheria.

Since Pulcheria was charged with her brother's education, she placed about him the most learned and virtuous teachers—but she made it her own responsibility to teach him the doctrines of the Faith and to incline him to sentiments of devotion, piety and a love of Christianity.

Pulcheria also supervised the education and religious development of her two younger sisters, who always wanted to imitate their older sister. Realizing that wicked tongues might speak falsely of her necessary contacts with the many men of the court, Pulcheria made a public vow of virginity. Her reasons for this vow were not only political ones, but arose also from virtue. Together with her sisters, who also made similar vows, the holy trio lived in love, charity and piety, devoting free time from the duties of their state to religious activities and to useful studies.

Pulcheria was extremely intelligent, being skilled in Greek and Latin, history and literature. She was also familiar with the fine arts and was a patroness of the sciences. The mature manner in which this young girl dispatched her duties bears consideration. The operation of the imperial palace, through her directions, was conducted in a systematic and orderly manner. When emergencies arose, she first prayed for Divine guidance and then asked the advice of the council, whose members were the wisest, most virtuous and most experienced persons of the Empire. In turn, these men readily acknowledged the

wisdom and prudence of Pulcheria's judgments. She made certain
that all her orders were executed with precision, and she prevented
revolts which ambition and jealousy invented to disturb the orderly
conduct of the Church and State. She established a lasting peace
with neighboring countries and abolished the remnants of idolatry
in several places. As Butler notes, "Never did virtue reign in the
Eastern Empire with greater lustre, never was the State more happy
or more flourishing or its name more respected, even among the
barbarians, than whilst the reins of the government were in the hands
of Pulcheria."

When her brother was 20 years old, Pulcheria considered it proper
for him to marry. Upon her prompting, his attention fell upon
Athenais, the daughter of an Athenian philosopher. When Athenais
came to court she gained the admiration of everyone by her beauty,
education and pleasant manner. Pulcheria judged her most worthy
to be the Emperor's consort, but there remained the matter of her
idolatrous upbringing. This problem was resolved when Athenais willingly accepted the True Faith, was baptized and adopted the Christian name, Eudocia. Two years after her marriage, Eudocia received
the royal title of "Augusta."

It was in the early years of this marriage that two principle achieve-
ments of St. Pulcheria and Theodosius were carried out. One was
the foundation or reorganization, in 425, of the University of Constantinople; the other achievement was the composition and publication of a code of law which became known as the Code of Theodosius.

After a time, members of the court, including Eudocia, developed
a resentment for Pulcheria's position and prestige. Chrysaphius, a
member of the court and a favorite of the Emperor, influenced both
Theodosius and Eudocia against Pulcheria, claiming that she had
too great an influence in the matters of government. Then, when
the Nestorian heresy took hold and was condemned at the Council
of Ephesus in 431, Pulcheria corresponded with St. Cyril of Alexandria about the matter and was successful in persuading Theodosius
to accept the condemnation. Since Theodosius had previously wavered in the matter, sometimes siding with Eudocia in her acceptance
of the false teaching, Eudocia became indignant at her husband's
final condemnation of the heresy.

As a means of retaliating against the successful influence of her
sister-in-law, Eudocia stirred up the lower elements among the

Nestorians to spread gross slanders about Pulcheria.

A further estrangement took place when Eudocia and Chrysaphius intrigued more strenuously against Pulcheria. False rumors were spread against her until finally her brother, who was unfortunately "weak of understanding," accepted his conniving wife's opinions and for a time believed all the false reports that were spread about his sister.

Theodosius was finally persuaded to order the Patriarch of Constantinople, St. Flavian, to make Pulcheria a deaconess of his church and so withdraw her from the court. When Theodosius insisted on obedience in the matter, St. Flavian warned Pulcheria to take care and to remain silent. Realizing the seriousness of the enemies' intent, Pulcheria retired to a country seat in the plains of Hebdomon, with the resolution to spend the remaining days of her life in prayer and seclusion.

For all her efforts to destroy the good name and influence of her sister-in-law, Eudocia was the one who suffered a reversal of fortune. Having used slander against Pulcheria, slander was her own undoing when she was falsely accused of infidelity with Paulinus, an officer of the court. Eudocia was subsequently banished and passed the remainder of her days in Jerusalem, where she is said to have died in holiness.

Pulcheria accepted her retreat from the court as a blessing and spent her time in prayer and good works. She made no complaints about her brother's ingratitude, of the empress whose jealousy caused her so much trouble, or the officers of the court who participated in intrigues against her. Pulcheria was content to spend the rest of her life in her peaceful and prayerful retreat, glad "both to forget the world and to be forgotten by it."

But a grave danger threatened both Church and State. Soon after Eudocia went into exile, Pulcheria returned to the court, where her brother and his retainers were now inclined to accept another heresy. Pope St. Leo the Great, in 449, appealed both to Pulcheria and Theodosius to reject Monophysitism—which Pulcheria wholeheartedly did—but her influence over her brother had been greatly weakened. Others attempted to dissuade Theodosius, but in the midst of their appeals, Theodosius suddenly died when he fell from his horse while hunting.

Now 51 years old, Pulcheria became the sole administrator of the Eastern Empire. To strengthen her position, she chose as her partner a wise statesman named Marcian who was zealous for the Catholic Faith and was both virtuous and charitable to the poor. He was a native of Thrace and a widower. Pulcheria felt that marriage would enhance Marcian's position and authority, and after Marcian consented to respect her vow of virginity, they were married.

The holy couple ruled together, while sharing the same views and sentiments which advanced the cause of religion and the just administration of the Empire. Their efforts to abolish heresy won the highest praise from Pope St. Leo the Great; their system of low taxation and little warfare earned the appreciation and respect of their subjects. Their partnership, unfortunately, lasted only three years, since in July of the year 453 Pulcheria died at the age of 54. She bequeathed her private fortune to religious and charitable causes, and her directions in this regard were faithfully executed.

Many praised the accomplishments of the virtuous Empress, including the members of the Council of Chalcedon who rejected the Monophysite heresy. The councilors hailed her as "guardian of the Faith, peacemaker, religious right-believer, a second St. Helen."

In writing to Marcian about Pulcheria, Pope St. Leo the Great declared that it was largely through Pulcheria's own efforts that truth had been vindicated against the errors both of Nestorius and the Monophysites. The Pope also expressed his appreciation for the benefits Pulcheria had bestowed on the Church, for her support of the papal legates, for the recall of the banished Catholic bishops and for the honorable burial of the body of the patriarch Flavian. She had also had the relics of St. John Chrysostom, who had died in exile, brought back to Constantinople for burial in the Church of the Apostles. She built churches, hospitals, houses for pilgrims, and gave rich gifts to various churches. Among the churches she built were three in honor of the Mother of God.

St. Pulcheria is venerated as a saint in the Greek and other oriental churches, as well as in the Latin Church. Her feast is given as September 10 in the *Roman Martryology*.

Chapter 185

BL. RALPH MILNER

d. 1591

As a husband and the father of seven children, Ralph Milner supported his family by farming near the City of Winchester, England. He was entirely illiterate and was raised as a Protestant who looked upon the sovereign of his country as the head of the Church of England. After observing the lives of the Catholics with whom he was acquainted and seeing how many of them refused to deny their faith, even though the denial would result in a heroic death, he was greatly inspired. He was eventually instructed in the Faith and was baptized, but on the very day of his First Holy Communion he was arrested for his beliefs. He was kept a prisoner for a number of years and was often released on parole. Since his guards trusted him, he was able to take advantage of his friendship with them to aid his fellow prisoners and to smuggle priests into the prison to administer the Sacraments to those who were closely confined.

Ralph Milner did not focus his activities only on relieving prisoners. Because of his knowledge of the countryside, he often guided missionary priests to areas where Catholics were in need of spiritual guidance. In this activity he became acquainted with Father Stanney, S.J., who afterward wrote the Saint's biography. According to Challoner, Father Stanney took notice that,

> Ralph Milner used to come once a month to the house where this priest resided, to conduct him about the villages, there to preach and administer the Sacraments to the poor; who also declares in his preface that he can testify that, ignorant as he [Ralph] was, he had, by the bright light of his virtues and by his fervent prayers, been, under God, the cause of the conversion of many to the Catholic Faith.

When Bl. Ralph broadened the areas of his activities, a secular priest, Fr. Roger Dickenson, came from Lincoln to assist Fr. Stanney. Fr. Dickenson was soon arrested, but was able to escape when his guards became intoxicated. The second time he was apprehended, both he and Ralph Milner were brought to trial: Fr. Dickenson for being a priest; Ralph Milner for assisting him.

At the trial, the judge had pity on Bl. Ralph, who was advanced in age and was the father of a large family. Seeking a pretext to set him free, the judge said that if Ralph Milner would consent to say his prayers in the nearby Protestant church, it would be taken as a gesture of his reconciliation with the Church of England and he would be free to live the rest of his years in peace. But since this act would serve as a renunciation of his Catholic faith, Bl. Ralph refused to do so. Challoner relates that Bl. Ralph answered, "Would your lordship then advise me, for the perishable trifles of this world, or for a wife and children, to lose my God? No, my Lord, I cannot approve or embrace a counsel so disagreeable to the maxims of the Gospel."

Challoner relates that his friends and ministers tried every argument to entice him to renounce his faith and thereby win his release.

> Even when he was at the very gallows, they ceased not to tempt him; and sent his seven children to him, to move him to relent by the sight of them; but his heart was too strongly fixed on God to be overcome by flesh and blood. He gave them, therefore, his last blessing, declaring aloud that he could wish them no greater happiness, than to die for the like cause for which he was going to die.

Both he and Fr. Roger Dickenson were executed at Winchester on July 7, 1591.

Chapter 186

BL. RAYMOND LULL

1233 - 1315

Born at Palma in Majorca about the year 1233, Raymond was the son of one of the military chiefs who in the first part of the thirteenth century succeeded in reconquering the island of Majorca from its Moslem invaders. He is described as having been wealthy, talented and ardent. He married young and had a son and a daughter. Even though he had a charming wife and a happy household, he was shameless in his pursuit of any young maiden that attracted him.

One night, about the year 1263, when he was busily composing a poem to his latest interest, he suddenly saw beside him the figure of Jesus Christ hanging on the Cross. The vision startled him to such an extent that he could not continue writing or shake off the effects, but had to take to his bed. It was only after the vision was renewed five separate times that his heart was touched and he experienced a complete conversion from his past sins and inclinations.

While reflecting on the words, "greater love than this no man hath, that a man lay down his life for his friends" (*John* 15:13), Raymond developed an extraordinary zeal to win the Moors to the service of Jesus Christ. To do this work, he realized that careful plans would have to be made and that he would have to sacrifice much—possibly even life itself. To obtain Divine guidance, he went on a pilgrimage to Compostela and to Roc Amadour. Upon returning home, he first provided for those who were dependent on him and then left for a period of seclusion and prayer. Next, he began acquiring the knowledge necessary for an intellectual crusade against the Moslem philosophy and religion. Nine years were spent in learning Arabic and in making other preliminary studies.

He eventually founded a school in Majorca where missionaries might study Arabic and Chaldean and be trained in all that might help them in their work. After placing the school under the guidance of the Friars Minor, he left for Rome in 1277. At Genoa he applied for membership in the Friars Preachers, but was refused, although he was permitted to become a Franciscan tertiary.

After a miraculous restoration of health in 1292, Raymond was carried on board a galley bound for Africa. He realized his dream of preaching in the streets of Tunis, but after imprisonment and rough treatment at the hands of the Moslems, he was forcibly deported. Arriving in Naples, he confided his plans to the Pope and appealed for his support, but received little response. A journey to Cyprus was also disappointing.

We next find Raymond Lull lecturing in Paris, but then, once again, he attempted to convert the Moors at Bugia in Barbary. As they did before, the Moors treated him poorly. They imprisoned him and then deported him once again. This time he suffered shipwreck before he reached Italy. Another appeal was made to the Pope and to the Council of Vienne in 1311, without satisfactory results. He again lectured at Paris and finally, on a third visit to Africa, he was stoned by the Saracens at Tunis and died of his injuries.

Although Bl. Raymond's life seems one of repeated disappointments, his literary activity was incredibly successful. Three hundred and thirteen different treatises are attributed to him, most of them in Latin, Catalan and Arabic. These include works on theology, philosophy, apologetics, science and pedagogy, philosophical novels, lyric poetry and mystical works. Many of his writings have been published in modern times, but a greater portion remains to be catalogued.

Five years before he died, Bl. Raymond summarized his life and struggles in this manner:

> I have been married and have had children; I have been rich and loved pleasures and the world. I have left all with a good heart for the glory of God, for the service of my fellow men, and to spread the holy Faith. I have learned Arabic and often visited the Saracens; for my faith I have been beaten and imprisoned; for 45 years I have endeavored to interest the heads of the Church and Christian rulers in the public good. And now, here I am old and poor, but my ideal is always the same and such it will remain until my death, please God.

At the time Bl. Raymond Lull was martyred for the Faith, he was over 80 years of age.

Chapter 187

ST. REGINA

d. 251

According to a French biography, Regina was the daughter of Clemens, a pagan citizen of Alise, in Burgundy. Since her mother died during her delivery, Regina was entrusted to the care of a Christian woman who baptized her and taught her the doctrines of the Faith.

Inspired by her love for Christ, Regina made a vow of chastity, promising that her affections would be reserved for God alone. When the time came for Regina to be returned to her father, he refused to receive her and drove her from his home after learning of her dedication to Christianity. After Regina returned to the woman who had cared for her during her youth, she found it necessary to support herself by tending sheep.

One day while the fifteen-year-old Regina was tending her flocks, she attracted the attention of Olybrius, the Prefect of Gaul. He expressed the desire to marry her, but Regina refused his proposal; nor would she listen to the attempted persuasions of her father, who was willing to accept her now that there was the prospect of a distinguished marriage.

Despite her refusal, Olybrius sent for her, and as she again rejected his proposal he became furious and had her placed in a dungeon. When she remained constant in her vow of virginity, Olybrius ordered her to be tortured. One account states that she was whipped and was then tortured with hot plates and burning pincers, as well as with iron combs. During her torment she continually praised God until finally Olybrius found it necessary to silence her by cutting her throat.

The relics of St. Regina were translated in the year 864 to the Abbey of Flavigny. A portion of her relics are still venerated at Alise-Sainte-Reine, where she suffered. In comparatively recent times the foundation of an ancient basilica which had been dedicated in her honor was found at Alise.

Chapter 188

ST. RICHARD

d. 722

This saint was an English prince who belonged to a family of saints. As a result of his marriage to Winna, Richard claimed St. Boniface as his nephew. Also, Richard's three children—sons Willibald and Wunibald, and daughter Walburga—are all honored as saints of the Church.

When Richard's son Willibald was a child and had fallen ill, those who tended him despaired of his recovery. Richard, by his fervent prayers, obtained the child's miraculous restoration to health when he placed Willibald at the foot of a great crucifix which stood in a public place in England.

Taking his two sons with him, Richard started out on a pilgrimage to Rome. He stayed for a time at Rouen and visited most of the holy places along the way, but he did not reach his destination. Richard died suddenly at Lucca, Italy in 722 and was buried there in the Church of San Frediano, where his relics still remain. Following the burial, his two sons continued the pilgrimage and prayed for their father at Roman shrines.

Richard's son Willibald continued on to the Holy Land and settled at Monte Casino while on his way home. The Pope, visiting Rome on another occasion, authorized the publication of Willibald's adventures, which is considered to be the first German guide book. When St. Boniface notified Gregory III that he needed help in evangelizing Germany, the Pope sent Willibald. In the year 741, Willibald was consecrated the first Bishop of Eichstätt. There he built a monastery, where the strict monastic rule was observed.

Richard's other son, Wunibald, after his ordination, founded in Heidenheim (in the diocese of Eichstätt) a double monastery where men and women, in separate living arrangements, observed the rule of St. Benedict. Wunibald governed the monks, while his sister,

Walburga, who had taken the veil in England, ruled as abbess of the nuns.

An unusual situation is observed with respect to the bones of St. Walburga. For four months each year, between two of the Saint's feast days, October 12 and February 15, a mysterious oil drips from the bones of the Saint. This has taken place for over 1,200 years. Thus far, science had been unable to produce an explanation for the occurrence.

St. Richard is mentioned in the *Roman Martyrology* on February 7.

Chapter 189

ST. RICHARD GWYN
(St. Richard White)

1537 - 1584

The first Welshman to suffer in his own land as the result of the persecution of Catholics by Queen Elizabeth I was St. Richard Gwyn, a schoolmaster. He was born at Llanidloes in the County of Montgomery about the year 1537. Little else is known of his life before the time that Queen Elizabeth ascended the throne.

Gwyn completed his studies at St. John's College at Cambridge, England, where he acquired a considerable reputation as a scholar. When his friend and patron, George Bullock, master of the college, had to resign his fellowship and all academic honors for the sake of his conscience, Gwyn returned to his native North Wales and began to teach school at various places in Flintshire and Denbighshire. An old account tells that, "His moderation and temperance were such that his enemies to this day could never charge him with any fault other than the following of his faith and conscience—which nowadays is accounted madness." He eventually married a virtuous lady named Catherine and became the father of six children, three of whom survived him.

Being a Catholic gentleman, he committed an error too common in those days, that while a Catholic at heart and in principle, he nevertheless outwardly conformed to the Protestant faith and attended their services. When missionaries from Douai, France arrived in Wales to reconcile people who, like Richard, had weakened their consciences, Richard was persuaded by them to confess his mistake and to courageously profess and practice the Catholic Faith. Queen Elizabeth and her ministers, on learning about the missionaries' successes, resolved to overcome their work by means of persecution. The first victim of this campaign was Richard Gwyn.

Because Richard had excused himself from the Protestant services on many occasions, his absences became so well-known that he took his family and left the area and successfully conducted schools in several other places. But in 1579, he was recognized in Wrexham by a vicar who had apostatized. Gwyn was denounced by the vicar, arrested and imprisoned in Ruthin jail, from which he later managed to escape.

In June of 1580, the Privy Council directed the Protestant bishops to be more vigilant in their dealings with Catholic recusants. The following month, Richard Gwyn was seized and brought before a magistrate, who sent him to Wrexham jail. During a court appearance he was offered his liberty if he would conform. Upon his refusal he was returned to jail, where he was secured with chains until the next session of the court.

The following May, when court was held at Wrexham, Judge Bromley was informed of Gwyn's previous participation in Protestant services and his present refusal to do so again. The judge then ordered that since Mr. Gwyn still refused to attend services, he should be taken there forcibly. Putting up as much resistance as he could, Gwyn loudly protested the violence done to him. And in the church itself, he rattled his chains and made such a disturbance that neither he, nor anyone else, could hear the minister. When Gwyn could not be silenced, the judge ordered that he be carried out and set in the stocks of the marketplace. In the meantime an indictment was drawn up against him for having "insolently and impiously" interrupted the minister and the people in the Divine worship. After a jury was impanelled, Mr. Gwyn was brought into the courtroom. When the clerk of the court began the indictment, his eyes weakened so that he could not continue reading. When the judge asked the clerk about his difficulty, he replied that he did not know, but that he could not see properly. The judge sneered, saying, "Take care lest the papists make a miracle of this."

The schoolmaster was returned to prison and was joined a short time later by two gentlemen, Mr. John Pugh and Mr. Robert Morris, who were also accused of failing to attend Protestant services. All three were arraigned for high treason and were sent from Wrexham jail to the Council of the Marches. Later in the year they suffered at Bewdley and Bridgenorth, where their jailers attempted to make them confess by whom they had been reconciled to the Catholic Church. Richard Gwyn and John Pugh courageously withstood their torments; Robert Morris weakened for a short time, but afterwards repented.

On October 11, 1584, the three men were brought to trial and indicted for high treason. Witnesses against them swore that the prisoners had said, in their hearing, that the Queen was not the head of the Church, but rather, the Pope was, and that the accused, Richard Gwyn, had attempted to reconcile Lewis Gronow to the Church of Rome. Gwyn denied any knowledge of Gronow and objected to the testimony, saying that the witnesses perjured themselves. No credence was given his claim, however.

As a last attempt to shake Richard Gwyn's resistance, the prosecutors brought into the courtroom Catherine Gwyn, who was carrying her youngest child in her arms. As the contemporary account of the trial tells, she surprised the court by declaring to the judge, "If you lack blood, you may take my life as well as my husband's; and if you will give the witnesses another bribe, they will bear evidence against me as well as they did against him." Infuriated at her remarks, the judge lost no time in instructing the jury. The twelve men deliberated and found Richard Gwyn and John Pugh guilty, but acquitted Robert Morris, who, to the surprise of the court, wept bitterly at being unable to suffer with his companions for so good a cause. Because of his behavior he was returned to prison, where he is believed to have died.

Later, one of the witnesses who had testified in court against the three prisoners made a public declaration that his evidence and that of the other two witnesses had been false, and that he had been paid by the Vicar of Wrexham and another person. John Pugh was reprieved, but Richard Gwyn suffered according to the sentence. He was hanged, cut down while still living, and his abdomen was opened. It is reported that while the hangman had his hands in the victim's bowels to remove them according to the sentence, the martyr, in his agony, was twice heard to pray, "Jesus, have mercy on me!" He was then beheaded and his body cut into quarters.

Having been imprisoned for four years, the martyr was executed at Wrexham, in Denbighshire, on October 17, 1584. His head and one of his quarters were set upon Denbigh Castle.

During his imprisonment Gwyn wrote a number of religious poems and a funeral ode in the Welsh language, all of which called on his countrymen to preserve the Catholic Faith. Richard Gwyn was beatified in 1929 and canonized by Pope Paul VI in 1970 with 39 other martyrs of England who died between the years 1535 and 1679. He is considered to be the protomartyr of Wales.

Chapter 190

BL. RICHARD HERST

d. 1628

The history of Bl. Richard Herst is said to be one of the most remarkable and unusual in the annals of the English and Welsh martyrs, since he was hanged after being falsely charged with willful murder.

He was born near Preston, in Lancashire, and was a successful and well-to-do farmer. But because Bl. Richard would not conform to the Anglican Church, of which Queen Elizabeth had claimed supremacy, the authorities called for his arrest. Sent to apprehend him was Christopher Norcross, who engaged the help of two men, Wilkinson and Dewhurst.

They found Bl. Richard plowing a field, and as Norcross handed him the warrant, Wilkinson struck at the humble farmer with a staff. A girl who was working in another part of the field, seeing this unwarranted attack, ran to summon her mistress, who came running out with a farmhand and another man by the name of Bullen, who was visiting at the time.

The process servers turned to meet the farmhand and the visitor and knocked them down. At almost the same time, the girl hit Dewhurst over the head. The process servers then ran away, but as Challoner relates, Dewhurst "partly on occasion of the blow, partly also to apply himself close to Wilkinson, made more haste than good speed, and ran so disorderly over the hard-ploughed lands as that he fell down and broke his leg." The fracture became infected, and thirteen days later Dewhurst died of gangrene, after having declared that his fall had been quite accidental.

Despite this deathbed declaration, Richard Herst was indicted for murder before Sir Henry Yelverton. During the trial, it was declared by two witnesses that Dewhurst's fall had been an accident, and that at the time the maid gave Dewhurst the blow upon the head, Richard

Herst was at least 30 yards away and had not given the girl any direction or encouragement to do such a thing. The jury who heard the few facts of the case delivered a verdict of not guilty. However, the judge was not satisfied with the verdict. Speaking privately with the foreman, he persuaded him to deliberate again and to bring back a verdict of guilty, since he felt that the defendant should be convicted "as an example."

Since the first charge brought against Richard Herst had been that he was a nonconformist, Bl. Richard's freedom was offered him if he would take the Oath of Supremacy, which had been condemned by the Holy See. Richard Herst refused to do so. A guilty verdict was promptly rendered, and a sentence of death was declared as punishment.

The day before he suffered, Bl. Richard was ordered to attend a service in a Protestant church. Since Richard refused to go, the High Sheriff ordered him to be dragged by force. While Richard Herst offered all the resistance he could, he was dragged over ragged and stony ground to the church. When he arrived he "cast himself upon the ground and thrust his fingers into his ears that he might not hear their doctrine." On returning to prison, he happily told all the Catholics along the way, "They have tortured my body, but I thank God they have not hurt my soul."

During the time of his confinement, Richard Herst wrote three letters to his confessor. In one of these letters, all of which are still preserved, Bl. Richard wrote,

> Although my flesh be timorous and fearful, I yet find great comfort in spirit in casting myself upon my sweet Saviour with a most fervent love, when I consider what He hath done and suffered for me, and my greatest desire is to suffer with Him. And I had rather choose to die a thousand deaths than to possess a kingdom and live in mortal sin; for there is nothing so hateful to me as sin, and that only for the love of my Saviour.

In another letter to his confessor he wrote, "I pray you remember my poor children." Richard Herst had six young children at the time, and one yet unborn.

Before leaving his cell on the day of his execution, he looked toward the castle and saw hanging there the head of the priest, Bl. Edmund Arrowsmith, who had died the day before. On being asked at what he was looking, Richard Herst answered, "I look at the head of that blessed martyr whom you have sent before to prepare the way for us."

As he was traveling to the place of execution, Bl. Richard was met in the street by Mr. King, the Vicar of the town, who questioned him about his faith. Richard Herst answered, "I believe according to the faith of the Holy Catholic Church." Bl. Richard carried with him a picture of Christ crucified on which he looked frequently, repeating short ejaculatory prayers as he did so. On reaching the scaffold, he paused to say a final prayer, but on seeing that the hangman was fumbling while trying to adjust the rope, Richard Herst called up to him, "Tom, I think I must come up and help thee."

Richard Herst died on August 29, 1628 and was beatified in 1929.

Chapter 191

ST. ROCH

1295 - 1327

According to the brief life of St. Roch which was written by Francis Diedo in 1478, the Saint was born in 1295, the son of the Governor of Montpellier, France. When he was 20 years old, he suffered the loss of both his parents. Inspired by grace, he gave his entire inheritance to the poor, garbed himself as a pilgrim and set out for Italy. St. Roch found the City of Aquapendente plague-stricken and immediately devoted himself to the care of the sick, curing many with a Sign of the Cross. He next visited Cesena, Rome, Mantua, Modena and Parma. At each place he cared for the sick, while disregarding his own welfare.

While ministering to the sick at Piacenza, he was stricken with the dreaded disease. Not wanting to be a burden to anyone, he dragged himself to a hut in the neighboring forest. There a dog found him, and somehow enticed its master to follow him to the Saint's humble shelter. The dog's owner, a man named Gothard, found the Saint and rendered him all the services that the Saint had so kindly ministered to the plague-stricken in the city. Upon his recovery, St. Roch decided that since the plague was then under control, he would return to France to nurse the injured at Montpellier, which was then engaged in a civil war.

Arriving at the city of his birth, he found that illness and penance had so altered his appearance that he was not recognized. He was apprehended as a spy and was sent to prison, where he languished for five years until his death in 1327 at the age of 32. When St. Roch's body was being prepared for burial, prison officials discovered the cross-shaped birthmark on his chest which identified him as the son of the former governor. He was accordingly given a public funeral, and numerous miracles at the time attested to his sanctity.

The popularity and veneration of the Saint grew rapidly, and he soon became the saint to be invoked against infectious diseases that afflict both man and beast. When the plague began to ravage the city where the Council of Constance (1414-1418) was being conducted, the Fathers of the Council ordered public prayers and a procession in honor of the Saint. Immediately, the plague disappeared so that their work could continue.

Pope Paul III instituted a confraternity under the invocation of the Saint, whose members were to have charge of the church and hospital which were erected during the pontificate of Alexander VI. The confraternity increased so rapidly that Pope Paul IV raised it to an archconfraternity. Afterward, the organization was favored by several pontiffs and was given a prelate of high rank to be its immediate superior.

According to Wadding, the relics of the Saint were carried to Venice in 1485 where they are still venerated, but smaller relics of the Saint are found worldwide.

In art, St. Roch is customarily depicted wearing the clothing of a pilgrim with a dog by his side. He is mentioned in the *Roman Martyrology*, and his feast is kept in many places on August 16.

Chapter 192

ST. ROSE OF VITERBO

1235 - 1252

As owners of a house and a plot of land, Rose's parents were not destitute, but are said to have lived in humble obscurity in Viterbo, Italy, some 40 miles north of Rome.

Rose was born to this hard-working couple about the year 1235 and displayed from babyhood an unusual goodness. At the age of seven she expressed the desire to live alone in a small room of her own so that she might pray undisturbed. When she was eight years old, Rose became seriously ill. On the vigil of the feast of St. John the Baptist she had a vision or dream of Our Lady, who told her that she was to enter the Third Order of St. Francis and live at home so as to give her neighbors a good example by both word and work. Rose soon recovered her health and was received as a Franciscan tertiary.

The political situation at the time became unsettled when Emperor Frederick II decided to make Rome the civil, as well as the ecclesiastical, capital of the world. With himself as administrator over all, his actions against Pope Gregory IX resulted in the Emperor's excommunication. As a result, Frederick set out to conquer the papal states, and in the year 1240 the Emperor actually occupied Viterbo and the surrounding regions.

Perhaps inspired by a sermon she heard, or by the vindictive words of the enemy, Rose, at the age of 12, began to courageously defy the enemy by walking up and down the streets while upbraiding the people for submitting to Frederick. She urged them to overthrow the enemy's garrison. Needless to say, the actions of the child drew a great deal of attention, and marvels are said to have accompanied her words.

Eventually, crowds would gather outside her house to get a glimpse of her. As a result, Rose's father became afraid of some unwelcomed retaliation and forbade Rose to leave the house. As enforcement of her father's order, Rose was threatened with a severe beating if she disobeyed. "If Jesus could be beaten for me, I can be beaten for Him. I do what He has told me to do, and I must not disobey Him," Rose replied gently.

After the parish priest expressed his approval of Rose's activities, her father relented and permitted Rose to resume her preaching in public. Aware that crowds were now listening to the twelve-year-old girl, those who sided with the Emperor became alarmed and asked that Rose be put to death as a danger to their ambitious endeavor. The officials, however, were fearful of the people if this should be done, and instead ordered that Rose and her parents be banished from the territory. The humble little family then left Viterbo for Soriano.

During their exile, Rose announced in early December the approaching death of Emperor Frederick II. On December 13, in fact, he died in Apulia. Without the main instigator of their endeavors, the enemy retired and peace was restored to Viterbo. The little family happily returned to their home and farmland.

Rose made an attempt to be accepted as a postulant at the convent of St. Mary of the Roses at Viterbo. The Abbess, however, refused to accept her. It has been speculated that the sisters did not want an "evangelical preacheress" among them. On hearing the Abbess' refusal, Rose said smilingly, "You will not have me now, but perhaps you will be more willing when I am dead."

Rose lived a contemplative life in her parents' house, where she died on March 6, 1252, being only 17 years old. She was buried in the Church of Santa Maria in Podio—but just as she had predicted, her body was removed six years later to the church of the convent of St. Mary of the Roses. This church was destroyed by fire in 1357, but her incorrupt body was unharmed and is now enshrined in the Monastero Clarisse S. Rosa in Viterbo.

Immediately after Rose's death, Pope Innocent IV ordered an inquiry with a view toward her canonization, but this did not take place until the year 1457.

In 1921 St. Rose's perfectly incorrupt heart was extracted and placed in a reliquary which is taken in procession through the city every year on the fourth of September, the feast day of the Saint. The incorrupt body of the young saint, who died over seven centuries ago, is exposed in a glass-sided casket for the veneration and edification of the faithful.

Chapter 193

ST. SABAS

d. 372

When Athanaric, a king of the Goths, raised a persecution against his Christian subjects, many Goths who had converted to Christianity were martyred. Of the 51 Gothic martyrs commemorated by the Greeks, the most famous is St. Sabas, who served as lector to the priest Sansala.

At the beginning of the persecution, the magistrates ordered that all Christians should offer a token sacrifice to the gods by eating meat that previously had been consecrated to the idols. Some pagans who had Christian relatives and friends whom they wished to save, persuaded certain officials to give these Christians meat that had not been offered to the gods.

St. Sabas spoke loudly against this hypocrisy. He refused to eat the meat himself and declared that those who did accept and eat the unconsecrated meat under these conditions were betrayers of the Faith. While a few Christians agreed with him, the greater part of the Christian community was so displeased with his opinion that they forced him to leave the city.

A year after St. Sabas was permitted to return, another persecution began. The Christian leaders of the town, still fearful of what would happen to them if they acknowledged their Christianity, offered to swear to the persecutors that there were no Christians in the town. St. Sabas could have left or kept quiet, but instead he waited until the oath was about to take place. Bravely presenting himself to the authorities he said, "Let no one swear for me; I am a Christian!" When the authorities learned that he had no worldly possessions except the clothes he wore, he was released with the remark: "Such a fellow can do us neither good nor harm."

A few years later, when the persecution again threatened the lives of Christians, soldiers broke into the lodging of the priest Sansala, with whom Sabas was staying. The priest was surprised in his sleep and was bound and thrown into a cart. Sabas was pulled from his pallet and was dragged through thorn bushes and whipped with sticks. Because the persecutors were determined to make him suffer still more, a rack was fashioned from the "axle-trees" of a cart. With his outstretched hands and feet bound to it, St. Sabas was tortured for a considerable part of the night. When his torturers finally decided to rest, a compassionate woman unfastened the Saint, but he refused to escape.

The next day, St. Sabas was suspended from the beam of a house. Later both Sabas and the priest were offered meat that had been offered to idols. When both men stoutly refused to touch it, Sabas was struck in the chest with a javelin. Since this did not kill him, orders were given that he should be drowned.

St. Sabas was subsequently taken to the banks of the Mussovo River, where his head was held under the water with a plank until he expired. According to a letter written on behalf of the local Christians to the church in Cappadocia very shortly after the martyrdom, St. Sabas' death appears to have taken place on April 12, 372, at the place now called Targoviste, northwest of Bucharest in Romania.

The Saint's body was drawn from the water and left on the shore, but it was recovered by the faithful and was sent by Junius Soranus, the Christian Duke of Scythia, to the Saint's country of Caesarea in Cappadocia, where St. Basil welcomed it.

Chapter 194

ST. SATURUS

d. c. 455

After renouncing the Catholic Faith which he had practiced since childhood, Genseric, King of the Vandals, began to persecute all his subjects who remained loyal to the Church.

Huneric, a nobleman, had as master of his household Saturus, a staunch Catholic. In order to comply with the directives of Genseric, to whom he owed allegiance, Huneric likewise persecuted Catholics who remained faithful and ordered St. Saturus to renounce his Church.

When Saturus refused, Huneric threatened to deprive him of his estate, his slaves, wife and children. Saturus' wife, fearful of losing her privileges and wealth, pleaded with her husband to comply, but he steadfastly refused to renounce the Catholic Faith for the comforts and material possessions of this world.

Huneric made good his threat by reducing Saturus to poverty, but as Victor of Vita commented, "Of his baptismal robe they could not rob him."

Saturus died about the year 455.

Chapter 195

ST. SERAPHINA

d. 1253

The memory of St. Seraphina (or Fina) is especially venerated in the old town of San Gimignano, Italy, where she was born. She is remembered there as a young girl who accepted great bodily sufferings with perfect resignation to the will of God.

Seraphina was born of respectable parents who had fallen into poverty. The child was pretty and attractive, modest and concerned for the poor, going so far as to give half her food to those who were less fortunate than herself. Even in her youth she became proficient in the household skills of sewing and spinning and was considered an able assistant to her mother.

While Seraphina was still quite young, her father died. At about the same time the beautiful young girl was attacked by a series of illnesses that left her unattractive and an object of pity. Her head, eyes, feet and internal organs were affected. Within a short time paralysis claimed her body. No doubt inspired to behave like Our Lord on the Cross, she would not allow a soft bed to be made for her. Instead, she chose to lay on a hard plank. Finding movement impossible, Seraphina lay on this board for six years in one position. Since there was constant contact with the wood, the plank eventually rotted and adhered to her skin, producing agonizing pain.

With the death of her father, Seraphina and her mother were reduced to abject poverty, which forced the mother to periodically leave the patient while she went begging or looking for work. While the mother was gone, the helpless Seraphina was forced to endure the presence of rats, which at times gnawed at her flesh or licked up her blood. Although in terrible pain, Seraphina always maintained a peaceful spirit, and while gazing upon the crucifix she was known to repeat countless times, "It is not my wounds but Thine, O Christ, that pain me."

As though poverty, sickness and paralysis were not enough of a burden, Seraphina had another to endure—the sudden death of her beloved and devoted mother. Seraphina was now completely destitute except for one devoted friend, Beldia, and a few neighbors, who gave her a minimum of attention due to their repugnance of her wounds.

Seraphina had a great devotion to St. Gregory the Great, who, she was told, had suffered from various diseases. She prayed fervently to this Saint that she might have patience in her affliction. Eight days before her death, as she lay alone and unattended, the Saint appeared to her and said, "Dear child, on my festival, God will give you rest." His prophetic words were realized. On the feast of St. Gregory in the year 1253, St. Seraphina died.

When the Saint's body was removed from the rotten board on which she had lain for so long, her neighbors declared that the wood was found to be covered with white violets which gave off a heavenly scent.

All the people of the city attended the funeral of the poor Saint, and many miracles were reported. One miracle in particular is said to have occurred as Seraphina lay dead. This miracle was in favor of her friend, Beldia, who had helped Seraphina after the death of her mother. While Beldia was standing in prayer beside the body of her friend, the corpse's hand began to rise. It clasped Beldia's injured arm, which was immediately cured.

White violets which bloom about the time of the Saint's feast day are still given the name of Santa Fina by the people of San Gimignano.

Seraphina is also called the "Saint of the Wallflowers," because these flowers reportedly sprang up on her coffin and on the towers of the town on the day of her death.

St. Seraphina is sometimes incorrectly identified as a Benedictine nun, but she belonged to no order and lived a life of seclusion in her own home.

St. Gregory the Great appears in a vision to St. Seraphina. She had prayed to him for patience in enduring the painful and disfiguring afflictions that had paralyzed her from childhood. Seraphina and her mother lived in abject poverty; when her mother left to beg or look for work, Seraphina was attacked by rats. But even the terrible pain she endured did not destroy the Saint's peaceful spirit. *(Painting by D. Ghirlandaio.)*

665

Ediz. Fontanelli, S. Gimignano/Plurigraf, Terni

All the people of San Gimignano, Italy attended the funeral of St. Seraphina. Many miracles were reported, including the immediate cure of the injured arm of Seraphina's only friend, Beldia. It is said that Beldia was standing in prayer beside Seraphina's body

666

St. Seraphina (d. 1253) is called "Saint of the Wallflowers" because flowers reportedly sprang up on her coffin and on the towers of the town the day she died.
She is pictured holding these flowers *(left)* and in the towers.

Chapter 196

ST. SERENUS

d. c. 307

Known as "The Gardener," St. Serenus was a Greek by birth who left all that he had to serve God in the ascetical life of celibacy, penance and prayer.

Upon reaching the area now known as Yugoslavia, he bought a garden, which he cultivated. Surrounded by the beauty and peace of the countryside, his body was nourished by the fruit and vegetables his garden produced while his soul benefited from his constant prayers and meditation.

During a persecution against the Christians, Serenus left his garden for a few months until peace was again established. Then one day after his return, he found a woman walking in the garden during the early afternoon, at an hour when people of stature were usually resting. When he courteously reminded her that it seemed an improper time for a woman of her position to be walking alone in the garden of an ascetic, the woman became insulted and furious. She immediately wrote to her husband, who belonged to the guards of the Emperor Maximian, and complained that she had been grievously offended by Serenus.

After receiving the letter, the woman's husband went to the Emperor to demand justice for his wife, who had been insulted in a distant land. He was given a letter addressed to the Governor of the province which would enable him to obtain satisfaction. In due time Serenus was brought before the Governor to reply to the charge made against his conduct.

In answer to the Governor's questions, Serenus acknowledged that he was a gardener and that he had never insulted a woman in his whole life. He remembered that a woman of stature had been found walking in his garden and that he had reminded the lady that it was an unseemly hour for a woman of position to be walking in the garden of an unmarried man.

Serenus answered the charge so sincerely that the woman's husband saw the situation from another point of view and asked that the charge of misconduct be dropped. But the Governor's suspicions were aroused in another area of the Saint's conduct.

Considering that Serenus was scrupulous in his dealings with the woman, he suspected that Serenus was a Christian and proceeded to question him. The Saint readily acknowledged that he was a Christian and that he was willing to suffer for the Faith. Without further questioning, St. Serenus was condemned to suffer death by decapitation. His martyrdom occurred about the year 307.

Chapter 197

BL. SERVULUS

d. 590

One Sexagesima Sunday, in the Basilica of St. Paul in Rome, St. Gregory the Great was preaching on the Gospel of the day, this being the parable of the sower whose seeds fell on rocks, thorns and good ground. The conclusion of the parable reads as follows: "But that [seed] on the good ground, are they who in a good and perfect heart, hearing the word, keep it, and bring forth fruit in patience." (*Luke* 8:15).

To illustrate this parable, the Saint told the story of Servulus, a holy invalid whose station for many years was near the Church of St. Clement. Many of St. Gregory's congregation had seen or known the holy beggar.

St. Gregory told the story again in his book called the *Dialogues*. All that we know of Bl. Servulus is given to us in Book IV, chapter 14 of that work. St. Gregory tells of the holy beggar in this manner:

> I remember that in my homily upon the Gospel, I told how in that porch which is in the way to St. Clement's Church there lay a certain man called Servulus, whom I doubt not but you also do remember who was poor in wealth, but rich in merits. This man had a long time been afflicted with sickness, for from the first time that I knew him, to the very last hour of his life, never can I remember but that he was sick of the palsy, and that so pitifully that he could not stand, nor sit up in his bed, neither was he ever able to put his hand into his mouth or to turn from one side to the other. His mother and brethren did serve and attend him, and what he got in alms, that by their hands he bestowed upon other poor people. Read he could not, yet did he buy the Holy Scriptures, which very carefully he caused such religious men as he entertained to read unto him. By means whereof, according to his capacity, though as I said he knew

670

not a letter of the book, yet did he fully learn the Holy Scripture. Very careful he was in his sickness always to give God thanks, and day and night to praise His Holy Name.

When the time was come in which God determined to reward this, his great patience, the pain of his body struck inwardly to his heart, which he feeling, and knowing that his last hour was not far off, called for all such strangers lodged in his house, desiring them to sing hymns with him for his last farewell and departure out of this life. As he was himself singing with them, all of a sudden he cried out aloud and bade them be silent saying, "Do ye not hear the great and wonderful music which is in Heaven?" And so while he lay giving of ear within himself to that divine harmony, his holy soul departed this mortal life, at which time all that were there present felt a most pleasant and fragrant smell...A monk of mine who was then present, and with many tears and faith to tell us that the sweetness of that smell never went away but that they felt it continually until the time of his burial.

St. Gregory the Great concludes his account of Blessed Servulus by observing that the memory of this poor sick beggar condemns those who, when blessed with good health and fortune, neither do good works nor suffer the least cross with noteworthy patience.

Chapter 198

BL. SIBYLLINA BISCOSSI

1287 - 1367

Born of humble parents in Pavia, Italy, Sibyllina Biscossi was orphaned at an early age. Before she was 10 years old, it became necessary for her to work as a servant girl; but two years later, as the result of a severe illness, she was rendered completely blind. Because Sibyllina was unable to perform any useful work, a community of Dominican tertiaries took pity on Sibyllina and permitted her to live with them. Intensely pious and suffering from the burden of her blindness, she felt convinced that if she prayed faithfully to St. Dominic her sight would be restored.

After a time, when her prayers were not answered, Sibyllina had a strange dream in which St. Dominic seemed to take her by the hand and lead her first through an area of darkness, where she sensed the presence of evil creatures, and then into an area of radiant light and peace. On awakening, it was not difficult for Sibyllina to understand that her blindness in this world would be rewarded with the sight of heavenly wonders. Thereafter she willingly accepted the hardships of her handicap.

When she was only 15 years old, Sibyllina arranged to live as a recluse in a room adjoining the Dominican church. There she practiced great austerity for 65 years, giving advice from the window of her cell to all those who were attracted by her reputation for holiness. Sibyllina was contemplative and knew the value of interior mortification of the will. She was favored with many heavenly revelations and was especially devoted to the Holy Ghost.

Uneducated as she was, Sibyllina spoke of Divine matters with such fluency and theological precision that many sinners repented and many others were converted.

Blessed Sibyllina possessed the singular gift of knowing when a consecrated Host was being carried past her window by a priest who was taking the Sacrament to the sick. On one occasion she warned a priest that the host he was carrying was not consecrated, which proved to be the case after the claim was investigated.

Sibyllina died on Friday, March 19, 1367, being in her 80th year. Owing to the many miracles and favors obtained through her intercession, she was beatified by Pope Pius IX in 1853.

Her body was found incorrupt at the time of the beatification and is enshrined in the Cathedral of Pavia.

Bl. Sibyllina Biscossi (1287-1367) was orphaned and began to work as a servant girl when nine years old. Two years later she became blind following a severe illness. Dominican tertiaries took care of her in Pavia, Italy, where she became a recluse. She is depicted here at far right.

674

The relics of Bl. Sibyllina, enshrined in the Cathedral of Pavia. Her body was found incorrupt at the time of her beatification in 1853. The beata had a reputation for holiness during her life; especially devoted to the Holy Ghost, she was a contemplative and was given many heavenly revelations. She also possessed the gift of knowing when a consecrated Host was being carried past her window to the sick. Many favors and miracles through her intercession have been reported.

Chapter 199

ST. SIGEBERT

630 - 656

The father of St. Sigebert was Dagobert I, King of France, who led such a sinful life that he was frequently rebuked by St. Amandus, Bishop of Maestricht. For the zeal with which he endeavored to convert Dagobert from his dissolute life, St. Amandus was banished from the realm.

If the holy Bishop was unable to succeed in this regard, it took a mere baby to win Dagobert from his evil ways. At the birth of his son, Sigebert, Dagobert was touched by an extraordinary grace and from that hour was completely converted to a life of virtue.

For the Baptism of the future Saint, Dagobert searched for the holiest prelate in the Kingdom to perform the ceremony. His choice fell to the banished St. Amandus, who was quickly recalled. When the Bishop arrived, Dagobert fell on his knees before him. He confessed his sins and promised amendment. The rite of Baptism was then performed with great ceremony at Orleans, with the godfather being Dagobert's brother, Charibert, King of Aquitaine.

Sigebert was a mere three years old when the doting father declared his son to be the King of Austrasia and gave him for his ministers the Archbishop of Cologne, St. Cunibert and Duke Adalgisilus. The person chosen to administer the whole Kingdom for the child King was Bl. Pepin of Landen, the mayor of the palace, who was a married man and the father of three children. Bl. Pepin, who is mentioned elsewhere in this volume, was also entrusted with the education of the young King.

When Dagobert's second son, Clovis II, was born in 634, the father allotted to him for his inheritance all the western part of France. Sigebert's territory of Austrasia consisted of the eastern part of France and parts of what are now Switzerland, Germany and Hungary.

After the death of Dagobert in 638, when Sigebert was eight years old and Clovis only four, the two brothers assumed their responsibilities, and with the help of their ministers who guided the youthful monarchs, they ruled their lands in perfect harmony and peace; the only war in which Sigebert was involved was an uprising in Thuringia, in which his army suffered.

Bl. Pepin of Landen, who trained young Sigebert, can be credited with molding the character of a saint who is also known to have reigned with perfect intelligence. Sigebert was assiduous in prayer, generous to the poor and conscientious in the exercise of Christian virtue. He endowed churches and hospitals and founded 12 monasteries. He was also a married man and the father of Dagobert II, who is also venerated as a saint.

It was with deep sorrow that the people of St. Sigebert's realm were informed of the untimely death of their virtuous king. Sigebert died in the year 656, during the eighteenth year of his reign and the twenty-sixth year of his life.

Chapter 200

ST. SIMON OF TRENT

d. 1475

In the Office for the feast of the Holy Innocents we read, "These children cry out their praises to the Lord; by their death they have proclaimed what they could not preach with their infant voices." St. Simon of Trent (Italy) likewise cries out his praises to the Lord, having also died in his innocence at the hands of unbelievers.

Simon of Trent was two and a half years old when he was kidnapped by non-believers who wanted to express their hatred for the Church by killing a Christian child.

One of the kidnappers, a man named Tobias, found Simon playing outside his home with no one guarding him. Simon was enticed away with kindness and was brought to the home of his abductor.

During the early hours of Good Friday, in the year 1475, the child's martyrdom began. His mouth was gagged, and he was held by the arms in the form of a cross. While in this position his tender body was pierced with awls and bodkins in blasphemous mockery of the sufferings of Jesus Christ. After an hour's torture, the child died. The body was kept for a short time before it was thrown into a canal. When the body was recovered, an investigation led to the arrest of suspects. After confessing their part in the crime, the child's murderers were severely punished.

The remains of little Simon were buried in St. Peter's Church at Trent, where many miracles took place. As a result, the title of saint was awarded to Simon, because of his tender age and the manner of his death.

Chapter 201

ST. SOLANGIA

d. 880

Born at Villemont, France, St. Solangia (Solange) was the child of pious parents who were vine-dressers. Although living in poor circumstances, she was blessed with some of Heaven's most beguiling gifts. She was sweet-tempered, lovable, charitable, industrious and extremely beautiful.

Reports of her beauty reached Bernard de la Gothie, the son of the Count of Poitiers. Bernard journeyed to meet Solangia and found her in the pasture, where she was minding her father's sheep. He immediately developed a great desire to have her for his wife and proposed marriage.

Solangia declined the offer, giving as her excuse the vow of virginity she had made at the age of seven. The nobleman expressed his disappointment and pleaded with her, describing the many benefits she was renouncing for herself and her poor family.

When Solangia continued to decline his proposal, Bernard decided to abduct her. Bernard caught her up and set her in the saddle before him, but Solangia resisted with such violence that she threw herself from his horse while it was crossing a stream. Although injured in the fall, she struggled to crawl to safety. The pride of the young nobleman was seriously wounded. Angry at seeing the girl attempting to escape him and furious at the rejection, he decapitated her with a blow from his sword. The year was 880.

The veneration paid to St. Solangia has remained active at the Church of St. Martin at Villemont, where the head of the Saint is reverently enshrined. Near her home, a field where she liked to pray received the name of Le Champ de Sainte Solangia.

In the past, during times of great calamity, the relics of the Saint have been taken in procession through the town of Bourges. Although the processions no longer take place, the Saint is still invoked in times of drought.

Chapter 202

ST. SOLOMON

d. 874

The few outstanding facts that are given us about the career of St. Solomon are accepted as substantially true by modern critical hagiographers. These facts reveal that he was a nephew of King Nominoius, the liberator of Brittany. After his uncle's death, his cousin Erispoius, King Nominoius' son, was declared the rightful heir, but Solomon, filled with envy, coveted the throne for himself.

To fulfill his prideful ambition, Solomon actually killed his cousin Erispoius. By means of this deliberate sin of murder Solomon became the King and ruler of all Brittany.

Although his sin disturbed his conscience and was well-known throughout his kingdom, Solomon's reign proved a glorious one in the eyes of the people, since he successfully defended his country from the Franks and the Northmen.

Later in life Solomon repented of the murder of his cousin and did penance for his crime. In addition to these penances, he became a great benefactor of religious houses. In 866 he transferred the remains of St. Maxentius to Brittany in order to save them from the Northmen, who were then troubling Aquitaine. He deposited the relics first in the Abbey of St. Saviour of Redon, and afterwards in the church of a monastery which he built at Plelan. In the charter of this new foundation he expressed his wish to be buried there.

In the year 874 St. Solomon was assassinated by some of his disgruntled subjects.

Chapter 203

ST. STEPHEN, KING OF HUNGARY

975 - 1038

The Magyars, who settled in Hungary during the last years of the ninth century, were a fierce and marauding people who first met Christianity in the course of their raids into Italy and France.

Almost a century later, their leader, Geza, realized the political necessity of Christianity for his country and married the Catholic Adelaide, sister of the Duke of Poland. Geza was eventually baptized, together with a number of his nobles; but this was largely a conversion of expediency, with the new Christians practicing the Faith outwardly, while privately retaining many of their pagan customs.

An exception was Geza's son, Vaik, who had been baptized at the same time as his father and had adopted the name of Stephen. Having been born in the year 975, he was only 10 years old at the time of his Baptism. He had not yet acquired pagan ways, undoubtedly because his Catholic mother had scrupulously guarded him against such influences, and with the same diligence had instructed him in the doctrines of the True Faith.

When Stephen was 20 years old he married Gisela, sister of Henry, the Duke of Bavaria, who is better known as the Holy Roman Emperor, St. Henry II. Two years later Stephen succeeded his father as Governor of the Magyars.

Since his people were then at peace with their neighbors, Stephen was able to turn his attention to the elimination of the idolatrous practices that still existed, and to the substitution of Christian devotions. To accomplish this, he welcomed a number of missionaries into the country. The German knights and priests who had settled in Hungary after his marriage also made numerous sincere converts, but many of the Magyars obstinately retained their superstitious practices and organized to defend idolatry through force of arms.

Stephen prepared for the confrontation by prayer and fasting, and with the help of German forces he thoroughly defeated the enemy. As a sign that God had triumphed over idolatry, Stephen built on the field of battle a great monastery in honor of St. Martin, to whom he had prayed before the battle. This monastery, known as the Archabbey of Martinsberg, or Pannonhalma, served for centuries as the motherhouse of the Hungarian Benedictine Congregation. With the defeat of the rebels, Stephen invited into his country many priests and religious from Germany, France and Italy. Their preaching and good example had a great influence over the people, who in time became conscientious followers of Christianity.

At the urging of his nobles, Stephen petitioned the papacy for the title of king, that with majesty and authority he might accomplish other deeds for the Church and the good of the people. This was granted by Pope Sylvester II, who provided the crown for Stephen's coronation that occurred on August 17, 1001.

After being endowed with royal dignity and with the Pope's benediction, Stephen divided the land into dioceses and archdioceses and built churches, religious houses and even hospices for pilgrims at Rome, Ravenna and Constantinople. His edicts concerning church tithes, and ordinances regarding the support of the clergy, attendance at Mass, observances of feasts and Church fasts were confirmed by the Pope.

Although occupied with building houses of worship, seeing to the support of the clergy and tending to matters of state, Stephen was always accessible to people of all ranks and listened to their complaints, especially those of the poor. For them he provided the necessities of life and even went around the country in disguise to discover the unfortunates who had been overlooked by his officers.

A story is told that one day, as St. Stephen was distributing alms, a group of beggars gathered around him and, not recognizing the King because of his humble clothing, they knocked him down, pulled at his beard and hair and snatched his purse—which contained enough money to relieve them and many others. Stephen humbly accepted this indignity and rejected the advice of his attendants that he should discontinue the practice of exposing himself in such a manner. Instead, he renewed his resolution never to refuse an alms to any of God's poor.

Stephen was not without troubles from rebels and invaders. In 1003 his Uncle Gyula, Prince of Transylvania, invaded his dominion and was defeated. In 1024 when his brother-in-law, the Emperor St. Henry II had died, his successor, Conrad II, intended to seize Henry's new See of Bamberg for his personal benefit, but Stephen was successful in defeating his plans.

And in 1025, Stephen had to subdue a revolt headed by a noble named Ajton, who was inclined to transfer his allegiance to the Eastern Emperor at Constantinople. Shortly after this trouble, Stephen had to resist an invasion of the Bessi from Bulgaria.

In 1031 Conrad, who was beginning to fear the growing power and influence of Hungary on the Bavarian border, marched against St. Stephen; however, the matter was settled by means of an agreement which prevented the loss of life.

It is no wonder that Stephen, with all the problems and responsibilities of his office, was looking forward to entrusting a part of the government to someone who was not only capable, but was also a sincere Christian. The person he had groomed to help, and later to succeed him, was his only son, Emeric. But in the year 1031, when some of the burdens of office were to be transferred, Emeric was accidentally killed while hunting bear. Stephen grieved for his son and cried, "God loved him, and therefore He has taken him away early."

The death of Emeric left Stephen without an heir, a situation that caused bitter disputes among members of his family over the matter of succession.

During the last years of Stephen's life, he was afflicted with a painful ailment and was sadly annoyed by the squabbling of at least five claimants. One was Peter, the son of Stephen's sister, Gisela. Described as an ambitious and cruel woman, Gisela had returned to the Hungarian court after the death of her husband, the Doge of Venice. She was determined that her son should rule and shamelessly took advantage of Stephen's sickness to forward her plans.

Two other claimants were Stephen's cousins, Andrew and Bela. These two went so far as to enter into a conspiracy to kill him. They engaged an assassin, who one night entered Stephen's bedroom. When he dropped his dagger, Stephen awakened and calmly observed, "If God be for me, who shall be against me?" Stephen's attendants apprehended the assassin, who implicated Andrew and Bela in the plot. All three were arrested, but Stephen pardoned and released them. It has been suggested that the episode had been planned by Gisela, who had hoped to prejudice Stephen against Andrew and Bela and thereby eliminate two of the rivals. Once again, Gisela interfered by removing Duke Basil by violence. Another claimant was advised by Peter to retreat or meet a similar treatment at the hands of his mother. In the end, Peter won the right of succession.

St. Stephen died at the age of 63 on the Feast of the Assumption in the year 1038. He was buried beside his son, St. Emeric, at Stuhl-weissenburg, which had been built by Stephen in honor of the Mother of God. Here at Stuhlweissenburg the kings of Hungary were afterwards both crowned and buried.

St. Stephen's tomb has been the site of many miracles. Forty-five years after his death, by order of Pope St. Gregory VII and at the request of King St. Ladislas, his relics were removed to Budapest, where they were placed in a chapel which bears his name within the great church of Our Lady at Buda (now known as the Cathedral of St. Stephen).

During the same year, 1083, Stephen was canonized by Pope St. Gregory VII. Innocent XI, in the year 1686, appointed September 2 as St. Stephen's feast day, although the Church now celebrates his feast on August 16.

Two outstanding relics of St. Stephen are carefully kept: the crown that was used at his coronation, and his incorrupt right hand. (For interesting details of both relics see the author's book, *Relics.*)

Hungary is privileged to have as its patron saints the Blessed Virgin under the title, "Great Lady of Hungary," and St. Stephen, who is also known as the "Apostolic King."

St. Stephen, King of Hungary (975-1038), the country's first king. St. Stephen defeated rival leaders, men who obstinately clung to idolatrous practices and opposed his Christianization policies, and thus he consolidated the country. Then, in response to a petition, St. Stephen received from the Pope the title of King—also receiving from him a splendid crown for the coronation, which took place in the year 1001. This monument to the Saint is located in Budapest.

Budapesti Szent Istvan Bazilika Plebania Hivatala

tended in charity to the poor. The holy King once allowed himself to be knocked down, humiliated and robbed by beggars as he distributed alms disguised in humble clothing. Then, rather than discontinuing this practice (as urged by his attendants), he renewed his resolve never to refuse alms to any of God's poor.

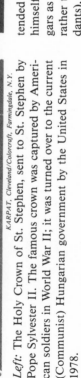

KARPAT, Cleveland/Colorcraft, Farmingdale, N.Y.

Left: The Holy Crown of St. Stephen, sent to St. Stephen by Pope Sylvester II. The famous crown was captured by American soldiers in World War II; it was turned over to the current (Communist) Hungarian government by the United States in 1978.

Right: The incorrupt right hand of St. Stephen, so often ex-

Chapter 204

BL. STILLA

d. 1141

Born at Abenberg, near Nuremburg, toward the end of the eleventh century, Bl. Stilla is believed to be related to the noble family of the Counts of Abenberg. This family gave many priests, bishops and holy men to the Church, notably Blessed Count Conrad I, Archbishop of Salzburg, who is believed to have been Stilla's brother.

On a hill adjoining her home, Stilla built a church at her own expense, which was consecrated and dedicated in honor of St. Peter in the year 1136. She visited this church every day and there, with the approval of Otto, Bishop of Bamberg, she took a vow of virginity.

She lived a virtuous life in her father's household, while dreaming that someday she would end her days in the monastery that she hoped to build beside the church. But death claimed Bl. Stilla about the year 1141, before her plans were realized.

Arrangements were made by her family to have her buried at Heilsbronn, where her brothers, who were monks, had built a Cistercian abbey. However, the two horses drawing the funeral cart refused to pull in that direction, turning always toward the church of St. Peter. There Bl. Stilla was buried in a grave that was adorned with her effigy. The tomb became a place of pilgrimage, and in 1897, on the grounds that her veneration antedated 1534, the Bishop of Eichstätt approved her cultus, which was eventually confirmed by Pope Pius XI in 1927.

The Bollandists list 55 exceptional miracles which have been acknowledged at Bl. Stilla's tomb by wax votive images.

Chapter 205

ST. SWITHIN WELLS

1536 - 1591

As the sixth son of Thomas Wells of Brambridge, England, Swithin was educated from his infancy in the ways of virtue. In his youth he engaged in innocent diversions, including hawking and hunting, yet he was always devout in prayer and dedicated to the True Faith. He is described as having been good-natured, courteous, generous, courageous, amiable and pleasant in conversation.

After he was instructed in the liberal sciences, Swithin traveled to Rome, partly to learn the Italian language and also to visit the holy places. After returning to England he was employed in noble houses, and for six years he gave himself "to a more profitable employment of training young gentlemen in virtue and learning," that is, he was a teacher in a boys' school at Monkton Farleigh in Wiltshire.

St. Swithin eventually married a good and pious woman, with whom he lived in an edifying manner. The couple had only one child, a daughter, Margaret.

Swithin moved to London in 1585 with his little family and there, for the next six years, he aided and hid priests. This was during the unfortunate time in British history when Queen Elizabeth was persecuting those who refused to acknowledge her as the head of the Church of England.

Swithin Wells always gave good example to his neighbors and was very successful in bringing heretics and schismatics to the Catholic Faith. He cautioned them not to indulge in worldly pleasures to such an extent that they would thereby neglect their prayers and devotions. He also encouraged them not to be fearful of professing their faith, but rather to despise all worldly things and, like him, to be continually advancing toward Heaven. He, himself, practiced what he instructed others to do. He professed his faith by permitting his home to be a harbor for priests, who came at all hours of the day.

Such visits by the clergy were considered an act of treason, to be punished by death. He is also known to have arranged lodging for priests where they could engage in catechetical instruction. Mr. Wells' activities became so well-known to the justices and other officials that it eventually became unsafe for anyone to be seen in his company.

In the last years of his life, Swithin Wells rented a house in Holborn, near Gray's Inn Fields, where he continued to provide assistance to a number of priests until the morning of November 8, 1591. On that day the Rev. Edmund Genings, who was a young priest, was celebrating Holy Mass in the home of Swithin and his wife, with a small group of people in attendance. In accordance with the October 18, 1591 royal proclamation which led to the stricter enforcement of the laws against Catholics in England, the celebrated priest-catcher, Topcliffe, arrived at the house with his officers. He arrested everyone in the house, including Mrs. Wells. Although Swithin Wells was not present at the time, he was arrested sometime later.

At the ensuing trial, the Rev. Edmund Genings was found guilty of being a priest, Swithin Wells of harboring priests, and Mrs. Wells of providing the conveniences and comforts of her home. The Rev. Genings was given the usual punishment—that he was to be hung, drawn and quartered. Swithin Wells was ordered to suffer a similar martyrdom. While waiting in prison for the sentence to be enforced, he wrote a letter to his brother-in-law, Mr. Gerard Morin. In this letter he explained:

> I have endured much pain, but the many future rewards in the heavenly payment make all pains seem to me a pleasure; and truly custom hath caused that it is now no grief to be debarred from company...I rejoice that thereby I have the better occasion, with prayer, to prepare myself to that happy end for which I was created and placed here by God...yet I am not alone. He is not alone who has Christ in his company. When I pray, I talk with God; when I read, He talketh to me; so that I am never alone. He is my chiefest companion and only comfort.

On the way to the place of execution, which was opposite to Gray's Inn Fields, near the place of his residence, Swithin saw an old friend in the crowd of onlookers and shouted to him, "Farewell, old friend! Farewell all hawking and hunting and old pasttimes—I am now going a better way!"

While Swithin Wells was standing at the scaffold awaiting his execution, the priest-catcher Topcliffe said to him, "See what your priests have brought you to." To this Swithin replied, "I am happy and thank God to have been allowed to have so many and such saint-like priests under my roof."

Swithin Wells was hanged and while still alive was cut down. When he was being drawn, that is, his viscera and heart were being cut from his body, he cried in agony, but the hangman said later that he heard Swithin invoke the aid of St. Gregory. Also suffering on the same day were priests and other laymen.

Mrs. Wells was also condemned for the same crime, of having harbored priests. She was to suffer the same sentence and was brought to the place of execution. However, after viewing the death of her husband she was remanded to Newgate prison, where she spent ten years in prayer and fasting. She died in prison in 1602. Their daughter, Margaret, eventually became a nun.

Swithin Wells was canonized by Pope Paul VI on October 25, 1970, together with 39 other English martyrs who died between 1535 and 1679.

Chapter 206

ST. SYNCLETICA

d. 400

Born in Alexandria, Egypt, of wealthy Macedonian parents, Syncletica was inclined toward virtue from childhood. Attracted by her great beauty and wealth, many young noblemen proposed marriage; but they were rejected because of the vow of virginity Syncletica had made in her youth. Her parents, at their death, left her the sole heir to their fortune, her two brothers having died earlier. Left in Syncletica's care was her sister, who was blind.

Wanting to abandon all material possessions for the love of God, Syncletica distributed her fortune among the poor, and with her sister she retired to an unused sepulchral chamber on the estate of a relative. Here, in the presence of a priest, she renewed her consecration to God and cut off her hair as a sign that she renounced the world. From then on, mortification and prayer were her chief occupations.

When Syncletica's virtue became known, many women came to ask her advice about temporal and spiritual matters. With zeal tempered by humility and many tears, Syncletica spoke to these women, encouraging them in their trials and urging them along the ways of holiness. Her words left a deep impression upon them. She often counseled them,

> O, how happy should we be, did we but take as much pains to gain Heaven and please God as worldlings do to heap up riches and perishable goods! By land they venture among thieves and robbers; at sea they expose themselves to the fury of winds and waves; they suffer shipwrecks and all perils; they attempt all, dare all, hazard all: but we, in serving so great a Master for so immense a good, are afraid of every contradiction.

While warning the women against the dangers and temptations of life, she was accustomed to say:

691

We must be continually upon our guard, for we are engaged in a perpetual war; unless we take care, the enemy will surprise us, when we are least upon our guard. A ship sometimes passes safe through hurricanes and tempests; yet if the pilot, even in relative calm, be not on the alert, a sudden gust may sink her. It does not signify whether the enemy clambers in by the window, or whether all at once he shakes the foundation, if at last he destroys the house. In this life we sail, as it were, in an unknown sea. We meet with rocks, shoals and currents; sometimes we are becalmed, and at other times we find ourselves tossed and buffeted by a storm. Thus we are never secure, never out of danger; and, if we fall asleep, are sure to perish. We have a most experienced pilot at the helm of our vessel, Jesus Christ, who will conduct us safe into the haven of salvation, if, by our supineness, we cause not our own ruin.

At other times she encouraged her listeners in the way of humility and virtue in the following words:

A treasure is secure so long as it remains concealed; but when once disclosed and laid open to every bold invader, it is presently rifled; so virtue is safe as long as it is secret, but if rashly exposed it but too often evaporates in smoke. By humility and contempt of the world, the soul, like an eagle, soars on high, above all transitory things, and swoops down victoriously on lions and dragons.

The virtue of the Saint and the good that was derived from her counsels were not lost to the devil, who tormented Syncletica in so many ways that she was considered another Job. The Saint's virtue, however, not only triumphed, but became even more illustrious.

In the 80th year of her life, the Saint was seized with an intense fever that did considerable damage to her lungs. At the same time that her lungs were infected, a cancer developed in her mouth. This not only devoured the flesh in that area, but it also afflicted the jaw and the larynx, robbing her of speech. With incredible patience and resignation to God's holy will, she permitted the physicians to pare away from her face the parts that were already dead. Because of these ministrations of the doctors and her frightful condition, she found no rest for the last three months of her life.

Although unable to speak, the Saint silently gave an example of virtue in the patient acceptance of life's trials. When the hour came for her death, Syncletica was surrounded by a heavenly light and was favored with consoling visions. Her death occurred in her eighty-fourth year.

The Greeks keep her festival on the fourth of January; the *Roman Martyrology* mentions her on the fifth of that month.

The biography of St. Syncletica is quoted in *Lives of the Fathers* by Rosweide, and in the writings of St. John Climacus, who was apparently acquainted with the Saint.

Chapter 207

STS. THARSILLA AND EMILIANA

d. 550

St. Gregory the Great's father, Senator Gordian, had three sisters: Gordiana, Emiliana and Tharsilla, who was the eldest. These aunts of St. Gregory led intensely religious lives in their father's house, which was located on the Clivus Scauri in Rome. Tharsilla and Emiliana were especially dedicated to the vocation they had chosen, that of remaining single women—but Gordiana, after a time, came to realize that God was calling her to another way of life and eventually married.

Tharsilla and Emiliana persevered in the vocation they had chosen and continued to care for their father's house, while spending all their free time in prayer, penance and spiritual conversation.

St. Gregory the Great, in Chapter 16 of his *Dialogues,* describes the life and death of his Aunt Tharsilla in this way:

> Sometime also, for the comfort of the soul that departs, there appears unto it the Author Himself of life, and Rewarder of all virtue. For proof where, I will here report that which I remember also to have spoken of in my homilies concerning my Aunt Tharsilla, who in the company of two others of her sisters, had for continuance in prayer, gravity of life, singularity in abstinence, arrived to the top of perfection. To this woman, Felix (Pope St. Felix III), my great grandfather, sometime Bishop of this see of Rome, appeared in vision, and showed her the habitation of everlasting light, speaking thus: "Come with me, and I will entertain you in this dwelling place of light." Shortly after, taken with an ague, she was brought to the last state, and as when noble men and women lie a-dying, many do visit them for the comfort of their friends. So divers both men and women, at the time of her departure were come, which stood round about her bed. At what time she suddenly, casting her eyes upward,

beheld our Saviour coming. Whereupon, looking earnestly upon Him, she cried out to them that were present, "Away, away. My Saviour Jesus is come." And so, fixing her eyes upon Him whom she beheld, her holy soul departed this life.

Such a wonderful fragrant smell ensued that the sweetness thereof gave evident testimony that the Author of all sweetness was there present.

Afterward, when her dead body, according to the manner, was made ready to be washed, they found that with long custom of prayer, the skin of her arms and knees were like a camel's become hard. And so her dead body gave sufficient testimony what her living spirit had continually practiced.

Tharsilla died on Christmas Eve, about the year 550. A few days later she appeared to her sister and invited Emiliana to celebrate the Epiphany with her in Heaven. Emiliana, in fact, died on January 5, the Epiphany then being observed on January 6.

Chapter 208

ST. THEOBALDUS

d. 1150

Regarded as the patron of cobblers and laborers, Theobaldus Roggeri is honored throughout the region of Piedmont, Italy, but especially at Vico, his birthplace, and at Alba, where he spent the greater part of his life. As the son of wealthy parents, he was provided with a good education—but the wealth and position of his family seemed to him to be inconsistent with the lowly state to which a Christian is called. For this reason he left his home and went to Alba, where he became apprenticed to a shoemaker. Theobaldus was so reliable, conscientious and proficient in his work that his master, on his deathbed, suggested that he marry the daughter of the house and assume control of the business.

Because of his vow of celibacy, Theobaldus declined to give the dying man an answer, but upon the man's death Theobaldus bid farewell to the widow and her daughter and left his earnings with them for their support. He then went on a pilgrimage to Compostela and the shrine of the Apostle, St. James Major. Upon his return to Alba, instead of resuming his trade, Theobaldus worked as a laborer, carrying sacks of corn and other merchandise.

His acts of charity and penance were numerous. While walking through the streets or alleys of the city, Theobaldus came into contact with sufferers of all kinds, whom he helped as best he could. Among other exercises he distributed two-thirds of his earnings to the poor, undertook severe fasts in spite of the strenuous character of his work, and as a penance he slept upon the bare ground. As a service to the Church he undertook, for the remainder of his life, to sweep and clean the Cathedral of St. Lawrence and tend the lamps.

After the Saint's death in 1150, a number of miracles contributed to his widespread veneration.

Chapter 209

ST. THEODOTA

d. 318

The Bollandists relate in the *Acta Sanctorum* that Theodota suffered at Plovdiv in Bulgeria, during the year 318.

When Agrippa was persecuting Christians, he commanded that the whole city should join him in offering sacrifice to Apollo during a festival held in the idol's honor. Many in the city complied with the order, but Theodota refused to participate. Previously a harlot, she had converted to Christianity.

When called before the authorities, St. Theodota answered that she had, indeed, been a sinner and would not commit another sin— much less the grievous sacrilege of offering sacrifice to a false god. Her steadfastness encouraged 750 Christians to refuse participation in the sacrifice.

As a punishment for Theodota's disobedience and because she had been the instrument that influenced so many to offend the god, Theodota was thrown into prison. There she lay for 20 days, praying for courage for herself and her fellow Christians. Called upon once more to answer for her refusal, she again admitted that she had been a harlot and had become a Christian, though she considered herself unworthy to bear that sacred name. Agrippa defiantly ordered that she be scourged.

When those who witnessed her agony urged her to obey the authorities and free herself, Theodota refused. During her scourging she cried, "I will never abandon the true God nor sacrifice to lifeless statues." She was then ordered to be racked and her body torn with an iron comb. Under these tortures Theodota continued to pray. The judge became enraged at her resolution and ordered that vinegar and salt should be poured into her wounds. When Theodota continued to pray, Agrippa next commanded the executioners to pull out her teeth, which they did with violence. Finally it was ordered

697

that she should be stoned to death.

When she was being led out of the city for her martyrdom, St. Theodota prayed: "O Christ, Who showed favor to Rahab the harlot and received the good thief, turn not Your mercy from me." In this way Theodota died a holy death.

Chapter 210

ST. THOMAS MORE

1478 - 1535

St. Thomas More's father was John More, an attorney, who was so highly respected that he was knighted and made a Judge of the Common Pleas. He was later honored as the Justice of the Court of King's Bench. Thomas' mother was Agnes Granger, who died while her son Thomas was still a child. Following his mother's death, Thomas, together with his brother and his two sisters, was placed in the care of a nurse, Mother Maud, whom he fondly remembered later in life.

Following the custom of the time, John More arranged for his son, who was then between 12 and 14 years old, to serve and be trained in one of the great houses in England. Thomas was fortunate that the place chosen for him was the house of John Morton, Archbishop of Canterbury and Lord Chancellor of England. The Archbishop was also a lawyer and scholar, as well as a diplomat and statesman. Under the Archbishop's guidance, and exposed to countless distinguished guests of the house, Thomas came to appreciate the authority and precepts of the Church and to sympathize with the poor and oppressed. He was also well-trained for public life and won countless friends in important positions. He also developed a natural wit, a kindly tact and an ease at speech-making.

Sometime after Thomas entered Oxford University to study for the bar, he, at 16, became greatly infatuated with a young lady who was 14. The attraction was mutual, but the girl's parents abruptly ended the matter. Following this first romance, Thomas experienced others. While the ladies seemed to have been attracted to his wit and charm, no scandal was ever lodged against his name.

Erasmus, who became a close friend, wrote of Thomas More, concerning the character of the future Saint:

He seems born and made for friendship, and is a most faithful friend. He so delights in the company and conversation of those whom he likes and trusts, that in this he finds the principal charm of life...Though he is rather too negligent of his own interests, no one is more diligent in those of his friends...He is so kind, so sweet-mannered, that he cheers the dullest spirit and lightens every misfortune. Since his boyhood he has so delighted in merriment that he seems to have been born to make jokes, yet he never carries this to the point of vulgarity, nor has he ever liked bitter pleasantries. If a retort is made against himself, even if it is ill-grounded, he likes it, from the pleasure he finds in witty repartees. He extracts enjoyment from everything, even from things that are most serious. If he converses with the learned and wise, he delights in their talent...With wonderful dexterity he accommodates himself to every disposition. His face is in harmony with his character, being always expressive of a pleasant and friendly cheerfulness and ready to break into smiles. To speak candidly, he is better adapted to merriment than to gravity or dignity, but he is never in the least degree tactless or coarse.

In addition to his law studies, Thomas read Greek philosophy and began to write Latin prose and verse. Concerning these verses, Beatus of Rheinau wrote:

Thomas More is in every way admirable. How sweetly and easily flow his verses! He writes the purest and clearest Latin, and everything is welded together with so happy a wit that I never read anything with greater pleasure. The Muses must have showered on this man all their gifts of humour, elegance and wit. He jokes, but never with malice, he laughs, but always without offense.

When Thomas began to show a great interest in classical studies, his father became so disappointed that his son was apparently deserting the family's traditional study of the law that he all but disinherited him and almost discontinued his allowance. When this occurred, Erasmus observed that John More was "in other respects a sensible and upright man."

For a time Thomas considered becoming a priest. He also thought of becoming a Franciscan friar or a Carthusian, but then decided upon the married state. To this end he became a welcomed visitor at the country home of Mr. John Colt, who had three daughters. William Roper writes that,

> More resorted to the house of one Master Colt, a gentleman of Essex, that had oft invited him thither, having three daughters whose honest conversations and virtuous education provoked him there specially to set his affection. And albeit his mind most served him to the second daughter, for that he thought her the fairest and best favoured, yet when he considered that it would be both great grief and some shame also to the eldest to see her younger sister preferred before her in marriage, he then of a certain pity, framed his fancy toward her and soon after married her.

Erasmus recorded an amusing story, which has been considered on good authority to refer to More and his wife, Jane.

> A young gentleman married a maiden of 17 years who had been educated in the country, and who, being inexperienced, he trusted to form easily in manners to his own humour. He began to instruct her in literature and music and by degrees to repeat the heads of sermons which she heard and generally to acquire the accomplishments he wished her to possess. Used at home to nothing but gossip and play, she at length refused to submit to further training, and when pressed about it threw herself down and beat her head on the ground as though she wished to die.
>
> Her husband concealed his vexation and carried her off for a holiday to her home. Out hunting with his father-in-law, he told his troubles and was urged to "use his authority and beat her!" He replied that he knew his power, but would much rather that she were persuaded, than come to these extremities. The father seized a proper moment, and looking severely on the girl, told her how homely she was, how disagreeable and how lucky to have a husband at all; yet he had found her the best-natured man in the world and she disobeyed him! She returned to her husband and threw herself on the ground, saying: "From this time forward you shall find me a different sort of person!" She kept her resolution and to her dying day, went readily and cheerfully about any duty, however simple, if her husband would have it so.

With the responsibilities of providing for his growing family, Thomas More applied himself to his professional work as a barrister. When defending widows and orphans, he refused all payments. Before long he became known as the most kind, just, skilled and popular attorney in London.

Thomas' home life was happy and prosperous. Little is known of his wife, Jane, except that she was a devoted mother and that she had developed into a delightful companion. But after only six years, Jane died unexpectedly, leaving four surviving children: Margaret, Elizabeth, Cecily and John. For her epitaph, Thomas wrote simply, "Dear Jane lies here, the little wife of Thomas More."

With four children to care for, the eldest being only five years old, Thomas More began almost at once the practical endeavor of finding a stepmother for them. Much to the surprise of his friends, he quickly decided upon a middle-aged widow. Within a few months Thomas married the widow, whom Erasmus describes as "no great beauty, nor yet young, but an active and careful housewife." At this time, More was 34 years old; his new wife, Alice Middleton, was seven years older. With the new wife came her daughter, Alice. Later Margaret Giggs joined the household, as did an adopted child, Margaret Clement.

While More acknowledged that Alice was an admirable mother to his children and a careful housekeeper, he accepted with good humor her many shortcomings. Several writers tell us what More had to virtuously contend with. They have described Alice as, "aged, blunt, and rude"; "spareful and given to niggardliness" and the "most loquacious, ignorant, and narrow-minded of women."

The virtue of St. Thomas is exemplified in a letter in which he excused his wife's faults in this manner: "I do not think it possible to live even with the best of wives, without some discomfort...this I would say with all the more confidence were it not that generally we make our wives worse by our own faults." On being asked why he chose small women for his wives, he jestingly replied, "If women were necessary evils, was it not wise to choose the smallest evil possible?" More overcame his difficulties with good humor and considerable tact, so that gradually his household became one of joy and comfort.

Erasmus wrote:

> He lives with his wife on as sweet and pleasant terms as if she had all the charms of youth...he guides his whole household,

in which there are no disturbances or quarrels. If any such arise, he immediately appeases it and sets all right again, never conceiving any enmity himself, nor making an enemy.

Only twice during his lifetime was St. Thomas More known to be angry.

After the publication of More's book, *Utopia,* King Henry VIII prevailed upon Thomas to enter the royal service. More's loyalty and patriotism finally overcame his reluctance, and he resolved to work for the good of his country. More was knighted, and was appointed one of the King's councillors, and then a Judge in the Court of Requests, which was otherwise known as the Poor Men's Court. More delighted in this position, since in it he could help the needy in their time of trouble.

Although busy with the Court and his duties to the King, More was always mindful of his religious obligations. He wrote that,

> delight and pleasure are to be found in spiritual exercises as labour and pain taken in prayer, alms-deeds, pilgrimage, fasting, discipline, tribulation, affliction...The best souls are they that have been travailed in spiritual business, and find most comfort therein.

Thomas More often cautioned his three daughters against pride and vanity and wrote:

> How delectable is that dainty damsel to the devil that taketh herself for fair, weening herself well-liked for her broad forehead, while the young man that beholdeth her, marketh more her crooked nose!...How proud is many a man over his neighbour, because the wool of his gown is finer! And yet as fine as it is, a poor sheep ware it on her back before it came upon his, and though it be his, is yet not so verily his as it was verily hers!...All that ever we have, of God we have received; riches, royalty, lordship, beauty, strength, learning, wit, body, soul and all. And almost all these things hath He but lent us. For all these must we depart, except our soul alone.

When members of his family were troubled he would say, "We may not look at our pleasures to go to Heaven in featherbeds; it is not the way; for Our Lord Himself went thither with great pain and by many tribulations...The servant may not look to be in better case than his master."

St. Thomas' home life was well-regulated and a model of pious living. On Sundays he attended church with all his household and even when he was Lord Chancellor, he continued to sing in the choir. At night all the family and servants met together for prayers; at meals, the Scriptures and a short commentary were read aloud by one of the children.

More had exceptional sympathy for women in labor, and when he heard that one of the village women was suffering, he would pray until word was brought of her safe delivery. His charity was boundless. He gave frequently and abundantly to those in need and would go through back lanes and inquire about the health and needs of the poor. He often invited his poorer neighbors to his table and received them with all respect and gladness. In his parish of Chelsea, he rented a house in which he gathered the infirm, the poor and the elderly. He maintained all these unfortunates at his own expense.

Another side of More's personality is shown in his hobby of collecting ancient coins and rare books as well as playing the lute and the viol. Objects of art were kept, not so much because of their value, but more for the quality of the workmanship. Among his treasures was a heart composed of amber in which a fly was imbedded. He likened the fly to friendship, which is kept imprisoned in the heart.

More's interests were turned to more serious matters when King Henry VIII decided to have his marriage to Catherine of Aragon declared null and invalid so that he might marry Anne Boleyn. Wolsey, as Lord Chancellor of England, visited the Pope on the King's behalf, but failed to obtain the desired annulment. Because of Wolsey's failure in this matter, he was forced to resign. Thomas More was then selected to replace him as Lord Chancellor.

More accepted the position after he obtained King Henry's promise that he could remain silent on the question of the divorce and remarriage. As Chancellor, More was the chief official adviser of the Crown, with functions both administrative and judicial. The Great Seal which he always kept on his person was used to authenticate acts of State and to acknowledge its bearer as the head of the English legal system.

When Henry VIII became infuriated with the Pope over the matter of his divorce, he manipulated Parliament and the House of Lords until finally there was a separation from Rome. Henry VIII then declared that he was the Supreme Head of the Church of England.

Thomas More was shocked that the King would claim this headship; moreover, he saw the evils to which this claim would lead. With a good conscience, Thomas More refused to acknowledge the King's divorce as being valid and resigned his position as Lord Chancellor after having served for only two years and seven months. As can be expected, the King was angry with Thomas for not agreeing with him, but he delayed his revenge for another time.

The loss of his office reduced More's income to a small pension. Having been generous to the poor, he was left with no savings on which to rely, nor did he own valuable property. In one aspect only was he favored, as he wrote to Erasmus:

> From the time of my boyhood, dearest Desiderius, I have longed that I might someday enjoy what I rejoice in your having always enjoyed—namely, that being free from public business, I might have some time to devote to God, prayer and myself. This, by the grace of a good God, and by the favour of an indulgent prince, I have at last obtained.

On March 30, 1534, the Act of Supremacy was enacted. It provided for the taking of an oath by all the King's subjects in which they acknowledged that his union with Catherine of Aragon had been an invalid marriage, that the King's union with Anne Boleyn was valid and that their offspring would be the legitimate heirs to the throne. The taking of the oath also involved the repudiation of "any foreign authority, prince or potentate." A refusal to take the oath was considered to be high treason. Many Catholics took the oath with the reservation, "so far as it be not contrary to the law of God."

When those who opposed the King were charged with treason and were imprisoned and beheaded, Thomas More knew that his time would also come. On April 12, 1534 he was ordered to appear before the commissioners for the purpose of taking the new oath. The next day the Saint attended Holy Mass, confessed and departed from his home for the last time. On appearing before the Commission, Thomas More refused to accept a repudiation of papal authority in England or to take the oath under any condition. The Commission gave him time to reconsider, but he did not change his mind. Therefore he was committed to the Tower.

At first the jailers treated the Saint with some leniency, permitting him visits from his beloved daughter, Margaret, and his wife. He was permitted to correspond with his friends, but later he was deprived of his chief consolation, his books and papers. His wife did not understand her husband's decision and wanted him to return home. Margaret tried to persuade her father to take the oath, but Thomas stood firm, gently calling her "Mother Eve" for her efforts to tempt him.

After 15 months of harsh imprisonment, Thomas' health was greatly impaired. Looking older than his 58 years, he was brought to stand trial on July 1, 1535. At the bar of the Court of King's Bench, in Westminster Hall, Thomas was charged with high treason and with maliciously attempting to deprive the King of his title of Supreme Head of the Church of England.

It is said that Thomas More could not defend the personal qualities of the Popes of his time, who were often openly criticized, but Thomas could not deny that the Pope was the visible head of the entire Church.

The guilty verdict was expected. Weeping at this time was Sir William Kingston, Constable of the Tower, who was Thomas' friend. William Roper, Thomas' son-in-law, wrote of this scene:

> There with a heavy heart, the tears running down his cheeks, William Kingston bade him farewell. Sir Thomas More, seeing him so sorrowful, comforted him with as good words as he could, saying "Good Master Kingston, trouble not yourself, but be of good cheer for I will pray for you and my good lady your wife, that we may meet in Heaven together, where we shall be merry for ever and ever."

Also meeting him with tearful farewells were members of his family.

The day before he died, the future Saint sent to his beloved daughter, Margaret, the hair shirt he had worn for many years as a penance. This he attempted to give her in secret, not wanting his wife, or others, to know of it.

Early in the morning of July 6, 1535, word was brought to the Saint that he was to be beheaded before nine o'clock. He thanked the messenger for his "good tidings" and remarked that he was most of all "bounded to his highness that it pleaseth him so shortly to rid me out of the miseries of this wretched world."

Upon arriving at the scaffold, his physical weakness was apparent when he asked for help in words that have become famous, "I pray you, Master Lieutenant, see me safe up; as for my coming down, let me shift for myself." After speaking a few words to the people, he asked for their prayers and begged them to pray to God for the King. He added, "I call you to witness, brothers, that I die in and for the Faith of the Catholic Church; the King's loyal servant, but God's first." After More encouraged the headsman, his head was placed on the block. He arranged his beard so that it would not be touched by the axe, saying, "for it at least had committed no treason."

The body of the Saint was interred for a time in the little chapel of St. Peter ad Vincula in the Tower. His head was exposed on a stake on London Bridge, where it remained for almost a month before his daughter, Margaret Roper, was able to claim it.

In the Anglican church of St. Dunstan, in Canterbury, Kent, is found the St. Nicholas or Roper Chapel. A marble slab located there informs the visitor that "Beneath this floor is the vault of the Roper family in which is interred the head of Sir Thomas More..." When the marble was placed on the floor of the chapel in 1932, the head of the Saint was believed to be in the vault. However, in 1978, which marked the 500th anniversary of the birth of Thomas More, an archaeological survey of the chapel was undertaken. This revealed that the skull of St. Thomas More was found "in a leaden casket in a niche in the North Wall."

Like St. Thomas Becket before him, who was Chancellor of England and keeper of the Great Seal, Thomas More also died for the doctrine of the Church by means of the blade. But unlike Thomas Becket, who was an Archbishop, Thomas More was a layman, and an exemplary husband and father. Another difference between the two is that while Thomas Becket was canonized soon after his death, Thomas More had to wait four hundred years, until 1935, to gain this distinction. In recent years, the lives of both Saints were portrayed in award-winning motion pictures: Thomas Becket in "Becket," and Thomas More in "A Man for All Seasons."

Photo by Franz Hanfstaengl, Munich/Schamoni

St. Thomas More (1478-1535), known for his wit, merriment and love for friends, resigned his high post of Lord Chancellor of England in response to King Henry VIII's usurpation of the Church's authority. He was imprisoned in the Tower of London. Convicted of treason because he could not accept King Henry VIII as head of the Church in England, the Saint was beheaded. *(Painting by Holbein.)*

708

Judges Postcards, Ltd., Hastings, England

St. Thomas More's first wife died around age 23, leaving him with four little children. Within a few months he remarried, taking to wife a middle-aged widow who proved a good mother to his children and a careful housekeeper, though she was difficult in other respects. Through good humor and much tact St. Thomas More established his household in peace and harmony. Pictured here is the Thomas More Window, St. Dunstan's (Anglican) Church, Canterbury. The window, installed in 1973, was the gift of various donors, including friends from St. Thomas Church, Kansas City, Missouri. *(Window designed and made by Lawrence Lee.)*

709

BENEATH THIS FLOOR
IS THE VAULT OF THE
ROPER FAMILY IN WHICH
IS INTERRED THE HEAD OF
SIR THOMAS MORE
OF ILLUSTRIOUS MEMORY
SOMETIME LORD CHANCELLOR
OF ENGLAND WHO WAS
BEHEADED ON TOWER HILL
6TH JULY 1535

ECCLESIA ANGLICANA LIBERA SIT

A.D. 1932

St. Thomas More Memorial Tablet in Roper Chapel (St. Nicholas Chapel) in St. Dunstan's Church, Canterbury. In 1978 an archaeological survey determined that the Saint's skull was not in this vault but rather "in a niche in the North Wall."

The Tower of London, where St. Thomas More was imprisoned for 15 months before being beheaded. At the scaffold he stated that he was dying as "the King's loyal servant, but God's first." *(Copper engraving by Wenzel Hollar, 1607-1677.)*

Chapter 211

BL. THOMAS PERCY

d. 1572

When Thomas Percy's father died a martyr at Tyburn for having denied the ecclesiastical supremacy of King Henry VIII, his two children, Thomas and Henry, were forcibly removed from the care of their mother, who was named "treasonable." They were placed in a number of foster homes, including that of Sir Thomas Tempest of Tong. In 1549, when Thomas came of age, the attainder under which he and Henry had suffered as a result of their father's actions was, to a certain extent, removed. They were "restored in blood," and shortly thereafter Thomas was knighted.

Three years later, during Queen Mary's reign, he regained his ancestral honors and lands. After being named Governor of Prudhoe Castle, Thomas Percy besieged and took Scarborough Castle from the rebel, Sir Thomas Stafford. This so pleased Queen Mary that she named Thomas Percy the Earl of Northumberland—an earldom to which his martyred father had been heir-presumptive. This title was given Thomas in consideration of his "noble descent, constancy in virtue, valour in arms, and other strong qualifications." Also given him at that time were the Baronies of Percy, Fitzpane, Plynings, Lucy and Bryan. He was installed at Whitehall with great pomp and soon was named Warden General of the Marches. In this capacity he served the Queen well in military and civil affairs on the Scottish border.

In 1558 he married Anne Somerset, daughter of the Earl of Worcester. She is described as a valiant woman who subsequently suffered much for the Faith.

After Elizabeth ascended the throne and was passing anti-Catholic measures in Parliament and laying the foundations of the Anglican Church, Thomas, who was known to be steadfastly loyal to the Catholic Church, was in the north, safely out of the turmoil. But for reasons not given, he soon resigned the wardenship and moved to the south. Queen Elizabeth favored the Earl and in 1563 gave him the Order of the Garter. When he was in the north, he played only a minor part in opposing the Queen and did so with considerable prudence. His lack of action and his acceptance of the Order of the Garter made him later express his dissatisfaction with his own behavior.

The north of England was still solidly Catholic. A Protestant observer said of Yorkshire that, "There were scarcely ten gentlemen of note that favour the Queen's proceedings in religion," and when Mary, Queen of Scots had to take refuge at Carlisle in 1568, she was soon regarded as the Catholic champion.

The following year—with the systematic persecution of the Catholics—those in the north, anticipating the excommunication of Elizabeth, were planning a campaign to liberate Queen Mary. The organizers of this rebellion were of the opinion that Mary should be the next heir to the throne so that she could "restore the Crown, the nobility, and the worship of God to their former estate."

Thomas had some misgivings about the project and made it clear that it was not a political endeavor, saying, "We are seeking, I imagine, the glory not of men but of God." He agreed to participate in the liberation, "to have some reformation in religion, or at the least some sufferance for men to use their conscience as they were disposed."

Thomas Percy, with the Earl of Westmoreland, wrote to Pope Pius V asking for advice; but before an answer was received from Rome, circumstances rushed them into action, against their better judgment. Their plan had become known to the authorities, and the two earls were summoned to appear before Elizabeth. A hasty meeting of the leaders was called at Brancepeth Castle. Although Thomas Percy disagreed, it was decided that the earls should ignore the summons. Instead, on November 14, the two earls marched into Durham at the head of their forces. The villagers welcomed them enthusiastically, and the cathedral was immediately restored to Catholic worship. Under the supervision of the Reverend William Holmes, altars were restored and decorated, and Protestant prayerbooks were destroyed.

On St. Andrew's feast day High Mass was sung in the cathedral, and on the following Sunday the Reverend Holmes publicly reconciled the huge congregation. After 11 years of forced apostasy, the people joyously greeted the celebration of Holy Mass. Under the banner depicting the Five Holy Wounds, Thomas Percy, with Bl.

Thomas Plumtree as chief chaplain, marched into Yorkshire and Wetherby, collecting recruits and encouraging the people. They turned again to the north, where they captured Hartlepool and Barnard Castle. This, however, was the limit of their success. At the end of a month, Elizabeth's troops, under the Earl of Sussex, forced the earls to see the futility of further combat. Thomas Percy and the Earl of Westmoreland sadly disbanded their men at Durham, and fled across the border into Scotland.

The Earl of Sussex took revenge on the people who had reverted to the public celebration of their faith, and hanged them by the hundreds. Escaping punishment was Thomas Percy's wife, who was one of the leading forces of the rebellion. She eventually came under the protection of Lord Home and died in exile at Namur.

Thomas Percy was captured by the Scottish regent, the Earl of Moray, and was imprisoned in Lochleven Castle for two and a half years while negotiations for his sale to the English government were being conducted. Dr. Nicholas Sander, a leading Catholic of the day, records that Thomas Percy bore his imprisonment and separation from his four small children and his wife with great patience. Thomas Percy, he wrote, observed all the fasts of the Church, spent a great deal of time in prayer and meditation, wrote a book of prayers which still exists, and emphatically refused an offer that he deny his faith in order to gain his pardon.

He was conducted to York and was lodged in the castle on August 21, 1572. He was offered a last chance to win his freedom on condition of apostasy, but he again refused. After being told he would die the next day, he spent all night in prayer. The next afternoon he was taken to the scaffold, where he told the people that he died a Catholic: "As for this new Church of England, I do not acknowledge it." He expressed sorrow that he had occasioned the death of so many as the result of the aborted rebellion, saying, "Yet I have no fear but that their souls have obtained the glory of Heaven." Following these words he was beheaded—to the sorrow of many, because, "Throughout his life he was beyond measure dear to the whole people." He was 44 years old. Thomas Percy was beatified with other English martyrs by Leo XIII in 1896.

His daughter Mary Percy founded the Benedictine convent at Brussels, from which nearly all the existing houses of Benedictine nuns in England are descended.

Chapter 212

BL. THOMAS SHERWOOD

d. 1578

Because we have contemporary documents, as well as an account of the life of Thomas Sherwood that was written by his brother, we are well informed concerning the life and death of this 27-year-old martyr. His father was Henry Sherwood, a woolen draper (a maker or dealer in cloth). His mother was Elizabeth, who in 30 years of marriage gave birth to 14 children.

Thomas Sherwood was born in London and was well-instructed in the Catholic Faith by his two devout parents. He attended school until his fifteenth year, when he was removed to help in his father's cloth business. In the *Acts of English Martyrs,* Pollen tells us that Thomas was

> of small learning, scarcely understanding the Latin tongue, but had much read books of controversies and devotion, and had used much to converse among Catholic priests, and by reason thereof, having a good wit and judgment, and withal being very devout and religious, he was able to give good counsel, as he did to many of the more ignorant sort, being much esteemed for his virtuous life and humble and modest behaviour: besides, God did give a special grace in his conversation, whereby together with his good example of life, he much moved and edified others. He was a man of little stature of body, yet of a healthful and good constitution, and very temperate in his diet.

After helping his father for a few years, Thomas felt himself called to the religious life. Because adherents to the Roman Catholic Church were being persecuted in England by Queen Elizabeth, Thomas Sherwood's parents permitted him to "pass the seas" to the seminary at Douai, France. Told by the priests that he must resume his studies, Thomas traveled back to London to make financial arrangements

715

for his support and tuition.

One morning, while walking down Chancery Lane in London, he met George Martin, the son of Lady Tregonwell (also Tregony). George Martin had seen Thomas many times at his mother's house in the company of a priest who was known as Mr. Stampe. Challoner suggests that George Martin resented Sherwood, believing that Mass was sometimes privately celebrated in his mother's home, and that Thomas Sherwood was arranging these meetings that placed his mother in jeopardy.

On seeing Thomas that morning, George Martin called for the constable and had his former friend arrested. While Thomas was standing before Mr. Fleetwood, the Recorder of London, George Martin testified that Sherwood was often in the company of priests and that he had even traveled across the seas to confer with traitors. The Recorder then asked Thomas what he thought of the Bull of Pius V and whether, if the Pope had excommunicated the Queen, she was then the lawful queen or not.

To this Sherwood answered according to his conscience, saying that if the Pope had indeed excommunicated the Queen, then he thought she could not be the lawful monarch—that he did not believe the Queen to be the head of the Church of England, and that this pre-eminence belonged to the Pope.

As to other questions asked of him regarding his journey to Douai, he would not answer. Having been betrayed by one whom he thought was a friend, Sherwood was committed to the Tower of London, where he was confined in a dark cell near the torture chamber. As soon as he was locked away, his lodgings were searched and plundered of all that he had, including money he had borrowed for the use of his father.

During the early days of his confinement he was harrassed and tortured in the hope that he would confess where he had heard Mass, or reveal the names of priests who were conducting these unlawful services. He was racked twice, but refused to answer any questions. As a result of the tortures, he lost the use of his legs. He was left without necessary clothing and was thrown into a filthy dungeon where his jailers thought the darkness, the stench, an insufficient amount of food and his nakedness would break his will.

Word of his sad condition reached Mr. Roper, the son-in-law of St. Thomas More, who offered the young prisoner some money for food. When the jailers refused to let their prisoner have the money, they did permit Mr. Roper to buy sixpence of straw for Thomas Sherwood to lie on.

In his book entitled *Torture in the Criminal Law of England,* Mr. Jardine gives us a description of the cell in which Thomas was confined:

> The cell was below high water mark and totally dark. As the tide flowed, innumerable rats, which infest the muddy banks of the Thames, were driven through the orifices of the walls into the dungeon. The alarm excited by the irruption of these loathsome creatures in the dark was the least part of the torture which the unfortunate captives had to undergo; instances are related, which humanity would gladly believe to be the exaggerations of Catholic partisans, where the flesh had been torn from the arms and legs of prisoners during sleep by the well-known voracity of these animals.

After a time the prisoner was interrogated by the Privy Council and by Gilbert Gerard, the Attorney General. Thomas Sherwood repeated the same statement he had made to the Recorder, that if the Queen had been excommunicated, then she could not be the lawful queen of England. What then occurred is given in the letter of the Lords of the Privy Council which reveals that the Lieutenant of the Tower and others were "to assay him (Sherwood) at the rack upon such articles as they shall think meet to minister unto him for discovering either of the persons or of further matters." That is, they wanted to obtain information that would convict other Catholics—information that Thomas Sherwood refused to give them even under severe torture.

Six months after his apprehension, Thomas was brought to trial. Part of the official record of his trial from the *Coram Rege Roll* (20 Eliz. rot. 3) reads as follows:

> Otherwise, to wit, in the term of St. Michael last part, before our Lady the Queen at Westminster, by the oath of 12 jurors, it was presented that Thomas Sherwood, late of London, yeoman, on the 20th of November, in the 20th year of the Lady Elizabeth, by the grace of God Queen of England, France and Ireland, Defender of the Faith...in the city of Westminster in the County of Middlesex, diabolically, maliciously, and

traitorously, compassing, imagining, thinking, devising, and intending the deprivation and deposition of the said Lady Queen Elizabeth, from her style honour, and royal title to the imperial crown of this kingdom of England, did, out of his own perverse and treacherous mind and imagination, maliciously, expressly, advisedly, directly and traitorously...say these false English words...to wit that "for so much as our Queen Elizabeth doth expressly disassent in Religion from the Catholic Faith, of which Catholic Faith, he sayeth that the Pope Gregory the Thirteenth that now is, is conserver, because he is God's General Vicar in earth: and therefore he affirmeth by express words that our said Queen Elizabeth is a schismatic and an heretic," to the very great scandal and derogation of the person of our Lady the Queen.

The Court records reveal the end of the trial in this manner:

The jury, therefore, then came before our Lady the Queen at Westminster, on Monday, the morrow of the Purification of Blessed Mary the Virgin...on which day Thomas Sherwood in his own proper person came before our Lady the Queen...under ward of the Lieutenant. The Sheriff returned the names of 12 jurymen, which jurymen having been impanelled and summoned for this, came to say truth about and over the premises. Who, having been elected, tried and sworn, say upon their oath that the aforesaid Thomas Sherwood is guilty of the several high treasons laid against him. Also that the self-same Thomas Sherwood hath no goods or chattels, land or tenements to their knowledge.

When the prisoner was asked if he could say anything for himself why the Court should not proceed judgment and execution of the verdict, Thomas "sayeth no otherwise than as he said above." The Attorney General, Gilbert Gerald, then ordered that,

Thomas Sherwood be led by the aforesaid Lieutenant unto the Tower of London, and thence be dragged through the midst of the City of London, directly unto the gallows of Tyburn, and upon the gallows there be hanged, and thrown living to the earth, and that his bowels be taken from his belly, and whilst he is alive be burnt, and that his head be cut off, and that his body be divided into four parts, and that his head and quarters be placed where our Lady the Queen please to assign them.

No one has preserved for us the details of Sherwood's conduct at the place of execution, but three weeks later, news of the death of this martyr reached the seminary at Douai. In the records of the seminary this notation is found:

> On the first of March (1578), Mr. Lowe returned to us from England, bringing news that a youth, by name (Thomas) Sherwood, had suffered for his confession of the Catholic Faith, not only imprisonment, but death itself. Amidst all his torments his exclamation had been, "Lord Jesus, I am not worthy to suffer this for Thee, much less to receive those rewards which Thou hast promised to those that confess Thee."

Having courageously endured a cruel imprisonment, chains, hunger, cold, stench, nakedness and the rack, Thomas Sherwood won the martyr's crown at Tyburn, London, on February 7, 1578, being only 27 years of age.

Chapter 213

ST. ULPHIA

d. 750

Under the direction of the aged hermit St. Domitius, St. Ulphia led the life of a solitary. According to legend, they both lived a short distance from the Church of Notre Dame in Amiens, France. Domitius, in passing, used to awaken Ulphia by knocking with his stick so that she might follow him to the church to attend Holy Mass. On one occasion the frogs had croaked so loudly during the greater part of the night that Ulphia had had little sleep. When St. Domitius had to persistently knock to awaken her, Ulphia accordingly forbade the frogs to croak again—and we are assured that in that locality they are silent even to this day.

After the death of Domitius, St. Ulphia was joined by a disciple named Aurea. For others who wished to follow her example, she founded a community at Amiens, but Ulphia eventually returned to her solitude.

Following her death in the year 750, St. Ulphia was buried at Amiens. When the magnificent Gothic cathedral was begun in the year 1220, it adopted the name of the little church of Notre Dame in which Ulphia and St. Domitius spent so many prayerful hours. In the year 1279, nine years after the cathedral's completion and more than five hundred years after her death, the remains of St. Ulphia were transferred to a worthy place within the great Cathedral of Amiens, where they are still found. The Cathedral of Amiens escaped serious injury during the two World Wars that devastated the city. During World War I it is estimated that 700 houses were lost; in World War II, the estimated number lost was 4,000.

Chapter 214

ST. VICTOR OF MARSEILLES

d. 304

When Emperor Maximian arrived at Marseilles, France, the flourishing Christian community became fearful of the persecution that was imminent. Victor, as a Christian officer in the Roman Army, went secretly at night to the homes of the faithful, inspiring them with contempt of a temporal death and the love of eternal life.

After a time his activities were discovered by the authorities, who ordered his arrest and arraignment before the prefects. These attempted to win him over to their pagan beliefs by telling him that he was serving Jesus Christ who was no more than a dead man, and that his promotion in the army and the favor of high authorities were at risk by this allegiance to a false religion.

Victor confronted his accusers by declaring that Jesus Christ was the Son of the true God, that He rose from the dead and reigns at God's right hand. The assembly responded to the words with shouts of rage, but because of Victor's high rank, the prefects did not know what punishment was appropriate and sent him to Maximian for sentencing.

The Emperor attempted to win him over with kindness, but when this failed, imprisonment and punishment were threatened. This, too, had no effect on Victor, who remained constant in his beliefs. Maximian at length commanded that Victor be bound hand and foot and dragged through the streets of the city, thinking that he would not only punish Victor, but that this would also serve as a warning and lesson to other Christians. The Emperor's treatment of Victor, and the Saint's courage during this trial, had an opposite effect, and only served to encourage the faithful.

Bruised and bloody from his ordeal, Victor was ordered to adore the Roman gods, but he refused and expressed his contempt for the gods and his love for Jesus Christ. One of the prefects, Asterius, then commanded him to be hoisted on a rack, on which he was stretched for a lengthy time. When Victor was finally taken down, he was thrown into a dungeon. But then a wonderful thing took place. At midnight Victor was visited by his Saviour, who was accompanied by angels. The prison was filled with a bright light, while heavenly voices were heard praising God. Three guards of the prison saw the light, and upon seeing the vision, fell to their knees and were instantly converted to the Faith. Their names are given as Alexander, Longinus and Felician. That same night they were secretly baptized.

Eventually Maximian learned about the conversion of the guards, and in a fury he ordered that they be beheaded. Encouraged during their last moments by Victor, the three soldiers were martyred while confessing their belief in Jesus Christ. Victor was tortured for his part in the conversion of the guards and was once again brought before the Emperor. He was commanded to offer sacrifice and to incense a statue of Jupiter, but Victor showed his contempt for the false god by kicking it with his foot. As punishment for this insult to Jupiter, Victor's foot was promptly chopped off by order of the Emperor. Victor was then sentenced to be crushed to death, but when this did not end his life, he was decapitated. The year was 304.

The bodies of the four martyrs were thrown into the sea, but were recovered by Christians who gave them a proper burial. Both St. Gregory of Tours and Venantius Fortunatus recorded that the tomb of St. Victor at Marseilles was one of the best-known places of pilgrimage on French soil. In the fifth century the Benedictines at Marseilles erected an abbey above the tomb of the martyrs. But, at the time of the Revolution of 1793, the relics were either misplaced or destroyed.

Chapter 215

BL. VILLANA DE BOTTI

d. 1360

The de Botti family of Florence was doubtless amazed by the devotions, fasts and austerities practiced by Villana while she was still a child—activities that are rarely practiced even by persons who are more advanced in age and virtue.

At the age of 13, she reputedly ran away from home to enter a convent, but she was refused admittance, apparently because of her tender years. To prevent Villana from leaving home again for such a purpose, her father, Andrea de Botti, a successful merchant, shortly afterward gave her in marriage to Rosso di Piero, who was also a merchant. The marriage is said to have been conducted against her will, but after the wedding Villana completely changed. She abandoned all her devout activities and gave herself to a life which was described by a biographer as being one of "pleasure and dissipation," while another calls her life "heartless and sinful." How long she engaged in this idle and worldly life we are not told, but apparently God had other plans for her.

One day, Villana was dressing for an evening's entertainment with friends. Her dress was considered sumptuous, jewels sparkled in her hair and adorned her very shoes. Before leaving her dressing room she went to the mirror to cast one last look at her image. One biographer claims that "God permitted the deformity of the soul within to become visible on the outward person." What Villana saw in the mirror was not her dazzling beauty, but a horrible demon. Her hair, which was bound with gold and jeweled chains, seemed a mass of coiled serpents; her face seemed horribly deformed; her eyes were red and fiery, and instead of her beautiful mouth, she saw the open jaws of a hellish monster. She ran to another mirror and then another, only to see the same horrible apparition. Grace touched her heart, and immediately she realized the sinfulness of her life. Villana tore away all the jewels and golden chains and left her home for the neighboring church of the Dominican fathers, Santa Maria Novella. Flinging herself at the feet of a holy friar, she made a tearful confession of her life. From then on she never reverted to worldly vanities.

When Villana returned home, she entered upon a rigorous course of penance which continued until her death. To atone for her past vanity she wore only simple clothes, and she devoted her time to prayer, penance and the care of the poor. Her childhood desire to enter religious life resurfaced, but her confessor advised against this and, in due time, accepted her as a member of the Dominican Third Order. As a secular member of this order, she advanced rapidly in the spiritual life.

While fulfilling her duties as wife and mistress of her household, Villana devoted all her remaining time to prayer, spiritual reading and relieving the poor. On one occasion she found a poor sick man lying in the road. She was somehow able to carry him on her shoulders to the hospital, where he mysteriously disappeared. As a mortification, and to benefit the poor, she often deprived herself of the necessities of life. After she was widowed, she increased her austerities and self-sacrifice and grew so rich in virtue that she was often found in ecstasy, particularly during Holy Mass or at spiritual conferences.

Villana suffered for a time from persecutions at the hands of neighbors when her honor was cruelly questioned. The devil himself also caused her great mental suffering. Once when Villana was struggling against a fierce temptation, St. Catherine the Martyr appeared to her with a beautiful crown in her hand, saying, "Be constant, my daughter, and behold the magnificent reward which awaits thee in Heaven." By this vision Villana understood that her time on earth was drawing to an end. As she lay on her deathbed after receiving the Last Rites, she asked for the reading of the Passion of Our Lord, and at the words, "Bowing His head He gave up the ghost," she crossed her hands on her breast and peacefully expired. The year was 1360.

Clothed in the habit of the Third Order of St. Dominic, her body was taken to Santa Maria Novella, where it became an object of veneration. To satisfy the devotion of the countless poor who had benefited from her charities, and the crowds of people who recognized her saintly virtues, Villana's body was left unburied for the space of 37 days. In 1824 the veneration paid to Villana was approved, and in 1829 Pope Leo XII presided over her beatification ceremony.

Chapter 216

ST. VLADIMIR

956 - 1015

St. Vladimir was the Grand Duke of Kiev and all Russia, and the grandson of St. Olga, who is considered to be the first Russian woman to accept Christianity. She was also the first Russian woman to be canonized.

Vladimir's father, Sviatoslav, the son of St. Olga, had two legitimate sons, Yaropolk and Oleg. Vladimir, the third son, was illegitimate, the child of a court favorite, Olga Malusha. Shortly before his death in 972, Vladimir's father divided his property among his three sons. The Grand Duchy of Kiev was given to Yaropolk; the land of Drevlani (now Galicia) was given to Oleg. When neither would journey to the ancient Russian capital of Novgorod, which threatened rebellion, this land was given to Vladimir.

Shortly after the father's death, war broke out between the two older brothers, Yaropolk and Oleg. Yaropolk conquered Oleg's forces and seized the Drevlanian territory. Oleg was not only dethroned, but also died during the struggle. On learning of this, Vladimir was afraid that Yaropolk would threaten him, as well, and so fled for help to the Varangians of Scandinavia. With Vladimir gone, Yaropolk conquered Vladimir's city of Novgorod, and united all the territories under his sceptre.

A few years later, Vladimir returned with a large force of mercenaries and reclaimed Novgorod. Growing bolder, he waged war against Yaropolk, defeated him and was instrumental in having him assassinated. With Yaropolk out of the way, Vladimir made himself ruler of the entire Kievan realm in the year 980.

Sometime after Yaropolk's death, Vladimir was accused of dragging Yaropolk's Christian widow from a convent, to which she had retired, and forcing her to marry him.

In spite of his grandmother's conversion to Christianity, Vladimir

725

was raised a heathen and indulged in the excesses which were available to a Russian prince at that time. Historians record that he engaged in "unbridled dissipation," and they name him a "flagrant polygamist." In addition to his wife, Ragnilda, he had five other wives and many female slaves. By these women he had ten sons and two daughters. Vladimir, however, was not the only Russian of the time to engage in polygamy. Constantin de Grunwald, in *Saints of Russia,* records that polygamy was widespread, especially among the wealthy.

Although there was an undercurrent of Christianity which was originally established among the eastern Slavs by St. Cyril and St. Methodius, Vladimir erected in Kiev many statues and shrines to the Slavic heathen gods. After doing battle in various regions, he planned a campaign against the Greco-Roman Empire, and in the course of this he became interested in Christianity. The *Chronicle of Nestor,* which was written by medieval monks, relates that he sent envoys to the neighboring countries for information concerning their religions. The envoys were unimpressed with the Jews of Khazar, the Germans with their Latin churches, and the Bulgarians who followed Mohammed, but they were particularly impressed with the Greek ritual of the great Church of St. Sophia of Constantinople. The envoys reported: "We came to the land of the Greeks, and we were led to the place where they serve their God, and we knew not whether we were in Heaven or on earth."

The envoys reminded Vladimir that his grandmother, Olga, had embraced the faith of the Byzantine Catholic Church. Vladimir also realized that civilization, which he wanted desperately for his people, was closely united to Christianity.

After he waged victorious campaigns against rebellious tribes and some of his neighbors, Vladimir's reputation increased. He understood the advantage and prestige to be derived from an alliance with one of the most powerful monarchs of the world, and sent envoys to Emperor Basil II at Constantinople. Vladimir offered to help the Emperor in defending against the advance of the Bulgarian armies and an uprising in Asia Minor.

As a reward, Vladimir asked for the Emperor's sister Anna in marriage. A threat to march on Constantinople was made if his proposal was refused. The Emperor replied that his sister was a Christian and could not marry a heathen, but if Vladimir were a Christian prince, and was successful in helping the Emperor in defending against his enemies, he would sanction the marriage.

Vladimir explained that he was already attracted to Christianity and agreed to be baptized. He received the Sacrament in the year 988. The Christianization of Russia is reckoned from that year. Following his Baptism, Vladimir married Princess Anna, who is said to have "bewailed her lot." Taking with him the relics of St. Clement, sacred vessels and images, he journeyed to Kiev with his new bride amid great pomp and celebration.

Upon arriving at Kiev, Vladimir saw to the conversion of his subjects and ordered the destruction of the statues of the gods. The wooden statue of the god Perum (the god of thunder and lightning) was torn from its pedestal and was dragged through the mud to the River Knieper, where it was thrown into the water. At Novgorod a resistance to Christianity was noted. Vladimir then sent Bishop Joachim with orders to tear down the statue of the god Perum that was in Novgorod, and to throw it into the River Volkhov. A popular legend relates that when this statue was being dragged in the mud, the devil entered into it and began to shout, "Woe is me!" As the wooden idol floated down the river under the main bridge, the idol threw away its staff and cried out once more, "The children of Novgorod will remember me!" The conversion of the city is said to have taken place without further incident.

The destruction of the idols was so impressive that the people readily followed the example of their monarch and accepted Christianity. It should be mentioned, however, that Christianity had already been secretly spread in Kiev and that the people only waited for an opportunity to publicly accept and acknowledge their faith. Vladimir not only reunited Russia, but he also opened it up to the Byzantine Catholic Church. As a result, missionaries, artists, architects and culture were firmly introduced into his capital of Kiev and spread throughout most of Russia.

Having once accepted Christianity, Vladimir was completely faithful to its practices. He put away his former wives and so educated his two sons of Anna that they are now venerated as St. Romanus and St. David, the names given them at their Baptism. They are also known as St. Boris and St. Gleb, the names they received at their birth.

Vladimir established churches and monasteries in several cities, and in 989 he erected the first stone church in Kiev, which is known as the Church of St. Mary Ever Virgin. In 996 he built the Church of the Transfiguration, which is also found in the City of Kiev. He abandoned his warlike career and devoted himself to the government of his people. He established schools, introduced ecclesiastical courts and became known for his mildness and for his zeal in spreading the Catholic Faith.

According to the *Chronicle of Nestor*, Vladimir extended his generosity to the poor in a most edifying manner. Whereas before his conversion Vladimir's court was known for its splendor and revelry, the *Chronicle* states that after his conversion, "He ordered all the poor and sick to come to his palace for food, drink and money. For those who were unable to come, he loaded carts with bread, meat, fish and honey and had them taken to the sick and the needy."

This interest in the needs of the sick and poor was extended by his example to all the cities and country districts of Russia. St. Vladimir is not only considered to be the first organizer of social assistance in Russia, but he is also known as the first educator of the country. Under Vladimir, Kiev became the great capital of Russia. It possessed the first Christian church, the first Christian school and had the first library in Russia.

After Vladimir's wife, Anna, died in 1011, his life became troubled by the activities of his older children. Also, we are told that his conscience was tortured by the memory of the crimes he had committed, particularly the murder of his brother, Yaropolk, and his dragging of Yaropolk's widow from the convent and marrying her.

Following the custom of his ancestors, he had parcelled out his kingdom among his children, giving the City of Novgorod to his eldest son Yaroslav, who then rebelled against Vladimir and refused to render him honor. In 1014 Vladimir prepared to journey to Novgorod to take the city away from his disobedient son. In the meantime, Yaroslav solicited the help of the Varangians against his father. While enroute to Novgorod, Vladimir became ill and died.

In the Russian Orthodox and Ruthenian Greek Catholic calendars, Vladimir's feast is celebrated on July 15. Because he was canonized before the Schism, he is also recognized by Rome as a saint of the Universal Church.

Although St. Olga, who ruled as regent for her infant son, received Baptism during her reign, her conversion did not affect the pagan faith of her subjects. However, Vladimir, her grandson, who became a Christian in the year 988, is considered to be the first Russian ruler, in his own right, to accept Baptism. His conversion produced so many converts among his people that he has since been called the "Baptizer of Russia." Throughout history he has carried the name Ravnoapostol, which means "equal to the Apostles."

Recognizing the Baptism of St. Vladimir in 988 as the year in which Christianity was introduced in Russia, in 1988 the Russian Orthodox Church launched a yearlong celebration of its 1,000th anniversary. In observance of this millennium, the Communist government of Russia permitted the publishing of 500,000 Bibles in the Russian and Ukrainian languages. They also restored to the Russian Orthodox Church in the Ukrainian capital of Kiev a cathedral which had been confiscated by the state 27 years ago. Attending a large celebration in the Cathedral of the Epiphany in Moscow were over 500 religious representatives from more than 100 countries. Also taking part was a high-ranking Vatican delegation.

St. Vladimir (956-1015), known as the "Baptizer of Russia" and as "Ravnoapostol," or "equal to the Apostles." Grandson of St. Olga, St. Vladimir is credited with the Christianization of his country. Raised a heathen, the young Vladimir killed his brother. For a time a "flagrant polygamist," Vladimir was baptized in 988 as part of his nuptial agreement to wed Anna, the sister of Emperor Basil II, who resided at Constantinople. Vladimir reformed his own life, giving up his former wives, and saw to the Christian conversion of his subjects, destroying many pagan idols and welcoming missionaries to Russia.

Chapter 217

ST. WENCESLAS

907 - 935

During a time when a national paganism was favored for Czecho-slovakia, Wenceslas' grandparents, the Duke and Duchess of Bohemia, as well as Wenceslas' father, Ratislav, converted to Christianity. They experienced the strong disapproval and criticism of powerful Czech families who were strongly opposed to the new religion.

Ratislav had married Drahomira—who had been baptized—but was actually in sympathy with the anti-Christians of the country. They were the parents of two sons, the future St. Wenceslas, born in 907, and Boleslas. It was probably at his father's insistence that Wenceslas, while still quite young, was placed in the care of his virtuous grandmother, St. Ludmila. The child was instructed by Ludmila and her chaplain in all the virtues which form the character of a Christian and a saint. He was later sent to a school of higher learning at Budec, where he made great progress in all the exercises suitable to his rank and future responsibilities.

After Wenceslas' father died, his mother, Drahomira, became regent for the young Wenceslas. She proceeded against the Christians and published an order forbidding priests and others who professed the Faith to teach or instruct children. She also placed pagans in responsible positions and tried every means to entice Wenceslas from his faith. Instigated by the non-Christian elements in the nobility, she developed a hatred and a consuming jealousy of her mother-in-law, Ludmila, because of her influence over Wenceslas. To prevent further influence, Drahomira sent two men to Ludmila's castle at Tetin with instructions to kill her. After burglarizing her castle, the men strangled Ludmila with her own veil.

The murder of his grandmother, coupled with other intrigues of Drahomira, led Wenceslas to assume control of the government in 922 in an attempt to end the internal struggles between the Christian and non-Christian factions in the country and to block the invasion of a neighboring tribe.

When non-Christians raised a huge party against him, Wenceslas thought he could secure peace for his country if he abdicated in favor of his brother, Boleslas. He also considered entering a monastery, but he postponed all these plans so that he could first complete the construction of the Church of St. Vitas for the enshrinement of an important relic of the Saint, which he had received from Emperor Henry I. This decision proved to be a fatal mistake.

Not knowing of Wenceslas' plan to abdicate, Boleslas sided with the opposing side against his brother and devised a plot to kill Wenceslas and succeed him. St. Wenceslas was then invited by Boleslas to visit him for the annual festivities honoring Sts. Cosmas and Damian. The morning after his arrival, Wenceslas was making his way to Mass through a private passage in the castle; there he met Boleslas, and stopped to thank him for his hospitality. "Yesterday I did my best to serve you fittingly," said Boleslas, "but this must be my service today," and he lunged at Wenceslas with a sword. The brothers struggled, but three co-conspirators ran in and helped in inflicting the fatal wound. As he lay dying at the chapel door, Wenceslas murmured, "Brother, may God forgive you." This took place in September in the year 935.

With miracles being reported at the tomb of Wenceslas, Boleslas became increasingly uneasy until finally, after three years, he had the body transferred to the Church of St. Vitas at Prague. At once Wenceslas was acclaimed by the people as a martyr who had given his life in upholding the Faith against pagan opposition.

The tomb became a place of pilgrimage, and at the beginning of the eleventh century, St. Wenceslas was already regarded as the national patron of the Czechs. He was officially awarded the patronage of Czechoslovakia at the time of his canonization. St. Wenceslas is the subject of the popular nineteenth century Christmas carol, "Good King Wenceslas." His feast is celebrated on September 28, the anniversary of the day of his death.

Chapter 218

ST. WERNHER

d. 1275

His age is not given, but St. Wernher is known to have been a child when he was abducted by non-Christians. Their purpose was to obtain possession of the Blessed Sacrament, or, at least, to use the blood of a Christian child for their magical or cultist rites.

It is believed that Wernher was seized after receiving Holy Communion on Maundy Thursday in the year 1275. He was hung by the heels in the hope that he would disgorge the wafer he had swallowed. When this failed, he was killed. His blood was drained before his body was carelessly thrown into a pit at Bacherach. When the boy's remains were discovered, the murderers were seized and executed for the crime.

Wernher was buried at Trier, where miracles soon occurred at his tomb. His feast was celebrated throughout Germany, but especially in the City of Trier, where the death of the little martyr was remembered with great sadness.

Chapter 219

BL. WILLIAM HOWARD

1614 - 1680

Directly descended from distinguished representatives of religion and art, Bl. William claims as his grandfather St. Philip Howard, the Earl of Arundel, who died in prison for the Faith in 1595. St. Philip's son, Thomas, who was born while his father was in prison, is recognized as the first great art collector of England and the father of our Bl. William Howard.

Born on November 30, 1614, William was educated in the Catholic Faith, and by the age of 14 he was made a Knight of the Bath at the coronation of King Charles I. When he was 23 years old he secretly married Mary Stafford, the Catholic sister of the last Baron Stafford. Soon afterward King Charles raised him to the rank of viscount.

Recognized as a loyal supporter of the King, William was entrusted by both Charles and Emperor Ferdinand with responsible assignments on the Continent, where he, like his father, indulged in the collection of fine art.

Upon the death of his father in 1646, William was thrust into a prolonged dispute with his eldest surviving brother, Earl Henry Frederick, over what remained of their inheritance. The Howard properties in England had been seized by Parliament, which greatly impoverished the family. This prompted Earl Henry Frederick to commence a series of unjust and vexing civil suits against his mother, during which he almost succeeded in robbing her of her dowry.

William, as her representative and defender, was involved in painful quarrels even after both mother and brother had passed away. His cousins and their agents continued against him for several years over the issue, which William continued as a matter of principle. In 1655 lawsuits were pending in Douai, Brussels and Amsterdam. While William fought for what was just and proper against scheming relatives who were vindictive and greedy, he was to be defended by his Benedictine confessor, Dom Maurus Corker, who wrote that William was "ever held to be of a generous disposition, very charitable, devout, addicted to sobriety, inoffensive in his words and a lover of justice."

In addition to court battles with his relatives, William had other troubles—these being literary friends of his father who were claiming manuscripts and rarities from the Arundel Collections. William successfully defended the collection, which created bitter enemies of the defeated claimants. They wrote bitter complaints against William, which found a permanent place in the diaries and works of distinguished writers.

When his lands were restored to William in 1660, "He lived in peace, plenty, and happiness, being blessed with a most virtuous lady to his wife, and many pious and dutiful children, in which state he remained till the sixty-sixth year of his age."

In 1678, Titus Oates created a false claim called the Popish Plot, in which he alleged that Catholics planned to assassinate Charles II, land a French army in England and turn the Government over to the Jesuits. The House of Commons apparently believed the tale, since countless Catholics were martyred as traitors to the Crown. Lord Stafford was included in the list of suspects who were supposed to have sided with the Pope against the English nation. It is believed that William was named because his age, simplicity and the previous differences with members of his family would make it comparatively easy to obtain a conviction.

On October 25 William was taken to the King's Bench Prison. From there he was transferred with others to the Tower. Two years elapsed before he was taken to trial. When he did appear before the House of Lords, who had assembled in Westminster Hall, the prosecutor's witnesses were such scoundrels as Dugdale, the Irish ex-Dominican Dennis, the apostate priest Smith, Tuberville and Oates himself. William Howard, being now in his late sixties, was somewhat deaf and could not properly hear all that the perjurers testified against him, yet Challoner writes that,

> These managers with all imaginable art and malice baited the good old gentleman for four whole days...but such was the force of truth and innocence and so good was his defense (notwithstanding the great fatigue of so many days' pleading and

all the eloquence employed against him), and brought such and so just exceptions against the witnesses and such proofs of their being perjured villains, that every unprejudiced man that will but read the memoirs of his trial, must agree that he was very unjustly condemned. However, such was the iniquity of the times and the aversion to his religion, he was found guilty by 55 lords and acquitted only by 31.

When the votes were counted and William was pronounced guilty of high treason, he replied, "God's Holy Name be praised for it. I confess I am surprised at it, for I did not expect it. But God's will be done, and your lordship's. I will not murmur at it. God forgive those who have falsely sworn against me."

After the Lord High Steward delivered an abusive speech against Catholics, William was sentenced to be hung, drawn and quartered. The King, however, disapproved of both the verdict and the sentence, but was successful only in changing the *manner* of execution (to beheading).

Dom Maurus Corker, Bl. William's confessor and fellow prisoner, wrote that William spent the three weeks before his execution "in serious reflection and fervent prayer, wherein he seemed to find a daily increase of courage and of comfort, as if the Divine Goodness intended to ripen him for martyrdom and give him a foretaste of Heaven."

William wrote his testament, of which several drafts are extant. In these he denied the charges against him by writing, "I hold the murder of one's sovereign a greater sin than anything since the Passion of our Saviour." He also wrote in moving terms of his grief, and his willingness to leave, for the sake of God, his "most deserving wife and most dutiful children. . . Receive, therefore, most dear Jesus, this voluntary oblation." He wrote to his children, and before dressing on the day of his death, he wrote a tender and loving letter to his wife.

On December 19, 1680, the day of William's death, several thousand people crowded on Tower Hill to witness the execution. Some are said to have paid a guinea for a favorable position.

After mounting the scaffold, William declared his innocence and expressed the opinion that he was being charged because of his religion. After praying aloud, he delivered a long discourse in which he professed his faith in all that the Catholic Church teaches. He exhorted all to pledge allegiance to their king in civil matters, and to give support to the Pope in matters of religion. He begged God to bless the crowd and to forgive his false accusers, as well as the executioner, who is identified as Jack Ketch. William Howard then kissed the block. He made the Sign of the Cross, and commended himself to the Divine Mercy before he adjusted his head for the axe. At the sight of the elderly gentleman being unjustly executed, many in the crowd took pity on him and called aloud for God to bless him.

Bl. William Howard was 66 years old at the time of his death on December 19, 1680. It was only in 1824 that Bl. William's title was awarded to Sir George William Stafford Jerningham, who became the eighth Lord Stafford. In 1929 Pope Pius XI beatified William Howard as a true martyr of the Church.

Chapter 220

ST. WILLIAM OF NORWICH

1132 - 1144

William, the son of Wenstan and Elviva, was born on Candlemas Day, probably in the year 1132, and was baptized in Haveringland Church. At the age of eight he began to learn the trade of a tanner, and in a few years he was employed in Norwich, England, where furs were in great demand for clothing and coverlets. William's trade brought him to the attention of wealthy Jews who lived under the King's protection near Norwich Castle. This district is now bounded by White Lion Street and the Haymarket. William made friends among the Jews, and although such mixed friendships were not unknown, they were unusual since the Jews were somewhat distrusted and generally only grudgingly tolerated by the Christians. For reasons not given, it seems that with the approach of the Lenten season in the year 1144, William's uncle forbade his association with his Jewish friends. This might have caused apprehension or resentment within the Jewish community.

For the remaining history of St. William of Norwich we are indebted to Thomas of Monmouth, who became a monk of the cathedral priory of Norwich. He investigated the matter and wrote the details of the murder of William in the second book of his *Vita en Passio.*

Thomas of Monmouth tells us that on Monday in Holy Week in the year 1144, William, who was then 12 years old, was lured away from his mother by someone who offered him employment in the archdeacon's household. A relative of the boy became suspicious of the whole story and followed William and his companion until he saw them enter the house of a Jew. William was never seen alive again.

The events that next transpired were later revealed by Jewish converts to Christianity and a servant of the house. Their accounts reveal that on Wednesday in Holy Week, after a service in the synagogue, the Jews meant to mock the Crucifixion, in contempt of Christ. They lacerated William's head with thorns, crucified him and pierced his side. On Holy Saturday, the 25th of March, Aelward Ded witnessed the Jew, Eleazar, and another man carrying a heavy sack to Mousehold, a wooded area near Norwich. When the sack was discovered a few hours later, it revealed William's mutilated body, which bore the clear signs of a violent death.

When word reached the Jewish community that the body had been found, they immediately went to the castle and placed themselves under the protection of the sheriff, who is said to have received a large bribe to guard them. The move was merely an act of prudence, since the boy's mother and relatives soon accused the Jews of the crime.

On Easter Monday the body was temporarily buried where it lay at Mousehold, and visits were frequently made there by young men and boys who had known the victim. A few days later the priest Godwin Sturt, William's uncle, formally accused the Jews at the Bishop's synod and then had the grave opened; the body was recognized as that of William.

Because of the nature of the wounds and the season of the year in which the Crucifixion had been re-enacted on the boy, the guilt of the Jews seemed confirmed. Since the Jews were then the King's men and under the protection of the sheriff, the Bishop, who had also brought charges, had no jurisdiction in the case. A number of bribes were known to have been offered to various individuals to suppress the story or drop the charges in the case. The only result was that the body of the boy martyr was removed on April 24 from Mousehold to the monks' cemetery at the Cathedral.

When Aelward Ded, who had discovered the body of the boy in the sack, was on his deathbed five years later, he told what he knew of the crime. As a result, Thomas of Monmouth, the monk chronicler, interviewed a Christian serving-woman who was employed in the house where the crime had been committed. She told how she had peered through a crack in a door and had caught sight of a boy fastened to a post. She had been ordered to bring hot water to her master, presumably to cleanse the body. She afterward found a boy's belt in the room and showed Thomas of Monmouth the marks of the martyrdom that were found in the room. Despite the evidence and the eye-witnesses, no one seems to have been brought to justice for the crime.

Due to the reports of miracles worked through the boy martyr's intercession, William of Turbeville, Bishop of Norwich (1146-1174), on four different occasions had the boy's remains transferred to more honorable places. The last transfer was to the Martyr's Chapel (now the Jesus Chapel) in Norwich Cathedral. Unfortunately, no trace of St. William's shrine remains, although its site is still known. In 1168 the Bishop erected a chapel in the woods where William's body had been discovered. The site of this chapel can still be visited.

Elias, Prior of the Cathedral (1146-1150), and some of the monks at first were skeptical about the miracles. However, the doubts of skeptics were overcome when miracles continued to take place, and when several monks had premonitory visions or dreams.

The boy from Haveringland became St. William, martyr, with a feast day on March 24.

Chapter 221

ST. WILLIAM OF ROCHESTER
(St. William of Perth)

d. 1201

Written by monks in 1516, the *Nova Legenda* reveals all that we know of St. William. This account reveals that he was a native of Perth, Scotland, and was a baker by trade. While still a young man he gave himself to piety and works of mercy and remained unmarried. Devoting himself entirely to the service of God, William was accustomed to set aside every tenth loaf for the poor. He attended Mass daily and was known as a man of great virtue.

One morning before it was light, as he was on his way to attend Holy Mass, William found an abandoned baby on the threshold of the church. Moved by pity, he gave the child to a good woman to nurse and care for at his expense. When the child was old enough, William took him into his household and later adopted him as his son. The name he gave the boy was Cokermay Doveni, which is Scottish for David the Foundling.

Having heard of the wonders that were taking place at the Shrine of St. Thomas Becket at Canterbury, William made a vow to visit this place of popular pilgrimage. When in 1201 he had saved a sufficient amount of money for the journey, he went to the church to hear Holy Mass and to have the priest bless his pilgrim's dress, his staff and wallet. With his adopted son, David, as his traveling companion, William set out for Canterbury to visit the tomb of St. Thomas Becket. Along the way they came to Rochester, where they spent a few days visiting the cathedral.

We do not know what changed David from the pious lad he had seemed to be. It has been speculated that he might have received a rebuke which he resented, or that he might not have wanted to undertake the pilgrimage. We do know that when William resumed his journey, David led him off the high-road, onto a deserted lane, where he struck his adopted father on the head and fled.

William's body was discovered by a mad woman who was accustomed to roam the countryside. She made a garland of wildflowers and put it on the head of the corpse. Returning after a time, she took the garland—which was tinged with the pilgrim's blood—and put it on her own head. The madness is said to have left her immediately. She went at once to the monks of the cathedral in Rochester to report the finding of the body and the circumstances of her cure. The monks had apparently known of the woman's lunacy before the miracle, since they and some of the people went to retrieve the wonder-working body for an honorable burial in the choir of the cathedral. It was very unusual for a layman to be buried there, since the area was reserved for the exclusive use of the monks. This is said to demonstrate the extraordinary nature of the woman's cure.

The miracles that were occurring at the tomb attracted the attention of countless pilgrims, who stopped there for prayer before moving on to visit the shrine of Thomas Becket. Because of the number of pilgrims to the shrine, their offerings were sufficient to defray the cost of rebuilding the whole east end of the cathedral. Among the distinguished people who have visited the tomb are King Edward I and Queen Philippa, who was the wife of Edward III.

Because of the great devotion shown the humble Scotsman and the many miracles occurring at William's tomb, the Bishop of Rochester, Lawrence de St. Martin, is said to have gone to Rome in 1256 to plead with the Pope for William's canonization. Later the same year, Pope Innocent IV pronounced the Church's recognition of William's sanctity. Eventually Pope Boniface IX in 1398 granted indulgences to penitents who visited St. William's altar at certain times of the year.

At the place where William was murdered, the monks built a little chantry chapel. In 1883 this gave way to the building of a hospital for infectious diseases. Until the 1940s, the site of the chapel was marked by a fragment of ancient flint-work built into the west boundary wall of the hospital grounds. The hospital that now stands on the site is called the Wisdom Hospice, which was named in commemoration of the woman who received her sanity through the intercession of St. William.

A medieval wall painting depicting St. William was discovered in the year 1883 in All Saints Church, Frindsbury, but this was later destroyed or hidden by some of the construction work that was done to the church. Fortunately, drawings and paintings were made of this medieval wall painting before it was lost.

Although the Shrine of St. William was destroyed at the time of the Reformation, his tomb is preserved against the north wall of the choir transept. In recent years the hospital, a church, a road and a school have been named for this Saint, whose memory is cherished in Rochester, England.

St. William of Rochester (d. 1201), a Scottish baker. The Saint was entirely devoted to the service of God. When he found an abandoned baby on the threshold of the church where he attended daily Mass, St. William took it upon himself to provide for the child. The adopted child later killed the Saint near Rochester, England, during a pilgrimage the two were making to the tomb of St. Thomas Becket. William's body was discovered by a mad woman, who miraculously regained her sanity by placing on her own head a garland of wildflowers she had put on the head of the corpse. The above painting is based on a fourteenth-century wallpainting that was discovered in All Saints Church, Frindsbury, in 1883. The original painting has been lost.

Chapter 222

BL. ZDISLAVA BERKA

d. 1252

Born in Leitmeritz (Litomerice) Czechoslovakia in the early part of the 13th century, Zdislava was pious as a child, and at the age of seven is known to have left home to live in the forest as a solitary. She spent only a short time in her retreat before she was found and returned home.

After some years, in spite of her great reluctance, Zdislava was forced by her family to marry a man who is said to have been noble and wealthy. Zdislava became the mother of four children, but her home life was unhappy due to the disposition of her husband, who treated her brutally. But by exercising extreme patience and gentleness, she was able to obtain a certain freedom in the practice of her devotions and her many works of charity. She made herself at all times the mother of the poor and especially of the fugitives who, during the troubled days of the Tartar invasion, approached her home at Gabal for assistance.

During the time of the invasion, Zdislava helped a sick and fevered mendicant, to whom she gave a bed in her home. When her husband returned and saw the repulsive condition of the religious, he became indignant at her hospitality and was prepared to eject the patient, when suddenly he found in the bed not the poor religious, but a figure of Christ Crucified. Deeply impressed by this miracle, Zdislava's husband relaxed certain restraints he had placed on his wife and permitted her to establish a Dominican priory at St. Lawrence, and to join the Dominican Third Order.

Zdislava is said to have had visions and ecstasies, and during those days of infrequent Communion, she is known to have received the Blessed Sacrament almost daily.

When Zdislava fell terminally ill, she consoled her children and her husband by saying that she hoped to help them more from the

Father's Kingdom than she had ever been able to do in this world. She died on January 1, 1252 and was buried in the Dominican Priory of St. Lawrence, which she had founded.

It is recorded that shortly after Zdislava's death she appeared in glory to her sorrowing husband, who had grown to appreciate the many virtues of his holy wife. This apparition greatly strengthened him in his conversion from a life of worldliness.

The veneration paid to Bl. Zdislava from the time of her death was approved by Pope St. Pius X in 1907.

Chapter 223

ST. ZITA

1218 - 1278

In spite of their difficult situation in life, Zita's pious parents gave their daughters such a fine example of Christian virtue that the elder girl became a Cistercian nun, and the younger girl became a saint.

Zita did not choose the religious life for herself. Instead, when she was only 12 years old, necessity prompted her to accept work as a servant. Her employer was Pagano di Fatinelli, a prosperous citizen who was in the wool and silk-weaving business. His property was at Lucca, only eight miles from Zita's native village of Monte Sagrati.

From the very beginning of her employment, Zita cultivated the habit of rising during the night for prayer. She also attended daily Mass at the Church of San Frediano, which was close to her new home. The good food with which she was provided was given to the poor, while she lived on scraps from the kitchen. Often she slept on the bare ground, her bed having been given over to a beggar.

For a number of years Zita suffered much from her fellow-servants, who disliked her way of life and regarded her industry as a silent reproach to themselves. They also resented her well-known dislike of sinful suggestions and foul language, as well as her exactitude in supplying for their deficiencies. For a time they were even successful in prejudicing her employers against her. All of these trials she tolerated with admirable patience, meekness, self-restraint and without complaint.

Once when a fellow-servant made dishonorable advances toward Zita, it became necessary for her to defend herself; as a result, she scratched the young man's face. When her master inquired about the cause of the man's injury, she made no excuse or explanation, apparently to protect the man from punishment.

Zita's patience and kindly manner soon overcame the hostility of

747

her fellow workers, and her mistress soon realized how fortunate she was to have Zita as a servant in her house. More responsible duties, including the care of the Fatinelli children, were entrusted to her. Eventually she was placed in charge of all the affairs of the house. In this position of command over the servants, she treated them all with kindness, never once seeking revenge for the ill-treatment she had formerly received from them. She was never severe except when there was a question of wrongdoing. She overlooked their shortcomings, and she took it upon herself to excuse or defend them to their employer.

During a time when food was scarce, Zita was driven by pity to give away her own food and to supply the poor with beans from her master's stock. One day, when he expressed his intention to inspect his store, Zita acknowledged to her mistress that she had made generous withdrawals from the supply. Fearful that he would demonstrate his violent temper on finding less than what he expected, Zita prayed fervently for a solution to her problem. To her unspeakable relief, the master found the supply intact. The only possible explanation was that the beans had been miraculously multiplied.

On another occasion, when Zita lingered at prayer, forgetful that it was baking day, she hurried to the kitchen, where to her surprise, she found that the loaves had been prepared and were ready for the oven.

Zita never wore shoes, and never wore new clothes, but rather only the poorest—even in cold weather. One bitterly cold Christmas Eve, when she refused to wear warmer clothes for the walk to Mass, her master threw over her shoulders his expensive fur coat, warning her not to lose it. At the entrance to the Church of San Frediano, Zita came upon the kneeling figure of a poor man who was suffering from the cold. Zita immediately took off the coat and placed it on the man, telling him that he might wear it until she came out of church. When the service was over, the man and the coat were nowhere to be found. Zita returned home to the reproaches of her master, who was understandably angry at his loss. A few hours later, when he was about to sit down to Christmas dinner, a stranger appeared at the door with the coat and handed it to Zita with a smile of gratitude. The master of the house saw the stranger for a moment before he disappeared from sight, leaving them with an unspeakable feeling of celestial joy. Since that day, the people of Lucca have given the name "The Angel Door" to the door of San Frediano where St. Zita met the stranger.

Between the years 1231 and 1234, when the City of Lucca lay under an interdict launched by Pope Gregory IX, Zita was obliged to walk into Pisan territory to receive Holy Communion. Since the times were dangerous, many feared for Zita's safety, but she was not concerned. Mysterious, but wonderful strangers befriended her, and on one occasion a beautiful lady accompanied her to the door of the house.

As the years passed, Zita became the friend and adviser of everyone in the household and was the only person who could manage the master's frequent rages. She found a measure of freedom from domestic duties and was permitted to visit the sick, the poor and prisoners. She was especially devoted to criminals who were awaiting execution and would spend hours in prayer on their behalf.

During her last illness many grieved, especially her master, who had grown fond of her. Zita died peacefully on April 27, 1278. She was 60 years of age and had served the Fatinelli family for 48 years. She was buried with all simplicity in the Church of San Frediano, where she had so often received the Sacraments.

Public veneration was shown to St. Zita immediately after her death. This veneration was approved by the Bishop of Lucca on May, 1278, just one month after her death.

Zita's coffin was opened in 1446, 1581 and 1651. Today the Saint's perfectly incorrupt body can be seen in a reliquary which is situated above and behind the main altar of the Church of San Frediano. On September 5, 1696, Pope Innocent XII confirmed the veneration paid to her, and on September 26, 1953, Zita was declared the patroness of domestic workers.

St. Zita always considered that she was serving God, rather than man, in the exact discharge of her domestic duties and was known to have said, "A servant is not pious if she is not industrious. Work-shy piety in people of our position is sham piety."

Els

Employed in domestic service all of her life, St. Zita (1218-1278) was at first persecuted by her fellow servants for her penances, hard work, and dislike of sinful
suggestions and foul language. But her kindness and meekness won them over. She
was eventually promoted to take charge of the household. Miracles attended St.
Zita's prayers and charities. For example, one time the Saint was surprised to find
that beans she had given to the poor, belonging to her master, were miraculously
replaced. On another occasion, when she spent time in prayer, forgetting that it
was baking day, she returned to find the loaves all prepared for baking.

The incorrupt body of St. Zita is protected in a glass-sided reliquary in the basilica of St. Frediano in Lucca, Italy. The Patroness of Domestic Workers used her little spare time in visiting the sick, the poor and prisoners. She prayed for hours on behalf of criminals awaiting execution. Public veneration was accorded St. Zita immediately after her death; she was canonized in 1696.

INDEX OF SAINTS

Their Lives and Difficulties

It is our prayer that this Index will be helpful to the lay members of the Church who are trying to live in a truly Christian manner while confronted by the many difficulties and temptations of the world. May these laymen draw courage and determination to endure or overcome their difficulties by examining the lives of the Secular Saints who also experienced countless trials, but who bravely surmounted them by turning to God and trusting in His holy will. Those who are enduring a particular trial or temptation can discover those saints who experienced a somewhat similar problem by examining the appropriate category of the Index, which is divided thus:

An apology might be made to those saints whose faults or sins are featured here. Since these are given with the sole intention of offering an example that might encourage the layman to overcome his difficulties and to advance in virtue, the Saints will, undoubtedly, excuse the exposure of their failings.

Through the Communion of Saints, we can claim these holy people as our blessed friends in Heaven. May they pray for us that we will profit by their example so that we, too, may overcome the dangers of this world and merit to join them someday in our heavenly homeland.

752

I

MARRIED SAINTS

MARRIED SAINTS: St. Adalbald of Ostrevant; St. Adelaide; Bl. Adrian Fortescue; Bl. Albert of Bergamo; Bl. Amadeus; Bl. Angela of Foligno; Bl. Anna Maria Taigi; St. Anne Lyne; St. Aurelius; Bl. Bartolo Longo; Bl. Blaesilla; Bl. Bonizella Piccolomini; Bl. Castora Gabrielli; St. Catherine of Genoa; Bl. Charles of Blois; Bl. Charles the Good; Bl. Claritus; St. Clotilde; St. Dagobert; Bl. Delphina; St. Dorothea of Montau; St. Edgar; St. Edward the Confessor; St. Edwin; St. Elizabeth of Hungary; St. Elizabeth of Portugal; St. Elzear; St. Fabiola; St. Ferdinand III; St. Gengulphus; St. Godelieve; St. Gorgonia; St. Gotteschalc; St. Gummarus; St. Guntramnus; St. Hedwig; St. Hedwig, Queen of Poland; Bl. Helen Duglioli; St. Helen of Sköfde; Bl. Helen of Udine; St. Helena; St. Henry; St. Hermengild; St. Homobonus; St. Hunna; Bl. Ida of Boulogne; St. Ida of Herzfeld; St. Isidore the Farmer; St. Ivetta; Bl. Jacoba; Bl. James Duckett; St. James Intercisus; Bl. Jeanne Marie de Maille; Bl. Joan of Aza; Bl. John Felton; Bl. John Storey; St. Joseph of Palestine; St. Julian the Hospitaller; St. Julitta; St. Ladislas; St. Leonidas; St. Leopold; Bl. Lodovica Albertoni; St. Louis Morbioli; St. Louis IX, King of France; Bl. Louis of Thuringia; St. Luchesius; St. Ludmila; St. Macrina the Elder; St. Margaret the Barefooted; St. Margaret of Scotland; St. Margaret Clitherow; Bl. Margaret Pole; St. Margaret Ward; Bl. Maria Christina of Savoy; St. Matilda; Bl. Michelina of Pesaro; St. Monica; St. Natalia; St. Nicholas of Flüe; St. Nonna; Bl. Novellone; St. Olaf; St. Olga; Bl. Paola Gambara-Costa; Bl. Pepin of Landen; St. Perpetua; Bl. Peter Tecelano; St. Pharaildis; St. Philip Howard; St. Polyeuctus; St. Prosper of Aquitaine; St. Pulcheria; Bl. Ralph Milner; Bl. Raymond Lull; St. Richard Gwyn; Bl. Richard Herst; St. Saturus; St. Sigebert; St. Stephen, King of Hungary; St. Swithin Wells; St. Thomas More; Bl. Thomas Percy; Bl. Villana de Botti; St. Vladimir; Bl.

William Howard; Bl. Zdislava Berka.

MARRIED YOUNG (19 years and under): St. Adelaide, 16; Bl. Amadeus, 18; St. Blaesilla, 19; St. Catherine of Genoa, 16; St. Clotilde, 18; St. Delphina, 15; St. Dorothea of Montau, 17; St. Elizabeth of Hungary, 14; St. Elizabeth of Portugal, 12; St. Elzear, 15; St. Hedwig, 12; St. Hedwig, Queen of Poland, 13 or 15; Bl. Helen of Udine, 15; Bl. Ida of Boulogne, 17; St. Ida of Herzfeld; St. Ivetta, 13; Bl. Joan of Aza; St. Louis IX, King of France, 19; Bl. Louis Morbioli; St. Margaret the Barefooted, 15; Bl. Michelina of Pesaro, 12; Bl. Paola Gambara-Costa, 12; Bl. Raymond Lull; Bl. Villana de Botti, 13 or 14.

MARRIAGES THAT WERE HAPPY, BUT BECAME UNHAPPY: Bl. Albert of Bergamo; St. Louis IX, King of France.

MARRIAGES THAT WERE UNHAPPY, BUT BECAME HAPPY: St. Catherine of Genoa; St. Dorothea of Montau; Bl. Paola Gambara-Costa; St. Philip Howard; Bl. Raymond Lull.

MARRIAGES THAT WERE DIFFICULT OR UNHAPPY: Bl. Anna Maria Taigi; Bl. Castora Gabrielli; St. Edward the Confessor; St. Fabiola; St. Gengulphus; St. Godelieve; St. Gummarus; Bl. Louis Morbioli; St. Margaret the Barefooted; St. Monica; Bl. Novellone; St. Pharaildis; Bl. Zdislava Berka.

MARRIED MEN

BAD-TEMPERED OR NAGGING WIFE: Bl. Albert of Bergamo; St. Gengulphus; St. Gummarus; Bl. Novellone; St. Thomas More.

CHILDLESS: Bl. Albert of Bergamo; Bl. Bartolo Longo; St. Gummarus; St. Henry; St. Julian the Hospitaller; Bl. Peter Tecelano.

COUPLES SEPARATED (amicably or otherwise): St. Edward the Confessor; St. Gengulphus; St. Gummarus; Bl. Louis Morbioli; St. Nicholas of Flüe; St. Philip Howard.

DISAPPOINTED IN LOVE (loved one but married another): St. Olaf; St. Thomas More.

DIVORCED: St. Guntramnus.

FORCED BROTHER'S WIDOW TO MARRY HIM (before his conversion): St. Vladimir.

IN-LAW PROBLEMS: St. Adalbald of Ostrevant, wife's family; St. Edward the Confessor, father-in-law and brothers-in-law; St.

Guntramnus, sisters-in-law; St. Henry, brothers-in-law.
MEDDLING WIFE: St. Louis IX, King of France.
NEGLECTED HIS WIFE (before conversion): St. Philip Howard.
MISTRESS (saint had this before conversion): St. Vladimir.
POLYGAMIST (before conversion): St. Vladimir.
UNFAITHFUL WIFE, saint who had: St. Gengulphus.
UNFAITHFUL TO THEIR WIVES (before conversion): Bl. Louis Morbioli; St. Philip Howard; Bl. Raymond Lull.
VOW OF CONTINENCE (after marriage): St. Elzear; St. Isidore the Farmer.

MARRIED WOMEN

ABUSED PHYSICALLY OR VERBALLY: Bl. Castora Gabrielli; St. Fabiola; St. Godelieve; St. Margaret the Barefooted; St. Monica; St. Pharaildis; Bl. Zdislava Berka.
CHILDLESS: St. Anne Lyne; Bl. Bonizella Piccolomini; St. Catherine of Genoa; Bl. Helen Duglioli.
DISAPPOINTED IN LOVE (loved one but married another): St. Hedwig, Queen of Poland.
DIVORCED: St. Fabiola; St. Helena.
DIFFICULT HUSBAND: Bl. Anna Maria Taigi; Bl. Castora Gabrielli; St. Catherine of Genoa; St. Dorothea of Montau; St. Fabiola; St. Hedwig, Queen of Poland; St. Margaret the Barefooted.
FORCED TO MARRY: St. Elzear; St. Hedwig, Queen of Poland; St. Ivetta; Bl. Lodovica Albertoni; Bl. Maria Christina of Savoy; Bl. Paola Gambara-Costa; St. Pharaildis; Bl. Villana de Botti.
HUSBAND MARRIED PREVIOUSLY: St. Adelaide; St. Margaret of Scotland; St. Matilda.
HUSBAND HAD MISTRESS: Bl. Paola Gambara-Costa.
ILLEGITIMATE CHILD (husband's child raised by saint): St. Catherine of Genoa; St. Elizabeth of Portugal.
IN-LAW PROBLEMS: St. Adelaide, daughter-in-law; Bl. Anna Maria Taigi, daughters-in-law; St. Elizabeth of Hungary, mother-in-law, sisters-in-law, brothers-in-law; St. Godelieve, mother-in-law; St. Helen of Sköfde, son-in-law; Bl. Jeanne Marie de Maille, husband's family; St. Ludmila, daughter-in-law; St. Monica, mother-in-law; St. Pulcheria, sister-in-law.

JEALOUS HUSBAND: Bl. Anna Maria Taigi; St. Elizabeth, Queen of Portugal; St. Hedwig, Queen of Poland.

NEGLECTED BY HUSBAND: St. Catherine of Genoa.

UNFAITHFUL HUSBAND: St. Catherine of Genoa; St. Elizabeth of Portugal; St. Fabiola; St. Monica; Bl. Paola Gambara-Costa.

VOW OF CONTINENCE (made during marriage): St. Catherine of Genoa; St. Hedwig.

VOW OF VIRGINITY MADE BEFORE MARRIAGE WAS RESPECTED AFTER MARRIAGE: St. Cecilia; Bl. Jeanne Marie de Maille; St. Pharaildis; St. Pulcheria.

II

WIDOWS AND WIDOWERS

WIDOWS: St. Adelaide; St. Angela of Foligno; St. Anne Lyne; St. Blaesilla; Bl. Bonizella Piccolomini; Bl. Castora Gabrielli; St. Catherine of Genoa; St. Clotilde; St. Dorothea of Montau; St. Elizabeth of Hungary; St. Elizabeth of Portugal; St. Fabiola; St. Felicitas; St. Hedwig; Bl. Helen Duglioli; St. Helen of Sköfde; Bl. Helen of Udine; Bl. Ida of Boulogne; St. Ida of Herzfeld; St. Ivetta; Bl. Jacoba; Bl. Jeanne Marie de Maille; St. Julitta; Bl. Lodovica Albertoni; St. Ludmila; St. Macrina the Elder; St. Margaret of Scotland; St. Margaret the Barefooted; St. Matilda; Bl. Michelina of Pesaro; St. Monica; St. Nonna; St. Olga; St. Pharaildis; Bl. Villana de Botti.

WIDOWERS: Bl. Adrian Fortescue; Bl. Albert of Bergamo; St. Edgar; St. Edwin; St. Ferdinand III; St. Joseph of Palestine; Bl. Novellone; Bl. Peter Tecelano; St. Thomas More; St. Vladimir.

SAINTS WHO MARRIED WIDOWERS: St. Margaret of Scotland; St. Pulcheria.

SAINTS WHO MARRIED WIDOWS: St. Edgar, King of England; Bl. James Duckett; St. Thomas More.

WIDOWS WHO RAISED CHILDREN ALONE: St. Elizabeth of Hungary; Bl. Jacoba; Bl. Margaret Pole.

WIDOW WHO REMARRIED: St. Adelaide.

WIDOWERS WHO REMARRIED: Bl. Adrian Fortescue; St. Edgar, King of England; St. Edwin; St. Ferdinand III; St. Joseph of Palestine; St. Thomas More.

YOUNG WIDOWS: St. Blaesilla; St. Ida of Herzfeld; St. Ivetta.

III

UNMARRIED SAINTS

BACHELOR SAINTS: St. Alexander; St. Benedict Joseph Labre; St. Benezet; St. Boniface of Tarsus; St. Caesarius; St. Casimir; Bl. Contardo Ferrini; St. Cuthman; Bl. Edward Coleman; St. Epipodius; St. Ethelbert; Bl. Ferdinand of Portugal; St. Gerald of Aurillac; Bl. Gerard of Monza; St. Guy of Anderlecht; Bl. Henry the Shoemaker; Bl. Henry of Treviso; St. John Rigby; St. Joseph Moscati; Bl. Marcel Callo; St. Marino; Ven. Matthew Talbot; St. Pantaleon; St. Roch; St. Serenus; St. Theobaldus; Bl. Thomas Sherwood.

UNMARRIED WOMEN SAINTS: St. Agatha; St. Alodia; St. Bibiana; St. Emiliana; St. Flora; St. Gudule; Bl. Isabella of France; Bl. Josefa Naval Girbes; St. Julitta; Bl. Kateri Tekakwitha; Bl. Margaret Fontana; Bl. Margaret of Castello; St. Margaret of Cortona; St. Mary; St. Nunilo; Ven. Pauline Jaricot; Bl. Pierina Morosini; St. Praxedes; Bl. Stilla; St. Syncletica; St. Tharsilla; St. Zita.

VOW OF CHASTITY OR VIRGINITY MADE BY UNMARRIED SAINTS: St. Agatha; St. Alodia; St. Gudule; St. Isabella of France; St. Joseph Moscati; Bl. Josefa Naval Girbes; Bl. Kateri Tekakwitha; Bl. Margaret Fontana; St. Nunilo; Ven. Pauline Jaricot; Bl. Pierina Morosini; St. Serenus; St. Stilla; St. Syncletica; St. Theobaldus.

IV

PARENTING

MOTHERS OF LARGE FAMILIES (5 children or more): St. Adelaide, 6; Bl. Angela of Foligno, several; Bl. Anna Maria Taigi, 7; St. Clotilde, 5; St. Dorothea of Montau, 9; St. Felicitas, 7; St. Hedwig, 7; Bl. Helen of Udine, several; St. Ivetta, 5; St. Margaret of Scotland, 8; Bl. Margaret Pole, 5; St. Matilda, 5.

MOTHERS (1-4 children): Bl. Castora Gabrielli, 1; St. Elizabeth of Hungary, 3; St. Elizabeth of Portugal, 2; St. Felicitas, 1; St. Gorgonia, 3; St. Hedwig, Queen of Poland, 1; St. Helen of Sköfde, 1; St. Helena, 1; St. Hunna, 1; St. Ida of Boulogne, 3; St. Ida of Herzfeld, 1; Bl. Jacoba, 2; Bl. Joan of Aza, 4; St. Julitta, 1; Bl. Lodovica Albertoni, 3; St. Ludmilla, 2; St. Macrina the Elder, 1; St. Margaret Clitherow, 3; Bl. Maria Christina of Savoy, 1; Bl. Michelina of Pesaro, 1; St. Monica, 3; St. Nonna, 3; St. Olga, 1; Bl. Paola Gambara-Costa; St. Perpetua, 1; Bl. Zdislava Berka, 4.

FATHERS OF LARGE FAMILIES (5 children or more): Bl. Adrian Fortescue, 5; Bl. Amadeus, 6; St. Dagobert, several; St. Edwin, 6; St. Ferdinand III, 13; St. Leonidas, 7; St. Leopold, 18; St. Louis IX, King of France, 11; St. Nicolas of Flüe, 10; Bl. Ralph Milner, 7; St. Richard Gwyn, 6; Bl. Richard Herst, 7; St. Vladimir, 14.

FATHERS (1-4 children): St. Adalbald of Ostrevant, 4; St. Aurelius, 2; St. Edgar, 3; St. Hermengild, 1; St. Isidore the Farmer, 1; Bl. James Duckett, 1; Bl. John Felton, 2; Bl. Louis of Thuringia, 3; St. Luchesius; St. Olaf, 1; Bl. Pepin of Landen, 3; St. Philip Howard, 2; St. Polyeuctus; Bl. Raymond Lull, 2; St. Richard, 3; St. Saturus; St. Sigebert, 2; St. Stephen, King of Hungary, 1; St. Swithin Wells, 1; St. Thomas More, 4; Bl. Thomas Percy, 4; Bl. William Howard.

ADOPTED CHILDREN (saints who adopted): St. Clotilde; Bl. Jeanne Marie de Maille; St. Thomas More; St. William of Rochester.

DEATH OF CHILDREN: Bl. Angela of Foligno, all 7 of her children; Bl. Anna Maria Taigi, 4 children; St. Clotilde, daughter died from husband's abuse; St. Dorothea of Montau, 8 children; St. Elizabeth of Hungary, 1 son; St. Felicitas, 1 child; St. Felicitas, 7 sons martyred; St. Hedwig, 3 children died in childhood, 3 as adults; St. Isidore the Farmer, 1 son; Bl. Jacoba, 2 sons and all her grandchildren; St. Julitta, 1 son; St. Leopold, 7 children; St. Louis IX, King of France, 2 children; St. Luchesius; St. Margaret of Scotland, 1 son; St. Matilda, 1 son; Bl. Michelina of Pesaro, 1 son; St. Nonna, 2 children; St. Perpetua, 1 child; St. Stephen, King of Hungary, 1 son.

DIED AFTER CHILDBIRTH: St. Hedwig, Queen of Poland; Bl. Maria Christina of Savoy.

DIFFICULTY WITH PARENTS (saints who had problems with their parents): Bl. Anna Maria Taigi; St. Casimir; Bl. Contardo Ferrini; St. Dymphna; St. Edward the Confessor; St. Ferdinand III; St. Germaine Cousin; St. Hermengild; St. Louis IX, King of France; Bl. Margaret of Castello; St. Margaret of Cortona; St. Regina; St. Wenceslas.

GAVE BIRTH IN PRISON: St. Felicitas.

GRANDMOTHERS WHO RAISED GRANDCHILDREN: St. Clotilde; St. Macrina.

GUARDIANS (saints who were guardians): St. Guntramnus; St. Joseph of Palestine.

ILLEGITIMATE CHILD (saints who had an illegitimate child before their conversion): St. Edgar, King of England; St. Margaret of Cortona.

PARENTS WERE DISINTERESTED IN THEM: St. Edward the Confessor; St. Germaine Cousin; Bl. Margaret of Castello.

POSSESSIVE OR DOMINEERING MOTHERS (saints who had troublesome mothers): Bl. Contardo Ferrini; St. Edward the Confessor; St. Louis IX, King of France.

SAINTS WHO WERE STEPPARENTS: St. Adelaide; St. Catherine of Genoa; St. Leopold; St. Thomas More.

SAINTS WHO HAD STEPPARENTS: St. Edward, King of England; St. Germaine Cousin; St. Hermengild; Bl. Lodovica Albertoni; St. Lufthild; St. Margaret of Cortona; St. Olaf; St. Philip Howard.

SAINTS WHO HAD TROUBLE WITH STEPPARENTS: St. Edward, King of England; St. Germaine Cousin; St. Hermengild; St. Lufthild; St. Margaret of Cortona; Sts. Nunilo and Alodia; St. Olaf.

YOUNG MOTHERS WHO LED A SINFUL LIFE BEFORE CONVERSION: Bl. Angela of Foligno; St. Margaret of Cortona.

V

CHILDHOOD

BORN IN PRISON: St. Mammas.

CHILD ABUSE (saints who experienced abuse during their childhood): St. Alodio; St. Germaine Cousin; St. Lufthild; Bl. Margaret of Castello; Bl. Maria Bartolomea Bagnesi; St. Nunilo.

DIED YOUNG: St. Agnes, 12; Bl. Antonia Mesina, 16; St. Arthelais, 16; St. Blaesilla, 20; Sts. Boris, 20, and Gleb; St. Cyricus, child; St. Dominic Savio, 14; St. Dymphna, 15; St. Edward, King of England, 17; St. Eulalia, 12; St. Godelieve, 21; St. Hallvard, adolescent; Little St. Hugh of Lincoln, child; Bl. James Bird, 19; St. Justus, 7; Ven. Laurence Humphrey, 20; St. Mammas; Bl. Margaret of Louvain, 18; St. Maria Goretti, 12; St. Pastor, 9; St. Pelagius, 13; St. Regina, 15; St. Rose of Viterbo, 17; St. Simon of Trent, 2; St. Solangia; St. Wernher; St. William of Norwich, 12.

FOSTER HOMES (saints who lived in foster homes): St. Edwin; Bl. Kateri Tekakwitha; Bl. Lodovica Albertoni; Bl. Maria Bartolomea Bagnesi; St. Pelagius; Bl. Thomas Percy.

ILLEGITIMATE: St. Vladimir.

KIDNAPPED CHILDREN: St. Arthelais; St. Dagobert; Little St. Hugh of Lincoln; St. Simon of Trent; St. Wernher; St. William of Norwich.

ORPHANED: St. Aurelius; St. Dagobert; Bl. Delphina; St. Drogo; Bl. Gerard of Monza; Bl. Kateri Tekakwitha; St. Mammas; St. Pulcheria; Bl. Sibyllina Biscossi.

POOR CIRCUMSTANCES (some saints who grew up in poor surroundings): Bl. Albert of Bergamo; Bl. Alpais; Bl. Anna Maria Taigi; Bl. Antonia Mesina; St. Dominic Savio; St. Dorothea of Montau; St. Drogo; St. Germaine Cousin; St. Guy of Anderlecht; St. Helena; Bl. Henry the Shoemaker; Bl. Henry of Treviso; St. Isidore the Farmer; Bl. Joan of Aza; St. Lydwine of Schiedam; Bl. Margaret of Castello; St. Maria Goretti; Ven. Matthew Talbot; St. Rose of Viterbo; St. Seraphina; St. Solangia; St. Zita.

RAISED BY GRANDMOTHER AND AUNTS: Bl. Lodovica Albertoni (4 households).

RAISED BY GUARDIAN: Bl. Jeanne de Maille; St. Mammas.

RAN AWAY FROM HOME: St. Alodia; St. Dymphna; St. Eulalia; Bl. Kateri Tekakwitha; St. Nunilo; Bl. Villana de Botti; Bl. Zdislava Berka.

REMOVED FROM PARENTS: St. Elizabeth of Hungary; St. Isidore the Farmer; Bl. Margaret of Castello; Bl. Thomas Percy; St. Wenceslas.

RESPONSIBILITIES WHEN YOUNG: Bl. Anna Maria Taigi; Bl. Antonia Mesina; St. Boris; St. Casimir; St. Edmund, King of England; St. Edward, King of England; St. Ferdinand III; St. Hedwig, Queen of Poland; Bl. Maria Bartolomea Bagnesi; St. Maria Goretti; Bl. Pierina Morosini; St. Pulcheria; St. Sigebert; St. Vladimir; St. Wenceslas.

TROUBLESOME DURING CHILDHOOD: St. Edgar, King of England; St. Guntramnus; Bl. Novellone; St. Olaf.

VI

DEATHS OF THE SAINTS

BETRAYED BY FRIEND: Bl. James Duckett; St. Oswin; Bl. Thomas Sherwood.
BETRAYED BY RELATIVES: St. Flora, brother; St. Pulcheria, sister-in-law.
BETRAYED BY SERVANT: St. Alexander; St. Epipodius; St. Philip Howard.
DIED FOR THE FAITH: Bl. Adrian Fortescue, d. 1539; St. Afra, d. 304; Sts. Agape, Chionia and Irene, d. 304; St. Agatha, d. 251; St. Agnes, d. 304 or 305; St. Alban, d. 209; St. Anne Lyne, d. 1601; Bl. Anthony Primaldi, d. 1480; Sts. Aurelius and Natalia, d. 852; St. Bibiana, d. 363; St. Blandina, d. 177; St. Boniface of Tarsus, d. 306; St. Cassian, d. 304; St. Cecilia, d. 177; St. Charles Lwanga and 21 Companions, d. 1885-1887; Sts. Cosmas and Damian, d. 303; St. Edmund, d. 870; Bl. Edward Coleman, d. 1678; St. Edwin, d. 633; Sts. Epipodius and Alexander, d. 178; St. Eulalia, d. 304; St. Felicitas, d. 203; Sts. Flora and Mary, d. 851; St. Genesius, d. 300; St. Helen of Sköfde, d. 12th century; St. Hermengild, d. 585; St. Hugh of Lincoln, d. 1255; Sts. Hyacinth and Protus, d. 257; Bl. James Bird, d. 1593; Bl. James Duckett, d. 1602; St. James Intercisus, d. 421; Bl. John Bodey, d. 1583; Bl. John Felton, d. 1570; St. John Rigby, d. 1600; Bl. John Slade, d. 1583; Bl. John Storey, d. 1571; St. Julia, d. 5th century; Sts. Julitta and Cyricus, d. 304; St. Julitta, d. 303; Sts. Justus and Pastor, d. 304; Ven. Laurence Humphrey, d. 1591; St. Leonidas, d. 202; Sts. Lucian and Marcian, d. 250; St. Mammas, d. 275; Bl. Marcel Callo, d. 1945; St. Marcellus, d. 298; St. Margaret Clitherow, d. 1586; Bl. Margaret Pole, d. 1541; St. Margaret Ward, d. 1588; St. Nicarete, d. 5th century; Ven. Nicholas Horner, d. 1590; Sts. Nunilo and Alodia, d. 851; St. Olaf, d. 1030; St. Pantaleon, d. 305; St. Pelagius, d. 925; Sts. Perpetua and Felicitas, d. 203; Sts. Philemon and Apollonius, d. 305; St. Philip

Howard, d. 1595; St. Pollio, d. 304; St. Polyeuctus, d. 259; St. Potamiana, d. 202; Bl. Ralph Milner, d. 1591; Bl. Raymond Lull, d. 1315; St. Richard Gwyn, d. 1584; Bl. Richard Herst, d. 1628; St. Sabas, d. 372; St. Serenus, d. 304 or 307; St. Simon of Trent, d. 1475; St. Swithin Wells, d. 1591; St. Theodota, d. 318; St. Thomas More, d. 1535; St. Thomas Percy, d. 1572; Bl. Thomas Sherwood, d. 1578; St. Wernher, d. 1275; Bl. William Howard, d. 1680; St. William of Norwich, d. 1144.

DIED FOR PURITY: St. Agatha; St. Agnes; Bl. Antonia Mesina; St. Dymphna; St. Maria Goretti; Bl. Pierina Morosini; St. Potamiana; St. Solangia.

DIED IN PRISON FROM SICKNESS: Bl. Ferdinand of Portugal; Bl. Marcel Callo.

GAVE LIFE FOR ANOTHER: St. Alban; St. Hallvard; St. Margaret Ward.

IMPRISONED FOR A TIME BEFORE MARTYRDOM: Bl. Adrian Fortescue; St. Alexander; St. Agatha; St. Agnes; St. Alodia; Bl. Edward Coleman; St. Epipodius; St. Felicitas; Bl. Ferdinand of Portugal; Bl. Flora; St. Gotteschalc; St. Hermengild; Bl. James Duckett; Bl. John Bodey; Bl. John Felton; St. John Rigby; Bl. John Slade; Bl. John Storey; St. Mammas; Bl. Marcel Callo; St. Margaret Clitherow; Bl. Margaret Pole; St. Margaret Ward; St. Mary; Ven. Nicholas Horner; St. Nunilo; St. Pelagius; St. Perpetua; St. Philip Howard; St. Polyeuctus; Bl. Ralph Milner; St. Regina; St. Richard Gwyn; Bl. Richard Herst; St. Roch; St. Swithin Wells; St. Thomas More; Bl. Thomas Percy; Bl. Thomas Sherwood; St. Victor of Marseilles; Bl. William Howard.

KILLED IN BATTLE: Bl. Charles of Blois; St. Edwin; St. Olaf.

KILLED HIS PARENTS BY MISTAKE: St. Julian the Hospitaller.

MURDER

MURDER ATTEMPTED AGAINST SAINTS: St. Edwin; St. Guntramnus; St. Ladislas; St. Stephen, King of Hungary.

SAINTS WHO WERE MURDERED: St. Charles the Good; St. Dagobert; Bl. Margaret of Louvain; St. Oswin.

SAINTS WHO MURDERED OR ORDERED A MURDER (before their conversion): St. Ceadwalla; St. Guntramnus; St. Solomon; St.

Vladimir.

SAINTS MURDERED BY IN-LAWS: St. Adalbald of Ostrevant; St. Ethelbert, by mother-in-law; St. Helen of Sköfde; St. Ludmilla.

SAINTS MURDERED BY RELATIVES: Sts. Boris and Gleb, brother; St. Dymphna, father; St. Edward, King of England, stepmother; St. Godelieve, husband; St. Hermengild, father; St. Oswin, cousin; St. Wenceslas, brother; St. William of Rochester, adopted son.

MURDERED BY STUDENTS: St. Cassian.

MURDERED BY WIFE'S LOVER: St. Gengulphus.

TORTURED (some of the saints who were tortured before dying): St. Agatha; St. Alban; St. Alexander; St. Anthony; St. Armogastes; St. Bibiana; St. Blandina; St. Charles Lwanga and Companions; St. Edmund; St. Epipodius; St. Eulalia of Merida; St. Eustace; St. Genesius; St. Hugh of Lincoln; St. James Intercisus; St. John; Bl. John Felton; St. John Rigby; St. Julia; St. Julitta; St. Mammas; St. Margaret Ward; Ven. Nicholas Horner; St. Pantaleon; St. Pelagius; St. Regina; St. Richard Gwyn; St. Sabas; St. Simon of Trent; St. Theodota; Bl. Thomas Sherwood; St. Victor of Marseilles; St. William of Norwich.

VII

GENERAL

ABANDONED: St. Elizabeth of Hungary; Bl. Ferdinand of Portugal; St. Flora; St. Germaine Cousin; Bl. Margaret of Castello; St. Pelagius.

ABUSED ADULTS: St. Elizabeth of Hungary endured the verbal abuse of her in-laws and members of the court; Bl. Maria Bartolomea Bagnesi was abused by her servant; Bl. Margaret of Castello, by parents, townspeople and children.

ACCUSED WRONGFULLY: St. Blandina; St. Dominic Savio; St. Elizabeth of Hungary; St. Elizabeth, Queen of Portugal; Bl. Edward Coleman; St. Helen of Sköfde; Bl. Kateri Tekakwitha; Ven. Laurence Humphrey; Bl. Margaret Pole; Bl. Margaret of Castello; St. Margaret of Cortona; St. Marino; St. Matilda; Bl. Paola Gambara-Costa; Ven. Pauline Jaricot; St. Philip Howard; St. Pulcheria; Bl. Richard Herst; St. Roch; St. Serenus; Bl. William Howard.

ALCOHOLISM (before conversion): Bl. Boniface of Tarsus; Ven. Matthew Talbot; St. Monica showed inclination toward alcoholism.

CARED FOR INCAPACITATED RELATIVE: Bl. Antonia Mesina, cared for her mother; St. Cuthman cared for his mother; St. Syncletica was responsible for her blind sister.

CONVERTS: St. Afra; St. Alban; St. Anne Lyne; St. Boniface of Tarsus; St. Ceadwalla; St. Charles Lwanga and Companions; Bl. Edward Coleman; St. Edwin; St. Flora; St. Genesius; St. Helena; St. Hermengild; Bl. James Bird; Bl. James Duckett; St. Joseph of Palestine; Bl. Kateri Tekakwitha; Ven. Laurence Humphrey; St. Lucian; St. Ludmila; St. Marcian; St. Margaret Clitherow; St. Natalia; St. Olga; St. Philemon; Bl. Ralph Milner; St. Theodota; St. Vladimir.

COURT (saints who were brought before the court for a civil matter): St. Julitta; Bl. William Howard.

CRITICISM (some of the saints who experienced criticism): Bl. Anna

Maria Taigi; Bl. Anthony Manzi; St. Benedict Joseph Labre; St. Elizabeth of Hungary; St. Elzear; St. Germaine Cousin; St. Isidore the Farmer; Bl. Jeanne Marie de Maille; Bl. Kateri Tekakwitha; Bl. Louis Morbioli; Bl. Margaret of Castello; St. Margaret of Ravenna; St. Matilda; Ven. Pauline Jaricot; St. Zita.

DEMON TROUBLE: Bl. Helen of Udine; St. Margaret of Fontana.

DENIED ENTRANCE TO RELIGIOUS LIFE: St. Benedict Joseph Labre; St. Henry; St. Joseph Moscati; Bl. Kateri Tekakwitha; Bl. Maria Bartolomea Bagnesi; St. Rose of Viterbo; Bl. Villana de Botti.

DISLIKED (some of the saints who were disliked): Bl. Anna Maria Taigi by her neighbors; Bl. Anthony Manzi, sisters and neighbors; Bl. Contardo Ferrini, classmates; St. Elzear, father's friend; Bl. Margaret of Castello, parents and others.

FIRED FROM JOB: St. Notburga.

FORCED TO LEAVE HOME (for various reasons): St. Anne Lyne; St. Edwin; St. Elizabeth of Hungary; St. Flora; St. Germaine Cousin; Bl. Jeanne Marie de Maille; St. Lufthild; St. Macrina the Elder; Bl. Marcel Callo; St. Regina.

HOMELESSNESS (some of the saints who experienced homelessness for various lengths of time): Bl. Albert of Bergamo; Bl. Anthony Manzi; St. Benedict Joseph Labre; St. Edwin; St. Elizabeth of Hungary; Bl. Louis Morbioli; St. Lufthild; Bl. Margaret of Castello; St. Margaret of Cortona.

HERMITS AND SOLITARIES: St. Dorothea of Montau; St. Drogo; St. Ivetta; Bl. John of Aza; Bl. Margaret of Castello; St. Mary of Egypt; St. Nicholas of Flüe; Bl. Novellone; St. Ulphia.

HUMILIATION (some of the saints who experienced humiliation): Bl. Amadeus; St. Armogastes; St. Edgar, King of England; St. Edward the Confessor; St. Gengulphus; St. Germaine Cousin; St. Helena; Bl. Jeanne Marie de Maille; Bl. Kateri Tekakwitha; Bl. Margaret of Castello; St. Margaret of Cortona; St. Matilda; St. Monica; Bl. Paola Gambara-Costa; Ven. Pauline Jaricot.

ILLITERATE: Bl. Margaret of Castello; Bl. Ralph Milner; Bl. Servulus.

KIDNAPPED ADULT: Bl. Margaret of Louvain was killed during kidnapping.

LEFT THE FAITH AND LATER RETURNED: Bl. Bartolo Longo; St. Gotteschalc; St. James Intercisus; Bl. John Storey; St. Luchesius;

St. Margaret of Cortona; Ven. Matthew Talbot; Bl. Novellone; St. Olaf; St. Pantaleon; St. Philip Howard; Bl. Villana de Botti.

FORMALLY RENOUNCED THE FAITH AND LATER RETURNED: St. Gotteschalc, St. James Intercisus; St. Philip Howard.

MENTAL CONDITION (saints who may have had psychological problems): St. Benedict Joseph Labre; St. Drogo; Bl. Helen of Udine; Bl. Jeanne Marie de Maille; Bl. Michelina of Pesaro.

SAINT WHO ENDURED ANOTHER'S MENTAL DISABILITY: St. Dymphna.

MISTAKES (some of the saints who made grave or foolish mistakes): Bl. Anthony Manzi; Bl. Ferdinand of Portugal; St. Guy of Anderlecht; St. Hermengild; St. Julian the Hospitaller; St. Louis IX, King of France; St. Ludmila; Ven. Pauline Jaricot; Bl. Thomas Percy; St. Wenceslas.

MULTIPLICATION OF FOOD: Bl. Paola Gambara-Costa; Bl. Novellone; Bl. Gerard of Monza; St. Zita.

MYSTICS: Bl. Alpais; Bl. Angela of Foligno; Bl. Anna Maria Taigi; St. Catherine of Genoa; St. Dominic Savio; St. Ivetta; Bl. Jeanne Marie de Maille; Bl. Lodovica Albertoni; St. Lydwine of Schiedam; Bl. Margaret of Castello.

NEGLECTED (some of the saints who experienced this): St. Edwin; St. Elizabeth of Hungary; St. Germaine Cousin; St. Godelieve; Bl. Margaret of Castello.

NURSING THE SICK (some of the saints who attended the sick): St. Catherine of Genoa; St. Elizabeth of Hungary; St. Fabiola; St. Gerard of Monza; St. Guy of Anderlecht; Bl. Henry the Shoemaker; St. Hunna; St. Ivetta; Bl. Jeanne Marie de Maille; St. Joseph Moscati; St. Julian the Hospitaller; St. Louis IX, King of France; Bl. Margaret of Castello; St. Margaret of Cortona; St. Matilda; St. Pantaleon; Bl. Peter Tecelano; St. Roch; Bl. Zdislava Berka.

BLACK MAGIC: St. Lucian and St. Marcian.

FIRE WORSHIPPERS: Sts. Anthony, Eustace and John.

PRIEST IN CHURCH OF SATAN: Bl. Bartolo Longo.

PENITENTS: St. Afra; Bl. Angela of Foligno; Bl. Bartolo Longo; Bl. Boniface of Tarsus; St. Edgar, King of England; St. Fabiola; St. Gotteschalc; St. Guntramnus; St. John Rigby; Bl. Louis Morbioli; St. Margaret of Cortona; St. Mary of Egypt; Ven. Matthew Talbot; Bl. Michelina of Pesaro; Bl. Novellone; St. Philip Howard;

St. Solomon; St. Theodota; Bl. Villana de Botti; St. Vladimir.

PERSONALITY WITHDRAWN: Bl. Contardo Ferrini.

PERSONALITY OUTGOING AND LIKEABLE: Bl. Marcel Callo.

POLITICAL PRISONERS: St. Adelaide; St. Charles of Blois; St. Louis IX, King of France.

PHYSICALLY UNATTRACTIVE: St. Drogo; St. Germaine Cousin; Bl. Henry of Treviso; Bl. Margaret of Castello.

POOR (some of the saints who helped the poor): Bl. Albert of Bergamo; Bl. Amadeus; Bl. Bonavita; Bl. Bonizella Piccolomini; Bl. Charles the Good; Sts. Cosmas and Damian; St. Elizabeth of Hungary; St. Elizabeth of Portugal; St. Fabiola; St. Gerard of Monza; St. Gorgonia; St. Guy; St. Hedwig; Bl. Helen Duglioli; St. Helen of Sköfde; Bl. Helen of Udine; Bl. Henry the Shoemaker; Bl. Henry of Treviso; St. Homobonus; St. Hunna; Bl. Ida of Boulogne; St. Ida of Herzfeld; Bl. Isabella of France; St. Isidore the Farmer; Bl. Jeanne Marie de Maille; St. Joseph Moscati; St. Julian the Hospitaller; Bl. Lodovica Albertoni; St. Louis IX, King of France; Bl. Louis of Thuringia; St. Luchesius; Bl. Margaret Fontana; Bl. Margaret of Castello; St. Margaret of Cortona; St. Margaret the Barefooted; St. Matilda; St. Nonna; St. Notburga; Bl. Novellone; Bl. Paola Gambara-Costa; Ven. Pauline Jaricot; St. Stephen, King of Hungary; St. Syncletica; St. Theobaldus; St. Thomas More; Bl. Villana de Botti; St. Vladimir; St. William of Rochester; Bl. Zdislava Berka; St. Zita.

POVERTY (saints who lived in poverty or were reduced to poverty): Bl. Anna Maria Taigi; St. Armogastes; St. Cuthman; St. Elizabeth of Hungary; Bl. Jeanne Marie de Maille; Bl. John Storey; St. Julia; Bl. Lodovica Albertoni; St. Macrina the Elder; Bl. Margaret of Castello; Ven. Matthew Talbot; Bl. Michelina of Pesaro; St. Regina; St. Saturus.

RAPE VICTIM: Bl. Pierina Morosini.

REJECTION (some of the saints who experienced rejection): St. Elizabeth of Hungary; St. Elizabeth of Portugal; St. Edward; St. Edwin; St. Ferdinand of Portugal; St. Germaine Cousin; St. Godelieve; St. Helena; Bl. Jeanne Marie de Maille; Bl. Margaret of Castello; St. Margaret of Cortona; Ven. Pauline Jaricot; St. Regina.

RIDICULE (some of the saints who experienced ridicule): Bl. Anthony Manzi; Bl. Bonavita; St. Elzear; St. Germaine Cousin;

Bl. Henry of Treviso; Bl. Jeanne Marie de Maille; Bl. Margaret of Castello; St. Nicholas Peregrinus; Ven. Pauline Jaricot; St. Zita.

SICK AND HANDICAPPED SAINTS: Bl. Alpais, invalid; Bl. Amadeus, epilepsy; Bl. Anna Maria Taigi, asthma, headaches, rheumatic troubles, hernia, earaches, partial blindness; St. Casimir, consumption; St. Drogo, hernia; Bl. Ferdinand of Portugal, various ailments; St. Gerald of Aurillac, blindness; St. Germaine Cousin, gland trouble, scrofulous condition and a lame arm; St. Gorgonia, unusual sickness; St. Henry, lame; Bl. Jeanne Marie de Maille, back trouble; Bl. Kateri Tekakwitha, headaches, weak and sensitive eyes; St. Louis IX, King of France, recurring malarial infection and skin disease; St. Lydwine of Schiedam, numerous and serious ailments; Bl. Margaret of Castello, blind, lame, hunchbacked and dwarfed; Bl. Margaret of Ravenna, blind; Bl. Maria Bartolomea Bagnesi, miscellaneous ailments; Ven. Nicholas Horner, amputated leg; St. Seraphina, paralysis and miscellaneous ailments; St. Servulus, invalid and palsy; Bl. Sibyllina Biscossi, blind; St. Syncletica, cancer.

SLANDER (some of the saints who experienced slander): St. Elzear; St. Pulcheria; Bl. Villana de Botti.

SUICIDE (was tempted to commit): Bl. Helen dei Cavalcanti.

TEMPER CORRECTED: St. Edward, King of England.

TEMPER (saints who endured another's): Bl. Anna Maria Taigi; Bl. Castora Gabrielli; St. Dorothea of Montau; Bl. Zdislava Berka.

TERTIARIES

ST. AUGUSTINE (HERMITS OF): Bl. Helen dei Cavalcanti.

CARMELITE: Bl. Josefa Naval Girbes; Bl. Louis Morbioli.

DOMINICAN: Bl. Adrian Fortescue; Bl. Albert of Bergamo; Bl. Margaret Fontana; Bl. Margaret of Castello; Bl. Maria Bartolomea Bagnesi; Bl. Villana de Botti; Bl. Zdislava Berka.

FRANCISCAN: Bl. Angela of Foligno; Bl. Bonavita; Bl. Castora Gabrielli; Bl. Contardo Ferrini; St. Delphina; St. Elizabeth of Hungary; St. Elizabeth of Portugal; St. Elzear; St. Ferdinand III; Bl. Jacoba; Bl. Jeanne Marie de Maille; Bl. Joan of Signa; Bl. Lodovica Albertoni; St. Louis IX, King of France; St. Luchesius; St. Margaret of Cortona; Ven. Matthew Talbot; Bl.

Michelina of Pesaro; Bl. Novellone; Bl. Peter Tecelano; Bl. Raymond Lull; St. Rose of Viterbo.
TRINITARIAN: Bl. Anna Maria Taigi.

TROUBLE WITH FAMILY MEMBERS

TROUBLE WITH MOTHERS: Bl. Anna Maria Taigi; Bl. Contardo Ferrini; St. Edward the Confessor; St. Louis IX, King of France; Bl. Margaret of Castello; St. Wenceslas.
TROUBLE WITH FATHERS: Bl. Anna Maria Taigi; St. Casimir; St. Dymphna; St. Ferdinand III; St. Germaine Cousin; St. Hermengild; Bl. Margaret of Castello; St. Margaret of Cortona; Ven. Matthew Talbot; St. Regina.
TROUBLE WITH SONS: Bl. Anna Maria Taigi; St. Clotilde; St. Elizabeth of Portugal; St. Hedwig; St. Matilda; St. Monica; St. Vladimir; St. William of Rochester.
TROUBLE WITH BROTHERS: St. Amadeus; Sts. Boris and Gleb; St. Flora; St. Guntramnus; Ven. Matthew Talbot; St. Pulcheria; St. Vladimir; St. Wenceslas.
TROUBLE WITH A SISTER: St. Stephen, King of Hungary.
TROUBLE WITH AN AUNT: Bl. Charles the Good.
TROUBLE WITH UNCLES: St. Stephen, King of Hungary.
TROUBLE WITH COUSINS: St. Ladislas; St. Oswin; St. Stephen, King of Hungary; Bl. William Howard.
TROUBLE WITH A STEPMOTHER: St. Edward, King of England; St. Germaine Cousin; St. Hermengild; St. Lufthild; St. Margaret of Cortona.
TROUBLE WITH A STEPFATHER: St. Nunilo and St. Alodia; St. Olaf.
TROUBLE WITH A STEPSON: St. Adelaide.
TROUBLE WITH IN-LAWS: St. Adalbald of Ostrevant, wife's family; St. Adelaide, daugher-in-law; Bl. Anna Maria Taigi, daughters-in-law; St. Edward the Confessor, father-in-law and brothers-in-law; St. Elizabeth of Hungary, mother-in-law, sisters-in-law, brothers-in-law; St. Godelieve, mother-in-law; St. Guntramnus; sisters-in-law; St. Helen of Sköfde, son-in-law and his family; St. Henry II, brothers-in-law; Bl. Jeanne Marie de Maille, husband's family; St. Ludmila, daughter-in-law; St. Monica, mother-in-law; St. Pulcheria, sister-in-law.

TROUBLE WITH FELLOW WORKERS: St. Isidore the Farmer; St. Zita.

UNFAIR ACTIONS EXPERIENCED BY SAINTS (some of the saints who were deprived of property, money or position): St. Adelaide; Bl. Albert of Bergamo; St. Anne Lyne; St. Armogastes; St. Bibiana; St. Ceadwalla; Bl. Charles of Blois; St. Dagobert; St. Edward the Confessor; St. Edwin; St. Elizabeth of Hungary; St. Hermengild; Bl. Jeanne Marie de Maille; St. Julia; St. Julitta; St. Macrina the Elder; Bl. Margaret Pole; Bl. Margaret of Castello; St. Matilda; Bl. Michelina of Pesaro; St. Olaf; Ven. Pauline Jaricot; St. Philip Howard; St. Saturus; Bl. Thomas Percy; Bl. Thomas Sherwood; St. Vladimir; Bl. William Howard.

WELFARE RECIPIENT: Ven. Pauline Jaricot.

VIII

OCCUPATIONS AND HOBBIES

ADMINISTRATOR: Bl. Pepin of Landen.

ART COLLECTOR: Bl. William Howard.

ATTORNEYS: Bl. Bartolo Longo; Bl. Contardo Ferrini; Bl. John Storey; St. Thomas More.

BAKER: St. William of Rochester.

BARON: St. Elzear.

BEGGAR: Bl. Servulus.

BLACKSMITH: Bl. Bonavita.

BRIDGE BUILDER: St. Benezet.

BUSINESS WOMAN: St. Margaret Clitherow.

BUTCHER SHOP (worked in): St. Margaret Clitherow.

CARVERS OF IMAGES: Bl. Louis Morbioli; St. Olaf.

CATTLE TENDER: Bl. Armogastes.

CENTURION: St. Marcellus.

CHURCH CLEANER: St. Theobaldus.

CLOTH DEALER: Bl. Thomas Sherwood.

COMB MAKER: Bl. Peter Tecelano.

COMEDIAN: St. Genesius.

COUNCILMEN: Bl. Contardo Ferrini; St. Nicholas of Flüe.

COUNTRY GENTLEMAN: Bl. Adrian Fortescue.

COUNTESSES: St. Elizabeth of Hungary (Landgravine); Bl. Ida of Boulogne.

COUNTS: St. Charles the Good; St. Gerald of Aurillac.

COURTIER: St. Gummarus.

CRUSADERS: Bl. Charles the Good; Bl. Ferdinand of Portugal; St. Louis IX, King of France; Bl. Louis of Thuringia.

DANCER: St. Philemon.

DEACON: St. Marino.

DUCHESSES: St. Hedwig; St. Ludmila.

DUKES: Bl. Amadeus; Bl. Charles of Blois; St. Henry; Bl. Pepin of Landen.

EMBROIDERY WORKER: Bl. Josefa Naval Girbes.

EMPEROR: St. Henry.

EMPRESSES: St. Adelaide; St. Helena; St. Pulcheria.

FARMERS: Bl. Albert of Bergamo; St. Isidore the Farmer; St. Nicholas of Flüe; Bl. Ralph Milner; Bl. Richard Herst.

FERRYMAN: St. Julian the Hospitaller.

FIELD WORKER: Bl. Alpais; St. Notburga.

GARDENER: St. Serenus.

GOVERNESS: Bl. Margaret Pole.

GUIDE TO THE HOLY LAND: St. Guy of Anderlecht.

HANDYMAN: Bl. Claritus.

HOSPITAL WORKERS: St. Catherine of Genoa; Bl. Gerard of Monza; St. Julian the Hospitaller.

HOUSEWIVES: Bl. Anna Marie Taigi; St. Anne Lyne; St. Dorothea of Montau; St. Gorgonia; Bl. Helen Duglioli; Bl. Helen of Udine; St. Margaret Clitherow; St. Nonna.

HUNTERS: St. Edward, King of England; St. Edward the Confessor; St. Oswin; St. Swithin Wells; St. Thomas More.

INNKEEPERS: St. Anne Lyne; St. Helena; Bl. Margaret of Louvain.

JUDGE: St. Nicholas of Flüe.

JUSTICE OF THE PEACE: Bl. Adrian Fortescue.

KINGS: St. Casimir; St. Dagobert; St. Edgar; St. Edmund; St. Edward; St. Edward the Confessor; St. Edwin; St. Ethelbert; St. Ferdinand; St. Guntramnus; St. Henry; St. Ladislas; St. Louis IX, King of France; St. Olaf; St. Oswin; St. Richard; St. Sigebert; St. Solomon; St. Stephen.

KNIGHTS: Bl. Charles the Good; St. Gengulphus; St. Julian the Hospitaller.

LABORERS: Bl. Henry of Treviso; St. Isidore the Farmer; Ven. Matthew Talbot; St. Theobaldus.

LANDGRAVE: Bl. Louis of Thuringia.

LEADER OF REBELLION: Bl. Thomas Percy.

LECTORS: St. Pollio; St. Sabas.

LINGUISTS: Bl. Contardo Ferrini; St. Gotteschalc.

LORD CHANCELLOR OF ENGLAND: St. Thomas More.

MAGISTRATE: St. Nicholas of Flüe.

MASTER OF HOUSEHOLD: St. Saturus.

MERCHANTS: St. Hallvard; St. Homobonus; St. Luchesius.

MIDWIFE: St. Margaret of Cortona.

MILL WORKER: Bl. Pierina Morosini.

MINER: Bl. Armogastes.

MOUNTAINEER: Bl. Contardo Ferrini.

MUSICIANS: St. Olaf; St. Philemon.

NEEDLEWORKERS (decorative sewing): Bl. Josefa Naval Girbes; Bl. Kateri Tekakwitha.

NURSES: Bl. Gerard of Monza; St. Nicarete (See also Nursed the Sick).

OCCULTISTS (before conversion): Bl. Bartolo Longo; Sts. John, Anthony and Eustace; St. Lucian and St. Marcian.

PHILOSOPHER: St. Leonidas.

PHYSICIANS: St. Caesarius; Sts. Cosmas and Damian; St. Joseph Moscati; St. Pantaleon.

PILGRIMS: Bl. Albert of Bergamo; Bl. Anthony Manzi; St. Benedict Joseph Labre; St. Davinus; St. Dorothea of Montau; St. Drogo; St. Guy of Anderlect; St. Nicholas Peregrinus; Bl. Novellone; St. Roch; St. Theobaldus; St. William of Rochester.

PRINCES: Sts. Boris and Gleb; St. Casimir; St. Ethelbert; Bl. Ferdinand of Portugal; St. Gotteschalc.

PROSTITUTES (before conversion): St. Afra; St. Mary of Egypt; St. Theodota.

PRINCESSES: St. Adelaide; St. Dymphna; Bl. Isabella of France.

PRISONERS (worked with): Bl. Bonavita; Bl. Jeanne Marie de Maille; St. Luchesius; St. Margaret Ward; Bl. Margaret of Castello; Bl. Ralph Milner.

PUBLISHER (dealer of books): Bl. James Duckett.

QUEENS: St. Clotilde; St. Elizabeth of Portugal; St. Hedwig;

St. Margaret of Scotland; Bl. Maria Christina of Savoy; St. Matilda.

ROMAN OFFICERS: St. Polyeuctus; St. Victor of Marseilles.

SATANIST (before conversion): Bl. Bartolo Longo.

SCHOLARS: Bl. John Bodey; St. Joseph Moscati; St. Philip Howard; St. Prosper of Aquitaine; St. Richard Gwyn.

SACRISTAN: St. Guy of Anderlecht.

SECRETARY: Bl. Edward Coleman.

SERVANTS: St. John Rigby; St. Notburga; Bl. Sibyllina Biscossi; St. Zita.

SEWING: Bl. Pierina Morosini; St. Seraphina.

SHEPHERDESSES: St. Germaine Cousin; Bl. Joan of Aza; St. Regina; St. Solangia.

SHEPHERDS: St. Cuthman; St. Drogo.

SHOEMAKERS: Bl. Anthony Primaldi; Bl. Henry the Shoemaker; Bl. Novellone; St. Theobaldus.

SLAVES: Bl. Blandina; St. Felicitas; Sts. Hyacinth and Protus; St. Julia; St. Potamiana.

SOLDIERS: St. Casimir; St. Ceadwalla; Bl. Charles of Blois; St. Edwin; St. Elzear; St. Ferdinand; St. Gotteschalc; St. Hermengild; St. James Intercisus; St. Ladislas; St. Leopold; St. Nicholas of Flüe; St. Olaf; St. Vladimir.

SPINNING: St. Seraphina.

STONEMASON: St. Marino.

STUDENTS: St. Dominic Savio; Sts. Justus and Pastor.

TAILOR: Ven. Nicholas Horner.

TANNER'S ASSISTANT: St. William of Norwich.

TEACHERS: St. Cassian; Bl. Contardo Ferrini; Bl. John Slade; Bl. Josefa Naval Girbes; St. Joseph Moscati; Bl. Louis Morbioli; St. Richard Gwyn; St. Swithin Wells.

WAITRESS: Bl. Margaret of Louvain.

WEAVING: Bl. Kateri Tekakwitha.

WRITERS: St. Prosper of Aquitaine; Bl. Raymond Lull; St. Thomas More.

BIBLIOGRAPHY

Albertson, S.J., Clinton. *Anglo-Saxon Saints and Heroes.* Fordham University Press. Bronx, New York. 1967.

Albin, The Rev. Hugh O. *The Parish Church of St. Dunstan.* Canterbury, Kent, England.

Arnold, Anneliese. *Hospice Built on Hallowed Ground.* Rochester, England. (Paper.)

Aston, Margaret. *The Fifteenth Century.* Harcourt, Brace & World, Inc. London. 1968.

Attwater, Donald. *Saints of the East.* P. J. Kenedy & Sons. New York. 1963.

Attwater. *Martyrs from St. Stephen to John Tung.* Sheed & Ward. New York. 1957.

Aurelius Augustinus, Saint. *St. Augustine's Confessions.* William Heinemann. London. 1931.

Ball, Ann. *Modern Saints—Their Lives and Faces.* TAN Books & Publishers, Inc. Rockford, Illinois. 1983.

Basil the Great, St. *Letters.* Volume II. Fathers of the Church, Inc. New York. 1955.

Bauer, Hermann. *St. Elisabeth Und Die Elisabethkirche Zu Marburg.* Marburg-Lahn. Buchdruckerei Hermann Bauer Verlag. 1964.

Beata Angela Da Foligno. Lettere Ai Discepoli. Edizioni Chiesa di San Francesco. Foligno, Italy. 1983.

Bechard, Henri. *Blessed Kateri Tekakwitha.* The Kateri Center. Caughnawaga, P.Q., Canada.

Beda Venerabilis. *The Ecclesiastical History of the English Nation.* J.M. Dent & Sons, Ltd. London, England. 1958.

Benedictine Monks of St. Augustine's Abbey, Ramsgate. *The Book of Saints.* Thomas Y. Crowell Company. New York. 1966.

Bessieres, S.J., Albert. *Wife, Mother and Mystic.* TAN Books & Publishers, Inc. Rockford, Illinois. 1952.

Blasucci, Antonio. *S. Francesco Visto Dalla Beata Angela Da Foligno.* Edizioni Chiesa di San Francesco. Foligno, Italy. 1985.

Blunt, Rev. Hugh Francis. *Great Wives and Mothers.* The Devin-Adair Company. New York. 1923.

Bouin, Rev. Paul. *The Uganda Martyrs.* The Regina Press. Turnhout, Belgium. 1965.

Brewer, E. Cobham. *A Dictionary of Miracles.* Cassell & Company, Ltd. New York. 1884.

Buehrle, Marie Cecilia. *Kateri of the Mohawks.* All Saints Press, Inc. New York. 1954.

Buehrle. *Saint Maria Goretti.* The Bruce Publishing Company. Milwaukee. 1950.

Butler, Alban; Thurston, S.J., Herbert; Attwater, Donald. *The Lives of the Saints.* 12 Volumes. P. J. Kenedy & Sons. New York. 1934.

Butler, N. V. Pierce. *A Book of British Saints.* The Faith Press, Ltd. London, England. 1957.

Camm, O.S.B., Dom Bede. *Forgotten Shrines*. MacDonald & Evans. London, England. 1936.

Caraman, S.J., Philip. *Margaret Clitherow*. The Catholic Truth Society. London, England. 1986.

The Catholic Encyclopedia. The Encyclopedia Press, Inc. New York. 1909.

Challoner, D.D., Richard. *Memoirs of Missionary Priests*. Burns, Oates and Washbourne, Ltd. London, England. 1924.

Chapter of St. Albans Cathedral. *A Visit to St. Albans Cathedral*. St. Albans, England. 1984.

Chioccioni, T.O.R.; P. Pietro. *Illustrated Guide to the Basilica of Saints Cosmas & Damian*. The Basilica of Saints Cosmas and Damian. Rome, Italy. 1973.

Clarke, James Freeman. *Events and Epochs in Religious History*. James R. Osgood & Co. Boston. 1883.

Colledge, O.S.B., Edmund; Walsh, S.J., James. *Following the Saints*. Good Will Publishers, Inc. Gastonia, North Carolina. 1970.

Conyngham, D. P. *Lives of the Irish Saints and Martyrs*. P. J. Kenedy & Sons. New York. 1870.

Coulton, G. G. *Life in the Middle Ages*. Cambridge University Press. London. 1967.

Cruz, Joan Carroll. *The Incorruptibles*. TAN Books and Publishers, Inc. Rockford, Illinois. 1977.

Cruz. *Relics*. Our Sunday Visitor, Inc. Huntington, Indiana. 1983.

Dahmus, Joseph. *Seven Medieval Kings*. Doubleday & Co., Inc. Garden City, New York. 1967.

Dahmus. *The Middle Ages*. Doubleday & Co., Inc. Garden City, New York. 1968.

De Bruges, Galbert. *Le Meurtre De Charles Le Bon*. Fonds Mercator-

Anvers. Antwerp, Belgium. 1987.

de Grunwald, Constantin. *Saints of Russia*. Hutchinson of London. London, England. 1960.

Delany, Selden P. *Married Saints*. The Newman Press. Westminster, Maryland. 1950.

Delehaye, Hippolyte. *The Legends of the Saints*. Fordham University Press. New York. 1962.

de Letter, S.J., P., translated by. *Ancient Christian Writers*. Prosper Aquitaine: Defense of St. Augustine. Volume 32. The Newman Press. Westminster, Maryland. 1963.

De Liguori, St. Alphonsus. *The Way of Salvation and of Perfection*. Redemptorist Fathers. Brooklyn, New York. 1926.

De Liguori, St. Alphonsus. *Victories of the Martyrs*. Redemptorist Fathers. Brooklyn, New York. 1935.

de Montalembert, Count. *The Life of Saint Elizabeth*. P. J. Kenedy & Sons. New York. 1886.

Der Selige Heinrich Von Bozen. Bozen. 1986.

de Sales, St. Francis. *Introduction to the Devout Life*. Harper & Brothers, Publishers. New York. 1950.

Dickens, A. G. *The English Reformation*. Schocken Books. New York. 1964.

Drane, Augusta Theodosia. *The Life of St. Dominic*. Burns & Oates, Ltd. New York. 1919.

Duckett, Eleanor. *The Wandering Saints of the Early Middle Ages*. W. W. Norton & Co., Inc. New York. 1959.

Eglise Fortifiee De Hunawihr. Edite par l'Association des Amis de l'Eglise Historique de Hunawihr. Alsace.

Englebert, Omer. *The Lives of the Saints*. Translated by Christopher and Anne Fremantle. Collier Books. New York. 1964.

Eusebius. *The Ecclesiastical History*.

William Heinemann, Ltd. London. 1926.

Fathers of the Church, Funeral Orations by St. Gregory Nazianzen and St. Ambrose. Volume 22. Fathers of the Church, Inc. New York. 1953.

Fathers of the Church, St. Basil Ascetical Works. Catholic University of America Press. Washington, D.C. 1962.

Favrais, Robert; Royer, Eugene. *Marcel Callo, Jociste et Martyr.* Supplement of Actualites Notre Temps. Coutances, France. August-September 1987.

Giovagnoll, Canon Anthony Francis. *The Life of Saint Margaret of Cortona.* Peter F. Cunningham. Philadelphia. 1858.

Gostling, Frances M. *The Lure of English Cathedrals.* Robert M. McBride & Co. New York. 1926.

Gregory the Great, St. *The Dialogues of S. Gregorie.* The Scholar Press. London, England. 1975.

Gueranger, Rev. Prosper. *Life of Saint Cecilia, Virgin and Martyr.* Peter F. Cunningham. Philadelphia.

Hartman, C. SS. R., Rev. Louis F., Editor. *Lives of Saints.* John J. Crawley & Co., Inc. New York. 1962.

Hieronymus, Saint Jerome. *Select Letters of St. Jerome.* William Heinemann, Ltd. London. 1933.

Historia Popular Da Rainha Santa Isabel, Protectora De Coimbra. 5th Edicao Revista e Anotada por Sebastiao Antunes Rodrigues. Grafica de Coimbra. Coimbra, Portugal. 1979.

Huysmans, J. K. *Saint Lydwine of Schiedam.* TAN Books & Publishers, Inc. Rockford, Illinois. 1979.

Iswolsky, Helene. *Christ in Russia.* The Bruce Publishing Co. Milwaukee. 1960.

Jones, Charles W. *Saints' Lives and Chronicles in Early England.* Cornell

University Press. Ithaca, New York. 1947.

Joseph Moscati, Professor of the University of Naples. Naples.

Karel de Goede, 1127-1977. Onthalcentrum. Brugge, Belgium. 1977.

Lamb, Harold. *The Crusades.* Doubleday & Co., Inc. Garden City, New York. 1931.

Larsen, Karen. *A History of Norway.* Princeton University Press. Princeton, New Jersey. 1948.

Larsson, Raymond E. *Saints at Prayer.* Coward-McCann, Inc. New York. 1942.

Lettere. *Nella Gloria Del Bernini.* Periodico Bimestrale della Causa di Beatificazione di Papa Giovanni e Pierini Morosini. November-December, 1987.

Lettere. *Pierina Morosini. Giovane Laica Martire.* Periodico Bimestrale della Causa di Beatificazione di Papa Giovanni e Pierina Morosini. Settembre-Ottobre, 1987.

Loades, D. M. *The Oxford Martyrs.* Stein and Day Publishers. New York. 1970.

L'Ortobene. Edizione Speciale. Nuoro, Italy. September 27, 1987. (Newspaper article.)

Macken, Rev. Thomas F. *The Canonisation of Saints.* M. H. Gill & Son, Ltd. Dublin. 1910.

Mann, Rev. Horace K. *The Lives of the Popes in the Early Middle Ages.* Volume V. Kegan, Paul, Trench, Trubner & Co., Ltd. London. 1925.

Mann. *The Lives of the Popes in the Middle Ages.* Volume XI. Kegan, Paul. Trench, Trubner & Co., Ltd. London. 1925.

Marion, Francis. *New African Saints.* Ancora Publishers. Milan, Italy. 1964.

Maurus of Mary Immaculate, C. P., Rev. *The Martyr of Le Ferriere, St. Mary*

Goretti. Scala Santa, Rome, Italy.

Melis, Mons. Giovanni. *Antonia Mesina Sugli Altari.* Editrice Stamperia Artistica-Sassari. Italy. 1987.

Murphy, S.S.J., Rev. Edward F. *Hand Clasps with the Holy.* Society of the Divine Saviour Publishing Dept. St. Hazianz, Wisconsin. 1941.

Neligan, Rev. William H. *Saintly Characters Recently Presented for Canonization.* P. J. Kenedy & Co. New York. 1859.

Newland, Mary Reed. *The Saints and Our Children.* P. J. Kenedy & Sons. New York. 1958.

O'Connell, Canon J. B., Editor. *The Roman Martyrology.* The Newman Press. Westminster, Maryland. 1962.

Pamphili, Eusebius. *The Ecclesiastical History.* Fathers of the Church. Catholic University of America Press. Washington, D.C. Volumes I and II. 1955.

Passionista, P. Fortunato. *La Beata Antonia Mesina.* Nettuno, Italy. 1987.

Pollen, John Hungerford. *Acts of English Martyrs.* Burns and Oates, Ltd. London. 1891.

Pope, Mrs. *The Lives of the Early Martyrs.* D. & J. Sadlier & Co. New York. 1856.

Previte-Orton, C. W. *The Shorter Cambridge Medieval History.* Cambridge University Press. Cambridge, Great Britain. 1971.

Procter, S.T.L., The Very Rev. Father. *Short Lives of the Dominican Saints.* Kegan, Paul, Trench, Trubner & Co., Ltd. London. 1901.

Purcell, Mary. *Matt Talbot and His Times.* Franciscan Herald Press. Chicago. 1977.

Riasanovsky, Nicholas V. *A History of Russia.* Oxford University Press. London. 1969.

Routh, E.M.G. *Sir Thomas More and*

His Friends, 1477-1535. Oxford University Press. London, England. 1934.

Salvatore, Prof. Lo Piccolo Don. *Pompei Città Mariana.* Plurigraf. Narni-Terni, Italy. 1974.

Sanna, Giovanni. *Martirio a Orgosolo, Antonia Mesina.* Editrice L'Ortobene. Nuoro, Italy. 1987.

Santa Margherita, Patrona Della Parrocchia di Cesolo. Cesolo, Italy. (Paper.)

Sante E Beate Umbre Tra Il XIII E Il XIV Secolo. Mostra Iconografica. Edizioni dell'Arquata-Foligno. Foligno, Italy. 1986.

Sharp, Mary. *A Guide to the Churches of Rome.* Chilton Books. New York. 1966.

Stenton, Sir Frank M. *Anglo-Saxon England.* Oxford University Press. London, England. 1943.

Stevenson, J., Editor. *A New Eusebius.* The Macmillan Company. New York. 1957.

Terzi, Ignazio. *Le Due Corone-Verginita e Martirio in Pierina Morosini.* Edizione Instituto Grafico Litostampa. Coordinazione a cura dell'Opera Barbarigo. Bergamo, Italy. 1984.

Trigg, Joseph Wilson. *Origen.* John Knox Press. Atlanta. 1983.

Undset, Sigrid. *Saga of Saints.* Longmans, Green & Co. New York. 1934.

Weiser, S.J., Francis X. *Kateri Tekakwitha.* The Kateri Center. Caughnawaga, P.O., Canada. 1972.

White, Helen C. *Tudor Book of Saints and Martyrs.* The University of Wisconsin Press. Madison, Wisconsin. 1963.

William of Norwich, (1132-1144.) Cathedral of Norwich. (Paper.)

Yonge, Charles Duke. *The Seven Heroines of Christendom.* W. Swan Sonnenschein & Co. London. 1883.

If you have enjoyed this book, consider making your next selection from among the following . . .

At your bookdealer or direct from the publisher.

Prices guaranteed through December 31, 1990.

Joan Carroll Cruz is a native of New Orleans and is the educational product of the School Sisters of Notre Dame. She attended grade school, high school and college under their tutelage. About her teachers Mrs. Cruz says, "I am especially indebted to the sisters who taught me for five years at the boarding school at St. Mary of the Pines in Chatawa, Mississippi. I cannot thank them enough for their dedication, their fine example and their religious fervor, which made such an impression on me." Mrs. Cruz has been a tertiary in the Discalced Carmelite Secular Order (Third Order) for the past 21 years; for eight years she served as Mistress of Formation (Novice Mistress). She is married to Louis Cruz, who owns a swimming pool repair and maintenance business.

Mrs. Cruz says that since her five children are now all young adults she has more time for writing, and she is immensely grateful for the invention of the word processor. Her books include *The Incorruptibles,* published in 1977 by TAN Books and Publishers, Inc.; *Desires of Thy Heart,* a novel with a strong Catholic theme published in hardcover by Tandem Press in 1977 and in paperback by Signet with an initial printing of 600,000 copies; *Relics,* published in 1983 by Our Sunday Visitor, Inc.; and *Eucharistic Miracles,* published in 1987 by TAN Books and Publishers, Inc. For her non-fiction books Mrs. Cruz depends heavily on information received from foreign shrines, churches, convents and monasteries. The material she receives requires the services of several translators. Mrs. Cruz is currently working on three projects.